Springer Series in Information Sciences 5

Editor: T. S. Huang

Springer Series in Information Sciences

Editors: King Sun Fu Thomas S. Huang Manfred R. Schroeder

Volume 1 **Content-Addressable Memories**
By T. Kohonen

Volume 2 **Fast Fourier Transform and Convolution Algorithms**
By H. J. Nussbaumer

Volume 3 **Algorithms and Devices for Pitch Determination of Speech Signals**
By W. Hess

Volume 4 **Pattern Analysis**
By H. Niemann

Volume 5 **Image Sequence Analysis**
Editor: T. S. Huang

Image Sequence Analysis

Editor: T. S. Huang

With Contributions by

J. K. Aggarwal E. Dubois Y. P. Hsu T. S. Huang
W. N. Martin H. H. Nagel B. Prasada B. M. Radig
M. S. Sabri W. Spiesberger M. Tasto R. Y. Tsai

With 125 Figures

Springer-Verlag Berlin Heidelberg New York 1981

Professor Thomas S. Huang

Department of Electrical Engineering and Coordinated Science Laboratory,
University of Illinois, Urbana, IL 61801, USA

Series Editors:

Professor King Sun Fu

School of Electrical Engineering, Purdue University,
West Lafayette, IN 47907, USA

Professor Thomas S. Huang

Department of Electrical Engineering and Coordinated Science Laboratory,
University of Illinois, Urbana, IL 61801, USA

Professor Dr. Manfred R. Schroeder

Drittes Physikalisches Institut, Universität Göttingen, Bürgerstraße 42–44,
D-3400 Göttingen, Fed. Rep. of Germany

ISBN 978-3-642-87039-2 ISBN 978-3-642-87037-8 (eBook)
DOI 10.1007/978-3-642-87037-8

Library of Congress Cataloging in Publication Data. Main entry under title: Image sequence analysis. (Springer series in information sciences; v. 5). Bibliography: p. Includes index. 1. Image processing. I. Huang, Thomas S., 1936– II. Agaarwal, J. K. (Jagdishkumar Keshoram), 1936– III. Series. TA1632.I483 621.36'7 81-13522 AACR2

Softcover reprint of the hardcover 1st edition 1981

Offset printing and bookbinding: Brühlsche Universitätsdruckerei, Giessen
2153/3130-543210

Preface

The processing of image sequences has a broad spectrum of important applications including target tracking, robot navigation, bandwidth compression of TV conferencing video signals, studying the motion of biological cells using microcinematography, cloud tracking, and highway traffic monitoring. Image sequence processing involves a large amount of data. However, because of the progress in computer, LSI, and VLSI technologies, we have now reached a stage when many useful processing tasks can be done in a reasonable amount of time. As a result, research and development activities in image sequence analysis have recently been growing at a rapid pace. An IEEE Computer Society Workshop on Computer Analysis of Time-Varying Imagery was held in Philadelphia, April 5-6, 1979. A related special issue of the IEEE Transactions on Pattern Analysis and Machine Intelligence was published in November 1980. The IEEE Computer magazine has also published a special issue on the subject in 1981.

The purpose of this book is to survey the field of image sequence analysis and to discuss in depth a number of important selected topics. The seven chapters fall into two categories. Chapters 2, 3, and 7 are comprehensive surveys on, respectively, the whole field of image sequence analysis, efficient coding of image sequences, and the processing of medical image sequences. In Chapters 1, 4, 5, and 6 the authors present mainly results of their own research on, respectively, motion estimation, noise reduction in image sequences, moving object extraction, and occlusion.

We hope that this volume will prove useful as a reference book for working scientists and engineers and as a supplementary textbook for regular and short courses on image and signal processing.

Urbana, Illinois
August 1981

Thomas S. Huang

Contents

List of Contributors

Aggarwal, Jagdish K.

Department of Electrical Engineering, University of Texas
Austin, TX 78712, USA

Dubois, Eric

INRS-Telecommunications, 3 Place du Commerce
Verdun, Québec, Canada H3E 1H6

Huang, Thomas S.

Department of Electrical Engineering and
Coordinated Science Laboratory, University of Illinois
Urbana, IL 61801, USA

Hsu, Yuan-Pei

Institute of Automation, Chinese Academy of Sciences
Beijing, People's Republic of China

Martin, Worthy N.

Department of Electrical Engineering, University of Texas
Austin, TX 78712, USA

Nagel, Hans-Helmut

Fachbereich Informatik, Universität Hamburg, Schlüterstraße 70
D-2000 Hamburg 13, Fed. Rep. of Germany

Prasada, Birendra

Bell Northern Research and INRS-Telecommunications
3 Place du Commerce
Verdun, Québec, Canada H3E 1H6

Radig, Bernd M.

Fachbereich Informatik, Universität Hamburg, Schlüterstraße 66-72
D-2000 Hamburg 13, Fed. Rep. of Germany

Sabri, M. Shaker

INRS-Telecommunications, 3 Place du Commerce
Verdun, Québec, Canada H3E 1H6

Spiesberger, Wolfgang

Scientific Control Systems GmbH, Oehleckering 40
D-2000 Hamburg 62, Fed. Rep. of Germany

Tasto, Manfred

Peter-Henlein-Straße 13
D-8560 Lauf a.d. Pegnitz, Fed. Rep. of Germany

Tsai, Roger Y.

Department of Electrical Engineering and
Coordinated Science Laboratory, University of Illinois
Urbana, IL 61801, USA

Chapter 1 Image Sequence Analysis: Motion Estimation

T. S. Huang and R. Y. Tsai

With 2 Figures

The processing of image sequences involving motion has become increasingly important. The following is a partial list of applications:

1) Military problems – Tracking of multitargets from video data. Measuring missile dynamics from video data. Target detection and recognition in Forward Looking Infrared (FLIR) image sequences.
2) Industrial problems – Dynamic monitoring of industrial processes. Dynamic robot vision.
3) Commercial problems – Bandwidth compression of TV conferencing and picture phone video signals.
4) Medical problems – Study of cell motion by microcinematography. Study of heart motion from X-ray movies.
5) Meteorology – Cloud tracking.
6) Transportation – Highway traffic monitoring.

Image sequence processing involves a large amount of data. However, because of the rapid progress in computer, LSI, and VLSI [1.1] technologies, we have now reached a stage when many useful processing tasks for image sequences can be done in a reasonable amount of time.

One of the most important issues in image sequence processing is motion estimation. In many image sequence processing problems, motion estimation is the key issue. For example, in efficient coding using DPCM in time, motion estimation and compensation can potentially improve the efficiency significantly. In reducing noise in image sequences by temporal filtering, registration of the object of interest from frame to frame is necessary, and registration is, in essence, equivalent to motion estimation. Finally, in tracking multiple targets (moving differently), motion estimation provides a powerful way of segmenting and identifying the individual targets.

Because of the importance of motion estimation, it will be the main concern of the present chapter. After a brief outline of the contents of the book in the next section, the remainder of this chapter is devoted to a discussion of motion estimation techniques.

1.1 Outline of Book

This book is divided into three parts. Part I contains two chapters (Chaps.1, 2). Chapter 1 by Huang and Tsai discusses techniques for motion estimation. In Chap.2, Nagel gives a comprehensive survey of past work in image sequence analysis. By examining applications in diverse fields, he observes the relationships among various techniques and tries to find common themes. Nagel concludes that the most important common problem in image sequence analysis is the modeling of the scene.

The three major areas in image processing are efficient coding, enhancement, and recognition. The four chapters (Chaps.3-6) in Part II describe results in image sequence processing in these areas. Chapter 3 by Dubois, Prasada, and Sabri reviews coding techniques for video signals which are to be displayed on a television screen for human viewing. In Chap.4, Huang and Hsu present results of two image sequence enhancement experiments where motion compensation was used before temporal noise filtering. Chapters 5 and 6 are concerned with object extraction and tracking in image sequences. In Chap.5, Radig presents a multilevel approach to the description of image sequences. He first extracts regions in each frame. Then, based on the attributes of the regions, he tries to link them in time. The important problem of multiple object occlusion is considered in Chap.6 by Aggarwal and Martin. Approaches to understanding occlusion using dot pattern analysis and edge and boundary analysis are described.

In Part III (Chap.7), Spiesberger and Tasto survey the applications of image sequence analysis to medicine. Three areas are discussed: the measurement of size, shape, volume, etc. as a function of time; functional imaging; and image enhancement. The emphasis is on X-ray images.

1.2 Estimation of Two-Dimensional Translation

A careful reading of Nagel's survey of image sequence analysis in Chap.2 will reveal that the analysis of image motion is still in its infancy. Most of the past work has been restricted to two-dimensional motion, especially translation. There have been three major approaches to estimating two-dimensional translation: i) Fourier method, ii) matching, and iii) method of differentials. We shall describe these approaches in the present section. Then in the remaining sections of this chapter, we shall discuss the extension of these approaches to estimating general two-dimensional and three-dimensional motion.

We shall assume throughout this chapter that we are working with two time-sequential images (frames) to find the amounts of motion the objects have undergone from one frame to the other.

1.2.1 The Fourier Method

The Fourier method is based on the property that if the Fourier transform of a function $f(X,Y)$ is $F(u,v)$, then the Fourier transform of $g(X,Y) = f(X-\Delta X, Y-\Delta Y)$ is $G(u,v) = F(u,v)\exp[-j2\pi(u\Delta X+v\Delta Y)]$. Here (X,Y) denote spatial coordinates, (u,v) spatial frequencies in cycles per unit length, $(\Delta X,\Delta Y)$ the amounts of two-dimensional translation, and $j = \sqrt{-1}$. The difference between the phase angles of the two Fourier transforms is

$$\Delta\varphi(u,v) = \angle G(u,v) - \angle F(u,v) = -2\pi(u\Delta X+v\Delta Y) \quad . \tag{1.1}$$

Therefore, if we calculate $\Delta\varphi$ at two frequency pairs (u,v), we can solve for ΔX and ΔY.

We can simplify the computation by working with the X and Y projections of f and g. Let

$$f_1(X) = \int_{-\infty}^{\infty} f(X,Y)dY \tag{1.2}$$

$$g_1(X) = \int_{-\infty}^{\infty} g(X,Y)dY \tag{1.3}$$

be the X projections, and denote their Fourier transforms by $F_1(u)$ and $G_1(u)$. Then it can readily be shown that

$$\Delta\varphi_1(u) = \angle G_1(u) - \angle F_1(u) = -2\pi u\Delta X \quad . \tag{1.4}$$

Thus, we can find ΔX by calculating $\Delta\varphi_1$ at only one value of the frequency u. Similarly, we can find ΔY by working with the Y projections of f and g.

Two remarks are in order. First, one has to be careful in calculating the phase difference in (1.1,4), because phase angles are not single valued. One can add integer multiples of 2π to them. If we simply use the principal values of $\angle G_1(u)$ and $\angle F_1(u)$ in (1.4), the resulting $\Delta\varphi_1$ may not be correct. One way to resolve this is the following. Let the size of the frame in the X direction be L, and let

$$\left|\frac{\Delta X}{L}\right| < \frac{1}{2k} \tag{1.5}$$

where k is a positive constant. Then from (1.4),

$$\left|\Delta\varphi_1\left(\frac{k}{L}\right)\right| = 2\pi \frac{k}{L} |\Delta X| < \pi \quad . \tag{1.6}$$

It is readily seen that the expression

$$\Delta\varphi_1 = (\angle G_1 + 2\pi n) - (\angle F_1 + 2\pi m) \quad ,$$

where n and m can be any integers, has a unique value if we demand that $|\Delta\varphi_1| < \pi$. Thus, if we know for example that the amount of translation in the X direction is less than half of the frame size, then we can estimate this amount by calculating $\Delta\varphi_1$ at frequencies $u \leq k/L$.

The second remark is that the Fourier method works only if we have an isolated moving object with a uniform (zero) background. If the background is stationary but not uniform, then g(X,Y) is no longer simply a shifted version of f(X,Y), and the Fourier method breaks down. However, in such a situation, one can still use the Fourier method if one is able to first segment out the moving object (by using frame differencing, for example) and set the background to zero.

1.2.2 Matching

Perhaps the most common example of matching methods is cross-correlation. More generally one sets up a cost function depending on f and g

$$C(\Delta X, \Delta Y) = \mathscr{F}\{f(X,Y), g(X,Y)\} \tag{1.7}$$

where

$$g(X,Y) = f(X-\Delta X, Y-\Delta Y) \tag{1.8}$$

and the function f(X,Y) usually represents a small block (window) in a larger image. Then one searches in the parameter space $(\Delta X, \Delta Y)$ for the minimum of C.

1.2.3 The Method of Differentials

The method of estimating two-dimensional translation using differentials was studied by ROCCA and CAFFORIO [1.2,3], LIMB and MURPHY [1.4], and NETRAVALI and ROBBINS [1.5]. The basic idea is to relate time differences to spatial differences.

Let $f_1(X,Y)$ and $f_2(X,Y)$ be the graylevels at spatial coordinates (X,Y) in two successive (time-sequential) frames. The time lapse Δt between the two frames is assumed small so that the amount of motion of any object in the scene is also small. At any given spatial location (X_0,Y_0) the time difference is

$$\Delta f(X_0,Y_0) \triangleq f_2(X_0,Y_0) - f_1(X_0,Y_0) \quad . \tag{1.9}$$

Assume the amount of two-dimensional translation is

$$\begin{aligned} \Delta X &= X_0' - X_0 \\ \Delta Y &= Y_0' - Y_0 \quad . \end{aligned} \tag{1.10}$$

Then, we have

$$\Delta f(X_0,Y_0) = f_2(X_0,Y_0) - f_2(X_0',Y_0') \quad . \tag{1.11}$$

The implicit assumption here is that any given point on the physical object appears in the two frames with the same graylevel. In many situations this assumption is reasonable if the motion between the two frames is small.

We expand $f_2(X_0',Y_0') = f_2(X_0+\Delta X, Y_0+\Delta Y)$ in (1.11) into a Taylor series and take only up to the linear terms (because of small motion) and get

$$\Delta f(X_0,Y_0) = -\Delta X \frac{\partial f}{\partial X}(X_0,Y_0) - \Delta Y \frac{\partial f}{\partial Y}(X_0,Y_0) \quad . \tag{1.12}$$

Equation (1.12) is the basic equation for estimating two-dimensional translations. At each point (X_0,Y_0) we can calculate Δf, and $(\partial f/\partial X, \partial f/\partial Y)$ (the latter by difference approximations), and get one linear equation with two unknowns ΔX and ΔY. If we have two spatially nearby points which we can assume to have the same motion, then by calculating Δf and $(\partial f/\partial X, \partial f/\partial Y)$, at each point we can get two linear equations. A unique solution to $(\Delta X, \Delta Y)$ will then be obtained, if the two equations are independent. In practice, one would use more than two neighboring points, and find the least-square solution.

1.3 Estimation of General Two-Dimensional Motion

All three approaches described in the preceding section can be extended to apply to the estimation of general two-dimensional motion which includes rotation and scaling in addition to translation. The extension of the matching approach is obvious. The only difference is that now the search space is four dimensional: $(\Delta X, \Delta Y, \vartheta, s)$ where ϑ is the rotation angle and s the scale factor. Therefore, the computational requirement is severe. As a result the matching approach becomes less attractive than the other two approaches.

In Sects.1.4,5 the differential approach will be used to estimate three-dimensional motion. General two-dimension motion will be treated there as a special case. Therefore, we shall describe only the Fourier approach in this section.

The major advantage of the Fourier approach over the matching approach is that in the frequency domain one can treat translation, rotation, and scaling separately. Most man-made objects contain sharp straight edges. A sharp straight edge gives rise to a line spectrum in the frequency domain. This line spectrum goes through the origin and is in a direction orthogonal to the original edge in the image. Therefore, the magnitude of the Fourier transform of a typical image contains several very distinct lines passing through the origin. Furthermore, remember the following two properties of two-dimensional Fourier transforms: i) a translation in the image domain does not change the magnitude of the Fourier transform; ii) a scaling of the image simply scales the Fourier transform in the opposite way.

Putting all these facts together, we can see how we treat translation, rotation, and scaling separately. First, we look at the magnitudes of the Fourier transforms of the two frames. Both will have similar distinct line structures (all lines being through the origin), but they differ by a rotational angle ϑ. By putting the magnitudes on top of each other (with the origins coincident) and rotating one magnitude with respect to the other, we can determine ϑ (the rotation angle at which the two line structures coincide). Then, comparing the two magnitudes along one of the line spectra, we can estimate the scale factor s. Note that both the search for ϑ and the search for s are one dimensional. Finally, the method described in Section 1.2.1 is used to determine the translation. We note that in determining ϑ, there is a 180° ambiguity. This ambiguity can be resolved by examining the phase angles.

1.4 Estimation of Three-Dimensional Motion: A Two-Step Method

We shall present a two-step method of estimating the parameters of general three-dimensional motion of rigid bodies based on two time-sequential per-

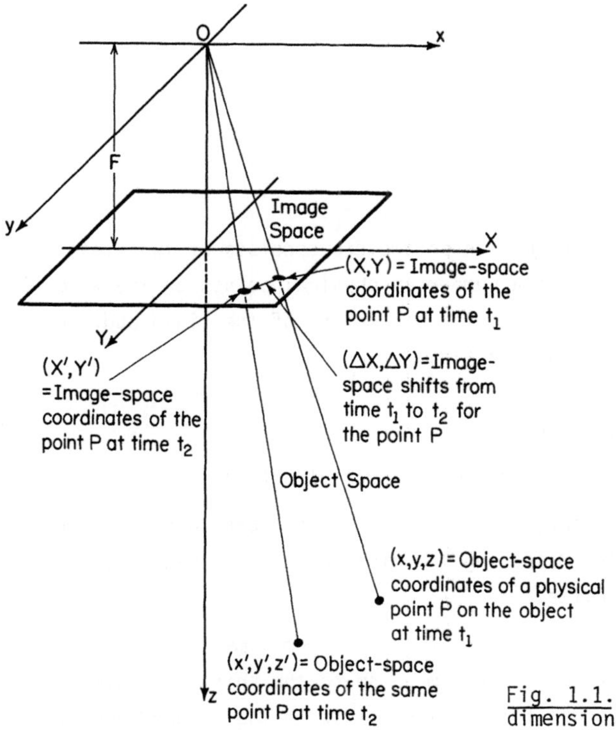

Fig. 1.1. Basic geometry for three-dimensional motion estimation

spective views. The first step is to estimate the image-space shifts of a number of points. Then, the second step is to determine the motion parameters from these shifts. The second step involves the solution of equations where the unknowns can be partitioned into two subsets appearing bilinearly.

An iterative method for solving such equations is suggested. In the special cases of three-dimensional translation and of two-dimensional motion with zooming, the equations become linear.

The geometry of the problem is sketched in Fig.1.1. The object-space coordinates are denoted by (x,y,z) and the image-space (perspective-view) coordinates by (X,Y). We have available two frames, i.e., time-sequential perspective views (at time t_1 and t_2) of a scene containing moving objects. Consider a particular physical point P on the surface of a rigid body in the scene. Let

$$
\begin{aligned}
(x,y,z) &= \text{object-space coordinates of P at time } t_1\\
(x',y',z') &= \text{object-space coordinates of P at time } t_2\\
(X,Y) &= \text{image-space coordinates of P at time } t_1\\
(X',Y') &= \text{image-space coordinates of P at time } t_2 \quad .
\end{aligned}
$$

We define

$$\Delta X \triangleq X' - X$$
$$\Delta Y \triangleq Y' - Y \tag{1.13}$$

as the image-space shifts of P from time t_1 to t_2.

Our method of estimating the motion parameters consists of two steps. First, the image-space shifts of a number of physical points on the same rigid body are estimated. Then, the motion parameters of the rigid body are determined from these image-space shifts.

1.4.1 Estimating Image-Space Shifts

The image-space shifts can be estimated in a variety of ways.

A) By a human operator. Looking at the two frames, one can identify corresponding pairs of points. Measuring the distance between each point pair gives the image-space shifts.

B) By cross-correlation. If the amount of motion from time t_1 to t_2 is small, then in a small neighborhood in the image space the shifts are almost constant (i.e., almost equal for all the points in the neighborhood). Therefore, the image-space shifts can be estimated by cross-correlation using a small window.

C) By the differential method. Again, assume the amount of motion is small from time t_1 to t_2. Then, the differential method of estimating two-dimensional translation described in Section 1.2.3 can be used for the image-space shifts. At each image point (X,Y) we have approximately

$$\Delta f = -\frac{\partial f}{\partial X}\Delta X - \frac{\partial f}{\partial Y}\Delta Y \tag{1.14}$$

where

$f_1(X,Y)$ = image intensity at (X,Y) and time t_1

$f_2(X,Y)$ = image intensity at (X,Y) and time t_2

$\left(\frac{\partial f}{\partial X},\frac{\partial f}{\partial Y}\right)$ = spatial gradient of $f_2(X,Y)$ at (X,Y)

and

Δf = frame difference at $(X,Y) = f_2(X,Y) - f_1(X,Y)$.

If a small number of nearby image points can be assumed to have the same shifts $(\Delta X,\Delta Y)$, then by calculating Δf and $(\partial f/\partial X,\partial f/\partial Y)$ at each point we can get a number of equations (1.14) and by solving them using least square we get an estimation of $(\Delta X,\Delta Y)$. We note in passing that HORN and SCHUNCK [1.6] considered the case where $(\Delta X,\Delta Y)$ are not constant but vary slowly.

1.4.2 Determining Motion Parameters: The Case of Three-Dimensional Translation

Before we examine the general case, let us look at the simpler case of pure (three-dimensional) translation.

Relationship Between Image-Space and Object-Space Coordinates

It is obvious from Fig.1.1 that

$$X = F\,\frac{x}{z}$$

$$Y = F\,\frac{y}{z}\ . \tag{1.15}$$

Basic Equations for Three-Dimensional Translation

Assume a rigid body has translated by $(\Delta x,\Delta y,\Delta z)$ in the object space between the two frames. Look at a particular physical point P on the rigid body. We have

$$\begin{aligned} x' &= x + \Delta x \\ y' &= y + \Delta y \\ z' &= z + \Delta z\ . \end{aligned} \tag{1.16}$$

From (1.15,16),

$$X' = \frac{F(x+\Delta x)}{z + \Delta z} = \frac{Xz + F\Delta x}{z + \Delta z}$$

$$Y' = \frac{F(y+\Delta y)}{z + \Delta z} = \frac{Yz + F\Delta y}{z + \Delta z}\ ,$$

whence

$$\begin{cases} \Delta X = X' - X = \dfrac{F\Delta x - X\Delta z}{z + \Delta z} = \dfrac{\Delta x' - X}{\bar{z} + 1} \\ \Delta Y = Y' - Y = \dfrac{F\Delta y - Y\Delta z}{z + \Delta z} = \dfrac{\Delta y' - Y}{\bar{z} + 1} \end{cases} \tag{1.17}$$

where

$$\Delta z' \triangleq \frac{\Delta z}{F}$$

$$\Delta x' \triangleq \frac{\Delta x}{\Delta z'}$$

$$\Delta y' \triangleq \frac{\Delta y}{\Delta z'}$$

$$\bar{z} = \frac{z}{\Delta z} \tag{1.18}$$

assuming $\Delta z \neq 0$.

Equations (1.17) are the basic equations relating the object-space translation to the image-space shifts. Suppose we have estimated the values of ΔX and ΔY at a particular image-space point (X,Y). Then in (1.17) the unknowns are $\Delta x'$, $\Delta y'$, and $\bar{z}$. It is obvious that we can determine Δx, Δy, and z only to within a proportionality constant (Δz), assuming $\Delta z \neq 0$. If $\Delta z = 0$, we can determine $\Delta x/z$ and $\Delta y/z$.

Solving (1.17)

From (1.17), we have

$$r \triangleq \frac{\Delta Y}{\Delta X} = \frac{\Delta y' - Y}{\Delta x' - X} \quad . \tag{1.19}$$

If we estimate the image-space shifts at 2 image-space points (corresponding to object-space points on the same rigid body), then using (1.19) we get 2 equations in the 2 unknowns $\Delta x'$ and $\Delta y'$. Since the equations are linear, it is a simple matter to solve them. Then the range or $\bar{z}$ value of each point can be obtained from (1.17).

More generally, in the presence of noise, we will take more than 2 image-space points and get more than 2 linear equations. Then we find the least-square solution for $\Delta x'$ and $\Delta y'$.

Graphical Interpretation

Graphically, (1.19) implies that a straight line with slope r and passing through the point $(\Delta x',\Delta y')$ in the X-Y plane is mapped into a straight line with the same slope r and passing through the origin in the ΔX-ΔY plane (Fig.1.2).

A graphical way of finding $\Delta x'$ and $\Delta y'$ is as follows. At 2 image-space points (X_1,Y_1) and (X_2,Y_2), we estimate the shifts and calculate the ratios

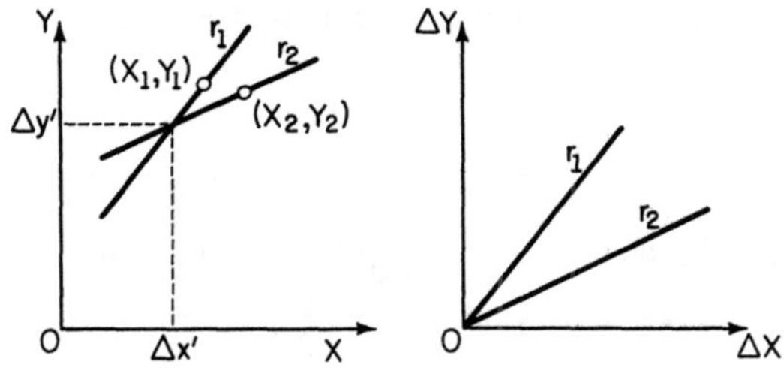

Fig. 1.2. Graphical method of estimating three-dimensional translation

r_1 and r_2. Then we draw a straight line through (X_1,Y_1) with slope r_1 and a second straight line through (X_2,Y_2) with slope r_2. The intersection of these two straight lines gives $(\Delta x',\Delta y')$. Then $\bar{z}_1$ and $\bar{z}_2$ can be determined from (1.17) if desired.

Note that in the case of no zooming, i.e., when $\Delta z = 0$, (1.17) becomes

$$\Delta X = F\frac{\Delta x}{z}$$

$$\Delta Y = F\frac{\Delta y}{z} \qquad (1.20)$$

and

$$r = \frac{\Delta Y}{\Delta X} = \frac{\Delta y}{\Delta x} \quad . \qquad (1.21)$$

Therefore, all points in the X-Y plane are mapped by (1.17) into a straighting line with slope $r = \Delta y/\Delta x$ and passing through the origin in the ΔX-ΔY plane.

Use of a Range Finder

Consider again the solution of (1.17) at a number of image-space points. If the range z at time t_1 of one of the physical points corresponding to these image points can be determined using a range finder, then Δx, Δy, Δz, and the ranges of all the other points can be found. This is obvious from (1.18).

1.4.3 Determining Motion Parameters: The General Three-Dimensional Case

Basic Equations for General Three-Dimensional Motion

Any three-dimensional motion of a rigid body can be decomposed into a rotation around an axis passing through the origin and a translation. We have

$$\begin{bmatrix} x' \\ y' \\ z' \end{bmatrix} = R\begin{bmatrix} x \\ y \\ z \end{bmatrix} + \begin{bmatrix} \Delta x \\ \Delta y \\ \Delta z \end{bmatrix} \qquad (1.22)$$

where $(\Delta x, \Delta y, \Delta z)$ is the amount of translation, and R is a rotation matrix [1.7]

$$R = \begin{bmatrix} n_1^2+(1-n_1^2)\cos\vartheta & n_1n_2(1-\cos\vartheta)-n_3\sin\vartheta & n_1n_3(1-\cos\vartheta)+n_2\sin\vartheta \\ n_1n_2(1-\cos\vartheta)+n_3\sin\vartheta & n_2^2+(1-n_2^2)\cos\vartheta & n_2n_3(1-\cos\vartheta)-n_1\sin\vartheta \\ n_1n_3(1-\cos\vartheta)-n_2\sin\vartheta & n_2n_3(1-\cos\vartheta)+n_1\sin\vartheta & n_3^2+(1-n_3^2)\cos\vartheta \end{bmatrix} \tag{1.23}$$

where n_1, n_2, and n_3 are the directional cosines of the axis of rotation

$$n_1^2 + n_2^2 + n_3^2 = 1 \tag{1.24}$$

and ϑ is the amount of rotation between the two frames.

Assume the amount of rotation, ϑ, is small. Then

$$R = \begin{bmatrix} 1 & -n_3\vartheta & n_2\vartheta \\ n_3\vartheta & 1 & -n_1\vartheta \\ -n_2\vartheta & n_1\vartheta & 1 \end{bmatrix} \quad . \tag{1.25}$$

And we have, using (1.15,22) and after some algebraic manipulation,

$$\Delta X = \frac{-(Fn_3Y-F^2n_2-n_2X^2+n_1XY)\vartheta\bar{z} + F\Delta x' - FX}{-(n_2X-n_1Y)\vartheta\bar{z} + F\bar{z} + F}$$

$$\Delta Y = \frac{-(-Fn_3X+F^2n_1+n_1Y^2-n_2XY)\vartheta\bar{z} + F\Delta y' - FY}{-(n_2X-n_1Y)\vartheta\bar{z} + F\bar{z} + F} \tag{1.26}$$

where the symbols are defined as in (1.18).

Let

$$\begin{aligned} \varphi_1 &\triangleq n_1\vartheta \\ \varphi_2 &\triangleq n_2\vartheta \\ \varphi_3 &\triangleq n_3\vartheta \end{aligned} \tag{1.27}$$

so that

$$\varphi_1^2 + \varphi_2^2 + \varphi_3^2 = \vartheta^2 \quad . \tag{1.28}$$

Then (1.26) becomes

$$\begin{cases} \Delta X = \dfrac{-[FY\varphi_3-(F^2+X^2)\varphi_2+XY\varphi_1]\bar{z} + F\Delta x' - FX}{-(\varphi_2X-\varphi_1Y)\bar{z} + F\bar{z} + F} \\ \Delta Y = \dfrac{-[-FX\varphi_3+(F^2+Y^2)\varphi_1-XY\varphi_2]\bar{z} + F\Delta y' - FY}{-(\varphi_2X-\varphi_1Y)\bar{z} + F\bar{z} + F} \end{cases} \quad . \tag{1.29}$$

Equations (1.26) or (1.29) are the basic equations for general three-dimensional motion.

Solving (1.29)

If we pick an image-space point and estimate the shifts, then (1.29) gives us 2 equations in the 6 unknowns,

$$\varphi_1,\ \varphi_2,\ \varphi_3,\ \Delta x',\ \Delta y' \text{ and } \bar{z} \quad .$$

Unfortunately, the equations are nonlinear.

Each new image-space point we pick gives us 2 new equations and one new unknown ($\bar{z}$). Therefore, we need a minimum of 5 image-space points. In that case, we have 10 nonlinear equations with 10 unknowns:

$$\varphi_1,\ \varphi_2,\ \varphi_3,\ \Delta x',\ \Delta y', \text{ and the 5 ranges } (\bar{z}) \quad .$$

We can of course take more points and find the least-square solution.

From φ_1, φ_2 and φ_3, we can find n_1, n_2, n_3 and ϑ by (1.27,28). Alternatively, canceling $\bar{z}$ in (1.29), we get

$$\frac{\Delta x' - X - \Delta X}{\Delta X(-\varphi_2X+\varphi_1Y+F)+[FY\varphi_3-(F^2+X^2)\varphi_2+XY\varphi_1]} = \frac{\Delta y' - Y - \Delta Y}{\Delta Y(-\varphi_2X+\varphi_1Y+F)+[-FX\varphi_3+(F^2+Y^2)\varphi_1-XY\varphi_2]} \quad . \tag{1.30}$$

The unknowns are φ_1, φ_2, φ_3, $\Delta x'$, and $\Delta y'$.

Picking a particular image-space point and estimating the shifts will give us one equation. To determine the 5 unknowns, we need at least 5 points. More generally, we will pick more than 5 image-space points and find the least-square solution. Then $\bar{z}$ can be found from (1.29).

In both approaches outlined above, the equations we get are bilinear in two subsets of unknowns. For example, in the second approach, the equations are bilinear in $\{\varphi_1,\varphi_2,\varphi_3\}$ and $\{\Delta x',\Delta y'\}$. To find the least-square solution of such equations, we may use the following iterative method. First, assume values for $\{\varphi_1,\varphi_2,\varphi_3\}$. Then the equations become linear in $\{\Delta x',\Delta y'\}$. Find the least-square solution for $\{\Delta x',\Delta y'\}$.

Substitute the solution into the original equations to get a set of linear equations in $\{\varphi_1,\varphi_2,\varphi_3\}$. Find the least-square solution for $\{\varphi_1,\varphi_2,\varphi_3\}$. Repeat the procedure until it converges to a solution for $\{\varphi_1,\varphi_2,\varphi_3,\Delta x',\Delta y'\}$.

The Special Case of "Two-Dimensional" Motion with Zooming

Assume all object points lie on a plane parallel to the image plane, i.e.,

$$z = \text{constant for all object points (at time } t_1) \quad . \tag{1.31}$$

And assume that the axis of rotation is perpendicular to the image plane, i.e.,

$$\begin{aligned} n_1 &= 0 \\ n_2 &= 0 \\ n_3 &= 1 \quad . \end{aligned} \tag{1.32}$$

Then, (1.26) becomes

$$\begin{aligned} X &= \frac{-Y\vartheta + F(\Delta x/z) - X(\Delta z/z)}{1 + \Delta z/z} \\ Y &= \frac{+X\vartheta + F(\Delta y/z) - Y(\Delta z/z)}{1 + \Delta z/z} \quad . \end{aligned} \tag{1.33}$$

The equations are linear in the 4 unknowns

$$\vartheta, \frac{\Delta x}{z}, \frac{\Delta y}{z} \text{ and } \frac{\Delta z}{z} \quad .$$

By estimating the image-space shifts at 2 or more points, we get 4 or more equations from (1.33). Then we can determine the least-square solution for the 4 unknowns.

1.5 Estimation of Three-Dimensional Motion: A Direct Method

We have presented a two-step method of estimating the parameters of general three-dimensional motion of rigid bodies based on two time-sequential perspective views. The first step is to estimate the image-space shifts of several points. Then the second step is to determine the motion parameters from these shifts. As discussed in Sect.1.4.1, the image-space shifts may be estimated in a number of ways. In particular the differential method can be used.

If the amount of motion between the two frames is small, then we may attempt to estimate the motion parameters directly using the differential method [1.8]. In the general three-dimensional motion case, what we do is to combine (1.14,29), to get

$$-\left[-\Delta fY+XY\frac{\partial f}{\partial X}+(F^2+Y^2)\frac{\partial f}{\partial Y}\right]\varphi_1\bar{z} - \left[\Delta fX-XY\frac{\partial f}{\partial Y}-(F^2+X^2)\frac{\partial f}{\partial X}\right]\varphi_2\bar{z}$$
$$-\left(FY\frac{\partial f}{\partial X}-FX\frac{\partial f}{\partial Y}\right)\varphi_3\bar{z} + F\Delta f\bar{z} + F\frac{\partial f}{\partial X}\Delta x' + F\frac{\partial f}{\partial Y}\Delta y' = FX\frac{\partial f}{\partial X} + FY\frac{\partial f}{\partial Y} - F\Delta f \quad . \tag{1.34}$$

The unknowns are φ_1, φ_2, φ_3, $\Delta x'$, $\Delta y'$, and $\bar{z}$.

However, if the geometry of the object surface is not known, then (1.34) cannot be used to find the unknowns.

The reason is that for each new image-space point we pick (and calculate Δf, $\partial f/\partial X$, $\partial f/\partial Y$), we introduce one new equation (1.34) and one new unknown $\bar{z}$. Therefore, the number of unknowns is always larger than the number of equations by 5. The problem becomes soluble if we can postulate a form for the object surface. For example. suppose we assume that all the image-space points we use correspond to physical object points lying on a plane

$$ax + by + cz = 1 \quad \text{at time } t_1 \quad . \tag{1.35}$$

From (1.15),

$$\bar{z} = \frac{1}{a'X + b'Y + \bar{c}} \tag{1.36}$$

where

$$\begin{aligned} a' &= a\Delta z' \\ b' &= b\Delta z' \\ \bar{c} &= c\Delta z \quad . \end{aligned} \tag{1.37}$$

Substituting (1.36) into (1.34), we will get an equation containing the 8 unknowns,

$$\varphi_1,\ \varphi_2,\ \varphi_3,\ \Delta x',\ \Delta y',\ a',\ b',\ \bar{c} \quad .$$

Therefore, if we pick 8 or more image-space points and calculate Δf, $\partial f/\partial X$, $\partial f/\partial Y$ at each, we will get 8 or more equations containing the 8 unknowns. Then we can find the least-square solution. Note that the equations are linear in $\{\varphi_1,\varphi_2,\varphi_3\}$ and bilinear in $\{\Delta x',\Delta y'\}$ and $\{a',b',\bar{c}\}$. Therefore, the iterative method described in Sect.1.4.3 can be used.

The method can be generalized to apply to object surfaces which are (or can be approximated as) piecewise planar. Picking 4 image-space points corresponding to 4 object-space points lying on a planar patch, we get 4 equations from (1.34) [together with (1.36)] with the unknowns

$$\varphi_1,\ \varphi_2,\ \varphi_3,\ \Delta x',\ \Delta y',\ a',\ b',\ \bar{c}\quad .$$

Picking an additional group of 4 points lying on a planar patch gives us 4 new equations and 3 new unknowns a', b' and $\bar{c}$.

Therefore, a total of 5 groups of 4 points (each group lying on a planar patch on the same rigid body) are needed to get 20 equations in 20 unknowns. In practice, more than 5 groups will be used and a least-square solution for the unknowns sought.

In the special case of two-dimensional motion with zooming, as considered at the end of Sect.1.4.3, (1.34) becomes

$$-\left(Y\frac{\partial f}{\partial X}-X\frac{\partial f}{\partial Y}\right)\vartheta+F\frac{\partial f}{\partial X}\left(\frac{\Delta x}{z}\right)+F\frac{\partial f}{\partial Y}\left(\frac{\Delta y}{z}\right)-\left(X\frac{\partial f}{\partial X}+Y\frac{\partial f}{\partial Y}+\Delta f\right)\left(\frac{\Delta z}{z}\right)=\Delta f\quad . \qquad (1.38)$$

This equation is linear in the 4 unknowns

$$\vartheta,\ \frac{\Delta x}{z},\ \frac{\Delta y}{z},\ \frac{\Delta z}{z}\quad .$$

Therefore, we can pick 4 or more image-space points and calculate Δf, $\partial f/\partial X$, $\partial f/\partial Y$ at each to get 4 or more equations, and then find the least-square solution. This special case was considered by NEWMANN [1.9] and by SCHALKOFF [1.10].

1.6 Summary

In this chapter, we have discussed several techniques for motion estimation. For two-dimensional translational motion, there are three approaches: Fourier method, matching, and the use of differentials. When the two-dimensional motion includes rotation and scaling in addition to translation, the matching approach becomes less attractive computationally than the other two approaches.

For general three-dimensional motion, one approach is to extend the method of differentials. An alternative approach is to use a two-step method. In the first step, we estimate the image-space shifts. Then, in the second step, the three-dimensional motion parameters are determined from these image-space shifts. The matching approach can, of course, be extended directly to apply to the three-dimensional problem. However, the dimensionality of the search space becomes very large and, therefore, the computational requirement impossible (unless very efficient search algorithms are found). The direct extension of the Fourier method to three dimensions does not seem possible.

As we mentioned earlier, motion analysis is still in its infancy. The techniques described in this chapter ignore many important factors, chief among which are radiometric considerations, occlusion, and deformable bodies. We have assumed that the graylevels of the two points in the two image frames corresponding to the same physical point on the object are the same. This may be approximately valid in many problems but completely false in others. What we need is to have a model of the three-dimensional scene with respect to its radiometric characteristics (reflective properties of the surfaces, illumination source, etc.). Then, we try to modify our motion estimation techniques to take account of this model. For example, in the methods for estimating three-dimensional motion described in Sect.1.5, the equations we get will now include additional parameters (unknowns) from the radiometric model. Deformable bodies can be handled similarly if simple models can be postulated for them. The problem of occlusion is more difficult to deal with. The use of some heuristics might be necessary. Here, a model of the scene will again help. So we have come back to Nagel's conclusion (which we mentioned in Sect.1.1): The most important problem in image sequence analysis is scene modeling.

In this chapter, we have discussed motion estimation techniques from a signal processing point of view, i.e., the techniques work at the picture element level. In many applications it might be advantageous to work at a higher level, i.e., to work with features extracted from the image frames [1.11]. One advantage is that we can try to choose features which are invariant to undesirable changes (radiometric, for example). We mention in this connection that in Chap.6 some solutions to the occlusion problem using key features are described.

Finally, we would like to point out that some of the motion estimation techniques discussed in this chapter are used in Chaps.3 and 4 for image coding and enhancement. In particular, Chap.4 includes some further discussions on the method of differentials.

Acknowledgement. The two-step method of estimating three-dimensional motion described in Sect.1.4 was developed during the authors' stay with the Signal Processing Group, Department of Electrical Engineering, Swiss Federal Institute of Technology – Lausanne, Summer Semester, 1980. The encouragement of Professor F. de Coulon and Professor M. Kunt of the Group are gratefully acknowledged. The work on the direct method of estimating three-dimensional motion and the various methods of estimating two-dimensional motion, described in Sects.1.3,4,6 was supported by the U.S. Army Research office under Contract DAAG-29-79-C-0200 at Purdue University.

References

1.1 D.F. Barbe (ed.): *Very Large Scale Integration VLSI. Fundamentals and Applications*, Springer Series in Electrophysics, Vol.5 (Springer, Berlin, Heidelberg, New York 1980)
1.2 F. Rocca: "TV Bandwidth Compression Utilizing Frame-to-Frame Correlation and Movement Compensation", in *Picture Bandwidth Compression*, ed. by T.S. Huang, O.J. Tretiak (Gordon and Breach, London 1972)
1.3 C. Cafforio, F. Rocca: "Tracking moving objects in TV images," Signal Proc. *1*, 133-140 (1979)
1.4 J. Limb, J. Murphy: Estimating the velocity of moving images in TV signals. Comput. Graph. Image Proc. *4*, 311-327 (1975)
1.5 A. Netravali, J. Robbins: Motion compensation TV coding: part 1. Bell Syst. Tech. J. *58*, 631-670 (1979)
1.6 B.K.P. Horn, B.G. Schunck: "Determining Optical Flow; AI Memo 572, M.I.T. (April 1980)
1.7 D.F. Rogers, J.A. Adams: *Mathematical Elements for Computer Graphics* (McGraw-Hill, New York 1976)
1.8 R.Y. Tsai, T.S. Huang: "Three-Dimensional Motion Estimation", Proc. First European Signal Processing Conference, Sept.16-19, 1980, Lausanne, Switzerland
1.9 T. Newman: "Video Target Tracking by Lie Algebra Techniques", Proc. Workshop on Automatic Missile Tracking, Redstone Arsenal, Alabama, Nov.1979
1.10 R.J. Schalkoff: "Algorithms for a Real-Time Automatic Video Tracking System", Ph.D. Thesis, Dept. of Elec. Engr., Univ. of Virginia, Charlottesville, VA (1979)
1.11 J.K. Cheng, T.S. Huang: "Matching of Relation Structures and Its Application to Image Processing"; Tech. Rpt., School of Elec. Engr., Purdue University (1981)

Chapter 2 Image Sequence Analysis: What Can We Learn from Applications?*

H. H. Nagel

The analysis of image sequences has only recently been recognized as a research area in its own right. A lot of isolated experience, however, had already been accumulated in various application-oriented investigations. It is the goal of this contribution to gather this experience in a coherent presentation, thus giving depth to an emerging discipline. The unifying idea underlying the organization of this review is an attempt to demonstrate that progress towards more automatic evaluation of image sequences has been intimately connected with improvements of the means to construct computer-internal descriptions - loosely called 'models' - of the depicted scene. This description has to take into account the spatial or temporal variations which are encountered throughout an image sequence. Attempts to describe the development of extractable subimages with time in a quantitative manner are abstracted from their application and presented in a separate chapter. A comprehensive bibliography, augmented by an author index, should facilitate access to the literature.

---

*This chapter has been reproduced in its self-contained form, and consequently does not stylistically conform to the other chapters in this volume. The chapter number 2 has been omitted within the chapter from headings and cross-references. The references are according to the name-date method and contain the section numbers where the references are cited. An index relating the authors cited to the entries in the list of references concludes the chapter.

1. Introduction

A digital image is obtained by quantizing the sensor signal from one or several spectral channels at each grid node of a two-dimensional raster. If this sampling process is extended to the third spatial dimension or to the time dimension we can organize the resulting samples as an image sequence. Digital image processing may be applied to study, e.g., the 3-D spatial variation of a density distribution obtained by computerized tomography. Likewise, one may study how a digital image varies with time due to motion of the sensor or of an object within the recorded scene. One may even sample simultaneously along the time and the three spatial dimensions in order to explore, for example, the time variation of a 3-D density distribution of a beating heart.

During the last decade, significant advances in digital sensor, storage, and processor technologies facilitated the sampling and evaluation of image sequences. The resulting growth in activities has been accompanied by the increasing realization that important methodological and conceptual parallels could be discerned between different application areas such as cloud tracking in satellite images and following an opaque bolus in x-ray film recorded for quantitative studies of blood circulation. How to isolate and track the image of a moving object and how to represent the results are questions which are studied now in their own right - generalizing from specific situations encountered in an application. This development has been reinforced by contact with research in physiology and psychology which attempts to explain the visual perception of moving objects - see, e.g., the book by ULLMAN 79 .

This trend is reflected by the recent literature. MARTIN and AGGARWAL 78 presented the first survey of attempts to evaluate time sequences of images. Their survey, however, does not include the literature about important areas such as x-ray image sequences and interframe coding. According to their subject title - dynamic scene analysis - these authors did not treat methodological similarities in the evaluation of time and spatial image sequences. In a short review, ONOE 78 discussed the problem of motion analysis based on digital image sequences from traffic scenes, cinemicrophotographies of living cells, animal behaviour, and cloud tracking in satellite images. A more comprehensive survey of the relevant work has been given by NAGEL 78b .

SCACCHI 79 discussed aspects of image sequence analysis in the context of the following question: given the current knowledge about visual information processing, what should be the attributes and the internal structure of a system which would exhibit a capability for visual motion perception? He relies on literature about human perception, image processing and artificial intelligence systems to sketch possible approaches and to identify problem areas for investigation. To put it colloquially, SCACCHI's presentation is 'model-driven', using this term as he defined it in his article: "When the system is being model-driven, the system relies on its existing knowledge to suggest or hypothesize the occurence of objects or events." In the current contribution, image sequence analysis is approached as a kind of exercise in conceptual clustering: numerous relevant articles from diverse application areas have been gathered and are presented in sufficient detail so that the commonalities in basic problems, processing techniques, and underlying concepts may become discernible. After this material has been exposed to the reader, the discussion will return to the relation between the current contribution and the presentation of SCACCHI 79.

1.1 Long-Range Implications of Image Sequence Analysis

Two basic problems are encountered by all investigations of the systematic variations between consecutive images from a sequence:

(a) How to decompose an image into segments with attributes such as greyvalue, size, shape, texture, etc. which remain (quasi-) invariant from one image frame to the next although not necessarily throughout an entire sequence. The isolation of such image segments has to cope with significant changes - for example in the relative configuration of such segments - and has to discriminate against insignificant changes due to noise.

(b) How to find a transformation which uses the smallest number of parameters to describe the observed changes throughout an image sequence.

The search for suitable transformations is based on two assumptions:

(aa) a scene depicted in the image sequence may be modeled in terms of separate objects which are related to the (quasi-) invariant image segments;

(ba) - in case of temporal image sequences - the observed time variations can be explained by relative motion between one or more such objects and the sensor or

(bb) - in case of spatial image sequences - the observed contour variations can be explained by the hypothesis that a locally smooth surface of well-defined spatial density distributions manifests itself in a sampling slice through the object configuration.

Modeling of the original scene is thus recognized to play an important role for the analysis of image sequences. The construction and application of computer-internal models is an area of research even for the static analysis of single images. Related activities are well presented in a book edited by HANSON and RISEMAN 78 . Diverse aspects of this research area have recently been discussed by NAGEL 79 .

Progress towards a compact description of variations in an analysed image sequence requires improved models of scene components and sensors, of their admissible relative configurations and motions. Proper choice of models based on the analysis of a subsequence may allow the prediction of individual image frames and frame-to-frame variations in the remaining sequence. By measuring how consistently and concisely vast amounts of input data can be described, the selection and adaptation of models can be evaluated within the image analysis system to a larger degree than in the case of single images.

Models eventually mediate actions external to the image analysis system proper - e.g., by describing an input image in terms familiar to a human viewer. Since the analysis of a single image offers less redundancy which can be exploited for system internal evaluation, the selection and adaptation of models has to be assessed outside of the image analysis system. In the single image approach, models are evaluated indirectly using the external actions mediated by these models. The possibility of evaluating models more thoroughly by exploiting the redundancy available during the analysis of image sequences is expected to contribute towards improved modeling for image analysis in general.

The development of systems for the analysis of image sequences is forced away from ad hoc assumptions towards the incorporation of more general concepts, especially about the 3-D structure of a scene. The concept of a surface patch in 3-D space can be based on the coordinated displacement of a connected set of pixels rather than on approximate constancy of the intensity within a subimage. To account in general for changes due to rotation about an axis parallel to the image plane, the concept of a 3-D volume has to be introduced. From there it is one step to the concept of a single rigid object which might be used in an attempt to explain a variety of changes. As a next step one may introduce several opaque rigid objects moving independently from each other along 3-D trajectories. Even if modeling has been restricted to convex objects, at this point one has to cope with occlusion. A further step would attempt to model a non rigid object as a flexible assembly of rigid subobjects.

The concepts mentioned so far are related to models of visible scene components. A different category of concepts - abstractions for object displacements and their time derivatives, for example as indicated by motion verbs - will have to be incorporated into advanced analysis systems for image sequences. The next higher level in complexity is the deduction of functions from observable time variations in spatial structures. Interactive systems are developed to facilitate the formation of new concepts by analysis of image sequences.

1.2 Scope of this Contribution

No periodical exists yet which specializes in problems related to the evaluation of image sequences. Since 1978, however, the situation has been improving. A session dedicated to this topic was arranged for the first time at the International Joint Conference on Pattern Recognition in Kyoto/Japan (November 7-10, 1978). The first workshop exclusively devoted to the computer analysis of time-varying imagery was organized at Philadelphia/PA in April 1979, sponsored by the University of Pennsylvania and the IEEE Computer Society. The successful contacts which have been established at these events between researchers from different application areas foster a continuation of this development, as is exemplified by dedicated sessions at the subsequent IEEE Conference on Pattern Recognition and Image Processing in Chicago/IL (August 6-8, 1979) and at the International Joint Conference on Artificial Intelligence in Tokyo/Japan (August 20-23, 1979).

During the work on this contribution it became necessary to restrict its scope. It was decided to emphasize a coherent presentation of application areas. This implied that important questions could not be treated in detail. Some of these are mentioned here to indicate the breadth of the field which would have to be considered according to the author's view on image sequence analysis:

* Interframe comparison techniques - some of these have been discussed in NAGEL 78b .

* Image matching - the reader is referred to a new chapter devoted to this topic in a forthcoming second edition of ROSENFELD and KAK 76. Some of these problems are also discussed in chapter 8 of HALL 79 .

* Human visual perception of temporal phenomena - the reader is referred to the recent book by ULLMAN 79 which also covers parts of the next subfield:

* 3-D modeling - this area will be discussed in a forthcoming article - see NAGEL 80 .

* A survey of sensor and processor technologies and their impact on the recording and analysis of image sequences.

* Questions concerning 'focus of attention' and plan formation, especially temporal plans.

* General problems related to the representation of knowledge and associated search methods such as they are investigated in artificial intelligence.

The wide scattering of articles across application oriented journals and conference proceedings presents difficulties for any attempt to cover exhaustively the potentially relevant literature. The material presented in this contribution has been gathered by a systematic search in periodicals, conference proceedings, and books about image processing. This search attempted to cover the image processing literature up to September 1979. References to various application areas were followed up whenever it appeared feasible. Since a primary literature search was impossible for all application areas, the effective cut-off date for the systematic search of application-oriented publications had to be prior to September 1979. More recent articles have been selectively quoted whenever it appeared suitable to illustrate the continuation of a development discussed in this contribution - provided it was directly accessible either in recent issues of journals or in the form of preprints or reprints made available by their authors.

2. Application Oriented Review

The trend towards explicit modeling of increasingly complex concepts is seen as a natural consequence of efforts to exploit the information offered by an image sequence. In the following sections, the accessible literature is reviewed placing emphasis both on the wide variety of actual applications and on the fact that common developments according to the considerations outlined in section 1.1 can already be recognized. Technical details will be sketched to the extent that a reader who is not specialized in the respective application area should be able to decide whether or not an approach might become relevant to him in the context of current - or future - developments. Publications discussing related applications or similar sources of input sequences are grouped together.

2.1 Coding of Image Sequences

A good introduction to image coding can be found in the recent textbooks by ROSENFELD and KAK 76 as well as GONZALEZ and WINTZ 77 . HALL 79 includes a discussion of interframe coding. A broader, well-illustrated introduction to this topic is given by PRATT 78 . A recent book edited by PRATT 79 treats image transmission techniques in depth. A large body of well organized knowledge has been accumulated about the coding of image sequences for bandwidth compression during transmission. Such coding techniques exploit the following premises:

* The similarity between successive frames

* Spatial resolution is automatically reduced proportional to the velocity of moving objects by the integrating effect of current TV-camera targets (if a different sensor will be used, this need no longer apply).

* Perceptible resolution loss in rapidly moving areas is tolerated by human perception as long as low to moderate motion is portrayed with good resolution.

* The TV-camera is not moved very often - if at all.

Since details about image coding can be found in the aforementioned publications, the following discussion is deliberately concentrated towards two goals:

- facilitating comparisons between image coding and other application areas;

- pointing out that successive improvements to interframe coding evaluate the input data in a manner which shows increasingly discernible relations to the semantics of the recorded scenes.

2.1.1 Coarse attributes of broadcast TV-frame sequences

Let D denote the fraction of pixels within a frame which change their intensity from the previous frame by more than a given threshold value. SEYLER 63+65a+65b has shown by extensive measurements on broadcast TV-frame sequences that the distribution of D could be well approximated by a gamma distribution - provided the sequence was long enough (> 10000 frames) and comprising many different scenes. Under these conditions, an average D of about 1/6 is obtained for a threshold set at 5 % of the maximum intensity. If the threshold is raised to 10 % the average D will drop to about 1/18. IINUMA et al. 75 reported similar measurements extended to color broadcast TV.

COLL and CHOMA 76 attempted to isolate transitions between scenes from continuous image activity in broadcast TV. They determined differences between corresponding intensities from frames separated by one third of a second . Scene switches could be identified as spikes in a diagram where the frame average of absolute intensity differences had been plotted as a function of time. These authors have shown that different broadcast TV programs had distinctive rates of scene switching and different bandwidth of continuous image activity. Higher bandwidth for the latter could be attributed to more violent motion of scene components or to panning as well as zooming of the TV camera.

Exploiting the 2-D spatial correlation rather than the frame average of absolute interframe differences should allow a more reliable determination of scene transitions. Checking such a sequence attribute could be useful in preventing misinterpretations during object tracking or change monitoring. Automatic detection of sudden scene transitions could be used, too, in order to prevent overloading of a coding system which exploits the high temporal correlation between consecutive TV frames from a continuous recording of a scene. This consideration motivated SEYLER and BUDRIKIS 59+65 to investigate how humans react to temporal suppression of spatial detail immediately after a scene change. Even critical viewers tolerated a spatial bandwidth reduction by a factor down to 0.05 - provided the full bandwidth (5 MHz) is restored within 0.3 to 0.8 second, depending on the spatial detail of the new scene.

2.1.2 Predefined frame segmentation

Computation of segment characteristics is simpler if a predefined segmentation - e.g. into square blocks of between 2 and 32 pixel edge length - is superimposed upon each frame from a sequence. 2-D image transformations of such predefined segments exploit the spatial correlation between adjacent pixels to compress the spatial intensity variations into a relatively small number of transform-domain coefficients.

HELLER 74 used a 4x4 Hadamard transform and transmitted the resulting coefficients with a fixed precision which had been selected for each coefficient according to its significance. Due to the usually high temporal correlation between adjacent TV frames, the transform coefficients do not change very much for corresponding segments from successive frames. In order to exploit this redundancy, the coded transform coefficients were only transmitted for every fourth segment within a frame. By suitably staggering the segments selected for transmission, the coded transform coefficients for each segment were transmitted every fourth frame. At the three intervening frames only the first three transform coefficients were updated, corresponding to the average intensity, a horizontal, and a vertical edge within the 4x4 segment. For these three coefficients, only the coarsely quantized differences between the current values and those most recently transmitted at the maximum predefined precision were sent. Frame memory requirements had been reduced from 128 down to 32 bits for each 4x4 segment by storing only the coded transform coefficients.

Although image quality appeared acceptable for stationary scenes at transmission rates down to 1 bit per pixel, nonstationary image areas showed disturbing effects at rates below 2 bits per pixel. Sending only coarsely quantized updates for three coefficients turned out to be insufficient for segments in nonstationary areas. A kind of frame repetition was used instead of the originally implemented transmission of coefficient differences in order to reduce the average rate from 2 bits down to 1 bit per pixel. Some other faults could be traced - see JONES 76 - to the fact that the fixed bit assignment did not allow the transmission of some occasionally large transform coefficient with sufficient precision. READER 75 pointed out that large coefficients are important despite their infrequent occurrence because they involve prominent features such as sharp high contrast edges - see also JONES 79. Adaptive coding is required to cope with such situations adequately - see PRATT 79 or HABIBI 77 for recent surveys on adaptive image coding.

The approaches to hybrid interframe coding investigated by ROESE and others differ from the work of HELLER and JONES in three aspects:

(i) The discrete cosine transform (DCT) or alternatively the Fourier transform (FT) was used on larger (16 x 16) segments.

(ii) Differential pulse code modulation (DPCM) techniques were employed to code the differences between corresponding transform coefficients from consecutive frames.

(iii) Rather than implementing the coder electronics, computer simulation experiments were performed which offered more freedom for experiments. Two series of 16 consecutive frames were digitized from 24 frames/sec motion pictures, with a resolution of 256x256x8 bit per frame.

With a DCT hybrid interframe coder at a transmission rate of 0.25 bit/pixel, ROESE and ROBINSON 75 obtained for a typical videotelephone "head and shoulder" scene an image quality which was comparable to the result of an intraframe coder requiring 2 bit/pixel. However, since performance of the hybrid interframe coder depends on exploiting temporal correlation, reduced levels of performance have to be anticipated for image sequences which are influenced by camera motion and therefore exhibit more changes between corresponding pixels from consecutive frames - see also ROESE et al. 77 .

In this context ROESE and ROBINSON 75 pointed out that certain kinds of camera motion such as panning yield an image sequence where successive frames differ essentially by a translation. In this case the Fourier transform appears theoretically attractive because the magnitude of the Fourier coefficients should remain essentially constant, the changes being reflected by a systematic variation of their phase factors. However, no practical experience with such an approach has been reported by them. HASKELL 74 suggested the application of such an approach not to the entire frame but only to the image of an object which was displaced from frame to frame by translational motion. However, the difficulties to reliably segment each frame into the moving object image and the stationary background let such an approach appear overly susceptible to noise. HASKELL 74 expected less difficulties if the Fourier coefficients were computed for interframe differences since then the segmentation problem would be circumvented. Provided the image of the moving object is displaced primarily by a translation, the Fourier coefficients obtained for successive frames should essentially differ by a phase shift only. This property would allow the transmission of the initial values of the Fourier coefficients and subsequently only the phase shifts. As another possibility, HASKELL 74 suggested that the expected phase shift be derived from an estimated displacement velocity of the nonstationary image component - see section 2.1.6 and 3.3. Using this phase shift together with the Fourier coefficients obtained from the current frame, the interframe differences related to this nonstationary image component could be estimated for the next frame and used as a predictor. Only deviations from interframe differences predicted in this manner needed to be transmitted. These ideas and experiences are in close analogy to investigations by ARKING, LO and ROSENFELD as well as LO and others - see ARKING et al. 75 - who attempted to obtain measurements of cloud displacement velocity from satellite images. It is not yet clear which additional conditions have to be obeyed in practice in order to derive reliable displacement estimates by analysing the phase shifts between corresponding Fourier coefficients from successive frames. However, in case the image sequence is obtained from a sensor moving along an approximately straight-line trajectory, the conditions are apparently favorable to pursue such an approach. PEARSON et al. 77 described a special purpose processor which estimated in real time the interframe displacement for two successive 128x128 videc images digitized at a rate of 30 images/sec. They extracted the phase-angle array from the cross-power spectrum and applied an inverse Fourier transform to it. If the second image would have been derived from the first one by a cyclical shift corresponding to the translation vector X, the inverse Fourier transform of the phase-angle array would result in a delta function at the location X. A search for the maximum in this inverse Fourier transform of the phase-angle array thus yielded an estimate of the displacement vector which appeared - according to PEARSON et al. 77 - to be fairly robust.

ROESE et al. 75 compared their hybrid interframe coders with a 3-D DCT transform coder applied to 16x16x16 pixel blocks from 16 consecutive frames and to a 3-D DPCM coder. At an average transmission rate of 1 bit/pixel, the hybrid DCT interframe coder yielded the smallest mean square coding error, the hybrid FT coder having only a slightly larger error. The 3-D DCT transform coder yielded larger errors than the hybrid coders but was still much better than the 3-D DPCM coder.

ROESE and PRATT 76 developed theoretical performance models for different interframe hybrid DCT/DPCM and 3-D DCT transform coders and substantiated their results by comparison with computer simulation experiments on the aforementioned test sequences.

ROESE et al. 77 refined this analysis and described a spatial adaptive technique whereby the parameters for the DPCM coding of each transform coefficient were derived from temporal difference statistics accumulated separately in each 16x16 segment for each coefficient during the coding process. For both the 3-D DCT transform coder and the adaptive hybrid DCT/DPCM coder no image degradation could be seen on their test sequences at rates down to 0.5 bit/pixel per frame.

Although coding efficiency increases with growing segment size, a pure interframe transform coder for blocks of 16x16x16 pixels appeared impractical. NATARAJAN and AHMED 77 studied a nonadaptive interframe transform coder based on DCT or alternatively Walsh-Hadamard transforms of 4x4x4 pixel blocks, using computer simulation experiments. They described a vector formalism which alleviated the time consuming address evaluations during computation of the 3-D transforms. They reported acceptable image quality while coding black/white broadcast TV pictures digitized into 416x476x6 bit per frame at a rate of 1 bit/pixel per frame.

KNAUER 75+76 described a real-time digital video processor to perform Hadamard transformations on 4x4x4 pixel blocks of video frames digitized into 512x525 pixels at 6 bit/pixel. The first coefficient of each 64-tuple reflects the average intensity in the 4x4x4 block whereas the remaining coefficients measure the relative variations within such a block along the horizontal, vertical, and temporal axis. Knauer adapted the quantization accuracy of the coding step to the amount of temporal variation determined for each block from the transform coefficients which reflect the changes along the time axis. At high temporal variations, an option giving high temporal and low spatial fidelity was used. At low temporal variations an option emphasizing high spatial fidelity at the expense of low temporal fidelity was activated. Acceptable subjective image quality has been reported with 1 bit/pixel per frame.

2.1.3 Towards variable spatial segmentation

LIMB 79 investigated attempts to formulate objective criteria which closely reflect human judgement on image quality. Further discussions of related topics can be found in SAKRISON 79 , RUBINSTEIN and LIMB 78 , LIMB and RUBINSTEIN 78 . According to LIMB 79, the visibility of distortions in relatively homogeneous image areas appears to influence human judgement to a large extent. This may explain why the root mean square error (RMSE) seems to be an acceptable objective image quality criterion for single images. Regarding image sequences, however, KNAUER and others have pointed out that mean square error and similar analytical measures do not model adequately the complex motion detection functions of the human eye. Similar observations caused investigations into the design of quantizers for real-time Hadamard transform coding at Bell Laboratories - see MOUNTS et al. 77 and NETRAVALI et al. 77 . Spatial correlation beyond the transformed 2x2 pixel segment was exploited to predict coefficients for neighboring segments. These authors demonstrated that predictions could be achieved which are better than the mere use of corresponding coefficients from the previous block .

STULLER and NETRAVALI 79 extended the inter-segment descriptor prediction into the time dimension in order to estimate displacement parameters for predefined transform coding segments. Inter-segment prediction of temporal or spatial descriptor values is but one possibility of exploiting the correlation between adjacent segments. An alternative is the aggregation of neighboring segments with similar descriptor values into clusters and then coding the cluster description. HILBERT 75 studied a clustering approach for coding of multispectral satellite images. HABIBI and SAMULON 75 investigated this approach and compared it with other coding methods - see, too, HABIBI 77 and the literature quoted there. As a rationale for spatially adaptive coding, HABIBI 77 formulated the observation that images in general depict combinations of objects which show up as image areas with varying degrees of visible edges and internal detail. Coding may adapt to the individual descriptor values determined for each predefined segment or for an aggregation of segments. If the predefined segments are small relative to the resulting clusters, the 2-D cluster shape may acquire importance as a descriptor and appropriate image segmentation becomes a dominant problem as in the case of pictorial pattern recognition and image understanding. The work of GUPTA and WINTZ 75 exemplified this use of segmentation both for coding and interpretation purposes. Although the work of COLEMAN and ANDREWS 79 has been performed in the context of image understanding projects, their basic assumptions and methodological approach can be seen as an extension of the ones discussed here.

If efficient coding is the goal, PRATT 78 categorized such approaches as feature coding. COOPER 74 described attempts to decompose images which may arise in teleconference or remote classroom situations into a hierarchy of subpicture clusters down to primitive descriptors such as circles, line segments, rectangles, ellipses, triangles and others. Efficient coding of these primitives and their relation in the hierarchy could be obtained at the price of considerable segmentation and classification efforts. COOPER 76 pursued these ideas further, specializing on line drawing images such as blackboard contents or charts. An analogous approach to the coding of satellite or aerial images with dominant line structures like roads, rivers, railway tracks, has been discussed by CHIEN and PETERSON 77 . The goal had been to achieve compression ratios of the order of 100 : 1 by using criteria which emphasized the image semantics rather than faithful reproduction of pictorial details. Neither the algorithms nor the required processing capacity are available yet to solve such tasks satisfactorily.

Recognition of edge structures, however, has been exploited for improved coding without pushing to the limits of pictorial pattern recognition or image understanding. KESKES et al. 79 recently reported new statistical measurements about edges in TV-pictures and included references to earlier work. SCHREIBER et al. 59 described separate encoding for high and low spatial frequency components in a 1-D TV-line signal. This approach has been extended to 2-D greyvalue TV images by GRAHAM 67 . The image should be subjected in parallel to a low-pass filter and an edge detector using a gradient or Laplacian operator. The results of both manipulations had to be encoded separately for transmission, applying methods adapted to the different characteristics of the two resulting images. The predominant 2-D continuity of edge elements could be exploited for efficient encoding of contours. Isolated edge elements and very short open contour segments were suppressed as irrelevant. At the receiver, the contour image had to be convolved with a suitably designed filter to produce a "synthetic highs" image which was subsequently combined with the low-pass picture to yield a reconstituted result.

This approach invites comparison with the recent investigations by MARR and coworkers - see MARR and POGGIO 79 , GRIMSON and MARR 79 , MARR et al. 79 . Both images from a stereo pair were subjected to a Gaussian spatial filter in order to limit spatial frequency variations. Zero crossings in the output of a subsequently applied Laplacian operator corresponded to edges in the filtered images. Location, orientation and greyvalue gradient attributes of such zero crossings were used as image descriptors which appeared to be well suited for matching between two images of a stereo pair. These operations were repeated using Gaussian bandpass filters with increasing frequency limits in order to gradually refine the stereo match from large disparities at low spatial resolution to small disparities at high resolution. Although no mathematical proof has yet been given that a 2-D image could be reconstructed from the image descriptors used for stereo matching, algorithms have been mentioned which performed such reconstructions for some test images. A judgement on the final merits of this approach should be postponed, however, until it has been applied by independent groups to real-world images. An extension of this approach to matches between temporal image pairs has been described recently by MARR and ULLMAN 79, BATALI and ULLMAN 79. It appears interesting to explore the application of such an approach to image coding.

If the low-pass filtered image is more or less homogeneous, it might be suppressed entirely. Such a modification of 2-D contour coding for binary pictures has been discussed by

SCHREIBER et al. 68 . GONZALEZ and WINTZ 77 described the relevant algorithms in more detail. ROBINSON 76+77 presented a design which combined several directional gradient operators with a connectivity analysis for edge elements found within a 3x3 pixel neighborhood after adaptive thresholding on the gradient magnitude. This design has been implemented for real-time processing of TV-frame sequences - see ROBINSON and REIS 77 . An extension of such a design to incorporate a low-pass filtered image has been discussed by these authors based on successive greyvalue averaging for pixel neighborhoods as given in a quartic picture tree (QPT) - see, e.g., PAVLIDIS 77 for an exposition of this data structure.

Edge elements may not only appear in the description of region boundaries, their spatial distribution - texture - can be an important characteristic of the interior of image segments. LIMB 69 explored adaptive coding based on the distinction between image areas with high and low detail, i.e. conceptually generalizing from the edge to the textured region. He introduced a hysteresis into the transition process from low-to high-detail regions and back. This resulted in larger aggregations with an accompanying reduction in the coding overhead to signal a transition. This hysteresis approach was applied later to improve the segmentation in the context of conditional replenishment coding - see CONNOR et al. 73 . In order to code large digitized images for efficient storage in an image data base, LABONTE 77 applied the same approach - separating the image into regions with high and low spatial detail. Low detail regions were aggregated using a processing structure based on a quartic picture tree (QPT). As a result, the spatial resolution of the coded version varied according to the spatial detail of the original image. A conceptually analogous approach to coding binary images for database applications has been reported by AOKI 79 . The image has been described as a set of rectangles covering uniform image areas and explicit point-to-point data outside these rectangles. The algorithm to find suitably large uniform rectangles employed a QPT datastructure.

Rather than transmitting the contour information to the receiver, ZSCHUNKE 77 evaluated a modified DPCM system proposed by him in 1973 which exploited the direction attribute in addition to the location attribute connected with contour elements. His proposal can be understood as a refinement of the

2-D spatial prediction investigated by CONNOR et al. 71 . An estimate of the contour direction based on edge elements detected in preceding TV lines has been used to adapt the prediction of a greyvalue transition in the current TV line. Since a coarse quantization step for the difference between predicted and actual greyvalue is acceptable at strong transitions, the contour element prediction has been used also to switch the quantizing characteristic of the DPCM coder. Fine quantization steps required for fairly homogeneous regions could be replaced by coarse steps at the predicted contour locations, thus alleviating the slope overloading. Computer simulations demonstrated that this approach had advantages for high contrast images with smoothly bent and long contours. BAUCH et al. 74 extended this proposal to interframe coding and suggested extrapolation from moving edge elements in the current frame to predict the displacement and amplitude for a moving element in the following frame.

An approach towards adaptive coding based on local contour predictions analogous to ZSCHUNKE 77 has been described by COHEN and ADOUL 76 . Their non linear prediction can be looked at as a 2-D variant of the approach by DUKHOVICH and O'NEAL 78 who applied an analogous technique to a three-dimensional prediction in raster space and time (see section 2.1.6). A thorough review of predictive coding techniques can be found in MUSMANN 79 .

2.1.4 Spatial segmentation based on temporal characteristics

Simultaneous minimization of visual quality degradation and spatial as well as temporal resolution places a premium on appropriate segmentation of image frames from a sequence into stationary and nonstationary components. The sustained efforts to reduce the transmission bandwidth for image sequences resulted in "moving object detectors" that became comparable to those developed in attempts towards semantic understanding of image sequences. Tracing this development for the class of "pixel change detection" interframe coders will provide the guideline for their discussion. All approaches considered here reconstitute displays of acceptable quality for scenes with small to moderate changes as they occur, e.g., in video telephone or TV-conferencing applications. Progress can be recognized from the gradual reduction of transmission bandwidth despite transition to finer image rasters.

The original conditional replenishment technique - see MOUNTS 69 - transmitted 8-bit PCM greyvalues for each pixel (171 lines per frame with 120 pixels per line) that differed by more than the given threshold from the corresponding pixel in the preceding frame. No aggregation of neighboring changed pixels into a one- or two-dimensional nonstationary image component was attempted. An average transmission rate of 1 bit per pixel could be achieved although the instantaneous rate would fluctuate considerably, thus necessitating substantial transmission buffers.

PEASE and LIMB 71 obviated such large transmission buffers by always sampling every other pixel within a scanline (staggering the sample positions from line to line and inverting the sampling pattern after every frame). They aggregated positions of significantly changed pixels within a scanline into a one-dimensional nonstationary segment. At the receiver, pixels at positions sampled in the current frame would be displayed at the updated intensity value. Pixels not sampled in the current frame would be displayed with the same intensity as used in the previous frame if they belonged to a stationary segment (lower temporal resolution). In nonstationary segments, however, intensities of pixels not sampled in the current frame would be linearly interpolated between the updated values of their two immediate neighbors within their scanline (lower spatial resolution).

Using estimated statistical distributions for three categories of greyvalue differences, BROFFERIO and ROCCA 77 classified the pixels within a video scanline into three segment types based on the best predictor of their greyvalues from those previously encountered. Greyvalues for pixels in background areas and those representing objects with negligible motion could be best predicted from pixels observed at the same raster position in the previous frame. Greyvalues for pixels belonging to object images which move with an already known velocity could be obtained by bicubic interpolation from earlier segments attributed to this object image. Greyvalues for remaining pixels were predicted from a neighbor that immediately preceded them in a scanline. Following this segmentation, the predictor sequence and the prediction errors had to be transmitted. In a simulation study they assumed that a single displacement vector was sufficient to characterize the translation of all nonstationary image components within the frame. Methods to estimate the displacement vector are discussed in sections 2.1.6 and 3. Their simulation results indicated that movement compensation offered the potential to halve the bit rate required for coding. This expectation seems to be slightly overoptimistic if it is compared with more recent results by NETRAVALI and coworkers as discussed in section 2.1.6.

These approaches did not attempt to exploit correlations between the stationary or nonstationary segments from neighboring scanlines. An attempt to extend the definition of a nonstationary segment to two dimensions vastly overshooted this secondary goal from a semantic point of view although it represented a further progress towards the primary goal of bandwidth compression. Rather than detecting tightly enclosed nonstationary segments within an image, an entire field (one of the two linewise interlaced half-frames) would be declared nonstationary if it contained 512 or more pixels (about 2 % of a field) which exhibited an intensity difference between frames of more than 15 (out of 256) greylevels - see LIMB and PEASE 71 . A switch from this "nonstationary field" mode back to the "stationary field" mode would occur after less than 512 pixels exceeded the intensity difference threshold of 15 greylevels in an even-numbered field of a nonstationary field series.

The average transmission rate of 1 bit per pixel obtained with the conditional replenishment coder of MOUNTS 69 initiated a search for methods to alleviate the concomitant transmission buffer problems by smoothing the large fluctuations of the instantaneous transmission rate. Among other techniques, CANDY et al. 71 clustered pixels within a scanline that exhibited significant interframe intensity differences into runs - i.e. 1-dimensional nonstationary segments. As the activity in the recorded scene grew, the runs would increase in length but not in number to any great degree. As another saving step a significant interframe intensity difference was ignored if it was isolated within a scanline by at least two preceding and two following pixels with no significant deviations from their greylevels in the previous frame.

Aggregation of changes into runs together with suppression of isolated changes could not, however, decrease fluctuations of the instantaneous transmission rate to the desired degree. If image nonstationarity - measured by the filled fraction of the transmission buffer - increased, the coder of CANDY et al. 71 could switch into other modes (in addition to the stationary and nonstationary segment modes) and reduce the spatial resolution by 2:1 horizontal subsampling. Moreover, the threshold for detecting significant changes would be raised in steps from 1.5 % to 3 % of the maximum intensity amplitude (from 4 to 7 out of 256 levels). A more detailed comparative discussion of the last four approaches by MOUNTS 69, PEASE and LIMB 71, LIMB and PEASE 71, and CANDY et al. 71 can be found in HASKELL et al. 72 .

In order to suppress uncorrelated interframe differences due to noise, CONNOR et al. 73 exploited the spatial and temporal correlations between interframe differences in nonstationary image areas at two levels. The first level filtered the interframe differences before subjecting them simultaneously to three different threshold functions. At the second level, the resulting significant changes were evaluated in the context of a 2-dimensional sliding mask environment around the pixel of interest. The exploitation of spatial and temporal correlation among interframe differences yielded three dissimilarity predicates at each rasterposition:

* a moving edge predicate;
* a conservative and
* a sensitive
  low-textured nonstationarity ("moving flat area") predicate.

The premise that nonstationary image components are spatially and temporally contiguous was exploited by CONNOR et al. 73 at the second level where each pixel was assigned to either the stationary or the nonstationary subcategory. This decision was based on the above predicate values in a sliding mask (3 lines wide by 8 rasterpositions long) environment around the pixel of interest by an N (= 4-9) out of M (= 24) vote. If the transmission buffer filled up - i. e. for "moderate" versus no or slow movement - interframe differences within nonstationary image components would only be transmitted for every other field. Linear interpolation between corresponding pixels of the two neighboring updated fields would be used to display pixels in nonstationary image areas of fields which were not updated. This conditional - i.e. dependent on the nonstationarity of the pixel in question - field interpolation is also called 'conditional vertical subsampling'. As such it represents still another way to exploit the spatial correlation of nonstationary image components - essentially the conditional version of a technique employed by LIMB and PEASE 71 for entire fields. Comparing this approach by CONNOR et al. 73 to the earlier one of CANDY et al. 71 we see as important differences the considerably improved "nonstationary component (moving area)" detector and the application of conditional field interpolation.

The ideas reflected in the design of this nonstationary component detector can be found in a number of subsequently published approaches to bandwidth compression of TV-frame sequences. A theoretical analysis of interframe differences in stationary and nonstationary areas has been presented by CONNOR and LIMB 74 . This is important for a good discrimination between slowly changing small subimages and noise. The observation that activity in a scene tends to be spatially coherent motivated HASKELL 76a to the following proposal: conditional replenishment coders should specify the position of nonstationary segments within a scanline relative to the nearest neighbor in the same or the preceding line. The use of variable length address codes could then lead to reduced transmission requirements for address information. However, since this constitutes only a small fraction of the transmitted information (less than 20 %) no substantial overall gains could be realized in this manner. Approaches based on movement compensation reduced the bit rate required for transmission of prediction errors to the extent that the addressing information became a significant fraction of the total bit rate - see the discussion of NETRAVALI and ROBBINS 79 in section 2.1.6. Under such conditions the suggestions of HASKELL 76a acquired practical importance.

2.1.5 Reduction of spatial bandwidth in moving subimages

Due to psycho physical effects in the human visual system and the intensity averaging for moving object images on a video camera target, reduction of spatial resolution might be accepted by a human observer for nonstationary image areas but not for stationary ones. KINUHATA et al. 78 exploited this phenomenon to switch a digital TV standards converter - e.g. PAL to NTSC - from a high spatial resolution mode in stationary image areas to a lower spatial resolution mode in nonstationary image areas. The latter mode avoided disturbing effects at the contours of moving object images. MIYAHARA 75 subjectively assessed the degradation of picture quality due to blur in subimages which corresponded to moving objects. Based on these investigations he estimated that the signal bandwidth could be reduced within moving subimages by a factor of 3.5. The displacement between two consecutive frames which could just be perceived in these experiments turned out to be about one third of the horizontal or vertical spacing between pixel centers. This happens to coincide with the estimated precision which should be achieved by an algorithm for determining the displacement velocity of moving object images in TV-frame sequences (see paragraph IV of CAFFORIO and ROCCA 76).

Similar observations by others had already resulted in the suggestion to exploit this effect for coding improvements. Conceptually, such suggestions represent an intermediate step between the qualitative observation of nonstationarity in time and the introduction of a quantitative displacement - i.e. velocity - attribute for nonstationary subimage areas.

LIPPEL 79 considered each frame of a PCM-coded video sequence as a stack of bit planes and suggested that the transmission rate could be reduced by temporal subsampling of individual bit planes. The temporal frequency for sampling each bit plane should decrease with decreasing significance of the corresponding bit position in the PCM code word for the intensity. 3-dimensional ordered dither should be added to the video signal prior to quantization in order to let the aliasing effects appear less objectionable to the human viewer.

ROCCA 69 investigated trading greyvalue resolution against spatial resolution for more compact transmission of nonstationary image components. GABOR and HILL 61 - see also JAESCHKE and OST 72 - proposed to reduce the resolution in nonstationary image areas by transmitting only every other frame and interpolating pixel values for dropped frames from the transmitted preceding and succeeding frames. THOMA 72 combined differential pulse code modulation (DPCM) with frame repetition in 2:1 dot interlace for videotelephone signals. FUKINUKI et al. 76 suggested a recursive filter which suppressed higher spatial frequencies in nonstationary image components and thereby reduced the prediction error by a factor of three without discernible visual quality degradation.

The number of intraframe as well as interframe differences within nonstationary areas tends to increase with growing displacement velocity of the subimage corresponding to a moving object. As WENDT 73 pointed out, the magnitude of interframe differences increases, too, whereas the magnitude of intraframe differences decreases with growing velocity - due to the greater correlation between neighboring pixels along the displacement direction. WENDT 73 was able to obtain good results with 4-bit intraframe DPCM coding for nonstationary subimages where 4-bit interframe DPCM yielded unsatisfactory results.

LIMB et al. 74 applied an algorithm similar to CONNOR et al. 73 for segmentation into nonstationary and stationary image areas, but transmitted updating information for nonstationary areas as intraframe differences. Using a variable wordlength code for these intraframe pixel-to-pixel differences had the tendency to decrease the transmission rate with growing displacement velocity because the pixel values became more similar in image areas corresponding to moving objects. This counterbalanced the size increase for the nonstationary image areas.

HASKELL and SCHMIDT 75 described a videotelephone coder explicitly designed for transmission of slowly changing graphics at a rate of 200 kbit/sec (0.1 bit/sec for the 1 MHz signal) - emphasizing high spatial resolution at the cost of temporal resolution. The 7-bit PCM input signal had been temporally filtered by averaging it with a frame-repeated signal. The approach of CANDY et al. 71 had been employed for segmentation into nonstationary versus stationary image areas. When the transmission buffer filled up, the adaptive linear predictive coder allowed the dropping of every other field, subsampling every other pixel within a line, and dropping every other frame without affecting its performance. This reduced the spatial resolution of nonstationary image areas in proportion to the amount of change and restored full resolution as quickly as possible after changes ceased.

Since the bandwidth of a videotelephone is insufficient for teleconference applications, HASKELL et al. 77 investigated the design of a coding system for a transmission rate of 1.5 Megabit/sec. They designed twelve control modes into their experimental interframe coder for 4-MHz monochrome NTSC signals (525 lines with 510 pixels each) from a high quality video camera (55 dB SNR). With such a large number of modes they investigated the combination of bit rate reduction techniques developed for interframe coding of 1-MHz videotelephone signals described in the preceding paragraph and some extensions thereof. They included conditional vertical in-field subsampling, predictive coding of interframe differences, and temporal filtering to blur "moving" image areas in proportion to their "velocity". The method employed by HASKELL et al. 77 to separate nonstationary from stationary image components slightly modified the approach reported by CONNOR et al. 73 .

A concise discussion of these investigations can be found in HASKELL 76b and HASKELL 79 .

YASUDA et al. 77 developed an interframe coder for the transmission of 4-MHz NTSC greyvalue as well as color signals based on predictive coding of interframe differences. The expected difference between the pixel of interest in the current frame and the corresponding one in the previous frame was assumed to be equal to the difference obtained between the corresponding predecessor pixels in this line. The deviation of the actual from the predicted difference was suitably quantized and transmitted using a variable wordlength code.

To realize further advantages from the use of a variable wordlength code, YASUDA et al. 77 introduced an "activity dependent" temporal filter: the observed interframe difference was multiplied by a factor between 0.5 and 1 where the precise actual value depended on the filled fraction of the transmission buffer. This blurred "moving" image areas in rough proportion to their "velocity" in the same manner - but to a larger degree - as the integrating effect of the camera target. Application of these techniques segment an image only implicitly into stationary and nonstationary components: substantial deviations from the predicted interframe differences tended to cluster at the transition zones between stationary and nonstationary image areas.

The bandwidth reduction achievable with these techniques alone was insufficient. If the transmission buffer filled up, the authors not only applied horizontal and vertical line subsampling, but in addition determined whether an interframe difference exceeded a threshold for a pixel group in a non updated line . Such a group (called a segment by YASUDA et al. 77) would be identified as nonstationary and its pixel values would be obtained at the receiver by averaging the updated vertical neighbors. Pixels in stationary groups of lines not updated would be repeated from the previous frame.

Based on earlier experiences - see HELLER 74 and JONES 76 - as well as a proposal by READER 75 , JONES 77 applied the conditional replenishment approach to the Hadamard transform coefficients of 8x8 segments rather than directly to the pixels. The coding of transmitted coefficients was adapted to the lower spatial resolution in nonstationary segments. High quality graphics and adequate motion rendition has been reported for teleconferencing and remote classroom situations.

The preceding discussion made no explicit distinction between a nonstationary image component and the image of a moving object. Even in the case where the scene illumination and the camera parameters remain constant, however, these notions are not equivalent: the nonstationary image component obtained by comparing two consecutive frames using change detection techniques comprises not only the image of a moving object but in addition the background uncovered by the displacement of the object. In the course of research to achieve bandwidth compression down to transmission rates of 64 kbits/sec for videotelephone signals, KLIE 78 suggested and implemented an ingenious idea to separate these two contributions to the nonstationary image component. To suppress aliasing errors due to subsampling along the time axis, he included a temporal low pass filter into his experimental setup (compare HASKELL et al. 77 , YASUDA et al. 77). Theoretical analysis of this configuration showed that the temporal low pass filter affected, too, the spatial frequency distribution within each frame. By appropriate choice of the filter parameters KLIE 78 could arrange that this "crosstalk" effect would be restricted to image areas representing objects with nonzero velocity whereas background area with zero velocity would not be affected - even if it were just uncovered by a moving object.

By comparing a signal that had been subjected to a temporal low pass filter with an appropriately delayed version of the unfiltered signal, KLIE 78 was able to derive a signal which deviated from zero only in the image area corresponding to a moving object. Converting this signal into a mask KLIE then separated the uncovered background within a nonstationary image component from the image of a moving object. Therefore, his "motion" detector differs from his "change" detector.

This approach assumed that the entire subimage corresponding to a moving object could be assigned to the nonstationary category by evaluation of interframe differences. The change detector of KLIE 78 consisted of a carefully balanced multiple threshold combination of several descriptors depending on one through five consecutive pixels within one scanline. Problems should therefore be expected in the following constellations:

(i) The image of the moving object contains homogeneous segments which extend along a scanline significantly longer than the frame-to-frame object image displacement along the scanline. Such a situation has been discussed in a slightly different context by JAIN and NAGEL 78+79 .

(ii) The displacement of a moving object subimage along a scanline is a small integer multiple of the wavelength for spatial frequency components which dominate the greyvalue distribution within this subimage (stroboscopic effects).

In such situations the change detector employed by KLIE 78 would have difficulties to properly classify the entire subimage of a moving object as nonstationary. Similar problems are to be expected for subimage displacements perpendicular to a scanline. However, further efforts are underway to overcome these difficulties (MUSMANN 80). The object image velocity evaluated by this approach depended - due to the temporal filtering - on more than just two consecutive frames. The different formalisms used by KLIE 78 and KNAUER 75+76 should not distract from the important parallelism in the systematic exploitation of the same basic assumptions underlying their approaches. The explicit determination of a 2-D frame-to-frame displacement - i.e. velocity - attribute for nonstationary image components can be understood as conceptual extensions of the approaches discussed in this paragraph.

2.1.6 Interframe coding based on movement compensation

Assume an image sequence comprises a stationary background in front of which an object image is translated from frame to frame by a 2-D displacement vector (dx, dy). Within the interior of this moving subimage, a pixel at position (x, y) in the previous frame constitutes a very good prediction for the pixel at position (x+dx, y+dy) in the current frame. Larger deviations from this prediction would only be expected for pixels in the vicinity of the subimage boundary.

ROCCA 69 suggested that this consideration be exploited in order to reduce the transmission rate by transmitting first the displacement vector and subsequently only the differences between the greyvalues predicted on this basis and the actual ones. To accommodate more general situations - e.g. more than one moving object or panning of the camera - ROCCA proposed to subdivide each frame into square segments of fixed size. The displacement vector for each segment had to be determined by a search for the maximum cross-correlation between the segment from the previous frame and segments from a neighborhood about its center in the current frame. HASKELL and LIMB 72 designed a similar approach and HASKELL 75 pointed out that a simple extension of a technique described by MANASSE 67 could also be used for such purposes.

Unless the exact position of the cross-correlation maximum would be interpolated, such a - computationally still too expensive - approach yields only integer values for the components of the displacement vector. A number of different proposals have been investigated which are based on the considerations outlined above. Such techniques developed for efficient transmission of TV frames exhibit striking analogies with approaches to visual object tracking and to understanding the behavior of moving objects recorded in image sequences. Therefore, the underlying concepts will be discussed for all these approaches together in a separate section. The following paragraphs are restricted to point out the implications for interframe coding.

ROCCA and ZANOLETTI 72 modeled a video image as a mosaic of polygonally bounded homogeneous zones with randomly varying size and greyvalue. They further assumed that such a mosaic changed slowly from frame to frame. They used this model to derive the average transmission rate for a movement compensation coder as a function of the size of homogeneous zones.

HASKELL 75 investigated the greyvalue prediction Pz for the current pixel Z formed as a linear combination from a set of 22 pixels Yi selected from a 5x5 environment centered around Z according to the following rules:

(i) no pixels from the corners of the 5x5 square;

(ii) from the current field - due to the usual raster scan sequence - only pixels within this environment to the left and above Z are encountered prior to Z and thus were taken into account;

(iii) from the immediately preceding field - i.e. half a frame period ago - all pixels within a 3x3 environment around Z were taken into account;

(iv) from the field a full frame period ago, all pixels within the 5x5 environment around Z except those in the corners were taken into account.

Apart from entropy measurements for different fixed linear combinations from the above pixel set, HASKELL 75 investigated the entropy for linear combinations with weighting coefficients adapted to the individual test frame pairs. In order to accommodate even displacement variations within a field, he subdivided a field into fixed blocks. The weighting coefficients for the linear combination used as predictor Pz were determined for each block separately by minimizing the square of the difference (Z-Pz) summed over all pixels within a block. Although HASKELL 75 had only frame pairs available for his experiments, his results clearly showed how the optimum weighting coefficients reflected the frame-to-frame displacement of the translated object image. The implications of these investigations are also discussed in HASKELL 76b and HASKELL 79 .

REIS et al. 76 described a noise-resistant low bit rate digital video link for remotely piloted vehicles (RPVs). It had been based on a digital implementation of a fast 2-D rationalized Haar transform using a combination of zonal and adaptive threshold compression techniques. Due to its simplicity, LIPPMANN 79 favored an approach rather similar to the fixed linear combination of HASKELL 75 for such an application. LIPPMANN 79 suggested that the central - i.e.

target - area of the field of view should be coded with a higher accuracy than the rest of the picture.

Although the approach of DUKHOVICH and O'NEAL 78 did not explicitly address movement compensation, it will be discussed here to compare it with the work of HASKELL 75 . DUKHOVICH and O'NEAL 78 defined an environment around the pixel Z similar to the one chosen by HASKELL 75. They embedded this environment into a 3-D coordinate system. The units for the two spatial and the time axes were defined in such a way that they could select three mutually orthogonal planes in the 3-D space all of which contained the pixel Z. Three categories of pixel combinations were investigated, each category containing pixels from only one of these three planes. Threshold decisions selected one predictor from each category as a so-called representative for that plane. A linear combination of these representatives was used as predictor for the intensity at Z. The weights in this linear combination were determined from the requirement that the mean squared prediction error within each block of 36x36 pixels in 8 consecutive frames had to be minimized. The key difference between this approach and the one by HASKELL 75 consisted in the fact that these authors used a nonlinear relationship in order to predict the intensity at position Z from those of its environment whereas HASKELL 75 employed a linear relationship. In a way, DUKHOVICH and O'NEAL 78 imposed a structure on the possible spatio-temporal greyvalue variations which were admitted as a basis for prediction of the intensity at Z. This concept is analogous to the one which forms the basis for the movement compensation coders to be discussed in the remaining part of this section.

LIMB and MURPHY 75a were the first to report on an implementation which determined the absolute frame-to-frame displacement of a single object translated with constant velocity parallel to the scanlines of a recording TV-camera. A slight modification of this circuit enabled them to determine the sign in addition to the magnitude of the velocity of the object image - see LIMB and MURPHY 75b . CAFFORIO and ROCCA 76 generalized this approach in order to determine both velocity components - parallel as well as perpendicular to the scanlines. Moreover, their approach enabled them to determine the velocity of more than a single moving object in the field of view, provided the object images were sufficiently large and moved with sufficiently different velocities. Their analysis suggested that spatial low-pass filtering of interframe differences should improve the velocity estimate which indeed could be demonstrated by computer simulations using digitized videotelephone signals.

FUKINUKI 78 had derived the same relation as CAFFORIO and ROCCA 76 to compute the frame-to-frame displacement from the intraframe greyvalue gradient and the interframe difference - see section 3.2 . A single displacement vector for the entire image of a moving object would be appropriate only in the rare situations of pure translation parallel to the image plane and negligible changes due to variations in perspective and illumination. Since a displacement vector derived under these assumptions might not result in optimal predictions for all pixel itensities, FUKINUKI 78 divided the image into fixed 16x16 pixel windows and used a mean-square - error approach to estimate a displacement vector individually for each window.

Considerable progress in this direction - improved coding due to spatially adapted displacement estimates for movement compensation - has been achieved in recent investigations of NETRAVALI and coworkers. Let the image of an object point have been observed at time t with the 2-D coordinate vector X in the image plane. Assume that object translation during a frame period Dt caused this position to be reached from an image plane location represented by a coordinate vector X-DX at time t-Dt. Provided the perspective projection and the object illumination remained essentially the same during this translation, the image intensity I(X-DX,t-Dt) should be a good predictor for the value of I(X,t). NETRAVALI and ROBBINS 79 introduced an estimate estDX for the frame-to-frame displacement at the pixel position X and defined the "Displaced Frame Difference" DFD by

$$DFD(X,estDX) = I(X,t) - I(X-estDX,t-Dt).$$

This scalar function of two vector variables, X and estDX, represents the movement compensated prediction error for the intensity at pixel position X. The corresponding temporal prediction not compensated for object motion had been denoted as "Frame Difference" FD with

$$FD(X) = I(X,t) - I(X,t-Dt).$$

NETRAVALI and ROBBINS 79 proposed to minimize the squared

prediction error SQUARE(DFD(X,estDX)) by suitable modification of estDX using a gradient descent procedure. Since applying this approach to each pixel until convergence would make any real-time implementation prohibitively expensive, they suggested that this approach be employed recursively while advancing according to the scanning order from pixel Xi-1 to Xi. They therefore updated estDXi - the estimated displacement vector at pixel position Xi - based on the preceding displacement estimate estDXi-1 derived for pixel position Xi-1 by subtracting a fraction epsilon of the gradient of the squared prediction error:

$$\begin{aligned} \mathrm{estDXi} = {} & \mathrm{estDXi{-}1} \\ & - (\mathrm{epsilon}/2) * \mathrm{GRAD}(\mathrm{SQUARE}(\mathrm{DFD}(\mathrm{Xi}, \mathrm{estDXi{-}1}))) \end{aligned}$$

where the gradient had to be taken with respect to estDXi-1. This could be simplified to

$$\begin{aligned} \mathrm{estDXi} = {} & \mathrm{estDXi{-}1} \\ & - \mathrm{epsilon} * \mathrm{SIGN}\ (\ \mathrm{DFD}\ (\ \mathrm{Xi}\ ,\ \mathrm{estDXi{-}1}\ )\ ) \\ & * \mathrm{SIGN}\ (\ \mathrm{grad}\ (\ \mathrm{I}\ (\mathrm{Xi}-[\mathrm{estDXi{-}1}]\ ,\ \mathrm{t{-}Dt})\ )\ ) \end{aligned}$$

with SIGN(Z) = Z / |Z| and [estDXi-1] representing estDXi-1 rounded to the nearest integer. The gradient in this case had to be taken with respect to X and had been approximated by element differences EDIF for the horizontal component and line differences LDIF for the vertical component. A 3-point linear interpolation was used to determine DFD(Xi,estDXi-1) for noninteger values of estDXi-1.

Displacement estimates estDX were updated only for pixel positions at which the frame difference FD(X) exceeded a higher threshold T2 (=3, with 255 as highest intensity) or the frame difference at X as well as some of its neighbors exceeded a lower threshold T1 = 1. If neither of these conditions were satisfied for the pixel Xi, the displacement estimated for the preceding pixel Xi-1 was assigned likewise to Xi. This corresponds to the hypothesis that pixel Xi belongs either to a stationary image component or to the homogeneous interior of a nonstationary image component.

The nonstationary image component was further segmented into

(i) compensible regions where movement compensated prediction was adequate and, therefore, no prediction error needed to be transmitted.

(ii) uncompensable regions where a prediction error had to be transmitted. This decision was taken if FD(X) > 3. To reduce the occurrence of isolated compensable pixels, runs of length 1, 2, or 3 of compensable pixels were bridged by declaring them uncompensable.

Simulation studies on several series of 64 consecutive digitized videotelephone frames with considerable activity - including camera panning - demonstrated that the movement compensated coder performed significantly better than a conditional replenishment coder, especially in highly nonstationary image areas. This is important because it helps to delay coder overloading. Compared to pure conditional replenishment coding, movement compensation reduced the average bit rate per field by about 30 - 40 %. This had the effect that the fraction of transmission rate required for addresses raised from about 15 - 30 % for a conditional replenishment coder to 50 - 65 % for the movement compensated coder. Under these circumstances the cluster addressing approach discussed by HASKELL 76a became significant.

ROBBINS and NETRAVALI 79 streamlined their approach further by two modifications.

(i) Let U, V, W denote three consecutive pixel positions within the preceding line of the same field that contained pixel X, V being vertically above X. FD(X) was chosen as prediction error at X

if $|DFD(U,estDV)| + |DFD(V,estDV)| + |DFD(W,estDV)|$ exceeded $FD(U) + FD(V) + FD(W)$,

otherwise DFD(X,estDV) was chosen.

The displacement estimate estDV for the pixel V vertically adjacent to X was used to reduce the timing constraints within the decision logic. This choice selected the smallest prediction error available.

(ii) The prediction error was only transmitted if it exceeded a certain threshold, i.e. for unpredictable pixels. Therefore, only two segment types had to be distinguished - namely segments with predictable or unpredictable pixels - with a consequent reduction in addressing information to be transmitted.

These modifications resulted in a bit rate reduction of 50-70 % for a rather active head-shoulder scene, compared to 30-40 % for the approach described by NETRAVALI and ROBBINS 79 and a bit rate of 100 % for conditional replenishment coding without movement compensation. For a videoframe sequence with violent motion, this approach yielded a bit rate reduction of 23 - 33 % compared with 15 - 25 % for the former approach. These figures could be further improved by making the decision between predictable and unpredictable slightly nonlocal, using in addition the prediction error of surrounding pixels already processed.

STULLER and NETRAVALI 79 extended the movement compensation approach to hybrid interframe/DPCM coding (compare section 2.1.2). The best predictor for the spatial transform coefficient of a block was no longer assumed to be the corresponding coefficient obtained for the same block of the previous frame. Within the image of a translating object it would be more appropriate to select as predictor the corresponding coefficient from a block positioned in the previous frame such that object translation could be compensated. The authors developed an algorithm which updated the displacement estimate recursively from coefficient to coefficient and verified it using a synthetical image. Since this algorithm is local in nature, it could be used to determine individual image displacements for several objects in the field of view. Provided the motion of an object image could be approximated by translation at least within the spatial dimensions of a transform block, this algorithm could cope with more complicated global movement of an extended object image. The performance of a coder based on this approach has been investigated by NETRAVALI and STULLER 79 .

2.1.7 Coding of color video sequences

An early implementation for frame-to-frame coding of NTSC color TV has been briefly mentioned by SCHAPHORST 69 .

IINUMA et al. 75 applied techniques very similar to those of CANDY et al. 71 and CONNOR et al. 73 - see section 2.1.4 - to investigate the transmission of regular 4-MHz NTSC color TV signals. The chrominance signal was extracted at a fifth of the sampling rate of the luminance signal, time compressed by a factor five and transmitted during the invisible period of a TV line in time division multiplex (TDM) with the luminance signal. The interframe coding techniques could be applied to the entire TDM signal as if it were a regular black/white video signal. For scenes with mostly moderate changes as in TV conferencing or videotelephone situations IINUMA et al. 75 obtained acceptable picture quality at a transmission bandwidth of 6.3 Mbit/s for color image sequences on a NTSC raster of 510 columns by 525 lines. YASUDA et al. 77 developed an interframe coder for transmission of 4-MHz NTSC color signals based on predictive coding of interframe differences - see section 2.1.5 where their corresponding approach to greyvalue video sequences has been discussed. The chrominance signals were treated similarly to the approach of IINUMA et al. 75 by subsampling, time compression and time division multiplex with the luminance signal. Measurements by YASUDA et al. 77 confirmed earlier investigations by IINUMA et al. 75 that the presence of the color signal increased the amount of information due to interframe differences within TV-image sequences from a variety of scenes by only 10 % of the information connected with luminance changes.

These approaches required the separation of the luminance component from the chrominance component since these components had to be processed in a different way. The usual filters employed for this separation let a residual chrominance component pass with the luminance component. If the interframe difference had been formed from the luminance component, the residual chrominance component was reinforced due to the 180 degree phase shift of the subcarrier whereas the luminance components in stationary image areas cancelled each other to a large extent. This effected a substantial contribution to the interframe difference which had to be evaluated for the discrimination between stationary and moving image areas and therefore resulted in an excessive number of pixels being declared as nonstationary. DUBOIS 79 proposed to pass the interframe difference signal through a chrominance-band rejection filter before further evaluation. Experiments employing this approach with a conditional replenishment coder as described by CANDY et al. 71 demonstrated that the reduction of the nonstationary area and improved prediction combined to decrease the bit rate by about 20 % without observable degradations in image quality. Different approaches to obtain good separation of a composite NTSC signal into luminance and chrominance components have been discussed by MAXEMCHUK and SHARMA 78 although these authors did not explore interframe coding.

ISHIGURO et al. 76 have chosen a different approach in order to use interframe coding for very high quality transmission of NTSC color TV signals at rates of 16-32 Mbit/sec. They separated the luminance and chrominance components by a reversible orthogonal transformation which converted the composite signal of two horizontal lines into a line sum - mainly corresponding to the luminance - and a line difference corresponding mainly to the chrominance signal. In this way they prevented that the chrominance signal remained in the frame difference due to sub-carrier phase reversal between successive frames. Moreover, the frame difference signal was subjected to a nonlinear filter which acted as a temporal low pass for small difference amplitudes, essentially suppressing random and feedback quantization noise. Larger frame differences - mainly caused by motion in the scene - would be left almost unaffected thus avoiding blur of moving objects. These techniques were combined with known ones such as variable length coding in order to bring the transmission down without visibly impairing image quality.

The observation that chrominance changes contributed only about 10 % to the transmission rate may be related to the observation by NETRAVALI and RUBINSTEIN 77 that noise is less visible around sharp spatial luminance transitions than around chrominance transitions. Apparently most chrominance transitions accompany luminance transitions. NETRAVALI 78 exploited this to adapt a filter for the chrominance component on the basis of a control signal derived from the luminance component. It will be interesting to compare these observations with experiences in the segmentation of color TV frames for interpretation purposes.

Further information about coding of color TV image sequences can be found in HASKELL 79 . HABIBI and BATSON 78 discussed the application of such techniques for video communication with the Space Shuttle. Intraframe coding approaches to color TV have been treated recently by OHIRA et al. 78 as well as SAWADA and KOTERA 78a+78b . FREI and BAXTER 77 discussed a distortion measure for color images. The earlier literature about coding of color TV has been very well surveyed by BAUCH et al. 74 and more recently by MUSMANN 79 .

2.1.8 Discussion

Four considerations suggest that scene analysis on image sequences may profit from paying closer attention to the work on interframe coding:

(i) The variety of techniques for comparing image frames and for segmenting them into nonstationary and stationary areas;

(ii) The fairly general assumptions about the contents of image sequences that form the basis for these approaches;

(iii) The efforts to establish objective quality criteria for judging the results of different approaches;

(iv) The possibility of a transfer of techniques from one field to the other. For example, in bandwidth compression experiments for color TV, chrominance changes contributed only about 10 % of the information that had to be transmitted due to luminance changes caused by motion (IINUMA et al. 75 , YASUDA et al. 77). Can the scene analysis of image sequences concentrate on luminance changes to a similar extent ?

Coding approaches for image sequences have been presented as a progression from the local, pixel oriented view without regard to the semantic content of images towards a more global, object oriented view. Efforts to improve interframe coding resulted in techniques for extracting a concise description for spatial and temporal variations in the greyvalues or colors of nonstationary segments and for delineating image areas which might represent a moving object. This kind of presentation has been based on the hypothesis that a link between coding and understanding image sequences is already discernible. Such a link is likely to facilitate the use of scene specific knowledge through internal computer models of depicted objects and their time variations for improved coding. As an example for this possibility, RIDSDALE and KULICK 79 investigated structural image models incorporating temporal information to achieve high data compression for storage and transmission of radiographic and optical image sequences of the human body.

2.2 Image Sequences from Airborne and Satellite Sensors

HORAN 78 outlined the diverse capabilities of a modern satellite for a broader audience. Aerial and satellite image sequences are routinely evaluated to find answers for a wide variety of questions. Their discussion will be organized according to decreasing spatial extent of the phenomena or objects which somehow characterize each problem area. First, phenomena concerning the atmosphere as well as ocean and land surfaces will be discussed, followed by mapping and surveillance problems, change detection and land use applications. Although the automatic visual navigation of airborne vehicles could constitute another subsection to be included here, not enough material is yet available.

2.2.1 Horizontal wind velocities derived from image sequences in the visual channel

Wind velocities are estimated from cloud displacements observed in a sequence of satellite images as regular input data to weather forecasting. A manual approach described in FUJITA 69 combined two or more copies each from a sequence of satellite images taken at 20-30 minute intervals over a period of 2-3 hours into a film loop which is continuously projected onto a digitizing tablet. An operator selected a cloud feature - like, e.g., the centroid of a cloud, of a hole in extended cloud cover, or of a cloud cluster, as well as brightness centers or prominent cloud edges - and marked its position in the projection of the initial and final frame from the filmloop, using the intermediate frames to securely track the selected features. The measured displacement of the selected feature had to be corrected for distortion and transformed to an earth surface coordinate system. On the hypothesis that positional changes of clouds were solely effected by horizontal winds, the resulting cloud feature displacement had to be converted into wind velocity.

Operational systems developed from this approach have been described by FUJITA et al. 69 , HUBERT and WHITNEY 71 , BRISTOR 72 . Since manual measurements were time consuming and susceptible to unsystematic errors, several techniques have been studied to perform the cloud displacement measurements automatically. LEESE et al. 70 + 71 implemented a cross-covariance search for the best match between 60x60 pixel subimages from two consecutive satellite picture frames. LEESE et al. 70 explored, too, a faster binary matching technique. Each satellite frame was converted into a binary "edge" picture by greylevel slicing and divided into 60x60 pixel windows. Each window from one frame was compared to windows within a certain search environment from the next frame using the percentage of coinciding binary edge elements as match score. A local cloud displacement was defined as the vector connecting the centers of the best match window pair. Since this approach turned out to depend critically on the equivalence of greylevel slices from two consecutive satellite images, it was later abandoned in favor of the cross-covariance match. This latter method was initially employed in an interactive approach where an operator selected windows dominated by a single cloud layer with a reasonably unique greyvalue pattern.

BRADFORD et al. 72 - see, too, BRISTOR 72 - developed this approach into a semiautomatic system for the determination of wind velocities from low level, single layer cloud displacements. For this purpose they had to include a procedure for registering satellite pictures to a high degree of precision and a quality control procedure which excluded automatic measurements incompatible with climatological knowledge about the geographical area under consideration. However, no procedure was available yet to employ meteorological knowledge about the short term developments for quality control. The results of this system were therefore edited by a meteorologist who removed measurements from unsuitable subimages.

LEESE et al. 70+71 as well as BRADFORD et al. 72 employed the fast Fourier transform (FFT) technique to compute the cross-covariance. BRADFORD et al. 72 used a 32x32 pixel window within a 64x64 pixel search area. Application of the FFT technique implied that the intensity function is periodic in the space domain, i.e. what moves out of the subwindow at one boundary must come in at the opposite boundary. ARKING et al. 75 determined that a violation of this implicit assumption did not appear to influence the optimum lag location and thus the displacement vector significantly. The investigations by LO 75 and others to exploit the Fourier transform phase shifts for the determination of cloud displacements did not yield reliable results - compare the discussions in connection with transform coding approaches in section 2.1.2.

SHENK and KREINS 70 determined centroid coordinates for interactively selected cloud segments and derived a cloud displacement vector as the one connecting corresponding centroids from two consecutive satellite pictures. The following approach employed clustering techniques to achieve essentially the same result. ENDLICH et al. 71 applied the ISODATA algorithm - see BALL and HALL 67 or the textbooks of DUDA and HART 73 , TOU and GONZALEZ 74 - to cluster interactively the 2-D intensity distribution within 120x120 pixel subwindows from a satellite image into about 10-20 clusters. The 2-D location and mean intensity of the cluster center was used as a descriptor for a cloud segment. Each cluster center was tentatively paired with all centers derived within the same subwindow from a satellite image recorded 30-90 minutes later. The differences between x and y components from these tentative pairings were histogrammed. A peak in these histograms was selected as indicative for the components of the cloud displacement vector in the subwindow studied. A dissimilarity or "fitting" function representing a linear combination of descriptor differences and their variances was used to select the best set of pairings. All cluster centers contributing to this set were removed and the procedure was iterated to search for other sets of pairings corresponding to different displacement vectors unless the dissimilarity function exceeded a threshold. As HALL 77 pointed out, this entire approach comprised two clustering procedures: a "static" one to derive descriptors representing cloud segments in each satellite picture and a "dynamic" one to match the resulting descriptor sets from frame to frame. It would be interesting to replace either or both of these clustering procedures by relaxation labeling techniques - see ROSENFELD 78 - and to compare the results.

Wind velocities derived from satellite pictures according to approaches outlined in the preceding paragraphs have been compared with each other - see, e.g., IZAWA and FUJITA 69 - and with other measurements by HUBERT and WHITNEY 71 , HASLER 73 , HASLER et al. 76 , BAUER 76 , SMITH and HASLER 76 . Provided the cloud segments used for displacement measurements had been carefully selected and all known systematic errors had been corrected, good agreement could be achieved. The most significant uncertainty was due to lack of knowledge about cloud height. Two or more cloud layers at different altitudes could result in wrong automatic measurements if the cloud motions differed in speed and direction. The automatic separation of cloud layers based on shape has been studied by AGGARWAL and DUDA 75 and based on brightness by LO 75 . A pattern recognition approach investigated the automatic classification of clouds into categories established by meteorologists in order to select the ones most suitable for reliable wind velocity determination even for high level cloud layers - see PARIKH 76a+76b+77 .

Presumably induced by his film loop observation, FUJITA 69 mentioned the possibility of differentiating various cloud layers on the basis of their different velocities. This idea to exploit displacement or motion attributes for segmenting images from a sequence into semantically meaningful image components has already been encountered in other areas as well. Local cloud features, however, are often neither well enough defined nor sufficiently stable to facilitate such an approach. O'ROURKE 80 suggested an investigation of the possibility to use optical flow determinations - such as they are described in section 3 - for cloud motion estimates. It is not inconceivable that a suitable analysis of velocity vector fields derived in that manner could contribute to an improved description - especially if the temporal consistency of such vector fields will be evaluated in the light of a suitable meteorological model (see section 2.2.3).

2.2.2 Image sequences including the infrared channel

Estimates of cloud temperature obtained by infrared sensors considerably improved the classification of cloud types and the separation of different cloud layers - see DECOTIIS and CONLAN 71 for a discussion of the problems involved and for references to the earlier literature. PICHEL et al. 76 investigated the generation of artificial stereo image pairs from multispectral satellite pictures for interactive cloud height determination.

SHENK and KREINS 70 used the technique described above to derive wind velocities from image pairs recorded in the infrared channel (3.5-4.1 micro-m) by a NIMBUS II satellite with a highly inclined orbit. The centroid of a cloud segment was computed as the spatial average of pixels having the lowest temperature - i.e. those which should represent the cloud top. The wind velocities derived in this way correlated reasonably well with observed wind velocities.

The semiautomatic approach described by BRADFORD et al. 72 had been extended into an operational system for the evaluation of multispectral images recorded in one infrared (10.5-12.6 micro-m) as well as several visual channels by geostationary satellites - see GREEN et al. 75 or NOVAK and YOUNG 76 . The editing step in this system still had to be performed by a meteorologist. The infrared image enabled him to distinguish between low, middle, and high clouds. Meteorological features such as cyclonic vortices, cold fronts, tropical disturbances, jet streams, and subtropical high- pressure systems could be identified in both the visual and infrared channel picture. Thus it became possible to assign a height estimate to cloud segments used for velocity determination (YOUNG 75). THOMASELL 76 investigated an automatic editing step based on infrared data in order to increase the internal consistency of wind velocity estimates derived by an operational system.

This approach has been further refined by HUGHES et al. 78 . Routine calibration of infrared intensity reading versus height was used to select an infrared intensity range which corresponded to cloud top heights not exceeding 3000 m. 16x16 pixel windows centered at predefined grid locations were only accepted for further processing if a minimum number of pixels within this range was exceeded. In this case a cross-correlation search was performed for the optimum match in a satellite picture recorded 30 minutes later. However, only pixels within the accepted infrared intensity range were allowed to contribute to the cross-correlation value and therefore to the displacement determination. Windows with insufficient low level clouds were thus excluded and spots of higher level clouds could not influence the displacement result. Experience has shown that the difficulties in determining cloud motion for a specific altitude are connected with the remaining incertainty in the relationship between the infrared measurements and the altitude. In order to speed up the cross-correlation search, the first displacement tests for each window were restricted to 11x11 lag values around an expected displacement. If a reliable correlation maximum could be identified within this restricted search area - which happened in about 75 % of all cases - no search was performed for the 17x17 displacements considered in the full 32x32 search window. HAASS and BRUBAKER 79 recently suggested that time could be saved in cross-correlation search by establishing a set of predictors comprising not only the centroid coordinates but in addition area size, brightness, and other descriptors for cloud segments. As mentioned previously, efforts to evaluate image sequences faster and more precisely result in the attempt to derive computer internal dynamic models of the real world phenomena being depicted.

The method described by ENDLICH et al. 71 has been developed into an automatic approach by WOLF et al. 77+79 . Pixels usable for cloud tracing were separated from background by a locally adapted intensity threshold in both channels. Since the ISODATA clustering algorithm had turned out to be too time consuming, 8 connected groups of cloud pixels were taken as cloud segments. For each segment the following descriptors were computed: size, center coordinates, average intensities in the visual and infrared channel, as well as the standard deviations of the x and y center coordinates as a coarse shape indicator. An empirical dissimilarity function based on these descriptors was used to score a possible pairing of cloud segments within a 120x70 pixel search window from two consecutive frames. For middle and high clouds better results were obtained when clustering was based on the infrared rather than visible data whereas the reverse was true for low level clouds. High displacement values required a first guess in order to cluster interframe pairings of cloud segments reliably. Alternatively, one could have reduced the resolution with a concomitant loss in the precision of the resulting displacement determination, possibly followed by a second more precise determination.

SMITH and REYNOLDS 76 compared IR height estimates with values obtained by geometric evaluation of the shift between cloud edges and shadows cast by these clouds. This approach is restricted to situations where the ground surface is known to be flat and the shadows are clearly visible, unobstructed by other clouds. Auto-correlation of interactively selected image windows was used to determine the apparent displacement. The IR height estimate, combined with known satellite position and sun angle, provided a start value in the auto-correlation search for a second maximum. Differences between cloud heights estimated from IR data, cloud/shadow edge geometry, and radar measurements varied between 2-4 km. Further investigations based on more data appeared to be required before attempts at explaining these differences seemed justified to the authors. A different geometric approach towards cloud height determination consists in the evaluation of stereo pairs of (sub-)images. This method has been investigated with subimages which had been extracted from the - almost - simultaneous overlapping coverage of the same area by two different geostationary satellites. Since the geometric conditions do not allow the application of this method to areas at higher latitudes, stereo pairs have been formed by evaluating successive images from polar satellites, using the - computable - satellite displacement between the successive recording of the same cloud surface. Detailed geometric considerations for such an approach as well as references to earlier publications about this topic can be found in LORENZ and SCHMIDT 79 .

2.2.3 Formation and refinement of meteorological and geological knowledge

The determination of wind velocities from practically simultaneous intensity recordings over large geographical areas - like, e.g., the Pacific Ocean - as well as the consistent accumulation of such data for periods extending over many days facilitated conceptual advances in understanding dynamical aspects of tropical circulation - see FUJITA et al. 69 . The study of meteorological phenomena extending over smaller spatial and temporal domains has also been fostered by the evaluation of image sequences. SIKDAR and SUOMI 72 , for example, described a simple technique for measuring transport of energy by convective clouds investigated in Applications Technology Satellite (ATS) images. Further examples can be found in FREEMAN 76 and HUBERT 76 . By careful comparison of low-cloud satellite wind estimates with those based on simultaneous observations from aircrafts, SMITH and HASLER 76 found evidence for regional differences. This might stimulate research to refine meteorological models. Of special interest are the relationships between observable spatial and temporal variations of intensities measured in the visible as well as infrared channels and the growth, displacement, and dissipation of clouds.

BAUER 76 compared wind velocity estimates derived from radiosondes and from cloud tracking in satellite image sequences. Both methods exhibited uncertainties of the order of 4-5 m/s and agreed with each other within this error margin. FUJITA et al. 75 estimated that the reproducibility of semiautomatic cloud displacement measurements corresponded to standard deviations of about 1 m/s for the speed and about 4 degree in the direction. HASLER et al. 76 as well as SUCHMAN and MARTIN 76 presented data supporting these estimates. Accuracy of wind estimates, however, appeared unlikely to be better than 2 m/s due to uncertainties in the physical and dynamical characteristics of cloud motion and hence in the conversion of cloud motion into wind velocities.

Progress towards more precise velocity estimates from cloud tracking requires the interaction between meteorologists who refine their knowledge about cloud dynamics and computer scientists who convert this knowledge into algorithms for objective evaluation and use in increasingly automatic operations. The work reported by PARIKH 76a+76b+77 as well as PARIKH and ROSENFELD 78 are examples of steps in the required direction. Selecting cloud formations which are unsuitable for reliable determination of wind velocities should be avoided. Infrared windows from satellite data were tentatively segmented by locating clusters of greyvalues in an infrared histogram. A multistage algorithm evaluated textural and tonal features which characterize meteorological properties of desired cloud patterns in order to classify the segments. Neighboring segments assigned to compatible classes could then be merged - compare this with the "semantic" region growing approach described by YAKIMOVSKY and FELDMAN 73 . The selected cloud formation should exhibit sufficiently uniform meteorological properties to enable a more reliable conversion of their displacement into wind velocity. Although PARIKH 76b mentioned that under favorable circumstances meteorologists might use displacement - i.e. temporal - characteristics to classify cloud segments, such attributes have not yet been incorporated into her approach. Further progress requires the incorporation of more meteorological knowledge about both the static and dynamic aspects of cloud formation, growth, and dissipation in order to fully exploit the information offered by multispectral satellite image sequences. A computerized expert systems approach seems to be appropriate if this situation is compared to other application areas - see, e.g., WATERMAN and HAYES-ROTH 78 or SRIDHARAN 78 .

A second incentive for analysing the variation of mesoscale cloud formations from picture to picture is connected with attempts to detect and track tornado thunderstorms and other kinds of severe bad weather constellations - see, e.g., FUJITA 69, IZAWA and FUJITA 69, HASLER 71, MILLER et al. 75 , and FREEMAN 76 .

ADLER and FENN 76 investigated the development of thunderstorms based on infrared satellite data recorded within a restricted picture area at 5 minute intervals. VIEZEE et al. 72 used kinematic computations on cloud motion in order to describe the development, location, and movement of a surface cyclone and to compare their computed displacement vectors with those extracted from satellite image sequences. The goal is to derive precise meteorological models for predicting which observable cloud and temperature constellations are likely to evolve into a thunderstorm. In order to determine thermodynamic instabilities leading to severe storms, KANAL and PARIKH 77 investigated a pattern recognition approach based on classification of cloud types and especially the evolution of their features with time. Characteristic temporal variations of the electromagnetic radiation have been recognized as important features for identification of storms not only in the visible and infrared part of the spectrum, but in other parts of the spectrum as well - see KRITIKOS and SHIUE 79 for microwaves, WANG and BURNS 76 for even longer wavelengths. A combination of infrared and microwave recording has been mentioned by YATES and BANDEEN 75 and tested in the meantime - see GRANTHAM et al. 77 , MYERS 78 , MOORE and FUNG 79 .

So far, only cloud translation parallel to the earth's surface has been discussed explicitly. A recent investigation by HAASS and BRUBAKER 79 has been concerned with attempts to estimate cloud rotation around a vertical axis. The contour of a cloud segment has been described as a polar coordinate envelope with respect to a polar coordinate system centered interactively within the cloud. 1-D cross-correlation of such envelopes from corresponding cloud segments in consecutive images has been suggested for determining cloud rotation. Reliable determination of cloud rotation could be another indicator for certain severe weather situations.

Sequences of infrared images allow the observation of the temperature at a fixed geographical location as a function of time. This opened the possibility of estimating vertical cloud motion (LO 75) and of studying clear air turbulances (HALL et al. 72) as well as time variations in the temperature of large sea surface areas - see LEESE and TARPLEY 75, WATERS 78. YATES and BANDEEN 75 mentioned in this context measurements of sea ice coverage. They pointed out that clouds and ice which are often indistinguishable in a single satellite image might nevertheless be separated by an interframe comparison of a picture sequence recorded on successive days: cloud patterns are dynamic whereas ice features are relatively stable within a day.

An especially illuminating example of the information to be extracted from a sequence of satellite images is the determination of thermal inertia from measured variations in the radiation temperature of the earth's surface at various times in the diurnal cycle. Thermal inertia is a volume rather than a surface property. Its measurement, therefore, permits discrimination among materials that may be indistinguishable when only surface reflectivity data are available. Thus, thermal inertia allows the determination of the boundary between materials with similar reflective properties but different thermal properties. As an additional possibility, a massive layer of material may be sensed through a thin surface layer of another material with different thermal properties - see WATSON 75 and KAHLE 76 . Similarly, a satellite equipped with an Electronically Scanned Microwave Radiometer (ESMR) has been used to measure soil moisture effects by observing the temperature cycle of soils - see YATES and BANDEEN 75.

It should be mentioned that the velocity of winds in direct contact with the ocean surface can be derived from radar back scatter recorded by airborne or satellite microwave sensors - see GRANTHAM et al. 77 , TOMIYASU 78 , MOORE and FUNG 79 .

Cloud displacements observed in image sequences from the planet Venus have been used to estimate wind velocities in the Venus atmosphere (LYNN 76).

2.2.4 Registration of images and production of mosaics

In order to obtain a reliable estimate for the wind velocity, the satellite images have to be registered precisely with each other via landmarks. They can be located automatically in each image by a hierarchical search procedure - see HALL et al. 72 , SMITH and PHILLIPS 72 , BRADFORD et al. 72 . All these approaches employed cross-correlation for template matching. The attitude stability of the ATS satellite over 3-4 days has been exploited by searching for a simultaneous alignment from a sequence of satellite images rather than aligning each image individually to the ground control points (SMITH and PHILLIPS 72).

Techniques based on locating exactly known ground control points in LANDSAT images have been perfected to correct absolute geometric errors to less than one pixel and relative errors between different images to better than one-fourth pixel (BERNSTEIN 76). This allowed a more precise determination of the satellite's attitude and trajectory by tracking ground control points in satellite image sequences (DOOLITTLE et al. 75 , MILLER et al. 75). Using 50 - 100 landmarks and interpolating cross-correlation values obtained at integer displacements, HUGHES et al. 78 reported interframe registration errors of less than 1/8 of a pixel for the infrared channel of the Geostationary Operational Environmental Satellite GOES-2. This corresponded to an uncertainty of about 1 km on the earth surface. Temporal (cloud cover, sun angle) and seasonal variations combined with different observation angles relative to the surface slope complicated the match between landmark template and scene image. HORN demonstrated that a detailed understanding of the entire image formation process - and not only its geometrical aspects - is required to obtain exact matching (HORN and BACHMAN 78 , HORN 78).

In many cases, no judiciously selected ground control point templates were available to assist in bringing images into registration. ANUTA 69+70 investigated cross-correlation techniques in order to register multispectral images recorded at the same time but by different sensors. He also discussed the application of these techniques for registering frames from a temporal image sequence.

Precise relative registration between images enabled the production of high-resolution mosaics and - if combined with pixel classification - of thematic maps. Unless the relative location of component images is at least approximately known, matching has to be attempted between all pairs of component images for all relative displacements which result in a reasonable overlap. This involves considerable search if many component images have to be assembled into a mosaic.

TANAKA et al. 78 described hierarchical matching based on a pyramid representation (see PAVLIDIS 77) for the component images. Gross registration at a coarse resolution of the pyramids was employed to reduce the window size for the subsequent search at a finer resolution level. An arrangement graph - see TANAKA et al. 77 - was built with component images as nodes and edges between all node pairs for which acceptable partial matches had been obtained. An edge had as an attribute the relative displacement vector corresponding to the best partial match between the component images involved. A triangle check on these displacement vectors insured the consistency of all tentative arrangements at each level of the pyramid representation before the search at the next-finer resolution could be started. The experiment reported by these authors admitted only rotation-free, square component images with identical dimensions. Normalized cross-correlation was used as a similarity function. Considerable savings in computation time have been reported.

Although in different contexts, hierarchical matching using a similar approach has been described by WONG and HALL 78+79 as well as HORN and BACHMAN 78 .

If sufficient knowledge about the viewing conditions for each frame and about the object is available, the transformations required for the registration of sections from different frames can be computed directly. GREEN 78 reported that an oblate spheroid model of the Mars - or other planets - in conjunction with space probe trajectories have been used to derive mosaics from several planets, combining images from Mariner space missions.

If the component images to be assembled into a mosaic had been recorded at different times, naturally occurring variations like haze or other phenomena might have resulted in tonal differences between neighboring component images. To avoid artificial edges at the seam lines, MILGRAM 75 applied a global greylevel adjustment after geometric registration. Within the overlap region of two component images, a seam point in each scanline was chosen which minimized the greylevel discontinuity. A final smoothing step averaged the remaining contrast over a neighborhood of the seampoint. Further improvements to these techniques have been described by MILGRAM 77b .

2.2.5 Change detection

ROSENFELD 61 appears to be the first who discussed the comparison of digitized images for automatic detection of changes in reconnaissance data. He distinguished three subtasks: (i) data registration; (ii) change detection and localization; (iii) change discrimination. The first of these subtasks has been treated in the preceding section. ROSENFELD 61 emphasized already the need to correct for relative radiometric distortions in addition to the geometric ones. He proceeded to discuss several correlation measures which quantified the similarity between descriptors based on points, lines, or areas from the two images to be compared. The third subtask is of special interest in the context of this survey. It involved the realization that - in addition to the information contained in the two digital images - extensive knowledge would be required about the sensors used, the scene depicted, and the purpose for which changes had to be identified. Knowledge of these kinds was implied by the discussion of criteria which could be used to discriminate changes of interest from other - neglectable - changes such as those, for example, caused by variations of shadows or clouds. It was not until a decade and a half later that PRICE 76 introduced knowledge sources relating to the change detection purpose ("matching and change detection knowledge") and to the scene domain ("segmentation knowledge") as explicit conceptual entities. Separate conceptual models for the sensor and for the scene illumination have been discussed by NAGEL 79 .

SHEPARD 64 again pointed out the importance of automatic change detection and discussed some of the problems of discriminating uninteresting changes. SWOBODA and GERDES 68 implemented a flying spot scanning system for automatic target recognition. They demonstrated the importance of the "inverse" problem: reliable automatic detection of targets despite significant background changes due to variations of sun angle, ground conditions etc. These authors considered it important to employ indicators about the background conditions - either extracted automatically or supplied by an operator - in order to compensate the influence of background variations on the features derived from a potential target subimage prior to the classification step.

PAOLANTONIO 69 suggested that two flying spot film readers be employed, using high precision cathode ray tubes for measuring at the same time the intensity of mission and reference exposures. Signals obtained by scanning corresponding points had to be subtracted. This difference should have been digitized and further evaluated by a computer program to suppress changes due to uninteresting effects, although no specific criteria or algorithms were mentioned.

A basically similar concept has been developed and implemented by LILLESTRAND 72 and ULSTAD 73 for detecting small differences between side-looking radar imagery recorded at different times along roughly the same flight path. LILLESTRAND 72 and ULSTAD 73 employed normalized cross-correlation as the similarity function, the descriptors being image subarrays of a size varying between 32x32 and 128x128 pixels. Since a rough registration of the two images could be assumed, descriptors were picked on a coarse grid of 16x16 locations for a 1000x1000 pixel archive image. The best match for each descriptor had to be found in a neighborhood around its grid position on the current image. After a map warp had been derived from interpolated locations for cross-correlation maxima, the mean transparency (greyvalue) and contrast of the images were adjusted (transparency rectification). The subsequent change detection employed two thresholds in a scatter diagram of corrected pixel value from the current image versus the pixel value from the archive image in order to classify the pixel as an unchanged feature, a feature added or a feature removed from the current image in comparison with the archive image. A conceptually similar approach aiming for real-time processing of radar signals rather than digitized photographic records has been reported recently by PUTRA and TOOLE 79 . Applying such an approach to other than side-looking radar images - e.g. aerial photographs - caused difficulties when effects such as variations in cast shadows due to differences in scene illumination could no longer be neglected.

Even for side-looking radar images, a mere thresholding of the difference signal obtained from two corresponding pixels was insufficient to distinguish between changes of interest and false alarms due to shadow differences or scintillations, i.e. differences in the radar signal returned by the same object but from slightly different aspect angles. A high threshold suppressed fine changes, a smaller one admitted too many false alarms. HENRIKSON 72 attempted to exploit an assumed difference between the spatial distribution of intensities around changes of interest versus changes due to false alarms. He evaluated several statistical descriptors derived from environments in the mission and reference frame at the location where a change had been detected. The most important test involved the correlation coefficient between these environments. Supplementary tests compared the mean and contrast for these environments, the slope of the regression line between the intensities from the two environments and the standard deviation of the joint distribution perpendicular to the regression line. This approach allowed the reduction of the threshold which defined a significant interframe difference and nevertheless reduced the number of false alarms. However, these rather general statistical descriptors are inadequate to model the large variety of attributes which might be exploited to distinguish between changes of interest and false alarms.

A more general approach than the preceding one is a test of whether or not intensity samples from a window in the mission image may have been drawn from the same distribution as the samples in the corresponding window of the reference image. EGHBALI 79 employed the Kolmogorov-Smirnov test to decide this question at a specified significance level for 16 x 16 pixel windows from registered LANDSAT images. Intensities in the windows had been corrected to exhibit the same mean and variance. Although this approach did not require knowledge of the intensity distribution from which samples were drawn, a test window comprising at least 100 pixels was necessary to comply with the conditions on which this test had been based. The result did not appear to depend critically on misregistrations by a few pixels. Although such a registration was an order of magnitude more crude than the one required for the earlier approaches - which worked towards a relative registration error of a quarter raster unit - the reported insensitivity is not extremely surprising in view of the large test area. The author suggested that scene dependent knowledge be exploited by testing for significant changes in the spectral channel which described best the situation prevailing at the time the reference image had been recorded.

KAWAMURA 71 also exploited scene dependent knowledge by his choice of descriptors for recognizing changes in aerial photographs caused by urban development. He performed an interactive similarity search by visually selecting nine pairs of corresponding points from two digitized aerial photographs in order to determine the coefficients of a higher order polynomial transformation which registered the images with respect to each other. The subsequent change detection has been based on three different descriptors, the first being represented by the greyvalues in sample cells of 32x32 pixels. The second descriptor was defined as the average self-information per intensity symbol. The third descriptor was given by the probability estimate of finding especially bright intensities which in an urban scene tend to be due to man-made objects such as rooftops, parking lots, streets, etc. The dissimilarity function used by KAWAMURA 71 was a polygonal approximation to a nonlinear discriminant surface in a three-dimensional feature space made up by the normalized cross-correlation coefficient, the average change in self-information per intensity symbol, and the average change in high-intensity probabilities, all derived for each sample cell in the two aerial images to be compared. The discriminant surface had been derived from training samples.

The basic assumption behind the approaches described so far is at first quite attractive: after appropriate geometric and radiometric transformations, the intensity difference between mission and reference image would be larger than some suitable threshold essentially at those locations which correspond to significant changes. As has been seen in the preceding presentation, rather involved postprocessing of changes isolated by such a procedure had to be invoked - based on judiciously chosen descriptors for the environment of intensity changes. KAWAMURA 71 already avoided a thresholded intensity difference as a way of focussing attention for further processing. Based on such considerations, several approaches have been developed which relied entirely on an expansion of the techniques previously used for "postprocessing". If suitable descriptors had been chosen, a much more concise and relevant representation of mission and reference image could be derived. The changes of interest should then be identified by comparing the descriptors of these images rather than the image signals themselves.

Images to be compared by PRICE 76 , PRICE and REDDY 75+77a+77b+79 were segmented into regions which were described by size, location, perimeter squared over area, orientation of the intrinsic ellipsis, color or intensity, as well as combinations of these features and relations between a region and its neighbors. Similarity search was performed by comparing the description for each region from one image with the description of every region from the other image. The absolute differences between feature values from the two regions to be compared were weighted by empirically determined coefficients and summed to yield the similarity function. To study these heuristics, images from a variety of sources (side-looking radar, aerial, and satellite images) have been investigated. It is important that the authors provided explicit means to introduce domain and task specific knowledge into the similarity search: each feature difference in the similarity function was multiplied by a strength factor which could be chosen by the user to reflect specific knowledge about the relevance of this feature for the current domain, task, or state of search.

The regions which best matched each other were used to determine a transformation that allowed the registration of the two images. User knowledge could be applied to determine the order in which region matches had to be attempted and when to modify strength factors so that certain features contributed to the similarity function after they could be evaluated properly based on previously established region matches. Exploiting these options, PRICE 78 gave examples where this symbolic registration approach allowed the registration of images that had been rotated with respect to each other by 90 or 180 degree around an axis perpendicular to the image plane.

PRICE and REDDY could compare images in more than one way. The first alternative consisted in comparing the actual feature values of best-match regions after registration, especially those features originally excluded from the similarity search. Another alternative consisted in searching for added or missing regions in the second as compared to the first image. These aspects have not yet been developed in detail in the published reports.

TRUITT et al. 76 investigated a system starting from the same considerations outlined above. They restricted themselves to three basic descriptor types which were suitable for real-time extraction. The first type consisted of straight line contours made up from edge elements for which the direction of the light to dark transition was recorded. The second type comprised small areas which were lighter or darker than their surrounding regions. The third descriptor type consisted of a set of statistical parameters used for texture classification. Registration was achieved by searching for endpoints of edges in the mission image around the endpoint location in the reference image. This assumed that images were already in approximate registration. The displacements obtained for matching endpoints were averaged for fine registration. Objects of interest for interframe comparison were taken to be represented by a collection of blobs and edges with a coherent relationship to one another - e.g. light and dark sides appropriately positioned. Changes were detected by comparing object descriptions extracted from mission and reference frames. Size and shape attributes of objects as well as a more global analysis step of clustering objects into spatially related target groups could be exploited for further discrimination. These techniques allowed more changes of interest to be found at a specified level of false alarms than thresholding intensity differences between corresponding pixels combined with some postprocessing as described earlier. Test results obtained by an implementation have been reported by TISDALE 77 .

It should be noted that the approaches of PRICE and REDDY as well as of TRUITT et al. attempt to model the spatial relationships between intensities or their gradients in order to characterize the interesting objects in the image. Earlier approaches did not select potential areas of change based on structural characteristics. The postprocessing step applied in some cases was restricted to estimating the structural similarities around suspected changes by correlation of windows extracted from mission and reference images. No discrimination based on a more detailed analysis of the greyvalue structure for each window had been attempted.

The idea of building a model for images of interesting objects observed throughout a sequence of images - with either the objects or the observer moving or both - has been mentioned by BULLOCK and DUDANI 76 as well as NAGEL 78a . According to BULLOCK 76+78 , simple local descriptors based on edge elements and their relationships represented a reasonable balance between conflicting demands for relative invariance and small computational complexity. The former demand excluded point features, the latter segmentation and interpretation of images prior to their comparison. BULLOCK 78 pointed out that the features used in their approach - and this applies, too, to the one reported by TRUITT et al. 76 - boiled down to what was called "general purpose models" by ZUCKER et al 75 .

It is not surprising that approaches to automatic photointerpretation relied essentially on the same feature set which has been used for low-level interframe comparison discussed in this section. An early exposition can be found in HOLMES 66 . A (hybrid) special purpose processor for real-time automatic screening of reconnaissance and surveillance imagery described by GEOKEZAS et al. 75 is a more recent example. Since these approaches were not concerned with interframe comparison, they will not be treated in greater detail although important aspects were strikingly similar to the systems discussed in this section.

2.2.6 Cover-type mapping based on time-varying imagery

HOFFER 78 proposed the mapping of "cover type" be distinguished from the mapping of "land use". The former can be derived from the analysis of multispectral remotely sensed images whereas the latter can be inferred from cover type with some reliability only if additional knowledge about the specific area to be mapped is available.

Although the majority of early applications - see e.g. NAGY 72 - evaluated individual satellite images, there existed already a variety of examples which depend on comparing two or more aerial/satellite images taken at different times (NAGY 72 , BERNSTEIN 76):

* growth of forests (GOLDBERG and KOURTZ 77)
* determination of shoreline erosion
* riparian formation
* monitoring condition of lakes
* predicting and assessing flood damage
* anticipating irrigation needs
* mapping of snow coverage (MILLER et al. 75).

Early considerations for improving crop classification by repeated analysis of the same ground area over a crop maturation period can be found in PARK 69 , ANUTA 70 , STEINER 70 , and SINCLAIR et al. 71 . Characteristic temporal variations in the spectral composition of remotely sensed radiation have to be exploited for more reliable yield estimates. ENGVALL et al. 77 employed this approach to check the reasonableness of a maximum likelihood classification for separating wheat from non-wheat. They compared this classification result at the end of a growing season to a decision derived from satellite images of the same areas taken at three different instants throughout the wheat growing season. HOFFER 78 discussed these questions in depth. MISRA and WHEELER 77+78 demonstrated this in the specific case of wheat. A different crop classification algorithm based on temporal attributes has been reported by KANEKO 78 . SWAIN 78 proposed a cascade classifier model based on a Bayesian approach in order to classify a pattern of multiple observations in a time-varying environment.

DUGGIN 77 has shown that reflectance or radiance measurements for different wheat fields depend significantly on the sun angle. Satellite measurements recorded at the same time of the day during a crop growth period have to be carefully corrected for sun angle variations before they are used to compute temporal attributes for crop classification.

Seasonal differences have also been exploited to achieve greater discrimination in cover types for land use determination in an urban area - see BRYANT 76 - or in rural areas - see HABERAECKER 78+79 .

2.2.7 Discussion

The pressure to develop adequate models for describing the input images and their time variation should have become obvious throughout the preceding discussion. It might be said that the desire for more appropriate interpretation of observable differences is the main source of modelling efforts with airborne or satellite imagery - in contrast to image coding where improvements to coding efficiency produce the driving forces. In actual practice, however, both aspects are present. The clustering approaches to satellite image bandwidth compression reported by HILBERT 75 as well as HABIBI and SAMULON 75 - see section 2.1.3 - are steps towards an object related image decomposition. On the other hand, availability of some models would facilitate the on-board processing of data from satellite mounted sensors. This could relieve the pressure to transmit huge amounts of unprocessed data - see, e.g., WILSON et al. 79 .

2.3 Medicine: Image Sequences of the Human Body

The medical field represents a rapidly expanding area of applications for the evaluation of image sequences recorded by ultrasound, optical, x-ray, and radio-isotope sensors. An attempt by a non-specialist to achieve anything close to complete coverage of the medical literature relevant in this context did not appear feasible. The following presentation should therefore be understood as a sampling of the literature to illustrate trends as I perceived them. Additional publications can be found, e.g., in the excellent book edited by HEINTZEN and BUERSCH 78 and the series of international conferences on computers in cardiology (proceedings available from IEEE).

Practically all image sequences to be discussed in the remainder of this section have been generated from x-ray or radioisotope sources. Ultrasound is another important source for medical image generation - see HAVLICE and TAENZER 79 . Spatial - see PRESTON 79 - as well as temporal ultrasonic image sequences - see KISSLO et al. 78 - have been recorded. Although these ultrasound images yield important information which complements that obtainable by angiographic or scintigraphic studies - see POPP 78 - the evaluation of ultrasonic images apparently still requires the immediate interpretation by a human expert - see LE CROISETTE and GAMMELL 78 . With few exceptions, no articles have been encountered so far which address themselves to the automatic evaluation - as opposed to computerized derivation - of ultrasonic image sequences. The approach of SCHUDY 79 for the determination of interior heart surfaces will be treated in sections 2.3.3 and 2.8.4. Regarding the preliminary results of PIERONI and COSTABILE 79 to outline the ultrasonic image of a foetus moving in its gestational sac, it appears too early to judge the applicability of their method. The introduction of phased array ultrasound sensors facilitated the recording of ultrasound image sequences with rates up to 60 frames/sec - see KISSLO et al. 78 , MACOVSKI 79 , and WALKER et al. 78 . This enables, for example, the noninvasive study of the beating heart. It can be expected that, after an exploratory period, algorithms for the automatic evaluation of such ultrasonic cardiac image sequences will be developed.

The mutual stimulation between technological developments and advances in the evaluation of image sequences has been especially strong in the area of medical applications. An example is the 'Dynamic Spatial Reconstructor' developed by WOOD and coworkers at the Mayo Clinic - see, e.g., JOHNSON et al. 76 and RITMAN et al. 78 - in order to record and evaluate series of 3-D tomograms of the human body at the rate of 60 Hz.

This should enable the analysis of dynamic phenomena such as ventricular wall motion of the beating human heart - see WOOD 76 . Preparatory experiments to digitize and record x-ray image data at video rates have been described by GILBERT et al. 76a+76b . GILBERT et al. 79 reported about the development of special purpose processors for such applications. Analogous developments for sequences of angiocardiograms have been described by KRUGER et al. 78 as well as BRENNECKE et al. 79a+79b . Another approach developed in order to analyse, e.g., the blood flow by angiography of liver and kidney has been described by HOEHNE et al. 78 , NICOLAE and HOEHNE 79 .

The derivation of spatial descriptions for organs has been treated in the context of spatial image sequences in section 2.8. The subsequent discussion has been organized to illustrate that advances in the evaluation of medical image sequences are not only influenced by improved facilities to sense and record data. These advances reflect, too, improved abilities to model - in a quantitative manner - parts of the body and some dynamic phenomena occurring in the human organism. Different techniques to extract the required mechanical and physiological data from image sequences are outlined in separate sections about blood circulation, heart motion, and metabolism of non-moving organs. In order to emphasize the increasing interaction between the evaluation of image sequences and quantitative - mechanical as well as physiological - models of various organs and organ functions, these aspects are discussed in a subsequent section. The construction of programs which attempt to classify the extracted data as normal or abnormal as well as more detailed diagnostic algorithms are seen as intermediate steps towards the derivation of such quantitative computer-internal models for the human body and its functions.

2.3.1 Preprocessing of image sequences

Early efforts have naturally been directed at improving the presentation of image sequences for human inspection. How the acquired data can be presented to a physician in an optimal manner is a research problem in its own right - see GALLAGHER et al. 77 .

The subtraction of x-ray images obtained before and after injection of roentgen-opaque material into the blood (angiography) enhances the resulting difference image for interpretation by a physician. Digitization of x-ray images facilitates the performance of nonlinear operations such as compensation for film characteristics during the determination of the difference image - see CHOW et al. 73 . Although digitized film images have to be aligned prior to subtraction, relative geometric distortions can usually be neglected. Therefore, the registration tends to be much less involved here than with satellite or airborne images. If an average of several digitized pre-injection images is subtracted from a post-injection image, image components not affected by the injection of roentgen-opaque material can be suppressed even more effectively - see CHOW and KANEKO 72 .

Provided the spatial, time and greyvalue resolution of TV recording is sufficient, alignment problems disappear. Recording cineangiographic image sequences on videotape rather than film enabled HEINTZEN and coworkers to investigate several modifications to this "image difference" technique. Just as CHOW and KANEKO 72, HEINTZEN and coworkers averaged the logarithm of (8 bit) intensity values at each position of a 256x256 raster, but only for video frames recorded at the same phase of the heart cycle, and - separately - for both periods prior and after injection of contrast material. The resulting synthetic pre-injection images were subtracted from the corresponding post-injection ones. Each such difference image was further subjected to intraframe enhancement techniques such as histogram equalization or linearization - see HEINTZEN et al. 75 , BRENNECKE et al. 76+77+78a+78b . The increased signal-to-noise ratio of such a phase-registered average was then exploited to obtain high - contrast difference images at a significantly smaller injection of roentgen-opaque material. Even if the contrast material had not been injected directly into, e.g., the left ventricle, the phase registered averaging produced a sufficiently enhanced difference image despite the dilution of contrast material resulting from the more remote, but less critical intravenous injection.

A different modification of such subtraction techniques consisted in storing 8 bit intensity values of a single digitized pre-injection video frame in a fast access memory and subtracting these background values in real time from video frames of cineangiocardiograms, recording only the intensity difference on videotape after rescaling by a factor in the range 2 - 8. A conventional videotape recorder could be used even for small intensity changes (due to reduced injection of contrast material) with a gain of about 6 dB in the signal-to-noise ratio compared to difference signals obtained from video tape recordings of regular angiocardiograms - see BRENNECKE et al. 76+77 .

Another special purpose processor system to perform similar subtraction operations in real time has been described by KRUGER et al. 78 .

2.3.2 Blood circulation studies

X-ray opaque material injected into the blood facilitates not only the discrimination of blood vessels from the surrounding tissue but also the study of blood flow. A short injection of such material - a bolus - does not dissolve immediately. Its travel with the blood may be recorded in a time series of single-plane x-ray images. Evaluation of such sequences may contribute to a quantitative understanding of blood circulation - either for general studies or for diagnostic purposes relating to a patient. LEDLEY 73 presented examples for this approach. HOEHNE et al. 78+79 nicely illustrated several techniques to extract quantitative information about the blood circulation in organs - as, e.g., the kidney - from a temporal image sequence. In order to make this information easily accessible to a physician, it is displayed in relation to the organ topology as a single so-called 'functional image': each pixel presents, for example, the arrival time of a bolus front at the corresponding location in the organ by means of a greyvalue or color code. Additional examples - especially regarding scintigraphic image sequences - as well as further references to the literature about functional images can be found in GALLAGHER et al. 77 and in HOLDEN 79 .

More details about studies of blood circulation by angiographic techniques can be found in part I of HEINTZEN and BUERSCH 78 .

Analogous approaches are being realized in ophthalmoscopy using radiation in the visible rather than x-ray energy range. The rear part of the human eye can be illuminated through the pupil and simultaneously imaged onto film or a TV sensor by a so-called fundus camera. If a fluorescent tracer is injected into a forearm vein it will reach the eye a few seconds later through the retinal artery. By appropriate illumination, light emission from this fluorescent material can be stimulated, marking its passage from the retinal arterioles through the capillary mesh and out through the retinal vein. Film recording of this process at about 20 frames/sec enables qualitative and quantitative evaluation of the blood circulation in the eye - see LEDLEY 73 :

* The physician attempts to detect anomalies such as incomplete filling of the capillary bed, leakages and blocked vessels for diagnostic purposes and to monitor treatment of eye diseases.

* The diameter of blood vessels in the eye can be measured as a function of time. In addition, blood flow rates and circulation times can be determined quantitatively by measuring the tracer dilution as a function of position and time.

It is expected that replacing photography by video recording in conjunction with fast automatic evaluation of digitized video frames will result in an instrument capable of sustained operation in a clinical environment - see McCORMICK et al. 76 , READ et al. 77 . This latter group digitized TV images in real time at a rate of 5-15 frames/sec over a period of 45 seconds for a total of about 300 frames. The resulting digitizings (256x256 pixels with 64 greylevels) were stored on a fast digital disk for subsequent analysis. The refined understanding of blood circulation in the eye which is expected from such quantitative studies of dynamic phenomena is considered as important as the immediate application of these techniques for diagnosis and treatment monitoring.

Another evaluation of image sequences - although on a time scale (one angiogram per year) different from the one discussed up to now - was concerned with the quantitative determination of atherosclerotic changes in the femoral artery of men who had experienced a myocardial infarction - see SELZER et al. 76 .

2.3.3 Delineating images of the heart for the study of dynamic shape variations

A temporal series of images may capture information about dynamic variations in organ position, size, and shape. These variations may be closely related to the function of the organ.

The ability to derive a detailed quantitative description of heart dynamics for an individual patient represents an eminently important goal. The left ventricle is that heart chamber whose contraction pumps the blood through the human body. A primary subgoal consists in the determination of the left ventricular volume as a function of time. In angiocardiography, x-ray opaque material is injected into the left ventricle and x-ray exposures are recorded at a rate of up to 60 frames per second. Originally, special film has been used. This technique is gradually being supplemented or replaced by recording on video-tape or video-disc. Since the ventricle had to be isolated and measured in a larger number of frames, the measurements were originally extracted by reliable - but slow - interactive contour tracing or by simple - but less robust - automatic approaches. Efforts to analyse the heart dynamics by isolation and tracking of special x-ray opaque markers surgically implanted into the heart wall were based on adaptive template matching - see GATTIS et al. 78 as well as GERBRANDS et al. 79 . The search area was predicted from marker coordinates determined in preceding frames. These techniques are not specific to cardiac image sequences - they will repeatedly be encountered for target tracking in biomedical (section 2.4) and behavioral (section 2.5) applications as well as in the analysis of image sequences from outdoor scenes (section 2.6).

DEJONG and SLAGER 75 described a rather flexible hybrid approach to extract the left ventricular contour in real time by adaptive thresholding of the analog video signal in two small expectation windows per video line, one window for the leading and one window for the trailing ventricle edge. The threshold level was adapted to the contour environment by taking into account the position and greyvalues of already accepted contour points as well as greyvalues from two sampling areas at either side of the contour. The centers of each expectation window in the subsequent line were taken to be the locations of the two contour points accepted in the current line. If no contour point could be accepted within an expectation window, provisions were available to extrapolate the contour in order to bridge difficult image regions. Improvements consisted in predicting the location of the expectation window from the direction of the last accurately detected contour portion. A linear contour extrapolation could be seen as analogy to the edge prediction investigated by ZSCHUNKE 77 for picture coding (see section 2.1.3).

LEDLEY 73 described a purely digital approach which was computationally cheaper although less robust. The left ventricle may be roughly approximated by an ellipsoid. The long axis of this ellipsoid extends between the apex of the heart and the center of the aortic valve through which the blood is pumped into the body. LEDLEY 73 analysed the greyvalue profile extracted from the image of the left ventricle along one or more lines perpendicular to the long axis. By choosing a suitable greyvalue threshold, the small axis of the approximating ellipsoid could be determined. The left ventricular volume could then be estimated from the measured projected lengths of long and small axes.

Since contour extraction is a problem in its own right which is well covered by textbooks on image processing and by an abundance of specialized articles, technical aspects of edge detection and tracking will not be treated in the following discussion. Interactive tracing of contours has been described - among others - by HEINTZEN et al. 75 as well as KRUGER and HUI 76.

Provided images of the beating heart have been recorded at sufficiently high frame rates - approaching 60 frames/sec - the ventricular contour will change smoothly from frame to frame. This knowledge has been exploited by more complex approaches to the determination of ventricular boundaries. Consecutively recorded single-plane x-ray images can be stacked chronologically on top of each other, accepting time as the third dimension. The variation of the left ventricular contour with time will then appear in this three-dimensional space as a smooth surface which can be located by a guided search such as it has been described by LIU 77 . A more detailed discussion of this method including conceptual extensions can be found in chapter 2.8.4.

REEVES et al. 79 recently proposed an interactive variant of this conceptual approach in order to replace the time consuming interactive tracing of ventricular contours in each frame of an angiographic image sequence. The surface representing the time variation of the left ventricular contour will be approximated using well known techniques from computer graphics - such as splines or Coon's patches. These approximations can describe complex surfaces with comparatively few parameters. The intersection curve of the approximated surface with a plane corresponding to a certain instant of time during the cardiac cycle is therefore expected to represent a reasonable approximation of the actual ventricular contour. This intersection curve would have to be generated in real time by a special purpose processor in order to be mixed with the video signal from a replay of the angiocardiographic image sequence. The operator could adjust interactively the parameters which determine the surface in order to achieve optimal overlap of the generated intersection curve with the dynamically changing ventricle contour throughout the heart cycle. As REEVES et al. 79 pointed out, their proposal represents an adaptation of the ideas described and implemented in the GALATEA system - see FUTRELLE 74 as well as FUTRELLE and POTEL 75 (compare section 2.4).

SCHUDY 79 reported about investigations to describe the interior heart surface by a linear superposition of spherical harmonic functions. He allowed the weighting coefficients to depend on time. This enabled him to approximate dynamic 3-D shape variations. SCHUDY 79 had to develop a special optimization procedure in order to determine the required coefficients from a temporal sequence of 3-D cardiac ultrasound data. The temporal and spatial smoothness of this time-dependent combination of spherical harmonics appeared to be well suited for interpolation of spatial and temporal irregularities in the raw data which were due to the measurement process as well as to the complicated internal structure of the heart.

ASHKAR and MODESTINO 78 described a heuristic search to extract object contours from noisy images. The continuation of a partial contour through a pixel to any of its unprocessed neighbors had to be evaluated based on a cumulative figure of merit derived from a heuristic weight function. In addition to local estimates for the edge strength, this weight function took into account a priori knowledge about a smoothly bending contour and about the expected contour shape. The latter information was represented by a contour prototype. The ventricle contour had to be traced interactively in the first frame in order to obtain a prototype for automatic analysis of the second frame. In subsequent frames, the contour extracted from the preceding frame would serve as prototype.

Another algorithm following a similar approach has been reported independently by EIHO et al. 78 . The heuristic search procedure described by CLAYTON et al. 74 for left ventricular boundary extraction is essentially a similar approach. It differs from the other ones in details of the heuristic weight function and in the fact that only five points on the ventricular boundary have to be marked interactively in the first frame - rather than the entire contour as required by the start procedure of the other two approaches.

Earlier experiences had shown that a fully automatic contour extraction by thresholding would have to incorporate a procedure for an adaptive local determination of threshold values. A powerful but computationally expensive approach has been developed by CHOW and KANEKO 72 . They searched a suitably enhanced digitized x-ray film image of the left ventricle for subregions with larger greyvalue variances. For such subregions, a mixture of two normal distributions was fitted to the corresponding greyvalue histogram. If an acceptable fit could be obtained for a subregion, a threshold was determined and used to classify the greyvalues of this subregion as either interior or exterior to the left ventricle. In this way CHOW and KANEKO 72 derived automatically a series of 25 left ventricular contours covering approximately one cardiac cycle. These authors processed each frame separately.

KANEKO and MANCINI 73 extended this approach in order to exploit the expected smooth frame-to-frame variation of the ventricular contour. They applied the method of CHOW and KANEKO 72 to the first frame in order to extract a reference boundary to start with. The reference boundary was divided into N boundary segments of equal length. Around each of these segments a small rectangular region was chosen in the subsequent frame, with long sides parallel to the corresponding segment of the reference boundary. A minimum squared error procedure was used to place a new straight line segment through the points of maximum intensity gradients within each rectangle. Connecting the midpoints of these new line segments from adjacent rectangles yielded the new boundary polygon which in turn served as reference boundary for the subsequent frame.

Due to heart contraction and contrast medium fluctuations, the intensity within the heart image area varies much more strongly with time - i.e. frame index - than outside this area. TASTO 74 defined the pixel of a computed image as the sum of absolute intensity differences at its rasterposition between all images in a sequence that are exactly K (chosen between 6 and 10) frames apart. Only pixels above the mean value for all pixels of this computed image were retained. After an iterative noise suppression step, the outer boundary of the resulting nonzero pixel grouping was taken as an initial estimate for the left ventricular contour.

A procedure described by TASTO 73 exploited this estimate together with coarse assumptions about the shape of the left ventricle in a search for boundary elements which exhibited a local maximum of the intensity gradient in the expected boundary area. A smooth connected boundary accepted in one frame served as boundary estimate for the subsequent frame. TASTO et al. 78 have compared several minor variations of this approach with each other and with manual contour determinations - in the latter case with acceptable results.

Another fully automatic approach has been described by SMALLING et al. 76 . These authors analysed greyvalue histograms from selected scanlines of the first frame of a sequence in order to determine a greyvalue threshold by which they could separate the left ventricle from background. This procedure was applied to various parts of the first frame to obtain locally adapted threshold values. The threshold values determined for the first frame were then used to process the remaining frames in a sequence although later experience recommended to update these threshold values continuously during progression through the image sequence. The boundary detection algorithm operated line by line, accepting a contour point if the intensity gradient along the scanline exceeded a gradient threshold and if the intensity - averaged over three successive pixels - exceeded the greyvalue threshold. The resulting contour was smoothed. After detection of the aortic valve position the ventricular boundary was converted into a closed contour by connecting the boundary across the aortic valve. The resulting closed contours were translated such that their centroids coincided and their long axes were aligned. This facilitated a comparison of consecutive contours in a search for abnormal motion of the ventricular boundary during a heart cycle.

Part II of the book edited by HEINTZEN and BUERSCH 78 contains a collection of more recent articles which described and evaluated interactive as well as automatic approaches to the analysis of angiocardiographic image sequences - including some of those outlined in the preceding paragraphs.

YACHIDA et al. 79a further refined the techniques for extracting information about the dynamics of the heart wall from a film recording of an angiocardiogram. They first condensed a picture digitized with 256x256 pixel resolution into a 64x64 picture. Areas in this 64x64 picture with high response to 3x3 directional gradient mask operators were selected for further processing. This represents an application of the 'planning' approach originally discussed by KELLY 71 . At each selected area, the gradient estimate was refined in the corresponding area of the higher resolution image, but only along the orientation of highest response observed in the condensed picture. A heuristic search then traced a polygonal approximation to the ventricular boundary through these areas by maximizing a cumulative figure of merit reflecting the a priori knowledge about the contour as well as measured edge strength and orientation. Further details about this approach to boundary detection can be found in YACHIDA et al. 79b .

The ventricle boundary extracted from one frame was used as a contour estimate guiding the search in the subsequent frame. Moreover, each new image frame was quickly evaluated to determine whether the contour had moved enough to warrant a more detailed analysis. This 'planning with respect to frame number (time)' reduced the number of frames to be analysed in detail to about 1/3 of the sequence on average and down to 1/16 at the end of an expansion or contraction period when the ventricular wall moves only rather slowly.

The approaches discussed so far extracted the boundary of the left ventricle from cine-angiocardiograms and presented the results as a series of contour lines - possibly centered and oriented to facilitate visual comparison. Radii from the center of gravity to points on the contour, the projected area of the left ventricle, and estimates for the ventricular volume as well as time derivatives of these quantities could be determined from the series of ventricular contours. However, no higher level description of shape or dynamic shape variation has been computed.

A long-term cooperation of physicians specializing in cardiology with computer scientists from the University of Toronto and McGill University at Montreal incorporated higher level cardiological knowledge into a system for the analysis of angiocardiographic image sequences - see TSOTSOS et al. 77+78+79a+79b . Their low level image processing for the extraction of ventricular contours might not yet be as sophisticated as that in other more recent approaches - such as, e.g., the one reported by YACHIDA et al. 79a+79b . However, TSOTSOS et al. provided a knowledge representation required to establish a connection between changes detectable at the pixel level of temporal image sequences on the one hand and the high level concepts on the other hand which categorize the dynamic behavior of a ventricle under study. Their system comprised an explicit shape representation for different segments of the ventricular contour. It attempted to classify the temporal displacement characteristics of ventricular contour segments into various normal and pathological categories. This categorization allowed the description of information extracted from an angiographic image sequence in terms familiar to cardiologists. Moreover, this knowledge representation was exploited to organize intermediate results in a form which facilitated the use of a priori and acquired knowledge in order to guide the evaluation of subsequent image frames or to reevaluate earlier hypotheses.

Injection of radioactive nuclei into a peripheral vein and subsequent recording of their decay gamma rays by a scintigraphic camera provide another way to obtain images of, e.g., the left ventricle. Although these scintigraphic images offer even less contrast than good x-ray images, HACHIMURA et al. 78 were able to determine the left ventricular contour in such scintigraphic image sequences. By detailed analysis of the left ventricular contour obtained at the end-diastole (maximal dilatation) and the end-systole (maximal contraction) they attempted to classify the observed left ventricular wall motion into a normal and an abnormal category.

2.3.4 Isolation of organs based on spectral and temporal pixel characteristics

The two preceding sections emphasized the analysis of image variations caused by mechanical phenomena - circulation of the blood and motion of the heart. The selective accumulation or depletion of chemical compounds in certain organs due to their metabolism can be exploited to obtain characteristic variations in the temporal and spectral composition of absorbed or emitted radiation.

If x-ray opaque material accumulates only slightly in those parts of the body which should be studied, the resulting change in contrast may be insufficient to outline the accumulation area against strongly absorbing background. However, the absorption coefficient of the background does not change very much with moderate variations of the x-ray beam energy whereas a contrast material may be selected which exhibits a marked change of its absorption coefficient in this energy range - see MISTRETTA et al. 73 . Under such conditions, KRUGER et al. 78 recorded images with quasimonoenergetic x-ray beams of different energy and subtracted these images from each other. The background absorption was cancelled and those image areas became visible where some contrast material with strong energy dependent absorption coefficient had accumulated. Automatic extraction of these regions in the difference image would have been possible by thresholding and subsequent smoothing to suppress 'pepper and salt' noise.

We may consider this approach as the evaluation of an image sequence comprising only two frames - namely the two absorption images recorded in different spectral channels corresponding to the different x-ray beam energies. An analogous approach may be applied to scintigraphic images obtained by recording the gamma rays from pharmaceuticals which have been 'labelled' with radionuclides. The spatial distribution of scintigraphic events reflects the selective accumulation of such radiopharmaceuticals in certain parts of the body such as liver and pancreas. The scintigraphic image of the liver normally overlaps that of the pancreas. If no radiopharmaceutical is available which accumulates exclusively in the pancreas, the latter organ may nevertheless be isolated by subtraction of two scintigraphic images recorded in different spectral channels as described, e.g., by GOSE et al. 75 .

Two pharmaceuticals were injected, both marked with a radionuclide which differed, however, in the energy of the emitted gamma ray. Let Ilp denote the intensity (counts) recorded from the radiopharmaceutical which accumulated in both liver and pancreas whereas the other radiopharmaceutical accumulated in the liver only. The corresponding intensity will be denoted by Il. If the liver cells accumulate both pharmaceuticals homogeneously throughout the entire organ and if other assumptions - no background radiation, equal absorption for both gamma rays despite their different energy - are justified, then the intensity in the liver region of the scintigraphic images should exhibit the same variation with the liver geometry for both spectral channels. Therefore, the ratio

$$R(i,j) = Ilp(i,j) / Il(i,j)$$

of the two spectral intensity components should be essentially independent of the rasterposition (i,j) - provided the rasterpositions are restricted to the image region which corresponds exclusively to the liver. If this restriction is relaxed and the ratio R(i,j) of the two spectral components is entered into a histogram for all rasterpositions (i,j) in the scintigraphic image, the R(i,j) obtained from the liver region are expected to cluster around some value R, thus leading to a peak in this histogram. The value R can therefore be detected by identifying the expected peak in the histogram.

Once R is known, the image of the spectral channel corresponding to gamma rays from the liver alone can be multiplied by R and subtracted from the spectral image corresponding to liver plus pancreas, yielding a difference image Ip(i,j) corresponding to the pancreas :

$$Ip(i,j) = Ilp(i,j) - R * Il(i,j)$$

In order to identify the expected peak in the histogram by an automatic histogram analysis, GOSE et al. 75 had to remove the background intensity and to smooth the images in both spectral channels. Using three radiopharmaceuticals, GOSE et al. 76 were able to isolate the images of liver, pancreas, and spleen from multispectral scintigraphic images.

The work of KRUGER et al. 78 and GOSE et al. 75+76 has been presented in somewhat greater detail because it should illustrate simple applications of a more general approach that has been extended from spectral to temporal image sequences. In the case of KRUGER et al. 78 , the spectral component images were combined linearly - using known weighting coefficients - in order to obtain a difference image within which the region corresponding to the organ of interest could be isolated by simple image processing procedures such as thresholding. GOSE et al. 75 again formed a linear combination of two spectral images in order to isolate the pancreas image region. In their case, however, the weighting coefficient R was unknown and had to be estimated from the two spectral component images by a clustering procedure. These authors exploited domain specific knowledge in order to combine the measurements in such a way that the clustering could be reduced to a one-dimensional search for the peak in a histogram. The same goal could be achieved by a cluster search in a two-dimensional histogram - a scatter-plot - of intensity recorded in one spectral channel versus intensity recorded at the same rasterlocation in the other spectral channel. The entries are expected to cluster around the origin - representing background events - or along straight lines through the origin. This is a consequence of assumptions outlined above - homogeneous accumulation of radiopharmaceuticals throughout the organ and no energy dependent absorption. The count or intensity recorded at a rasterlocation which corresponds to the scintigraphic image of exactly one organ will thus be proportional to a geometric factor which is identical in both spectral channels. The corresponding entries into the scatter-plot disperse along a line because this geometric factor may vary from rasterposition to rasterposition. The slope of this line is determined by the administered doses of radiopharmaceuticals, by their accumulation rate in an organ, and by the decay rates of the radioisotopes, i.e. parameters which are independent of the organ's geometry. By using intensity values from interactively selected test regions in a dual-channel scintigraphic image, GOSE et al. 76 illustrated that these elongated clusters corresponding to liver, pancreas, and spleen could be identified in such a scatter-plot in addition to the background cluster near the origin.

In order to prepare the conceptual transfer of this approach from spectral to temporal image sequences - with many more frames per sequence - let us assume that a scintigraphic image of the liver+pancreas area would be recorded in three spectral channels. In all three spectral channels, the same geometric factor relates the constant spatial density of radiopharmaceuticals within an organ to the decay count recorded at a certain rasterposition in the scintigraphic image. Therefore, as in the two-dimensional case, the decay event counts (intensity values) from one organ should disperse in the three-dimensional scatter-plot along a line through the origin. If there are two organs which do not overlap completely when viewed from the scintigraphic sensor, then two such line like clusters can be expected.

All pixels at which gamma rays from the area of overlapping organs are counted should exhibit intensity values which are positive linear combinations of values from the two lines corresponding to the 'pure organ' situation. Their entries into the three-dimensional scatter-plot should therefore fall onto or close to the plane defined by the two linear clusters corresponding to each organ. A principal component analysis followed by a selection of the eigenvectors connected with large eigenvalues yields a description for this plane because the scatter perpendicular to this plane should be small - being due to noise only. This approach can obviously be generalized to situations where data about n different organs are recorded in d different spectral channels - provided d is at least as great as n. After having performed a principal component analysis, the eigenvalues which significantly exceed the value to be attributed to noise are selected - see, e.g., DUDA and HART 73 (section 6.12) for an analysis of a related question. Let us assume that this decision can be made sufficiently reliable. The number of these large eigenvalues corresponds to the number of different organs - barring degenerate cases where several organs exhibit the same characteristics. The eigenvectors connected with these eigenvalues span the subspace in which the clusters corresponding to the different organs have to be found. Once these clusters have been identified, their spectral characteristics are known and can be used to extract the image of the corresponding organs in exact analogy to the simple cases discussed at the beginning of this section.

This approach will now be transferred from spectral to temporal image sequences. GOSE et al. 76 demonstrated by illustrative examples how different temporal characteristics in the uptake and elimination of radiopharmaceuticals could be exploited in order to isolate the image of a single organ. A linear combination of suitable frames - interactively selected from a temporal sequence of scintigraphic images - yielded a computed frame from which the desired organ image could be extracted by simple thresholding and smoothing procedures.

Each temporal sample - i.e. each frame - takes on the role of a spectral channel in the preceding exposition of the method. ROSE et al. 79 discussed a semiautomatic approach to isolate several overlapping organs from each other in a temporal sequence of 13 scintigraphic images condensed into 32x32 pixel frames. A window comprising 5x19 pixels was selected from each frame. The eigenvalues of the covariance matrix corresponding to the 95x13 (pixels x frames) data matrix were determined by singular value decomposition. Phantom experiments yielded an estimate for the magnitude of an eigenvalue corresponding to noise. Based on this comparison value, an automatic selection procedure would have had to accept about 4-6 of the eigenvalues obtained from the patient data as significantly larger than the noise value. The authors expected four dominant independent temporal characteristics, one each for the blood, the soft tissue, the liver, and the gallbladder. Since the data had been normalized to zero mean value, these four independent temporal characteristics would be confined to a three-dimensional subspace of the 13-dimensional dataspace (one dimension for each of the 13 frames in the temporal sequence!). This three-dimensional subspace was determined by the three eigenvectors connected with the three largest eigenvalues. An interactive search in this three-dimensional subspace isolated four clusters, one for each of the four independent temporal characteristics. Each of the four cluster centers was represented by a specific linear combination of the three eigenvectors spanning the subspace or - equivalently - by a certain linear combination of the 13 temporal frames. The weighting coefficient of a certain frame in the linear combination representing, e.g., the liver cluster reflected the relative activity of the liver at that instant of time. The concept developped so far implied that the temporal variation at each pixel position in the 5x19 pixel window had to be represented as a linear combination of the four temporal characteristics for blood, soft tissue, liver, and gallbladder

- with positive coefficients since the decay events from radionuclides cannot cancel each other. Linear programming was used to obtain these coefficients for each pixel in every frame since a least square approach might have resulted in unrealistic negative coefficients for certain pixels. Once the coefficients were determined for all pixels, the original image sequence had been decomposed into four temporal sequences which represented separately the image of liver, gallbladder, soft tissue, and blood as a function of time.

Although some interaction had still been required to obtain this decomposition - notably the decision to retain a three-dimensional subspace and the identification of four clusters in this subspace - the general thrust of this approach should have become clear. ROSE et al. 79 discussed several possibilities to replace the remaining interactive steps by algorithms. More importantly, they pointed out that this approach could be used for different application areas such as the evaluation of aerial or satellite image sequences where contributions from overlapping, (partially) transparent emitters would have to be separated on the basis of their different time characteristics. Thermal inertia (see section 2.2.3) or mixed vegetation (see section 2.2.6) are examples for such situations.

2.3.5 Quantitative description, categorization, and modeling of organ functions

The possibility to use temporal image sequences for recording and visualization of dynamic processes in the human body has been demonstrated. Direct display of the recorded image sequence for scrutiny by a human expert is but a first step in the analysis of this information. Organ properties such as volume, surface, or circumference along different surface curves can be determined quantitatively as described, e.g., by HEINTZEN et al. 75 , SMALLING et al. 76 , or in the contributions to HEINTZEN and BUERSCH 78 . Such quantitative descriptors reflect the organ function more directly than the image sequence itself and therefore represent a more appropriate basis for an expert decision about whether the organ functions normally or - if not - what the defect might be.

A next subgoal consists in assigning extracted shapes and dynamic shape variations automatically to categories which correspond to a normal function of the isolated organ or to various pathological situations. The computer-internal representation of these categories runs the full gamut of pattern recognition techniques. A classification approach based on Fourier coefficients derived from a decomposition of the organ contours into spatial frequencies is one of these possibilities, applied by HACHIMURA et al. 78 . Dynamic effects can be represented by functional images in a manner which preserves the topological relations of the organ image. Therefore, functional images offer a suitable basis for classification approaches regarding structure and function of certain stationary organs - see HOEHNE et al. 79 , HOLDEN 79 , and especially the examples discussed by GALLAGHER et al. 77 .

NEJDL et al. 78 described a complex algorithm for automated diagnosis of lung ventilation and perfusion - based on similar parametric representations derived from scintigraphic image sequences of the lung. In a first step - the ventilation study - the patient breathed air containing radioactive xenon for a defined time interval. Scintigraphic images - recorded during this interval and after a defined period later - enabled the identification of lung areas which accepted or released air at an abnormal rate. Without moving the patient, a radiopharmaceutical was then injected into the blood. Again, a scintigraphic image sequence facilitated the quantitative study of blood circulation in the lung - in spatial correlation with the earlier ventilation study. The classification result of their algorithmic analysis for lung defects compared well with the diagnosis of expert physicians.

A principal component analysis of temporal image sequences - see the second half of section 2.3.4 - has been employed by SCHMIDLIN et al. 76 not only to isolate kidney images for over hundred patients but - in addition - to classify the isolated organs as normal or abnormal.

Efforts on the evaluation of image sequences from the human body have been presented in the preceding paragraphs as a progression through the following phases:

(1) inspection;
(2) preprocessing to facilitate inspection;
(3) extraction and presentation of quantitative properties;
(4) classification of measurements into normal/abnormal categories;
(5) attempts to integrate the different quantitative results into a consistent description of the organ, its function and its interaction with the environment.

This latter phase proceeds gradually to the development of quantitative computer-internal models of the organ and its function. Examples for this development will only be mentioned here because medical and physiological aspects would dominate a more detailed presentation and their discussion would thus stray beyond the scope of this survey.

Regarding the left ventricle, the reader is referred to the survey of RACKLEY 76 as well as the work reported by HEINTZEN et al. 75 , by TSOTSOS et al. 79a+79b , and further articles in HEINTZEN and BUERSCH 78 . Similar studies of the right ventricle can be found in LANGE et al. 76 . A mechanical analysis of the heart is under development which employs finite-element-analysis methods to describe the three-dimensional dynamic distribution of stress and strain on the cardiac muscle - see, e.g., JOHNSON et al. 76 and WOOD 76 for further references.

Investigations of quantitative models are not restricted to the heart. GALLAGHER et al. 77 reported about a complex compartmental model of renal function developed by DeGRAZIA in 1973.

Analogous efforts are concerned with the quantitative description of gastric activity. Apart from a study of emptying times - see, e.g., GALLAGHER et al. 77 - complex motions have to be analysed. GAUDEAU et al. 79 reported attempts to separate passive motion caused by the activity of heart and lungs from intrinsic gastric waves which are intricately connected with the stomach function. Such contractions and relaxations can possibly be quantified by a sophisticated shape analysis on radiographic image sequences.

2.3.6 Body surface potential maps

Medical image sequences quite different in origin and structure from the ones discussed so far can be derived by recording the electric potential on a large number - approximately 200 - of locations on the skin of a patient as a function of time. The spatial and temporal variation of this potential is connected to the heart excitation and may allow a more reliable diagnosis of certain heart abnormalities than the electrocardiogram (ECG) or the vectorcardiogram (VCG). A concise introduction - including references to the history of this question - can be found in PIERONI and NARASIMHAN 74 . More recently THOMAS et al. 79 reported about similar work.

PIERONI 76+79 looked for a compact representation of characteristic variations during such an image sequence which could comprise of the order of 300 frames per heart cycle. The body surface potential may deviate from zero potential towards both polarities. PIERONI restricted his analysis to two subsets of sample locations where the potential dropped to zero either from negative values or from positive ones. If the body potential is conceived to be plotted as a function of the two-dimensional arrangement of sample point positions, the subsets selected by PIERONI corresponded to contour lines obtained by intersecting the potential function with the plane of zero potential. Adjacent sample points where the potential dropped to zero from the same polarity were connected to form 'chainlets'. These were classified into several categories, based on shape, position, and orientation. A heuristic transition table indicated acceptable transformations of a chainlet from one frame into a 'related' chainlet extracted from the subsequent frame. The temporal evolution of chainlet transformations was expected to reflect - at least in a phenomenological manner - characteristic aspects of the dynamics of body surface potentials.

Since the derivation and classification of chainlets appeared to be strongly influenced by noise effects, PIERONI and FREEMAN 78 adopted a slightly different approach. A four-direction chain code was used to represent the boundary of areas in the 2-D arrangement of sample point positions for which the body surface potential was negative. The shapes of such blob-like areas were then matched to a family of templates derived from the union of partially overlapping rectangles. These templates reflected a few basic shapes obtained by removing corners from a rectangle containing the boundary curve. If these templates are compared to the basic shapes of a defined 'order' as introduced by BRIBIESCA and GUZMAN 78+79 , it appears attractive to investigate the shape numbers introduced by the latter authors in order to characterize the boundary curves.

A histogram of shape complexity - taken by PIERONI and FREEMAN 78 to be given by the number of corner-smoothing operations required to arrive at one of the template shapes - versus frame number constituted the phenomenological representation of the dynamics in this latter approach. No frame-to-frame matching was required. The relevance of this representation to medical diagnosis remained an open question. It is not inconceivable that progress in the automated evaluation of these image sequences has been handicapped by a lack of even a crude qualitative model about how the measured body surface potential should vary and how it might be related to specific heart abnormalities. PIERONI attacked the problem to analyse a temporal sequence of body surface potential maps by reducing it to contourline matching. It should be interesting to study the adaptation of other techniques for frame-to-frame curve matching to this problem area. A syntactic approach has recently been reported by FAN and FU 79 which appears to be a candidate for a more detailed investigation in this direction.

2.3.7 Studying the pupil of the human eye

A quantitative investigation of the expansion and contraction of the human pupil can give the ophthalmologist important help for diagnosis and treatment monitoring. The patient is seated in a darkened room so that his pupils open widely. A pupil - illuminated by an infrared light-emitting diode - is recorded using an infrared-sensitive video camera. Periodically - about once every six seconds - a bright flash of visible light causes the pupil to contract. The instantaneous boundary of the pupil is determined during this contraction and subsequent re expansion process from a series of consecutive IR TV frames. By recording many such sequences it becomes possible to isolate frames where lid movements influenced the determination of the pupil contour. After these frames have been removed, the remaining images are averaged for corresponding phases of the repeatedly recorded contraction and expansion cycles of the pupil.

The resulting temporal sequence of pupil contours can be conceived as time samples from an - approximately - cylindrical surface in a three-dimensional space constituted by the two coordinate axes in the TV-target plane and the time axis. Applying a gradient operator to this surface yields an estimate of contraction and expansion speed for the pupil reaction to the flash. Azimuthal inhomogeneities in the contraction of the pupil may be described quantitatively by integrating the actual pupil radius in a certain direction over time and by plotting the resulting integral as a function of the azimuthal angle. Similarly, the area, circumference, and other attributes of the pupil image may be extracted from the recorded image sequences and studied as a function of time - see SCHULTES et al. 79 .

2.4 Biomedical Applications

Two conceptual tasks can be distinguished in biomedical investigations of image sequences from microscope observations. One approach analyses positional changes as being due to movement of microbes, cells, or subcellular particles. This allows the study of transportation as well as stimulus-response phenomena. The other approach investigates size and shape changes, studying growth and transformation phenomena.

DAVENPORT et al. 70 studied the stimulus-response behavior of microorganisms moving in a wet-slide preparation under a microscope using image sequences recorded on videotape. GREAVES 75 described a system which transformed the video signals from such a tape recording into a binary picture using an interactively determined threshold. A thinning algorithm reduced the image of each organism to a single point. A time-ordered list of such point coordinates represented a "bugpath". An interactive system enabled the researcher to compute properties of a bugpath such as the velocity or mean direction and to aggregate data from many quantitative evaluations into a description of the observed stimulus-response behavior.

Although starting from a completely different biomedical investigation, LEVINE and YOUSSEF 78b , LEVINE et al. 79 ended up solving a tracking problem analogous to those already mentioned. It had been reported that lymphocytes tend to move toward pre-malignant or regressive tumor cells whereas they seem to move away from malignant cells. The motion of lymphocytes appears to be influenced by chemicals that are emitted by invasive cells. In order to obtain statistically reliable quantitative observations about this so-called chemotaxis, large number of lymphocytes had to be tracked in time-lapse cinemicrophotographs recorded at 20 second intervals over a period of 1-2 hours. GREENE and BARNES 77 mechanically tracked one cell at a time by positioning the microscope stage according to a control signal derived from a five unit photodiode array. LEVINE and YOUSSEF 78a designed a computer controlled system to achieve the same goal by evaluating time-lapse TV images.

According to LEVINE et al. 79, this experimental device might be employed to scan a proliferating cell in order to trace the genealogies of selected cells.

In a similar tracking problem, TAKAGI and SAKAUE 78 had to determine the paths of granules in a cultivated, living pancreatic cell recorded by time-lapse cinemicrophotography at 1 second intervals for 5 - 10 minutes. These granules carry insulin from ribosomes where it is produced to the cell membrane. Analysing the motion of these granules may therefore contribute to a better understanding of hormone production mechanisms. Although the greylevel of granules was much darker than that of the cell background, the large number of such granules and their widely varying motion pattern complicated the tracking.

In order to study processes in the membrane and interior of stationary or moving cells, attempts have been started for measuring the size and shape variations of observed cells - see LEVINE et al. 79 . LIPKIN et al. 79 described possible extensions of such an approach to study morphologically discernible cell activities, and how these are influenced by environmental carcinogens. In a similar approach, ARIKI 78 , ARIKI et al. 78 developed an interactive system to analyse the morphogenetic movement - see ROBERTSON and COHEN 72 - of a dissociated cell of Xenopus laevis, a protozoon. An elaborate interactive facility is required not only to facilitate handling of unexpected variation in the raw data during the course of an experiment, but even more to support the concept formation when measurements of dynamic entities have to be evaluated. This latter aspect has been emphasized, e.g., for the evaluation of time-lapse cinemicrophotography of developing organisms such as cellular slime molds - see FUTRELLE 74 , FUTRELLE and POTEL 75 , POTEL and SAYRE 76+77 .

Further examples for the application of such an interactive system can be found in POTEL and MACKAY 79 as well as POTEL et al. 79 . FUTRELLE and CHENG 79 as well as POTEL and MACKAY 79 described a facility to dynamically overlay computer graphic displays and film by registered projection onto the same screen. This considerably simplified a check on correct interactive input of data and especially the tracking and data recording of dynamic phenomena. The approach towards interactive determination of cardiac wall motion discussed by REEVES et al. 79 is an extension of these techniques - see section 2.3.3.

During design, implementation, and improvement of these interactive systems, experience has been gathered with the design of datastructures suitable for accepting the interactive measurements and for the creation of dynamic displays based on such data - see FUTRELLE and SPECKERT 78 , FUTRELLE and CHENG 79 , POTEL and MACKAY 79 , POTEL et al. 79 , and SAYRE 79 . These experiences and concepts for the design of sequence descriptions should be investigated - just as the work of TSOTSOS 80 - if datastructures for the representation of dynamic phenomena have to be designed for advanced image sequence analysis systems.

GLASER 68 described an experimental apparatus to record the growth of bacterial colonies on petri dishes by taking photographs about once every hour on 35 mm film and to analyse such films using a flying-spot scanner. Organisms had to be identified on the basis of their growth rate and of their appearance under particular growth conditions. More details about the intraframe image analysis employed in these experiments have recently been reported by COUCH et al. 79 whereas the sequence aspects have only be mentioned again.

2.5 Behavioral Studies

The automatic analysis of image sequences recorded from scenes with humans or animals offer the potential to acquire large amounts of quantitative observations for behavioral studies. Up to now, most situations of interest to behaviorists are not yet amenable to automatic evaluation unless the data gathering is restricted to positional variations of markers which can be easily identified and tracked within the image sequence. LAPPALAINEN and TERVONEN 75 described a set-up with two TV cameras which enabled a computer to read the coordinates of a few white markers on dark background detected by a thresholding circuit for each TV frame. However, no attempts had been made to track and interprete these coordinate measurements by computer.

Analysis of human gait poses difficult problems. Facilities for measuring the temporal changes in the relative configuration of limbs and the human torso offer the possibility to check and refine quantitative models for human locomotion. Recent studies - see CHENG 74 and RAHMANI 79 - used a TV camera to determine the projected coordinates of six lights which had been fixed at limbs and joints of a person walking in a darkened room. Under these conditions, thresholding the intensity allowed the identification of the images of these lights in each video frame. CHEN 79 investigated the realization of a more complex system consisting of three TV cameras and a force plate, the latter one used to measure the forces conveyed by a foot of a walking person to the floor. The arrangement of three cameras should enable the determination of 3-D spatial coordinates of lights on all sides of the human body. No complex image analysis was intended. References to earlier work on human gait analysis can be found in the theses by CHEN 79 and RAHMANI 79. The latter one contains various approaches to construct quantitative models of human locomotion. A very simplified stick-figure representation for a moving human body has been discussed by SAYRE 79 .

SPECKERT 76 analysed two short films showing a cat in a treadmill. Round white markers had been attached to the skin of the cat quite near to joints. The images of these markers were identified in each frame and tracked from frame to frame. Based on an interactive evaluation of the resulting trajectory measurements, attempts to describe quantitatively the locomotion of a cat in different gaits were discussed.

In another example, the object localization capability has been investigated for a certain kind of fish which tends to hover among inanimate objects such as rock or grass common to its habitat. Despite the fact that plants may sway slowly, such fishes attempt to maintain their position relative to these plants. In order to study the mechanisms enabling such behavior, UTER 77 employed an overhead camera to observe one such fish between two rods swinging sideways in an aquarium. Although thresholding the signal from a single selected TV line yielded data of interest to his experiment, UTER 77 exploited only in a most rudimentary fashion the flexibility that the analysis of image sequences offers for observation of behavior. LUBINSKI et al. 77 described a set-up for observing fishes in a vat which relied on an intensity threshold approach similar to UTER 77. However, these authors extracted a coordinate pair representing the object location. A 2-D window within the field of view could be specified to which recording was then restricted. Nevertheless, a more sophisticated approach is necessary in order to obtain data useful for realistic behavioral studies.

YACHIDA et al. 78 observed fishes swimming in a vat by an overhead TV camera connected to a videotape recorder to study their behavior under a variety of stimuli such as lights or tones. About 8 frames per second were recorded for periods between 2 and 30 seconds, resulting in sequences of 20-250 frames. A sophisticated image analysis allowed the identification of the often motion-blurred images of fishes, the modeling of the shape of these images, and to employment of shape prediction in order to disambiguate situations where one fish occluded another.

2.6 Object Tracking in Outdoor Scenes

Solution approaches to problems in this area could be categorized, e.g., according to application or technical aspects like the significance of real-time constraints. The truly important characteristics, however, are the methods by which attributes of the object, its trajectory, and its acceleration as well as attributes of its environment, can be identified from an image sequence and exploited for the tracking task. If real-time constraints at the timescale of seconds or less have to be obeyed, the attributes available must allow a quick and reliable discrimination between the environment and the object to be tracked. In such situations, the position of the object image centroid - or any other well-defined reference point connected with the object image - has to be estimated. Control techniques are employed to keep this position centered in the field of view. Such approaches will be discussed in a following subsection on target tracking. There are other situations where more emphasis is placed on simultaneous tracking of a multitude of objects in order to determine their number and identity, possibly even to study their interactions based on their recorded trajectories. The larger number of objects to be tracked is usually accompanied by greater variations in the object attributes. Moreover, ambiguities might arise due to clustering of moving objects or trajectory intersections. Therefore, more detailed descriptors for each object have to be derived from the image sequence and the analysis becomes more involved. Monitoring of vehicular traffic offers a number of illustrating examples for this latter category.

2.6.1 Traffic monitoring

WOLFERTS 73a+73b+74 described an operational semi-automatic image processing system for determination of vehicle velocities from time-lapsed aerial film recording of street scenes. In addition to the velocity, the vehicle type - car, truck, bus, etc. - could be identified and vehicle behavior for a variety of quickly changing traffic situations could be observed. The image of a vehicle to be tracked had to be selected interactively by an operator. Cross-correlation was used to track this vehicle image in subsequent frames. A flying-spot scanner digitized the film with 6-bit greyvalue resolution on a 256x256 pixel raster for 20 mm x 20 mm windows. A related approach has been sketched by KANADE and OHTA 74 .

Thorough explorative studies with a similar interactive flying-spot system for the evaluation of street traffic films have been reported by RAUDSEPS 75 . Concerning the conceptual insights to be gained from such evaluations, he distinguished between "macroscopic" and "microscopic" aspects of traffic situations. The former aspects refer to mean vehicle velocity, vehicle density, flow rate in vehicles/hour, distribution of traffic by lanes, by vehicle type etc. These aspects could potentially be measured using, e.g., induction loops. Microscopic aspects were defined by RAUDSEPS 75 as being related to actions of an individual vehicle or configurations of a few vehicles and included headway between individual vehicles, lane-changing, overtaking, and others. Evaluation of image sequences seems to offer special advantages for the investigation of such microscopic traffic aspects. For example, HANSCOM 73 evaluated - by visual inspection - time-lapse film recordings of highway traffic at a complex intersection in order to quantitate erratic driver behaviour before and after improving a route-guidance sign. CRIBBINS 73 reported about analogous investigations.

Since it should be possible to restrict the number of microscopic aspects required for the analysis of normal traffic situations, it might be illuminating to design a frame-like description for each microscopic aspect analogous to the motion descriptors designed by TSOTSOS for left ventricular wall motion - see TSOTSOS 77+80 , TSOTSOS et al. 79a+79b and earlier reports quoted there. It might be useful to emphasize the difference between the knowledge-driven approach suggested here and the one described by AGIN 79 . The latter one is restricted to the evaluation of a single image. The context for the analysis of the image - especially the identification and classification of vehicles in aerial photographs of road scenes - is provided by sophisticated integration of three different kinds of knowledge:

(i) knowledge about the problem domain in the form of "road expert" routines;
(ii) knowledge about the site depicted in the form of a geographical database;
(iii) knowledge about the particular conditions prevailing at the time the photograph had been taken.

All of this represents static knowledge whereas the extension suggested above refers to the exploitation of knowledge about the dynamic aspects of road situations. A truly robust system will have to incorporate knowledge about static as well as dynamic aspects. The motivation to develop a knowledge-driven approach combining the static and dynamic aspects increases when the evaluation of TV-frame sequences rather than film is considered. It is encouraging to see that trends in this direction become clearly discernible in the recent literature.

First attempts to employ TV-frame recording for traffic analysis have been reported by ONOE et al. 73 . An image recorded on a solid-state video storage tube was subtracted from subsequent TV frames of the same street scene. Provided no distortions and noise would occur, the difference image would show a large change signal in regions where a car had been displaced between the two frames compared. ONOE et al. 73 demonstrated this approach for estimating the velocity of two cars. To reduce the processing time required, ONOE and OHBA 76 restricted the analysis to pixels selectively digitized along the image of lanes to be studied. Following some preprocessing, it was decided that vehicles were present at all pixels where the intensity differed by more than a threshold from a corrected average of pixel intensities sampled along lane images. In essence, this is a rather preliminary version of the approach reported by QUAM 78 and AGIN 79 who also attempted to identify vehicles as significant deviations from the predicted road surface appearance. As AGIN 79 demonstrated, there are many pitfalls connected with such an approach. The design of a reliable vehicle counting and identification system to be operated in real time on TV input requires the careful consideration of many aspects - e.g., lighting conditions, properties of street surface and TV cameras, etc. - as investigated by RUEENAUFER 76 .

He oriented the video scanlines parallel to the projected vehicle displacement. A rectangular window parallel to the scanlines was selected interactively such that it covered a section of a traffic lane and preferably some zone free from street traffic on at least one side of the lane. The window was divided into 5 x 5 subwindows, each comprising 5 x 5 pixels on a 256x256 raster. A reference frame without a vehicle in the window was chosen by a human operator. Intensity averages over a subwindow from later frames were compared to corresponding intensity averages from the reference frame. Since a raster unit was equivalent to about 0.2 m on a vehicle, a single subwindow did not cover the entire vehicle image in a direction perpendicular to its displacement. The five neighboring rows of subwindows taken together, however, extended beyond the vehicle image. Intensity averages from subwindows not affected by a vehicle image could be used to monitor slow variations in the background intensity due to changes in the scene illumination by, e.g., shadows of wandering clouds. This enabled compensation of changes in the road background intensities for subwindows covering the traffic lane proper. Phase shifts between comparable intensity differences from subwindows along the displacement direction of vehicle images could be used to determine the vehicle's velocity. The number of adjacent subwindows within a row for which the mean intensity differed significantly from that of the reference frame allowed the estimation of the vehicle length and thus the vehicle type (car, van, truck/bus).

JONES 74 - see also CHIEN and JONES 75 - attempted to apply real-time tracking techniques investigated in the context of visual feedback for automatic manipulators to vehicle tracking in TV signals from street scenes. Moving objects were detected using an image difference technique and tracked on the basis of prominent greyvalue, edge, or texture features found within a predefined window centered at the image position of the assumed moving object. Steps towards a considerably more refined analysis - although not yet applied to traffic scenes - have been reported by CHIEN et al. 79 and JACOBUS 79 .

GERLACH 79 successfully combined several techniques in order to achieve a significantly improved robustness for tracking single vehicles in road scenes recorded by a ground-based TV camera. An interactively selected window around the vehicle image to be tracked was crosscorrelated with a suitably selected search area of subsequent TV frames. As long as the cross-correlation maximum remained higher than a threshold, the reference subimage was updated using the intensities within the areas in subsequent frames which corresponded to the optimum match of the reference subimage. Appropriately weighting the pixel intensities from the reference subimage and the current frame allowed the controlling of the rate at which the reference subimage adapted to the changing appearance of the object as well as the foreground and background covered by the reference window. Since the object image remained essentially centered in the reference window whereas the foreground and background changed from frame to frame, this adaptation resulted in a blurr of the background contribution. This effect was exploited to obtain a coarse estimate of the object image. Spatial differentiation of the reference subimage resulted in larger gradients at the object boundaries whereas only small gradients were to be expected in the background surrounding the object image in the reference subimage. Therefore, all pixels were considered to be background when working from the reference window boundary inwards until the first significant gradient had been encountered. Only the pixels of the remaining "object mask" within the reference subimage were used for subsequent correlations thus reducing the influence of background variation on the cross-correlation maximum. (A conceptually similar approach has been applied by GARDNER et al. 77 in order to extract an aircraft silhouette from series of tracking windows showing the aircraft in a cloudy environment.

Moreover, the difference between subimages around the object location detected in consecutive frames was evaluated. Since the object image should have appeared in roughly identical positions with respect to the subimages from which the difference was computed, larger differences were expected to be due to foreground components partially occluding the object or to especially prominent background structures. These differences shifted from frame to frame relative to the reference window boundary which remained centered on the object to be tracked. An analysis of these shifting contributions in the sequence of difference images allowed their classification as foreground or background components - see BACH et al. 78. The corresponding pixels were excluded from the "object mask" used to control the cross-correlation of the reference subimage with the search area in the next frame.

This approach represents a successful attempt to obtain a more reliable tracking method by integrating several techniques in order to derive an improved internal description of the object image to be tracked. Several of these techniques had been investigated earlier by NAGEL 78a as well as JAIN et al. 77 , JAIN and NAGEL 77+78+79 , DRESCHLER and NAGEL 78 . In these cases TV-image sequences from downtown street intersection scenes had been investigated as a method of studying the principle problems of image sequence analysis, as opposed to an intent to design operational systems.

It should be pointed out that successful experience with automatic tracking of vehicles in TV-signals from street traffic scenes might possibly be employed to support tracking of boats and ships in a radar surveillance system as, e.g., described by HILKE 73 for the port of Hamburg and the 50 mile stretch of the Elbe river between Hamburg and the North Sea.

2.6.2 Target tracking

The most advanced among the real-time video tracking systems reported so far in the open literature appears to be GILBERT et al. 78+80 . The goal was to keep a missile image centered in the field of view of a TV-camera. Azimuth, elevation, and zoom of this TV-camera could be mechanically controlled by three signals derived from processing the TV-image sequence. A fourth control signal rotated the image sensed by the TV-camera electronically in order to align the missile image orientation vertically. The missile plume could thus be assumed to show up below the missile target itself.

Each pixel within a tracking window around the currently assumed missile image location was classified based on its intensity value as corresponding either to the missile target, the missile plume, or the foreground and background due to mountains, sky, or clouds. Postulating that such a categorization is always possible in the immediate vicinity of the missile image, the exact thresholds used to discriminate between these three classes were continuously adapted. For this purpose, intensity histograms obtained from prespecified subwindows around the current estimate of the missile target image location had to be evaluated, taking into account the relative sizes of image areas for the target, the plume, and the background.

The binary mask corresponding to pixels classified as missile target was projected in parallel both to the horizontal and vertical window edge. These projections were analysed using area quantization techniques. Size and shape descriptors obtained in this way for the missile target image mask were compared with adaptively updated stored descriptors and exploited to estimate the confidence that the image processing results indeed defined the current location of the missile target. If this confidence dropped below a threshold, no updating of size and shape descriptors for missile target image and tracking window occurred in order to prevent incorrect adaptation during periods when the target had been lost due to sunglare or due to rapid changes in cloud formations or background scenery. In such situations, predictions based on earlier but more reliable estimates had to be employed to specify these parameters as well as the control signals for the TV camera. An analogous preventive strategy has been found necessary by GERLACH 79 . GILBERT et al. 80 tested their approach by computer simulations using digitized video fields from video-tape recordings of typical tracking sequences. A hardware implementation has been reported to conform to the projected performance for all required subsystems.

LANDZETTEL and HIRZINGER 79 decomposed the real-time tracking problem into two parts, only one of which had to be performed at video rates. They assumed that a rectangular window with sides parallel and perpendicular to the video scanlines had been positioned interactively such that it enclosed the object to be tracked. For each video scanline segment contained in the window, an analog comparator determined the first occurrence where the video signal exceeded the threshold and the last occurrence where it dropped below the threshold. Only the coordinates of these points - the location of the object contour - were transferred to a microprocessor. The ensueing reduction in data rate enabled the second part of the tracking process to update the position of each side of the tracking window and the threshold value if required. The decision logic of this updating algorithm took several situations into account, for example the possibility that the object to be tracked could be occluded partially or completely. In such situations, the edges of the tracking window were repositioned according to predictions based on the recent motion history. Standard situations such as the partial occlusion of a horizontally moving object were handled by assuming that the object image did not move vertically. Therefore, the height of the sides delimiting the tracking window in the vertical direction were kept constant for a while despite the fact that the vertical extension of the object image changed due to the partial occlusion. A small number of similar heuristics covered most of the situations which resulted in failures for trackers relying exclusively on contrast. The video camera could be panned and tilted in real time by control signals derived from the tracking window displacement so that the object image tended to remain centered in the field of view. In this approach, the object image is modelled only in a most rudimentary way - by updating the threshold for the analog comparator. The flexibility and robustness of this approach must be attributed to the fact that the decision logic attempted to identify typical situations which might occur in the course of object tracking. The tracking algorithm then attempted to react in an appropriate manner to each situation identified. One might say that in this approach it is not the object image which is modelled - as in the approaches of GILBERT et al. 78+80 or GERLACH 79 - but a possible sequence of characteristic states which might be encountered while tracking an object.

A rather different approach towards - eventually real-time - video tracking of aircrafts has been explored by WALLACE and MITCHELL 79 . Based on the assumption that the aircraft image can be completely extracted from each video frame - for example by a thresholding operation - , the closed outer contour of an isolated aircraft image was represented by suitably normalized Fourier descriptors. A library of such normalized Fourier contour descriptors had been derived for six different aircrafts. About 150 different projections of each aircraft were taken into account in this library, covering a reasonable sample of possible aircraft orientations with respect to the tracking video camera. A heuristic dissimilarity function was employed to classify the contour of an aircraft extracted from a video image by comparing its descriptors to those of each library entry. The absolute values of the differences in real and imaginary parts for corresponding normalized Fourier descriptors were summed to obtain the dissimilarity function. The normalized Fourier descriptors had been defined in such a way that a contour of an aircraft projection not directly contained in the library could be linearly interpolated between the closest neighbors in the projection library.

WALLACE et al. 79 discussed an alternative for shape descriptors which could be used even for partial contours. However, this alternative has not yet been investigated for tracking purposes.

The tracking algorithm comprised two phases - the target acquisition and the tracking phase proper. The target acquisition phase compared the extracted contour via its associated normalized Fourier descriptors with all entries in the library. A match identified not only the aircraft type, but in addition it provided an estimate of the aircraft orientation relative to the video camera. In the tracking phase, only 3-5 neighboring contour descriptor sets were used for comparison, thus drastically reducing the search effort by exploitation of the continuity assumption. If this prediction turned out to be unsuitable, the target acquisition phase could be reentered. This possibility increased the robustness of the approach because a misclassification regarding aircraft type or orientation could be identified and corrected as soon as more reliable contour data would become available in the course of the tracking process.

This approach emphasizes shape rather than intensity characteristics. The knowledge about objects to be tracked is represented by the algorithm for derivation of normalized Fourier shape descriptors, by the library of coded shape templates as well as the associated dissimilarity function, and by the template interpolation algorithm. No interframe comparison takes place. The prediction of neighboring templates is only used to reduce the search effort. One has to contrast this template-based '3-D movement analysis' with an approach which incorporates the laws of 3-D perspective projection and light reflection and which, therefore, can compute the possible transformation of one object image into a subsequent one as well as relate the current aircraft attitude to its trajectory in space. The authors pointed out, however, that the information about the aircraft orientation associated with each frame could be exploited to check whether or not the recorded temporal sequence of aircraft positions and orientations would be compatible with the aerodynamics of the aircraft type in question.

Earlier attempts to track object images in series of TV frames have been restricted to simulations which were mostly based on unrealistic simple assumptions about the structure of input video sequences. The target descriptors are rather similar to the attributes employed for discrimination between relevant and irrelevant changes in change detection as well as the automatic screening approaches discussed at the end of section 2.2.5.

WINSOR and THOMAS 73 described a hybrid processor for real-time target tracking in video images. The intensity information extracted from a tracking window was condensed into a binary signature. This was subsequently correlated with a reference signature in order to obtain a control signal which adjusted the camera line of sight to keep the target centered in the field of view. The reference signature could be updated. No details about the signature were given.

GROMMES and YI 74 assumed four different fixed intensities to represent sky, clouds, target aircraft body, and target tail plume, respectively in a 50x50 pixel field of view. They determined the first and second coordinate moments of the targetmask - i.e. the centroid coordinates and their variance - to derive simulated control signals for pan and tilt of a hypothetical TV camera. Since pixels corresponding to the target body were assumed to be unambiguously identifiable based solely on their intensity, interframe matching or further structural analysis were not required.

MILSTEIN and LAZICKY 77+78 investigated statistical methods in simulated tracking studies. Airplane target intensities were assumed to be normally distributed with fixed mean and variance. Background intensities were likewise assumed to be normally distributed with a fixed mean - lower than for the airplane target - and a fixed variance. Three different statistical descriptors were computed for 20x20 pixel windows in a 100x100 pixel field of view: (i) a rank test based on comparison with a learning sample set; (ii) a likelihood function; (iii) the average intensity. The target was assumed to remain in the previous window or to shift into one of the eight neighboring windows around the previous one. Under these conditions, assuming that the target was in the window with the highest average intensity turned out to be almost as reliable as the test for the highest value of the airplane likelihood. The rank test failed when correlation had been introduced between the intensities of adjacent background pixels. Neither of these approaches employed any interframe comparisons although the restrictions on successive target positions introduced some correlation between frames.

WINKLER and VATTRODT 78a+78b used a conspicuousness detector in an interactive system approach to track object images that exhibited a local maximum of conspicuousness within an enclosing rectangle. This detector represented an improvement of an earlier version developed by WINKLER 75 on the basis of combinatorial analysis. The window position was updated from frame to frame to be centered around the current location of maximum conspicuousness subject to constraints derived from physical laws governing the motion of observed real-world objects. The advantage of this approach compared to cross-correlation search using greyvalue templates consisted in less expensive computations and the fact that no template needed to be stored and updated.

Interframe matching of subimages for tracking purposes has been investigated by MOSKOWITZ 64 on the basis of cross-correlation and moment descriptors. MCVEY and WOOLARD 79 discussed the derivation of TV-camera control signals for object tracking using cross-correlation. SCHALKOFF 79 , SCHALKOFF and MCVEY 79 developed an algorithm to determine the 2-D displacement and affine transformations - rotation and dilatation - of an object image between consecutive video frames. Their approach has been based on the following assumptions:

(i) the object image could be reliable separated from the background;

(ii) the object image would be large and compact enough such that pixels in its boundary area constituted only a small fraction of all its pixels;

(iii) the greyvalues in the object image would exhibit a significant variation although restricted to lower spatial frequency components.

Their approach is closely related to methods developed for movement compensation in interframe coding - see section 2.1.6 - and will be discussed separately in section 3.2.

Starting from a study on tracking simulated clouds that partially occlude each other - see AGGARWAL and DUDA 75 -, AGGARWAL and coworkers concentrated on the problem of modeling the image of a partially occluded object and using the derived model to track the object through partial or even complete occlusion. These authors began with binary images, progressing by systematically relaxing the constraints placed on object contours. AGGARWAL and DUDA 75 required polygonal boundaries. CHOW and AGGARWAL 77 admitted non-polygonal boundaries subject to the constraint that object images were observed unoccluded for at least two frames in order to estimate their contour and displacement velocity. Area centroid coordinates, length and orientation of principle axes were used to describe object images for the purpose of interframe matching. MARTIN and AGGARWAL 79a+79b developed an internal representation based on straight and curved line segments which together formed an object contour. This approach enabled tracking individual boundary segments thus allowing the decomposition of the contour of two overlapping object images during the tracking process into boundary parts related to the component objects. These first three approaches were concerned only with plane objects having identical greyvalues against a well contrasting background such that no internal edge would be recognized within the image of overlapping objects. The study of ROACH and AGGARWAL 79 extended these investigations to the case where internal edges were taken into account, modeling objects in a 3-D blocksworld.

MCINTOSH 79 reported on investigations to improve the tracking reliability even under adverse circumstances such as those encountered by airborne sensors rapidly approaching a moving target which had to be tracked. Image differencing techniques have been explored to detect and track a moving object within the field of view. Preliminary results indicated that considerable work will have to be invested to reliably model the multitude of systematic variations which may occur under these circumstances from frame to frame. This implies both the task of discriminating the moving target of interest as well as the problem of deriving appropriate descriptors for its image which could be used for interframe matching. Investigations in this direction - although not yet for real-time applications - have been reported by BULLOCK and DUDANI 76 , BULLOCK 78 .

Provided the problem has been solved - perhaps interactively - of which image components have to be tracked, sequential estimation theory (Kalman filtering) could be employed to put the tracking process on a firm statistical basis. Investigations towards this goal have been reported by FUTRELLE and SPECKERT 78 .

Another method is discussed by MILGRAM 77 . This author applied dynamic programming to organize the search for a consistent description of regions that have to be tracked throughout a sequence of image frames. There appears to be a close methodological relation between this dynamic programming approach by MILGRAM 77 and other approaches. DRESCHLER and NAGEL 78 used a minimum spanning tree to establish the "best" connection between descriptor sets for regions derived from a video frame sequence. RADIG 78a+78b+78c adapted for this purpose a search technique developed by LOWERRE 76 for speech recognition and subsequently modified into "beam search" for image interpretation by RUBIN 78 , RUBIN and REDDY 77 . The idea common to all these approaches is the consideration to base the tracking decisions on more global information about the sequences rather than on a single pair of descriptor sets derived from two frames. For a discussion of this consideration see DRESCHLER and NAGEL 78.

2.7 Industrial Automation and Robotics

Application of visual sensors to industrial automation appears to be dominated still by the evaluation of single images (DODD and ROSSOL 79 , NITZAN and ROSEN 76 , ROSEN and NITZAN 77). NEUMANN 78 studied the tracking of an object on a simulated conveyor belt by instantiating 2-D relational models based on straight line contour approximations to images of a scene that contained a moving object.

DAVIES and SMITH 79 determined relative displacements between parts of a gas turbine engine as a function of various operating conditions. Reference subimages dominated by the picture of parts under study were interactively selected in the first frame of a sequence of high-energy x-ray images. The corresponding location in subsequent frames was determined by search for a cross-correlation peak.

HERNAN and JIMENEZ 79 accumulated statistic measurements on the formation and disappearance of blobs in the turbulent mixing layer between high speed parallel streams of different gases. Image processing techniques were applied to digitized frames from high speed film recordings of these experiments in order to isolate and classify blob boundaries. Ellipses were fitted to blobs and subsequently used to track a blob from frame to frame until it disappeared by coalescence with other ones.

If tracking has to be performed under real-time constraints, one reverts to registering greyvalue or binary templates or to the identification of a feature that is characteristic for the object in question and can be easily isolated within a search window. Employing such techniques, UNO et al. 76 reported on using a TV camera to detect the position of bolts and reenforcement ribs on moving steel moulds by a TV camera in order to control a manipulator. UNO et al. 76 inspected every video frame only within one or a few windows at fixed locations and measured how well a feature of an object that moved horizontally through the field of view of the video camera fitted into the window. Provided this measure was smaller than a given template dissimilarity threshold, the displacement between the object feature and the window center was determined. If this displacement was positive for one frame and became negative for the subsequent frame, the feature in question had passed the window center. An interframe comparison was performed only indirectly by detecting the sign change of valid displacement measures. The number of rasterpositions within a subwindow varied between 448 and 1280 depending on the feature in question. The effective image area in this case contained 320 x 240 pixels.

Visual feedback can become important for versatile mechanical manipulators which should operate with tight tolerances for certain tasks. SHIRAI and INOUE 73 reported about such experiences. JONES 74 , CHIEN and JONES 75 investigated real-time tracking techniques to study the application of fast visual feedback to industrial automation. GIMELFARB et al. 75 reported analogous studies which, however, had not been extended to real-time processing. BIRK et al. 77 investigated means to correct workpiece orientation by an industrial manipulator using visual feedback. They derived values for simple features like centroid coordinates, area, and principle axes from binary images of the workpiece recorded by two TV cameras. These values were compared to reference values obtained during a learning phase in order to estimate the initial workpiece position and orientation. Corrections to workpiece orientation were derived from changes in the values of these features obtained from subsequent image frames when the manipulator transported the workpiece along a calculated safe trajectory to a machine fixture. Control considerations in the context of visual feedback have been discussed, too, by BONNELL and HUHNS 79 .

ESKENAZI and CUNNINGHAM 77 described a real-time tracking capability based on greyvalue correlation by using the video sensing and processing set-up developed for the JPL navigable-robot project. By simultaneously tracking the same object in two stereo image sequences, ESKENAZI and CUNNINGHAM 77+78 were able to determine the object's 3-D trajectory. Using this technique to track a stationary object from a moving robot, the robot's trajectory can be determined in order to guide its navigation and to adjust the pan and tilt of a stereo camera assembly on the robot for keeping the reference object in the field of view.

The research on navigable robots is an important source of experience about the evaluation of image sequences. WILLIAMS 76 described the experimental set-up for the vision system of the JPL navigable robot. The navigation system for this robot has been based on facilities to build a terrain model of the robot environment by evaluating a series of video images obtained at different locations along the robot trajectory - see THOMPSON 77. A scanning laser range finder (LEWIS and JOHNSTON 77) and stereo vision (LEVINE et al. 73 , O'HANDLEY 73 , YAKIMOVSKY and CUNNINGHAM 78) yielded additional information to improve the modeling of the robot environment. The terrain model must be used to navigate this robot - see MILLER 77 as well as GIRALT et al. 79 for analogous considerations in case of another robot project. The interaction between planning, execution of the plan, and updating of the environment model due to new visual input during the execution steps has been discussed by KUIPERS 79 .

MORAVEC 77 reported results about the Stanford navigable robot which used a less costly and therefore less elaborate set-up. GENNERY 77a+77b developed a stereo vision system for this Stanford robot with encouraging results. The image recorded by a video camera fixed to the robot had to be transmitted to a stationary computer via a radio-link. This transmission deteriorated the image data so that no reliable navigation beyond a few meters appeared possible. MORAVEC 79 modified this set-up by mounting the video-camera on a slide which could be translated perpendicular to the line-of-sight of the camera in precisely controllable steps. By this method, a sequence of stereo images with precisely known camera displacements could be recorded from a stationary robot, using the same camera and thus avoiding recalibration. Moreover, frame-to-frame matches within such a stereo image sequence could rely on small disparities between object images - as has been pointed out by NEVATIA 76 . This technique yielded a more reliable object image correspondence between the terminal frames of the stereo sequence. Based on these stereo measurements, a more reliable model of the robot environment could be derived in the form of a map. The robot trajectory could be planned and executed using this map - see MORAVEC 79 .

Fast obstacle avoidance based on hybrid processing of video signals from a stereo-camera arrangement has been reported by TSUGAWA et al. 79 . However, no explicit plans of the environment were derived from the video data and rather straight-forward algorithms were employed in order to control a motor car by signals derived from the stereo-camera set-up mounted at the car front. Efforts to identify moving pedestrians on a sidewalk in the context of such an autonomous vehicle experiment have been reported by TSUKIJAMA and SHIRAI 79 . In order to comply with stringent reaction time constraints, gross heuristics had to be employed.

In general, projects on navigable robots force the development of environment models from a sequence of video images. Such models need not be restricted to a map containing the location and possibly the extent of an obstacle - without further classification. GENNERY 79 reported an attempt to cluster 3-D point coordinates extracted from stereo measurements by a Mars probe into objects which were approximated as ellipsoids. Since these models must be suitable to plan and control the robot trajectory - see LOZANO-PEREZ and WESLEY 79 -, such endeavours will be subject to immediate tests thus providing very healthy feedback on the modeling process, too. Moreover, such projects press towards reasonably fast heuristics and implementations. They therefore can be seen as complementary to approaches that model the environment with more elaborate techniques in order to obtain more details or to investigate more generally applicable methods.

2.8 Spatial Image Sequences

If one considers an image sequence as a stack of image frames, the applications discussed so far implied the time as the dimension along which image frames had been stacked. Differences between consecutive images had therefore been attributed to time-dependent variations in the recorded scene, its illumination or its position relative to the recording camera.

However, the stacking dimension can just as well represent a spatial dimension. Each frame is an image of a particular slice through a 3-D spatial arrangement of objects. The slices can be real ones - obtained by cutting a preparation - or virtual ones, e.g. the focussed section of a preparation in a microscope or the sample plane obtained by computerized tomography from x-ray or ultrasound recordings. The basic task in all these cases consists in forming an adequate 3-D spatial concept of the object arrangement depicted by the recorded succession of slices. According to SOROKA 79a , not much is known about how this task is solved by man. It appears that solving this task can be eased considerably if the images from a series of spatial slices are presented in quick succession as a cinefilm. CHRISTIANSEN and SEDERBERG 78 mentioned that this approach for visualizing the spatial organisation of the human brain from microtome slices had been applied already in 1967 at the University of California at San Diego. Another early reference to such an approach encountered during the literature search for this survey is a quotation of WELLS 69 by ROBINSON 72 . There, a series of echograms had been presented as a motion film in such an order that they merge and provide the viewer with the impression of advancing through the image. LEVINTHAL and WARE 72 reported similar experiences for image sequences about the morphology of the central nervous system of simple animals recorded by an electron microscope (see also the discussion in REDDY et al. 73). An analogous procedure has been advocated for visualizing the spatial extent of a tumor from computerized tomography data - see GLENN et al. 77.

In these cases, spatial sequences have been converted to time sequences in order to facilitate the perception of spatial structures. The statement that such a conversion from spatial to time sequences seems to offer an advantage for human perception could be interpreted in the following way: the ability to infer the spatial structure of the environment from a sequence of visual sensings by a moving observer is more important for human survival than the ability to infer spatial relationships from a sequence of spatial slices. This question, however, will not be pursued further because this survey has been deliberately restricted to the analysis of image sequences by machines. More references to this line of thought can be found in SHEPARD 79 .

Spatial image sequences are often derived by methods whose treatment is outside of the scope of this chapter. Computerized tomography has recently been surveyed by, e.g., KAK 79 . Literature about electron microscope images can be found in the survey by HAWKES 78 .

The discussion of publications about spatial image sequences will be organized according to the influence which explicit spatial models of the imaged structures exert on the processing.

2.8.1 No explicit models: presentation of images from spatial slices

A manual technique has been described by DUNN 72 who provides, too, references to the earlier literature.

A microscope with high magnification has a shallow depth of focus, only a few microns thick. The part of a structure which appears sharp under a microscope could be thought of as a thin virtual slice through the preparation being viewed. However, such a virtual slice has no well-defined boundaries in depth - in contrast to real microtome slices. Therefore, prominent structures from neighboring virtual slices can be seen as blurred images. WEINSTEIN and CASTLEMAN 72 digitized microscope images from a preparation in a series of consecutive virtual slices taken at increasing depth of the focal plane. In order to enhance the structures which were in focus at a given depth within the preparation, suitably filtered images recorded at the next higher and lower depth setting were subtracted from the image to be enhanced. The residual effects of structures from neighboring virtual slices could thus be removed in good approximation. This approach is also discussed by ROSENFELD and KAK 76 , p. 187. Related approaches in analog or hybrid image processing have been discussed by HAEUSLER 72+77.

WALL and KARSPECK 76 applied a different approach to increase the apparent focal depth of a microscope. Each image from a series of consecutive virtual slices - called optical sections by these authors - from a lung tissue preparation was digitized and divided into square subregions with a sidelength of 10 pixels. The magnitude of greylevel differences between neighboring interior pixels from each subregion was summed as an estimate of the average greylevel gradient. A composite image was constructed as a mosaic of subregions from images of different virtual slices. At each subregion position, the subregion with the highest estimate for the average gradient was included into the composite image. This criterion did not take into account the smooth variation of the imaged structure and therefore occasionally resulted in a checkerboard effect. As an improvement of this approach, the authors assembled a reconstruction map indicating the virtual slice number which yielded the highest average gradient estimate for each subregion position. This reconstruction map was subsequently smoothed using a 5x5 uniform weight averaging filter. On the basis of this smoothed reconstruction map it was decided from which virtual slice the subregion had to be selected for inclusion into the final mosaic.

Pulse-echo 2-D ultrasound echoscopy provides an image of a virtual slice through a patient's body. A set of serial cross sections can be obtained which represent a spatial image sequence based on transverse ultrasonic echograms. ROBINSON 72 discussed several methods to interpolate between neighboring virtual slices in order to derive the image for a virtual slice not directly recorded. Extending this approach, he computed density values for a spatial grid which allowed resampling to derive images of virtual slices at any orientation.

Computerized tomography (CT) reconstructs the density distribution in a cross section of a body from x-ray recordings - another possibility of deriving the image of a virtual slice. Application of this technique for a number of more or less closely spaced parallel virtual slices yields a genuine 3-D spatial density distribution. This offers the opportunity to compute the image of a virtual slice which has not been directly obtained by CT reconstruction, in analogy to the approach of ROBINSON 72. Starting from a sequence of 12 consecutive transverse CT cross sections of a human brain, PETERS 75 derived images for frontal sections in which a physician could assess the position and extension of a brain tumor more easily than in transverse cross sections. Further examples have been discussed, e.g., by HUANG and LEDLEY 75 as well as by GLENN et al. 77 . An arbitrary virtual slice through part of a body - not only the brain - may be selected if this part has been covered by a sequence of CT cross sections. Such an ability can be of considerable advantage not only for diagnostic purposes, but likewise for the preparation of surgery and the evaluation of radiation treatment plans. HSI and LEE 78 described techniques to reduce the time required for computing an arbitrary slice, based on an interpolation algorithm reported by LEE and MOZLEY 76 . TAMURA et al. 78 describe a specialized processing system to compute and display the image of an arbitrary virtual slice from a sequence of ultrasonic or x-ray tomograms.

An analogous approach has been used by BAJCSY and WINSTON 78 with respect to a stack of digitized radiographs from real serial sections of a cat's brain in order to visualize the relative rate of glucose consumption in this brain.

O'ROURKE 80 pointed out the similarity between slice-slice interpolation and key-frame to key-frame interpolation in computer animation of graphic displays. Both interpolation processes make minimal assumptions about the semantic content of the images. They rather are based on the assumption that the input images have been suitably selected for interpolation.

2.8.2 Isolation, tracking, and representation of line-like features in 3-D space

The approaches discussed in the preceding section burdened the human viewer with the entire task

* of isolating an object image in the visual data presented,
* of identifying and tracking an object from slice to slice,
* of deriving spatial attributes for an object, and
* of determining the spatial relationships between different objects.

Steps towards an algorithmic approach to cope with these subtasks are the isolation, tracking, and representation of 3-D line-like structures. The dendrite system of certain neurons or the spatial arrangement of the central nervous system in simple animals may serve as examples for structures falling into this category. Statistically reliable quantitative information about the morphology of certain neurons or neuron assemblies may yield important clues regarding the detailed function of individual nerve cells and how it is effected - see LEVINTHAL and WARE 72 or REDDY et al. 73 .

After suitable preparation, a nerve cell may be separated from its surrounding in a microscope image on the basis of its greyvalue or color. WEINSTEIN and CASTLEMAN 72 planned to develop their system towards automatic tracking of nerve cells. LEVINTHAL and WARE 72 described an interactive measurement system for electron and optical microscope images of microtome slices from a preparation containing the central nervous system of a simple animal. The image of each slice had been interactively aligned with those of preceding slices and subsequently been photographed on cinefilm. An operator could instruct the computerized measurement system to select a frame and to accept the coordinates of a cursor set onto a nerve cell slice visible in that frame. Identifying and tracking a nerve cell from frame to frame was the task of the operator. The computer executed the commands issued by the operator and performed the storage and bookkeeping operations for measurements and associated labeling information. Together with each 2-D measurement within an image, the frame - i.e. microtome slice - number was recorded as the third spatial coordinate. This enabled a subsequently activated evaluation program to convert the recorded raw data into a tree structure reflecting the true 3-D topology of branch and termination points for individual nerve cells within a 3-D compound structure of such cells. The resulting data structure can be considered a good example for the concept of "sequence description" discussed by NAGEL 78b . Based on this sequence description, various projection and stereo image displays could be generated to facilitate visualization of the nerve cell structure.

GARVEY et al. 73 exploited the shallow depth of focus associated with high magnification optical microscopy to automate the tedious task of dendrite tracking. The microscope image could be digitized by a TV camera. The greyvalues were recorded along a semicircle around an interactively selected start point on a dendrite. Plotting the measured greyvalues versus the arclength along the semicircle yielded a bump if the continuation of the dendrite had been crossed. The raster coordinates of the point where such a bump reached its extremum had to be combined with the microscope stage coordinates to determine the projected position of the dendrite continuation. The depth of the microscope focal plane within the preparation could be adjusted under computer control until the extremum of the bump became as great as possible. In this manner, the third coordinate of the continuation point on the dendrite could be determined. If the bump complied with certain criteria defining a reliably detected continuation of the dendrite, the measured point was accepted and used in turn as a center for a new semicircle thus proceeding with the 3-D tracking of this dendrite. In order to detect a dendrite branching, the greyvalue measurements along a semicircle were scrutinized to identify additional bumps. In case of difficulties the tracking algorithm prompted operator interaction.

A different approach towards automatic tracking of neurons has been reported by REDDY et al. 73 . Intracellular stain injection allows the selective colouring of a single nerve cell. A preparation containing a nerve cell treated in this manner had been sliced by a microtome. Each slice had been imaged using high power fluorescent photomicrography. In such an image, the cross section through a stain-filled nerve cell appeared as a bright blob. Digitization of these image frames enabled the application of standard image processing techniques such as the determination of 2-D intensity gradients, thresholding, edge following, etc., in order to extract the regions corresponding to cross sections through a particular nerve cell or other structures of interest. A search procedure attempted to match corresponding regions from frame to frame, in order to align images from adjacent slices - see, too, REDDY and RUBIN 78 - and to track a nerve cell or other parts of interest in 3-D space. All these steps could be replaced or corrected by operator interaction. Based on these reults, a sequence description could be built which represented nerve cells by variable-diameter straight-line tubes and surfaces of more extended structures like a ganglion by triangular or irregular strips. This representation could be used in conjunction with standard computer graphic techniques to display the entire assembly under arbitrarily specifiable viewing conditions. Moreover, quantitative data about the topology or other attributes like surface area or volume of these structures could be derived.

Certain elongated neurons extend throughout a considerable volume although their interior comprises only a small fraction of the volume required to faithfully cover their 3-D structure. Representation of such a neuron at the full experimental resolution by flagging unit cubes in a 3-D grid may require more storage than available. REDDY and RUBIN 78 investigated a recursive divide and conquer strategy based on nested, arbitrarily oriented parallelepipeds in order to reduce the overall storage requirements. A local coordinate system is associated with each parallelepiped. At each nesting level, the location and orientation of every enclosed parallelepiped is given by a separate coordinate transform which relates the associated local coordinate system to the one of the enclosing parallelepiped. The authors pointed out that this approach does not only offer considerable flexibility for storage and display of complicated 3-D object models but, in addition, facilitates modeling component motion by admission of explicit time dependency for certain of these coordinate transformations.

A three-dimensional representation of line-like structures at a larger scale than used for nerve fibres has been studied by RUBIN and SAYRE 78 . These authors identified corresponding image points of the brain vasculature in two angiograms taken at different orientation of the skull. By measuring the image locations in both views not only for a series of such vasculature points but also for images of lead shot taped to the skull as reference points, the 3-D coordinates of vasculature points could be reconstructed. This corresponds to a wide angle stereo reconstruction. The 3-D coordinates of the x-ray source and of the image plane in the camera had to be determined from known 3-D positions of lead shot in a phantom and the images of these calibration points. By using linear interpolation in space between the 3-D reconstructed vascular points - see SAYRE et al. 79 - selected portions of the brain vasculature could be displayed as they would appear from an arbitrary viewing position.

Apart from this spatial visualization of the vasculature, an important additional option was investigated by RUBIN and SAYRE 78 - see also SAYRE et al. 79 . The density difference between blood and brain tissue is often not sufficient to allow a differentiation between these components in a computed brain tomogram. Thus one could either see the spatial distribution of brain tissue, but not the vasculature, by looking at displays of brain tomograms - or one could look at a brain angiogram to see the vasculature, but then the brain tissue could not be related to the vasculature in detail. RUBIN and SAYRE 78 combined their method of 3-D representation for the vasculature with images derived from computed brain tomograms. They recorded two angiographic images and a series of brain tomograms from the same patient, with lead shot taped to the patient's skull for calibration purposes. Measuring the images of lead shot in the angiograms as well as in the tomograms, they were able to determine the coordinate transformation from the 3-D reconstruction of the vasculature into the coordinate frame of the spatial sequence of brain tomograms. With this transformation known, they could overlay a display of an arbitrary slice through the 3-D representation of the vasculature obtained from the angiographic images with a corresponding slice through the 3-D tomogram as discussed in section 2.8.1. In this manner, the advantages of both medical imaging approaches can be combined. This applies, of course, not only to the brain but to other parts of the body as well.

2.8.3 Object surfaces derived from contour measurements in a series of slices

The approach towards representation of a 3-D structure described by REDDY et al. 73 exhibited a mixed characteristic. Dendritic branches were represented by straight-line tubes, emphasizing their line-like character, whereas the comparatively large external surface of the ganglion was represented by strip patches. This approach - as well as the ones to be discussed in the following - conceptually decomposes a 3-D preparation into several distinct objects of interest embedded in some surrounding substance of less interest. Each object comprises a well-defined volume of material with specific properties and a well-defined surface which separates this material from the surrounding substance. Slicing through the preparation exhibits the interior of these objects, with a more or less well defined contour delimiting the object interior against the surrounding substance. Extraction of these contours from a sequence of slices and interpolation between corresponding contours from adjacent slices yields an approximation to the object surface. Based on such approximate reconstruction, object attributes such as volume, surface area, shape descriptors, etc., can be determined quantitatively. In addition, the surface approximation allows the computation of displays of the object as it would appear from randomly selectable view points. Standard techniques of computer graphics such as removal of hidden lines and surfaces, perspective projection, shading, and colouring may be applied to enhance visualization of the 3-D structure. Moreover, these quantitative object models may be exploited in order to derive radiation treatment plans. In the remainder of this section, a number of increasingly sophisticated approaches will be discussed which derive a 3-D object description by interpolating a surface between object contours extracted from a series of real or virtual slices.

In the system of VEEN and PEACHEY 77 - see also PEACHEY et al. 76 - an operator traced the contour of interesting objects in the image of each slice. The contour trace was digitized. Operator selected reference points in each image were digitized, too, in order to facilitate alignment of different images with respect to each other. The contour extracted from a slice was displayed as if a slab had been cut according to this contour form from a layer of sheets, the number of sheets being proportional to the slice thickness. Each sheet was slightly displaced with respect to the preceding one - depending on the view point selected for the presentation - and hidden lines were removed. Although this approach represents a considerable help for the 3-D visualization of, e.g., component structure in a yeast cell, no computer internal surface approximation had been derived for the different components.

CHRISTIANSEN and SEDERBERG 78 also started by handtracing contours in a series of photographic images from microtome slices of a human brain. Node points in each contour were selected by a human operator such that straight-line connections between successive node points would yield an acceptable polygonal approximation to each closed contour trace. The authors then went beyond the approach of PEACHEY et al. 76 by semiautomatic interpolation of a polyhedron surface in 3-D space. The rectangles enclosing the polygons extracted from two consecutive slice images were mapped onto a unit square. Applying the same mapping to the enclosed polygons yielded transformed polygons with roughly the same center and size. Numbering of consecutive nodes must yield the same sense of rotation for each polygon. Numbering had to start with those nodes which represented the nearest neighbors among pairs of nodes from two transformed polygons derived from two adjacent slices. These start nodes were connected to obtain the first side of a triangle. The second side could be either of the two lines which connected a start node with the next node on its polygon. Among these two alternatives the node with the shorter diagonal connection to the node on the other polygon was chosen. The resulting diagonal was then taken as the first side of a new triangle which had to be completed by using the same criterion of shortest diagonal connection. This approach allowed the construction of a polyhedron surface from triangular tiles which interpolated between the object contours extracted from adjacent slices. This algorithm had been extended to cope with some of the situations where a single closed contour had to be connected with two smaller closed contours extracted from the adjacent slice. In some cases a point could be introduced automatically between the two adjacent slices such that the surface would split there into two separate branches - or join two separate branches into a single one. The relative simplicity of this entire approach was made possible by embedding it into an interactive system where the user would provide the correct decisions in more complicated situations.

The "Three-Dimensional Reconstruction and Display (THREAD)" system reported by MAZIOTTA and HUANG 76 required less operator interaction to locate contours in each slice image. Only the left-most point on the boundary of the object of interest had to be indicated by the operator, together with three alignment points. The contour was then traced by a simple contour following algorithm. The operator could manually edit the resulting contour if necessary. The operator then had to specify a rate at which equally spaced nodes for a polygonal contour approximation were selected from the contour points. The surface interpolation between contour approximations from adjacent slices was constructed from rectangular tiles - see WILLEY et al. 73 for an earlier use of this approach: each of two consecutive nodes on one contour approximation was connected by a straight line with a corresponding node from the nearest pair of consecutive nodes on the contour approximation extracted from the adjacent slice. This technique has been applied to construct a surface for visualizing, e.g., a nucleolus of a neuron based on a series of digitized photographs from electron microscope images of microtome slices as well as a brain tumor isolated by evaluation of computerized tomography data.

The approaches described in the preceding two paragraphs relied on simple heuristic algorithms, supported by user interaction, in order to approximate contours from adjacent slices by polygons and to interpolate a polyhedron surface between these polygons. KEPPEL 75 started from given polygonal contours in two adjacent slices, assuming random distribution of node points along each contour. Interpolation of a polyhedral surface between successive contour polygons by triangulation required an answer to the question of which nodes should be connected to form a triangle. KEPPEL treated this question as a graph search problem. Since his basic solution was applicable to convex contour sections, the node set of a polygonal contour had to be decomposed into subsets corresponding to convex and concave contour parts which were treated separately. The triangulation between entire contours consisting of convex and concave parts was derived from the intermediate results for these parts. The graph search was guided by an objective function based on the following postulate: the optimal surface approximation between two closed convex polygonal contours is a triangulation maximizing the volume of a polyhedron which comprises the contour nodes as verticles.

FUCHS et al. 77 reported a general algorithm to construct a surface over a set of consecutive cross-sectional contours by triangulation. Constructing such a surface section between a pair of consecutive contours has been reduced to the problem of finding certain minimal cost cycles in a directed toroidal graph. This search could be effected by a new fast algorithm. Their approach does not rely on a specific heuristic thus offering considerable freedom in the choice of an optimization criterion. The authors demonstrated their approach by constructing the minimal area triangulation surface for contour data describing a human head.

Their approach has been used by SHANTZ and McCANN 78 in order to construct a surface description for dendrites from several interacting neurons. They started by handtracing the outer boundaries of dendrites in a sequence of microtome slice images obtained by an electron microscope. The digitized contour traces were recorded by a computer together with bookkeeping information. An algorithm reduced the chain encoded boundary traces to a polygonal approximation, retaining few boundary points in boundary sections with small curvature and more points in sections with higher curvature. These polygons represented their input to the surface reconstruction algorithm of FUCHS et al. 77 . Apart from the fact that SHANTZ and McCANN applied an advanced algorithm for automatic construction of a surface from contour data, these authors discussed the question of organizing their data using a semantic net structure to represent objects and relations between objects. This constituted an example where a higher level sequence description for a spatial image sequence would be organized to allow access by concepts. It must be seen as a parallel to endeavours to provide conceptual access to sequence descriptions for time sequences such as, e.g., discussed by TSOTSOS et al. 79 .

The approach described by SUNGUROFF and GREENBERG 78 applied a simple gradient detector and edge follower in order to automatically extract object contours from virtual slice images obtained by computerized tomography. User interaction, however, was still available if necessary. The cross-sectional contours were represented by B splines. These contours were not required to come from parallel planes. Any combination of open or closed contour curves could be admitted. Deviating from the triangulation approach discussed in preceding paragraphs, these authors used cardinal splines to interpolate a surface between contour sections because this allowed the representation of complex shapes with a minimum amount of data. The authors used the resulting surfaces not only for display purposes. They presented examples for using these surface models to derive radiation treatment plans. The importance of 3-D models for radiation treatment plans has been emphasized, e.g., by REINSTEIN et al. 78 . KELLY et al. 78 employed the algorithm of FUCHS et al. 77 for their 3-D radiation treatment planning program.

As far as modeling object surfaces based on spatial image sequences is concerned, the gap to advanced techniques has been closed. The remaining difficulties are related to the problem of reliably extracting the relevant contours from the image sequences. The recent work by HALL and HWANG 79 on segmentation of computerized tomography images could be seen as another step towards the fully automatic extraction of object surface descriptions from spatial image sequences.

2.8.4 Surface detection in samples on a 3-D grid

If the spatial distance between consecutive - real or virtual - slices becomes comparable to the diameter of the sampling area which corresponds to a pixel in the 2-D image of a slice, a sequence of 2-D digitized images represents the results of sampling a volume at regular 3-D grid positions. Under such conditions, edge detection in 2-D images may be generalized by operating directly in the 3-D grid arrangement of samples in order to detect the surfaces which separate different objects in space from each other. LIU 77 developed such an algorithm in analogy to a 2-D boundary generation approach based on Robert's cross operator (see, e.g., PRATT 78 , p. 487). The intensity value of a pixel was associated with the center of the raster square. The lower right corner of the raster square was designated as the - point-like (0-D) - boundary element for this pixel. Application of Robert's cross operator assigned a gradient value to each boundary element. Starting from an interactively selected position, a search attempted to connect boundary elements with high gradient value into a region boundary. If the maximum of the gradient values among all unprocessed boundary elements in the neighborhood of the current search point dropped below a threshold, a backtrack mechanism had to be activated. The search would be terminated by some heuristic criterion.

In analogy to this approach, LIU 77 associated each density sample with the center of a cubic volume element or 'voxel' at the grid location selected by three index values. Three edges meeting at a specified corner of the cube were designated as the - line-like (1-D) - boundary elements associated with each voxel. In the 3-D case, each line-like boundary element was common to four adjacent voxels. A gradient component was assigned to each boundary element. This gradient component was computed as the sum of the two absolute density differences between the diagonal voxel pairs which had just this boundary element in common. Starting from an interactively specified location, a search procedure in analogy to the 2-D case sketched above attempted to continue each boundary element by selecting one or at most two neighbors with as high a gradient value as possible. In order to avoid the generation of a thin twisting surface, the search would proceed in a breadth-first fashion. The voxel face connecting two accepted boundary elements represented one surface element. The set of all square surface elements derived in this way constituted the desired surface.

Applying this approach to computerized tomography data in order to isolate, e.g., human organs may yield surfaces which comprise between 10000 and 25000 square faces - see HERMAN 79 . Due to this large number of faces, the usual approach for the display of polyhedrons with shading and removal of hidden surfaces requires too much time. HERMAN and LIU 79 reduced the time for computing a display by exploiting the fact that all possible faces can be organized into pairs with orientations restricted to the three coordinate axes. Moreover, the distance between the image plane and a face - required for elimination of hidden surfaces - needed to be computed only for the center of each face. ARTZY 79 described a further speed-up for display computations in such cases.

Recent developments open the possibility of deriving computerized tomography data for a significant fraction of the human body within 1/60 of a second - see, e.g., RITMAN et al. 78 . The resulting time sequence of 3-D data may be treated as a set of samples in a 4-dimensional space. Even moving organs such as the human heart may be recorded with sufficient spatial and temporal resolution to study the dynamics of ventricular wall motion in detail. At such resolutions, the ventricular wall does not change abruptly. This premise - although less well satisfied for his temporal sequences of 3-D ultrasound cardiac data - formed the basis for investigations by SCHUDY 79 to derive an approximate description of dynamic 3-D shape variations of the interior heart wall by a linear superposition of spherical harmonic functions with time dependent weighting coefficients (see section 2.3.3). HERMAN and LIU 78 exploited this knowledge about temporal continuity to improve the segmentation of 64x64 pixel virtual cross sections through an intact heart and lung area obtained by computerized tomography at twelve different times during a pulmonary cycle. Whereas the segmentation of each individual image could not separate the right and left lung images at certain times in the pulmonary cycle, application of the 3-D version of LIU's algorithm to the entire stack of 12 cross sections detected the left lung boundary correctly in all images. HERMAN and LIU 78 extended this approach by generalizing the algorithm of LIU 77 from three to four dimensions. They introduced the notion of a 'hypervoxel' to represent the density of a voxel at a certain time t. The six square surface elements of this hypervoxel assumed the role of line-like boundary elements in LIU's algorithm. The resulting boundary consisted of cubes connecting the selected square surface boundary elements associated with high values of the density gradient. In this way the continuity of changes in an organ surface may be exploited to identify this surface more reliably.

A further generalization of this approach to higher dimensions has been discussed by HERMAN et al. 79 .

HERMAN 79 reported another variant of the approach to directly detect the boundary surface in a 3-D arrangement of density samples. He assumed that each voxel within the object volume of interest exhibits a density value between specified limits. A face separating a voxel with density value in between these limits from a voxel with density value outside these limits must be part of the surface bounding the object. Each face of this surface shared an edge with one of its four neighboring faces in the surface. Two edges of each face were designated as incoming, the remaining two edges as outgoing ones. The entire surface was mapped into a directed graph, with faces mapping into nodes and adjacency relations mapping into edges. HERMAN 79 reported that - based on this mapping - the surface detection problem could be transformed into a binary tree traversal problem.

LIU 77 as well as HERMAN 79 selected voxel faces associated with high density gradients and constructed the desired surface by concatenating such faces at shared edges. The density gradient was estimated very locally - based on two or four volume elements - and the local surface orientation was restricted to the direction of the three coordinate axes. ZUCKER and HUMMEL 79 developed an operator to determine the optimal planar surface element separating two parts of a test volume containing a 3-D step transition between two density values. Their operator has to be applied to test volumes of

3x3x3 or 5x5x5 elements, thus estimating the density gradient in a less local manner than in the preceding cases. Since no explicit restrictions were placed on the orientation of the planar surface elements, a smooth transition in surface orientation could be described. However, since all surface elements were assumed to be of same size, the set of accepted surface elements would not constitute a locally continuous surface because the edges of adjacent surface elements need not to coincide as in the approaches of LIU 77 and HERMAN 79. This might complicate the computation of quantitative attributes like volume or surface area for the objects bounded by the surface approximation. However, ZUCKER and HUMMEL pointed out that acceptable displays could be derived from their surface representation if the sample density is high compared to the extension of the interesting object. They discussed several measures for assessing the quality of their surface approximation to the inhomogeneous density distribution.

2.8.5 Volume growing

The surface detection discussed in the preceding section and the volume growing to be discussed now correspond to a generalization of edge finding and region growing techniques, respectively, as they are known from segmentation approaches to 2-D images. Volume growing consists in aggregating volume elements which form a connected set and are similar according to some criterion. HERMAN et al. 79 discussed ways to extend the notions of adjacency and connectivity for discrete sample sets to three- and higher dimensional spaces.

BAJCSY and WINSTON 78 applied a volume growing technique to derive a 3-D representation for certain cerebral structures from a sequence of digitized autoradiographic images obtained from serial sections of a cat's brain. The density associated with each volume element corresponded to the relative rate of glucose consumption in that part of the brain. The volume growing process was based on 3-D connectivity and local similarity of density values between connected volume elements. Since the density gradient might not always allow the separation of the desired parts of the brain from other structures, anatomic knowledge has to be made available in order to avoid wrong decisions during the volume growing process.

Straight-forward volume growing as sketched by BAJCSY and WINSTON 78 can require considerable computer time unless the entire 3-D set of samples can be accommodated in a random access memory and a compact object has to be isolated. Often these conditions cannot be satisfied. To cope with such situations, RHODES et al. 78 developed an algorithm which decomposed the volume growing approach into two parts. One part consisted of a 2-D region growing algorithm developed by YAKIMOVSKY and CUNNINGHAM 76 . This algorithm proceeded by a breadth-first search starting in the 8 neighborhood of seed pixels which had to be supplied interactively for the first 2-D image of a sequence. Once region growing around all available seed pixels in the current image had terminated, candidate seed pixels were generated automatically for the adjacent images in the sequence. This seed pixel transfer between consecutive images can be described easily if one considers the image sequence number as the third grid coordinate value for each pixel and conceives each pixel as a voxel. The set of candidate seed pixels in image k+1 (or k-1) comprises all voxels which share an edge or a face with a voxel corresponding to a pixel accepted as part of a region in image k. Candidate seed pixels would be dropped from this set when their rasterposition in image k+1 (or k-1) was encountered during a region growing process that had started from a seed pixel already accepted in image k+1 (or k-1).

The other part of the algorithm developed by RHODES et al. 78 consisted of a control strategy for the decision which image from the sequence should be processed next. The goal was to completely isolate all desired objects with a minimum number of examinations for each image from the sequence. Since an extended object may well bend back into unprocessed parts of images already examined, a simple consecutive search through all images in the sequence may fail to identify the full extend of more complicated objects. The control strategy was based on search methods for AND/OR graphs developed for problem solving in the area of artificial intelligence. The authors presented test results for a plexiglass phantom and a human bronchial tree extracted from a 3-D sample set of computerized tomography data.

2.8.6 Deriving descriptions based on volume primitives

The approaches discussed so far isolated an object from its environment in a spatial image sequence by deriving its bounding surface or by identifying the volume elements constituting its volume. In the case of more complicated objects, such an elementary representation might not be sufficient, e.g., to characterize the object automatically. One way to achieve such a goal would be a decomposition of the isolated object into parts, followed by an exploration of structural relationships between those parts. This structural analysis can be simplified by the assumption that the parts must correspond to one or a small number of volume primitives, especially if easily manageable generic descriptions are available for such volume primitives. The generalized cone or generalized cylinder introduced by BINFORD 71 represents one of these volume primitives.

SOROKA and BAJCSY 76 investigated the possibility of using a generalized cylinder already in the procedure to isolate an object from a spatial sequence of images. Several questions associated with this approach to model building have been formulated by BAJCSY and SOROKA 77 . SOROKA and BAJCSY 78 described an algorithm for extraction of elliptical cylinders from a spatial sequence of binary images. Elliptical cylinders are a subset of generalized cylinders, obtained by sweeping an elliptical cross section along a straight line - the axis - perpendicular to the plane of the cross section. Figures in the binary image of a slice were crudely categorized either as ellipse or as complex. Adjacent slices were then examined in an attempt to continue 2-D figures into 3-D cylinders. An elliptical figure would either be matched to an already hypothesized elliptical cylinder or - in case of matching failure - would be considered as the starting cross section of a new cylinder. A complex figure would be split if part of it could be matched to a cross section predicted by extrapolating an already hypothesized cylinder from an adjacent slice image.

SOROKA 79c compared this approach to another one which attempted to hypothesize elliptical cylinders based on figures from only a few non-adjacent slice images and to verify these hypotheses by examining intermediate slice images. More details about both alternatives can be found in SOROKA 79a + 79b .

Both approaches have been tested with simulated data as well as some binary slice images derived from computerized tomography data. No clear-cut advantage could be stated for either approach.

Generally, acceptable cylinder representations could be extracted if an elongated object had been sliced almost perpendicular to its long axis and if the cross section was similar to an ellipse. Difficulties arose, e.g., at the end of a cylinder terminated by a plane. Oblique slices through the terminal part of such a cylinder could not be approximated adequately by an ellipse. Moreover, only slices perpendicular to the three mutually orthogonal coordinate axes were taken into account. This complicated tracking objects with a long curved axis like, e.g., a helix or a torus.

It appears advisable, therefore, to extend the set of volume primitives beyond elliptical cylinders, to incorporate a more sophisticated shape analysis of figures in each image of a sequence, and to provide facilities for tracking through space along curved axes. This approach by BAJCSY and SOROKA is significant, however, because it provided the first attempt for structural analysis of object descriptions derived from spatial image sequences.

2.8.7 Estimating parameters of spatial models by statistical evaluation of planar sections (stereology)

Often a detailed 3-D description of each object that might be isolated in a spatial image sequence containing many similar objects would require more data processing capacity than available - provided an algorithmic determination is already possible at all. In certain disciplines - e.g. cytology - it is of considerable interest to estimate at least the average value of surface area, volume, or other attributes for a large population of objects like cells or cell constituents observable in light- or electron-microscope images. Measurements in 2-D images of microsections can be related to 3-D attributes of spatial microstructures by postulating that the objects of interest can be modeled as simple geometric bodies like spheres, discs or cylinders. However, stereology uses these volume primitives in a probabilistic approach - as opposed to the deterministic one outlined in the preceding section: objects are supposed to be randomly distributed, randomly oriented, and randomly intercepted by stereological test procedures such as sections, test lines, or test points. For a general introduction to stereology see UNDERWOOD 70 . The quantitative determination of 3-D attributes from planar sections have been discussed by, e.g., LINDBERG 76 and UNDERWOOD 76 . The relations between 3-D attributes and the parameters which can be measured in a 2-D image have been derived mostly by postulating that the imaged slice has vanishing thickness. WEIBEL 76 presented correction factors for the different volume primitives which compensate for the fact that such postulates cannot be met. Moreover, he discussed other situations which may adversely influence the correctness of estimates obtained by quantitative stereology.

According to WEIBEL 76 , application of stereological methods to subcellular structures required in most cases that the objects of interest had to be identified and measured by trained investigators. In less complicated images such as lung tissue photomicrographs, the lung tissue could be separated from the background by a judicious thresholding procedure. Exploratory results for the automatic estimation of the internal lung surface area have been reported by LEVINE et al. 70 . Later, TOU et al. 78 developed an algorithm for the automatic extraction of stereological parameters to characterize the lung tissue. Further improvements to this approach have been reported by TOU and FERNG 78 as well as by TOU and LIU 79 .

2.8.8 Discussion

Technical parallels in the processing of spatial and temporal image sequences cannot be overlooked. The alignment problem has to be solved for images of microtome slices just as for satellite images. Tracking object images poses similar problems, be it in space or in time. In this context, an observation by COLLAN 76 should be mentioned who investigated the human ability to track a cell from slice to slice through a sequence of images for various distances between slices. It turned out that the reliability with which an object could be identified in the image of a neighboring slice decreased significantly once the inter-slice distance exceeded about 1/10 of the object diameter. It might be worthwhile to study the factors influencing this result and to evaluate such experiences during the development of algorithms for interframe comparison in image sequences.

The role of object modeling is even more evident for spatial image sequences than it is for temporal ones. This may be due to the fact that generating static displays from computer-internal models of objects and their environment has been pursued by more people for a longer time than the generation of dynamic displays. Computer graphics derives an image from a computer-internal object description. The analysis of spatial image sequences is the inverse operation: derivation of a computer-internal object description - the model - from a sequence of 2-D images. An illustrating - although not yet economically relevant - application of this approach outside medicine has been given by HERMAN 79 who generated a display of a fan from a description which had been extracted from 3-D computerized tomography image sequences recorded from this fan.

This relation between models, computer graphics, and image sequence analysis carries over from spatial to temporal image sequences. It becomes especially obvious in the (4-D) case of time sequences of spatial image sequences to be generated by the 'Dynamic Spatial Reconstructor' - see RITMAN et al. 78 - or in efforts to derive a model of the moving heart surface from ultrasound data - see SCHUDY 79 . The role of 3-D representations both for computer vision as well as for computer graphics has been emphasized by BADLER and BAJCSY 78 . Investigations in this direction by BOURNE 78 , BAJCSY and BOURNE 78 as well as O'ROURKE and BADLER 79 must be mentioned in this context.

It might be asked whether the analysis of image sequences and stereology have much in common - apart from using digitized images of slices. Stereology is probabilistic in nature whereas practically all other approaches treated in this chapter strived for an accurate description of an individual object of interest. Both areas of research - the established one, stereology, as well as the emerging one, evaluation of spatial image sequences - move in the same direction: computer-internal models of real-world objects under scrutiny have to be improved qualitatively as well as quantitatively. Structural analysis decomposes objects into more primitive parts and records the spatial relationships between these parts. The volume primitives employed are similar or identical: discs, spheres, cylinders. It is conceivable that the currently existing differences between stereology and the deterministic analysis of spatial image sequences with respect to methodology and emphasis may be bridged in the future. Both areas will profit from progress in algorithmic segmentation and shape analysis for single images as well as progress in matching segments or aggregates of segments from frame to frame in a spatial image sequence.

This should not be seen as a mere technological development only, essentially mediated by faster data processing. It has conceptual implications. WEIBEL 76 quoted de Duve succinctly stating a driving concept of modern cell biology: functions of a cell may be associated with a particular structural element and therefore the attempt must be made to identify such an association. Stereology should push structural analysis to the stage where a quantitative correlation could be established between cell structure and cell function, the latter one being indicated by biochemical activities. If we replace spatial image sequences by temporal ones, unraveling of associations between function and dynamic changes in structural appearance plays an analogous role. This can be exemplified by the subject of a recent workshop: roentger video techniques for dynamic studies of structure and function of the heart and circulation - see HEINTZEN and BUERSCH 78 .

3. Modeling Temporal Variations of Image Functions Caused by Moving Objects

Various approaches have been reported to derive a quantitative model for the temporal variations in an image sequence, based on the assumption that these variations are caused by a moving object. These approaches attempted to approximate the image function without regard to the actual 3-D variations in the scene. Moreover, a number of rather restrictive assumptions had to be made in order to derive quantitative relations. Some of these restrictions could be relaxed a bit at the price of a more complicated mathematical treatment. Despite all obvious shortcomings, it appeared useful to present a coherent exposition of the various approaches. In order to achieve this goal, several approaches discussed in section 2.1.6 on movement compensation are reformulated here to integrate them into a more general context.

3.1 Estimating the Translation for Video Images of Moving Objects

Let us assume that the image intensity is given as a continous function $I(x, y, t)$. Its Taylor series starts as

$$I(x+Dx,\ y+Dy,\ t+Dt) = I(x, y, t) + (\partial I/dx) * Dx + (dI/dy) * Dy + (\partial I/\partial t) * Dt \quad \ldots\ldots\ldots\ldots (1)$$

If the image of a moving object after the time interval Dt resulted from a translation (Dx, Dy), then both sides in the first line of this equation should be equal, yielding

$$-\ (dI/\partial t) = (dI/dx) * Vx + (dI/\partial y) * Vy$$

with velocity estimates

$$Vx = (Dx/Dt) \quad \text{and} \quad Vy = (Dy/Dt)$$

LIMB and MURPHY 75a measured the absolute value of the velocity for an object image which was displaced parallel to the scanlines (Vy = 0):

$$Abs(dI/dt) = Abs(dI/dx) * Abs(Vx)$$

In a digital picture function, the time derivative is approximated by the interframe difference and the horizontal gradient component by the intraframe difference between two pixels within a scanline. Dividing the magnitudes of these differences, obtained for just one pixel within the moving object image, will yield only an unreliable estimate for Abs(Vx). Therefore, LIMB and MURPHY 75a added these absolute differences for all pixels of the moving object image in two accumulators and obtained:

Abs(Vx) = (Sum of absolute interframe differences) /
(Sum of absolute intraframe element differences)

They reported measurements for three objects in front of a textured, well contrasting background with image sizes varying between about 1/2 down to 1/32 of a videotelephone image area. These object images were translated uniformly along the horizontal at speeds between 0.5 and 4 pixels/frame. The speed measurements obtained by this approach agreed well up to velocities of 2.5 pixels/frame with the expected value for all three object sizes. At higher displacement rates the results for different object sizes began to deviate from each other and increased less than proportional to the real speed. The pixels corresponding to the image of the moving object were separated from stationary background using the technique of PEASE and LIMB 71 .

LIMB and MURPHY 75a measured the speed for an object displaced along directions that deviated up to a right angle from the scanline by rotating the camera around the optical axis. The result depended only weakly on this angle because the spatial gradient of the intensity within this object image was distributed more or less uniformly over all directions. In such a situation the element-to-element difference derived within a scanline could be used to estimate the average gradient.

Using a generalization of this approach, LIMB and MURPHY 75b determined in real time the magnitude and the sign of the velocity component along scanlines for a single moving object image. To understand their method, let us assume initially that the object image is displaced along scanlines and that its intensity distribution perpendicular to the scanline direction is constant, i.e. $V_y = 0$ and $(dI/dy) = 0$. Then the sign bit of V_x is equal to the exclusive OR between the sign bits of the interframe (i.e. dI/dt) and the intraframe (i.e. dI/dx) difference for each pixel of the moving object image. Thus, the original approach has to be modified only by accumulating the interframe differences taking into account the sign obtained in this manner (rather than only their magnitudes) :

$$V_x = (\text{Sum of interframe differences}) / (\text{Sum of magnitudes of intraframe differences})$$

If we relax the simplifying restrictions on intensity distribution and displacement velocity of the moving object image, but still restrict ourselves to determining only the element-to-element difference within a scanline, then we neglect in effect the bracketed term on the right hand side of

$$-(dI/dt)_{parallel} - (dI/dt)_{normal} = (dI/dx)*V_x + [(dI/dy)*V_y] .$$

The lefthand side has been split conceptually into contributions to the interframe difference from displacements parallel and normal to the scanline. Provided the intensity variations within the nonstationary image area along these two directions are uncorrelated, the exclusive OR of sign bits from the total interframe difference (dI/dt) and the within-line element-to-element difference (dI/dx) will not be strongly correlated with the sign of the interframe difference arising only from motion normal to the scanline, i.e. $(dI/dt)_{normal}$. Forming the sum of total interframe differences with this sign will therefore effectively cancel the contributions from $(dI/dt)_{normal}$. LIMB and MURPHY 75b demonstrated for one of their moving object images that this condition was satisfied.

To separate the nonstationary image component from the stationary background they used a segmentation procedure analogous to the one described by CONNOR et al. 73 although without filters. LIMB and MURPHY 75b derived the entity used as (dI/dx) for a raster position by averaging the corresponding intraframe differences from the previous and the current frame. If objects were translated in front of a plain background they obtained satisfactory measurements for the horizontal velocity component within the range of 0.25 to 3.5 pixels/frame for object sizes between about 1/64 to 1/2 the videotelephone image area, almost independently of the actual vertical velocity. However, objects moving in front of significantly textured background led to satisfactory measurements only for velocity components up to 2.5 pixels/frame. This effect could be traced to the fact that contributions due to noise and transition zones between nonstationary and stationary image components did not cancel when the magnitude of intraframe differences were accumulated as an estimate for (dI/dx).

CAFFORIO and ROCCA 76 generalized this method to determine both velocity components for image displacements between -3 and +3 pixels per frame period. Quantizing speed measurements into bins of 0.2 pixels/frame representative for their experiments yielded a 30x30 raster in the (Vx, Vy) plane considered. The differential quotients in equation (1) were replaced by the corresponding inter- and intraframe differences yielding a linear relation between Vx and Vy for each pixel within a nonstationary image area. The authors incremented a hit counter for each bin in the (Vx, Vy) plane hit by the line Vy = f(Vx). The intersections between such lines clustered at the displacement velocity (Vx, Vy) of a moving object image. This technique can be considered as an analogy to the Hough transform - see DUDA and HART 73 , p.335. The authors presented velocity measurements in the range mentioned above for a single object image that covered about 60 % of the visible frame area (128x128 pixels). They extended their approach to measure the velocity components for two object images - simultaneously displaced at different velocities - by searching for two distinct peaks in the histogram accumulated over the rastered (Vx, Vy) plane. Each of these two object images covered about 1/3 of the visible frame area.

Segmentation into stationary and nonstationary image areas was performed based on a two-state Markov model for explaining the sequence of observed interframe differences along a scanline, considering interframe differences as zero-mean independent Laplacian variates. Each pixel was assigned to the stationary or nonstationary state using the Viterbi algorithm - see FORNEY 73 - to minimize a total cost estimate for transitions among such assignments along a scanline.

Velocity measurements obtained by the method of CAFFORIO and ROCCA 76 began to deviate from the true image displacement rate above 2.5 pixels/frame. However, using low-pass filtering of interframe differences, these authors obtained results that vary linearly with the true displacement rate - slightly better than comparison measurements by the same authors using the method of LIMB and MURPHY 75b. The article of CAFFORIO and ROCCA 76 comprised a theoretical analysis of the minimum size for a moving object image and the appropriate raster size for the (Vx, Vy)-plane histogram to achieve a required statistical accuracy in the velocity determination.

CAFFORIO and ROCCA 79 modified their equations in order to take noise effects into account. An experimental implementation of their new approach enabled them to demonstrate that noise introduces a bias into the displacement estimates. This bias can be controlled to some extent by low-pass filtering.

FENNEMA and THOMPSON 79 applied basically the same method as CAFFORIO and ROCCA 76 to determine the displacement rate per frame for the images of two and three moving objects in a scene observed at two different times. The images were digitized into 8-bit greyvalues on a 128x128 raster. Like CAFFORIO and ROCCA 76, FENNEMA and THOMPSON 79 subjected both images to a low-pass spatial filter in order to reduce the effect of noise and step edges in the intensity distribution before the spatial gradients were estimated by a (3x3) Sobel operator. They excluded all raster positions at which the magnitude of the interframe difference remained smaller than a threshold from contributing to the velocity-plane histogram. No further attempt was made at this stage to segment the frames into stationary and nonstationary areas. However, FENNEMA and THOMPSON 79 required additionally that the gradients estimated at the same pixel position in both frames differed by less than a threshold, otherwise the gradients estimated at this raster position would be excluded from consideration. In this manner FENNEMA and THOMPSON solved the problem which of the two spatial gradients estimated from the frames involved should be used (LIMB and MURPHY 75b solved this problem by averaging the corresponding intraframe differences). The polar coordinate raster employed by these authors for rastering the velocity plane appeared unnecessarily complicated compared to the rectangular (Vx, Vy) raster used by CAFFORIO and ROCCA 76.

The essential difference between FENNEMA and THOMPSON 79 and earlier approaches to velocity measurements must be seen in the method with which these authors designed their computer internal description of the image sequence. In a first pass, they assigned a pixel to the stationary component if the gradients estimated at that position were excluded from contributing to the velocity-plane frequency histogram. Otherwise, a pixel was assigned to the nonstationary image component with a histogram peak position in the velocity plane closest to the velocity curve derived by equation (1) from the gradient estimates for this pixel. A second pass then reassigned each pixel to the image component represented most frequently among its neighbors. Contrary to the previous approaches, FENNEMA and THOMPSON 79 segmented each frame based upon the velocity measurement obtained for a pixel and its environment. Their sequence description thus included not only the velocity components of moving object images but in addition a data structure representing separately the image of each moving object. As attempted earlier by POTTER 75a+75b+77 , the velocity estimate has been used as an attribute upon which region growing - see BRICE and FENNEMA 70 - was based as a method of segmenting the images. Similar considerations have recently been published by MARR and ULLMAN 79 and - in a different form - by MAITRE 79 . This has to be contrasted with approaches that first segment an image relying exclusively on data from a single frame and then estimate the segment velocity by evaluating the displacement of a successfully matched segment from a neighboring frame in a sequence - see the discussion in section 3.3.

THOMPSON 79 refined this region growing aspect. In a first step, each image frame had to be segmented into primitive regions based solely on the greyvalues of this frame. A second step started from velocity estimates for pixels derived according to FENNEMA and THOMPSON 79 and attempted to assign a velocity value to each primitive region. If a considerable fraction of pixels along the boundary of a primitive region exhibited a sizeable velocity component perpendicular to the local boundary direction and if the distribution of velocity estimates along this boundary was dominated by one peak then the velocity of this peak center was assigned to the primitive region. Otherwise the primitive region was labelled as having an undefined velocity. A third step merged regions provided their greyvalue characteristics as well as their velocity attributes were compatible. This third phase allowed the extension of a more reliable velocity estimate - derived from image areas with a strong grey value gradient - into the interior of agglomerated homogeneous regions where the original velocity estimates were less certain. The final fourth phase assumed that velocity attributes could be trusted enough to cluster neighboring regions based exclusively on the similarity of their velocity attributes. Thus regions with different greyvalue characteristics could be merged into the image of a moving object identified by a single velocity. The concept to identify images of moving objects based on the assumption that all their parts undergo a common frame-to-frame displacement is the same as discussed by NAGEL 78a . Preliminary tests of the approach by THOMPSON 79 on series of two to three photographs digitized into 8 bit greyvalues on a 100x100 pixel raster have shown that further work in this direction appears promising. In this context the work by JAIN et al. 79 must be mentioned where an attempt was made to derive a mask covering the image of a moving object in each frame of an image sequence by starting their analysis at those pixels which exhibited a significant frame-to-frame greyvalue difference. MARR and ULLMAN 79 as well as BATALI and ULLMAN 79 recently published analogous results derived from two random dot patterns where the dots within a rectangular window had been shifted from one frame to the next with respect to the remaining dots - see section 3.3 .

3.2 Including Image Plane Rotation and Scale Changes into the Displacement Characteristic

SCHALKOFF 79 , SCHALKOFF and MCVEY 79 recently reported a significantly improved theoretical analysis by extending the line of thought discussed so far in this chapter for applications in target tracking - see section 2.6.2. Their analysis will be presented here in a slightly modified form in order to facilitate a comparison with other approaches and a discussion of the implications.

Let I(X,t) denote the intensity measured at the time t in a sensor location represented by the 2-D coordinate vector X' = (x,y) where the apostrophe indicates transposition of vectors or matrices. The image I(X,t) is decomposed into two contributions - one from the background, denoted by BI(X,t), and another one representing the image OI(X,t) of a moving object. The background image BI should not vary with time. The concept underlying the following discussion assumes that one image frame has been picked from the sequence and that the object image OI has been isolated in this frame. This OI should then serve as a time-independent model for the object image - implying that the partial derivative of OI with respect to time t is identically zero. OI and BI are combined to form I by using a binary object mask OM which has the value 1 for all pixel positions corresponding to the object and 0 elsewhere:

$$I = OI * OM + [1-OM] * BI$$

OI as well as OM are defined in the coordinate system corresponding to the frame from which OI and OM have been extracted. The 2-D position vector in this coordinate system - henceforth denoted as 'object coordinate system' - will be written in the following as Y. In this case, it is assumed that OM does not depend explicitly on time - just like OI. It should be noted that the different approaches of NAGEL 78a , JAIN et al. 77 , JAIN and NAGEL 79 , FENNEMA and THOMPSON 79 , JAIN et al. 79 , THOMPSON 79, GERLACH 79 , all represent experimental attempts to derive such a mask OM from an image sequence.

In order to model the time variation of I(X,t) caused by the moving object, a linear time dependent mapping from the sensor coordinate system X into the object coordinate system Y is assumed:

$$Y(X,t) = A(t) * X - DX(t) \tag{2}$$

where the matrix A with possibly time-varying coefficients represents a general affine transformation and DX = (Dx,Dy)' represents the translation of the Y-origin with respect to the X-origin. If t0 corresponds to the frame from which OI and OM have been extracted we have, of course, Y(X,t0) = X. Using these conventions, I(X,t) can be expressed as

$$\begin{aligned} I(X,t) = {} & OI(Y(X,t)) * OM(Y(X,t)) \\ & + BI(X,t) * [1-OM(Y(X,t))] \end{aligned} \tag{3}$$

The subsequent discussion will be restricted to an image area entirely covered by OM(Y(X,t)) = 1, i.e. the interior of the moving object image. This restriction is discussed further in section 3.3. The change of intensity I during a time interval Dt can then be given by

$$
\begin{aligned}
I(X,t+Dt)-I(X,t) &= Dt*(d/dt)I(X,t) \\
&= Dt * (d/dt)OI(Y(X,t)) * OM(Y(X,t)) \\
&\quad + Dt * OI(Y(X,t)) * (d/dt)OM(Y(X,t))
\end{aligned} \tag{4}
$$

The time derivatives on the right hand side are given by

$$
\begin{aligned}
(d/dt)OI(Y(X,t)) &= GRAD'OI(Y(X,t)) * (d/dt)Y(X,t); \\
(d/dt)OM(Y(X,t)) &= GRAD'OM(Y(X,t)) * (d/dt)Y(X,t).
\end{aligned}
$$

Since we restricted ourselves to the interior of the moving object image, GRAD'OM(Y(X,t)) will be zero for all Y to be considered here - i.e. the second of these expressions can be dropped. The time derivative of Y(X,t) will be approximated as

$$
\begin{aligned}
Dt*(d/dt)Y(X,t) &= Y(X,t+Dt)-Y(X,t) \\
&= [A(t+Dt)-A(t)] * X - [DX(t+Dt)-DX(t)] \\
&= DA(t,Dt) * X - DDX(t,Dt)
\end{aligned} \tag{5}
$$

where it is assumed that the elements of

$$
DA(t,Dt) = \begin{bmatrix} a(t,Dt) & b(t,Dt) \\ c(t,Dt) & d(t,Dt) \end{bmatrix}
$$

as well as

$$
DDX(t,Dt) = (DDx(t,Dt) , DDy(t,Dt))'
$$

go to zero at least linearly with Dt. The 2-D sensor is assumed to be rastered, with grid positions Xi = (xi,yi)' numbered according to some linear order, e.g. a linewise noninterlaced scanning order. If we introduce the abbreviation

$$
DIi(t,Dt) = I(Xi,t+Dt) - I(Xi,t)
$$

we may write - suppressing momentarily the explicit notation of the time dependance - equation (4) in the form

$$
DIi = GRAD'OI(A*Xi-DX) * [DA * Xi - DDX] \tag{6}
$$

For each pixel position Xi we can determine DIi from the interframe difference and GRAD'OI(A*Xi-DX) by measuring the spatial gradient of the greyvalue function within the interior of the moving object image in one image frame. Since DA as well as DDX can be assumed to be constant - if not for the entire moving object image, then at least for more than six pixels -, we obtain an overdetermined system of equations for the six unknown elements of DA and DDX. In order to solve the resulting estimation problem explicitly, SCHALKOFF and MCVEY made a further simplification: the general affine transformation A(t) had been restricted to a rotation in the image plane and a common scale factor.

$$A = s * \begin{bmatrix} \cos(\text{theta}) & -\sin(\text{theta}) \\ \sin(\text{theta}) & \cos(\text{theta}) \end{bmatrix}.$$

This reduced the number of parameters to be estimated from six to four: the two components of DDX = (DDx, DDy)' and the two parameters specifying DA

$$DA = \begin{bmatrix} s*\cos(\text{theta})-1 & -s*\sin(\text{theta}) \\ s*\sin(\text{theta}) & s*\cos(\text{theta})-1 \end{bmatrix}$$

$$= \begin{bmatrix} a & -c \\ c & a \end{bmatrix}.$$

Remember that - according to the definition of DA(t,Dt) in equation (5) - all elements of DA vanish with vanishing Dt because in this case the scale change s between the transformations at time t and t+Dt will approach 1 and the rotation angle theta will approach zero.

With OIi = OI (A(t) * Xi - DX(t)) one obtains

$$DIi = GRAD'OIi * \begin{bmatrix} a*xi - c*yi - DDx \\ c*xi + a*yi - DDy \end{bmatrix} \qquad (7)$$

which can be rearranged into

```
DIi =  [xi*GRADxOIi + yi*GRADyOIi] *  a
     + [xi*GRADyOIi - yi*GRADxOIi] *  c
                    -    GRADxOIi  *  DDx
                    -    GRADyOIi  *  DDy.
```

Introducing the notation

```
Fi1 = xi * GRADxOIi  +  yi * GRADyOIi
Fi2 = xi * GRADyOIi  -  yi * GRADxOIi
Gi1 =     -GRADxOIi
Gi2 =     -GRADyOIi
```

and E = (E1 , E2)' with E1=a and E2=c yields

```
DIi = (Fi1, Fi2, Gi1, Gi2) * (E1, E2, DDx, DDy)'   .    (8)
```

The four unknown elements of the parameter vector (a, c, DDx, DDy)' have to be estimated by minimizing the squared difference between DIi and its right hand side representation over a suitably chosen subset of pixels i within the image of a moving object. Reasonable choices for such a subset could be the entire interior of the moving object image or a quadratic window entirely contained in the moving object image, similar to predefined segments for transform coding.

SCHALKOFF and MCVEY employed a pseudoinverse formalism to derive a solution for the components of E and DDX whereas here a different solution approach has been derived in order to obtain the desired result in a form more suitable for further discussions.

The index i is henceforth used as a row index, i.e. (DIi), (Fi1), (Fi2), (Gi1), (Gi2) are considered as column vectors with i running from 1 to the number N of pixels in the subset. The minimization problem then takes the form

```
Sum over i of SQR(Fi*E + Gi*DDX - DIi) = Minimum .
```

Equating the partial derivatives of the left hand side with respect to the components of E and DDX to zero yields the following system of matrix equations

```
F'*F * E  +  F'*G * DDX  =  F'*DI
                                          (9)
G'*F * E  +  G'*G * DDX  =  G'*DI
```

$$\text{with} \quad F'*DI = \begin{bmatrix} Fi1'*DIi \\ Fi2'*DIi \end{bmatrix}$$

and, e.g., the upper right element of the square 2x2 matrix $F'*G$ being given by $Fi1'*Gi2$ with summation over the index i being implied. To solve this set of four linear equations with the four unknowns $(E1, E2, DDx, DDy)'$, the following matrix identity (derived in analogy to a formula given by DORNY 75 , p. 32) will be used:

$$\begin{bmatrix} P & Q \\ R & S \end{bmatrix}^{-1} = \begin{bmatrix} [P-Q*S^{-1}*R]^{-1} & -[P-Q*S^{-1}*R]^{-1}*Q*S^{-1} \\ -S^{-1}*R*[P-Q*S^{-1}*R]^{-1} & S^{-1}+S^{-1}*R*[P-Q*S^{-1}*R]^{-1}*Q*S^{-1} \end{bmatrix}$$

With

$$P = F'*F \qquad Q = F'*G$$
$$R = G'*F \qquad S = G'*G$$

and the pseudoinverse $G'' = [G'*G]^{-1}*G'$ we obtain

$$[P-Q*S^{-1}*R]^{-1} = [F'*F - F'*G*G''*F]^{-1} \quad .$$

With this expression and Id to denote the identity matrix, the solutions for the system of equations (9) can be written as

$$estE = [F'*(Id-G*G'')*F]^{-1} * F' * (Id-G*G'') * DI \tag{10}$$

$$estDDX = G''*DI - G''*F*[F'*(Id-G*G'')*F]^{-1} * F' * (Id-G*G'') * DI \tag{11}$$

or, substituting the solution for estE into the one for estDDX

estDDX = G" * DI - G" * F * estE (11a)

This important result will now be discussed regarding different aspects. Remember that the elements of E specify the free parameters of the transformation A which has been restricted to a plane rotation and a scale factor. Assume for a moment that the motion of the object image is dominated by the frame-to-frame translation represented by DDX = (DDx, DDy)'. Then the components of estE will be negligible and we obtain the estimate

estDDX = G" * DI

The 2 x 2 matrix G' * G is given by

$$G'*G = \begin{bmatrix} [(GRADxOIi) * (GRADxOIi)] & [(GRADxOIi) * (GRADyOIi)] \\ [(GRADxOIi) * (GRADyOIi)] & [(GRADyOIi) * (GRADyOIi)] \end{bmatrix}$$

where - as in the following - summation over identical indices i or j appearing in a bracketed term is implied. Since this matrix can be explicitly inverted, one obtains

$$\begin{aligned} estDDX &= G"*DI \\ &= [G'*G]^{-1} * G' * DI \\ &= [1/det(G'*G)] * \end{aligned}$$

$$\begin{bmatrix} -[(GRADyOIi)*(GRADyOIi)]*[(GRADxOIj)*(DIj)] \\ +[(GRADxOIi)*(GRADyOIi)]*[(GRADyOIj)*(DIj)] \\ \\ [(GRADxOIi)*(GRADyOIi)]*[(GRADxOIj)*(DIj)] \\ -[(GRADxOIi)*(GRADxOIi)]*[(GRADyOIj)*(DIj)] \end{bmatrix}$$

which is the result derived by CAFFORIO and ROCCA 76+79 , FUKINUKI 78 as well as NETRAVALI and ROBBINS 79 .

Comparing their result with the one obtained above, one immediately recognizes that the estimate estDDX = G"*DI is biased unless the second term G"*F*estE in the full expression for estDDX is zero due to an accidental vanishing of the matrix product G"*F. No bias, of course, is introduced into estDDX if the interframe intensity differences have been caused by a pure translation of the object image. In this case - see equation (13a) and the discussion following it - estE vanishes justifiably and not only accidentally !

The expression given above for estDDX will now be transformed into the one given by SCHALKOFF and MCVEY 79.

$$\begin{aligned} \mathrm{estDDX} &= G''*(\mathrm{Id}-F*[F'*(\mathrm{Id}-G*G'')*F]^{-1}*F'*(\mathrm{Id}-G*G''))*\mathrm{DI} \\ &= [G'*(\mathrm{Id}-F*F'')*G]^{-1}*[G'*(\mathrm{Id}-F*F'')*G]*G'' \\ &\qquad *(\mathrm{Id}-F*[F'*(\mathrm{Id}-G*G'')*F]^{-1}*F'*(\mathrm{Id}-G*G''))*\mathrm{DI}\,. \end{aligned}$$

Using $G'GG'' = G'$ we obtain

$$\begin{aligned} \mathrm{estDDX} &= [G'*(\mathrm{Id}-F*F'')*G]^{-1}*G'*(\mathrm{Id}-F*F''*G*G'') \\ &\qquad *[\mathrm{Id}-F*[F'*(\mathrm{Id}-G*G'')*F]^{-1}*F'*(\mathrm{Id}-G*G''))*\mathrm{DI}\,. \end{aligned}$$

Since $(\mathrm{Id}-F*F''*G*G'')*F = F*(\mathrm{Id}-F''*G*G''*F)$

and $[F'*(\mathrm{Id}-G*G'')*F]^{-1} = [\mathrm{Id}-F''*G*G''*F]^{-1}*[F'*F]^{-1}$

we obtain

$$\begin{aligned} \mathrm{estDDX} &= [G'*(\mathrm{Id}-F*F'')*G]^{-1} * G' * \\ &\qquad (\ \mathrm{Id}-F*F''*G*G''-F*[\mathrm{Id}-F''*G*G''*F]*[\mathrm{Id}-F''*G*G''*F]^{-1} \\ &\qquad * F'' * (\mathrm{Id}-G*G'')\ ) * \mathrm{DI} \end{aligned}$$

which yields

$$\mathrm{estDDX} = [G'*(\mathrm{Id}-F*F'')*G]^{-1}*G'*(\mathrm{Id}-F*F'')*\mathrm{DI}\ . \tag{12}$$

Similar transformations yield

$$\begin{aligned} \mathrm{estE} &= F'' * \mathrm{DI} \\ &\quad - F''*G*[G'*(\mathrm{Id}-F*F'')*G]^{-1}*G'*(\mathrm{Id}-F*F'')*\mathrm{DI} \end{aligned} \tag{13}$$

which can be expressed as

$$\text{estE} = F'' * (DI - G * \text{estDDX}) \qquad (13a)$$

This last expression for estE shows that the parameters specifying an incremental frame-to-frame rotation and scale change of the image of a moving object will vanish to the extent that all observable interframe intensity differences DIi within a window can be computed from a common shift vector estDDX.

SCHALKOFF 79 solved the set of N equations

$$DIi = (Fi, Gi) * (E, DDX)' \qquad i = 1,2,\ldots,N \qquad (14)$$

by

$$\begin{bmatrix} \text{estE} \\ \text{estDDX} \end{bmatrix} = \begin{bmatrix} F'' - F''*G*H'' \\ H'' \end{bmatrix} * DI \qquad (15)$$

with $H = (Id-F*F'') * G$ and $H'' = [H'*H]^{-1} *H'$.

SCHALKOFF 79 made use of a less well known formula by CLINE 64 to derive the pseudoinverse of a partitioned matrix (F G) where the submatrices F and G have the same number of columns. The equivalence of estDDX = H"*DI with equation (12) can be seen if the identities

$$(F*F'')' = F*F'' \quad \text{and} \quad (Id-F*F'')'*(Id-F*F'') = (Id-F*F'')$$

are used to evaluate H'*H. Similarly, the equivalence of SCHALKOFF's result for estE with equation (13) can be shown.

3.3 Discussion

A plane rotation of the object image around a point Z = (Zx,Zy) different from the origin can be expressed as the additive combination of a rotation around the origin and an additional translation depending on Z. It will be interesting to see whether the technique outlined above could be used to estimate the rotation of cloud configurations in satellite image sequences of tornado thunderstorms. This approach could turn out to be a useful complement to the one investigated by HAASS and BRUBAKER 79 - see section 2.2.3.

This approach by SCHALKOFF and MCVEY 79 is important because it shows to what extent the greyvalue variations observable in image sequences can already be modeled. The model represented by equations (2) and (3) had to be simplified further in order to arrive at a closed solution for the four parameters which are used to describe the 2-D motion of an object image. Despite these simplifications, this model offers the opportunity to at least discuss specific assumptions and point out connections with other considerations.

It will have to be verified using actual data from TV or satellite sensors whether the introduction of rotation and dilatation parameters - i.e. the components of E - represents a consistent improvement for the description of moving object images. Unless the conditions are known where this is the case, it does not make sense to attempt the determination of all four parameters for the affine transformation A in the form originally introduced in equation (2).

Furthermore, it will have to be investigated to what extent the use of approximate digital operators for determination of GRAD OI(Y(X,t)) influences the reliability of the results for estDDX and estE. So far, no precise tests have been performed. Recent investigations of several digital gradient operators - see, e.g., BROOKS 78a as well as ABDOU and PRATT 79 - make it appear unlikely that every gradient operator or even the simple intraframe intensity difference between two neighboring pixels should be equally suitable.

In this context the suggestion by CAFFORIO and ROCCA 76+79 as well as FENNEMA and THOMPSON 79 should be mentioned: they subject the image to a low-pass filter before a translation vector for a moving object image is estimated. In the interior of the image of a moving object, this low-pass filtering should ensure that the intensity does not exhibit a significant nonlinear variation over the spatial extent of the digital gradient operator. SCHALKOFF and MCVEY 79 specifically excluded the boundary area of the moving object image because there the assumption of a linear intensity variation is definitely wrong.

Low-pass filtering of the entire image would alleviate this problem. Moreover, it appears necessary to investigate - by studying real-world image sequences - the bias in displacement estimates due to noise (see CAFFORIO and ROCCA 79) or due to oversimplifying assumptions for the estimation methods.

Although the moving object mask OM(Y) essentially disappeared due to later restrictions, it may nevertheless be useful to consider its role in the attempt to model the greyvalue variations within an image sequence. Its appearance corresponds to the hidden surface problem of computer graphics, i.e. it reflects the 3-D nature of the scene. Moreover, the mask OM(Y) could be used in an attempt to extend the object tracking from 2-D to 3-D - apart from the occlusion problem. The object mask represents the silhouette of the object. MARR 77 evaluated the contour line of an object in a single image to infer the 3-D object shape under certain assumptions. It appears promising to combine the knowledge about the 2-D translation, rotation, and scale change of a moving object image - estimated by the techniques outlined above - with the time variation of the contour of the object mask OM(Y(X,t)) in order to increase the constraints on possible 3-D object shape and motion interpretations. The investigations reported by BAKER 77 could be seen as early attempts in this direction.

POTTER 75a+75b+77 attempted to match greylevel transitions from frame to frame in order to obtain local displacement estimates which could then be exploited to segment each image frame. This approach has recently been pursued further by MARTIN and AGGARWAL 79b as well as KORN and WEDLICH 79a+79b . These authors fitted straight line segments to edge elements in order to obtain more reliable contour segments. This, in effect, represents a complementary approach to the one discussed in the preceding section: displacement estimates are based here on greyvalue transitions with high spatial frequency content rather than on lower spatial frequencies which have to dominate the greyvalue transitions in the interior of nonstationary image components in order to justify the approximations discussed in the preceding section. MARTIN and AGGARWAL 79b - see section 2.6.2 - treated only contours in binarized images. They employed a shape matching procedure for contour segments which offered the possibility to decompose the contour into parts related to different overlapping noncontrasting objects. KORN and WEDLICH 79a+79b employed a clustering procedure in a scatter plot of displacement vector components in order to identify maxima which could be attributed to the joint displacement of a group of straight-line contour segments.

Another possibility to estimate interframe displacements has been studied by MARR and ULLMAN 79 . They estimated the displacement direction from the time derivative of the zero crossings which had been located in the output of an Laplacian operator applied to a convolution of the image with a Gaussian filter. This approach seems to be attractive as a potential explanation for the low-level processes in the human visual system. First results for random dot patterns have been reported by these authors as well as in BATALI and ULLMAN 79.

For the sake of completeness, other approaches for estimating interframe displacements of subimages should be mentioned here. The possibility to exploit the phase correlation method has been discussed in section 2.1.2. It appears worthwhile to investigate to what extend the technique described by PEARSON et al. 77 will yield results compatible with those obtained by the approach of SCHALKOFF and MCVEY 79 . Furthermore, the pixel-recursive approach studied by NETRAVALI and ROBBINS 79 , ROBBINS and NETRAVALI 79 as well as the coefficient-recursive approach for transformed images as discussed by NETRAVALI and STULLER 79 , STULLER and NETRAVALI 79 should be compared to the other approaches regarding computational expenses versus susceptibility to noise and estimation bias.

The straightforward cross-correlation search originally suggested by ROCCA 69 for displacement estimation is computationally unattractive in comparison with the other approaches. The earliest approach to displacement estimation is contained in the article by MOSKOWITZ 64 . However, no results of this approach for real-world image sequences have been found in the literature.

The prime motivation for the rather extensive discussion of approaches to estimate displacement, rotation, and scale changes for the image of a moving object has been twofold. First, such attempts clearly transcend the area of coding applications, and the techniques developed in different application areas are based on the same assumptions. Second, despite many restrictions of the currently available approaches, one should realize the steady improvements from the results reported 1975 by LIMB and MURPHY to the recent analysis

4. Conclusion

Some - not all - aspects of the analysis of image sequences have been reviewed in the preceding sections in order to provide the reader with background information to judge the following considerations.

The wide variety of applications demonstrates that it would be a mistake to reduce the analysis of image sequences to some subproblem such as 'visual motion perception' or the 'occlusion problem'. Spatial image sequences as well as temporal characteristics of spatially constant phenomena such as the accumulation and wash-out of radioisotopes from certain organs represent examples to the contrary. A theory for the evaluation of image sequences will have to offer a rather wide spectrum of concepts and descriptive tools in order to cope with available input data. In view of this consideration, it appears questionable whether we know already enough to sketch the structure of 'intelligent systems' which should be capable of analysing image sequences. Such schemas are useful because they attempt to chart a vast area and thus provide a preliminary framework within which detailed research results can be assessed. It is only argued here that one should be careful with any explicit or implicit claims about presenting the definite structure. The discrepancy between the information contained in image sequences and the fraction which we know to extract automatically is still too great. This caution may be reinforced by the consideration that several important aspects of image sequence analysis - see section 1.2 - had to be omitted from this review. It could well be, therefore, that the discrepancy between the real extent of the problem and our knowledge to cope with it may be even greater.

Apart from this precaution, what could be gained by the preceding review ? It is hoped that the conceptual and technical parallels in the evaluation of image sequences from various application areas have become more discernible. This might facilitate the transfer of solution approaches and techniques from one application area to another - especially with respect to the various questions discussed in section 1.

Moreover, it can be recognized that the development of some application areas - such as the evaluation of satellite image sequences for the derivation of wind velocity estimates or the evaluation of angiographic image sequences in medicine - may have a future analogon in certain other areas, for example the evaluation of image sequences from ultrasound sources or in behavioural studies.

The possibility to make such an analogous development plausible has been the reason to include interactive approaches into the review. It extended the period throughout which the development of an application area could be discussed and thus broadened the basis for a comparison. However, there is even more to it. Automatic approaches have been restricted to a fairly low level of evaluation. The transition from the processing of pixel attributes, edge elements, blobs, and regions to high level abstractions related to a specific application has been based on rather domain specific connections. There is a huge gap in intermediate concepts, in related data structures, and in algorithms for their manipulation which should provide a gradual transition in the level of abstraction from the pixel to the questions of interest for an application. Some interactive systems have developped from mere operator intervention to a research environment for the investigation of such intermediate level concepts. This is necessary in order to gain experience with such general concepts as 'event', 'interval', etc. which eventually have to be incorporated in a system for the evaluation of image sequences. Examples for such a development can be found in the work of ARIKI et al., FUTRELLE, POTEL, SAYRE, TSOTSOS, and others discussed in section 2.4. Transfer of such investigations to other application areas may result in the gradual emergence of intermediate level abstractions which are fairly independent of individual applications.

In addition to this formalization of concepts, there are technical questions which appear in more or less the same form in different application areas. 2-D vector fields of interframe displacements, for example, have to be determined for motion compensated bandwidth compression as well as for cloud velocity determination. It will be interesting to see whether the formalism discussed in section 3 can be put to use in the evaluation of satellite image series.

A similar, if not more obvious, example is the alignment or frame-to-frame registration problem. It is encountered in the evaluation of satellite image sequences for the estimation of cloud displacement velocity or for the construction of mosaics, in the registration of digitized film images from the beating heart or from behavioural studies as well as in the registration of images from microtome slices. In all these cases, control points, edges, or regions had to be selected from one image and to be compared to suitable candidates in other images. The selection of such control features has mostly been based on domain specific knowledge, either by performing it interactively, or by providing predefined data and algorithms to extract the relevant image segments. It is an important research problem to investigate whether this domain specific a-priori knowledge about what constitutes an appropriate control segment for interframe alignment can be replaced by an automatic selection procedure. This procedure would have to evaluate an entire image sequence - rather than only two frames - in order to isolate corresponding image segments in each frame. The next step would be an attempt to use corresponding image segments in order to determine the parameters of an interframe mapping. Such a mapping would be acceptable if the remaining discrepancies between aligned image frames could be attributed to a small number of potential explanations. This set of causes can be divided into two subsets, one of which comprises the domain-specific explanations. These should be consolidated into a computer-internal model of the situation which yielded the image sequence to be analysed.

The other subset comprises the general concepts and rules which have been discussed in section 1.1 : the concepts of a surface and a volume in three-dimensional space, the dynamics of such bodies, the variability in scene illumination and associated effects, as well as how the position and attitude of the observer influences his view of the scene. The so-called 'occlusion problem' is but one aspect of the required 3-D modeling. The treatment of temporal and spatial image sequences offers various examples. Moreover, the complementary role of image sequence analysis and dynamic computer graphics becomes obvious: dynamic computer graphics derives an image sequence from a dynamic computer-internal representation of a scene whereas the analysis of image sequences has to result in a computer-internal description of the scene and its development with time. Although the same remark can be made regarding the analysis of a single image and static computer graphics, the extension to image sequences emphasizes one very important aspect: the role of general transformations and their invariances for image analysis. Translation, rotation, perspective projection from variable viewing positions are general concepts which can be exploited to explain observed frame-to-frame variations. In addition to these geometric laws, radiometric ones must be used to explain not only the shape, but also the intensity variations on curved surfaces. It must be anticipated that progress in the evaluation of image sequences will be connected with the ability to put these general laws to use.

Exploitation of these laws and their invariances will unify processing aspects for diverse application areas, with respect to temporal, spatio-temporal, and spatial image sequences. Processing of stereo image combinations will appear as a subproblem, as exemplified by the work on motion parallax and navigable robots (see section 2.7).

Should a multispectral image be considered as an image sequence, emphasizing the 'spectral' dimension ? The real question appears to be whether or not one might gain from taking this point of view - and this question cannot be answered yet. There seem to be no transformations in the spectral dimension which have invariances closely related to common experiences - such as size or shape for translation. Moreover, usually the spectrum is sampled only in few broad bands. Not much evidence is available that techniques related to geometric transformations can be transferred to the spectral dimension. However, treating temporal sequences of measurements in analogy to spectral features has been applied in the evaluation of scintigraphic image sequences - see section 2.3.4. So it appears useful to leave this question open for a while.

Throughout this review, attention has been drawn to the interaction between the evaluation of image sequences and the improvement of quantitative models to describe complex phenomena in the application domain. Prominent examples are meteorological models or the investigations about relations between structure and function in angiographic, scintigraphic, or neurological studies.

This review covered a wide range of applications in an attempt to demonstrate that commonalities can be recognized. This applies to lower level image processing approaches as well as to the investigation of concepts at an intermediate level of abstraction. Moreover, it appears that more algorithmic oriented - as opposed to purely interactive - approaches to the evaluation of image sequences develop in evolutionary steps which appear analogous across application domains. It may be justified, therefore, to shift the emphasis away from the investigation of solutions to specific application problems towards a more general formulation of problems and solution approaches. In other words, the analysis of image sequences emerges as a discipline with fundamental coherence and broad appeal to basic research as well as a wide spectrum of applications.

5. Acknowledgements

I thank B. Neumann, B. Radig, and J. O'Rourke for many discussions about this subject and for their very helpful comments on a preliminary version of this article. The help of G. Hille, B. Radig, and especially Mrs. R. Jancke during the text editing and printing is gratefully acknowledged. Mrs. E. Criegee, the librarian of our department, managed to provide copies of a large number of articles which were not available at libraries in Hamburg. If the bibliography should turn out to be useful, please think high of her help to obtain the articles as well as the help of Mrs. R. Jancke to edit the references. A. Rosenfeld kindly provided me with an advance copy of a new chapter from the forthcoming second edition of 'Digital Image Processing'. Many other authors made reprints or preprints of their articles available. In this context I want to thank R. Brennecke / Universitaet Kiel and B.K.P. Horn / MIT, Cambridge/MA for repeatedly providing me with literature by other authors which I could not obtain without their help. Finally, my thanks are due to T.S. Huang who encouraged me to finish this review despite the fact that it took me much longer than both of us had anticipated - the bibliography quadrupled in the course of writing this contribution !

6. References

Abbreviations :

IJCAI = International Joint Conference on Artificial Intelligence
IJCAI-69 : Washington/DC , USA , May 7-9, 1969
IJCAI-71 : London / UK , September 1-3, 1971
IJCAI-73 : Stanford/CA , USA , August 20-23, 1973
IJCAI-75 : Tbilisi/Georgia, USSR , September 3-8, 1975
IJCAI-77 : Cambridge/MA, USA , August 22-25, 1977
IJCAI-79 : Tokyo/Japan , August 20-23, 1979

IJCPR = International Joint Conference on Pattern Recognition
IJCPR-73 : Washington/DC , USA , Oct. 30 - Nov. 1 , 1973
IJCPR-74 : Copenhagen / Denmark , August 13-15, 1974
IJCPR-76 : Coronado/CA , USA , November 8-11, 1976
IJCPR-78 : Kyoto / Japan , November 7-10, 1978

WCATVI-79 = IEEE Workshop on Computer Analysis of Time-Varying Imagery, Philadelphia/PA, USA, April 5-6, 1979

The numbers following the ==> pointer after a reference keyword represent the section where this reference is discussed. If the same number appears more than once, this reference is discussed in different contexts in the same section .

Abdou and Pratt 79 ==> 3.3;
Quantitative Design and Evaluation of Enhancement/ Thresholding Edge Detectors
I.E. Abdou and W.K. Pratt
Proc. IEEE 67 (1979) 753-763

Adler and Fenn 76 ==> 2.2.3;
Thunderstorm Monitoring from a Geosynchronous Satellite
R.F. Adler and D.D. Fenn
7th Conference on Aerospace and Aeronautical Meteorology (1976) pp. 307-311

Aggarwal and Duda 75 ==> 2.2.1; 2.6.2;
Computer Analysis of Moving Polygonal Images
J.K. Aggarwal and R.O. Duda
IEEE Trans. Computers C-24 (1975) 966-976

Agin 79 ==>2.6.1;
Knowledge-Based Detection and Classification of Vehicles and Other Objects in Aerial Road Images
G.J. Agin
Proc. Image Understanding Workshop, L.S. Baumann (ed.) Palo Alto/CA, April 24-25, 1979, pp. 66-71
Science Applications, Inc., Arlington/VA 22209

Anuta 69 ==> 2.2.4;
Digital Registration of Multispectral Video Imagery
P.E. Anuta
SPIE J. 7 (1969) 168-175

Anuta 70 ==> 2.2.4; 2.2.6;
Spatial Registration of Multispectral and Multitemporal Digital Imagery Using Fast Fourier Transform Techniques
P.E. Anuta
IEEE Trans. on Geoscience Electronics GE-8 (1970) 353-368

Aoki 79 ==> 2.1.3;
Rectangular Region Coding for Image Data Compression
M. Aoki
Pattern Recognition 11 (1979) 297-312

Ariki 78 ==> 2.4; 4;
A System for Analyzing Time-Varying Image Patterns
Y. Ariki
Department of Information Science Technical Report (1978)
Faculty of Engineering, Kyoto University, Kyoto

Ariki et al. 78 ==> 2.4; 4;
An Interactive Image Modeling and Tracing System for Moving Pictures
Y. Ariki, T. Kanade, and T. Sakai
IJCPR-78 Nov. 7-10, 1978 Kyoto/Japan, pp. 681-685

Arking et al. 75 ==> 2.1.2; 2.2.1;
An Evaluation of Fourier Transform Techniques for Cloud Motion Estimation
A.A. Arking, R.C. Lo, and A. Rosenfeld
TR-351 (January 1975) Computer Science Department, University of Maryland, College Park/MD

Artzy 79 ==> 2.8.4
Display of Three-Dimensional Information in Computed Tomography
E. Artzy
Computer Graphics and Image Processing 9 (1979) 196-198

Ashkar and Modestino 78 ==> 2.3.3;
The Contour Extraction Problem with Biomedical Applications
G.P. Ashkar and J.W. Modestino
Computer Graphics and Image Processing 7 (1978) 331-355

Bach et al. 78 ==> 2.6.1;
Detektion bewegter Objekte in 2-dimensionalen Bildszenen
S. Bach, H. Gerlach und H. Kazmierczak
Bericht 58 (Maerz 1978)
Forschungsinstitut fuer Informationsverarbeitung und Mustererkennung, Karlsruhe/Germany

Badler and Bajcsy 78 ==> 2.8.8;
Three-Dimensional Representations for Computer Graphics and Computer Vision
N.I. Badler and R. Bajcsy
Proc. SIGGRAPH '78, R.L. Phillips (ed.)
Atlanta/GA, August 23-25, 1978,
Computer Graphics 12 (1978) 153-160

Badler and O'Rourke 79 ==> 2.8.8;
Representation of Articulable, Quasi-Rigid, Three-Dimensional Objects
N.I. Badler and J. O'Rourke
Proc. NSF Workshop on the Representation of Three-Dimensional Objects
R. Bajcsy (ed.), Philadelphia/PA, May 1-2, 1979

Bajcsy and Bourne 78 ==> 2.8.8;
Representation of Knowledge in Computer Vision Systems: A Comparative Analysis of Pattern Recognition and Artificial Intelligence Approaches with Applications to Reconstruction of 3-D Objects
R. Bajcsy and D.A. Bourne
MS-CIS-78-38 (1978)
Department of Computer and Information Science
University of Pennsylvania, Philadelphia/PA

Bajcsy and Soroka 77 ==> 2.8.6;
Steps Towards the Representation of Complex
Three-Dimensional Objects
R.K. Bajcsy and B.I. Soroka
IJCAI-77, p. 596
Bajcsy and Winston 78 ==> 2.8.1; 2.8.5;
A Computer System for Reconstruction and
Display of the Macrostructure of Brain
from Radiographs of Serial Sections
R. Bajcsy and I. Winston
Proc. BIOSIGMA '78, Paris/France, April 1978
also MS-CIS-78-33
Computer and Information Science Department
University of Pennsylvania, Philadelphia/PA
Baker 77 ==> 3.3;
Three-Dimensional Modelling
H.H. Baker
IJCAI-77, pp. 649-655
Ball and Hall 67 ==> 2.2.1;
A Clustering Technique for Summarizing Multivariate Data
G.H. Ball and D.J. Hall
Behavioral Science 12 (1967) 153-155
Batali and Ullman 79 ==> 2.1.3; 3.1; 3.3;
Motion Detection and Analysis
J. Batali and S. Ullman
Proc. Image Understanding Workshop, pp. 69-75
L.S. Baumann (ed.), Los Angeles/CA, Nov. 7-8, 1979
Science Applications, Inc., Arlington/VA 22209
Bauch et al. 74 ==> 2.1.3; 2.1.7;
Picture Coding
H.H. Bauch, H. Haeberle, H.G. Musmann, H. Ohnsorge,
G.A. Wengenroth, and H.J. Woite
IEEE Trans. Communications COM-22 (1974) 1158-1167
Bauer 76 ==> 2.2.1; 2.2.3;
A Comparison of Cloud Motion Winds with
Coinciding Radiosonde Winds
K.G. Bauer
Monthly Weather Review 104 (1976) 922-931
Bernstein 76 ==> 2.2.4; 2.2.6;
Digital Image Processing of Earth Observation Sensor Data
R. Bernstein
IBM Journal of Research and Development 20 (1976) 40-57
Binford 71 ==> 2.8.6;
Visual Perception by Computer
T.O. Binford
presented to IEEE Conference on Systems and Control
(Dec. 1971), Miami/Florida
Birk et al. 77 ==> 2.7;
Workpiece Orientation Correction with a Robot
Arm Using Visual Information
J.R. Birk, R.B. Kelley, and V.V. Badami
IJCAI-77, p. 758
Bonnell and Huhns 79 ==> 2.7;
Theory of Image Control
R.D. Bonnell and M.N. Huhns

Bourne 78 ==> 2.8.8;
Three Dimensional Picture Processing and its
Use in Bio-Medical Applications
D.A. Bourne
SPIE, Los Angeles 1978

Bradford et al. 72 ==> 2.2.1; 2.2.2; 2.2.4;
An Experimental Model for the Automated Detection,
Measurement, and Quality Control of Low-Level
Cloud Motion Vectors from Geosynchronous Satellite Data
R. Bradford, J.A. Leese, and C.S. Novak
Proc. 8th Int. Symposium on Remote Sensing of
Environment, October 2-6, 1972, pp. 441-462
University of Michigan, Ann Arbor/Michigan

Brennecke et al. 76 ==> 2.3.1; 2.3.1;
Digital Processing of Video-angiocardiographic
Image Series Using a Minicomputer
R. Brennecke, T.K. Brown, J. Buersch, and P.H. Heintzen
Proc. IEEE Conference on Computers
in Cardiology, St. Louis/MO 1976, pp. 255-260

Brennecke et al. 77 ==> 2.3.1; 2.3.1;
Computerized Video-Image Preprocessing
with Applications to Cardio-Angiographic
Roentgen-Image-Series
R. Brennecke, T.K. Brown, J. Buersch, and P.H. Heintzen
GI/NTG Fachtagung Digitale Bildverarbeitung
Muenchen, 28.-30. Maerz 1977, (H.-H. Nagel, ed.)
Informatik Fachberichte 8 (1977) 244-262
Springer Verlag Berlin-Heidelberg-New York, 1977

Brennecke et al. 78a ==> 2.3.1;
A Digital System for Roentgen Video Image Processing
R. Brennecke, T.K. Brown, J. Buersch, and P.H. Heintzen
in: Heintzen and Buersch 78, pp. 150-157

Brennecke et al. 78b ==> 2.3.1;
Improved Digital Real-Time Processing and
Storage Techniques with Application to
Intravenous Contrast Angiography
R. Brennecke, H.J. Hahne, K. Moldenhauer,
J.H. Buersch, and P.H. Heintzen
Proc. Computers in Cardiology 1978, pp. 191-194

Brennecke et al. 79a ==> 2.3;
ISAAC: a Digital Computer System for Acquisition
and Analysis of Time-Varying Imagery
R. Brennecke, H.J. Hahne , K. Moldenhauer,
and P.H. Heintzen
WCATVI-79, pp. 119-120

Brennecke et al. 79b ==> 2.3;
A Special Purpose Processor for Digital
Angiocardiography - Design and Application
R. Brennecke, H.J. Hahne, K. Moldenhauer,
J.H. Buersch, and P.H. Heintzen
Proc. Computers in Cardiology 1979
IEEE Computer Society, Long Beach/CA

Bribiesca and Guzman 78 ==> 2.3.6;
Shape Description and Shape Similarity
Measurement for Two-Dimensional Regions
E. Bribiesca and A. Guzman
IJCPR-78, pp. 608-612

Bribiesca and Guzman 79 ==> 2.3.6;
How to Describe Pure Form and How to Measure Differences in Shapes Using Shape Numbers
E. Bribiesca and A. Guzman
IEEE Conference on Pattern Recognition and Image Processing, Chicago/IL, August 6-8, 1979, pp. 427-436

Brice and Fennema 70 ==> 3.1;
Scene Analysis Using Regions
C.R. Brice and C.L. Fennema
Artificial Intelligence 1 (1970) 205-226

Bristor 72 ==> 2.2.1;
Extracting Atmospheric Wind Estimates from Geostationary Satellite Image Data
C.L. Bristor
Proc. Symposium on Computer Image Processing and Recognition, (A.J. Carlson, ed.), Columbia/Missouri (August 1972), pp. 2-1-1 through 2-1-6

Bristor 75
Central Processing and Analysis of Geostationary Satellite Data
C.L. Bristor (ed.)
NOAA Technical Memorandum NESS 64, U.S. Department of Commerce, Washington, D.C. (March 1975)

Brofferio and Rocca 77 ==> 2.1.4;
Interframe Redundancy Reduction of Video Signals Generated by Translating Objects
S. Brofferio and F. Rocca
IEEE Trans. Communications COM-25 (1977) 448-455

Brooks 78 ==> 3.3;
Rationalizing Edge Detectors
M.J. Brooks
Computer Graphics and Image Processing 8 (1978) 277-285

Bryant 76 ==> 2.2.6;
Integration of Socioeconomic Data and Remotely Sensed Imagery for Land Use Applications
N.A. Bryant
in: Green et al. 76, pp. 9-1 through 9-8

Bullock 76 ==> 2.2.5;
Finding Structure in Outdoor Scenes
B.L. Bullock
in: Pattern Recognition and Artificial Intelligence
C.H. Chen (ed.)
Academic Press, New York 1976, pp. 61-85

Bullock 78 ==> 2.2.5; 2.6.2;
The Necessity for a Theory of Specialized Vision
B.L. Bullock
in: Computer Vision Systems
A.R. Hanson and E.M. Riseman (eds.)
Academic Press, New York 1978, pp. 27-35

Bullock and Dudani 76 ==> 2.2.5; 2.6.2;
FOOTPRINTS: a Representation for Restricted Motion in Outdoor Scenes
B.L. Bullock and S.A. Dudani
IJCPR-76, pp. 429-430

Cafforio and Rocca 76 ==> 2.1.5; 2.1.6; 3.1; 3.2; 3.3;
Methods for Measuring Small Displacements of Television Images
C. Cafforio and F. Rocca
IEEE Trans. Information Theory IT-22 (1976) 573-579

Cafforio and Rocca 79 ==> 3.1; 3.2; 3.3; 3.3;
Tracking Moving Objects in Television Images
C. Cafforio and F. Rocca
Signal Processing 1 (1979) 133-140

Candy et al. 71 ==> 2.1.4; 2.1.5; 2.1.7; 2.1.7;
Transmitting Television as Clusters of Frame-to-Frame Differences
J.C. Candy, M.A. Franke, B.G. Haskell, and F.W. Mounts
Bell System Techn. J. 50 (1971) 1889-1917

Chen 79 ==> 2.5;
A Minicomputer-Multiple Microprocessor System for Gait Analysis Using Television and Force Plate Data
H.J. Chen
Ph.D. Thesis (August 1979)
Department of Electrical Engineering,
The Ohio State University, Columbus/OH

Cheng 74 ==> 2.5;
Computer-Television Analysis of Biped Locomotion
I.-S. Cheng
Ph.D. Thesis (December 1974)
Department of Electrical Engineering,
The Ohio State University, Columbus/OH

Chien and Jones 75 ==> 2.6.1; 2.7;
Acquisition of Moving Objects and Hand-Eye Coordination
R.T. Chien and V.C. Jones
IJCAI-75, pp. 737-741

Chien and Peterson 77 ==> 2.1.3;
Image Compression with Feature Extraction and Reconstruction
R.T. Chien and L.J. Peterson
Proc. IEEE Workshop on Picture Data Description and Management, April 21-22, 1977, Chicago/Ill., pp. 96-99
see also
Image Compression and Reconstruction Using Feature Extraction
R.T. Chien and L.J. Peterson
IJCAI-77, p. 658

Chien et al. 79 ==> 2.6.1;
Motion Detection and Analysis with Intermediate-Level Primitives
R.T. Chien, C.J. Jacobus, and J.M. Selander
WCATVI-79, pp. 23-24

Chow and Aggarwal 77 ==> 2.6.2;
Computer Analysis of Planar Curvilinear Moving Images
W.K. Chow and J.K. Aggarwal
IEEE Trans. Computers C-26 (1977) 179-185

Chow and Kaneko 72 ==> 2.3.1; 2.3.3; 2.3.3;
Automatic Boundary Detection of the Left Ventricle from Cineangiograms
C.K. Chow and T. Kaneko
Computers and Biomedical Research 5 (1972) 388-410

Chow et al. 73 ==> 2.3.1;
X-Ray Image Subtraction by Digital Means
C.K. Chow, S.K. Hilal, and K.E. Niebuhr
IBM J. Res. Develop. 17 (1973) 206 -218

Christiansen and Sederberg 78 ==> 2.8; 2.8.3;
Conversion of Complex Contour Line Definitions
into Polygonal Element Mosaics
H.N. Christiansen and T.W. Sederberg
Proc. SIGGRAPH '78 , R.L. Philips (ed.)
Atlanta/GA, August 23-25, 1978
Computer Graphics 12 (1978) 187-192
Clayton et al. 74 ==> 2.3.3;
Left Ventricular Videometry
P.D. Clayton, L.D. Harris, S.R. Rumel, and H.R. Warner
Comp. Biomed. Res. 7 (1974) 369-379
Cline 64 ==> 3.2;
Representations for the Generalized Inverse
of a Partitioned Matrix
R.E. Cline
SIAM Journal 12 (1964) 588-600
Cohen and Adoul 76 ==> 2.1.3;
Adaptive Differential Coding of Picture Signals Based
on Local Contour Prediction
P. Cohen and J.P. Adoul
National Telecommunications Conference Record
1976, pp. 6.1-1 to 6.1-5
Coleman and Andrews 79 ==> 2.1.3;
Image Segmentation by Clustering
G.B. Coleman and H.C. Andrews
Proc. IEEE 67 (1979) 773-785
Coll and Choma 76 ==> 2.1.1;
Image Activity Characteristics in Broadcast
Television
D.C. Coll and G.K. Choma
IEEE Trans. Communications COM-24 (1976) 1201-1206
Collan 76 ==> 2.8.8;
Combined Light and Electron Microscopy of Serially
Sectioned Cells and Tissues
Y. Collan
Proc. 4th Int. Congress for Stereology
Gaithersburg/MD, Sept. 4-9, 1975
NBS, Washington/DC 1976, pp. 375-378
Connor and Limb 74 ==> 2.1.4;
Properties of Frame-Difference Signals Generated
by Moving Images
D.J. Connor and J.O. Limb
IEEE Trans. on Communications COM-22 (1974) 1564-1575
Connor et al. 71 ==> 2.1.3;
Television Coding Using Two-Dimensional Spatial
Prediction
D.J. Connor, R.F.W. Pease, and W.G. Scholes
Bell System Technical Journal BSTJ 50 (1971) 1049-1061
Connor et al. 73 ==> 2.1.3; 2.1.4; 2.1.5; 2.1.7; 3;
A Frame-to-Frame Picturephone Coder for Signals
Containing Differential Quantizing Noise
D.J. Connor, B.G. Haskell, F.W. Mounts,
Bell System Techn. J. 52 (1973) 35-51
Cooper 74 ==> 2.1.3;
Feature Selection and Super Data Compression for
Pictures Occurring in Remote Conference and
Classroom Communications
D.B. Cooper
IJCPR-74, pp. 111-115

Cooper 76 ==> 2.1.3;
Super High Compression of Line Drawing Data
D.B. Cooper
IJCPR-76, pp. 638-642
Couch et al. 79 ==> 2.4;
Analysis of Images of Colonies of Tissue
Culture Cells and Microorganisms
J.L. Couch, M.W. Konrad, and D.A. Glaser
IEEE Conference on Pattern Recognition and Image
Processing, Chicago/IL, August 6-8, 1979, pp. 473-478
Cribbins 73 ==> 2.6.1;
Use of Multiple Time-Lapse Cameras for Traffic Studies
P.D. Cribbins
Proc. SPIE 37 (1973) 53-58
Davenport et al. 70 ==> 2.4;
The Investigation of the Behavior of Microorganisms
by Computerized Television
D. Davenport, G.J. Culler, J.O.B. Greaves,
R.B. Forward, and W.G. Hand
IEEE Trans. Biomedical Eng. BME-17 (1970) 230-237
Davies and Smith 79 ==> 2.7;
Digital Analysis of Internal Machine Part
Motion in a Time Series of Radiographs
D.L. Davies and P.H. Smith
WCATVI-79, pp. 128-130
DeCotiis and Conlan 71 ==> 2.2.2;
Cloud Information in Three Spatial Dimensions
Using IR Thermal Imagery and Vertical Temperature
Profile Data
A.G. DeCotiis and E. Conlan
Proc. 7th Int. Symposium on Remote Sensing of
the Environment, Ann Arbor/MI 1971, pp. 595-606
DeJong and Slager 75 ==> 2.3.3;
Automatic Detection of the Left Ventricular
Outline in Angiographs Using Television Signal
Processing Techniques
L.P. DeJong and C.J. Slager
IEEE Trans. Biomedical Engineering BME-22 (1975) 230-237
Dodd and Rossol 79 ==> 2.7;
Computer Vision and Sensor-Based Robots
G.G. Dodd and L. Rossol
Plenum Press New York 1979
Doolittle et al. 75 ==> 2.2.4;
Attitude Determination Support for the SMS/GOES Satellites
R.C. Doolittle, J. Ellickson, and J.R. DeMeo
paper no. 3 (pp. 26-32) in Bristor 75
Dorny 75 ==> 3.2;
Vector Space Approach to Models and Optimization
C.N. Dorny
J. Wiley and Sons, New York/NY 1975
Dreschler and Nagel 78 ==> 2.6.1; 2.6.2;
Using "Affinity" for Extracting Images of Moving
Objects from TV-Frame Sequences
L. Dreschler and H.-H. Nagel
IfI-HH-B-44/78 (February 1978)
Dubois 79 ==> 2.1.7;
Effects of Digital Demodulation on Component
Coding of NTSC Color Signals
E. Dubois
IEEE Trans. Communications COM-27 (1979) 1342-1348

Duda and Hart 73 ==> 2.2.1; 2.3.4;
Pattern Classification and Scene Analysis
R.O. Duda and P.E. Hart
John Wiley & Sons, New York, 1973

Duggin 77 ==> 2.2.6;
Likely Effects of Solar Elevation on the Quantification of Changes in Vegetation with Maturity Using Sequential LANDSAT Images
M.J. Duggin
Applied Optics 16 (1977) 521-523

Dukhovich and O'Neal 78 ==> 2.1.3; 2.1.6;
A Three-Dimensional Spatial Non-Linear Predictor for Television
I.J. Dukhovich and J.B. O'Neal
IEEE Trans. Communications COM-26 (1978) 578-583

Dunn 72 ==> 2.8.1;
Graphic Three-Dimensional Representations from Serial Sections
R.F. Dunn
J. Microscopy 96 (1972) 301-307

Eghbali 79 ==> 2.2.5;
K-S Test for Detecting Changes from LANDSAT Imagery Data
H.J. Eghbali
IEEE Trans. Systems, Man, and Cybernetics SMC-9 (1979) 17-23

Eiho et al. 78 ==> 2.3.3;
Automatic Processing of Cineangiographic Images of Left Ventricle
S. Eiho, M. Kuwahara, M. Fujita, S. Sasayama, and C. Kawai
IJCPR-78, pp. 740-743

Endlich et al. 71 ==> 2.2.1; 2.2.2;
Use of a Pattern Recognition Technique for Determining Cloud Motions from Sequences of Satellite Photographs
R.M. Endlich, D.E. Wolf, D.J. Hall, and A.E. Brain
J. of Applied Meteorology 10 (1971) 105-117

Engvall et al. 77 ==> 2.2.6;
Pattern Recognition of LANDSAT Data Based Upon Temporal Trend Analysis
J.L. Engvall, J.D. Tubbs, and Q.A. Holmes
Remote Sensing of Environment 6 (1977) 303-314

Eskenazi and Cunningham 77 ==> 2.7;
A Random Access Picture Digitizer, Display, and Memory System
R. Eskenazi and R.T. Cunningham
IJCAI-77, pp. 769-770

Eskenazi and Cunningham 78 ==> 2.7;
Real-Time Tracking of Moving Objects in TV Images
R. Eskenazi and R.T. Cunningham
IEEE Workshop on Pattern Recognition and Artificial Intelligence, Princeton/NJ, April 12-14, 1978, pp. 4-6

Fan and Fu 79 ==> 2.3.6;
A Syntactic Approach to Time Varying Image Analysis
T.I. Fan and K.S. Fu
Computer Graphics and Image Processing 11 (1979) 138-149
see, too : IEEE Conference on Pattern Recognition and Image Processing, Chicago/IL, August 6-8, 1979, pp. 638-645

Fennema and Thompson 79 ==> 3.1; 3.2; 3.3; 3.3;
Velocity Determination in Scenes Containing Several Moving Objects
C.L. Fennema and W.B. Thompson
Computer Graphics and Image Processing 9 (1979) 301-315

Forney 73 ==> 3.1;
The Viterbi Algorithm
G.D. Forney, Jr.
Proc. IEEE 61 (1973) 268-276

Freeman 76 ==> 2.2.3; 2.2.3;
Use of a Model of Mesoscale Flow to Aid the Determination of Winds from a Geostationary Satellite
J.C. Freeman
Proc. Symposium on Meteorological Observations from Space: Their Contribution to the First GARP Global Experiment, Philadelphia/PA
June 8-10, 1976, pp. 248-251

Frei and Baxter 77 ==> 2.1.7;
Rate-Distortion Coding Simulation for Color Images
W. Frei and B. Baxter
IEEE Trans. Communications COM-25 (1977) 1385-1392

Fuchs et al. 77 ==> 2.8.3; 2.8.3; 2.8.3;
Optimal Surface Reconstruction from Planar Contours
H. Fuchs, Z.M. Kedem, and S.P. Uselton
C.ACM 20 (1977) 693-702

Fujita 69 ==> 2.2.1; 2.2.1; 2.2.3;
Present Status of Cloud Velocity Computations from the ATS I and ATS III Satellites
T.T. Fujita
Space Research IX, pp. 557-570,
North Holland Publ. Co., Amsterdam 1969

Fujita et al. 69 ==> 2.2.1; 2.2.3;
Formation and Structure of Anticyclones Caused by Large-Scale Cross-Equatorial Flows Determined by ATS-I Photographs
T.T. Fujita, K. Watanabe, and T. Izawa
J. of Applied Meteorology 8 (1969) 649-667

Fujita et al. 75 ==> 2.2.3;
Satellite-Tracked Cumulus Velocities
T.T. Fujita, E.W. Pearl, and W.E. Shenk
J. of Applied Meteorology 14 (1975) 407-413

Fukinuki 78 ==> 2.1.6; 3.2;
Measurement of Movement and Velocity of Moving Objects with Picture Signals
T. Fukinuki
Record of Technical Group on Image Technology of the Institute of Electronics and Communications Engineers (IECE) of Japan
October 29, 1978 (IE 78-67, pp. 35-41)

Fukinuki et al. 76 ==> 2.1.5;
Improvement of Inter-Frame Predictive Coding of TV-Signals by Utilizing Visual Properties for Moving Objects
T. Fukinuki, H. Yoshigi, and K. Fukushima
Trans. of the IECE of Japan E 59 (Sept. 1976) 28-29 and 59-A (1976) 764-771 (the latter in Japanese)

Futrelle 74 ==> 2.3.3; 2.4; 4;
GALATEA: Interactive Graphics for the Analysis of Moving Images
R.P. Futrelle
Proc. IFIP-74 (J.L. Rosenfeld, ed.)
North-Holland Publ. Co., Amsterdam 1974, pp. 712-716
Futrelle and Cheng 79 ==> 2.4; 4;
Data Abstractions for the Description of Complex Ongoing Activities - the Design of a Moving Image Analysis System
R.P. Futrelle and W.K. Cheng
WCATVI-79, pp. 131-133
Futrelle and Potel 75 ==> 2.3.3; 2.4; 4;
The System Design for GALATEA, an Interactive Real-Time Computer Graphics System for Movie and Video Analysis
R.P. Futrelle and M.J. Potel
Computers and Graphics 1 (1975) 115-121
Futrelle and Speckert 78 ==> 2.4; 2.6.2;
Extraction of Motion Data by Interactive Image Processing
R.P. Futrelle and G.C. Speckert
Proc. IEEE Conference on Pattern Recognition and Image Processing
Chicago/Ill., May 31 - June 2, 1978, pp. 405-408
Gabor and Hill 61 ==> 2.1.5;
Television Band Compression by Contour Interpolation
D. Gabor and P.C.J. Hill
Proc. Inst. Elect. Eng. 108 part B (1961) 303-324
Gallagher et al. 77 ==> 2.3.1; 2.3.2; 2.3.5; 2.3.5; 2.3.5;
Image Processing and Pattern Recognition in Nuclear Medicine
J.H. Gallagher, D.F. Preston, R.G. Robinson, W.F. Herrin, W. Servoss, and S. Fritz
IEEE Conference on Pattern Recognition and Image Processing, Troy/NY, June 6-8, 1977, pp. 55-60
Gardner et al. 77 ==> 2.6.1;
Extraction of an Aircraft Silhouette when the Aircraft is Moving across the Background
G.Y. Gardner, J. Mendelsohn, and M.R. Wohlers
Proc. 7th Annual Automatic Pattern Recognition Symposium, College Park/MD, May 23-24, 1977
Electronic Industries Association, Washington/DC 1977, pp. 329-342
Garvey et al. 73 ==> 2.8.2;
Automated Three-Dimensional Dendrite Tracking System
C.F. Garvey, J.H. Young, Jr., P.D. Coleman, and W. Simon
Electroencephalogr. Clin. Neurophysiol. 35 (Aug. 1973) 199-204
Gattis et al. 78 ==> 2.3.3;
Techniques for Automatic Extraction of the Location of Surgically Implanted Markers from Radiographic Images of the Heart
J.L. Gattis, N.M. Schmitt, and A.P. Frankowski
IJCPR-78, pp. 857-859

Gaudeau et al. 79 ==> 2.3.5;
Squelettisation et Anamorphose dans l'Etude de la Dynamique des Deformations des Structures: Application a l'Analyse de la Motricite Gastrique
C. Gaudeau, M. Boiron, and J. Thouvenot
Proc. 2eme Congres AFCET-IRIA Reconnaissance des Formes et Intelligence Artificielle, September 12-14, 1979, Toulouse/France, vol. III, pp. 57-63

Gennery 77a ==> 2.7;
A Stereo Vision System for an Autonomous Vehicle
D.B. Gennery
IJCAI-77, pp. 576-582

Gennery 77b ==> 2.7;
A Stereo Vision System
D.B. Gennery
Proc. Image Understanding Workshop, L.S. Baumann (ed.) Palo Alto/CA, Oct. 20-21, 1977
Science Applications, Inc., Arlington/VA, pp. 31-46

Gennery 79 ==> 2.7;
Object Detection and Measurement Using Stereo Vision
D.B. Gennery
IJCAI-79, pp. 320-327

Geokezas et al. 75 ==> 2.2.5;
A Real-Time Imagery Screener
M. Geokezas, R. Jennewine, and G.D. Swanlund
Fifth Annual Symposium on Automatic Imagery Pattern Recognition, College Park/MD, April 17-18, 1975, pp. 55-86
Electronic Industries Association, Washington/DC 1975

Gerbrands et al. 79 ==> 2.3.3;
Computer Analysis of Moving Radiopaque Markers from X-Ray Cinefilms
J.J. Gerbrands, F.Booman, and J.H.C. Reiber
Computer Graphics and Image Processing 11 (1979) 35-48

Gerlach 79 ==> 2.6.1; 2.6.2; 2.6.2; 3.2;
Digitale Bildfolgenauswertung zum Wiederfinden von Objekten in natuerlicher Umgebung
H. Gerlach
in: Angewandte Szenenanalyse, J.P. Foith (ed.)
Informatik Fachberichte 20, pp. 199-207
Springer Verlag, Berlin-Heidelberg-New York 1979

Gilbert et al. 76a ==> 2.3;
A Real-Time Hardware System for Digital Processing of Wide-Band Video Images
B.K. Gilbert, M.T. Storma, C.E. James, L.W. Hobrock, E.S. Yang, K.C. Ballard, and E.H. Wood
IEEE Trans. Computers C-25 (1976) 1089-1100

Gilbert et al. 76b ==> 2.3;
A Programmable Dynamic Memory Allocation System for Input/Output Digital Data into Standard Computer Memories at 40 Megasamples/s
B.K. Gilbert, M.T. Storma, K.C. Ballard, L.W. Hobrock, C.E. James, and E.H. Wood
IEEE Trans. Computers C-25 (1976) 1101-1108

Gilbert et al. 78 ==> 2.6.2; 2.6.2;
A Real-Time Video Tracking System Using Image Processing Techniques
A.L. Gilbert, M.K. Giles, G.M. Flachs, R.B. Rogers, and Y. Hsun U
IJCPR-78 Nov. 7-10, 1978 Kyoto/Japan, pp. 1111-1115

Gilbert et al. 79 ==> 2.3;
Implementation of Computation-Intensive Reconstruction
Algorithms for X-Ray Computed Tomography
B.K. Gilbert, L.D. Harris, R.D. Beistadt,
R.A. Robb, and D.E. Atkins
IEEE Conference on Pattern Recognition and Image Processing,
Chicago/IL, August 6-8, 1979, pp. 256-264
Gilbert et al. 80 ==> 2.6.2; 2.6.2;
A Real-Time Video Tracking System
A.L. Gilbert, M.K. Giles, G.M. Flachs,
R.B. Rogers, and Y.Hsun U
IEEE Trans. Pattern Analysis and Machine
Intelligence PAMI-2 (1980) 47-56
Gimelfarb et al. 75 ==> 2.7;
A "Hand-Eye" Robot Simulation System
G. Gimelfarb, E. Kushner, V. Rybak
IJCAI-75, pp. 766-770
Giralt et al. 79 ==> 2.7;
A Multi-Level Planning and Navigation System for a
Mobile Robot : A First Approach to HILARE
G. Giralt, R. Sobek, and R. Chatila
IJCAI-79, pp. 335-337
Glaser 68 ==> 2.4;
An Automated System for Growth and Analysis
of Bacterial Colonies
D.A. Glaser
in: Image Processing in Biological Science
University of California Press, San Francisco
and Los Angeles/CA 1968, pp. 57-74
Glenn et al. 77 ==> 2.8; 2.8.1;
Alternative Display Formats for Computed
Tomography (CT) Data
W.V. Glenn, Jr., K.R. Davis, G.N. Larsen,
and S.J. Dwyer, III
in: Current Concepts in Radiology, vol. 3, pp. 88-124
E.J. Potchen (ed.), C.V. Mosby, St. Louis/MO 1977
Goldberg and Kourtz 77 ==> 2.2.6;
The Use of LANDSAT Imagery for Forestry Mapping:
Description of a Proposed Operational System
M. Goldberg and P. Kourtz
Proc. IEEE Workshop on Picture Data Description
and Management, Chicago/Ill., April 21-22, 1977, pp. 61-63
Gonzalez and Wintz 77 ==> 2.1; 2.1.3;
Digital Image Processing
R.C. Gonzalez and P. Wintz
Addison-Wesley Publ. Co., Reading/MA 1977
Gose et al. 75 ==> 2.3.4;
Dual Isotope Imaging: Automated Liver-Pancreas Subtraction
E.E. Gose, S. Shponka, W.E. Barnes, and E. Kaplan
Proc. Joint Int. Conference on Computer Graphics,
Pattern Recognition and Data Structure, Los Angeles/CA
May 14-16, 1975, pp. 65-67
Gose et al. 76 ==> 2.3.4; 2.3.4; 2.3.4;
Object Detection in Multiple Images
E.E. Gose, J.S. Arnold, W.E. Barnes, S. Shponka,
I. Nejdl, and E. Kaplan
IJCPR-76, pp. 531-537

Graham 67 ==> 2.1.3;
Image Transmission by Two-Dimensional Contour Coding
D.N. Graham
Proc. IEEE 55 (1967) 336-346
Grantham et al. 77 ==> 2.2.3; 2.2.3;
The SeaSat-A Satellite Scatterometer
W.L. Grantham, E.M. Bracalente, W.L. Jones, and J.W. Johnson
IEEE J. Oceanic Eng. OE-2 (1977) 200-206
Greaves 75 ==> 2.4;
The Bugsystem: The Software Structure for the Reduction of Quantized Video Data of Moving Organisms
J.O.B. Greaves
Proc. IEEE 63 (1975) 1415-1425
Green 78 ==> 2.2.4;
Applications of Digital Image Processing Techniques to Problems of Data Registration and Correlation
W.B. Green
Proc. NCC, AFIPS 47 (1978) 141-149
Green et al. 75 ==> 2.2.2;
The Automatic Extraction of Wind Estimates from VISSR Data
R. Green, G. Hughes, C. Novak, and R. Schreitz
paper no. 12 (pp. 94-110) in Bristor 75
Green et al. 76
Proceedings
CALTEC/JPL Conference on Image Processing Technology, Data Sources and Software for Commercial and Scientific Applications
W.B. Green, G.H. Redmann, F.C. Billingsley, R.B. Gilmore (eds.)
Cal. Institute of Technology, Pasadena/CA
November 3-5, 1976
Greene and Barnes 77 ==> 2.4;
System for Automatically Tracking White Blood Cells
F.M. Greene, Jr., and F.S. Barnes
Rev. Sci. Instruments 48 (1977) 602-604
Grimson and Marr 79 ==> 2.1.3;
A Computer Implementation of a Theory of Human Stereo Vision
W.E.L. Grimson and D. Marr
Proc. Image Understanding Workshop, pp. 41-47
L.S. Baumann (ed.), Palo Alto/CA, April 24-25, 1979
Science Applications, Inc., Arlington/VA 22209
Grommes and Yi 74 ==> 2.6.2;
Analysis and Simulation of a Video Tracking System
R.J. Grommes and C.J. Yi
Proc. IEEE Systems, Man, and Cybernetics Conference
Dallas/TX 1974, pp. 93-98
Gupta and Wintz 75 ==> 2.1.3;
A Boundary Finding Algorithm and its Application
J.N. Gupta and P.A. Wintz
IEEE Trans. on Circuits and Systems
CAS-22 (1975) 351-362
Haass and Brubaker 79 ==> 2.2.2; 2.2.3; 3.3;
Estimation of Lateral and Rotational Cloud Displacement from Satellite Pictures
U. Haass and T.A. Brubaker
WCATVI-79, pp. 103-104

Haberaecker 78 ==> 2.2.6;
Untersuchungen zur Klassifizierung multispektraler Bilddaten aus der Fernerkundung
P. Haberaecker
Dr.-Ing. Dissertation (July 1978)
Fachbereich Verkehrswesen, Technische Universitaet Berlin/Germany

Haberaecker 79 ==> 2.2.6;
On the Classification of Multitemporal Image Data
P. Haberaecker
The Institute of Physics Conference Series, No. 44, pp. 231-237 (1979)

Habibi 77 ==> 2.1.2; 2.1.3;
Survey of Adaptive Image Coding Techniques
A. Habibi
IEEE Trans. Communications COM-25 (1977) 1275-1284

Habibi and Batson 78 ==> 2.1.7;
Potential Digitization/Compression Techniques for Shuttle Video
A. Habibi and B.H. Batson
IEEE Trans. Communications COM-26 (1978) 1671-1682

Habibi and Samulon 75 ==> 2.1.3; 2.2.7;
Bandwidth Compression of Multispectral Data
A. Habibi and A.S. Samulon
Proc. SPIE 66 (August 1975) 23-35

Hachimura et al. 78 ==> 2.3.3; 2.3.5;
Left Ventricular Contour Extraction from Radioisotope Angiocardiograms and Classification of Left Ventricular Wall Motion
K. Hachimura, M. Kuwahara, and M. Kinoshita
IJCPR-78 Nov. 7-10, 1978 Kyoto/Japan, pp. 911-913

Haeusler 72 ==> 2.8.1;
A Method to Increase the Depth of Focus by Two Step Image Processing
G. Haeusler
Optics Communication 6 (1972) 38-42

Haeusler 77 ==> 2.8.1;
Optical Software Survey
G. Haeusler
Optica Acta 24 (1977) 965-977

Hall 77 ==> 2.2.1;
An Adaptive Process for Tracking Clouds from Satellite Images
D.J. Hall
in: Image Science Mathematics
C.O. Wilde and E. Barrett (eds.)
Western Periodicals Corp., North Hollywood/CA 1977, pp. 118-122

Hall 79 ==> 1; 2.1;
Computer Image Processing and Recognition
E.L. Hall
Academic Press New York/NY 1979

Hall and Hwang 79 ==> 2.8.3;
Object Location in Computed Tomography Images Using Global Local Segmentation
E.L. Hall and J.J. Hwang
IEEE Conference on Pattern Recognition and Image Processing Chicago/IL, August 6-8, 1979, pp. 344-352

Hall et al. 72 ==> 2.2.3; 2.2.4;
Objective Methods for Registering Landmarks and Determining Cloud Motions from Satellite Data
D.J. Hall, R.M. Endlich, D.E. Wolf, and A.E. Brain
IEEE Trans. Computers C-21 (1972) 768-776

Hanscom 73 ==> 2.6.1;
An Evaluation of Diagrammatic Signing Using Time-Lapse Photography
F.R. Hanscom
Proc. SPIE 37 (1973) 7-14

Hanson and Riseman 78 ==> 1;
Computer Vision Systems
A.R. Hanson and E.M. Riseman (eds.)
Academic Press New York 1978

Haskell 74 ==> 2.1.2;
Frame-to-Frame Coding of Television Pictures Using Two-Dimensional Fourier Transforms
B.G. Haskell
IEEE Trans. Information Theory IT-20 (1974) 119-120

Haskell 75 ==> 2.1.6;
Entropy Measurements for Nonadaptive and Adaptive, Frame-to-Frame, Linear Predictive Coding of Videotelephone Signals
B.G. Haskell
Bell System Techn. J. 54 (1975) 1155-1174

Haskell 76a ==> 2.1.4; 2.1.6;
Differential Addressing of Clusters of Changed Picture Elements for Interframe Coding of Videotelephone Signals
B.G. Haskell
IEEE Trans. Communications COM-24 (1976) 140-144

Haskell 76b ==> 2.1.5; 2.1.6;
Interframe Coding of Monochrome Television - a Review
B.G. Haskell
SPIE 87 (1976) 212-221

Haskell 79 ==> 2.1.5; 2.1.6; 2.1.7;
Frame Replenishment Coding of Television
B.G. Haskell
in: Image Transmission Techniques, W.K. Pratt (ed.)
Academic Press, New York 1979, pp. 189-219

Haskell and Limb 72 ==> 2.1.6;
Predictive Video Encoding Using Measured Subject Velocity
U.S. Patent 3.632.865
B.G. Haskell and J.O. Limb

Haskell and Schmidt 75 ==> 2.1.5;
A Low-Bit-Rate Interframe Coder for Videotelephone
B.G. Haskell and R.L. Schmidt
Bell System Techn. J. 54 (1975) 1475-1495

Haskell et al. 72 ==> 2.1.4;
Interframe Coding of Videotelephone Pictures
B.G. Haskell, F.W. Mounts, and J.C. Candy
Proc. IEEE 60 (1972) 792-800

Haskell et al. 77 ==> 2.1.5;
Interframe Coding of 525-Line, Monochrome Television at 1.5 Mbits/s
B.G. Haskell, P.L. Gordon, R.L. Schmidt, and J.V. Scattaglia
IEEE Trans. Communications COM-25 (1977) 1339-1348

Hasler 71 ==> 2.2.3;
Tropical Cloud Clusters Analyzed Using Techniques for Obtaining Wind, Divergence, and Vorticity Fields from Geostationary Satellite Pictures
A.F. Hasler
Ph.D. Thesis (1971)
University of Wisconsin, Madison/Wisconsin

Hasler 73 ==> 2.2.1;
A Verification Experiment Comparing Cloud Motion Wind Estimates with Aircraft Winds
A.F. Hasler
Int. Conference on Meteorological Satellites
Paris, May 21-24, 1973, pp. 59-63

Hasler et al. 76 ==> 2.2.1; 2.2.3;
Wind Estimates from Cloud Motions: Phase 1 of an In Situ Aircraft Verification Experiment
A.F. Hasler, W. Shenk, and W. Skillman
J. Applied Meteorology 15 (1976) 10-15

Havlice and Taenzer 79 ==> 2.3;
Medical Ultrasonic Imaging : An Overview of Principles and Instrumentation
J.F. Havlice and J.C. Taenzer
Proc. IEEE 67 (1979) 620-641

Hawkes 78 ==> 2.8;
Electron Image Processing: A Survey
P.W. Hawkes
Computer Graphics and Image Processing 8 (1978) 406-446

Heintzen and Buersch 78 ==> 2.3; 2.3.2; 2.3.3; 2.3.3; 2.3.5; 2.3.5; 2.8.8;
Roentgen-Video-Techniques for Dynamic Studies of Structure and Function of the Heart and Circulation
P.H. Heintzen and J.H. Buersch (eds.)
Georg Thieme Verlag, Stuttgart 1978

Heintzen et al. 75 ==> 2.3.1; 2.3.3; 2.3.5; 2.3.5;
Automated Video-Angiocardiographic Image Analysis
P.H. Heintzen, R. Brennecke, J.H. Buersch, P. Lange, V. Malerczyk, K. Moldenhauer, and D. Onnasch
IEEE Computer 8, no. 7 (July 1975) 55-64

Heller 74 ==> 2.1.2; 2.1.5;
A Real Time Hadamard Transform Video Compression System Using Frame-to-Frame Differencing
J.A. Heller
Proc. Nat. Telecommunications Conference, San Diego, 1974, pp. 77-82

Henrikson 72 ==> 2.2.5;
Techniques and Applications of Digital Change Detection
P.J. Henrikson
Proc. Symposium on Computer Image Processing and Recognition, A.J. Carlson (ed.)
Columbia/Missouri, August 1972, p.r 6-1-1 through 6-1-10

Herman 79 ==> 2.8.4; 2.8.4; 2.8.8;
Representation of 3-D Surfaces by a Large Number of Simple Surface Elements
G.T. Herman
Proc. NSF Workshop on the Representation of Three-Dimensional Objects
R. Bajcsy (ed.), Philadelphia/PA, May 1-2, 1979

Herman and Liu 78 ==> 2.8.4;
Dynamic Boundary Surface Detection
G.T. Herman and H.K. Liu
Computer Graphics and Image Processing 7 (1978) 130-138
see also: Proc. Symposium on Computer-Aided
Diagnosis of Medical Images, J. Sklansky (ed.)
Coronado/CA, November 11, 1976, pp. 27-32
Herman and Liu 79 ==> 2.8.4;
Three-Dimensional Display of Human Organs from
Computed Tomograms
G.T. Herman and H.K. Liu
Computer Graphics and Image Processing 9 (1979) 1-21
Herman et al. 79 ==> 2.8.4; 2.8.5;
Detection of Changing Boundaries in Two and
Three Dimensions
G.T. Herman, S.N. Srihari, and J.K. Udupa
WCATVI-79, pp. 14-16
Hernan and Jimenez 79 ==> 2.7;
Automatic Analysis of Movies in Fluid Mechanics
M.A. Hernan and J. Jimenez
WCATVI-79, pp. 134-135
Hilbert 75 ==> 2.1.3; 2.2.7;
Joint Classification and Data Compression of
Multidimensional Information Sources - Application to ERTS
E.E. Hilbert
Conference Record vol. II, International Conference
on Communications, June 1975, pp. 27-6 through 27-11
Hilke 73 ==> 2.6.1;
Landradaranlagen fuer die Schiffsicherung
O. Hilke
in: Funksysteme fuer Ortung und Navigation und ihre
Anwendung in der Verkehrssicherung
E. Kramar (Hrsgb.)
Verlag Berliner Union GmbH Stuttgart und
W. Kohlhammer GmbH Stuttgart 1973
Hoffer 78 ==> 2.2.6;
Biological and Physical Considerations in Applying
Computer-Aided Analysis Techniques to Remote Sensor Data
R.M. Hoffer
in: Remote Sensing: The Quantitative Approach,
P.H. Swain and S.H. Davis (ed.)
McGraw-Hill Inc. New York 1978, chapter V
Hoehne et al. 78 ==> 2.3.2;
Encoding and Analysis of X-Ray Image Series
K.H. Hoehne, M. Boehm, and G.C. Nicolae
IJCPR-78, pp. 743-746
Hoehne et al. 79 ==> 2.3; 2.3.2; 2.3.5;
The Processing of X-Ray Image Sequences
K.H. Hoehne, M. Boehm, and G.C. Nicolae
in: Advances in Digital Image Processing, P. Stuck.. (ed.)
Plenum Press New York/NY 1979, pp. 147-163
Holden 79 ==> 2.3.2; 2.3.5;
Functional Imaging: Applications in Three
Radiological Modalities
J.E. Holden
IEEE Conference on Pattern Recognition and Image Processing
Chicago/IL, August 6-8, 1979, pp. 368-375

Holmes 66 ==> 2.2.5;
Automatic Photointerpretation and Target Location
W.S. Holmes
Proc. IEEE 54 (1966) 1679-1686
Horan 78 ==> 2.2;
Nimbus: the Vanguard of Remote Sensing
J.J. Horan
IEEE Spectrum 15, No. 11 (Nov. 1978) 36-43
Horn 78 ==> 2.2.4;
Vision
B.K.P. Horn
AISB/GI-78 Conference on Artificial Intelligence
Hamburg, July 18-20, 1978, pp. 147-163
Horn and Bachman 78 ==> 2.2.4; 2.2.4;
Using Synthetic Images to Register Real Images with
Surface Models
B.K.P. Horn and B.C. Bachman
C. ACM 21 (1978) 914-924
Hsi and Lee 78 ==> 2.8.1;
Reconstruction of an Oblique Viewing Plane from
Transaxial Scanning X-Ray Tomographic Data
P.C. Hsi and Chin-Hwa Lee
IEEE Conference on Pattern Recognition and Image
Processing Chicago/IL, May 31 -June 2, 1978, pp. 210-213
Huang and Ledley 75 ==> 2.8.1;
Three-Dimensional Image Reconstruction from
In Vivo Consecutive Transversal Axial Sections
H.K. Huang and R.S. Ledley
Computers in Biology and Medicine 5 (1975) 165-170
Hubert 76 ==> 2.2.3;
The Relation Between Cloud Pattern Motion and Wind Shear
L.F. Hubert
Monthly Weather Review 104 (1976) 1167-1171
Hubert and Whitney 71 ==> 2.2.1; 2.2.1;
Wind Estimation from Geostationary-Satellite Pictures
L.F. Hubert and L.F. Whitney
Monthly Weather Review 99 (1971) 665-672
Hughes et al. 78 ==> 2.2.2; 2.2.4;
Automated Techniques for the Detection and
Displacement Measurement of Selected Cloud Imagery
Observed in Geostationary Satellite Data
G. Hughes, C. Novak, and R. Schreitz
Proc. 8th Annual Automatic Imagery Pattern
Recognition Symposium, R.A. Kirsch and R.N. Nagel (eds.)
Gaithersburg/MD, April 3-4, 1978, pp. 81-90
Electronic Industries Association, Washington/DC 1978
Iinuma et al. 75 ==> 2.1.1; 2.1.7; 2.1.8;
Interframe Coding for 4-MHz Color Television Signals
K. Iinuma, Y. Iijima, T. Ishiguro, H. Kaneko, and
S. Shigaki
IEEE Trans. on Communications COM-23 (1975) 1461-1466
Ishiguro et al. 76 ==> 2.1.7;
Composite Interframe Coding of NTSC Color Television Signals
T. Ishiguro, K. Iinuma, Y. Iijima, T. Koga,
S. Azami, and T. Mune
1976 National Telecommunications Conference Record
Dallas/TX, Nov. 1976, pp. 6.4-1 to 6.4-5

Izawa and Fujita 69 ==> 2.2.1; 2.2.3;
Relationship between Observed Winds and Cloud Velocities Determined from Pictures Obtained by the ESSA III, ESSA V and ATS I Satellites
T. Izawa and T. Fujita
Space Research IX, pp. 571-579
North Holland Publ. Co., Amsterdam 1969

Jacobus 79 ==> 2.6.1;
Visual Recognition of Artifacts by Computer
Ch.J. Jacobus
Ph.D. Thesis (July 1979)
Department of Electrical Engineering
University of Illinois, Urbana-Champaign/IL

Jaeschke and Ost 72 ==> 2.1.5;
Bandbreitenreduktion durch verringerte Bildwechselrate
F. Jaeschke and J. Ost
Radio Mentor 38 (1972) 110-113

Jain and Nagel 77 ==> 2.6.1;
Analysing a Real World Scene Sequence Using Fuzziness
R. Jain and H.-.H. Nagel
IEEE Conference on Decision and Control, New Orleans, Dec. 7-9, 1977

Jain and Nagel 78 ==> 2.1.5; 2.6.1;
On a Motion Analysis Process for Image Sequences from Real World Scenes
R. Jain and H.-H. Nagel
IEEE Workshop on Pattern Recognition and Artificial Intelligence, Princeton, N.J., April 12-14, 1978
(available as report IfI-HH-B-48/78)

Jain and Nagel 79 ==> 2.1.5; 2.6.1; 3.2;
On the Analysis of Accumulative Difference Pictures from Image Sequences of Real World Scenes
R. Jain and H.-H. Nagel
IEEE Trans. Pattern Analysis and Machine Intelligence PAMI-1 (1979) 206-214

Jain et al. 77 ==> 2.6.1; 3.2;
Separating Non-Stationary from Stationary Scene Components in a Sequence of Real World TV-Images
R. Jain, D. Militzer, and H.-H. Nagel
IJCAI-77, 612-618 and
IfI-HH-B-32/77 (March 1977)
Institut fuer Informatik, Universitaet Hamburg

Jain et al. 79 ==> 3.1; 3.2;
Segmentation through the Detection of Changes due to Motion
R. Jain, W.N. Martin, and J.K. Aggarwal
Computer Graphics and Image Processing 11 (1979) 13-34

Johnson et al. 76 ==> 2.3;
Bioimage Synthesis and Analysis from x-Ray, Gamma, Optical, and Ultrasound Energy
S.A. Johnson, R.A. Robb, E.L. Ritman, B.K. Gilbert, J.F. Greenleaf, L.D. Harris, M.J. Berggren, R. Sturm, P.A. Chevalier, R.M. Heethar, E.H.Wood, G.T. Herman, and Y.C. Pao
in: Digital Processing of Biomedical Images
K. Preston, jr., and M. Onoe (eds.)
Plenum Press, New York 1976, pp. 203-226

Jones 74 ==> 2.6.1; 2.7;
Tracking: An Approach to Dynamic Vision and Hand-Eye Coordination
V.C. Jones
Ph.D. Thesis, Electrical Engineering, Graduate College of the University of Illinois at Urbana-Champaign (1974), Coordinated Science Laboratory R-696 (1975)

Jones 76 ==> 2.1.2; 2.1.5;
A Real-Time Adaptive Hadamard Transform Video Compressor
H.W. Jones
SPIE 87 (1976) 2-9

Jones 77 ==> 2.1.5;
A Conditional Replenishment Hadamard Video Compressor
H.W. Jones
SPIE 119 (1977) 91-98

Jones 79 ==> 2.1.2;
A Comparison of Theoretical and Experimental Video Compression Designs
H.W. Jones
IEEE Trans. Electromagnetic Compatibility EMC-21 (1979) 50-56

Kahle 76 ==> 2.2.3;
Derivation of a Thermal Inertia Image from Remotely Sensed Data
A.B. Kahle
in: Green et al. 76, pp. 11-1 through 11-8

Kak 79 ==> 2.8;
Computerized Tomography with X-Ray, Emission, and Ultrasound Sources
A.C. Kak
Proc. IEEE 67 (1979) 1245-1272

Kanade and Ohta 74 ==> 2.6.1;
Picture Processing Laboratory and its Applications
T. Kanade and Y. Ohta
Proc. IFIP-74 (J.L. Rosenfeld, ed.)
North-Holland Publ. Co., Amsterdam 1974, pp. 738-742

Kanal and Parikh 77 ==> 2.2.3;
Severe Storm Pattern Recognition from Meteorological Satellite Data: a Report on Current Status and Prospects
L.N. Kanal and J.A. Parikh
Research and Development Technical Report ECOM-77-3, Atmospheric Sciences Lab., US Army Electronics Command, White Sands Missile Range/NM (March 1, 1977)

Kaneko 78 ==> 2.2.6;
Crop Classification Using Time Features Computed from Multi-Temporal Multi-Spectral Data
T. Kaneko
IJCPR-78, pp. 943-945

Kaneko and Mancini 73 ==> 2.3.3;
Straight-Line Approximation for the Boundary of the Left Ventricular Chamber from a Cardiac Cineangiogram
T. Kaneko and P. Mancini
IEEE Trans. Biomedical Eng. BME-20 (1973) 413-416

Kawamura 71 ==> 2.2.5;
Automatic Recognition of Changes in Urban Development from Aerial Photographs
J.G. Kawamura
IEEE Trans. Systems, Man, and Cyb. SMC-1 (1971) 230-239

Kelly 71 ==> 2.3.3;
Edge Detection in Pictures by Computer Using Planning
M.D. Kelly
Machine Intelligence 6 (B. Meltzer, D. Michie, eds.),
Edinburgh University Press, 1971, pp. 379-409

Kelly et al. 78 ==> 2.8.3;
CT and Radiation Therapy Planning
J.C. Kelly, P.N. Cook, H. Cox, S.J. Dwyer,
R.W. Conners, and C.A. Harlow
IEEE Conference on Pattern Recognition and Image
Processing, Chicago/Ill., May 31 - June 2, 1978, pp. 205-209

Keppel 75 ==> 2.8.3;
Approximating Complex Surfaces by Triangulation
of Contour Lines
E. Keppel
IBM J. Research and Development 19 (1975) 2-11

Keskes et al. 79 ==> 2.1.3;
Statistical Study of Edges in TV Pictures
N. Keskes, F. Kretz, and H. Maitre
IEEE Trans. Communications COM-27 (1979) 1239-1247

Kinuhata et al. 78 ==> 2.1.5;
Digital Standards Converter by Adaptive
Intra-Frame Line Interpolation
K. Kinuhata, H. Sasaki, H. Yamamoto, and K. Amano
IEEE Trans. Communications COM-26 (1978) 1413-1420

Kisslo et al. 78 ==> 2.3; 2.3;
Techniques for Real-Time Two-Dimensional Echocardiography
J.A. Kisslo, O.T. von Ramm, and F.L. Thurstone
in: Clinical Echocardiography
M.N. Kotler and B.M. Segal (eds.)
F.A. Davis Co., Philadelphia/PA 1978, pp. 21-38

Klie 78 ==> 2.1.5;
Codierung von Fernsehsignalen fuer niedrige
Uebertragungsbitraten
J. Klie
Dissertation, Juni 1978
Lehrstuhl fuer Theoretische Nachrichtentechnik
und Informationsverarbeitung, Techn. Universitaet
Hannover, D-3000 Hannover 1

Knauer 75 ==> 2.1.2; 2.1.3; 2.1.5;
Real-Time Video Compression Algorithm for Hadamard
Transform Processing
S.C. Knauer
Proc. SPIE 66 (August 1975) 58-69

Knauer 76 ==> 2.1.2; 2.1.3, 2.1.5;
Real-Time Video Compression Algorithm for Hadamard
Transform Processing
S.C. Knauer
IEEE Trans. Electromagnetic Compatibility
EMC-18 (1976) 28-36

Korn and Wedlich 79a ==> 3.3;
Motion Detection within a Natural Scene
Picked up by a Moving Optical Sensor
A. Korn and G. Wedlich
WCATVI-79, pp. 36-37

Korn and Wedlich 79b ==> 3.3;
Zur Detektion von Relativbewegungen in
bewegten natuerlichen Szenen
A. Korn and G. Wedlich
in: Angewandte Szenenanalyse, J.P. Foith (ed.)

Informatik Fachberichte 20, pp. 224-237
Springer Verlag, Berlin-Heidelberg-New York 1979
Kritikos and Shiue 79 ==> 2.2.3;
Microwave Sensing from Orbit
H.N. Kritikos and J. Shiue
IEEE Spectrum 16 (August 1979) 34-41
Kruger and Hui 76 ==> 2.3.3;
A Terminal/Time Share Based Method for Interactive
Left Ventricular Volume Estimation
R.P. Kruger and S. Hui
IEEE Trans. Systems, Man, and Cybernetics
SMC-6 (1976) 134-138
Kruger et al. 78 ==> 2.3; 2.3.1; 2.3.4;
A Digital Video Image Processor for Real-Time
X-Ray Subtraction Imaging
R.A. Kruger, C.A. Mistretta, J. Lancaster,
T.L. Houk, M. Goodsitt, C.G. Shaw, S.J. Riederer,
J. Hicks, J. Sackett, A.B. Crummy, and D. Fleming
Optical Engineering 17 (1978) 652-657
Kuipers 79 ==> 2.7;
Commonsense Knowledge of Space : Learning from Experience
B. Kuipers
IJCAI-79, pp. 499-501
LaBonte 77 ==> 2.1.3;
Two-Dimensional Image Coding by Micro-Adaptive
Picture Sequencing (MAPS)
A.E. LaBonte
Proc. SPIE 119 (1977) 99-106
Landzettel and Hirzinger 79 ==> 2.6.2;
Konzept und Realisierung eines mit Kontrastauswertung
arbeitenden TV-Trackers
K. Landzettel and G. Hirzinger
in: Angewandte Szenenanalyse, J.P. Foith (ed.)
Informatik Fachberichte 20, p. 222
Springer Verlag, Berlin-Heidelberg-New York 1979
Lange et al. 76 ==> 2.3.5;
The Analysis of Size, Shape, and Contraction Pattern
of the Right Ventricle from Angiocardiograms
P. Lange, D. Onnasch, K. Moldenhauer, V. Malerczyk,
F.L. Farr, G. Huettig, and P.H. Heintzen
Eur. J. Cardiology 4/Suppl. (1976) 153-168
Lappalainen and Tervonen 75 ==> 2.5;
Instrumentation of Movement Analysis by
Raster-Scanned Image Source
P. Lappalainen and M. Tervonen
IEEE Trans. Instrumentation and Measurement
IM-24 (1975) 217-221
Ledley 73 ==> 2.3.2; 2.3.2; 2.3.3;
Some Clinical Applications of Pattern Recognition
R.S. Ledley
IJCPR-73, pp. 89-112
Le Croisette and Gammell 78 ==> 2.3;
Signal Processing in Ultrasound
D.H. Le Croisette and P.M. Gammell
Proc. SPIE 167 (1978) 135-141
Lee and Mozley 76 ==> 2.8.1;
Coronal or Sagittal Plane Reconstruction of Transaxial
Scanning X-Ray Tomography

C.-H. Lee and J.M. Mozley
Proc. Symposium on Computer-Aided Diagnosis of Medical Images
J. Sklansky (ed.), Coronado/CA, November 11, 1976, pp.61-65

Leese and Tarpley 75 ==> 2.2.3;
Sea Surface Temperature from VISSR Data
J.A. Leese and J.D. Tarpley
paper no. 15 (pp. 128-132) in Bristor 75

Leese et al. 70 ==> 2.2.1;
The Determination of Cloud Pattern Motions from Geosynchronous Satellite Image Data
J.A. Leese, C.S. Novak, and V.R. Taylor
Pattern Recognition 2 (1970) 279-292

Leese et al. 71 ==> 2.2.1;
An Automated Technique for Obtaining Cloud Motion from Geosynchronous Satellite Data Using Cross-Correlation
J.A. Leese, C.S. Novak, and B.B. Clark
J. of Applied Meteorology 10 (1971) 118-132

Levine and Youssef 78a ==> 2.4;
A Real-Time Laboratory Device for Tracking and Quantifying Blood Cell Movement
M.D. Levine and Y.M. Youssef
Report No. 78-2R (January 1978)
Dept. Electrical Engineering, McGill University, Montreal

Levine and Youssef 78b ==> 2.4;
An Automatic Picture Processing Method for Tracking and Quantifying the Dynamics of Blood Cell Motion
M.D. Levine and Y.M. Youssef
Report No. 78-4R (February 1978)
Dept. Electrical Engineering, McGill University, Montreal
presented at 4th Int. Congress of Cybernetics and Systems, Amsterdam, August 21-25, 1978

Levine et al. 70 ==> 2.8.7
Automated Measurement of the Internal Surface Area of the Human Lung
M.D. Levine, M.L. Reisch, and W.M. Thurlbeck
IEEE Trans. Bio-Medical Engineering BME-17 (1970) 254-262

Levine et al. 73 ==> 2.7;
Computer Determination of Depth Maps
M.D. Levine, D.A. O'Handley, G.M. Yagi
Computer Graphics and Image Processing 2 (1973) 131-150

Levine et al. 79 ==> 2.4; 2.4;
Cell Movements: Its Characterization and Analysis
M.D. Levine, Y.M. Youssef, and F. Ferrie
WCATVI-79, pp. 93-95

Levinthal and Ware 72 ==> 2.8; 2.8.2; 2.8.2;
Three Dimensional Reconstruction from Serial Sections
C. Levinthal and R. Ware
Nature 236 (1972) 207-210

Lewis and Johnston 77 ==> 2.7;
A Scanning Laser Rangefinder for a Robot Vehicle
R.A. Lewis and A.R. Johnston
IJCAI-77, pp. 762-768

Lillestrand 72 ==> 2.2.5;
Techniques for Change Detection
R.L. Lillestrand
IEEE Trans. Computers C-21 (1972) 654-659

Limb 69 ==> 2.1.3;
Adaptive Encoding of Picture Signals
J.O. Limb

Symposium on Picture Bandwidth Compression MIT, April 1969
T.S. Huang and O.J. Tretiak (eds.)
Gordon and Breach, New York/NY 1972, pp. 341-382
Limb 79 ==> 2.1.3;
Distortion Criteria of the Human Viewer
J.O. Limb
IEEE Trans. Systems, Man, and Cybernetics
SCM-9 (1979) 778-793
Limb and Murphy 75a ==> 2.1.6; 3.1;
Measuring the Speed of Moving Objects from Television Signals
J.O. Limb and J.A. Murphy
IEEE Trans. Communications COM-23 (1975) 474-478
Limb and Murphy 75b ==> 2.1.6; 3.1;
Estimating the Velocity of Moving Images in Television Signals
J.O. Limb and J.A. Murphy
Computer Graphics and Image Processing 4 (1975) 311-327
Limb and Pease 71 ==> 2.1.4; 3;
A Simple Interframe Coder for Video Telephony
J.O. Limb and R.F.W. Pease
Bell System Techn. J. 50 (1971) 1877-1888
Limb and Rubinstein 78 ==> 2.1.3;
On the Design of Quantizers for DPCM Coders:
A Functional Relationship Between Visibility,
Probability and Masking
J.O. Limb and C.B. Rubinstein
IEEE Trans. Communications COM-26 (1978) 573-578
Limb et al. 74 ==> 2.1.5;
Combining Intra-Frame and Frame-to-Frame
Coding for Television
J.O. Limb, R.F.W. Pease, and K.A. Walsh
Bell System Techn. J. 53 (1974) 1137-1173
Lindberg 76 ==> 2.8.7;
Volumetric Determinations of Cells and Cell
Organelles from Two-Dimensional Transsections
L.G. Lindberg
Proc. 4th Int. Congress for Stereology, pp. 359-362
Gaithersburg/MD, Sept. 4-9, 1975, NBS, Washington/DC 1976
Lipkin et al. 79 ==> 2.4;
Digital Analysis of Living Cell Image Sequences
in Support of Cytotoxicity-Carcinogenesis Research
L.E. Lipkin, P. Lemkin, and M. Wade
WCATVI-79, p. 25
Lippel 79 ==> 2.1.5;
Bit-Plane Analysis of Digitized Moving Pictures
B. Lippel
WCATVI-79, pp. 79-81
Lippmann 79 ==> 2.1.6;
Techniques of DPCM Picture Coding for RPV TV
R. Lippmann
IEEE Int. Conference on Communications
Boston/MA, June 10-13, 1979
Liu 77 ==> 2.3.3; 2.8.4;
Two- and Three-Dimensional Boundary Detection
H.K. Liu
Computer Graphics and Image Processing 6 (1977) 123-134
Lo 75 ==> 2.2.1; 2.2.1; 2.2.3;
The Application of a Thresholding Technique in Cloud
Motion Estimation from Satellite Observations
R.C. Lo
TR-357 (February 1975)
Computer Science Department, University of Maryland,
College Park/MD

Lorenz and Schmidt 79 ==> 2.2.2;
Verfahren zur stereoskopischen Wolkenanalyse aus dem Weltraum
D. Lorenz und E. Schmidt
Bildmessung und Luftbildwesen 47 (1979) 1-14

Lowerre 76 ==> 2.6.2;
The HARPY Speech Recognition System
B.T. Lowerre
Ph.D.Thesis, Dept. Comp.Sc. (April 1976)
Carnegie-Mellon University, Pittsburgh / PA

Lozano-Perez and Wesley 79 ==> 2.7;
An Algorithm for Planning Collision-Free Paths Among Polyhedral Obstacles
T. Lozano-Perez and M.A. Wesley
CACM 22 (1979) 560-570

Lubinski et al. 77 ==> 2.5;
Microprocessor-Based Interface Converts Video Signals for Object Tracking
K.S. Lubinski, K.L. Dickson, and J. Cairns, Jr.
Computer Design (Dec. 1977) 81-87

Lynn 76 ==> 2.2.3;
Recent Applications of Digital Processing to Planetary Science
D.J. Lynn
in: Green et al. 76, pp. 13-1 through 13-16

Macovski 79 ==> 2.3;
Ultrasonic Imaging Using Arrays
A. Macovski
Proc. IEEE 67 (1979) 484-495

Maitre 79 ==> 3.1;
Considerations sur l'Evolution Spatio-Temporelle de Segments d'Images
H. Maitre
Proc. 2eme Congres AFCET-IRIA Reconnaissance des Formes et Intelligence Artificielle, September 12-14, 1979 Toulouse/France, vol. II, pp. 151-157

Manasse 67 ==> 2.1.6;
Directional Correlation - A Technique to Reduce Bandwidth in PCM Television Transmissions
F.K. Manasse
IEEE Trans. Communications COM-15 (1967) 204-208

Marr 77 ==> 3.3;
Analysis of Occluding Contour
D. Marr
Proc. Royal Soc. B 197 (1977) 441-475

Marr and Poggio 79 ==> 2.1.3;
A Computational Theory of Human Stereo Vision
D. Marr and T. Poggio
Proc. Royal Society London B 204 (1979) 301-308

Marr and Ullman 79 ==> 2.1.3; 3.1; 3.1; 3.3;
Directional Selectivity and its Use in Early Visual Processing
D. Marr and S. Ullman
A.I. Memo 524 (June 1979)
Artificial Intelligence Laboratory, MIT, Cambridge/MA

Marr et al. 79 ==> 2.1.3;
Bandpass Channels, Zero-Crossings, and Early Visual Information Processing
D. Marr, S. Ullman, and T. Poggio
J. Opt. Soc. Am. 69 (1979) 914-916
Martin and Aggarwal 78 ==> 1;
Survey: Dynamic Scene Analysis
W.N. Martin and J.K. Aggarwal
Computer Graphics and Image Processing 7 (1978) 356-374
Martin and Aggarwal 79a ==> 2.6.2;
Occlusion in Dynamic Scene Analysis
W.N. Martin and J.K. Aggarwal
WCATVI-79, pp. 49-50
Martin and Aggarwal 79b ==> 2.6.2; 3.3;
Computer Analysis of Dynamic Scenes Containing Curvilinear Figures
W.N. Martin and J.K. Aggarwal
Pattern Recognition 11 (1979) 169-178
Maxemchuk and Sharma 78 ==> 2.1.7;
Separation of NTSC Signals by Minimum Square Error Filters and Adaptive Filters
N.F. Maxemchuk and D.K. Sharma
IEEE Trans. Communications COM-26 (1978) 583-593
Maziotta and Huang 76 ==> 2.8.3;
THREAD (Three-Dimensional Reconstruction and Display) with Biomedical Application in Neuron Ultrastructure and Computerized Tomography
J.C. Maziotta and H.K. Huang
Proc. NCC AFIPS 45 (1976) pp. 241-250
McCormick et al. 76 ==> 2.3.2;
Image Processing in Television Ophthalmoscopy
B.H. McCormick, J.S. Read, R.T. Borovec, and R.C. Amendola
in: Digital Processing of Biomedical Images
K. Preston, Jr., and M. Onoe (eds.)
Plenum Publishing Co., New York 1976 , pp. 399-424
McIntosh 79 ==> 2.6.2;
Moving Target Detection by Imaging Missile Seekers
D.M. McIntosh
WCATVI-79, p. 105
McVey and Woolard 79 ==> 2.6.2;
A Perturbation Method for Obtaining Control Signals in an Image Tracking System
E.S. McVey and W.B. Woolard, Jr.
Proc. 1979 Joint Automatic Control Conference
Milgram 75 ==> 2.2.4;
Computer Methods for Creating Photomosaics
D.L. Milgram
IEEE Trans. Computers C-24 (1975) 1113-1119
Milgram 77a ==> 2.6.2;
Region Tracking Using Dynamic Programming
D.L. Milgram
TR-539 (May 1977), Computer Science Center, University of Maryland, College Park/MD
see, too, WCATVI-79, p. 13
Milgram 77b ==> 2.2.4;
Adaptive Techniques for Photomosaicking
D.L. Milgram
IEEE Trans. Computers C-26 (1977) 1175-1180

Miller 77 ==> 2.7;
Autonomous Guidance and Control of a Roving Robot
J.A. Miller
IJCAI-77, pp. 759-760
Miller et al. 75 ==> 2.2.3; 2.2.4; 2.2.6;
Further Outlook for GOES
D.B. Miller, J.A. Leese, and C.L. Bristor
paper no. 18 (pp. 146-150) in Bristor 75
Milstein and Lazicky 77 ==> 2.6.2;
Algorithms to Track a Moving Object
L.B. Milstein and T. Lazicky
IEEE Conference on Pattern Recognition and
Image Processing, Troy/NY, June 6-8, 1977,
pp. 148-152
Milstein and Lazicky 78 ==> 2.6.2;
Statistical Tests for Image Tracking
L.B. Milstein and T. Lazicky
Computer Graphics and Image Processing 7 (1978) 413-424
Misra and Wheeler 77 ==> 2.2.6;
Classification of Landsat Data to Recognize Wheat
P.N. Misra and S.G. Wheeler
IEEE Conference on Pattern Recognition and
Image Processing, Troy/NY, June 6-8, 1977, pp. 280-288
Misra and Wheeler 78 ==> 2.2.6;
Crop Classification with LANDSAT Multispectral
Scanner Data
P.N. Misra and S.G. Wheeler
Pattern Recognition 10 (1978) 1-13
Mistretta et al. 73 ==> 2.3.4;
Absorption Edge Fluoroscopy Using Quasi-monoenergetic
X-ray Beams
C.A. Mistretta, M.G. Ort, F. Kelcz,
J.R. Cameron, M.P. Siedband, and A.B. Crummy
Invest. Radiol. 8 (1973) 402-412
Miyahara 75 ==> 2.1.5;
Analysis of Perception of Motion in Television Signals
and its Application to Bandwidth Compression
M. Miyahara
IEEE Trans. on Communications COM-23 (1975) 761-768
Moore and Fung 79 ==> 2.2.3; 2.2.3;
Radar Determination of Winds at Sea
R.K. Moore and A.K. Fung
Proc. IEEE 67 (1979) 1504-1521
Moravec 77 ==> 2.7;
Towards Automatic Visual Obstacle Avoidance
H.P. Moravec
IJCAI-77, p. 584
Moravec 79 ==> 2.7;
Visual Mapping by a Robot Rover
H.P. Moravec
IJCAI-79, pp. 598-600
Moskowitz 64 ==> 2.6.2; 3.3;
Terminal Guidance by Pattern Recognition -
A New Approach
S. Moskowitz
IEEE Trans. Aerospace and Navigational
Electronics (1964) 254-265

Mounts 69 ==> 2.1.4;
A Video Encoding System with Conditional Picture-Element Replenishment
F.W. Mounts
Bell System Techn. J. 48 (1969) 2545-2554

Mounts et al. 77 ==> 2.1.3;
Design of Quantizers for Real-Time Hadamard Transform Coding of Pictures
F.W. Mounts, A.N. Netravali, and B. Prasada
Bell System Technical Journal 56 (1977) 21-48

Musmann 79 ==> 2.1.3; 2.1.7;
Predictive Image Coding
H.G. Musmann
in: Image Transmission Techniques
W.K. Pratt (ed.)
Academic Press, New York 1979, pp. 73-112

Musmann 80 ==> 2.1.5;
Private Communication, February 1980

Myers 78 ==> 2.2.3;
Studying the Oceans from Space
W. Myers
IEEE Computer 11, No. 8 (August 1978) 68-75

Nagel 78a ==> 2.2.5; 2.6.1; 3.1; 3.2;
Formation of an Object Concept by Analysis of Systematic Time Variations in the Optically Perceptible Environment
H.-H. Nagel
Computer Graphics and Image Processing 7 (1978) 149-194

Nagel 78b ==> 1; 2.8.2;
Analysis Techniques for Image Sequences
H.-H. Nagel
IJCPR-78, pp. 186-211

Nagel 79 ==> 1; 2.2.5;
Ueber die Repraesentation von Wissen zur Auswertung von Bildern
H.-H. Nagel
in: Angewandte Szenenanalyse, J.P. Foith (ed.)
Informatik Fachberichte 20, pp. 3-21
Springer Verlag, Berlin-Heidelberg-New York 1979

Nagel 80 ==> 1;
From Digital Picture Processing to Image Analysis
H.-H. Nagel
Proc. International Conference on Image Analysis and Processing, V. Cantoni (ed.),
Pavia/Italy, October 22-24, 1980, pp. 27-40

Nagy 72 ==> 2.2.6;
Digital Image Processing Activities in Remote Sensing for Earth Resources
G. Nagy
Proc. IEEE 60 (1972) 1177-1200

Natarajan and Ahmed 77 ==> 2.1.2;
On Interframe Transform Coding
T.R. Natarajan and N. Ahmed
IEEE Trans. Communications COM-25 (1977) 1323-1329

Nejdl et al. 78 ==> 2.3.5;
Computer Aided Diagnosis from Lung Ventilation and Perfusion Scintigrams
I.F. Nejdl, E.E. Gose, and E. Kaplan
IJPCR-78, pp. 914-918

Netravali 78 ==> 2.1.7;
Noise Removal from Chrominance Components
of a Color Television Signal
A.N. Netravali
IEEE Trans. Communications COM-26 (1978) 1318-1321
Netravali and Robbins 79 ==> 2.1.4; 2.1.4; 2.1.6; 3.2; 3.3;
Motion Compensated Television Coding: Part 1
A.N. Netravali and J.D. Robbins
Bell System Technical J. 58 (1979) 631-670
Netravali and Rubinstein 77 ==> 2.1.7;
Quantization of Color Signals
A.N. Netravali and C.B. Rubinstein
Proc. IEEE 65 (1977) 1177-1187
Netravali and Stuller 79 ==> 2.1.4; 2.1.6; 3.3;
Motion-Compensated Transform Coding
A.N. Netravali and J.A. Stuller
Bell System Technical Journal 58 (1979) 1703-1718
see, too : Proc. IEEE Conference on Pattern Recognition and
Image Processing, Chicago/IL, August 6-8, 1979 pp. 561-567
Netravali et al. 77 ==> 2.1.3;
Some Experiments in Adaptive and Predictive
Hadamard Transform Coding of Pictures
A.N. Netravali, B. Prasada, and F.W. Mounts
Bell System Technical J. 56 (1977) 1531-1547
Neumann 78 ==> 2.7;
Interpretation of Imperfect Object Contours
for Identification and Tracking
B. Neumann
IJCPR-78 Nov. 7-10, 1978 Kyoto/Japan, pp. 691-693
Nevatia 76 ==> 2.7;
Depth Measurement by Motion Stereo
R. Nevatia
Computer Graphics and Image Processing 5 (1976) 203-214
Nicolae and Hoehne 79 ==> 2.3;
Multiprocessor System for the Real-Time
Digital Processing of Video-Image Series
G.C. Nicolae and K.H. Hoehne
Elektronische Rechenanlagen 21 (1979) 171-183
Nitzan and Rosen 76 ==> 2.7;
Programmable Industrial Automation
D. Nitzan and Ch.A. Rosen
IEEE Trans. Computers C-25 (1976) 1259-1270
Novak and Young 76 ==> 2.2.2;
The Operational Processing of Wind Estimates
from Cloud Motions
C. Novak and M. Young
Proc. Symposium Meteorological Observations from
Space: Their Contribution to the First GARP Global
Experiment, 1976, pp. 214-221
O'Handley 73 ==> 2.7;
Scene Analysis in Support of a Mars Rover
D.A. O'Handley
Computer Graphics and Image Processing 2 (1973) 281-297
Ohira et al. 78 ==> 2.1.7;
Orthogonal Transform Coding System for NTSC
Color Television Signals
T. Ohira, M. Hayakawa, and K. Matsumoto
IEEE Trans. Communications COM-26 (1978) 1454-1463

Onoe 78 ==> 1;
Digital Image Processing for Motion Analysis
M. Onoe
Proc. 13th Int. Congress High Speed
Photography and Photonics (Aug. 1978)
Onoe and Ohba 76 ==> 2.6.1;
Digital Image Analysis of Traffic Flow
M. Onoe and K. Ohba
IJCPR-76, 803-808
Onoe et al. 73 ==> 2.6.1;
Computer Analysis of Traffic Flow Observed
by Subtractive Television
M. Onoe, N. Hamano, K. Ohba
Computer Graphics and Image Processing 2 (1973) 377-392
O'Rourke 80 ==> 2.2.1;
private communication 1980
O'Rourke and Badler 79 ==> 2.8.8;
An Image Analysis System for Human Motion
J. O'Rourke and N. Badler
WCATVI-79, pp. 61-63
Paolantonio 69 ==> 2.2.5;
Difference Measurements in Automatic
Photointerpretation of Surveillance Maps
A. Paolantonio
Information Display 6 (March/April 1969) 41-44
Parikh 76a ==> 2.2.1; 2.2.3;
Cloud Pattern Classification from Visible and
Infrared Data
JoAnn Parikh
TR-442 (February 1976) Computer Science Center
University of Maryland, College Park/MD
Parikh 76b ==> 2.2.1; 2.2.3; 2.2.3;
An Approach to Selection of Wind Tracers from Tropical
Maritime Geosynchronous Satellite Cloud Imagery
JoAnn Parikh
TR-450 (March 1976)
Computer Science Department, University of Maryland,
College Park/MD
Parikh 77 ==> 2.2.1; 2.2.3;
A Comparative Study of Cloud Classification
Techniques
JoAnn Parikh
Remote Sensing of Environment 6 (1977) 67-81
Parikh and Rosenfeld 78 ==> 2.2.3;
Automatic Segmentation and Classification
of Infrared Meteorological Satellite Data
J.A. Parikh and A. Rosenfeld
IEEE Trans. Systems, Man, and Cybernetics
SMC-8 (1978) 736-743
Park 69 ==> 2.2.6;
Remote Sensing of Time Dependent Phenomena
A.B. Park
Proc. 6th Int. Symp. Remote Sens. Environ.
(Ann Arbor/Michigan, 1969) 1227-1236
Pavlidis 77 ==> 2.1.3; 2.2.4;
Structural Pattern Recognition
T. Pavlidis
Springer Verlag Berlin-Heidelberg-New York 1977

Peachey et al. 76 ==> 2.8.3;
Three-Dimensional Reconstruction from Serial High Voltage Electron Micrographs
L.D. Peachey, C.H. Damsky, and A. Veen
Proc. 4th Int. Congress for Stereology, pp. 207-210
Gaithersburg/MD, Sept. 4-9, 1975, NBS, Washington/DC 1976

Pearson et al. 77 ==> 2.1.2; 3.3;
Video-Rate Image Correlation Processor
J.J. Pearson, D.C. Hines, Jr., S. Golosman, and C.D. Kuglin
Proc. SPIE 119 (IOCC 1977) pp. 197-205

Pease and Limb 71 ==> 2.1.4; 3.1;
Exchange of Spatial and Temporal Resolution in Television Coding
R.F.W. Pease and J.O. Limb
Bell System Techn. J. 50 (1971) 191-200

Peters 75 ==> 2.8.1;
Enhanced Display of Three-Dimensional Data from Computerized X-Ray Tomograms
T.M. Peters
Computers in Biology and Medicine 5 (1975) 49-52

Pichel et al. 76 ==> 2.2.2;
Artificial Stereo: A Generalized Computer Algorithm for Combining Multi-Channel Image Data
W.G. Pichel, R.L. Brower, D.R. Brandman, and R.J. Moy
Proc. 4th Int. Congress for Stereology, pp. 219-220
Gaithersburg/MD, Sept. 4-9, 1975, NBS, Washington/DC, 1976

Pieroni 76 ==> 2.3.6;
A Method for Analyzing Dynamic Processes Represented by Chains of Maps
G.G. Pieroni
IJCPR-76, pp. 325-333

Pieroni 79 ==> 2.3.6;
A Method for Analyzing Dynamic Processes Represented by Sequences of Maps
G.G. Pieroni
Computer Graphics and Image Processing 10 (1979) 375-387

Pieroni and Costabile 79 ==> 2.3;
Experiments in Dynamic Segmentation
G.G. Pieroni and M.F. Costabile
IEEE Conference on Pattern Recognition and Image Processing, Chicago/IL, August 6-8, 1979, pp. 300-307

Pieroni and Freeman 78 ==> 2.3.6;
On the Analysis of Dynamic Map Data
G.G. Pieroni and H. Freeman
IJCPR-78, pp. 731-734

Pieroni and Narasimhan 74 ==> 2.3.6;
Cardiac Potential Map Analysis and Description
G.G. Pieroni and R. Narasimhan
IJCPR-74, pp. 276-280

Popp 78 ==> 2.3;
Clinical Applications of New Echocardiographic Techniques
R.L. Popp
Proc. SPIE 167 (1978) 143-150

Potel and MacKay 79 ==> 2.4;
Interactive Graphics Input Tools for Motion Analysis
M.J. Potel and St.A. MacKay
WCATVI-79, pp. 125-127

Potel and Sayre 76 ==> 2.4; 4;
Interacting with the GALATEA Film Analysis System
M.J. Potel and R.E. Sayre
Proc. SIGGRAPH '76
ACM SIGGRAPH Computer Graphics 10 (July 1976) 52-59
Potel and Sayre 77 ==> 2.4;
Motion Analysis with Vector Graphics
M.J. Potel and R.E. Sayre
Proc. IEEE Workshop on Picture Data Description
and Management, Chicago/Ill., April 21-22, 1977
pp. 184-186
Potel et al. 79 ==> 2.4; 2.4; 4;
Graphics Input Tools for Interactive Motion Analysis
M.J. Potel, R.E. Sayre, and S.A. MacKay
preprint 1979 (to be published)
Potter 75a ==> 3.1; 3.3;
Velocity as a Cue to Segmentation
J. Potter
IEEE Trans. Systems, Man and Cybernetics,
SCM-5 (1975) 390-394
Potter 75b ==> 3.1; 3.3;
Scene Segmentation by Velocity Measurements Obtained
with a Cross-Shaped Template
J. Potter
IJCAI-75, 803-810
Tbilisi, Georgia/USSR, September 3-8, 1975
Potter 77 ==> 3.1; 3.3;
Scene Segmentation Using Motion Information
J.L. Potter
Computer Graphics and Image Processing 6 (1977) 558-581
Pratt 78 ==> 2.1; 2.1.3;
Digital Image Processing
W.K. Pratt
Wiley, New York 1978
Pratt 79 ==> 2.1; 2.1.2;
Image Transmission Techniques
W.K. Pratt (ed.)
Academic Press New York/NY 1979
Preston 79 ==> 2.3;
Biomedical Image Processing
K. Preston, Jr.
in: Advances in Digital Image Processing, P. Stucki (ed.)
Plenum Press Publ. Co., New York/NY 1979, pp.125-146
Price 76 ==> 2.2.5; 2.2.5;
Change Detection and Analysis in Multi-Spectral Images
K.E. Price
Ph.D. Thesis, December 18, 1976
Department of Computer Science, Carnegie-Mellon
University, Pittsburgh/PA
Price 78 ==> 2.2.5;
Symbolic Matching and Analysis with Substantial
Changes in Orientation
K.E. Price
Proc. Image Understanding Workshop, pp. 93-99
Cambridge/MA, May 3-4, 1978, L.S. Baumann (ed.)
Science Applications, Inc., Arlington/VA
Price and Reddy 75 ==> 2.2.5;
Change Detection in Multi-Sensor Images
K. Price and D.R. Reddy

Tenth International Symposium on Remote Sensing of Environment
Ann Arbor, Michigan, October 1975

Price and Reddy 77a ==> 2.2.5;
Symbolic Image Registration and Change Detection
K. Price and D.R. Reddy
Proc. Image Understanding Workshop. pp. 28-31
Minneapolis/MN, April 20, 1977
Science Applications, Inc., Arlington/VA

Price and Reddy 77b ==> 2.2.5;
Change Detection and Analysis in Multispectral Images
K.E. Price and R. Reddy
IJCAI-77, pp. 619-625

Price and Reddy 79 ==> 2.2.5;
Matching Segments of Images
K. Price and R. Reddy
IEEE Trans. Pattern Analysis and Machine Intelligence PAMI-1 (1979) 110-116

Putra and Toole 79 ==> 2.2.5;
Automatic Digital Change Detection on SAT Imagery
T.P. Putra and J.W. Toole
WCATVI-79, p. 7

Quam 78 ==> 2.6.1;
Road Tracking and Anomaly Detection in Aerial Imagery
L.H. Quam
Proc. Image Understanding Workshop, pp. 51-55
L.S. Baumann (ed.), Cambridge/MA, May 3-4, 1978
Science Applications, Inc., Arlington/VA

Rackley 76 ==> 2.3.5;
Quantitative Evaluation of Left Ventricular Function by Radiographic Techniques
C.E. Rackley
Circulation 54 (1976) 862-879

Radig 78a ==> 2.6.2;
Auswertung von digitisierten Fernsehbildern zur Beschreibung bewegter Objekte
B. Radig
Dissertation, Fachbereich Informatik (Maerz 1978), Universitaet Hamburg

Radig 78b ==> 2.6.2;
Parameterized Region Extracting for the Description of Moving Objects
B. Radig
AISB/GI Conference on Artificial Intelligence
July 18-20, 1978, Hamburg, pp. 263-272

Radig 78c ==> 2.6.2;
Description of Moving Objects Based on Parameterized Region Extracting
B. Radig
IJCPR-78 Nov. 7-10, 1978 Kyoto/Japan, pp. 723-725

Rahmani 79 ==> 2.5;
An Experimental Study of Planar Models for Human Gait Utilizing On-line Computer Analysis of Television and Force Plate Data
S. Rahmani
Ph.D. Thesis (June 1979)
Department of Electrical Engineering
The Ohio State University, Columbus/OH

Raudseps 75 ==> 2.6.1;
Automatic Extraction of Highway Traffic Data from Aerial Photographs
J.G. Raudseps
DOT-TSC-FHWA-75-1
US Dept. of Transportation, Transportation Systems Center, Kendall Square, Cambridge/MA 1975

Read et al. 77 ==> 2.3.2;
The Television Ophthalmoscope Image Processor
J.S. Read, R.T. Borovec, R.C. Amendola, A.C. Petersen, M.H. Goldbaum, M. Kottow, B.H. McCormick, and M.F. Goldberg
Proc. IEEE Workshop on Picture Data Description and Management, Chicao/Ill., April 21-22, 1977, pp. 64-67

Reader 75 ==> 2.1.2; 2.1.5;
Intraframe and Interframe Adaptive Transform Coding
C. Reader
Proc. SPIE 66 (1975) 108-117

Reddy and Rubin 78 ==> 2.8.2; 2.8.2;
Representation of Three-Dimensional Objects
D.R. Reddy and S. Rubin
Computer Science Department, April 1978
Carnegie-Mellon University, Pittsburgh/PA

Reddy et al. 73 ==> 2.8; 2.8.2; 2.8.2; 2.8.3;
Computer Analysis of Neuronal Structure
D.R. Reddy, W.J. Davis, R.B. Ohlander, and D.J. Bihary
in: Intracellular Staining in Neurobiology (S.B. Kater and C. Nicholson, eds.)
Springer Verlag, New York-Heidelberg-Berlin 1973, pp. 227-253

Reeves et al. 79 ==> 2.3.3; 2.4;
Interactive Computer-Aided Analysis of Cardiac Motion Sequences
W. Reeves, R. Baecker, H.D. Covvey, D. Miller, and D. Galloway
WCATVI-79, pp. 64-65

Reinstein et al. 78 ==> 2.8.3;
A Computer-Assisted Three-Dimensional Treatment Planning System
L.E. Reinstein, D. McShan, B.M. Webber, and A.S. Glicksman
Radiology 127 (1978) 259-264

Reis et al. 76 ==> 2.1.6;
Adaptive Haar Transform Video Bandwidth Reduction System for the RPVs
J.J. Reis, R.T. Lynch, and J. Butman
20th Annual Meeting SPIE San Diego/CA, August 23-27, 1976
Proc. SPIE 87 (1976) 24-35

Rhodes et al. 78 ==> 2.8.5;
Three Dimensional Structure Isolation Using Parallel Image Planes
M.L. Rhodes, W.V. Glenn, and A. Klinger
IJCPR-78, pp. 584-591

Ridsdale and Kulick 79 ==> 2.1.8;
The Digital Encoding of Radiographic Motion Pictures: a Structural Approach
G.J. Ridsdale and J.H. Kulick
WCATVI-79, pp. 84-86

Ritman et al. 78 ==> 2.3; 2.8.4; 2.8.8;
Needs, Requirements and Design of a High Temporal Resolution Synchronous Cylindrical Whole-Body Transaxial Scanner for Simultaneous Study of the Structure and Function of the Heart and Circulation
E.L. Ritman, R.E. Sturm, R.A. Robb, and E.H. Wood
in: Roentgen-Video-Techniques, pp. 271-284
P.H. Heintzen and J.H. Buersch (eds.),
Georg Thieme Publishers, Stuttgart/Germany 1978

Roach and Aggarwal 79 ==> 2.6.2;
Computer Tracking of Objects Moving in Space
J. Roach and J.K. Aggarwal
IEEE Trans. Pattern Analysis and Machine Intelligence PAMI-1 (1979) 127-135

Robbins and Netravali 79 ==> 2.1.4; 2.1.6; 3.3;
Interframe Television Coding Using Movement Compensation
J.D. Robbins and A.N. Netravali
International Conference on Communications
June 1979, IEEE publication CH 1435-7/79
pp. 23.4.1 - 23.4.5

Robertson and Cohen 72 ==> 2.4;
Control of Developing Fields
A. Robertson and M.H. Cohen
Ann. Rev. Biophys. Bioeng. 1 (1972) 409-464

Robinson 72 ==> 2.8; 2.8.1;
Display of Three-Dimensional Ultrasonic Data for Medical Diagnosis
D.E. Robinson
J. Acoust. Soc. Am. 52 (1972) 673-687

Robinson 76 ==> 2.1.3;
Detection and Coding of Edges Using Directional Masks
G.S. Robinson
Proc. SPIE 87 (1976) 117-125

Robinson 77 ==> 2.1.3;
Edge Detection by Compass Gradient Masks
G.S. Robinson
Computer Graphics and Image Processing 6 (1977) 492-501

Robinson and Reis 77 ==> 2.1.3;
A Real-Time Edge Processing Unit
G.S. Robinson and J.J. Reis
Proc. IEEE Workshop on Picture Data Description and Management, Chicago/IL, April 21-22, 1977, pp. 155-164

Rocca 69 ==> 2.1.5; 2.1.6; 3.3;
Television Bandwidth Compression Utilizing Frame-to-Frame Correlation and Movement Compensation
F. Rocca
Symposium on Picture Bandwidth Compression
MIT, Cambridge/MA, April 1969
(T.S. Huang and O.J. Tretiak, eds.)
Gordon and Breach, New York 1972, pp. 675-693

Rocca and Zanoletti 72 ==> 2.1.6;
Television Bandwidth Compression via Movement Compensation on a Model of the Random Video Process
F. Rocca and S. Zanoletti
IEEE Trans. Communications COM-20 (1972) 960-965

Roese and Pratt 76 ==> 2.1.2;
Theoretical Performance Models for Interframe
Transform and Hybrid Transform/DPCM Coders
J.A. Roese and W.K. Pratt
Proc. SPIE 87 (August 1976) 172-179

Roese and Robinson 75 ==> 2.1.2;
Combined Spatial and Temporal Coding of
Digital Image Sequences
J.A. Roese and G.S. Robinson
Proc. SPIE 66 (1975) 172-180

Roese et al. 75 ==> 2.1.2;
Interframe Transform Coding and Predictive Coding
Methods
J.A. Roese, W.K. Pratt, G.S. Robinson, and A. Habibi
Proc. 1975 Intern. Conf. on Communications
ICC-75, vol. II, paper 23, pp. 17-21 (June 16-18, 1975)

Roese et al. 77 ==> 2.1.2; 2.1.2;
Interframe Cosine Transform Image Coding
J.A. Roese, W.V. Pratt, and G.S. Robinson
IEEE Trans. Communications COM-25 (1977) 1329-1339

Rose et al. 79 ==> 2.3.4;
The Use of Image Sequences to Discriminate
between Overlapping Radioactive Objects which
Differ in Their Dynamic Behavior
W.H. Rose, E.E. Gose, W.E. Barnes, E. Kaplan,
and J.S. Arnold
WCATVI-79, p. 96

Rosen and Nitzan 77 ==> 2.7;
Use of Sensors in Programmable Automation
C.A. Rosen and D. Nitzan
Computer 10 (December 77) 12-23

Rosenfeld 61 ==> 2.2.5;
Automatic Detection of Changes in Reconnaissance Data
A. Rosenfeld
Proc. 5th Conv. Mil. Electron. 1961, pp. 492-499

Rosenfeld 78 ==> 2.2.1;
Relaxation Methods in Image Processing and Analysis
A. Rosenfeld
IJCPR-78, pp. 181-185

Rosenfeld and Kak 76 ==> 1; 2.1; 2.8.1;
Digital Picture Processing
A. Rosenfeld and A.C. Kak
Academic Press, New York, 1976

Rubin 78 ==> 2.6.2;
The ARGOS Image Understanding System
St. Rubin
Report (Nov. 1978)
Department of Computer Science
Carnegie-Mellon University, Pittsburgh/PA

Rubin and Reddy 77 ==> 2.6.2;
The Locus Model of Search and it's Use
in Image Interpretation
S.M. Rubin and R. Reddy
IJCAI-77, pp. 590-595

Rubin and Sayre 78 ==> 2.8.2; 2.8.2;
A Computer-Aided Technique for Overlaying Cerebral
Angiograms onto Computed Tomograms
J.M. Rubin and R.E. Sayre
Investigative Radiology 13 (1978) 362-367

Rubinstein and Limb 78 ==> 2.1.3;
On the Design of Quantizers for DPCM Coders:
Influence of the Subjective Testing Methodology
C.B. Rubinstein and J.O. Limb
IEEE Trans. Communications COM-26 (1978) 565-572
Rueenaufer 76 ==> 2.6.1
Untersuchungen zur Ermittlung von Moeglichkeiten und
Grenzen der Einbeziehung des elektronischen Fernsehens
in die Analyse des Strassenverkehrsablaufs
P. Rueenaufer
Dissertation, Fakultaet fuer Elektrotechnik,
Rhein.-Westf. Techn. Hochschule Aachen (Dec. 1976)
Sakrison 79 ==> 2.1.3;
Image Coding Applications of Vision Models
D.J. Sakrison
in: Image Transmission Techniques
W.K. Pratt (ed.)
Academic Press, New York 1979, pp. 21-71
Sawada and Kotera 78a ==> 2.1.7;
A 32 Mbit/s Component Separation DPCM Coding
System for NTSC Color TV
K. Sawada and H. Kotera
IEEE Trans. Communications COM-26 (1978) 458-465
Sawada and Kotera 78b ==> 2.1.7;
32 Mbit/s Transmission of NTSC Color TV Signals
by Composite DPCM Coding
K. Sawada and H. Kotera
IEEE Trans. Communications COM-26 (1978) 1432-1439
Sayre 79 ==> 2.4; 2.5;
Three-Dimensional Motion Analysis, with one
Foot on the Ground
R.E. Sayre
WCATVI-79, pp. 136-137
Sayre et al. 79 ==> 2.8.2; 2.8.2;
Quantitative Three-Dimensional Angiograms: Applications,
Including Augmentation of Computed Tomograms
R.E. Sayre, J.M. Rubin, E.E. Duda, and N.J. Patronas
Proc. Sixth Conference on Computer Applications in
Radiology and Computer-Aided Analysis of Radiological
Images, Newport Beach/CA, June 19-21, 1979
Scacchi 79 ==> 1;
Visual Motion Perception by Intelligent Systems
W. Scacchi
IEEE Conference on Pattern Recognition and Image
Processing, Chicago/IL, August 6-8, 1979, pp. 646-652
Schalkoff 79 ==> 2.6.2; 3.2; 3.2;
Algorithms for a Real-Time Automatic Video Tracking
System
R.J. Schalkoff
Ph.D. Thesis (May 1979)
Dept. Electrical Engineering, Univ. of Virginia
Charlottesville/VA
Schalkoff and McVey 79 ==> 2.6.2; 3.2; 3.3; 3.3;
Algorithm Development for Real-Time Automatic Video
Tracking Systems
R.J. Schalkoff and E.S. McVey
Proc. 3rd International Computer Software and Applications
Conference, Chicago/IL, November 1979, pp. 504-511

Schaphorst 69 ==> 2.1.7;
Frame to Frame Coding to N.T.S.C. Color TV
R. Schaphorst
Symposium on Picture Bandwidth Compression
MIT, Cambridge/MA, April 1969
(T.S. Huang and O.J. Tretiak, eds.)
Gordon and Breach, New York 1972

Schmidlin et al. 76 ==> 2.3.5;
Evaluation of Dynamic Studies by Means of Factor Analysis
P. Schmidlin, J. Clorius, R. Kubesch, and K. Dreikorn
Proc. International Symposium on Medical Radionuclide Imaging
Los Angeles/CA, October 25-29, 1976 IAEA 1977

Schreiber et al. 59 ==> 2.1.3;
Synthetic Highs: An Experimental TV Bandwidth
Reduction System
W.F. Schreiber, C.F. Knapp, and N.D. Kay
J. Soc. Motion Pict. and Telev. Eng. 68 (1959) 525-537

Schreiber et al. 68 ==> 2.1.3;
Contour Coding of Images
W.F. Schreiber, T.S. Huang, and J.O.Tretiak
WESCON Tech. Papers, session 8
(August 1968)

Schudy 79 ==> 2.3; 2.3.3; 2.8.4; 2.8.8;
Towards an Anatomical Model of Heart Motion
as Seen in Cardiac Ultrasound Data
R.B. Schudy
WCATVI-79, p. 87-89

Schultes et al. 79 ==> 2.3.7;
Verarbeitung von Bildsequenzen bei der
ortsaufloesenden Pupillographie
N. Schultes, D. Doepfer, H. Baldauf, M. Mertz
in: Angewandte Szenenanalyse, J.P. Foith (ed.)
Informatik Fachberichte 20, pp. 289-292
Springer Verlag, Berlin-Heidelberg-New York 1979

Selzer et al. 76 ==> 2.3.2;
Computer Analysis of Cardiovascular Imagery
R.H. Selzer, D.H. Blankenhorn, D.W. Crawford,
S.H. Brooks, and R. Barndt, jr.
in: Green et al. 76, pp. 6-1 through 6-20

Seyler 63 ==> 2.1.1;
Real-time Recording of Television Frame
Difference Areas
A.J. Seyler
Proc. IEEE (Corresp) 51 (1963) 478-480

Seyler 65a ==> 2.1.1;
Statistics of Television Frame Differences
A.J. Seyler
Proc. IEEE 53 (1965) 2127-2128

Seyler 65b ==> 2.1.1;
Probability Distributions of Television Frame
Differences
A.J. Seyler
Proc. Inst. Radio Electron. Eng. (Australia)
(Nov. 1965) pp. 355-366

Seyler and Budrikis 59 ==> 2.1.1;
Measurements of Temporal Adaptation to Spatial
Detail Vision
A.J. Seyler and Z.L. Budrikis
Nature 184 (1959) 1215-1217

Seyler and Budrikis 65 ==> 2.1.1;
Detail Perception after Scene Changes in Television Image Presentations
A.J. Seyler and Z.L. Budrikis
IEEE Trans. Inform. Theory IT-11 (1965) 31-43

Shantz and McCann 78 ==> 2.8.3;
Computational Morphology: Three-Dimensional Computer Graphics for Electron Microscopy
M.J. Shantz and G.D. McCann
IEEE Trans. Biomedical Eng. BME-25 (1978) 99-103

Shenk and Kreins 70 ==> 2.2.1; 2.2.2;
A Comparison Between Observed Winds and Cloud Motions Derived from Satellite Infrared Measurements
W.E. Shenk and E.R. Kreins
J. of Applied Meteorology 9 (1970) 702-710

Shepard 64 ==> 2.2.5;
A Concept of Change Detection
J.R. Shepard
Photogrammetric Engineering 30 (1964) 648-651

Shepard 79 ==> 2.8;
Connections between the Representation of Shapes and of their Spatial Transformations
R.N. Shepard
Proc. Workshop on the Representation of Three-Dimensional Objects, R.Bajcsy (ed.), University of Pennsylvania, Philadelphia/PA, May 1-2, 1979, pp. N-1 through N-20

Shirai and Inoue 73 ==> 2.7;
Guiding a Robot by Visual Feedback in Assembling Tasks
Y. Shirai and H. Inoue
Pattern Recognition 5 (1973) 99-108

Sikdar and Suomi 72 ==> 2.2.3;
On the Remote Sensing of Mesoscale Tropical Convection Intensity from a Geostationary Satellite
D.N. Sikdar and V.E. Suomi
J. Applied Meteorology 11 (1972) 37-43

Sinclair et al. 71 ==> 2.2.6;
Reflectance and Internal Structure of Leaves from Several Crops during a Growing Season
T.R. Sinclair, R.M. Hoffer, and M.M. Schreiber
Agronomy Journal 63 (1971) 864-868

Smalling et al. 76 ==> 2.3.3; 2.3.5;
Digital Boundary Detection, Volumetric and Wall Motion Analysis of Left Ventricular Cine Angiograms
R.W. Smalling, M.H. Skolnick, D. Myers, R. Shabetai, J.C. Cole, and D. Johnston
Comput. Biol. Med. 6 (1976) 78-85

Smith and Hasler 76 ==> 2.2.1; 2.2.3;
A Comparison of Low-Cloud Satellite Wind Estimates with Analyses Based on Aircraft Observations in a Disturbed Tropical Regime
C.L. Smith and A.F. Hasler
Monthly Weather Review 104 (1976) 702-708

Smith and Phillips 72 ==> 2.2.4; 2.2.4;
Automated Cloud Tracking Using Precisely Aligned Digital ATS Pictures
E.A. Smith and D.R. Phillips
IEEE Trans. Computers C-21 (1972) 715-729

Smith and Reynolds 76 ==> 2.2.2;
Comparison of Cloud Top Height Determinations from Three Independent Sources: Satellite IR Measurements, Satellite Viewed Cloud Shadows, Radar
E.A. Smith and D. W. Reynolds
Proc. Symposium on Meteorological Observations from Space: Their Contribution to the First GARP Global Experiment, Philadelphia/PA June 8-10, 1976, pp. 237-244

Soroka 79a ==> 2.8; 2.8.6;
Understanding Objects from Slices: Extracting Generalized Cylinder Descriptions from Serial Slices
B.I. Soroka
TR-79-1 (March 1979)
Department of Computer Science
University of Kansas, Lawrence/KS 66045

Soroka 79b ==> 2.8.6;
Generalized Cylinders and Serial Sections
B.I. Soroka
Proc.NSF Workshop on the Representation of Three-Dimensional Objects, R. Bajcsy (ed.)
University of Pennsylvania, Philadelphia/PA, May 1-2, 1979

Soroka 79c ==> 2.8.6;
Generalized Cylinders from Parallel Slices
B.I. Soroka
IEEE Conference on Pattern Recognition and Image Processing, Chicago/IL, August 6-8, 1979, pp. 421-426

Soroka and Bajcsy 76 ==> 2.8.6;
Generalized Cylinders from Serial Sections
B.I. Soroka and R.K. Bajcsy
IJCPR-76, pp. 734-735

Soroka and Bajcsy 78 ==> 2.8.6;
A Program for Describing Complex Three-Dimensional Objects Using Generalized Cylinders as Primitives
B.I. Soroka and R.K. Bajcsy
IEEE Conference on Pattern Recognition and Image Processing, Chicago/IL, May 31-June 2, 1978, pp. 331-339

Speckert 76 ==> 2.5;
A Computerized Look at Cat Locomotion or One Way to Scan a Cat
G. Speckert
AI Memo 374 (July 1976)
Artificial Intelligence Laboratory, MIT, Cambridge/MA

Sridharan 78 ==> 2.2.3;
Special Issue on Applications to the Sciences and Medicine
N.S. Sridharan (ed.)
Artificial Intelligence 11 (1978) 1-195

Steiner 70 ==> 2.2.6;
Time Dimension for Crop Surveys from Space
D. Steiner
Photogrammetric Eng. 36 (1970) 187-194

Stuller and Netravali 79 ==> 2.1.3; 2.1.6; 3.3;
Transform Domain Motion Estimation
J.A. Stuller and A.N. Netravali
Bell System Technical Journal 58 (1979) 1673-1702
see, too : WCATVI-79, p. 82

Suchman and Martin 76 ==> 2.2.3;
Wind Sets from SMS Images: An Assessment of
Quality for GATE
D. Suchman and D.W. Martin
J. Applied Meteorology 15 (1976) 1265-1278
Sunguroff and Greenberg 78 ==> 2.8.3;
Computer Generated Images for Medical Applications
A. Sunguroff and D. Greenberg
Proc. SIGGRAPH 78, R.L. Phillips (ed.)
Atlanta/GA, Aug. 23-25, 1978
Computer Graphics 12 (1978) 196-202
Swain 78 ==> 2.2.6;
Bayesian Classification in a Time-Varying
Environment
P.H. Swain
IEEE Trans. Systems, Man, and Cybernetics
SMC-8 (1978) 879-883
Swoboda and Gerdes 68 ==> 2.2.5;
A System for Demonstrating the Effects of
Changing Background on Automatic Target Recognition
W. Swoboda and J.W. Gerdes
in: Pictorial Pattern Recognition
G.C. Cheng et al. (eds.), pp. 33-43
Thompson Book Co., Washington/DC 1968
Takagi and Sakaue 78 ==> 2.4;
The Analysis of Moving Granules in a Pancreatic
Cell by Digital Moving Image Processing
M. Takagi and K. Sakaue
IJCPR-78 Nov. 7-10,1978 Kyoto/Japan, pp. 735-739
Tamura et al. 78 ==> 2.8.1;
Specialized Processing System for Three-Dimensional
Display Based on Serial Tomograms
S. Tamura, K. Tanaka, K. Yoshida, J. Hiramoto,
K. Hirano, and M. Matsumoto
IJCPR-78, pp. 851-853
Tanaka et al. 77 ==> 2.2.4;
On Assembling Subpictures into a Mosaic Picture
M. Tanaka, S. Tamura, and K. Tanaka
IEEE Trans. Systems, Man, and Cybernetics
SMC-7 (1977) 42-48
Tanaka et al. 78 ==> 2.2.4;
Picture Assembly Using a Hierarchical
Partial-Matching Technique
M. Tanaka, S. Tamura, and K. Tanaka
IEEE Trans. Systems, Man, and Cybernetics
SMC-8 (1978) 812-819
Tasto 73 ==> 2.3.3;
Guided Boundary Detection for Left Ventricular
Volume Measurements
M. Tasto
IJCPR-73, pp. 119-124
Tasto 74 ==> 2.3.3;
Motion Extraction for Left Ventricular Volume
Measurement
M. Tasto
IEEE Trans. Biomedical Engineering BME-21 (1974) 207-213

Tasto et al. 78 ==> 2.3.3;
Comparison of Manual versus Computer
Determination of Left Ventricular Boundaries
from X-Ray Cineangiocardiograms
M. Tasto, M. Felgendreher, W. Spiesberger,
and P. Spiller
in: Heintzen and Buersch 78, pp. 168-183
Thoma 72 ==> 2.1.5;
Video Transmission Network with Intraframe
DPCM and Optional Interframe Coding
W. Thoma
Proc. Int. Conf. Communications, Philadelphia/PA
June 1972, pp. 39-1 through 39-6
Thomas et al. 79 ==> 2.3.6;
Body Surface Potential Maps: Processing the
Sequence of Images
C.W. Thomas, R. Plonsey, and J. Liebman
WCATVI-79, p. 97
Thomasell 76 ==> 2.2.2;
Objective Editing of Automated, Low Level Cloud
Motion Vectors from Geostationary Satellites
A. Thomasell, Jr.
Proc. Symposium Meteorological Observations from
Space: Their Contribution to the First GARP
Global Experiment, 1976, pp. 222-225
Thompson 77 ==> 2.7;
The Navigation System of the JPL Robot
A.M. Thompson
IJCAI-77, pp. 749-757
Thompson 79 ==> 3.1; 3.2;
Combining Motion and Contrast for Segmentation
W.B. Thompson
Technical Report 79-7 (March 1979)
Computer Science Department, University of Minnesota
Minneapolis/Minnesota 55455
see, too, WCATVI-79, pp. 27-28
Tisdale 77 ==> 2.2.5;
A Digital Image Processor for Automatic Target
Cueing, Navigation, and Change Detection
G.E. Tisdale
Proc. SPIE 101 (1977) 112-119
Tomiyasu 78 ==> 2.2.3;
Tutorial Review of Synthetic-Aperture Radar
(SAR) with Applications to Imaging of the
Ocean Surface
K. Tomiyasu
Proc. IEEE 66 (1978) 563-583
Tou and Ferng 78 ==> 2.8.7;
Computer Analysis of Network Pictures
J.T. Tou and W.M. Ferng
IJCPR-78, pp. 630-634
Tou and Gonzalez 74 ==> 2.2.1;
Pattern Recognition Principles
J.T. Tou and R.C. Gonzalez
Addison-Wesley Publ. Co., Reading/MA, 1974
Tou and Liu 79 ==> 2.8.7;
An Approach to Computer Processing of Lung
Tissue Micrographs
J.T. Tou and H.H. Liu

Proc. IEEE Conference on Pattern Recognition and
Image Processing, Chicago/IL, August 6-8, 1979,
pp. 453-459
Tou et al. 78 ==> 2.8.7;
Computer Analysis of Stereological Parameters
from Lung Tissue
J.T. Tou, C.S. Cheng, M. Fisher, and M. Ferng
Proc. IEEE Conference on Pattern Recognition
and Image Processing, Chicago/IL,
May 31 - June 2, 1978, pp. 379-384
Truitt et al. 76 ==> 2.2.5; 2.2.5;
A Change Detection and Classification System
for Side-Look Radar Images
T.P. Truitt, D.T. Bisell, and G.E. Tisdale
Proc.Nat. Aerospace and Electronics Conference,
Dayton/Ohio (May 1976), pp. 533-538
see also: IEEE Trans. Aerospace and Electronics Systems
AES-12 (1976) 423
Tsotsos 77 ==> 2.6.1;
Some Notes on Motion Understanding
J.K. Tsotsos
IJCAI-77, p. 611
Tsotsos 80 ==> 2.4; 2.6.1; 4;
A Framework for Visual Motion Understanding
J.K. Tsotsos
Technical Report CSRG-114 (June 1980), University of Torontc
Department of Computer Science, Toronto/Canada
Tsotsos et al. 77 ==> 2.3.3;
An Interactive Knowledge-Based Systems
Approach to Cardiac Image Description and
Analysis
J.K. Tsotsos, R. Baecker, H.D. Covvey,
W. Reeves, J. Mylopoulos, and E.D. Wigle
Proc. IEEE Computers in Cardiology
October 1977, Rotterdam, pp. 377-384
Tsotsos et al. 78 ==> 2.3.3;
Gross and Segmental Motion Analysis in Dynamic
Cardiac Imagery
J.K. Tsotsos, H.D. Covvey, J. Mylopoulos,
and E.D. Wigle
Proc. 2nd Annual Symposium on Computer
Application in Medical Care, pp. 45-48
F.H. Orthner (ed.)
November 5-7, 1978, Washington/D.C.
Tsotsos et al. 79a ==> 2.3.3; 2.3.3; 2.3.5; 2.6.1; 2.8
A Framework for Visual Motion Understanding
J.K. Tsotsos, J. Mylopoulos, H.D. Covvey,
and S.W. Zucker
WCATVI-79, pp. 56-58
Tsotsos et al. 79b ==> 2.3.3; 2.3.5; 2.6.1;
ALVEN: A Study on Motion Understanding by Computer
J.K. Tsotsos, J. Mylopoulos, H.D. Covvey,
and S.W. Zucker
IJCAI-79, pp. 890-892
Tsugawa et al. 79 ==> 2.7;
An Automobile with Artificial Intelligence
S. Tsugawa, T. Yatabe, T. Hirose, and S. Matsumoto
IJCAI-79, pp. 893-895

Ullman 79 ==> 1;
The Interpretation of Visual Motion
S. Ullman
The MIT Press, Cambridge/MA, 1979
Ulstad 73 ==> 2.2.5;
An Algorithm for Estimating Small Scale Differences between Two Digital Images
M.S. Ulstad
Pattern Recognition 5 (1973) 323-333
Underwood 70 ==> 2.8.7;
Quantitative Stereology
E.E. Underwood
Addison-Wesley Publ. Co., Reading/MA 1970
Underwood 76 ==> 2.8.7;
Three-Dimensional Shape Parameters from Planar Sections
E.E. Underwood
Proc. 4th Int. Congress for Stereology, pp. 91-92
Gaithersburg/MD, Sept. 4-9, 1975, NBS, Washington/DC 1976
Uno et al. 76 ==> 2.7;
A Method of Real-Time Recognition of Moving Objects and its Application
T. Uno, M. Ejiri, and T. Tokunaga
Pattern Recognition 8 (1976) 201-208
Uter 77 ==> 2.5;
A Real-Time Video System for Tracking One-Dimensional Movements of Two Objects
T.G. Uter
IEEE Trans. Biomedical Eng. BME-24 (1977) 75-78
Veen and Peachey 77 ==> 2.8.3;
TROTS: a Computer Graphics System for Three-Dimensional Reconstruction from Serial Sections
A. Veen and L.D. Peachey
Computers and Graphics 2 (1977) 135-150
Viezee et al. 72 ==> 2.2.3;
A Sample Computation of Kinematic Properties from Cloud Motion Vectors
W. Viezee, S.M. Serebreny, R.L.Mancuso, and W.E. Shenk
J. Applied Meteorology 11 (1972) 731-741
Walker et al. 78 ==> 2.3;
High Resolution Dynamic Ultrasonic Imaging
J.T. Walker, A.L. Susal, and J.D. Meindl
Proc. SPIE 152 (1978) 54-58
Wall and Karspeck 76 ==> 2.8.1;
Texture Directed Image Compositing for FOCUS
R.J. Wall and M.H. Karspeck
in: Green et al. 76, pp. 7-1 through 7-4
Wallace and Mitchell 79 ==> 2.6.2;
Real-Time Analysis of Three-Dimensional Movement Using Fourier Descriptors
T.P. Wallace and O.R. Mitchell
WCATVI-79, pp. 32-33
Wallace et al. 79 ==> 2.6.2;
Three-Dimensional Shape Analysis Using Local Shape Descriptors
T.P. Wallace, O.R. Mitchell, and K. Fukunaga
IEEE Conference on Pattern Recognition and Image Processing, Chicago/IL, August 6-8, 1979, pp. 292-299

Wang and Burns 76 ==> 2.2.3;
Classifikation and Machine Recognition of Severe Weather Patterns
P.P. Wang and R.C. Burns
IJCPR-76, pp. 198-204

Waterman and Hayes-Roth 78 ==> 2.2.3;
Pattern-Directed Inference Systems
D.A. Waterman and F. Hayes-Roth
Academic Press, New York/NY 1978

Waters 78 ==> 2.2.3;
Time Compositing of Meteorological Satellite Data for Ocean Current Identification
M.P. Waters, III
Proc. 8th Annual Automatic Imagery Pattern Recognition Symposium, R.A. Kirsch and R.N. Nagel (eds.) Gaithersburg/MD, April 3-4, 1978, Electronics Industries Association, Washington/DC 1978, pp. 59-65

Watson 75 ==> 2.2.3;
Geologic Applications of Thermal Infrared Images
K. Watson
Proc. IEEE 63 (1975) 128-137

Weibel 76 ==> 2.8.7; 2.8.7; 2.8.8;
Progress, Success and Problems in Applying Stereology in Biological Research
E.R. Weibel
Proc. 4th Int. Congress for Stereology, pp. 341-350 Gaithersburg/MD, Sept. 4-9, 1975, NBS, Washington/DC 1976

Weinstein and Castleman 72 ==> 2.8.1; 2.8.2;
Reconstruction 3-D Specimens from 2-D Section Images
M. Weinstein and K.R. Castleman
Proc. SPIE 26 (1972) 131-137

Wells 69 ==> 2.8;
Physical Principles of Ultrasonic Diagnosis
P.N.J. Wells
Academic Press, New York/NY 1969

Wendt 73 ==> 2.1.5;
Interframe-Codierung fuer Videosignale
H. Wendt
Internat. Electron. Rundschau 27 (1973) 2-7

Willey et al. 73 ==> 2.8.3;
Computer Graphics in Three Dimensions for Perspective Reconstruction of Brain Ultrastructure
T.J. Willey, R.L. Schultz, and A.H. Gott
IEEE Trans. Biomed. Eng. BME-20 (1973) 288-291

Williams 76 ==> 2.7;
The Robot's Eyes: Vision System for the JPL Robotic Project
D.S. Williams
pp. 14-1 through 14-6 in Green et al. 76

Wilson et al. 79 ==> 2.2.7;
Adaptive Remote Sensing Technology for Feature Recognition and Tracking
R.G. Wilson, W.E. Sivertson, Jr., and G.F. Bullock
IEEE Conference on Pattern Recognition and Image Processing, Chicago/IL, August 6-8, 1979, pp. 623-629

Winkler 75 ==> 2.6.2;
Ein kombinatorisches Auffaelligkeitsmass
G. Winkler
Mitteilungen des Instituts fuer Informationsverarbeitung in Technik und Biologie 1975, Karlsruhe/Germany, pp. 8-13

Winkler and Vattrodt 78a ==> 2.6.2
Measures for Conspicuousness of Images
G. Winkler and K. Vattrodt
Computer Graphics and Image Processing 8 (1978) 355-368
Winkler and Vattrodt 78b ==> 2.6.2;
Masze fuer die Auffaelligkeit in Bildern
G. Winkler and K. Vattrodt
DAGM Symposium Bildverarbeitung und
Mustererkennung, E. Triendl (ed.)
Informatik Fachberichte vol. 17, pp. 237-242
Springer Verlag Berlin-Heidelberg-New York 1978
Winsor and Thomas 73 ==> 2.6.2;
TVAC - A Television Area Correlator Tracking System
C.A. Winsor and F.J. Thomas
25th Annual Southwestern Conference and Exhibition
Record, April 1973, pp. 501-504
Wolf et al. 77 ==> 2.2.2;
Experiments in Automatic Cloud Tracking Using
SMS-GOES Data
D.E. Wolf, D.J. Hall, and R.M. Endlich
J. Applied Meteorology 16 (1977) 1219-1230
Wolf et al. 79 ==> 2.2.2;
An Automatic Method for Determining Cloud Motions
from Pictures Taken by Geosynchronous Weather
Satellites
D.E. Wolf, D.J. Hall, and R.M. Endlich
WCATVI-79, pp. 101-102
Wolferts 73a ==> 2.6.1;
Ein interaktives Verfahren zur teilautomatischen
Auswertung von Luftbildern fuer Verkehrsanalysen
K. Wolferts
Proc. NTG/GI Fachtagung Cognitive Verfahren und Systeme,
Th. Einsele, W. Giloi, H.-H. Nagel (eds.)
Hamburg, April 11-13, 1973
Lecture Notes Economics and Mathem. Systems vol. 83
Springer Verlag Berlin-Heidelberg-New York 1973, pp.307-331
Wolferts 73b ==> 2.6.1;
Teilautomatisches Verfahren zur Bildauswertung
verkehrstechnischer Beobachtungen
K. Wolferts
Dissertation, Fakultaet fuer Bauingenieur- und
Vermessungswesen, Universitaet Karlsruhe (July 1973)
Wolferts 74 ==> 2.6.1;
Special Problems in Interactive Image Processing for
Traffic Analysis
K. Wolferts
IJCPR-74, pp. 1-2
Copenhagen, August 13-15, 1974
Wong and Hall 78 ==> 2.2.4;
Sequential Hierarchical Scene Matching
R.Y. Wong and E.L. Hall
IEEE Trans. Computers C-27 (1978) 359-366
Wong and Hall 79 ==> 2.2.4;
Performance Comparison of Scene Matching Techniques
R.Y. Wong and E.L. Hall
IEEE Trans. Pattern Analysis and Machine Intelligence
PAMI-1 (1979) 325-330

Wood 76 ==> 2.3
New Horizons for Study of the Cardiopulmonary
and Circulatory Systems
E.H. Wood
Chest 69 (1976) 394-408
Yachida et al. 78 ==> 2.5;
Automatic Motion Analysis System of Moving
Objects from the Records of Natural Processes
M. Yachida, M. Asada, and S. Tsuji
IJCPR-78 Nov. 7-10, 1978 Kyoto/Japan, pp. 726-730
Yachida et al. 79a ==> 2.3.3; 2.3.3;
Efficient Analysis of Noisy Dynamic Pictures
Using Plan
M. Yachida, M. Ikeda, and S. Tsuji
WCATVI-79, pp. 90-92
Yachida et al. 79b ==> 2.3.3; 2.3.3;
Plan-Guided Analysis of Noisy Dynamic Images
M. Yachida, M. Ikeda, and S. Tsuji
IJCAI-79, pp. 978-983
Yakimovsky and Cunningham 76 ==> 2.8.5;
On the Problem of Embedding Picture Elements in Regions
Y. Yakimovsky and R. Cunningham
Techn. Memo 33-774, Jet Propulsion Lab.,
Cal. Inst. of Technology, Pasadena/Cal. 1976
Yakimovsky and Cunningham 78 ==> 2.7;
A System for Extracting Three-Dimensional Measurements
from a Stereo-Pair of TV-Cameras
Y. Yakimovsky and R.T. Cunningham
Computer Graphics and Image Processing 7 (1978) 195-210
Yakimovsky and Feldman 73 ==> 2.2.3;
A Semantics-Based Decision Theory Region Analyser
Y. Yakimovsky and J.A. Feldman
IJCAI-73, pp. 580-588
Yasuda et al. 77 ==> 2.1.5; 2.1.7; 2.1.8;
Transmitting 4-MHz TV Signals by Combinational
Difference Coding
H. Yasuda, H. Kuroda, H. Kawanishi, F. Kanaya,
and H. Hashimoto
IEEE Trans. Communications COM-25 (1977) 508-516
Yates and Bandeen 75 ==> 2.2.3; 2.2.3; 2.2.3;
Meteorological Applications of Remote Sensing
from Satellites
H.W. Yates and W.R. Bandeen
Proc. IEEE 63 (1975) 148-163
Young 75 ==> 2.2.2;
The GOES Wind Operation
M.T. Young
paper no. 13 (pp. 111-121) in Bristor 75
Zschunke 77 ==> 2.1.3; 2.1.3; 2.3.3;
DPCM Picture Coding with Adaptive Prediction
W. Zschunke
IEEE Trans. Communications COM-25 (1977) 1295-1302
Zucker and Hummel 79 ==> 2.8.4;
An Optimal Three-Dimensional Edge Operator
S.W. Zucker and R.A. Hummel
IEEE Conference on Pattern Recognition and Image Processing
Chicago/IL, August 6-8, 1979, pp. 162-168

Zucker et al. 75 ==> 2.2.5;
General Purpose Models: Expectations About the Unexpected
S.W. Zucker, A. Rosenfeld, and L.S. Davis
IJCAI-75, pp. 716-721

7. Author Index

McCormick, B.H.	McCormick et al. 76
	Read et al. 77
McIntosh, D.M.	McIntosh 79
McShan, D.	Reinstein et al. 78
McVey, E.S.	Schalkoff and McVey 79
	McVey and Woolard 79
Meindl, J.D.	Walker et al. 78
Mendelsohn, J.	Gardner et al. 77
Mertz, M.	Schultes et al. 79
Milgram, D.L.	Milgram 75 + 77a + 77b
Militzer, D.	Jain et al. 77
Miller, D.	Reeves et al. 79
Miller, D.B.	Miller et al. 75
Miller, J.A.	Miller 77
Milstein, L.B.	Milstein and Lazicky 77 + 78
Misra, P.N.	Misra and Wheeler 77 + 78
Mistretta, C.A.	Mistretta et al. 73
	Kruger et al. 78
Mitchell, O.R.	Wallace and Mitchell 79
	Wallace et al. 79
Miyahara, M.	Miyahara 75
Modestino, J.W.	Ashkar and Modestino 78
Moldenhauer, K.	Brennecke et al. 78b + 79a + 79b
	Heintzen et al. 75
	Lange et al. 76
Moore, R.K.	Moore and Fung 79
Moravec, H.P.	Moravec 77 + 79
Moskowitz, S.	Moskowitz 64
Mounts, F.W.	Haskell et al. 72
	Connor et al. 73
	Candy et al. 71
	Netravali et al. 77
	Mounts 69
	Mounts et al. 77
Moy, R.J.	Pichel et al. 76
Mozley, J.M.	Lee and Mozley 76
Mune, T.	Ishiguro et al. 76
Murphy, J.A.	Limb and Murphy 75a + 75b
Musmann, H.G.	Bauch et al. 74
	Musmann 79 + 80
Myers, D.	Smalling et al. 76
Myers, W.	Myers 78
Mylopoulos, J.	Tsotsos et al. 77 + 78 + 79a + 79b
Nagel, H.-H.	Dreschler and Nagel 78
	Jain and Nagel 77 + 78 + 79
	Jain et al. 77
	Nagel 78a + 78b + 79 + 80
Nagy, G.	Nagy 72
Narasimhan, R.	Pieroni and Narasimhan 74
Natarajan, T.R.	Natarajan and Ahmed 77
Nejdl, I.F.	Gose et al. 76
	Nejdl et al. 78
Netravali, A.N.	Netravali 78
	Netravali and Robbins 79
	Netravali and Rubinstein 77
	Netravali and Stuller 79
	Netravali et al. 77
	Robbins et Netravali 79
	Stuller and Netravali 79
	Mounts et al. 77

Chapter 3 Image Sequence Coding

E. Dubois, B. Prasada, and M. S. Sabri

With 26 Figures

The scope of this chapter encompasses the coding of video signals, both black and white and color, to be displayed on a television screen for human viewing. Discussions of image sequences derived from radar, infrared, and acoustic sources as well as image sequence coding for automatic tracking of objects have been excluded.

3.1 Overview

The NTSC (National Television System Committee) color signal sampled at 10.7 MHz (3 times the color subcarrier frequency), and linearly quantized to 256 levels, gives a data rate of 85.6 Mb/s. It is well known [3.1] that the television signal has a large amount of redundancy. It is also known [3.2-4] that the capacity of the human eye-brain mechanism is several orders of magnitude below 85 Mb/s. Since the cost of digital processing is decreasing much faster than the cost of communications, it is both technically feasible and economically attractive to code the video signal to obtain data compression.

There are a number of applications where such coding might be used. These include point-to-point transmission of commercial television programs, satellite transmission, and video teleconferencing. In these applications, the cost of the transmission facility, type of picture material normally encountered and required quality dictate the amount of bandwidth compression that can reasonably be aimed for. This may range from compression factors of two or three for high-quality entertainment television to factors of fifteen or more for video conferencing.

The redundancy in a scene manifests itself as spatial and temporal correlation. Intraframe coders exploit the former, while interframe coders exploit both. Thus, in general, interframe coding subsumes intraframe coding techniques. In addition to the exploitation of redundancy in the signal, it is also possible to reduce the transmission rate by introducing greater coding degradations in those areas of the picture where human visual sensitivity is low and to reproduce accurately those areas where the visual sensitivity is high. For example, in interframe coding, advantage should be taken of the reduced spatial resolution requirements for moving objects in a scene as compared to stationary objects.

The problem of coding for a given application, thus, is to exploit the statistical and spectral properties of the input pictures, the psychovisual properties of the viewer, and his sensitivity to certain distortions for that specific application, to reduce the transmission rate.

The problem of encoding has been formulated by Shannon as the source coding problem with a fidelity criterion in the general framework of information theory [3.5,6]. Shannon has defined the rate distortion function R(D) of a discrete source, which measures the amount of information needed to specify the output with certain distortion D, defined as the expected loss of fidelity. The expectation is taken over an assumed probability distribution on the source. A typical rate distortion function is shown in Fig.3.1.

At zero distortion, the rate approaches the entropy of the source. As distortion D increases, there is a corresponding decrease in the rate. This theory does provide a bound on attainable performance, and hence useful insights in the evaluation of coding techniques; however, its potential utility has been limited by several factors. Video signal statistics are not precisely known; they do not normally satisfy the condition of stationarity and ergodicity. Further, it is rare that one can obtain an analytically tractable and yet subjectively meaningful fidelity criterion.

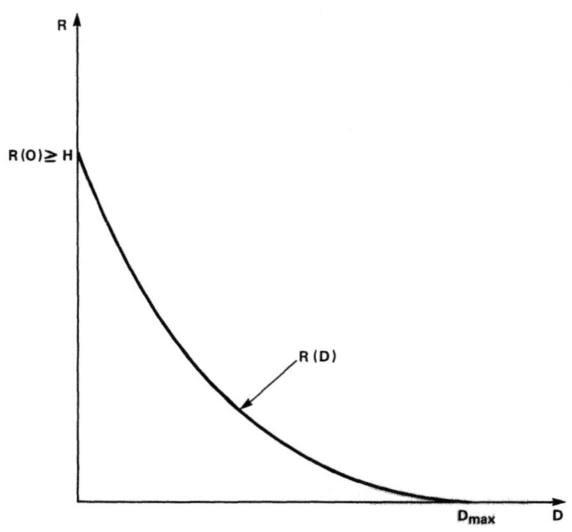

Fig. 3.1. Typical rate distortion function

Interframe coders utilize the similarity between successive frames of a television signal, especially in stationary areas. They also attempt to effect the most favorable exchange between amplitude, spatial, and temporal resolution. The simplest way to exploit the similarity between successive frames is to transmit only changed areas from one frame to another. Since the changed area will be dependent on the size and speed of the moving objects in the scene, a coder of this kind must have a buffer to smooth out the data rate. Due to cost considerations and the perceptual effect of delays, the size of the buffer must be restricted so that it can smooth the data over only a few fields. The coder, thus, has to be constrained to generate a more or less fixed number of bits in every field. It is important in the design of such coders to have several modes of operation. As the activity in a scene increases, the coder switches to modes which provide decreased accuracy of description in a manner least objectionable to the human viewer. Thus one obtains a minimum and graceful degradation in the signal quality while keeping the average bit rate constant. Such coders are called multimode interframe coders.

The art of interframe coding then is to effect the best trade-off between bit rate, cost, and quality for a given application by introducing coding errors (in spatial, amplitude, or temporal domain) where they are least visible. These aspects will be studied in detail in the rest of this chapter.

The characterization of the source (the television signal) and the receiver (the human viewer) is first developed in Sects.3.2,3. Emphasis is placed on three-dimensional spatiotemporal descriptions of signal properties (correlations, spectrum) and relevant psychovisual properties of the viewer, and their implications to coding.

This is followed by a discussion of predictive coding, with special emphasis on coding of the quantized prediction error, which is of central importance in interframe coding. A detailed description of movement-compensated predictive coding is also presented. Transform domain coding and hybrid coding are then discussed. These coding techniques comprise Sects.3.4-6.

Multimode coders are discussed in Sect.3.7. The basic principle of graceful degradation of signal quality and techniques used to achieve this are presented. An illustrative example is discussed.

The problem of coding color signals is treated in Sect.3.8. The effect of the introduction of color, in both component and composite signal form, on previously described techniques is pointed out.

The chapter closes with discussion of current trends. A brief description of the digital video sequence store (DVS), a general purpose simulator for interframe coding studies, is given in the Appendix.

3.2 The Television Signal

3.2.1 The Digital Television Signal

a) *Scanning*

The task of an image communication system is to transmit a three-dimensional time-varying image. To accomplish this over a conventional communication channel, it is necessary to sample this three-dimensional signal and map the samples into a one-dimensional signal for transmission. There are many ways that this can be done, but the technique universally used in television is rectilinear scanning, and we will restrict the discussion to this method.

Rectilinear scanning consists of sampling the moving image in temporal and vertical dimensions by successively transmitting N lines of an image during a period of T_f seconds. The number of lines per frame depends on the spatial bandwidth of the signal and the desired spatial resolution, while the frame repetition rate $(1/T_{fr})$ is governed by requirements of adequate motion rendition and freedom from flicker. Thus, these parameters depend on both the signal properties, and viewer requirements. It has been found that, while approximately 25 pictures per second are required to depict smooth motion, at least 50 pictures per second are necessary to eliminate flicker. (It should be noted that flicker is due to nonideal signal reconstruction in the receiver.) The technique used in television to equalize the disparity between these two figures is 2:1 line interlace. In this method each frame is divided into two fields; every second line is scanned in one field period, and the remaining lines are scanned in the next field period. The commonly used field frequencies are 60 Hz and 50 Hz, resulting in 30 or 25 pictures per second, which is adequate for good motion rendition. Further, in the interlaced picture there is no large area flicker at 30 or 25 Hz, but rather there is a less objectionable interline flicker.

b) *Spectrum of Scanned Signal*

The spectrum of the scanned signal, treated as a one-dimensional signal, has been considered by MERTZ and GRAY [3.7] and FRANKS [3.8]. However, in analysis and processing of the video signal, it is much more natural and profitable to treat the signal in its three-dimensional form, and to deal with the three-dimensional spectrum. Since the scanning consists of vertical and temporal sampling, this spectrum is simply obtained by replicating the three-dimensional spectrum of the original continuous scene in the vertical and temporal frequency dimensions with an appropriate modification to account for interlace.

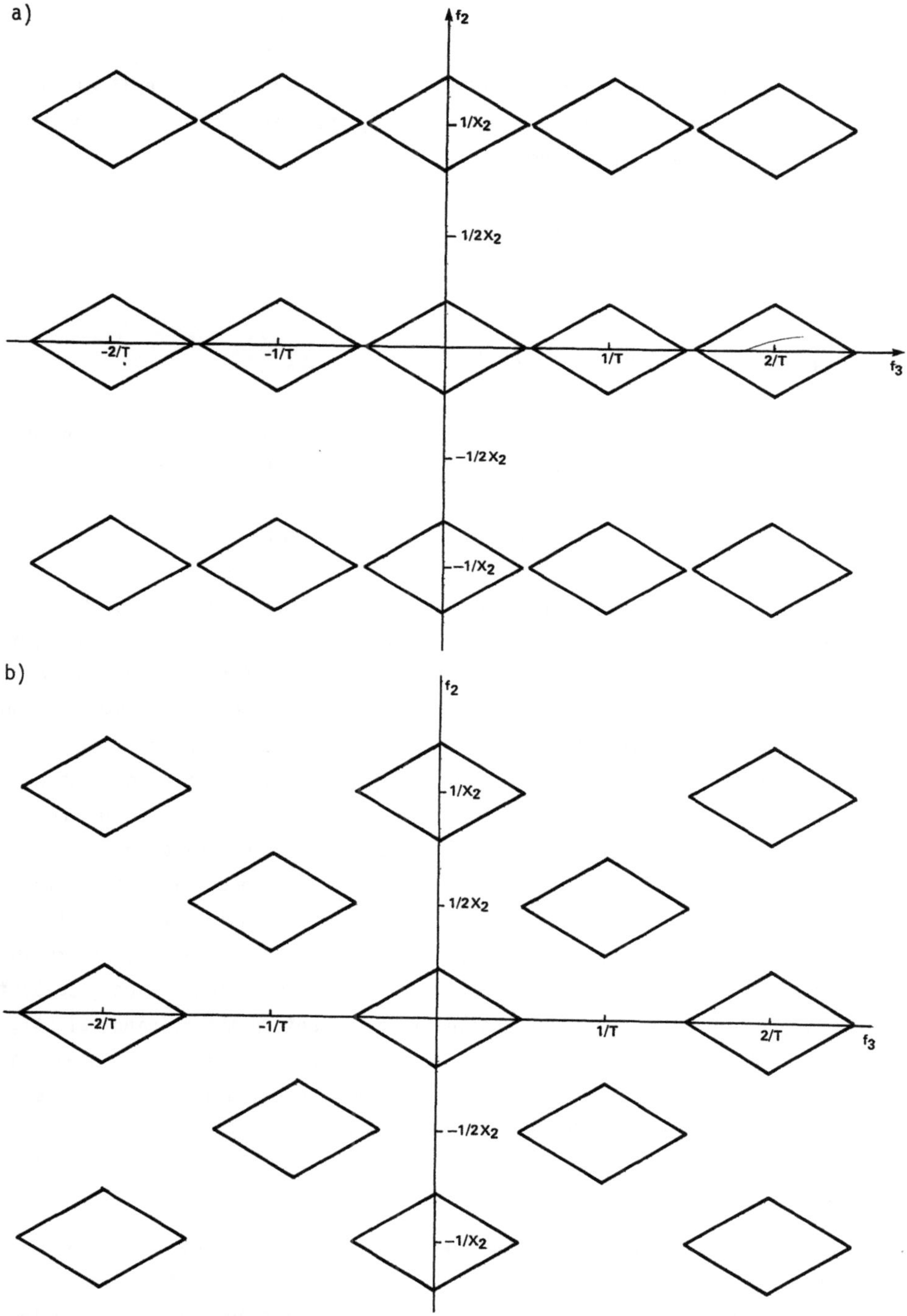

Fig. 3.2a,b. Vertical temporal spectrum of scanned video signal. (a) Sequential scanning, (b) 2:1 line-interlaced scanning

Specifically, let $u_a(x_1,x_2,t)$ be the continuous scene, where x_1 and x_2 are horizontal and vertical spatial dimensions and t is time, and $S_{u_a}(f_1,f_2,f_3)$ the power spectral density of this signal. If u_a is sampled in vertical and temporal dimensions with sampling intervals X_2 and T to obtain the sequentially scanned (noninterlaced) signal

$$u(x_1,m_2,m_3) = u_a(x_1,m_2X_2,m_3T) \quad ,$$

its spectrum is given by

$$S_u(f_1,f_2,f_3) = \frac{1}{TX_2} \sum_{r=-\infty}^{\infty} \sum_{s=-\infty}^{\infty} S_{u_a}\left(f_1,f_2+\frac{r}{X_2},f_3+\frac{s}{T}\right) \quad .$$

Thus, S_{u_a} is repeated in vertical and temporal frequency dimensions with period $1/X_2$ and $1/T$, respectively. If u_a is band limited, such that

$$S_{u_a}(f_1,f_2,f_3) = 0 \qquad |f_2| > 1/2X_2 \quad , \quad |f_3| > 1/2T$$

then there is no overlap or aliasing introduced by the scanning, and the original scene could, in principle, be reconstructed exactly by an ideal two-dimensional low-pass filter. This is in fact the task of the television receiver. This situation is illustrated in Fig.3.2a which shows a cross section of the three-dimensional spectrum of the scanned signal in the f_2f_3 plane.

Interlace can be accounted for by multiplying the noninterlaced scanned signal by a modulating waveform which is zero in every second line in one field, and in every other line in the second field and one elsewhere [3.9], such as $[1+(-1)^{m_2+m_3}]/2$. The resulting spatiotemporal spectrum is shown in Fig.3.2b. We see that if the signal does not simultaneously have both high spatial and temporal frequencies, aliasing will not occur. Since it is known that the human visual system has poor response at these frequencies (see Sect. 3.3.1), even if such higher frequencies were present in the original signal, they could be filtered out without affecting picture quality. This shows that line interlace can allow the same quality of reproduction as noninterlaced scanning with a lower spatiotemporal sampling rate.

c) *Sampling*

Henceforth, it will be assumed that the original analog video signal is obtained by 2:1 line interlaced scanning. It has been noted that the signal is sampled in vertical and temporal dimensions and continuous in the horizontal dimension. Furthermore these vertical and temporal sampling intervals are generally predetermined by the particular TV standard in a country and hence the digital system designer has little control over them. To obtain a digital signal, it is now necessary to sample and quantize the video signal in the horizontal dimension. Assuming uniform spacing of samples in the horizontal dimension, the system designer has the flexibility to choose the horizontal sampling frequency as well as the spatial and horizontal-temporal projections of the sampling pattern. The minimum sample rate would be obtained by choosing the sampling pattern so that the number of samples per unit volume is minimized subject to the absence of aliasing [3.10]. This would in general lead to a nonrectangular sampling as is already the case for the vertical-temporal pattern. The effect of this sampling is the replication of the three-dimensional spectrum of Fig.3.2b in the horizontal frequency dimension but with possible vertical and temporal offsets due to the sampling pattern.

The simplest technique for analyzing such a nonrectangular sampling is to decompose the sampling grid into a superposition of rectangular grids. Thus, the sampled waveform can be expressed

$$u(x_1,x_2,t) = u_a(x_1,x_2,t)d(x_1,x_2,t)$$

where $d(x_1,x_2,t)$ is a three-dimensional array of delta functions positioned on the sampling grid. For a superposition of rectangular grids,

$$\begin{aligned} d(x_1,x_2,t) = &\sum_{i_1=-\infty}^{\infty}\sum_{i_2=-\infty}^{\infty}\sum_{i_3=-\infty}^{\infty} \delta(x_1-i_1X_1,x_2-i_2X_2,t-i_3T) \\ &+ \delta\left[x_1-(i_1+\alpha_1)X_1,x_2-(i_2+\alpha_2)X_2,t-(i_3+\alpha_3)T\right] \end{aligned}$$

where $0<\alpha_i<1$ defines the offset between the two grids, and X_1, X_2, T are the basic sampling intervals for the rectangular grids. The spectrum of the sampled waveform is given by

$$U(f_1,f_2,f_3) = U_a(f_1,f_2,f_3) * D(f_1,f_2,f_3)$$

where $*$ denotes three-dimensional convolution, and

$$\begin{aligned} D(f_1,f_2,f_3) = &\frac{1}{X_1X_2T}\sum_{k_1=-\infty}^{\infty}\sum_{k_2=-\infty}^{\infty}\sum_{k_3=-\infty}^{\infty} \delta(f_1-k_1/X_1,f_2-k_2/X_2,f_3-k_3/T) \\ &\cdot \left\{1+\exp[-j2\pi(\alpha_1k_1+\alpha_2k_2+\alpha_3k_3)]\right\} \quad . \end{aligned}$$

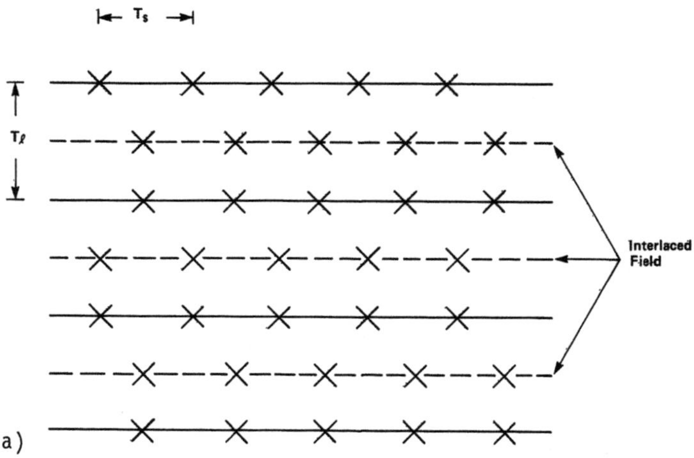

a)

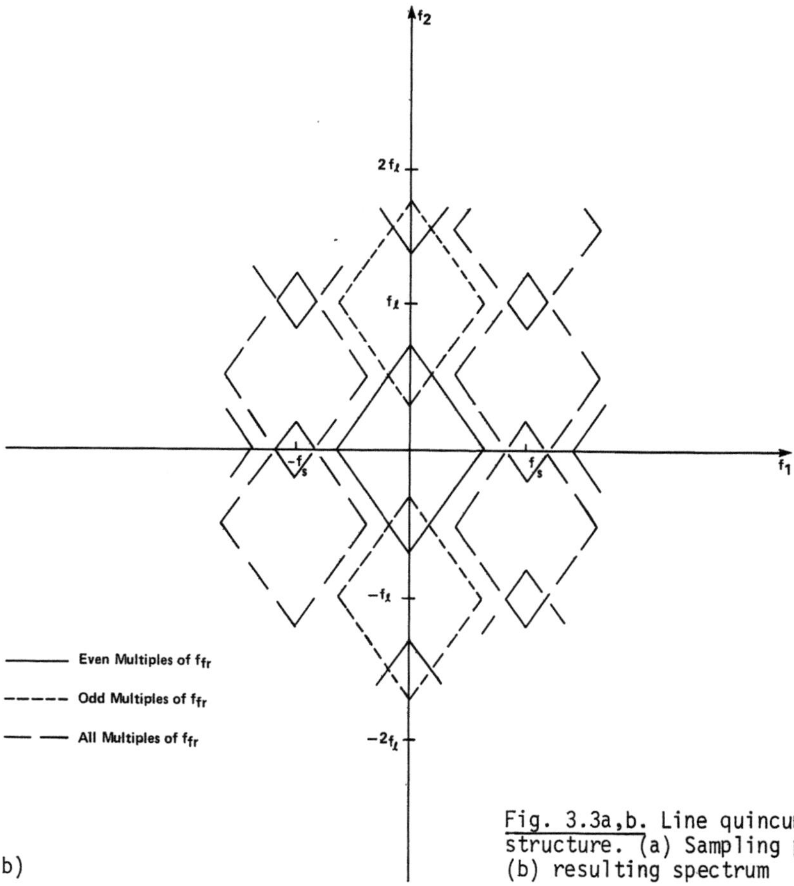

b)

Fig. 3.3a,b. Line quincunx sampling structure. (a) Sampling pattern, (b) resulting spectrum

This causes the spectrum to be replicated with a basic period of $1/X_1, 1/X_2$, $1/T$ with these replications being multiplied by the term $\{1+\exp[-j2\pi(\alpha_1 k_1+\alpha_2 k_2+\alpha_3 k_3)]\}$ which causes them to cancel for certain values of k_1, k_2, k_3, depending on α_1, α_2, and α_3.

Practical considerations often introduce certain constraints. For example, to avoid the need for complicated temporal filters requiring many frame memories, the horizontal-temporal projection of the sampling pattern should be rectangular. SABATIER and KRETZ [3.11] have studied several sampling patterns satisfying this constraint, and have found a structure referred to as line quincunx, shown in Fig.3.3, to give good results. This pattern is the superposition of four rectangular grids having a basic period of T_s, $2T_\ell$, T_{fr}. Figure 3.3b shows the spatial projection of the spectrum for a signal sampled with this structure. Solid components are at even multiples of f_{fr}, dotted components are at odd multiples of f_{fr}. The original spectrum is reproduced unaliased and can be recovered by a suitable three-dimensional filtering. In practice, a spatial filter is used to eliminate the components at $(\pm f_s, \pm f_\ell/2)$ and the task of eliminating components at $(0, \pm f_\ell)$ is left to the television receiver.

3.2.2 Characterization of the Sampled Video Signal

It will be assumed that the video signal has been sampled above the Nyquist rate in a suitable sampling pattern and quantized with a sufficient number of levels (usually 7 or 8 bits per pel) so that the digitization is transparent to the viewer. In order to be able to transmit or store this digital video signal efficiently, it is essential that it be accurately characterized. This is generally attempted by specifying a stochastic image model. Many such models have been proposed, but none are successful in accurately characterizing the full gamut of natural moving scenes. However, some simplified models have been successful in allowing various specific properties of the video signal to be utilized for efficient coding.

The general three-dimensional stochastic process $u(x_1, x_2, t)$ is completely specified by the joint probability densities

$$p(u_1, u_2, \ldots, u_J, \underline{x_1}, \underline{x_2}, \ldots, \underline{x_J})$$

for all sets of J sample points [3.12]. Here $\underline{x}$ denotes the point (x_1, x_2, t). However, such high-order joint probability density functions for images are not known. Many coding techniques exploit only certain known and easily obtainable properties of image statistics, such as first- and second-order moments, and statistics of differential signals.

In general, the amplitude histogram of an image is rather irregular, with peaks in high- and low-luminance regions. When averaged over a large class of images, this gives a density which is approximately uniform. Thus, the first-order probability density is of little direct use. The autocovariance function of an image (assume a wide sense stationary image process) is given by

$$R_u(\underline{\tau}) = E[(u(\underline{x})-m)(u(\underline{x}+\underline{\tau})-m)]$$

where $m = E[u]$. Models for the autocovariance function which have been found to be useful are the exponential functions

$$R_1(\underline{\tau}) = \exp(-k_1|\tau_1|-k_2|\tau_2|-k_3|\tau_3|) \tag{3.1}$$

and

$$R_2(\underline{\tau}) = \exp(-\sqrt{k_1\tau_1^2+k_2\tau_2^2} - k_3|\tau_3|) \quad . \tag{3.2}$$

Note that the model (3.1) is separable in all dimensions while (3.2) is non-separable spatially. The spatially separable model is often more appropriate for scenes of man-made objects with many horizontal and vertical edges, while a circularly symmetric model may be better for "natural scenes". Such models may be used for the design of predictive coders as discussed in Sect.3.4.

It is often easier to characterize certain differential signals such as those used in predictive coding. For example, a good estimate of the probability density of a signal is essential for efficient quantizing. Various models such as Laplacian and Gamma densities have been found to fit the differential signals encountered in predictive coders. This will be discussed further in Sect.3.4.

The assumption of stationarity for image signals is very weak. In fact, scenes are composed of many objects, some of which may be textured, others of constant intensity, some moving, others fixed. Models which can account for this structure would be of great utility. Some attempts at arriving at such models include the Yan and Sakrison two-component model [3.13], in which the image is assumed to be composed of the sum of a piecewise linear function, and a residual textural component. The residual component is more accurately representable as a stationary process.

Successful models for time-varying imagery must account for the fact that the scene is composed of many objects, some of which change their position from frame to frame. In such a model, the dynamic component of the scene could be described by a displacement field rather than by actual image intensities at each frame. It is hypothesized that this displacement field could be more economically represented than the actual image field. This model is the basis for movement-compensated coders discussed in Sect.3.5.

3.3 Some Relevant Psychovisual Properties of the Viewer

To understand the fidelity requirements for interframe coding, a knowledge of the relevant properties of vision is required. Extensive literature is available on the psychophysics of vision. However, it does not provide us at this time with a clear insight into the process of perception. In this section, we will discuss some work that is directly relevant to the coding of television image sequences.

For coding of television pictures with very low distortion the degradation due to coding will be near the visual threshold. Thus, threshold data will be useful. On the other hand, suprathreshold data are more applicable to the coding of television pictures in applications where visible distortion can be tolerated for short periods of time, e.g., in video-conferencing situations. An extensive bibliography of papers relative to psychovisual properties can be found in [3.14].

We will now study the linear behavior of the visual system in terms of filtering and the nonlinear effects of masking by suprathreshold edges.

3.3.1 Spatiotemporal Response of the Human Visual System

Studies have been made to obtain the response of the human visual system to inputs which vary both as a function of space and time. ROBSON [3.15] and KELLY [3.16] have used flickering gratings that are characterized by

$$L = L_0[1+m\cos(2\pi u_0 x)\cos(2\pi f_0 t)]$$

where L_0 is the average luminance, u_0 the spatial frequency, and f_0 the temporal frequency. Figure 3.4 shows a linearly scaled perspective view of a surface, to which Robson's data shown in Fig.3.5 approximates [3.17]. Even though the surface has been drawn over all four quadrants, the measurement corresponds only to positive frequencies. The plot has been made on the as-

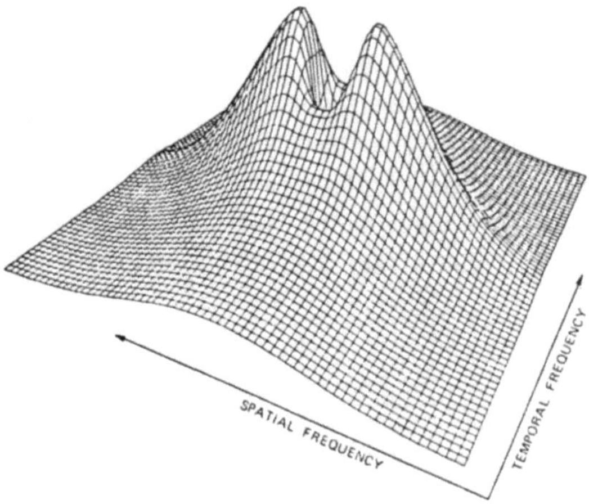

Fig. 3.4. Perspective view of spatiotemporal frequency response [3.17]

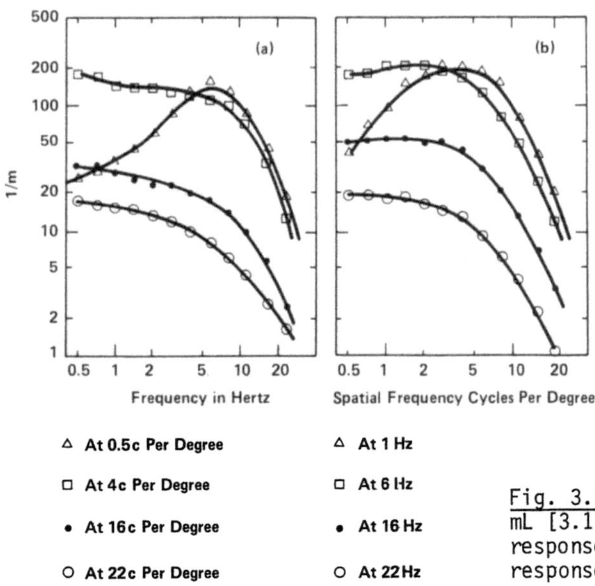

Fig. 3.5a,b. Robson's data at 6.3 mL [3.17]. (a) Temporal frequency response, (b) spatial frequency response

sumption of quadrantal symmetry. It can be seen from the plot that the spatiotemporal response is not separable into a product of spatial and temporal responses. Thus, based on a linear system model, the human visual system can be represented by a three-dimensional bandpass filter which has the highest response at a spatial frequency of 5 c/deg and zero temporal frequency at a given level of adaptation (6.3 mL). The cutoff bandwidth is 10 c/deg in the spatial frequency and about 10 Hz in the temporal dimension.

Examination of the perspective plot indicates certain other interesting features. At high temporal frequencies, the spatial contrast sensitivity is reduced, indicating that the sensitivity of the human visual system is low to fine spatial detail in rapidly moving objects. Similarly, at high spatial frequencies, there is an overall decrease in flicker sensitivity. Interlaced scanning takes advantage of this.

3.3.2 Perception in Moving Areas

The behavior of the human visual system is quite different in the tracking and nontracking mode. If an image can be tracked, the retinal integration is minimized and the spatial resolution requirement in the moving area is high. However, if an object cannot be easily tracked, then the human visual system can tolerate a loss of spatial resolution. These conclusions are supported by a study of MIYAHARA [3.18]. Most of the movements encountered on the television screen, such as head or hand movements, cannot be easily tracked.

3.3.3 Temporal Masking

An interesting experiment has been reported by SEYLER and BUDRIKIS [3.19] on detail perception after scene changes in television image presentations. They have found that the human observer does not perceive a temporary reduction of spatial detail after scene changes. In their experiment, the bandwidth of the broadcast television signal was reduced from 5 MHz to 250 kHz at each scene change by means of an electronic variable bandwidth low-pass filter. It was found that an average recovery time of 780 ms was acceptable. From the initial bandwidth of 250 kHz, the final bandwidth of 5 MHz was achieved in 780 ms with an exponential increase of bandwidth with time. The experiment has implications for interframe coding and the size of buffer storage in such systems.

Recently, masking provided by a moving object on the newly exposed background in a television picture has been studied [3.20]. A series of experiments has been performed using a natural scene as a background and a synthetic moving object. In these experiments, the spatial resolution of newly exposed background is reduced in a controlled manner. Results indicate that the moving object provides significant masking on the newly exposed background.

3.3.4 Exchange of Spatial, Temporal, and Amplitude Resolution

In setting television standards, the resolution required in the spatial domain is determined using still pictures. The amplitude resolution is based on no visible difference between an original nonmoving test chart and the quantized version. The temporal resolution is determined by the flicker requirements. It is well known that for adequate representation of the pictures, the viewer does not require the upper bound of resolution in all three domains simultaneously. For example in a television scene, the nonmoving parts of the picture require low temporal resolution and high spatial resolution. The moving parts require high temporal resolution and low spatial resolution. Several examples of exchange of spatial and temporal resolution are present in the literature [3.21-23]. Similarly, by taking advantage of the spatial masking properties, the amplitude resolution can be lowered in areas of a picture requiring high spatial resolution [3.24]. At this time sufficient information is not available for a systematic and subjectively optimum exchange of resolution in the three domains.

3.4 Predictive Coding

3.4.1 Philosophy of Predictive Coding

Predictive coding schemes exploit the redundancy in the input video signal in order to reduce the transmission rate (or storage requirements) required to communicate (or store) these signals with a given fidelity. Due to the correlation between neighboring (in space and time) elements of the signal, a given sample value can be predicted from previously transmitted samples. The most common form of predictive coding is differential pulse code modulation (DPCM). The basic DPCM coder/decoder (Codec) structure is illustrated in Fig.3.6. The prediction error is quantized within the loop and transmitted.

It is easily seen from Fig.3.6 that in the absence of transmission errors, and with identical predictors at transmitter and receiver, the reconstruction

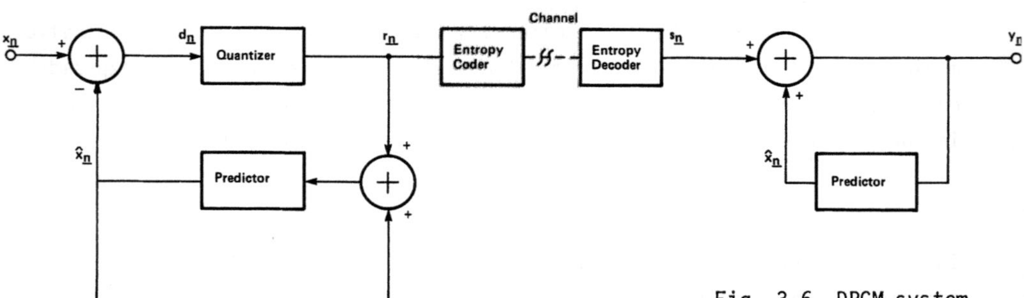

Fig. 3.6. DPCM system

error $y_n - x_n$ is equal to the error caused by quantizing the prediction error, i.e., $r_n - d_n$. The quantizer should be designed to match the statistics of the prediction error d_n. If the predictor is improved, thus decreasing the variance of the prediction error, then for a fixed number of quantization levels, the variance of the quantization error can be reduced, improving the fidelity with which the input is reconstructed. Conversely, for a given fidelity, fewer quantization levels are required, thus reducing the required transmission rate.

The statistics of the prediction error signal d_n are not highly sensitive to the presence of the quantizer in the loop. Hence the predictor can first be designed assuming no quantization (and hence a linear system), and then a quantizer designed to match the statistics of the resulting prediction error. If desired, these steps can be repeated with this quantizer now in the loop. This approach, although perhaps suboptimal, allows one to consider the predictor and quantizer design problems separately.

3.4.2 Predictor Design

The predictor of Fig.3.6 can be an arbitrary function of previously transmitted pels. The simplest and most widely used predictors are fixed linear predictors. These work well for images which can be satisfactorily modeled as samples of a stationary random process. Since this is in general not the case, adaptive linear predictors and nonlinear predictors can lead to better results. The fact that the image in general consists of moving objects on a fixed background has led to the concept of movement-compensated prediction, to be discussed in Sect.3.5.

The performance of any component of a predictive coder can only be judged by its effect on the final transmission rate, subject to a given quality. Thus, the design of a predictor depends on the fidelity criterion used. If this fidelity criterion is mean-squared error, then under reasonable conditions the bit rate increases monotonically with mean-square prediction error. Thus, the mean-square prediction error is generally used to evaluate the effectiveness of a predictor. The ratio of signal variance to prediction error variance gives a measure of prediction gain. However, the actual relation between bit rate and mean-square prediction error is not linear, and the bit-rate reduction achieved by reducing the mean-square prediction error depends on the quantization scheme and resulting fidelity. Since the mean-square-error criterion does not accurately reflect the human viewer's fidelity requirements, two predictors which yield about the same mean-square prediction error can result in markedly different subjective quality.

An alternative performance criterion used to evaluate predictors is differential entropy of the prediction error d. In the case where d has density $P_\sigma = P_1(d/\sigma)/\sigma$ (i.e., the effect of changing the predictor simply scales the density), then

$$h(P_\sigma) = -\int_{-\infty}^{\infty} P_\sigma(x)\,\log[P_\sigma(x)]dx$$

$$= -\int_{-\infty}^{\infty} P_1(x)\,\log[P_1(x)]dx + \log\sigma = h(P_1) + \log\sigma \quad .$$

Thus, in this case mean-square prediction error and differential entropy are monotonically related, and the predictor which minimizes one also minimizes the other. This argument does not necessarily carry over if changing the predictor changes the distribution of d by other than a scaling.

a) *Linear Predictors*

Let $\{u_{\underline{n}-\underline{i}}\}$, $\underline{i}\in I$ be a set of previously transmitted pels in the neighborhood of $u_{\underline{n}}$. The set I specifies the set of pels to be used for the prediction. Note that $\underline{0}\notin I$. Figure 3.7 shows a typical set I, comprising pels in three consecutive fields. A linear prediction of $u_{\underline{n}}$ based on $\{u_{\underline{n}-\underline{i}}\}$ is

$$\hat{u}_{\underline{n}} = \sum_{\underline{i}\in I} a_{\underline{n}}(\underline{i})u_{\underline{n}-\underline{i}} \quad . \tag{3.3}$$

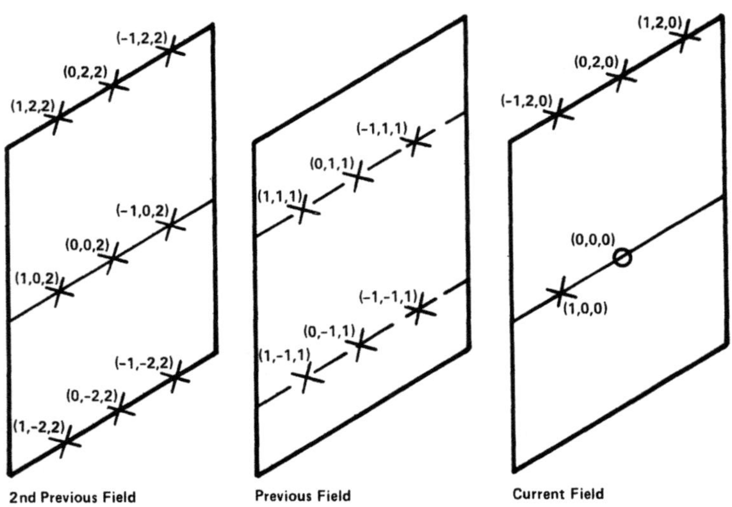

Fig. 3.7. Pels in neighborhood of current pel used to form prediction

This prediction is said to be fixed or time invariant if $a_n(\underline{i})$ is independent of $\underline{n}$. The best mean-square predictor is obtained by choosing $a_n(\underline{i})$ to minimize $E[\hat{u}_n-u_n]^2$. If u_n is a sample of a wide sense stationary process, a fixed predictor results, with coefficients given by the solution to the normal equations

$$\sum_{\underline{i}\varepsilon I} a(\underline{i})R_u(\underline{i}-\underline{k}) = R_u(\underline{k}) \qquad \underline{k}\ \varepsilon\ I \quad . \tag{3.4}$$

Using these coefficients, the mean-square error is

$$R_u(0) - \sum_{\underline{i}\varepsilon I} a(\underline{i})R_u(\underline{i}) \quad . \tag{3.5}$$

Since $R_u(\underline{0}) = \sigma_u^2$, then $\sum_{\underline{i}\varepsilon I} a_i R_u(\underline{i})$ represents the reduction in the variance of the transmitted signal due to the prediction, and is a measure of the prediction gain.

The decoder in Fig.3.6 is in general a three-dimensional recursive digital filter. In a practical implementation, it is necessary that this filter be stable. Although stability is assured for a one-dimensional prediction, WOODS [3.25] has demonstrated that the minimum mean-square-error predictor in two dimensions (and thus by implication also in three dimensions) can result in an unstable decoder. This could perhaps be avoided by choosing the $a(\underline{i})$ to minimize the mean-square error subject to a constraint ensuring stability.

O'NEAL [3.26] has studied some one- and two-dimensional minimum mean-square-error predictors. He found that good performance is obtained by basing the prediction on only two pels, the previous horizontally and vertically adjacent elements. For the pictures he studied (head and shoulders scenes) prediction gains of 7 to 12 dB were obtained. Little further could be gained by using more pels in the same field to form the prediction. HASKELL [3.27] studied three-dimensional linear predictors, using 22 pels in the current and two previous fields, solving (3.4) for each field. However, only moving area pels were included in the computation, and the resulting mean-square prediction error was not reported, so it is difficult to assess the further gains, although his results seem to indicate approximately 7 or 8 dB additional prediction gain.

In practice, the picture statistics are not stationary and (3.4) must be solved for each picture. Although Haskell obtained good results by solving (3.4) for each field, the resulting computation would be prohibitive in a real-time coding situation. Thus, various simple, fixed predictors are generally used.

Table 3.1. Common predictors for interframe coders $\hat{x}(\underline{n}) = \sum_{\underline{i} \in I} a(\underline{i}) x(\underline{n}-\underline{i})$

Transmitted signal $x - \hat{x}$	Predictor Set I	Predictor Coefficients $a(\underline{i})$
Frame difference	(0,0,2)	1
Element difference	(1,0,0)	1
Element difference of frame difference	(1,0,0),(0,0,2),(1,0,2)	1,1,-1
Line difference of frame difference	(0,2,0),(0,0,2),(0,2,2)	1,1,-1
Field difference	(0,1,1),(0,-1,1)	1/2,1/2
Element difference of field difference	(1,0,0),(0,1,1),(0,-1,1) (1,1,1),(1,-1,1)	1,1/2,1/2,-1/2,-1/2

HASKELL [3.27] studied the performance of a number of such fixed predictors on scenes with varying amount of motion. As before, the performance criterion was entropy of the prediction error signal. These predictors are most easily described in terms of the transmitted signal, for example, frame difference when using previous frame prediction. Table 3.1 lists the predictors studied by Haskell. Refer to Fig.3.7 for the relative locations of the pels used in the prediction. As one would expect, frame difference prediction performs well in areas with little motion, while intrafield predictors such as element difference do better when there is greater motion. The combinational intra-inter-field schemes are better than either of these and tend to be less sensitive to the amount of motion. Of the predictors studied by Haskell, element difference of field difference gave the best performance.

b) *Nonlinear Predictors*

The fact that images are not stationary and in fact contain many edges and contours has led to the use of nonlinear predictors. These predictors attempt to determine the direction of contours in the image, and choose the prediction accordingly. The prediction is still a function of previously transmitted pels, but this function is now nonlinear. The basic idea is illustrated by the following simple interframe predictor. Let $\underline{i}_1 = (1,0,0)$, $\underline{i}_2 = (0,0,2)$, $\underline{i}_3 = (1,0,2)$ (see Fig.3.7). Then

$$\hat{u}(\underline{n}) = \begin{cases} u(\underline{n}-\underline{i}_1) & \text{if} \quad |u(\underline{n}-\underline{i}_1)-u(\underline{n}-\underline{i}_3)| > |u(\underline{n}-\underline{i}_2)-u(\underline{n}-\underline{i}_3)| \\ u(\underline{n}-\underline{i}_2) & \text{otherwise} \quad . \end{cases} \tag{3.6}$$

Thus, $u(\underline{n}-\underline{i}_1)$, the previous element, is used as the prediction if there is significant motion near $u(\underline{n})$, while $u(\underline{n}-\underline{i}_2)$, the previous frame, is used if there is none. Intraframe predictors of this type have been proposed by GRAHAM [3.28], CONNOR et al. [3.29] and ZSCHUNKE [3.30].

A more complex three-dimensional nonlinear predictor has been proposed by DUKHOVICH and O'NEAL [3.31]. Three representative nonlinear predictors, S_1, S_2, S_3, of the type given by (3.6) are obtained in three planes (passing through the points [(0,0,0),(1,0,0),(0,1,1)], [(0,0,0),(1,0,0),(0,-1,1)] and [(0,0,0),(0,2,0),(0,0,2)]). The prediction is then formed as a linear combination of S_1, S_2 and S_3, i.e.,

$$\hat{u} = \alpha_1 S_1 + \alpha_2 S_2 + \alpha_3 S_3 \quad . \tag{3.7}$$

The α_i are then chosen to minimize the mean-square prediction error. They found that the optimal α_i are insensitive to changing image statistics, and thus predetermined fixed values can be used (they found α_1=.36, α_2=.37, α_3=.27). This prediction gave a 2 to 3 dB increase in prediction gain over a fixed best linear mean-square predictor based on pels at (1,0,0), (0,1,1), (0,-1,1). Presumably, this latter predictor must be optimized more frequently.

3.4.3 Quantization

Having selected a prediction strategy, the next step in the design of a predictive coder is to obtain the input-output characteristic for the quantizer. This quantizer may be fixed or it may be allowed to adapt to local picture properties. The design of the quantizer is also influenced by the code assignment procedure used to transmit the quantized prediction error. The general principle of quantizer design is to minimize some measure of picture distortion subject to a constraint on the transmission rate, given the type of code assignment that will be done.

A typical quantizing characteristic is shown in Fig.3.8. The input x to the quantizer may be continuous, or finely quantized with a uniform quantizer, such as when the input to the coder is a PCM signal. The output y takes on a discrete set of levels y_i, such that

$$Q(x) = y_i \qquad \text{where } x_i < x \leqq x_{i+1} \quad .$$

The y_i are referred to as representative levels, while the x_i are known as decision levels.

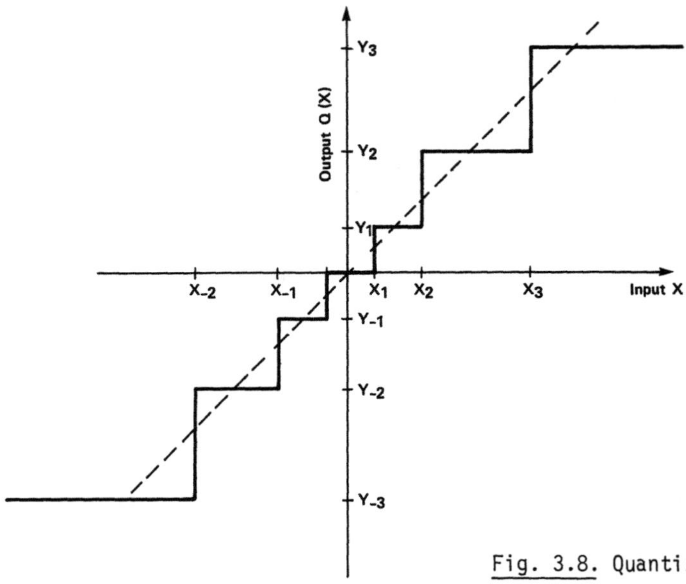

Fig. 3.8. Quantizer characteristic

If a fixed rate code is used to code the levels y_i, then a constraint on the transmission rate is in essence a constraint on the number of quantization levels. For N levels, the rate is $\log_2 N$ bits/pel. However, if N is not a power of 2, a block coding scheme will be required to achieve this. If variable-length code words are to be used, the transmission rate can be made close to the entropy of the quantizer output. The problem is thus to choose the quantizer representative and decision levels in order to minimize the expected distortion, subject to a constraint on either the number of levels, or the entropy of the quantizer output.

The major difficulty with this approach is the choice of a suitable subjective distortion criterion. The criterion most widely used is mean-square error $E[Q(x)-x]^2$, in which case the quantizer design problem is easily solved if the probability density function for the quantizer input (in our case the prediction error) is known. For the case of a fixed number of quantizer levels, MAX [3.32] has shown that the optimal quantizer is specified by

$$x_i = (y_{i-1}+y_i)/2$$

and

$$y_i = \int_{x_i}^{x_{i+1}} x p(x) dx \Big/ \int_{x_i}^{x_{i+1}} p(x) dx \quad . \tag{3.8}$$

Thus, the decision levels lie midway between representative levels, while representative levels are at the centroid of a quantizing interval. Given the probability density, levels which satisfy (3.8) can be determined numerically.

If the constraint is on output entropy, the quantizers are much less companded. Asymptotically, when the quantizing interval is small, uniform quantizers are optimal [3.33]. In the low-bit-rate region, which is of greater practical importance, this is not exactly so. However, experimental results show that uniform quantizers are near optimal at all rates [3.34] for probability density functions of practical interest, and exactly optimal for exponential and Laplacian densities.

Although mean-square error correlates reasonably well with perceived distortion, especially at small distortions, the mean-square-error criterion does not reflect many properties of the human visual system which could be utilized by a coder. An important example is the masking of quantization noise by features in the image such as edges. We note that the mean-square-error criterion is independent of the input, and depends only on the error. Some work has been done by several authors on quantizers which minimize a measure of "visibility" of quantization noise for intraframe prediction [3.35] as well as for a weighted mean-square-error criterion [3.36], but little work has been done for three-dimensional predictors, such as those of Table 3.1.

Greater scope for improvement over the fixed quantizers discussed previously is possible by the use of adaptive quantizers. The adaptation can be based on statistical, and/or psychovisual criteria, and can involve switching between a number of fixed quantizers, or changing the basic step size of a given quantizer. For example, in areas of the picture where there is very little activity, a fine quantizer can be used, and in areas with more activity, the quantization can be coarser [3.24,37].

3.4.4 Code Assignment

As mentioned previously, the processes of code assignment and quantization are interdependent. In particular the optimal quantization characteristic strongly depends on the code assignment to be used, either fixed or variable length. The two processes may interact dynamically as will be seen later.

The most common code assignment techniques used in interframe coding are variable-word-length coding and run-length coding. The latter is used in some form in virtually all interframe predictive coders, while the former is becoming increasingly more common.

a) *Variable-Word-Length Coding*

The principle of variable-word-length coding is simple. Assuming that the output levels of the quantizer are not equiprobable, code words of short length can be assigned to the most probable levels and words of longer length to the less probable levels. This results in a lower average word length than can be obtained by a fixed-length code.

The code with the minimum average code word length is the Huffman code [3.38]. This is a uniquely decodable (comma-free) code with average code word length bounded by

$$H \leq \bar{\ell} < H + 1$$

where H is the entropy of the quantizer output. Although the exact probability mass function for the quantizer output must be known to construct the Huffman code, it has been found that good performance can be obtained if the code is designed over an ensemble of pictures. There exist alternatives to the Huffman code with almost as good performance which are much more easily instrumentable [3.39].

Because the coder puts out information at a variable rate, a buffer must be provided to smooth the rate of information for transmission over a fixed-rate channel. The capacity of the buffer must be large enough to accommodate the peak output which occurs in periods of great activity. This problem is more acute when the run-length coding techniques of the next section are used, and is discussed in more detail there.

b) *Run-Length Coding*

In most television scenes, and particularly in video-conference scenes, much of the picture comprising background and other fixed objects does not change from one frame to the next. Hence predictors based on the frame-difference signal will yield zero prediction error in a significant fraction of the picture, generally in large connected regions. If this stationary area is large enough, it is more efficient to code the lengths of these runs than the actual prediction error at each pel. In effect, information is only being transmitted for the moving area while the stationary area is updated from the previous frame. Hence, this scheme is known as conditional replenishment, a term first used by MOUNTS [3.40]. Variations of this procedure have been used in most interframe coders described in the literature.

Due to input noise and quantization noise, many points in stationary areas will not have zero prediction errors. These isolated points tend to break up the runs and reduce the effectiveness of the run-length coding. For this reason, "noise-suppression" techniques are used to force the quantized prediction error to be zero at hypothesized noise points in the stationary area. In its most elaborate form, the coder would contain a segmenter which divides the scene into changed and unchanged areas. The quantized prediction error would be forced to zero in the areas determined to be unchanged. In practice, simple techniques prove quite adequate for this noise suppression. For example, a pel can be considered to be a moving area pel if the frame difference at that point exceeds a threshold, while one of four vertically adjacent elements and one of four horizontally adjacent elements also simultaneously exceed a threshold [3.48]. Otherwise the pel is considered to be in an unchanged area. This effectively eliminates isolated noise points. However, if the signal-to-noise ratio is low, more sophisticated techniques may be required [3.41].

As with the quantized prediction error, one can use either words of fixed length or variable length to transmit the run lengths. Due to the nonuniform probability of run lengths, the variable-length code can yield a reduction in this addressing overhead.

If a fixed-length code is used to transmit run lengths, then it may not be effective to run length code short runs of insignificant changes. Consider a run of insignificant changes of length ℓ_0 embedded in a longer run of significant changes. Two code words are necessary to identify this run in the longer run. Thus, if run lengths are coded with n_r bits and quantizer output "0" is coded with n_0 bits, then run-length coding the run of insignificant changes is inefficient for run lengths shorter than $\ell_0 = 2n_r/n_0$.

Transmitting the actual prediction errors for runs of insignificant changes shorter than ℓ_0 is known as gap bridging. In general, if variable-length codes are used to transmit run lengths, short runs have low addressing costs, and gap bridging is not useful, i.e., it pays to address all runs.

The positions of run lengths are correlated from line to line and from frame to frame. Thus, differential addressing schemes, which address positions of runs with respect to corresponding runs in previously transmitted lines, can give additional savings. HASKELL [3.42] found that savings of about 50 percent in coding the runs could be achieved. However, the actual reduction in bit rate depends on the relative amount of information required to code runs and to code the values of significant changes.

As mentioned previously, these variable-length codes and run-length codes put out information at a variable rate, and thus a buffer is required to smooth out the rate before presentation to a fixed-rate channel. To avoid the possibility of buffer overflow in the case of sustained periods of high activity, inordinately large buffers would be required. Besides the high cost, this would lead to subjectively objectionable delays. Thus, when using reasonably sized buffers, techniques are required to avoid the disastrous consequences of buffer overflow. This has led to the adaptive or multimode coders, which are discussed in Sect.3.7. In periods of high activity, when the buffer is starting to fill, the coding algorithm is changed in order to "gracefully degrade" the picture quality while avoiding buffer overflow. For example, the threshold in the noise-suppression circuit can be increased so that a smaller area is detected as having changed. Section 3.7 discusses several techniques that are used in multimode coders.

3.5 Movement-Compensated Prediction

3.5.1 General

A time-varying image to be transmitted consists in general of a number of objects with different motion superimposed on a background. If the camera is fixed, the background is stationary, while in the case of panning, it moves with approximately uniform velocity. In either case, with the exception of newly exposed background and foreground caused by motion, each pel is present in the previous field, displaced by an amount dependent on the motion of the given object. Hence, if the displacement field of the image is known, a very good prediction of the current field can be obtained by shifting and interpolating the parts of the previous field (or frame) which have moved. This forms the basis for the schemes known as movement-compensated predictive coding. The goal is to obtain improvement over the performance obtainable with the fixed predictors of Table 3.1 by basing the prediction on a more realistic model of the input signal.

The basic technique consists of the following elements:

1) estimation of the displacement field for the image; a simplified approach to estimating the displacement field is to i) segment the image into fixed background and into objects with different, but uniform, displacement, ii) estimate the displacement for each such object;
2) use of the displacement estimates to generate a movement-compensated prediction (this involves interpolation of the previous field or frame); and

3) coding of the prediction error and side information (segmentation and displacement estimates).

A block diagram of a movement-compensated predictive coder is shown in Fig. 3.9. In addition to forming the input for the predictive loop, the input signal is also fed to a segmenter and displacement estimator. The segmentation information is made available to the displacement estimator, so that an estimate will be confined to a single object or region. It is conceivable that the segmenter and displacement estimator could interact, recursively improving the estimate of the displacement field. The segmentation and displacement estimation are both used to control the predictor.

For fixed objects and background, the displacement is zero, and the best prediction is clearly the previous frame element. In moving areas, the prediction is the output of an interpolating filter, whose parameters are determined by the displacement estimation. If rigid body motion is assumed, the displacement can be specified by a translation and a rotation about an arbitrary point in the object. Hence, three additional parameters must be transmitted for each region. If the regions are sufficiently large, the overhead due to these parameters will be small. Often an assumption of translational

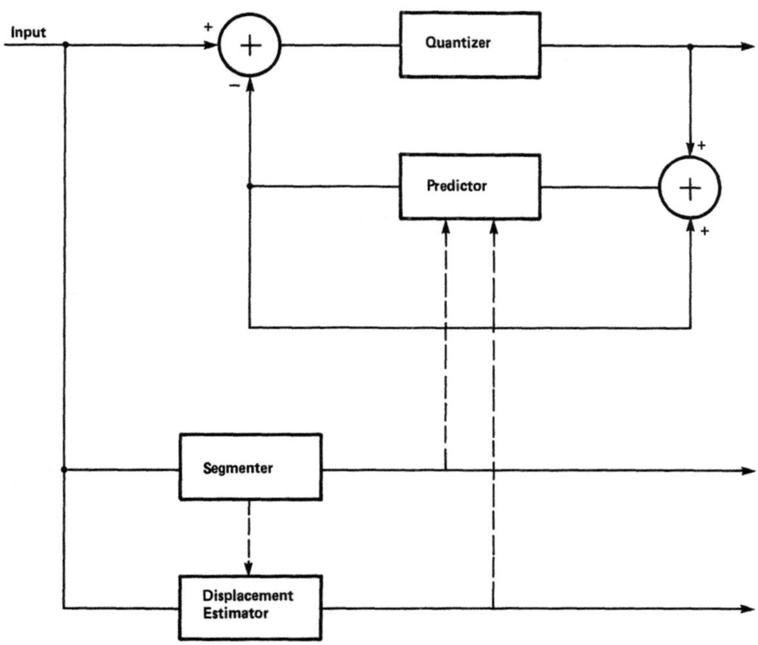

Fig. 3.9. Movement-compensated predictive coder

motion only is made, so that only two additonal parameters per region need be transmitted. It is possible that the segmenter also identifies newly exposed areas, in which case an intrafield predictor could be used for these areas.

This formulation is quite general. In practice, the segmentation of an image into different moving objects is quite difficult, especially for real-time implementation. Two simplified approaches which avoid such a segmentation have been proposed. The first divides the image into rectangular blocks, where it is assumed that each block contains a single object moving on a fixed background. Thus, it is only necessary to segment the block into changed and unchanged areas, and estimate the displacement for the moving area. In the second method, the displacement at each pel is recursively estimated, given the estimate at the previous pel. This technique can be implemented in such a way that no displacement information need be transmitted.

3.5.2 Block-Structured Movement-Compensated Coders

Block-structured coders have been proposed by HASKELL [3.27], NINOMIYA [3.43], and BROFFERIO et al. [3.44]. In this technique, the scene is divided into rectangular blocks, and a single shift is estimated for that block. The block may or may not be segmented into changed and stationary areas. The previous frame (or field) is shifted, and interpolated if nonintegral displacement estimates are allowed, to form the prediction for that block. Various aspects of this structure will now be discussed in more detail.

a) *Displacement Estimation*

There are two main classes of methods for estimating translational displacements: correlation or matching techniques, and differential methods. For an object in translational motion, with velocity $\underline{v} = (v_1, v_2)$, the image luminance satisfies

$$u(\underline{x},t) = u[\underline{x}-\underline{v}(t-t_0),t_0] \tag{3.9}$$

for an arbitrary reference time t_0. In particular, if τ is the time interval between frames

$$u(\underline{x},t_0+\tau) = u(\underline{x}-\underline{v}\tau,t_0) \tag{3.10}$$

where $\underline{d} = \tau\underline{v}$ is the displacement which occurs in one frame interval.

The matching techniques attempt to choose $\underline{d}$ from a set of possible displacements $\mathcal{D}$ to minimize some measure of the difference between the current frame and the previous frame displaced by $\underline{d}$. Thus, $\hat{\underline{d}}$ is the value which solves

$$\min_{\underline{d}\,\varepsilon\,\mathcal{D}} \sum_{\underline{x}\,\varepsilon\,\mathrm{MA}} N[u(\underline{x},t_0+\tau)-u(\underline{x}-\underline{d},t_0)] \tag{3.11}$$

where MA denotes the moving area.

N(.) is a nonnegative increasing function which serves as a distance measure. Common examples are $N(x)=|x|$ and $N(x)=x^2$. NINOMIYA [3.43] has proposed a threshold function suitable for high-speed real-time application

$$N(x) = \begin{cases} 1 & |x| \geq T \\ 0 & |x| < T \end{cases} \tag{3.12}$$

for some threshold T. These techniques require much computation, since (3.11) must be evaluated for each $\underline{d}\,\varepsilon\,\mathcal{D}$. There is thus a trade-off between accuracy and computation, and in practice, only a relatively small number of *integral* displacements have been used.

The differential techniques can be derived by differentiating (3.9) with respect to time

$$\frac{\partial u(\underline{x},t)}{\partial t} = -\underline{v}\cdot\nabla_{\underline{x}}\, u(\underline{x},t) \quad . \tag{3.13}$$

If the derivatives involved are approximated by finite differences, (3.13) becomes

$$\Delta_T(\underline{x},t) \approx -\underline{v}\cdot\Delta_{\underline{x}}\,(\underline{x},t) \quad . \tag{3.14}$$

The velocity estimate is obtained by choosing $\underline{v}$, which gives the best mean-square fit to (3.14) over the moving area, i.e., which minimizes

$$C = \sum_{\underline{x}\,\varepsilon\,\mathrm{MA}} [\Delta_T(\underline{x},t)+\underline{v}\cdot\Delta_{\underline{x}}(\underline{x},t)]^2 \quad . \tag{3.15}$$

By setting $\nabla_{\underline{v}}C=0$, one obtains

$$\hat{\underline{v}} = -\Big[\sum_{\underline{x}\,\varepsilon\,\mathrm{MA}} \Delta_{\underline{x}}(\underline{x},t)\Delta_{\underline{x}}(\underline{x},t)^T\Big]^{-1} \sum_{\underline{x}\,\varepsilon\,\mathrm{MA}} \Delta_T(\underline{x}t)\Delta_{\underline{x}}(\underline{x},t) \quad . \tag{3.16}$$

This estimator was first obtained by CAFFORIO and ROCCA [3.45].

Figure 3.10 shows the results obtained using this algorithm. A single field of a head and shoulders image was shifted by integral displacements,

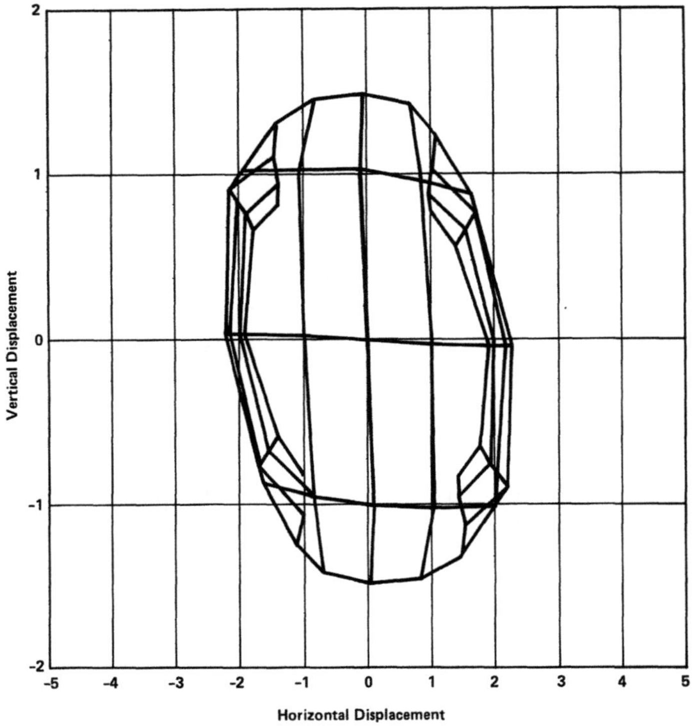

Fig. 3.10. Performance of Cafforio and Rocca displacement estimation algorithm

and the displacement was estimated as above. The frame difference is used to estimate the temporal derivative, while the average of central differences in the two frames is used to estimate the spatial gradient. The true displacements are the grid points of the rectangular grid, while the estimates are shown on the superimposed pattern, which is a deformation of this grid. Reasonable results are obtained for horizontal shifts in the range -2 to +2 pels and vertical shifts between -1 and +1 lines. For larger displacements, the algorithm breaks down. This is because the frame difference does not adequately approximate the temporal derivative. The performance for large displacements can be improved by low-pass filtering the image to eliminate frequency components with a period shorter than the maximum expected displacement. An example is shown in Fig.3.11, where the image has been filtered by taking the average of a 3-line by 5-pel block centered on the given pel prior to evaluating (3.16).

Evidently the performance for large displacements has been greatly improved, at the expense of the accuracy at small displacements. An alternative

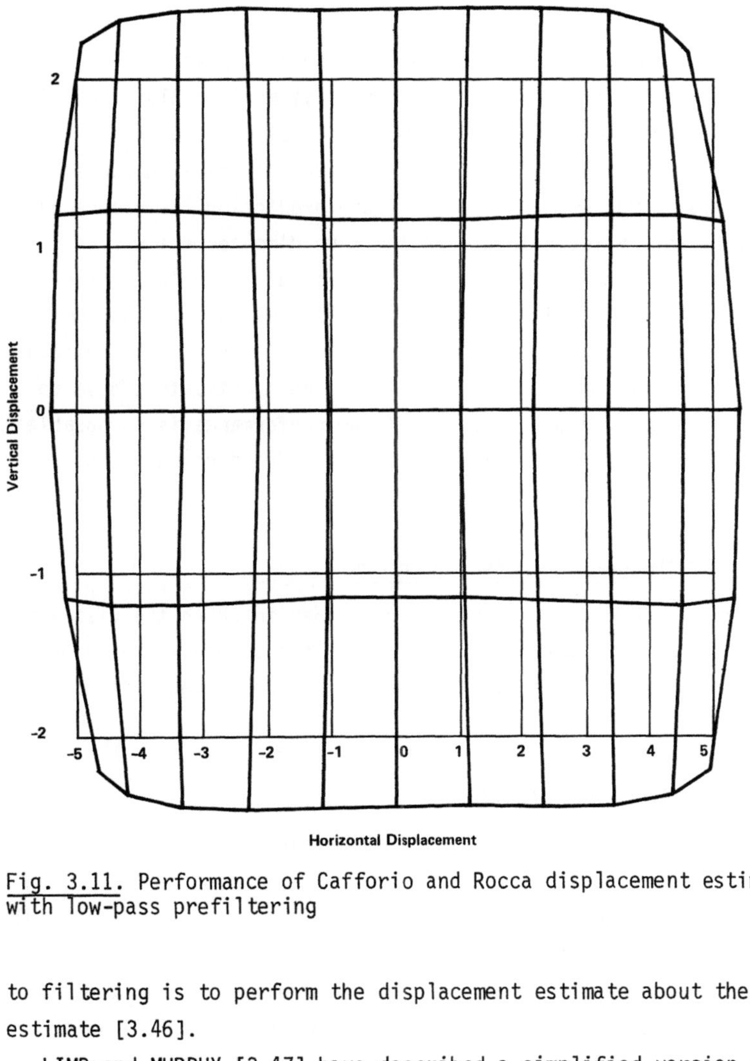

Fig. 3.11. Performance of Cafforio and Rocca displacement estimation algorithm with low-pass prefiltering

to filtering is to perform the displacement estimate about the previous frame estimate [3.46].

LIMB and MURPHY [3.47] have described a simplified version of this estimator which gives almost the same performance,

$$\hat{\underline{v}} = -\begin{bmatrix} \sum_{\underline{x}\varepsilon MA} \Delta_T(\underline{x},t)\ \mathrm{sign}[\Delta_{x_1}(\underline{x},t)] \Big/ \sum_{\underline{x}\varepsilon MA} |\Delta_{x_1}(\underline{x},t)| \\ \sum_{\underline{x}\varepsilon MA} \Delta_T(\underline{x},t)\ \mathrm{sign}[\Delta_{x_2}(\underline{x},t)] \Big/ \sum_{\underline{x}\varepsilon MA} |\Delta_{x_2}(\underline{x},t)| \end{bmatrix} \tag{3.17}$$

where $\underline{x} = (x_1, x_2)$.

b) *Results*

Several block-structured coders of this type have been simulated. HASKELL [3.27] simulated a scheme in which the scene was divided into blocks of 27 pels × 16 lines. He used a matching technique over a set of 17 possible integral displacements, with $N(x) = |x|$. On the average this gave entropies approximately 1 bit/pel smaller than previous frame prediction. As can be expected, best performance was obtained when the true displacement was an integral number of pels, in scenes containing one single translational displacement. NINOMIYA [3.43] has implemented in real time a similar scheme, using the threshold norm (3.12). He also reported savings of about 1 bit/pel.

Detailed studies using the differential displacement estimators have not been published, although indications are that the performance is comparable to or better than the matching techniques, at much reduced computational complexity.

3.5.3 Pel-Recursive Movement-Compensated Coders

NETRAVALI and ROBBINS [3.48,49] have proposed a coder in which the displacement estimate is recursively updated at each pel. This update is based only on previously transmitted pels, so that no explicit displacement estimate need be transmitted.

a) *Pel-Recursive Displacement Estimation*

Define the displaced frame difference, with displacement $\underline{d}$,

$$D(x,t,\underline{d}) = u(\underline{x},t) - u(\underline{x}-\underline{d},t-\tau) \quad . \tag{3.18}$$

If the object has translated by an amount $\underline{d}$ in one frame, then $D(\underline{x},t,\underline{d}) = 0$. The basis of the pel-recursive estimator is to adjust $\hat{\underline{d}}$ at each pel in order to reduce $|D(\underline{x},t,\hat{\underline{d}})|$. This is done by changing $\hat{\underline{d}}$ in the direction of the negative gradient

$$\hat{\underline{d}}^i = \hat{\underline{d}}^{i-1} - \frac{\varepsilon}{2} \nabla_{\underline{d}}[D(\underline{x},t,\hat{\underline{d}}^{i-1})]^2 \tag{3.19}$$

where $\hat{\underline{d}}^i$ is the displacement estimate at pel i of some scanning sequence. Using (3.18) gives

$$\hat{\underline{d}}^i = \hat{\underline{d}}^{i-1} - \varepsilon D(\underline{x},t,\hat{\underline{d}}^{i-1}) \nabla_{\underline{x}} u(\underline{x}-\hat{\underline{d}}^{i-1},t-\tau) \quad . \tag{3.20}$$

Since $u(\underline{x},t)$ is only defined at sampling instants, interpolation must be used to evaluate $D(\underline{x},t,\hat{d})$ and $\nabla_x(\underline{x}-\hat{\underline{d}},t-\tau)$. Netravali and Robbins found it adequate to use linear interpolation to evaluate $u(\underline{x}-\hat{\underline{d}},t-\tau)$, and $\nabla_x(\underline{x}-[\hat{\underline{d}}],t-\tau)$ to estimate the gradient, where $[\hat{\underline{d}}]$ is $\hat{\underline{d}}$ rounded to the nearest grid point. Use of this algorithm, with $\varepsilon = 1/1024$ led to a reduction in entropy of 1 to 1.5 bits/pel, for the displaced-frame difference, with respect to simple frame difference.

b) *Coder Operation*

In order that the displacement estimate need not be transmitted, a given pel is coded using the displacement estimate for a previously transmitted pel. Two obvious choices are the horizontally and vertically adjacent pels. The scene is first segmented into changed and stationary areas. The displacement estimation does not proceed in stationary areas; a displacement of zero is assumed and the previous frame element is used as prediction. Using a 35-level quantizer, NETRAVALI and ROBBINS [3.48] found that this scheme gave a decrease in the bit rate in the range of 20-50 percent for a wide class of scenes. They also investigated many simplifications involving accuracy required in the computation of the gradient and updating of the displacement estimate. These simplifications were found to only marginally degrade the performance.

3.5.4 Code Assignment

To gain full benefits from movement compensation, a proper code assignment must be done. For the coders described in the previous sections, this involves addressing the moving and stationary areas and coding the movement-compensated prediction error in moving areas. If the movement compensation has been successful, many of the quantized prediction errors will be zero, and run-length coding of the moving area as well will be profitable. However, there is an additional complication over conventional predictive coding where there are only two states to be coded (significant and insignificant changes) and run lengths are sufficient. There are now three states: stationary areas, insignificant compensated prediction errors, and significant compensated prediction errors. Thus, besides the run lengths, an identification for the state of the next run length must be provided. Thus specific code words could be reserved to serve this purpose. The results of NETRAVALI and ROBBINS [3.48], quoted in the previous section, include such a tristate run-length coding.

An alternative to the tristate encoding is to run length code only significant and insignificant prediction errors. The decision as to which prediction to use (i.e., previous frame or displaced previous frame) can be based on previously transmitted information, so that no side information giving this decision need be transmitted. For example, ROBBINS and NETRAVALI [3.49] have selected the prediction based on the best prediction for the three adjacent pels in the previous line. They found that this method further reduces the bit rate over the tristate coding by between 10 and 50 percent depending on the scene.

3.6 Transform Coding

3.6.1 General

One- and two-dimensional transform coding techniques have been used to reduce the spatial redundancy in video signals and images [3.12,50,51]. In order to incorporate the temporal redundancy reduction, three-dimensional transforms can be used [3.52-54].

The basic three-dimensional transform coding system is shown in Fig.3.12. The image sequence is subdivided into three-dimensional blocks each of size $N_1 \times N_2 \times N_3$ pels. A unitary transformation process is performed on each block. Thus if $u(i_1,i_2,i_3)$ is the input block (array), the transformed array $U(k_1,k_2,k_3)$ is given by

$$U(k_1,k_2,k_3) = \sum_{i_1=0}^{N_1-1} \sum_{i_2=0}^{N_2-1} \sum_{i_3=0}^{N_3-1} A(k_1,i_1,k_2,i_2,k_3,i_3)u(i_1,i_2,i_3) \tag{3.21}$$

$$k_1 = 0,N_1-1 \quad , \quad k_2 = 0,N_2-1 \quad , \quad k_3 = 0,N_3-1$$

where $A(k_1,i_1,k_2,i_2,k_3,i_3)$ is the unitary transform kernel.

As a result of this transformation process, most of the energy within the block can be compacted into only few transform coefficients. The transform coefficients are coded and transmitted over the channel. At the receiver, the coefficients are decoded and an inverse transform process is performed to restore the image block to the spatiotemporal domain, i.e.,

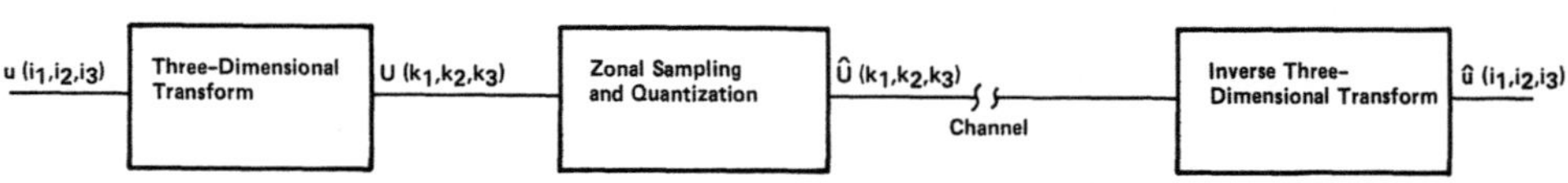

Fig. 3.12. General three-dimensional transform coding system

$$\hat{u}(i_1,i_2,i_3) = \sum_{k_1=0}^{N_1-1} \sum_{k_2=0}^{N_2-1} \sum_{k_3=0}^{N_3-1} A^{-1}(k_1,i_1,k_2,i_2,k_3,i_3)\hat{U}(k_1,k_2,k_3) \qquad (3.22)$$

$$i_1 = 0,N_1-1 \quad , \quad i_2 = 0,N_2-1 \quad , \quad i_3 = 0,N_3-1$$

where $\hat{U}(k_1,k_2,k_3)$ are the quantized (coded) transform coefficients and $\hat{u}(i_1,i_2,i_3)$ are the reconstructed pel values.

3.6.2 Coding of the Transform Coefficients

The first step in coding the transform coefficients is zonal sampling, where some of the transform coefficients are preselected for quantization and transmission. The remaining coefficients are not transmitted. At the receiver these coefficients can be set to zero or estimated to have some value based on the transmitted coefficients. There exist several criteria to perform this zonal sampling. The ideal approach is to use a subjective criterion, where the transform coefficients that are to be transmitted are chosen based on subjective evaluation experiments. However, due to the large number of possibilities, such an approach is impractical. A more popular approach is based on the energy in the transform coefficient, i.e., coefficients with larger energy are retained and those with small or negligible energy are dropped. Once the transform coefficients are selected, each coefficient is quantized using a number of bits dependent on the energy of the transform coefficient.

For each transform coefficient, a minimum mean-square-error quantizer can be designed, as described in Sect.3.4.3. This normally requires the knowledge of the probability density functions for each of the coefficients or an adequate model for them. For example, ROESE et al. [3.52], using the discrete cosine transform, modeled the probability density of the d.c. coefficient as a Rayleigh density and the remaining coefficients were modeled as Gaussian.

Other models have also been used for the Walsh-Hadamard transform [3.54]. More accurate descriptions of the probability densities of each transform coefficient can be obtained by actual measurements, either by real-time hardware or simulation using a wide range of video signals.

The above approach employs only the statistical properties of the transform coefficients. However, significant gains can be realized by incorporating the perceptual importance of the transform coefficients. For example, MOUNTS et al. [3.55] have developed a methodology to obtain subjectively optimum quantizers for 2×2×2 Hadamard transformed coefficients.

3.6.3 Types of Transform

There exist several unitary transforms which have been studied for picture coding. The optimum transform, in a least-mean-square sense is the Karhunen-Loeve (KL) transform. However, due to the large amount of computation as well as other limitations in implementing this transform [3.12,50], its use is currently impractical. Other transforms, such as discrete cosine, Hadamard, Fourier and slant transforms, have been studied. The choice between these "suboptimum" transforms is governed by the trade-off between implementation complexity and performance.

The transforms which are currently used are separable in the three dimensions, i.e., the three-dimensional transform can be implemented as a cascade of three one-dimensional transforms. There is clearly no restriction that the same type of transform be used in all three dimensions. For example, in [3.56] a two-dimensional slant transform was used spatially and a one-dimensional Hadamard transform was used in the temporal direction. At this time, it is not clear which is the best choice of transforms in each dimension.

3.6.4 Adaptive Coding of Transform Coefficients

In transform coding, a number of bits is usually allocated to each block. In fixed techniques these bits are preallocated to the transform coefficients. However, since the activity within a block may vary widely from one block to the next, fixed techniques do not utilize the available number of bits efficiently. Savings in the number of bits or improvement in quality can result from using adaptive techniques.

The simplest method of adaptation is threshold sampling [3.12,50], where transform coefficients whose value are below a prespecified threshold are dropped. Another adaptive technique involves the distribution of the number of bits available based on local activity within the block. For example, in stationary areas of the image sequence, fewer bits are allocated to transform coefficients representing temporal activity, and in moving areas, fewer bits are allocated to coefficients representing spatial activity.

3.6.5 Hybrid Transform / DPCM Coding

One of the problems associated with three-dimensional transform coding techniques is the large amount of storage required at both the receiver and transmitter. The hybrid transform DPCM [3.12,57,58] gives a partial remedy for this problem.

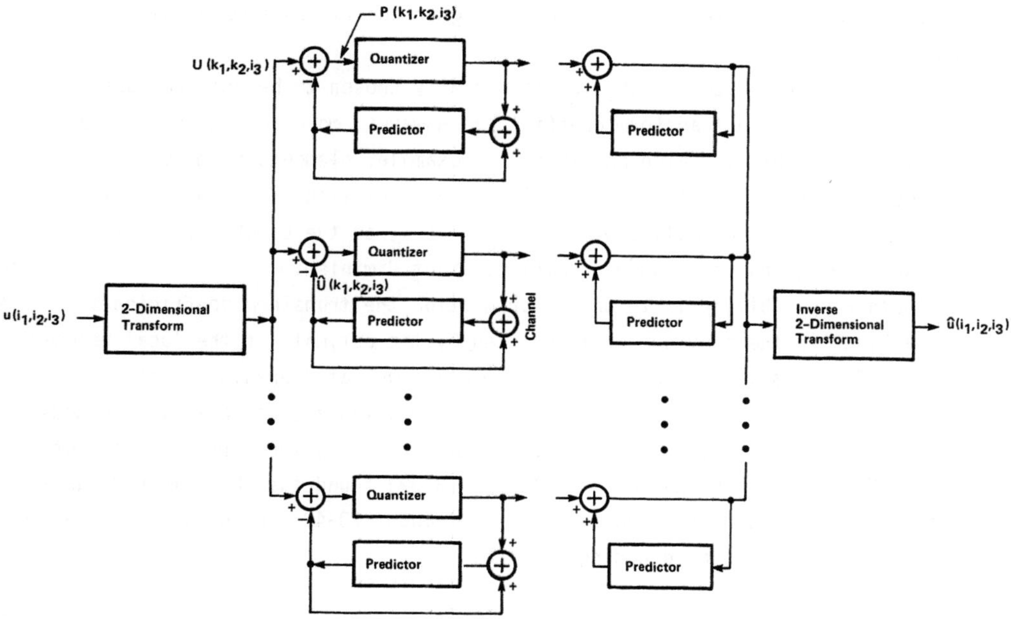

Fig. 3.13. Hybrid transform / DPCM system

A block diagram of the basic interframe hybrid coder is shown in Fig.3.13. A two-dimensional transform is performed on each block, and predictive coding (DPCM) is applied in the temporal direction. The result of the 2-D transform is

$$U(k_1,k_2,i_3) = \sum_{i_1=0}^{N_1-1} \sum_{i_2=0}^{N_2-1} u(i_1,i_2,i_3)A(k_1,i_1,k_2,i_2) \tag{3.24}$$

where $A(k_1,i_1,k_2,i_2)$ represents the two-dimensional transform kernel. At each spatial frequency (k_1,k_2) a prediction $\hat{U}(k_1,k_2,i_3)$ is performed.

The prediction error is given by

$$P(k_1,k_2,i_3) = U(k_1,k_2,i_3) - \hat{U}(k_1,k_2,i_3) \quad .$$

This prediction error is quantized using a finite number of levels dependent on the energy of the prediction error at frequency (k_1,k_2). The quantizer representative levels (and thresholds) are chosen in a way similar to that used in the three-dimensional transform case. In general, not all the transform coefficients need to be coded by DPCM. In [3.58] only the d.c. coefficients were coded using DPCM, while the higher coefficients were quantized and transmitted directly.

The predicted value $\hat{U}(k_1,k_2,i_3)$ is normally chosen to be the previous frame reconstructed transform coefficient. However, more sophisticated prediction algorithms are also possible. For example, elements from spatially adjacent blocks can also be used to form the prediction. This approach is only attractive when small block sizes are used; as the block size is increased, the gains using such predictors might diminish.

Another possibility is to use as prediction the transform coefficients for a block in the previous frame shifted by the estimate of the local velocity [3.59]. This is similar to the movement-compensated prediction of Sect. 3.5. The displacement estimate can be obtained using the differential methods described in Sect.3.5.2a or by a modification of the pel-recursive method of Sect.3.5.3a [3.60]. NETRAVALI and STULLER [3.59] found that both methods gave comparable results, providing a decrease of about 20-40 percent in bit rate over uncompensated hybrid coding.

3.7 Multimode Coders

3.7.1 Overview

This section addresses in more detail the adaptive or multimode predictive coders introduced in Sect.3.4.4. When using the variable-length codes and run-length codes described in that section, information is put out at a variable rate. To transmit this data over a fixed-rate channel, a buffer is required to smooth the information rate. Since the size of the buffer is limited by constraints on cost and perceptual effects of delay, peaks of activity in the image signal can cause this buffer to overflow. To avoid this, it is necessary to adapt the coder operation to the amount of motion, providing for a gradual and graceful degradation of quality as the amount of activity increases. Depending on the desired transmission rate, it may be possible under conditions of moderate motion to utilize various psychovisual properties, as described in Sect.3.3, so that the adaptation can occur without introducing visible degradations (e.g., spatial subsampling in moving areas). However, for violent motion, visible degradation may be unavoidable. It must be decided, for the application in question, to what extent visible degradations can be tolerated.

Ideally, the mode of operation should depend on the actual characteristics of the signal which produce the nonuniform information rate, i.e., percentage

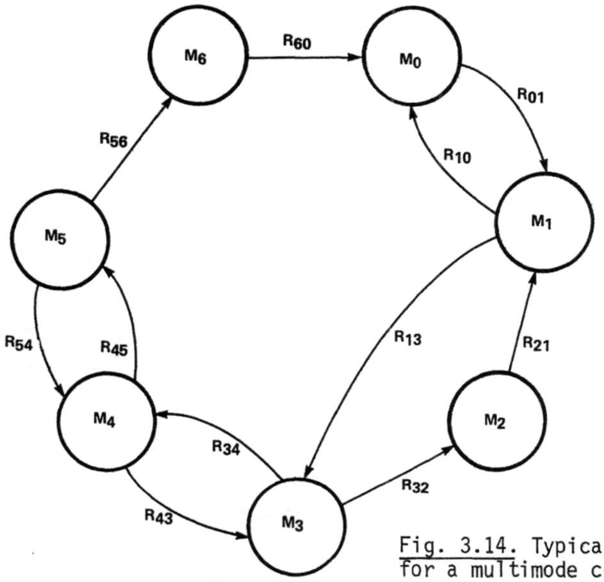

Fig. 3.14. Typical state transition diagram for a multimode coder

of frame moving, velocity of motion, amount of spatial detail, etc. However, most multimode coders which have been proposed base the decision on a single parameter, the buffer memory occupancy. The operation of a multimode coder is best illustrated by means of a state transition diagram, as shown in Fig. 3.14. The modes of operation are indicated by $M_0,M_1...M_n$, each mode representing a specific choice of coder parameters (sampling rates, quantizer levels, thresholds, etc.), while R_{ij} represent state transition rules (e.g., buffer memory occupancy changes from below T_i to above T_i). In general, most transitions are not permitted, and transitions are between adjacent, or nearly adjacent modes, as in Fig.3.14.

M_1 is referred to as the main mode of operation, designed for "typical" image statistics, and giving full available resolution and best picture quality. M_0 is an "underflow" mode, which ensures that the buffer does not empty, perhaps by transmitting full resolution 8-bit PCM. A refresh mode may also be considered in order to limit the propagation of channel errors. Modes M_2, $M_3,...,M_n$ are referred to as "overflow modes", invoked successively in periods of increased picture activity. A number of specific techniques used in overflow modes of operation will now be discussed.

3.7.2 Techniques Used in Multimode Coding

a) *Subsampling*

The spatial and temporal sampling rates in television are sufficiently low that any systematic decrease in these rates would result in visible impairments. However, as discussed in Sect.3.3.2, the viewer has reduced resolution requirements for rapidly moving objects, so that such regions may be sampled at a lower rate without introducing visible distortions. However, to avoid aliasing, which would be visible, the signal should be properly band limited prior to subsampling. Camera integration can perform part of this band limiting; the integration of the camera pick-up tube automatically band limits the signal in the spatial domain to some extent in moving areas. The temporal masking effects described in Sect.3.3.3 can be used by introducing spatial subsampling after gross temporal changes such as scene changes. If the image activity necessitates spatial and temporal subsampling above these thresholds, visible loss of resolution will result.

The choice of the subsampling pattern is of importance. The effects of sampling patterns have been discussed in Sect.3.2.1. Proper choice of the subsampling pattern will minimize aliasing caused by subsampling, and thus less severe two-dimensional band limiting can be performed, reducing the loss of resolution. The quality of the reconstructed signal also depends on the interpolation algorithm used at the receiver.

The types of subsampling generally employed are horizontal, vertical, field (which is vertical-temporal subsampling), and frame subsampling (temporal only) [e.g., 3.23,61,62]. If suitable pre-band-limiting is not performed, the aliasing resulting from spatiotemporal subsampling will be seen as raggedness of edges and jerky motion. Due to the cost of frame stores, the temporal interpolation is usually done with only one or two frames (i.e., repeating and linear interpolation).

The subsampling ratio need not be fixed. It is possible to adaptively drop the maximum number of samples, so that reconstruction error is less than some threshold. This threshold can be increased in higher overflow modes. Alternatively, the interpolation error can be quantized and transmitted, with the quantization becoming coarser in higher modes.

b) *Temporal Filtering*

Temporal filtering has threefold use in interframe coders: reduction of aliasing effects if temporal subsampling is used, reduction of the bit rate by reducing the frame difference values, and noise suppression by properly rounding or truncating small frame difference signals.

Temporal filtering can be incorporated as a prefilter [3.63,64] or as an integral part of the predictive loop [3.23,62,65,66]. The use of a prefilter has the advantage that such a filter can be designed to have a linear phase response (constant delay), hence avoiding picture degradations caused by phase nonlinearity. However, since a unit temporal delay corresponds to a frame memory, use of temporal filtering as an integral part of the predictive loop alleviates the need for extra memory, as it uses the same memory required for prediciton. Two types of temporal filtering have been used, linear and nonlinear. We shall concentrate on the temporal filter as an integral part of the interframe coder.

Figure 3.15 shows a basic interframe predictive coder which incorporates temporal filtering. A multiplier α, less than or equal to unity, is inserted prior to the quantizer. If the quantization noise is modeled as an additive noise $q(\underline{n})$, uncorrelated with the signal, then the output $y(\underline{n})$ of the receiver is given by

$$y(\underline{n}) = \alpha[x(\underline{n})-h(\underline{n})*y(\underline{n})] + q(\underline{n}) + h(\underline{n}) * y(\underline{n}) \qquad (3.25)$$

where $x(\underline{n})$ is the input signal, $h(\underline{n})$ is the impulse response of the predictor, and "*" denotes convolution. Alternatively (3.25) is described in the frequency domain as

$$Y(\underline{z}) = \frac{\alpha X(\underline{z})}{1-(1-\alpha)H_p(\underline{z})} + \frac{Q(\underline{z})}{1-(1-\alpha)H_p(\underline{z})} \qquad (3.26)$$

where $\underline{z} = (z_1,z_2,z_3)$, $z_i = \exp(-j\omega_i T_i)$.

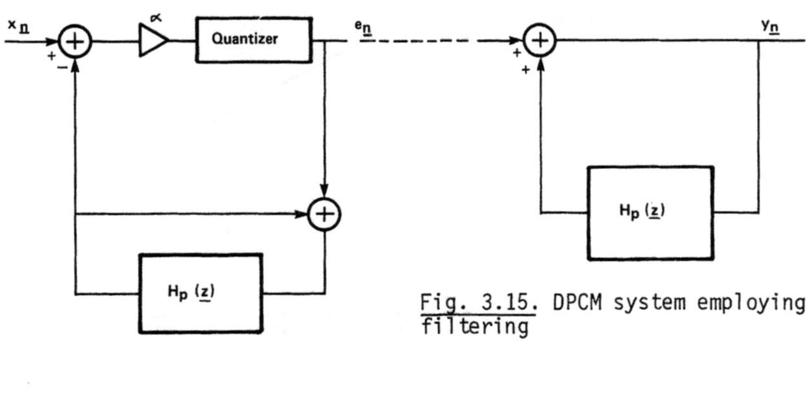

Fig. 3.15. DPCM system employing temporal filtering

It can be seen from (3.26) that for $\alpha < 1$, there is a spatiotemporal filtering of both the signal and quantization noise. This is a low-pass filtering which blurs the signal and attenuates high-frequency noise. The effects of linear temporal filtering on the output quantization noise have been studied [3.66]. It has been shown that if a uniform quantizer is used, an increase in the output quantization noise would result in addition to the undesired quantization noise spectrum shaping (the opposite of what is desired based on the spatiotemporal sensitivity data of Sect.3.3.1). However, if a nonuniform quantizer is used, a reduction in the output quantization noise would, in general, result.

When variable-word-length coding is used in conjunction with the interframe predictive coder, the inner quantization levels are assigned a smaller number of bits than the outer levels. The temporal filter multiplier α reduces the prediction error signal and hence forces it to use the inner quantizer levels, resulting in a reduction of the bit rate. However it should be noted that two opposing effects are at work. On one hand, the bit rate is reduced due to the attenuation of the prediction error signal. On the other hand, poorer predic-

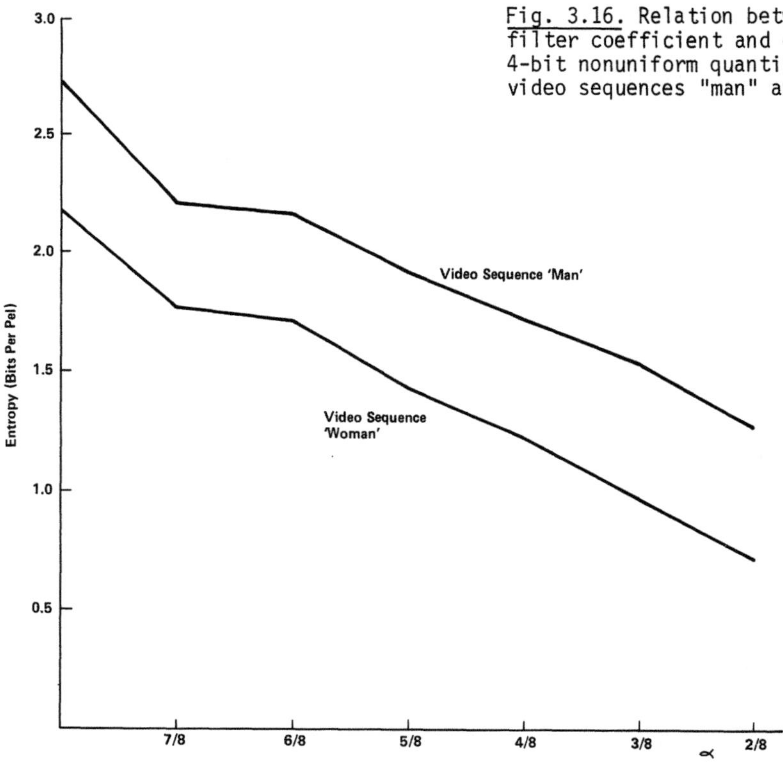

Fig. 3.16. Relation between temporal filter coefficient and entropy using 4-bit nonuniform quantizer for two video sequences "man" and "woman"

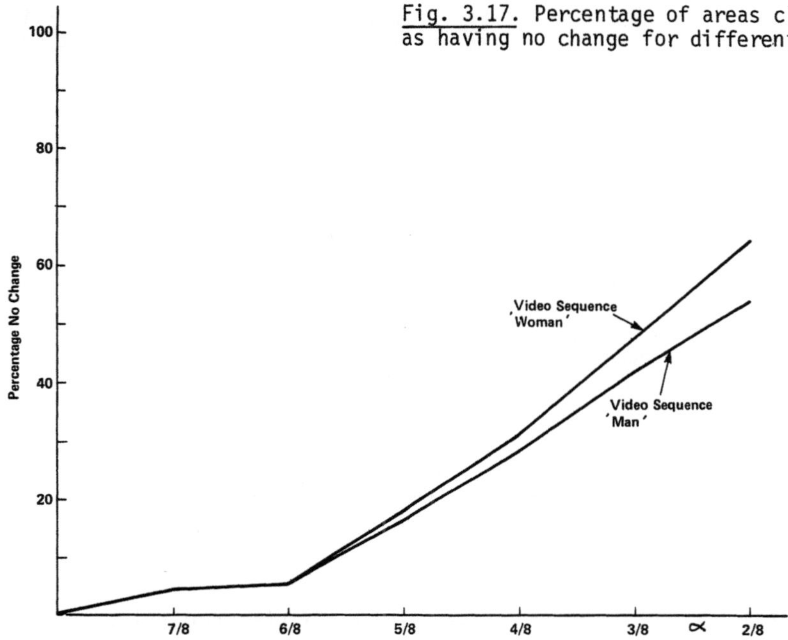

Fig. 3.17. Percentage of areas classified as having no change for different values of α

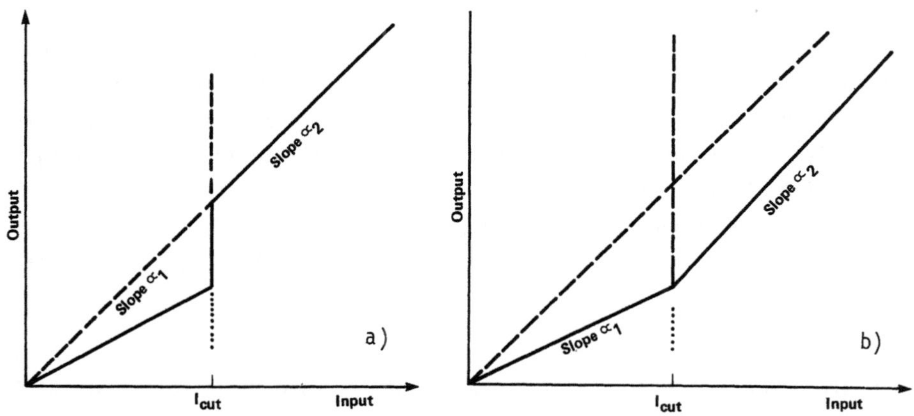

Fig. 3.18a,b. Two types of nonlinear characteristics (a) NL_1, (b) NL_2

tion results which offsets this gain to some degree. The temporal filtering also causes areas classified as having changed from one frame to the next to decrease. In Fig.3.16 the measured entropy versus α for two video sequences are shown, and in Fig.3.17 the percentage of changing areas is also shown for different values of α. These curves make clear the effect of temporal filtering on reducing the bit rate, but of course at the expense of quality. It

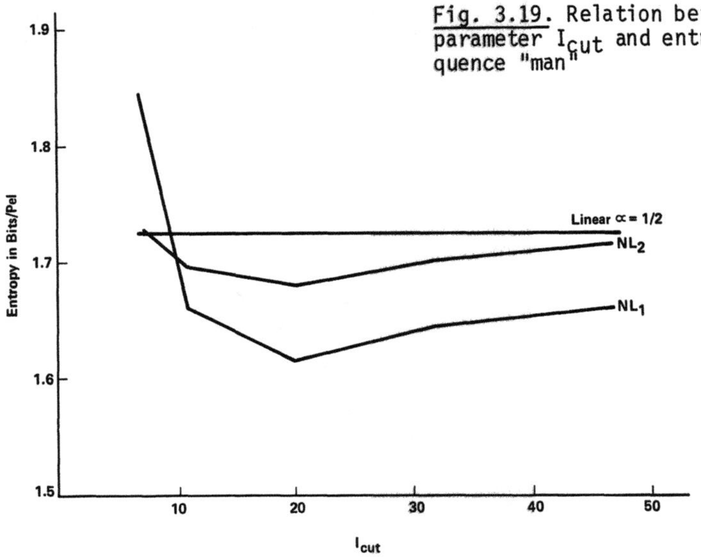

Fig. 3.19. Relation between nonlinearity parameter I_{cut} and entropy for video sequence "man"

should be noted that the low-pass filtering also affects input noise, and thus actually improves quality in this respect.

Instead of using a constant coefficient α independent of the frame difference signal, a nonlinear temporal filter can be used. Examples of two types of nonlinearities which have been used in multimode coders are shown in Fig. 3.18. Figure 3.19 gives a comparison of entropy for the linear temporal filtering with $\alpha = 1/2$ and the two types of nonlinear filtering, as a function of the point of discontinuity.

In general, nonlinear temporal filtering is more effective than linear temporal filtering in terms of bit-rate reduction as well as picture quality.

c) *Change of Thresholds*

There are several thresholding functions that are used in different parts of a multimode coder. Change of these thresholds would have an impact on the bit rate. For example, in the conditional replenishment systems, thresholds used to classify image areas as changing or stationary can be varied, the higher the thresholds the lower the bit rate. However, high thresholds give rise to some image impairments such as the dirty-window effect. Another example of threshold variations is in noise-suppression techniques, where increasing the threshold would cause more isolated pel changes to be removed.

d) *Switched Quantizers*

In this case more than one quantization law is used. Such quantization laws may have varying numbers of levels and also may be made to better match the signal characteristics. Switching between such quantizers is based on local picture properties as well as the buffer memory occupancy.

3.7.3 Choice and Ordering of Modes of Operation

As mentioned ealier, a multimode coder should be able to handle any video signal to assure its continuous operation. In lower modes of operation the coder should be able to provide the full available resolution both in changing and stationary areas. As picture activity increases, higher order modes are invoked in such a way as to gracefully and progressively degrade the signal to maintain a constant average bit rate while handling an increasing amount of picture activity.

Ideally speaking, the larger the number of operating modes, the more flexibility the designer has and hence the better the overall picture quality that can be obtained. However, the overall complexity of the coder increases, and the problem of optimizing the coding parameters becomes more difficult. On the other hand, if the number of operating modes is too small, switching between modes causes objectionable abrupt changes in quality.

For each mode M_i of operation, a coding strategy is first chosen. Normally it involves the use of one or more of the data reduction techniques described in the previous sections. For a given image, operating the coder in a higher mode results in a reduction in bit rate and possibly a concurrent degradation in picture quality. The transition rules R_{ij} are normally based on the buffer memory occupancy. As the buffer memory occupancy exceeds T_i, the coder switches operation from mode M_i to M_{i+1}. If the buffer memory falls below a safe threshold T_i^-, the coder is switched from mode M_{i+1} to M_i. Normally T_i is chosen greater than T_i^-, i.e., a hysteresis is built into the process to prevent the coder from oscillating between modes. The buffer memory occupancy criterion is by no means an optimum decision rule for switching modes, additional criteria can also be established.

There are some restrictions as to where and when to switch to a higher mode of operation. Such restrictions are imposed by picture quality and by system constraints. If the switching to a higher mode of operation requires horizontal or vertical subsampling in the moving area only, switching is allowed anywhere, However in temporal subsampling with field/frame repeat or interpolation, the switching is normally done on a frame or field basis. For example, frame repeat is allowed on the whole frame and not part of it, to prevent picture break up. Temporal filtering is normally carried out on a line-by-line basis. By restricting where to switch, the overhead information (if required) is reduced and more uniformity in quality is achieved.

In addition to the above modes of operation, an update of the picture material should be carried out. Normally in interframe coders, a few lines per frame are directly transmitted by PCM. This cleans up the picture from residual impairments due to coding and limits the propagation of transmission channel errors. Sequential update gives rise to a problem of nonuniform quality which can be seen as a visible crawling pattern, especially in the higher modes of operation. To alleviate this, coarser PCM quantization may be used. However this can reduce quality in the low modes of operation. A more promising approach is the use of pseudorandom update, where picture lines are updated in a pseudorandom fashion under the constraint that all frame lines are updated within a given period of time.

In addition to protection of buffer overflow by switching to higher modes of operation, buffer underflow protection is also necessary. This protection can be realized in several ways. One approach is to transmit PCM values to the buffer. Another approach is to insert in the buffer some dummy information bits, resulting in inefficient utilization of the channel capacity. For both cases some overhead information must be supplied to the receiver. Optimization of a multimode coder involves the adjustments of a large number of parameters. Moreover, most of these parameters are interdependent. In addition, the quantity being optimized, picture quality is highly subjective. Thus simulation either by software or hardware together with subjective testing plays an important role in the design and optimization of a multimode coder.

3.7.4 Multimode Coder Example

Many multimode coders have been described in the literature (e.g., [3.23,61, 62,65]). To illustrate the general principles described above, this section briefly describes a multimode interframe coder for coding monochrome NTSC video signals for transmission at 1.5 Mbit/s [3.23]. The coder is in fact constructed as a real-time simulator under minicomputer control, allowing some flexibility in changing parameters to optimize performance. The coder utilizes a combination of predictive DPCM coding and the conditional replenishment. There are 12 modes of operation in which one or more of the following techniques are used:

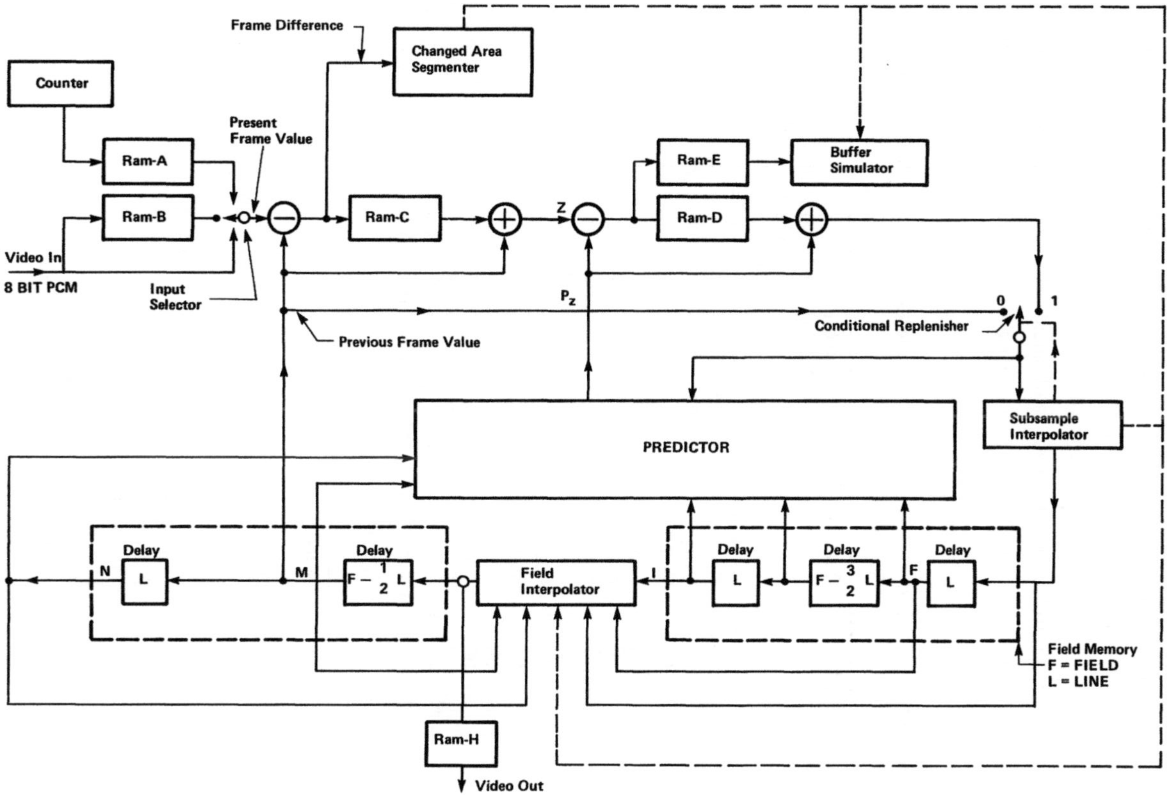

Fig. 3.20. Real-time coder simulation system [3.23]

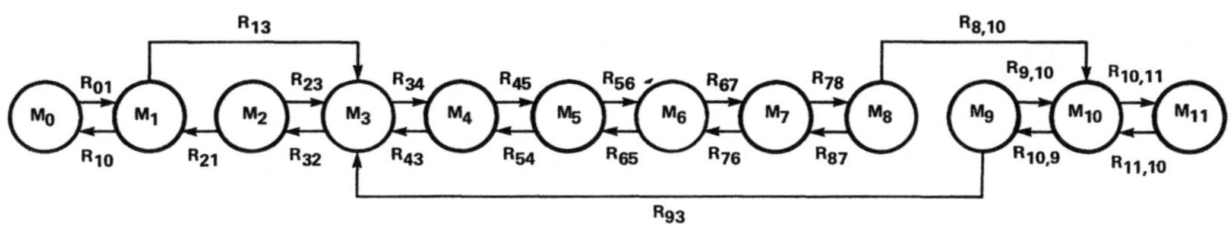

Fig. 3.21. State transition diagram for Haskell's 1.5 Mb/s coder

1) linear and nonlinear temporal filtering,
2) horizontal, vertical, and temporal subsampling,
3) isolated pel change suppression (noise suppression),
4) switched quantizers, fine and coarse.

A basic block diagram of the real-time hardware simulator is shown in Fig. 3.20. Not shown are the A/D, D/A and the minicomputer system. Random access memories are used to preprocess the digital video signal and to implement the temporal filter and quantizers. In the changed area segmenter, a digital low-pass filter is used to remove the high-frequency noise as much as possible. Two alterable thresholds T_1 and T_2 are used. Differences greater than or equal to T_2 are classified as significant changes, and those less than or equal to T_1 are classified as insignificant changes; however, differences greater than

Table 3.2. Parameters of coding modes. Lower order modes are for low movement; higher order modes are for rapid movement

Mode (i)	Buffer thresholds Lower	Upper	Quantizer	Segmenter Filter	Thresholds (Scale 0 to 225) T_1	T_2
0	0	6400	Fine	FA	1	6
1	1600	38400	Fine	FA[1]	1	6
2	8192	38400	Fine	FB	3	5
3	3200	38400	Fine	FA	1	3
4	3200	51200	Fine	FA	2	3
5	3200	54400	Fine	FC	2	3
6	32000	70400	Coarse	FD	2	3
7	32000	83200	Coarse	FD	2	3
8	32000	96000	Coarse	FD	2	3
9	32000	100000	Fine	FA	1	3
10	64000	99200	Coarse	FD	2	3
11	64000	100000	Coarse	FD	2	3

1 For noisy input signals segmenter filter FE is used in mode 1

Mode (i)	Temporal filter α	Subsampling
0	.75	None
1	.75	None
2	.75	None
3	.75	Field
4	.625	Field
5	.625	Field, H
6	.625	Field, H
7	Nonlinear	Field, H
8	Nonlinear	Field, H, V
9	.75	Field
10	Nonlinear	Field, H, V, Frame
11		Field, H, V, Frame

Table 3.3. Segmenter frame difference filter unit impulse responses; filter length = 5 pels

Frame differences Filter	Impulse response (successive pels)				
FA	.0625	.125	.25	.125	.0625
FB	.0625	.0625	.25	.0625	.0625
FC	.125	.125	.25	.125	.125
FD	.25	.125	.25	.125	.25
FE	.25	.25	.25	.25	.25

Table 3.4. DPCM quantizer output levels (on a 9-bit scale -255 to 255) and variable word lengths of code words. The 5-bit code word 00000 is reserved for indicating end of a cluster of significant changes. Threshold values are half-way between representative levels

Quantizer	Output levels and code word lengths						
Fine	Levels	0	±3	±8	±16	±27	±42
	Bits	1	2,3	4,7	7,8	8,8	8,8
Coarse	Levels		±3	±12	±24		
	Bits		1,2	3,4	6,6		

T_1 and less than T_2 undergo isolated pel rejection before being classified. Gap bridging is also used to increase the efficiency of addressing moving areas.

Both linear and nonlinear temporal filtering are also used. The predictive DPCM coder is capable of implementing several interframe prediction algorithms, and a variable-word-length coder is also included. Figure 3.21 shows the state transition diagram for this coder. The description of the modes and transition rules are shown in Table 3.2. Tables 3.3,4 give the impulse response for the low-pass filter in the segmenter and the quantizer level assignments, respectively.

In the lower order modes of operation, best attainable picture quality is obtained. As the amount of activity in the signal increases, field subsampling and more temporal filtering are used together with varying the segmentation thresholds. Further increased activity forces the coder to use coarser quantization, nonlinear temporal filtering, and subsampling in the three dimensions.

Note that a hysteresis is built into the transition rules to prevent oscillating between modes. In addition, the switching between modes is allowed only at specific instances. For example, mode 2 is entered only from mode 3 during the vertical blanking interval after an odd field. However, switching from mode 3 to mode 4 is allowed any time.

3.8 Color Coding

The color video signal consists of three components, red, green, and blue, combined to form the composite color video signal. This section presents a brief discussion of the implications of color on coding of image sequences. A detailed review of color coding is given in [3.67].

3.8.1 The NTSC Composite Video Signal

In the NTSC color television system, the T.V. camera supplies simultaneous red, green, and blue signals representing the objects being televised. Through a matrix transformation, the RGB signals are transformed into the luminance signal Y and two chrominance signals I and Q. The matrix transformation is given by

$$\begin{bmatrix} Y \\ I \\ Q \end{bmatrix} = \begin{bmatrix} 0.30 & 0.59 & 0.11 \\ 0.60 & -0.28 & -0.32 \\ 0.21 & -0.52 & 0.31 \end{bmatrix} \begin{bmatrix} R \\ G \\ B \end{bmatrix} \quad . \tag{3.27}$$

The chrominance signals I and Q are band limited to 1.5 MHz and 0.8 MHz, respectively, then are quadrature modulated by the color subcarrier signal at 3.58 MHz (455 $f_\ell/2$, where f_ℓ is the line frequency). The modulated chrominance signals are added to the luminance signal Y to form the composite signal

$$u(t) = y(t) + i(t)\cos(2\pi f_{sc} t+\varphi) + q(t)\sin(2\pi f_{sc} t+\varphi) \quad . \tag{3.28}$$

3.8.2 Three-Dimensional Spectrum of the NTSC Composite Signal

As with monochrome signals, the efficient coding and processing of color video signals require the understanding of the three-dimensional spectrum of the signal, particularly in the way the luminance and chrominance bands are interrelated [3.68,69]. The one-dimensional spectrum commonly used in television engineering does not provide sufficient insight for many multidimensional processes.

Because the color subcarrier frequency f_{sc} is an odd multiple of half the line frequency f_ℓ and half the frame frequency f_{fr}, the phase of the subcarrier changes by 180° from line to line and from frame to frame. Figure 3.22 shows the phase relationships for a 2:1 line-interlaced sampling grid. A three-dimensional composite NTSC signal which is consistent with Fig.3.22 is

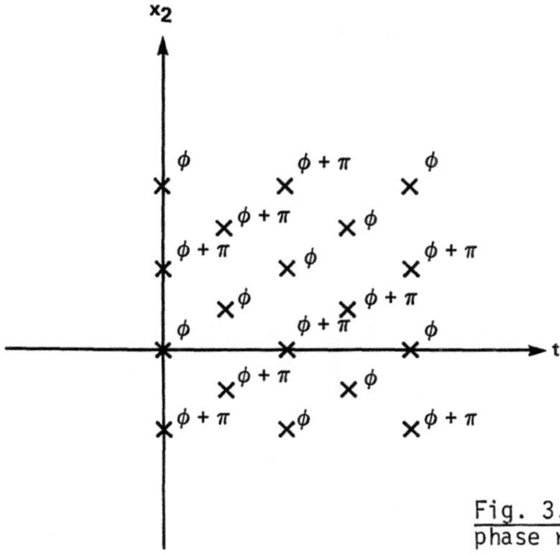

Fig. 3.22. Vertical temporal chrominance phase relationship for NTSC color signal

$$u(x_1,x_2,t) = y(x_1,x_2,t) + i(x_1,x_2,t)\cos(2\pi f_{sc}x_1+\varphi)\cos[\pi(f_{fr}t-f_\ell x_2)] + q(x_1,x_2,t)\sin(2\pi f_{sc}x_1+\varphi)\cos[\pi(f_{fr}t-f_\ell x_2)] \quad . \qquad (3.29)$$

The spectrum of the NTSC signal is obtained by replicating the spectrum of the signal given by (3.29) in the vertical-temporal frequency plane in the manner depicted in Fig.3.2b. This spectrum is shown in Fig.3.23. In the temporal-vertical plane (Fig.3.23a), the luminance signal is clustered at multiples of the frame frequency (30 Hz) temporally and multiples of the line frequency vertically in a checkerboard pattern. The chrominance signal is clustered at odd multiples of half the frame frequency temporally and odd multiples of half the line frequency vertically. In the horizontal-vertical plane (Fig.3.23b), the luminance is clustered at multiples of the line frequency vertically and extends horizontally to 4.25 MHz (approximately). The chrominance is clustered at odd multiples of half the line frequency vertically, and at f_{sc} horizontally.

To obtain a digital video signal, sampling in the horizontal direction is required. Two factors affect the resulting spectrum of the sampled signal: the sampling frequency and the sampling pattern. The horizontal sampling frequency is normally related to the line or color subcarrier frequencies. Again, as for the monochrome case, although the vertical-temporal sampling pattern is fixed, the spatial and horizontal-temporal projections remain to be chosen.

Careful choice of the sampling patterns allows for reduction of data rate by reducing the sampling frequency, while avoiding aliasing errors, by prop-

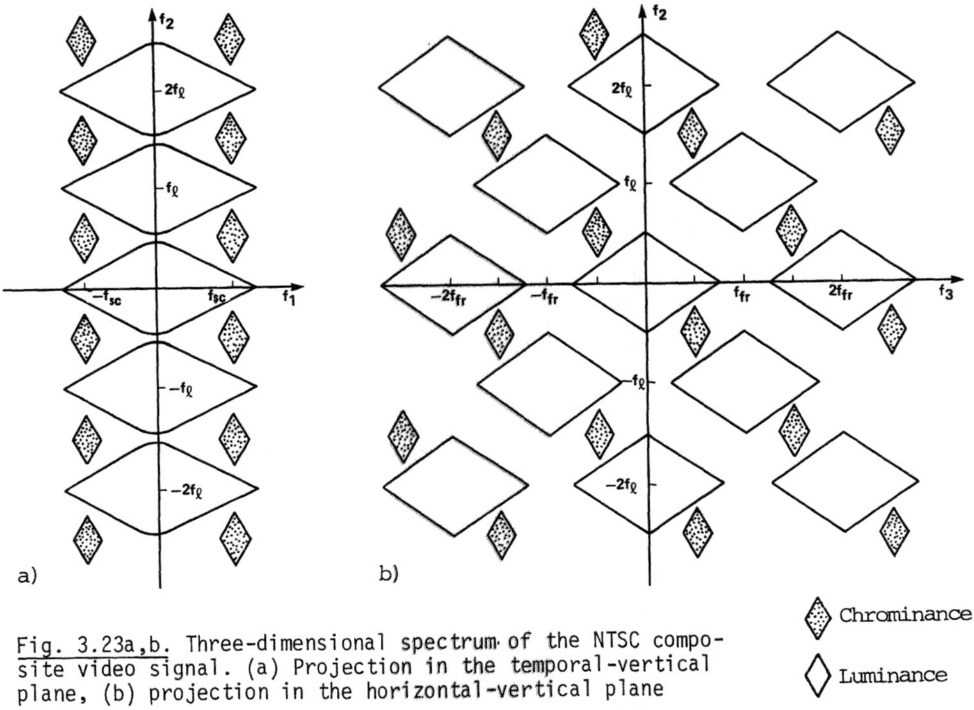

Fig. 3.23a,b. Three-dimensional spectrum of the NTSC composite video signal. (a) Projection in the temporal-vertical plane, (b) projection in the horizontal-vertical plane

erly interleaving luminance and chrominance information in three-dimensional frequency space. To illustrate this point, consider a sampling of the composite video signal at twice the color subcarrier frequency ($2\ f_{sc} \simeq 7.16$ MHz). Three possible spatial sampling patterns, aligned, checkerboard, and double checkerboard, are shown in Fig.3.24. The resulting spatial spectrum is shown in Fig.3.25 for each of the sampling patterns. Note that for the aligned pattern, serious aliasing results for both luminance and chrominance. For the checkerboard pattern, overlap between the luminance and chrominance results. For both cases, aliasing cannot be removed by postfiltering. However, for the double checkerboard pattern, the luminance and chrominance are replicated without overlap, so that the original signal can be reconstructed by a suitablve two-dimensional low-pass filter. More flexibility can be obtained if we allow specification of the sampling pattern in the temporal-horizontal plane, and use of three-dimensional filters.

3.8.3 Predictive Coding

There are two basic approaches to coding the NTSC color signal. The first is component coding. The composite NTSC color signal is separeted into its three

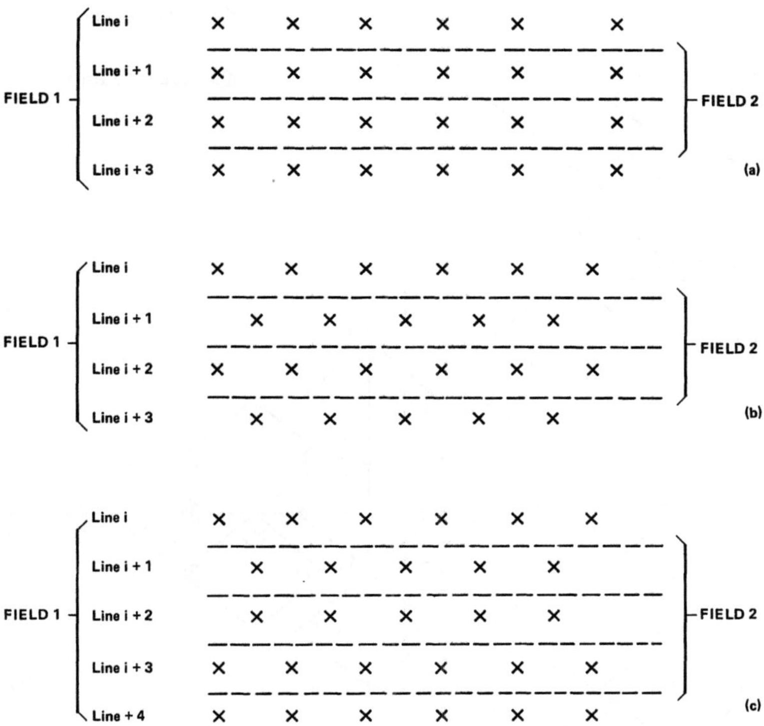

Fig. 3.24a–c. Three possible sampling patterns at sampling frequency $f_s = 2f_{sc}$. (a) Aligned; (b) checkerboard; (c) double checkerboard

components, e.g., Y, I, and Q, using analog or digital filtering techniques. Each component is coded separately utilizing its distinct spectral, statistical, and perceptual properties. For this case, standard monochrome coding techniques discussed earlier are directly applicable, although use may be made of the correlation between components.

Problems of residual chrominance in the luminance signal due to imperfect filtering cause the performance of the interframe coder to be degraded, especially in the segmentation of stationary and changing areas of the picture. The problem can be largely eliminated by filtering the frame difference signal with a chrominance rejection filter prior to segmentation [3.70]. With previous frame prediction, best results are obtained if this filter is placed within the DPCM loop.

The second approach is the direct processing and coding of the composite signal. However, due to the distinct properties of the composite signal, straightforward application of the monochrome techniques is not possible. In

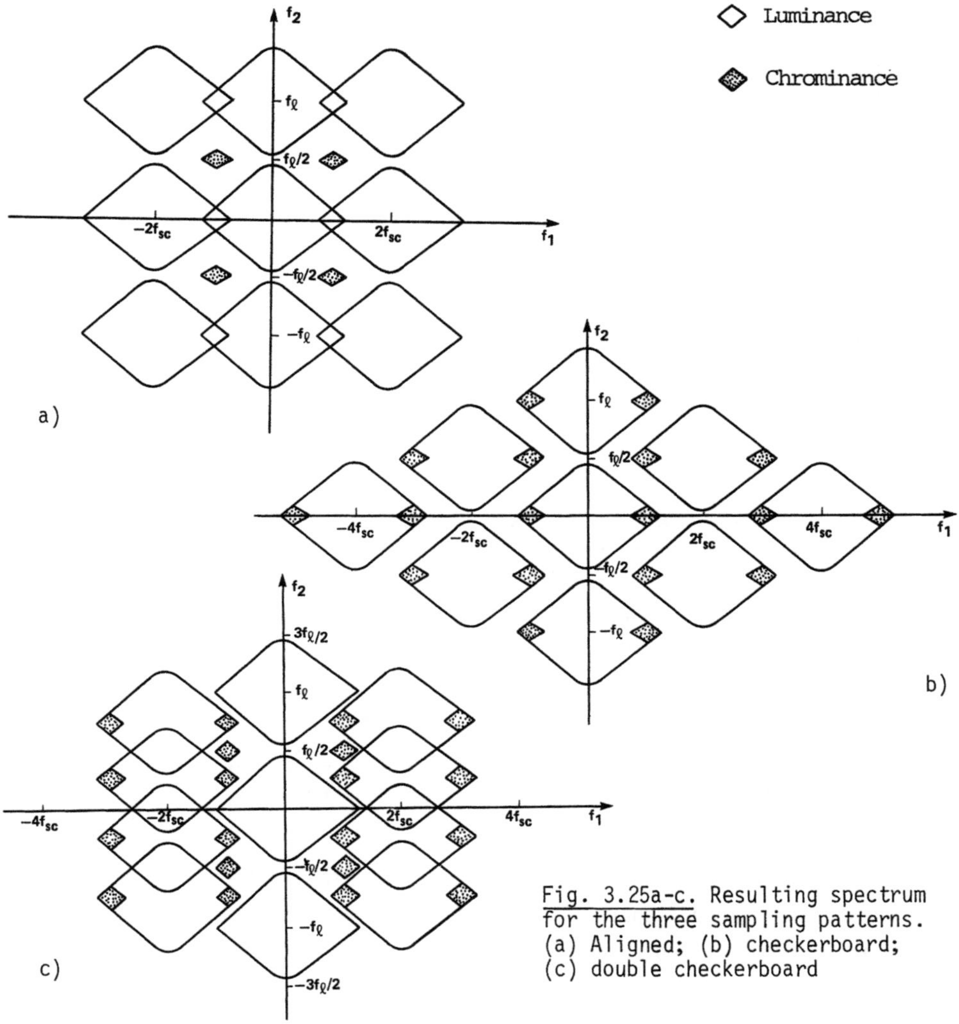

Fig. 3.25a-c. Resulting spectrum for the three sampling patterns. (a) Aligned; (b) checkerboard; (c) double checkerboard

particular, the relationship of the phase of the color subcarrier for the pels used to form the prediction must be taken into account.

Direct interframe coding of the composite signal is possible using an approach similar to the spatial chrominance-corrected predictor [3.71]. A simple interframe chrominance-corrected predictor is the second previous frame element. Unfortunately the performance of this predictor is poor and two frame memories are required at both receiver and transmitter. In a more general chrominance-corrected predictor, elements in three-dimensional neighborhood are used to form the prediction. This process involves the partial or full separation of the luminance and chrominance components and reconstruction of the predicted value with the correct chrominance phase. Normally this task is achieved inside the predictor. When using a chrominance-corrected interframe predictor together with conditional replenishment (or a variation of it), the phase of the chrominance signal in the stationary area has to be inverted for correct display at the receiver. It is also possible to preinvert the phase of the chrominance signal every second frame prior to predictive coding. Standard monochrome techniques are directly applicable in this case. A post-processor is required after the receiver to reconstruct the correct signal phase.

3.9 Concluding Remarks

A considerable amount of work on interframe coding has been done in the past decade, culminating in the construction and marketing of several interframe coders for NTSC signals operating in the 15-22 Mbit/s range [3.62,65]. Efforts to reduce the bit rate have gone as far as investigating the possibility of transmitting video-conference signals at 64 kb/s [3.64].

However, there is yet much that remains to be done, in utilizing both viewer and source properties. Some research areas include development of systematic procedures for effecting a subjectively optimal exchange of spatial, temporal, and amplitude resolution. This would have an important impact on the design of multimode coders. Another important problem is the transmission of an image by means of its displacement field. Techniques for estimating an arbitrary (but appropriately characterized) displacement field, and using this to code the image field must be developed. Section 3.5 has presented some rudimentary steps in this direction. It is hoped that solutions to the above problems lead toward the basic information-theoretical goal of image coding: matching the source output rate to the receiver's capacity to accept information.

Appendix A: A Digital Television Sequence Store (DVS)

DVS is a general purpose simulation facility for processing television pictures, especially moving sequences. It provides facilities for real-time acquisition and display of digitized color (NTSC) or black and white sequences. It operates in a non-real-time processing environment providing the user random access to the stored data and the flexibility to simulate different processing algorithms. The processed sequences can be displayed in real time and compared.

The system design concept of DVS [3.72] involves the use of several moving-head, removable-pack, disk drives operated in parallel to provide the necessary bit-rate capability. A semiconductor buffer memory, which has a high-speed port to accept digitized video and a low-speed port to communicate with the disk, is associated with each disk drive. The current implementation of DVS at BNR/INRS Signal Processing Laboratory permits a maximum sequence length of 80 seconds and can record/display a 256×212 subarray of the entire frame. However, the DVS has been designed in a modular fashion, allowing expansion in terms of increased data rate (resulting in increased window size on the picture) and/or increased storage capacity (resulting in longer sequences).

The DVS is supported by a PDP 11/34 computer operating under RSX-11D in a multiuser environment.

A.1 Capabilities

The NTSC composite signal can be sampled at 2, 3, or 4 times the color subcarrier frequency (7.2, 10.7, or 14.3 MHz) and can be linearly quantized up to 256 levels (8 bits). The system can easily be enhanced to accommodate other sampling frequencies below 15 MHz.

The DVS has two modes of recording. In one mode, it records a video sequence of a predetermined length starting at a given time. In the second mode, DVS simulates a recording loop continuously recording the last n seconds of video ($n \leq 80$ s). The recording process can be stopped at any time to preserve the last n seconds of recording. The first mode is useful for automatic sampling of broadcast material, while the second mode is useful in capturing an event after it has occurred. DVS is also capable of recording every m^{th} frame of a sequence.

There are several display modes. The DVS can display a sequence of predefined length either repetitively or in "palindromic" mode. In the latter mode, an arbitrary subsequence of a recorded sequence is repetitively displayed, first in the forward direction and then the reverse direction. This makes it possible to present motion without abrupt discontinuity at the end and beginning of the sequence. DVS has facilities for slow-motion display as well as for stepping through video frames one by one. An important display feature of DVS is the capability to switch back and forth between two sequences without seeing transient effects on the monitor.

For non-real-time processing of video data, the user has random access to the recorded data.

A.2 The System

A block diagram of DVS is shown in Fig.3.26. This is a two-disk configuration of DVS. The disks used are CDC 9762-1 80 Mbyte storage module drives (SMD's). These drives have a burst transfer rate of about 1.2 Mbytes/s. Each disk is provided with a high-speed semiconductor buffer memory of 256 kbytes.

The General Video Controller (GVC) includes the digital video switch which connects one buffer memory to either the A/D or D/A converter, the digital time-base generator and the analog television interface. The GVC has an interface to the PDP 11/34 through which it receives control information and transfer timing information.

Each Field Storage Unit (FSU) consists of the semiconductor buffer with high-speed video port, a Computer Bus (Channel) Interface, a disk adapter, a disk controller and a disk drive. The channel interface links the computer to both the buffer and the disk adapter.

The analog video signal is connected to the video ports of the high-speed semiconductor buffer memories via the GVC. The incoming digitized video windows are switched from one buffer memory to another in a cyclical fashion. This "round-robin" mode of operation makes the disks work in parallel and doubles the transfer rate. In the particular implementation, six field windows (1/10 s) are sent before the video input stream is switched to the other

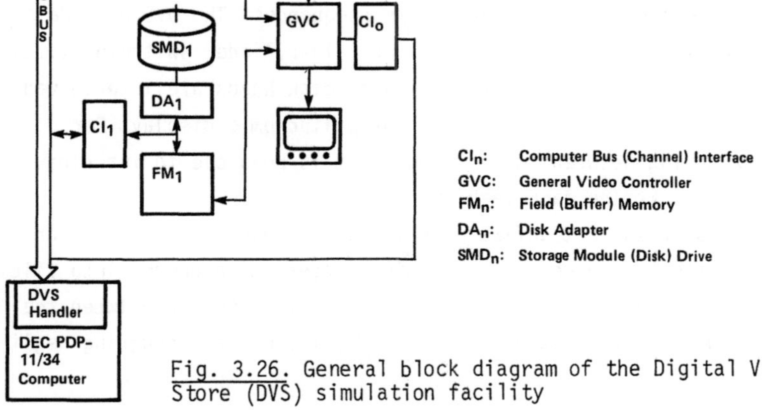

Fig. 3.26. General block diagram of the Digital Video Sequence Store (DVS) simulation facility

buffer. The disk transfer "start up" delay is thus incurred every 1/10 s instead of every 1/60 s, thus increasing the throughput and providing a larger window.

A.3 Software

DVS has a comprehensive support software package resident in the host computer. DVS has been integrated in the multiuser environment by means of a device handler, which is a special task under RSX-11/D. The handler provides the software interface between a particular hardware device and the application program using that device.

DVS software support can be subdivided into four basic functions

1) data base management,
2) real-time system control,
3) data processing support, and
4) system maintenance and calibration.

DVS has been designed to support several users. At any time, only one user can access DVS; however each user can have one or more VISTAs (visual information storage area) defined on the disk. The data base management system of DVS provides the users with the following facilities:

a) user segregation and data security,
b) dynamic resource allocation,
c) archiving facility,
d) simple user interface, and
e) access to physical parameter information.

The software for real-time system control provides the user with convenient facilities for recording video sequences in predefined areas in the file system and for subsequent display of sequences/subsequences. The DVS disk data format has been devised to minimize the cylinder-to-cylinder switching time. The fields recorded during the forward motion of disk heads are interleaved with those recorded during the return trip for palindromic display. For "glitch-free" switching between two sequences, it is possible to interleave two or more sequences in the same fashion.

The data processing support software provides a convenient facility for reading data from stored sequences and writing processed sequences into file areas. Under the control of the user, video data is transferred between the computer and DVS using direct memory access (DMA) techniques incurring negligible CPU overhead.

The system maintenance and calibration software provides facilities that aid in monitoring the integrity of some of the key components and permit adjustment of system variables to comply with user-defined specifications or with predefined default values. Work is in progress to incorporate a local video processor in the FSU to enhance the processing power.

References

3.1 E.R. Kretzmer: Statistics of television signals. Bell Syst. Tech. J. *31*, 751 (1952)
3.2 G.C. Sziklai: Some studies on the speed of visual perception. IRE Trans. IT-*2*, 125 (1956)
3.3 J.R. Pierce, J.E. Karlin: Reading rates and the information rate of a human channel. Bell Syst. Tech. J. *36*, 497 (1957)
3.4 H. Jacobson: The informational capacity of the human eye. Science *113*, 292 (1951)
3.5 C.E. Shannon: "Coding Theorem for Discrete Source with a Fidelity Criterion", in *Information and Decision Processes*, ed. by R.E. Machol (McGraw-Hill, New York 1960) pp.93-126
3.6 T. Berger: *Rate Distortion Theory: A Mathematical Basis for Data Compression* (Prentice-Hall, Englewood Cliffs, NJ 1971)
3.7 P. Mertz, F. Gray: A theory of scanning and its relation to the characteristics of the transmitted signal in telephotography and television. Bell Syst. Tech. J. *13*, 464 (1934)
3.8 L.E. Franks: A model for the random video process. Bell Syst. Tech. J. *45*, 609 (1966)
3.9 D. Pearson: *Transmission and Display of Pictorial Information* (Wiley, New York 1975)
3.10 D.P. Petersen, D. Middleton: Sampling and reconstruction of wave-number limited functions in n-dimensional Euclidean spaces. Inf. Control *5*, 279 (1962)
3.11 J. Sabatier, F. Kretz: Sampling the components of 625-line colour television signals. Eur. Broadcast. Union Rev. Tech. *171*, 2 (1978)
3.12 W.K. Pratt: *Digital Image Processing* (Wiley, New York 1978)
3.13 J.K. Yan, D.J. Sakrison: Encoding of images based on a two-component source model. IEEE Trans. COM-*25*, 1315 (1977)
3.14 A.N. Netravali, J.O. Limb: Picture coding: a review. Proc. IEEE *68*, 366-406 (1980)
3.15 J.G. Robson: Spatial and temporal contrast-sensitivity functions of the visual system. J. Opt. Soc. Am. *56*, 1141 (1966)
3.16 D.H. Kelly: Adaptation effects on spatio-temporal sine-wave thresholds. Vision Res. *12*, 89 (1972)
3.17 Z.L. Budrikis: Model approximations to visual spatio-temporal sine-wave threshold data. Bell Syst. Tech. J. *52*, 1643 (1973)
3.18 M. Miyahara: Analysis of perception of motion in television signals and its application to bandwidth compression. IEEE Trans. COM-*23*, 761 (1975)
3.19 A.J. Seyler, Z.L. Budrikis: Detail perception after scene changes in television image presentations. IEEE Trans. IT-*11*, 31 (1965)
3.20 Y. Ninomiya, B. Presada: "Some Qualitative Results on Temporal Masking in Television Pictures", Picture Coding Symposium, Ipswich, England, July, 1979
3.21 R.F.W. Pease, J.O. Limb: Exchange of spatial and temporal resolution in television coding. Bell Syst. Tech. J. *50*, 191 (1971)

3.22 J.O. Limb, R.F.W. Pease: A simple interframe coder for video telephony. Bell Syst. Tech. J. *50*, 1877 (1971)
3.23 B.G. Haskell, P.L. Gordon, R.L. Schmidt, J.V. Scattaglia: Interframe coding of 525-line monochrome television at 1.5 Mbits/s. IEEE Trans. COM-*25*, 1339 (1977)
3.24 A.N. Netravali, B. Prasada: Adaptive quantization of picture signals using spatial masking. Proc. IEEE *65*, 536 (1977)
3.25 J.W. Woods: Stability of DPCM coders for television. IEEE Trans. COM-*23*, 845 (1975)
3.26 J.B. O'Neal: Predictive quantizing systems (differential pulse code modulation) for the transmission of television signals. Bell Syst. Tech. J. *45*, 689 (1966)
3.27 B.G. Haskell: Entropy measurements for non-adaptive and adaptive frame-to-frame linear predictive coding of video telephone signals. Bell Syst. Tech. J. *54*, 1155 (1975)
3.28 R.E. Graham: Predictive quantizing of television signals. IRE Wescon Conv. Rec. *2*, Pt.4, 147 (1958)
3.29 D.J. Connor, R.F.W. Pease, W.G. Scholes: Television coding using two-dimensional spatial prediction. Bell Syst. Tech. J. *50*, 1049 (1971)
3.30 W. Zschunke: DPCM picture coding with adaptive prediction. IEEE Trans. COM-*25*, 1295 (1977)
3.31 I.J. Dukhovich, J.B. O'Neal: A three-dimensional spatial non-linear predictor for television. IEEE Trans. COM-*26*, 578 (1978)
3.32 J. Max: Quantizing for minimum distortion. IRE Trans. IT-*6*, 7 (1960)
3.33 H. Gish, J.N. Pierce: Asymptotically efficient quantizing. IEEE Trans. IT-*14*, 676 (1968)
3.34 P. Noll, R. Zelinski: Bounds on quantizer performance in the low bit-rate region. IEEE Trans. COM-*26*, 300 (1978)
3.35 A.N. Netravali: On quantizers for DPCM coding of picture signals. IEEE Trans. IT-*23*, 360 (1977)
3.36 J.O. Limb: Source receiver encoding of television signals. Proc. IEEE *55*, 364 (1967)
3.37 B. Prasada, A.N. Netravali, A. Kobran: Adaptive companding of picture signals in a predictive coder. IEEE Trans. COM-*26*, 161 (1978)
3.38 D.A. Huffman: A method for construction of minimum redundancy codes. Proc. IRE *40*, 1098 (1952)
3.39 T.S. Huang: "Easily Implementable Suboptimum Runlength Codes", Proc. Int. Conf. on Commun., San Francisco, CA, 1975, p.7-8
3.40 F.W. Mounts: Video encoding system with conditional picture element replenishment. Bell Syst. Tech. J. *48*, 2545 (1969)
3.41 J.O. Limb, R.F.W. Pease, K.A. Walsh: Combining intraframe and frame-to-frame coding for television. Bell Syst. Tech. J. *53*, 1137 (1974)
3.42 B.G. Haskell: Differential addressing of clusters of changed picture elements for interframe coding of video telephone signals. IEEE Trans. COM-*24*, 140 (1976)
3.43 Y. Ninomiya: "Motion-Correction in Interframe Coding Systems, Image Engineering Group Meeting", Record IE-78-6 (1978) [in Japanese]
3.44 S. Brofferio, C. Cafforio, P. DelRe, G. Quaglia: Redundancy reduction of video signals using movement compensation. Alta Freq. *43*, 836 (1974)
3.45 C. Cafforio, F. Rocca: Methods for measuring small displacements of television images. IEEE Trans. IT-*22*, 573 (1976)
3.46 C. Cafforio, F. Rocca: Tracking moving objects in television images. Signal Proc. *1*, 133 (1979)
3.47 J.O. Limb, J.A. Murphy: Estimating the velocity of moving images in television signals. Comp. Graph. Image Proc. *4*, 311 (1975)
3.48 A.N. Netravali, J.D. Robbins: Motion-compensated television coding: part I. Bell Syst. Tech. J. *58*, 631 (1979)
3.49 J.D. Robbins, A.N. Netravali: "Interframe Television Coding Using Movement Compensation", Proc. Int. Commun. Conf. 23.4.1 (1979)

3.50 P. Wintz: Transform picture coding. Proc. IEEE *60*, 809 (1972)
3.51 H.J. Landau, D. Slepian: Some computer experiments in picture processing for bandwidth reduction. Bell Syst. Tech. J. *50*, 1525 (1971)
3.52 J.A. Roese, W.K. Pratt, G.S. Robinson: Interframe cosine transform image coding. IEEE Trans. COM-*25*, 1329 (1977)
3.53 S.C. Knauer: Real-time video compression algorithm for Hadamard transform processing. IEEE Trans. EMC-*18*, 28 (1976)
3.54 T.R. Natarajan, N. Ahmed: On interframe transform coding. IEEE Trans. COM-*25*, 1323 (1977)
3.55 F.W. Mounts, A.N. Netravali, B. Prasada: Design of quantizers for real-time Hadamard-transform coding of pictures. Bell Syst. Tech. J. *56*, 21 (1977)
3.56 K. Shibata: "Three-Dimensional Orthogonal Transform Coding of NTSC Colour Signals", Picture Coding Symposium, Tokyo, August, 1977
3.57 A. Habibi: Hybrid coding of pictorial data. IEEE Trans. COM-*22*, 614 (1974)
3.58 J.A. Heller: "A Real-Time Hadamard Transform Video Compression System Using Frame-to-Frame Differencing", Proc. Nat. Telecom. Conf., San Diego, CA, 1974, p.77
3.59 A.N. Netravali, J.A. Stuller: Motion-compensated transform coding. Bell Syst. Tech. J. *58*, 1703-1718 (1979)
3.60 J.A. Stuller, A.N. Netravali: Transform domain motion estimation. Bell Syst. Tech. J. *58*, 1673-1702 (1979)
3.61 J.C. Candy, M.A. Franke, B.G. Haskell, F.W. Mounts: Transmitting television as clusters of frame-to-frame differences. Bell Syst. Tech. J. *50*, 1889 (1971)
3.62 I. Ishiguro, K. Iinuma, Y. Iijima, T. Koga, S. Azami, T. Mune: "Composite Interframe Coding of NTSC Color Television Signals", Proc. Nat. Telecomm. Conf., Dallas, TE, 1976, p.6.4-1
3.63 H. Kawanishi, H. Yasuda, H. Kuroda: "An Experimental Inter-Multiframe Coder", Picture Coding Symposium, Tokyo, August 1977
3.64 J. Klie: Codierung von Videosignalen für eine Übertragungsrate von 64 Kbit/sec., NTG Fachberichte *65*, 131 (1978)
3.65 H. Yasuda, H. Kuroda, H. Kawanishi, F. Kanaya, H. Hashimoto: Transmitting 4 MHz TV signals by combinational difference coding. IEEE Trans. COM-*25*, 508 (1977)
3.66 M.S. Sabri: "Linear and Nonlinear Temporal Filtering of NTSC Video Signals", Picture Coding Symposium, Ipswich, England, July 1979
3.67 J.O. Limb, C.B. Rubinstein, J.E. Thompson: Digital coding of color video signals — a review. IEEE Trans. COM-*25*, 1349 (1977)
3.68 E. Dubois, M.S. Sabri: "Multi-Dimensional Spectra of Sampled NTSC Colour Signals with Application to Coding", Picture Coding Symposium, Ipswich, England, July 1979
3.69 J.O. Drewery: The filtering of luminance and chrominance signals to avoid cross-colour in a PAL colour system. BBC Eng. *105*, 8 (1976)
3.70 E. Dubois: Effects of digital demodulation on component coding of NTSC color signals. IEEE Trans. COM-*27*, 1342 (1979)
3.71 J.E. Thompson: Differential encoding of composite color television signals using chrominance-corrected prediction. IEEE Trans. COM-*22*, 1106 (1974)
3.72 R. Johnston, J. Mastronardi, G. Mony: A digital television sequence store. IEEE Trans. COM-*26*, 594 (1978)

Chapter 4 Image Sequence Enhancement

T. S. Huang and Y. P. Hsu

With 20 Figures

Although the restoration and enhancement of single images have been studied extensively [4.1], there have been very few results in the literature on the restoration and enhancement of image sequences. In Chap.3 of this book, noise reduction in image sequences is discussed in connection with interframe coding. In Chap.7, motion deblurring is briefly mentioned.

In the present chapter, we shall present in some detail results of two experiments in reducing image sequence noise by motion-compensated temporal filtering. In the first experiment, motion estimation is done by a simple matching technique, while in the second experiment, it is done by the method of differentials (discussed in Chap.1).

We might mention that many image sequences collected by visible, infrared, and other scanners are corrupted by random and burst noise (including line dropout). Reducing the noise will not only improve the visual appearance of the sequence but also facilitate automatic target detection, recognition, and tracking.

4.1 Temporal Filtering

To reduce noise in image sequences, we can apply three-dimensional filters, the three dimensions being the two spatial coordinates (x and y) and the time coordinate (t). However, to focus our attention on the time dimension, we use only temporal filters in the experiments described in this chapter.

4.1.1 Straight Temporal Filtering

Let $f_k(i,j)$ denote the gray level of the ij^{th} picture element (i^{th} row, j^{th} column) of the kth frame of the image sequence, and $g_k(i,j)$ that of the corresponding picture element in the filtered image sequence. A nonrecursive straight temporal filter over (2K+1) frames is defined by

$$g_k(i,j) = F\left\{f_{k-K}(i,j), f_{k-K+1}(i,j), \ldots, f_k(i,j), \ldots, f_{k+K}(i,j)\right\} \quad . \tag{4.1}$$

Two examples are

i) Linear time-invariant filtering

$$F\left\{x_{k-K}, x_{k-K+1}, \ldots, x_k, x_{k+1}, \ldots, x_{k+K}\right\} = \sum_{m=-K}^{K} a_m x_{k+m} \tag{4.2}$$

where a_m are constants. When all the a_m's are equal, we have the case of averaging.

ii) Median filtering

$$F\left\{x_{k-K}, \ldots, x_k, \ldots, x_{k+K}\right\} = \text{Median}\ (x_{k-K}, \ldots, x_k, \ldots, x_{k+K}) \quad . \tag{4.3}$$

A recursive straight temporal filter is defined by

$$g_k(i,j) = F\left\{f_{k-K}(i,j), f_{k-K+1}(i,j), \ldots, f_k(i,j); \right.$$
$$\left. g_{k-M}(i,j), g_{k-M+1}(i,j), \ldots, g_{k-1}(i,j)\right\} \tag{4.4}$$

where K and M are positive integers. Two examples are

iii) Linear time-invariant filtering

$$F\left\{x_{k-K}, \ldots, x_k; y_{k-M}, \ldots, y_{k-1}\right\} = \sum_{n=-K}^{0} a_n x_{k+n} + \sum_{m=-M}^{-1} b_m y_{k+m} \tag{4.5}$$

where a_n and b_m are constants.

iv) Median filtering

$$F\left\{x_{k-K}, \ldots, x_k; y_{k-M}, \ldots, y_{k-1}\right\} = \text{Median}\ (y_{k-M}, y_{k-M+1}, \ldots, y_{k-1}, x_k) \quad . \tag{4.6}$$

Note that for white Gaussian random noise, averaging in the temporal direction over N frames will reduce the noise variance by a factor of N. Median filtering will reduce the noise variance by a factor of only $2N/\pi$. However, for reducing salt-and-pepper noise and burst noise (including line dropout), median filtering is much more effective [4.2].

4.1.2 Motion-Compensated Temporal Filtering

Both averaging and median filtering (in the temporal direction) will degrade (blur) moving objects. To reduce this degrading effect, we propose to estimate the direction of motion at each picture element and then do the filtering along that direction.

We shall consider the nonrecursive filtering case, the recursive case being entirely similar. To obtain the filtered point $g_k(i,j)$, we track the object point located at the ij^{th} element of the kth frame over the (2K+1) frames to be used in the filter expression (4.1). Let the coordinates of this object point in the $(k+m)^{th}$ frame be $\underline{u}_{k+m}$, $m=-K,-K+1,\ldots,-1,0,1,\ldots,K-1,K$. Thus $\underline{u}_k=(i,j)$. The filtering is defined by

$$g_k(i,j) = F\left\{f_{k-K}(\underline{u}_{k-K}),\ldots,f_k(i,j),\ldots,f_{k+K}(\underline{u}_{k+K})\right\} \quad . \tag{4.7}$$

Two examples are

v) Nonrecursive linear time-invariant filtering, motion compensated, and

vi) Nonrecursive median filtering, motion compensated.

4.2 Temporal Filtering with Motion Compensation by Matching

In Sects.4.2,3 we report two temporal filtering experiments. In the first experiment, filters i), ii), v), and vi) of Sect.4.1 are used with $(2K+1)=3$, and $a_m=1/3$. Motion estimation is done by a simple matching method.

4.2.1 Motion Estimation by Matching

The motion was estimated in the following way. The sample variances are calculated for the 9 triplets $\{f_{k-1}(i-m,j-n),f_k(i,j),f_{k+1}(i+m,j+n)\}$ for $\{n=0;\ m=0,\pm1,\pm2,\pm3\}$ and $\{m=0;n=\pm1\}$.

The triplet with the smallest variance is taken as the direction of motion. For example, if the variance is smallest for $n=0;\ m=2$, then

$$\begin{aligned}\underline{u}_{k-1} &= (i-2,j)\\ \underline{u}_k &= (i,j)\\ \underline{u}_{k+1} &= (i+2,j)\end{aligned}$$

and the linear filter output will be

$$g_k(i,j) = \frac{1}{3}f_{k-1}(i-2,j) + \frac{1}{3}f_k(i,j) + \frac{1}{3}f_{k+1}(i+2,j) \quad .$$

4.2.2 Experimental Results of Filtering

The experimental results were obtained by computer simulation using the Digital Video Store System [4.3] at INRS Telecommunication. Three input sequences

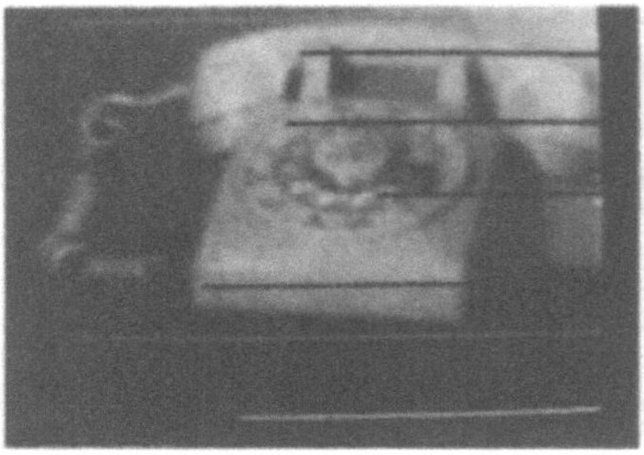

a)

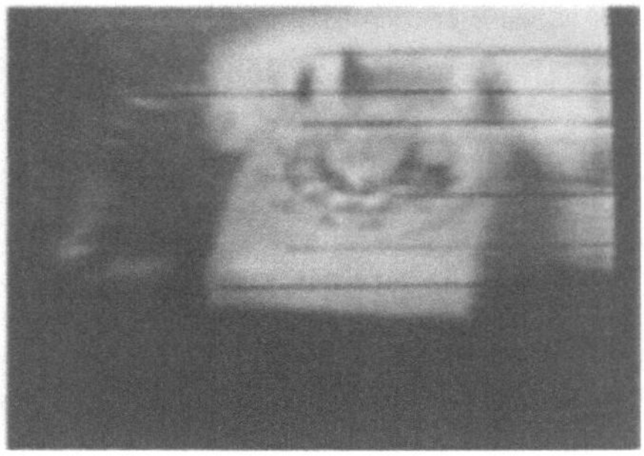

b)

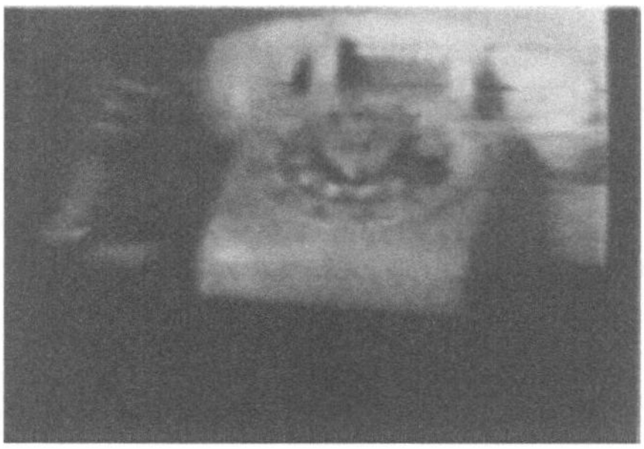

c)

Fig. 4.1a-c. Temporal filtering of a zooming sequence. (a) A frame from the original sequence containing Gaussian noise and line dropout. (b) A frame from the linearly filtered sequence. The temporal linear smoothing was over 3 frames. (c) A frame from the median-filtered sequence. The median was taken temporally over 3 frames

were used, a) panning, b) zooming, and c) conductor. Each frame contains approximately 256×256 samples with 8 bits per sample.

Four temporal filters were applied to each of these 3 sequences. These are filters i), ii), v), and vi) as described earlier.

The filtered results were recorded on a video tape. Here we can show only still frame results.

In Fig.4.1, some still frame results of temporal filtering of the "zooming" sequence are shown. Figure 4.1a shows a frame of the original sequence (before filtering) which contains Gaussian noise and line dropout. Figures 4.1b, c show still frames of the filtered sequences using filters i) and ii), respectively. Still-frame results of temporary filtering of the "conductor" sequence are shown in Fig.4.2. Figure 4.2a shows a frame of the original sequence. Figures 4.2b-e show still frames of the filtered sequences using filters i), ii), v), and vi), respectively.

4.2.3 Discussions

The performance of the temporal filters can be compared only by viewing the filtered sequences on a TV monitor. However, the following general conclusions can be stated.

a)

d)

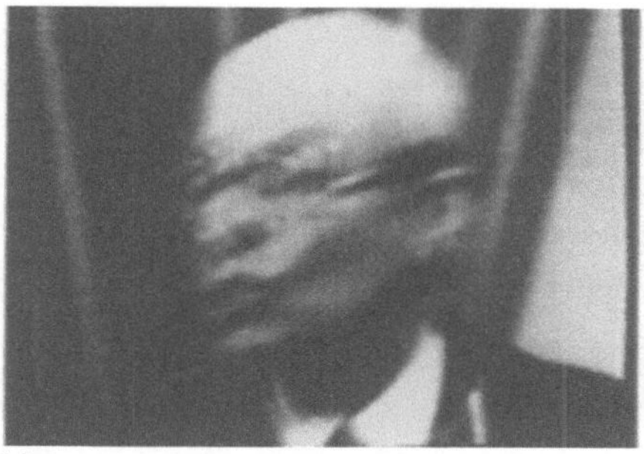

b)

e)

c)

Fig. 4.2a-e. Temporal filtering of the image sequence "conductor". (a) A frame from the original sequence. (b) A frame from the linearly filtered sequence. (c) A frame from the median-filtered sequence. (d) A frame from the motion-compensated linearly filtered sequence. (e) A frame from the motion-compensated median filtered sequence

1) In both the linear and the median filtering case, motion compensation helps greatly.
2) Overall, the motion-compensated median filter performs the best (in terms of reducing noise and preserving motion).
3) Edges of slow-moving large objects are preserved remarkably well by median filtering even without motion compensation.

4.3 Temporal Filtering with Motion Compensation by the Method of Differentials

In the second experiment, filters i) and v) of Sect.4.1 are used with a_m = constant and $2K+1=5$. Motion estimation is done by the method of differentials. We assume the motion to be purely two-dimensional translation.

4.3.1 Motion Estimation by the Method of Differentials

The method of differentials was discussed in Chap.1 (see also [4.4-6]). Since the notation we shall use here is slightly different from that in Chap.1, we will briefly rederive (1.12).

Let the luminance functions of two consecutive frames of images taken at the times t_1 and t_2 be $I_1(x,y)$ and $I_2(x,y)$, respectively, $\underline{S}=(S_x,S_y)$ the shift vector of the object in the image during the time interval $[t_1,t_2]$, and x and y the spatial coordinates in the image plane. Then we have

$$I_2(x,y) = I_1(x-S_x,y-S_y) \quad . \tag{4.8}$$

The frame-difference signal ΔI_1 is defined as

$$\begin{aligned}\Delta I_1(x,y) &\triangleq I_1(x,y) - I_2(x,y) = I_1(x,y) - I_1(x-S_x,y-S_y)\\ &= \frac{\partial I_1(x,y)}{\partial x} S_x + \frac{\partial I_1(x,y)}{\partial y} S_y + \varepsilon\end{aligned} \tag{4.9}$$

where $\partial I_1/\partial x$ and $\partial I_1/\partial y$ are the two components of the gradient of $I_1(x,y)$. In (4.9), ε represents the higher order terms in the Taylor series expansion of $I_1(x,y)$. Equation (4.9) establishes an approximate relationship between the frame difference signal, the spatial gradient, and the shift when the higher order terms in ε can be ignored. In the following discussion, we assume ε can be ignored.

At each picture element (pixel), we have an equation (4.9). To determine S_x and S_y, we solve simultaneous equations arising from a number of pixels in a common neighborhood. We write these equations in matrix form

$$[I] = [G][S] \tag{4.10}$$

where [I] is the frame difference column matrix, [G] the gradient matrix, and [S] the column vector of shifts. Because the gradient matrix [G] is generally not square but rectangular, its inverse does not exist. Our approach is to take the pseudoinverse of [G] to solve (4.10) [4.7]. Thus, assuming $[G]^T[G]$ is nonsingular (where T denotes matrix transposition), we have

$$[S] = \left[[G]^T[G]\right]^{-1}[G]^T[I] \quad . \tag{4.11}$$

As far as temporal filtering is concerned, we need to estimate the motion pixelwise to take account of the fact that the scene may contain many objects moving with different velocities. For application to temporal noise filtering, the motion information in areas containing edges are the most important while it is less important in areas which contain fairly uniform gray-level variations.

In the temporal filtering algorithm to be described in Sect.4.3.3, the following method is used for obtaining the pixelwise motion estimation. First, a block is taken from the upper left corner of the image, the size of the block taken is as small as possible; then we use (4.11) to estimate the shift over this block, and take the estimate as the estimated value of motion of the center of the block. Then, the block is shifted one pixel at a time, and the above process is repeated until all pixels in the image are estimated. As we shall see, the accuracy of estimation of motion using this approach is good even under noisy conditions. The estimated motion information is then incorporated in the filtering algorithm for motion compensation.

Before we report the results of temporal filtering, we examine various factors influencing the accuracy of motion estimation.

4.3.2 Various Factors Influencing Motion Estimation

a) *Presmoothing*

The linear relationship of (4.9) is not always satisfied in real images because of the sharpness of the edges. The edge of an object in an image forms a sharp transition between areas with different gray levels. The sharper the edge, the narrower the transition zone it covers. If the shift of an edge is greater than the width of the transition zone that it covers, the linear relationship will not hold. Figure 4.3 shows this situation in the one-dimensional case, the two-dimensional case being similar. In Fig.4.3a, the edge before shifting is represented by a solid line, and the shifted one by a dash line. The transition zone is less than one sampling interval (pixel) but the shift equals 2 pixels. At the position x_0, the frame difference signal is equal to zero and the gradient signal equals g_1, so that (4.9) fails in this case. But in Fig.4.3b, the edge transition zone covers 5 pixels, and the

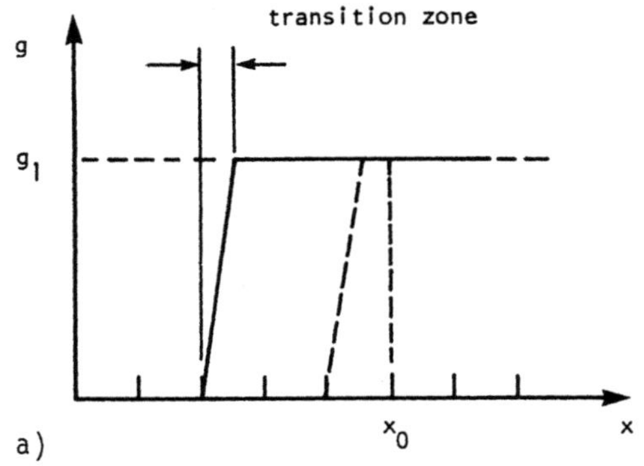

Fig. 4.3a,b. Effect of edge sharpness on motion estimation. (a) Sharp edge case. The shift is greater than the width of the transition zone. No point can satisfy (4.9). (b) Inclined edge. The shift is much less than the width of the transition of the edge. So most of pixels on the edge will satisfy (4.9)

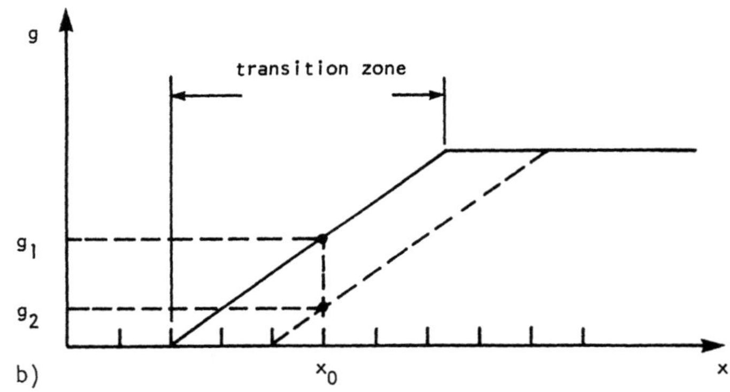

shift of the edge is still 2 pixels. At x_0, the frame difference signal equals g_1-g_2, and the gradient signal equals g_2, so that the linear relationship holds. Unfortunately, in many images we have edges like that in Fig.4.3a. One way to remedy this situation is to presmooth the image before using (4.11). We smooth it by replacing a pixel by its local average (over a small neighborhood). Figure 4.4a shows the effect of smoothing window size on the accuracy of estimation. The smoothing process is inserted before the calculation of the gradient and the frame difference. The abscissa represents the actual shift values (which are known) and the ordinate represents the estimated shift values. From the curves in Fig.4.4a we see that the error of estimation is getting greater when the smoothing window size becomes smaller. This is the case especially when the shift is large. The block size used here to solve (4.11) is 64×64. The smoothing window size tested is from 1×1 up to 11×11 pixels, where 1×1 means no smoothing is applied. An alternative presentation of the effect of smoothing window size is shown in Fig.4.4b. Here the known shift is 1 pixel. We use the ratio S_{known}/S_{est} to represent the effect of smoothing, where S_{known} is the known shift and S_{est} is the estimated shift.

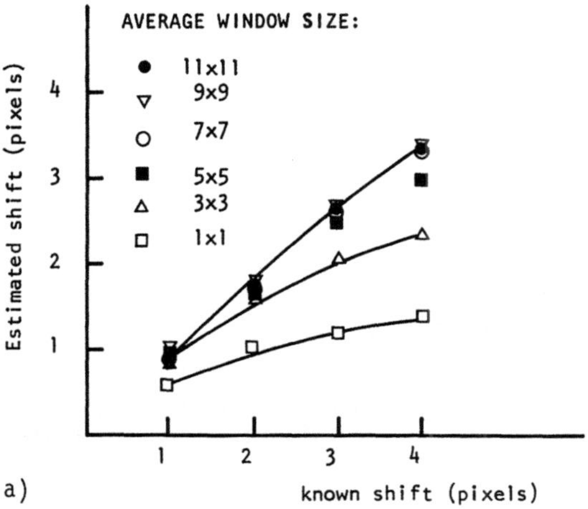

a)

Fig. 4.4a,b. Effect of smoothing window size on motion estimation

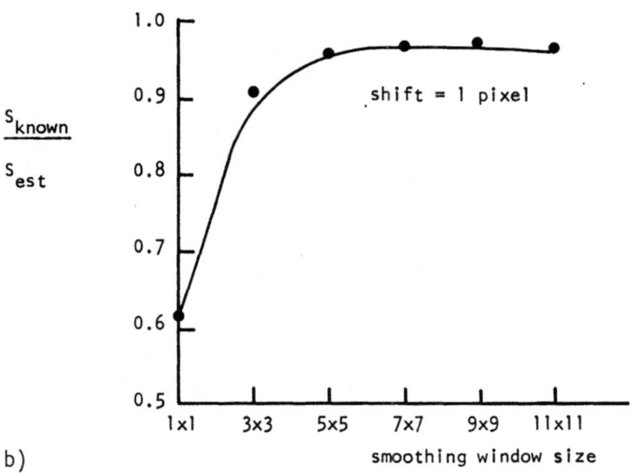

b)

The improvement of accuracy of estimation is obvious even when the smallest smoothing window size (3×3 pixels) is applied in this 1 pixel shift case. The image used in Figs.4.4a,b is a part of a girl's face (see Fig.4.6a). The results for other images are similar.

b) *Edge Density*

Edge density refers to the number of edges per unit spatial length. The more details an image area contains, the higher the density will be. In a dense case, if the shift of an edge is equal to or larger than the transition zone that it covers, the position of a shifted edge in the current frame may correspond to the position of a neighboring edge in the preceding frame. The

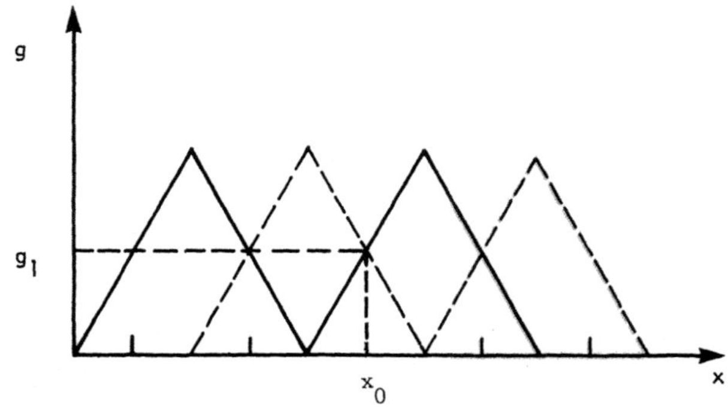

Fig. 4.5. The position of a shifted edge in the current frame (dashed line) may correspond to the position of a neighboring edge in the preceding frame (solid line)

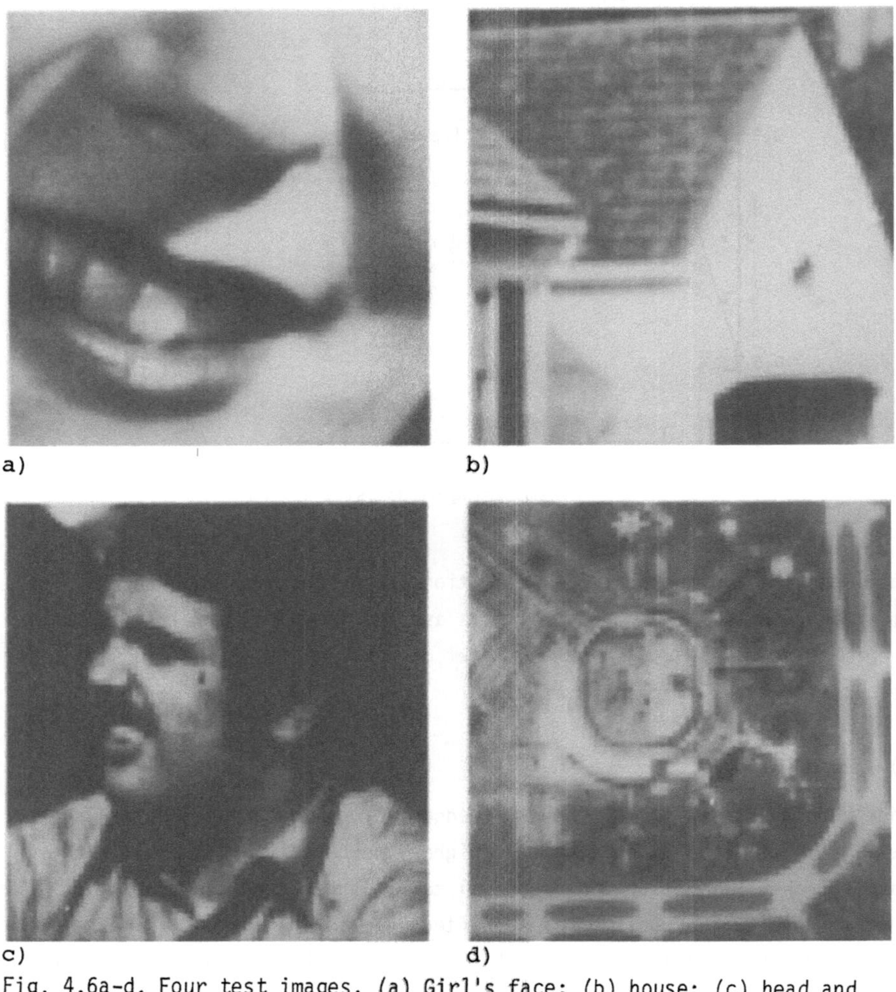

Fig. 4.6a-d. Four test images. (a) Girl's face; (b) house; (c) head and shoulder; (d) airport

frame difference signal may now be the difference between different edges. For example, in Fig.4.5, the edges occur one right after another. At the position x_0, the frame difference signal will be equal to the difference between the gray levels of the ascending edge and that of its neighboring descending edge. This violates the premise of (4.9), which requires the frame difference signal and the gradient signal to be calculated on the same edge. In this case, we could not find adequate points that satisfy (4.9) in a quite wide range. Figure 4.6 shows four different images with varying amounts of details. Figure 4.6a is a part of a girl's face with moderate edge density, the results of Fig.4.4 come out from this picture. Figure 4.6b is a part of a house, some areas (roof) are full of details and some (wall) are almost uniformly gray. Figure 4.6c is a person (head and shoulder) which contains many areas with small gray-level variations. Figure 4.6d is a part of an airport, which contains much detail. The effects of different edge density on estimation is shown in Fig.4.7. In Fig.4.7, the abscissa represents the known shift between the frames, the ordinate represents the relative estimated value S_{known}/S_{est} just as in Fig.4.4b. The circles represent the results of Fig.4.6a, the triangles represent the results of Fig.4.6b, the shaded-in squares represent the results of Fig.4.6c, the squares represent the results of Fig.4.6d. High accuracy of estimation is obtained for the image in Fig.4.6a which is of moderate edge density. Here most of the points at the edges satisfy the linear relationship in (4.9). The lowest accuracy occurs for the image of Fig.4.6d. Because of its fine detail, the relative error of the estimation is getting larger for the case of larger shift, notwithstanding the application of smooth-

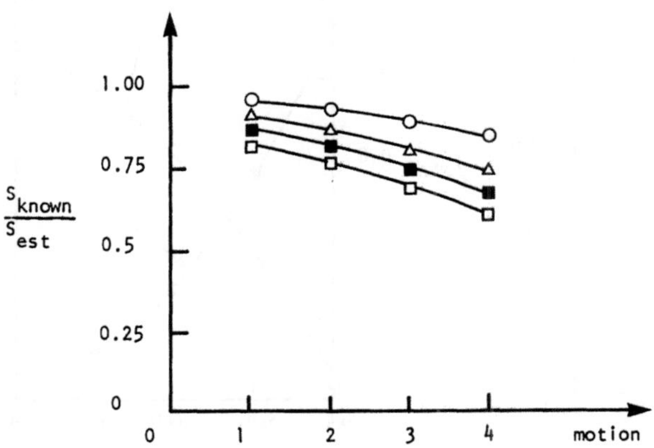

Fig. 4.7. Effect of edge density on motion estimation. Block size 64 × 64. Smoothing window size 11 × 11. o: Results from Fig.4.6a; Δ: results from Fig.4.6b; ■: results from Fig.4.6c; □: results from Fig.4.6d

ing before calculating S_{est}. The accuracy of estimation obtained with the other two images is somewhere in between. Areas with slow gray-level variations present a problem for motion estimation. However, in application to noise reduction, what is important is the motion information over the areas containing edges. We do not care about the areas with uniform gray levels or slow gray-level variations.

c) *Block Size*

In general, the distribution of edges in an image is not uniform, i.e., the edge density in an image is different from part to part. In the results presented in Sects.4.3.2a,b, the motion estimation was done globally over an entire 64×64 image. However, as mentioned earlier, for application to temporal filtering we need to estimate the motion pixelwise. Can the accuracy of estimation be retained if the block size used to estimate the motion is reduced? To find out we divide the 64×64 image into 1×1, 2×2, 4×4, 8×8, and 16×16 blocks; then the size of each block is 64×64, 32×32, 16×16, 8×8, and 4×4 pixels, respectively. If the 4×4 block size is used, there will be 16×16 estimates for the entire image, if the 8×8 block size is used, there will be 8×8 estimates for the entire image, etc. We then average the estimates at each block size level. The averaged values and the variances of estimation at each block size level are used for comparison. Two images are

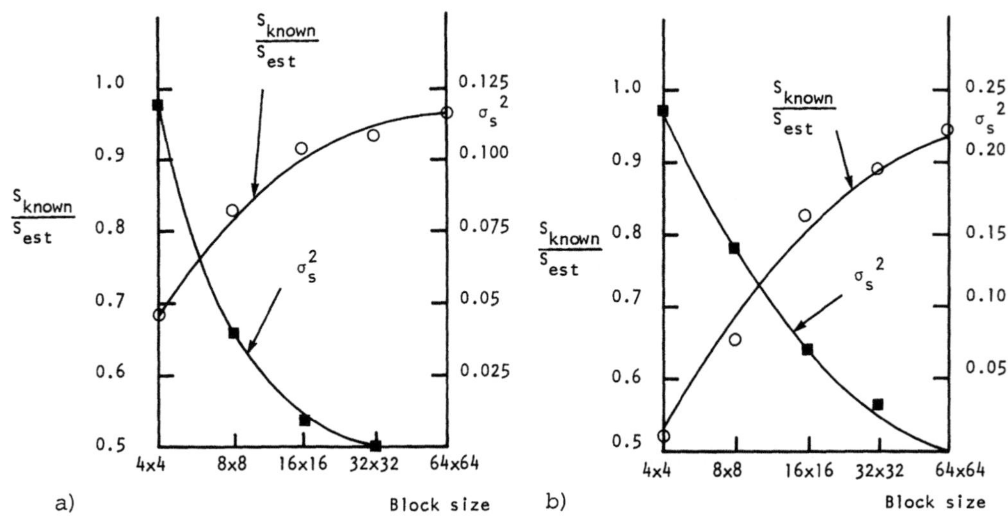

Fig. 4.8a,b. Effect of block size on motion estimation accuracy. (a) For image in Fig.4.6a; (b) for image in Fig.4.6b

used (Fig.4.6a,b). The results are shown in Fig.4.8. Figure 4.8a contains the results of the image of Fig.4.6a, and Fig.4.8b the results of the image of Fig.4.6b. There are two curves in each figure. One is the average value of relative estimation S_{known}/S_{est}, the other is the variance of the estimation σ_S^2. From Fig.4.8 we see that as the block size becomes smaller, the variance of the estimates gets higher, and the error of the average of the estimation greater. Note that the variance of the estimation of the image of the girl's face is almost half as big as that of the image of the house, and the variance of the estimation of the former is less than 0.05 when the 8×8 block size is used. This is because the girl's face is of moderate edge density so that most of the blocks include some adequate edge information. In the image of the house, there is much detail on the roof, while on the wall, large uniform gray-level areas exist. Thus, when the block size gets smaller, many blocks may not include any edge information, or may be too full of details so that the estimated values of shifts differ considerably from the true values.

d) *Noise*

The results in Sects.4.3.2a-c were obtained under noiseless conditions. It is expected that the error of estimation will be larger when some amount of noise exists in the image. The deterioration of the estimation, however, will be reduced due to the presmoothing process in the estimating algorithm. Figure 4.9 shows the results for different amounts of noise in the image. In this figure, the abscissa represents the standard deviation of the noise added to

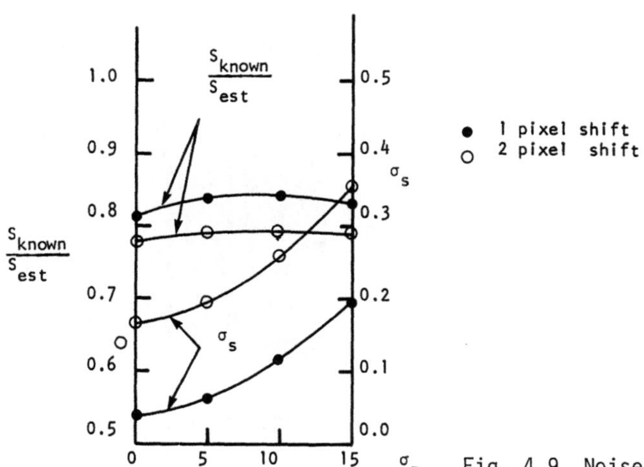

Fig. 4.9. Noise effects

the image (the image gray level ranges from 0 to 255), and the ordinates are the average relative estimate and its standard deviation. The smoothing window size used is 11×11 pixels. The algorithm used here to estimate the shift pixelwise was described at the end of Sect.4.3.1; the block size of 9×9 is selected according to the results of Sect.4.3.2c. The effect of the amount of noise on the average estimates is small, but the effect is greater on the

a) b) c)

Fig. 4.10a-c. Estimable region in black. Original image is Fig.4.6a. (a) Shift = 1 pixel, $\sigma_n = 15$; (b) shift = 2 pixels, $\sigma_n = 10$; (c) shift = 1 pixel, $\sigma_n = 0$

a) b) c)

Fig. 4.11a-c. Estimable region in black. Original image is Fig.4.6b. (a) Shift = 1 pixel, $\sigma_n = 15$; (b) shift = 2 pixels, $\sigma_n = 10$; (c) shift = 1 pixel, $\sigma_n = 0$

a) b) c)

Fig. 4.12a-c. Estimable region in black. Original image is Fig.4.6c. (a) Shift = 1 pixel, $\sigma_n = 15$; (b) shift = 2 pixels, $\sigma_n = 10$; (c) shift = 1 pixel, $\sigma_n = 0$

standard deviation of the estimates. The image used for getting the results is Fig.4.6a. Figures 4.10-12 show the results from the three images in Fig. 4.6a-c with different amounts of noise and shift added to them. The black area in each image represents the region in which the estimation errors are within a reasonable range (less than 20%). As will be seen in these figures, most of the regions that contain edges are "estimable". Of course, as the amount of noise or the shift is increased, the size of the "estimable" area is decreased.

e) *Estimation of Subpixel Motion*

One of the advantages of the differential method is its ability to estimate shifts which are less than 1 pixel, i.e., S_x and S_y in (4.9) need not be larger than 1 pixel and need not be integers.

Two successive frames for testing were generated by subsampling an 512×512 original image, the subsampling interval being 4 pixels in both directions. The subsampling of the first frame begins from the 1st column and the 1st row, and that of the second frame begins from the 2nd column and the 2nd row of the original image. The shift between these two frames is then 0.25 pixels in both the horizontal and the vertical directions. These two frames are shown in Fig.4.13a.

a)

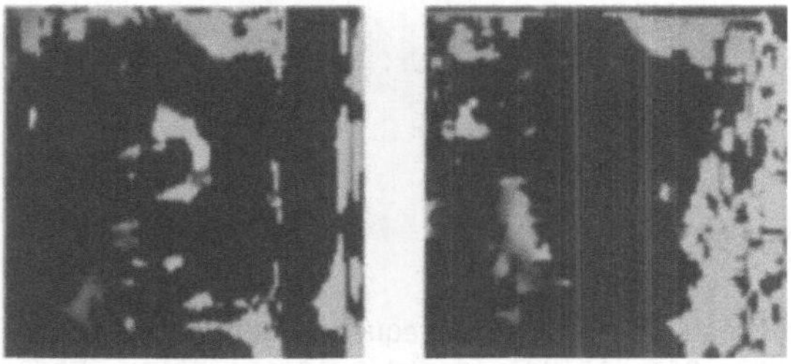

b)

Fig. 4.13a,b. Subpixel motion estimation. (a) Test image pair; (b) black regions represent pixels where the estimation error is less than 20%. Left and right pictures are for x and y shifts, respectively

After estimating the motion pixel by pixel in both spatial directions, we labeled with black spots those pixels where the estimations are close to the original shift values (errors smaller than 20%). These results are shown in Fig.4.13b.

Note that most of the areas containing edges are estimable, while some areas with slow gray-level variations are "nonestimable".

4.3.3 Experimental Results of Filtering

The two filters i) and v) of Sect.4.1 are used in our experiment with $a_m = 1/5$ and $2K+1 = 5$.

Five groups of image sequences (with 64×64 pixels per frame) were used. Each sequence of the first three groups was generated on the computer by shifting a single image repeatedly. The shift from one frame to the next is either 1 or 2 pixels. The three original images used to generate these three groups of sequences are Figs.4.6a-c. The fourth and fifth groups of image sequences were taken by a vidicon camera. Each of the two scenes contains two objects moving with different velocities. Zero mean white Gaussian noise of various amounts (σ_n=10, 15, and 20) were added to these sequences.

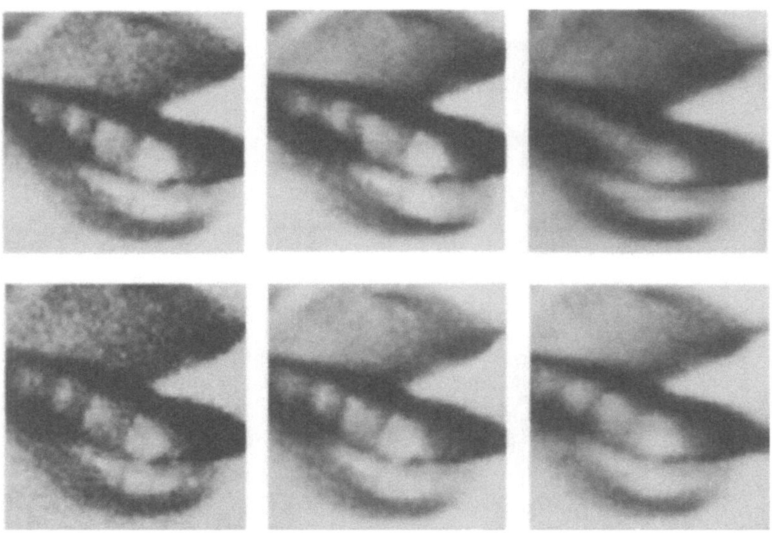

a)

b)

Fig. 4.14a,b. Temporal filtering results for image sequence generated from Fig.4.6a. In both (a) and (b), the left picture is the original noisy image, the middle picture is the filtered image with motion compensation, and the right picture is the filtered image without motion compensation. (a) Shift = 2 pixels, $\sigma_n = 10$; (b) shift = 1 pixel, $\sigma_n = 15$

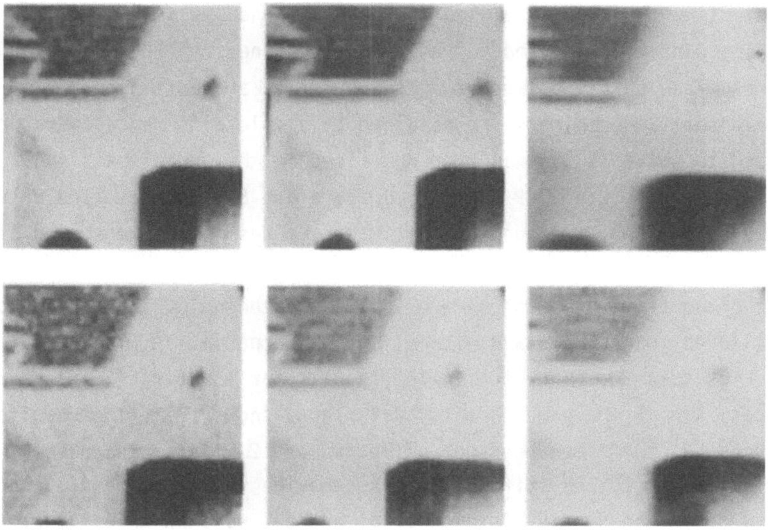

a)

b)

Fig. 4.15a,b. Temporal filtering results for image sequence generated from Fig.4.6b. In both (a) and (b), the left picture is the original noisy image, the middle picture is the filtered image with motion compensation, and the right picture is the filtered image without motion compensation. (a) Shift = 2 pixels, $\sigma_n = 10$; (b) shift = 1 pixel, $\sigma_n = 15$

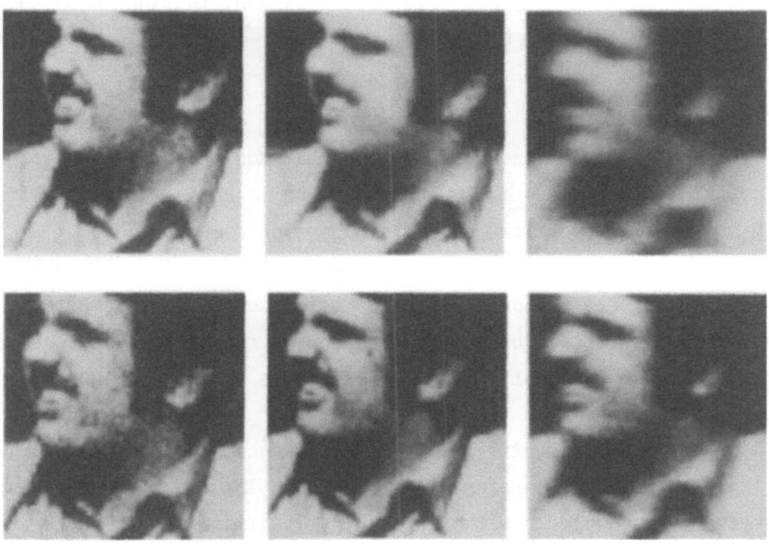

a)

b)

Fig. 4.16a,b. Temporal filtering results for image sequence generated from Fig.4.6c. In both (a) and (b), the left picture is the original noisy image, the middle picture is the filtered image with motion compensation, and the right picture is the filtered image without motion compensation. (a) Shift = 2 pixels, $\sigma_n = 10$; (b) shift = 1 pixel, $\sigma_n = 15$

The motion estimation algorithm used for each sequence is as follows. An 11×11 smoothing window is applied to reduce the sharpness of the edges in the five frames. Then shifts between successive frames are estimated. Frame differences and spatial gradients are obtained by simple difference operators. The method used to solve (4.11) has been described at the end of Sect.4.3.1. The block size used here was 9×9 pixels. So there are 64×64 estimated values for each frame pair. Then, we round the estimated values to integers, and use them for motion compensation.

Finally, the two filters i) and v) are applied to the noisy image sequence to get the filtered images with and without motion compensation. The results are shown in Figs.4.14-20. Figures 4.14-16 (results for the first 3 groups of image sequences) are of the same format. Each figure shows filtering results on two sequences: a) shift between successive frames = 2 pixels, and noise standard deviation $\sigma_n = 10$; b) shift between successive frames = 1 pixel, and noise standard deviation $\sigma_n = 15$. In each of a) and b), we show an original unfiltered image frame, and filtered frames with and without motion compensation.

In Figs.4.17-20, filtering results on the fourth and the fifth groups of image sequences are shown. Each group contains two sequences with noise standard deviations $\sigma_n = 15$ and 20, respectively. Here, instead of only one original frame, 5 frames of each original sequence are shown, together with the filtered frames with and without motion compensation.

4.3.4 Discussions

It is seen from the results of the last section that most edges in the images are preserved if the filter with motion compensation is used, while the edges are seriously blurred if the filter used has no motion compensation.

We note that in areas with slow gray-level variations, the estimated shifts are not accurate. However, in applications to motion-compensated temporal filtering this is not critical, because in areas with slow gray-level changes a large estimation error will not introduce noticeable distortion in the filtered image.

The method of differentials utilizes frame differences and spatial gradients in small neighborhoods. Therefore it can be used to deal with scenes involving several moving objects with different velocities. The approach can also be used for cases where the shifts are less than 1 pixel.

We note that the estimation accuracy can be improved by an iterative process. For example, if the true shift between the $(k-1)^{th}$ and the kth frames is 4 pixels and the first estimated value is 3 pixels, we shift back the kth

Fig.4.17a

Fig.4.17b.

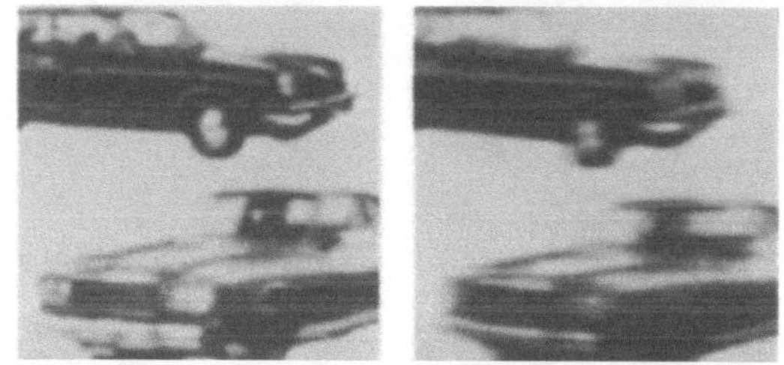

Fig.4.18b.

Fig.4.18a.

Fig. 4.17a,b. Temporal filtering results of image sequence containing two moving objects with different velocities. $\sigma_n = 15$. (a) Five frames of original noisy sequence; (b) filtered images — the left with motion compensation, the right without

Fig. 4.18a,b. Temporal filtering results of image sequence containing two moving objects with different velocities. $\sigma_n = 20$. (a) Five frames of original noisy sequence; (b) filtered images — the left with motion compensation, the right without

Fig.4.19a.

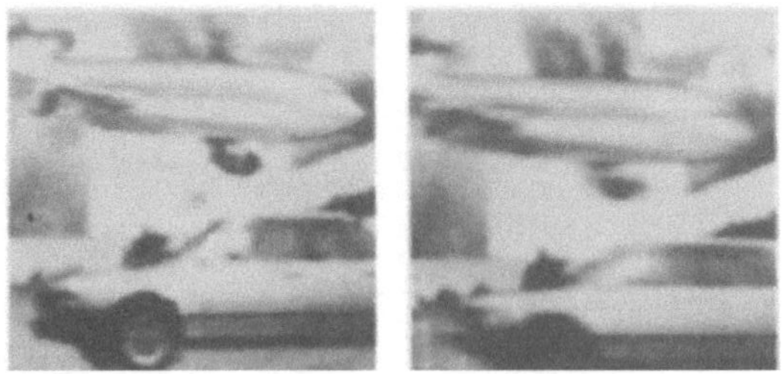

Fig4.19b.

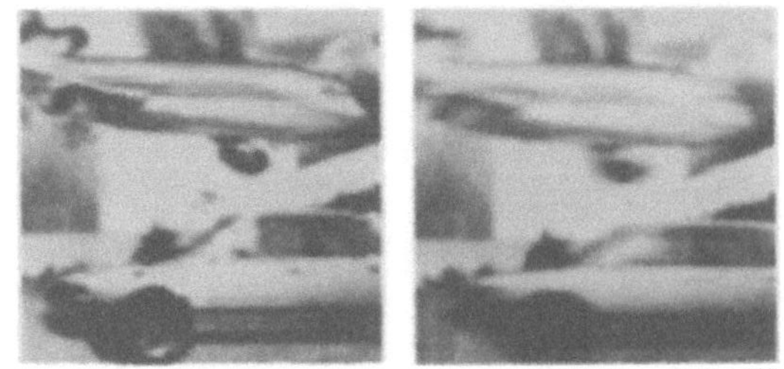

Fig.4.20b.

Fig.4.20a.

Fig. 4.19a,b. Temporal filtering results of image sequence containing two moving objects with different velocities against a stationary background. $\sigma_n = 10$. (a) Five frames of original noisy sequence; (b) filtered images – the left with motion compensation, the right without

Fig. 4.20a,b. Temporal filtering results of image sequence containing two moving objects with different velocities against a stationary background. $\sigma_n = 15$. (a) Five frames of original noisy sequence; (b) filtered images – the left with motion compensation, the right without frame by 3 pixels. Then, we estimate the shift between the $(k-1)^{th}$ frame and the shifted k^{th} frame. Because the shift between these two frames now becomes $4-3=1$ pixel, the estimated value may be, say, 0.95 pixel. The final estimate is then equal to $3+0.95=3.95$ pixels.

4.4 Summary

In this chapter we have presented two experiments in image sequence noise reduction using motion-compensated temporal filtering. Both of these experiments have the same main goal: to demonstrate that temporal filtering with motion compensation preserves image edge sharpness much better than without motion compensation.

However, the secondary goals of these two experiments are different. In the first experiment, we have shown that temporal median filtering can be superior to temporal averaging in many cases. In the second experiment, we have studied in detail the use of the method of differentials in motion estimation. It is seen that this method has many advantages including its capability in estimating motion locally and its computational efficiency.

Acknowledgement. The work reported in Sect.4.2 was carried out by TSH at INRS-Telecommunications, University of Quebec, where he was a Visiting Professor during the Summer Semester of 1979. The encouragement of Prof. M.L. Blostein, Director of INRS, and Prof. B Prasada, Head of the video communication group is greatly appreciated. The author also wishes to thank Profs. E. Dubois and S. Sabri for their invaluable help.

The work reported in Sect.4.3 was performed by the authors at Purdue University, West Lafayette, Indiana.

References

4.1 B.R. Frieden: "Image Restoration and Enhancement", in *Picture Processing and Digital Filtering*, ed. by T.S. Huang, 2nd ed. (Springer, Berlin, Heidelberg, New York 1979) Chap.5
4.2 B. Justuson: "Median Filters: Statistical Properties", in *Two-Dimensional Digital Signal Processing II: Transforms and Median Filters*, ed. by T.S. Huang (Springer, Berlin, Heidelberg, New York 1981)
4.3 R. Johnson, J. Mastronardi, G. Mony: A digital television sequence store, IEEE Trans. COM-*26*, 594-600 (1978)
4.4 J. Limb, J. Murphy: Estimating the velocity of moving images in tv signals. Comp. Graph. Image Proc. *4*, 311-327 (1975)
4.5 A. Netravali, J. Robbins: Motion compensation tv coding; part I. Bell Syst. Tech. J. *58*, 631-670 (1979)
4.6 C. Cafforio, F. Rocca: Tracking moving objects in tv images. Signal Proc. *1*, 133-140 (April 1979)
4.7 A. Albert: *Regression and the Moore-Penrose Pseudoinverse* (Academic, New York 1972)

Chapter 5 Image Region Extraction of Moving Objects

B. M. Radig

With 29 Figures

A sequence of TV frames is recorded from a real-world scene. In order to determine the motion attributes of objects, the segmentation of these digitized frames has to provide a reliable symbolic description for each image. For this purpose a hierarchy of relational structures is computed. Each grey-value matrix is transformed into a graph. Each node contains the coefficients of a small plane which approximates the image function in a local window. The arcs are initialized to the undirected binary adjacency relation. A constraint filter computes node- and arc-consistent subgraphs according to a specified parameter set by removing arcs which join incompatible neighbors. Isolated subgraphs are regarded as regions, their features are calculated essentially as distributions of node coefficients and differences thereof along arcs.

These features are compared in order to calculate similarity values for pairs of regions from different frames. The similarity values accomplish tracing an individual region through the sequence. The features reflect the interior structure of regions and are insensitive to changes of shape. In most cases regions can be traced even if they are partially occluded in some frames.

Generic object prototypes are formulated as parameter sets and geometrical constraints between the regions extracted by their application. Region attributes can be easily converted to parameter values. This supports a planning component of the system which directs the search for other regions in the same or the next frame according to the results of the region extraction process so far. Thus, the system is able to adapt prototypes by learning from their instances. It can search for missing members of a group of regions belonging to the same object, and it is able to focus its search on predicted object locations in subsequent frames.

Due to its flexibility and robustness in tracing objects this system may serve as a frontend of a knowledge-based analysis system for image sequences.

5.1 Overview

The history of the analysis of image sequences which record moving objects seems to be about ten years old. The earliest references in NAGEL's survey [5.1] are dated from 1969. Measurement of cloud velocity was one of the fundamental problems at the beginning [5.2]. This domain was not the only special one; other domains have been set up to study special problems in dynamic image analysis. ULLMAN [5.3] displayed dot and line patterns in order to study the physiological mechanism of motion reception. Homogeneous planar objects moving in front of a contrasting homogeneous background have been employed in order to study occlusion [5.4-6]. Familiar blocks-world objects ease the study of motion in space [5.7] or three-dimensional reconstruction by motion stereo [5.8].

As in static scene analysis real-world images are a challenge in dynamic analysis, too. Here I think of domains which are not controlled by the experimentalist but are only observed by him. Traffic scenes — as a typical real-world situation — exhibit actions which impose a multitude of difficulties for analysis, and whose participating objects are complicated with respect to their surface structure. They are easy to observe; in our case we let a TV camera look down from our laboratory window. First publications on this domain are [5.9,10].

In real-world scene sequences the question arises at what level of abstraction the images should be compared, what the items should be which are linked from frame to frame. WOLFERTS, for instance, cross-correlated subsections which enclose the cars; their exact positions are determined by the maximal correlation value. An operator, originally described by MORAVEC [5.11], which selects conspicious points was used by BARNARD and THOMPSON [5.12] in order to determine vehicle displacements. They linked those points whose frame-to-frame correspondence is determined by a relaxation technique. On a similar low level of abstraction, POTTER [5.13] computed velocity fields, comparing attributes of regularly scattered cross-shaped templates. Comparison of somewhat higher level symbols — of edge segments, straight lines, vertices, regions — can be found in restricted (artificial) scene domains [5.6-8,14,15a, 15b]. There, the use of such symbols is obvious.

Real-world moving objects are mostly analysed in terms of simple models like rectangles in [5.16], statistical parameters in [5.17], homogeneous regions in [5.18,19], or simple shape templates as in [5.20]. A richer description of images is found in [5.21], but PRICE's sequences are degenerated to image pairs; his aim is detection of changes. In this work one can see some of the dangers which come with a sophisticated repertoire. How is the following situation to be handled? [Ref.5.22, p.623]

If the recognition procedure were given the segments which were extracted, several errors might be expected because of the segmentations. Several ships are broken into two regions and these may be recognized as two individual ships or as no ships. Also some of the piers are broken into several pieces and some of these pieces may resemble a ship more than a pier.

Coming back to the question of the appropriate conceptual level on which to compare descriptions of real-world images, there is no definite answer. To extract the semantics of an object movement, as BADLER [5.23] did from artificially generated line drawings, is as well justified as the attempt to explain why at a certain location a pixel changed its value (grey or color component) a certain amount from one frame to the next. I can only state my preference for starting correlation of descriptive units on an intermediate level. The low-level approaches ignore the complexity of reasons why pixel values may change. They are, by their methodology, restricted to simple motion, such as pure translation parallel to the image plane, or fail if an object stops. High-level approaches which independently analyse each image of a sequence with methods from the repertoire of static scene analysis, ignore the advantage of a possible grouping of symbols to object candidates (structure from motion [5.3]) utilizing the knowledge of their movement in the image plane (e.g., [5.24,25]) or even their reconstructed motion in the original space (e.g., [5.26]). I prefer to establish a correspondence between symbols which are generated by a segmentation process and whose features are insensitive to those distortions in object projections which usually hinder the establishment of correspondence links.

5.1.1 Symbolic Description

The required segmentation process should be insensitive to all the kinds of noise which appear in TV images (Sect.5.2.2). Noise reduction can be done by averaging over small patches of the image, or by applying some edge-preserving smoothing operation like the one of NAGAO and MATSUYAMA [5.27]. My attention was drawn to a method published by HOLDERMANN and KAZMIERCZAK [5.28]. They approximated the image function locally with small planes computed by a least-squares fit. This seemed to me a good compromise between smoothing and keeping enough information about the image. Later a few other authors, e.g., [5.14,29-32], utilized directional derivatives. O'GORMAN [5.33] proposed Walsh-function expansion in order to determine edge response and angle. BROOKS [5.34] and HARALICK [5.35] gave a mathematical treatment of surface-fitting and orthogonal-basis applications for step edges.

My first attempt in processing the matrix of plane approximations was to extract line structures by thinning [5.36,37], tracing [5.28] or search [5.38]. However, the results of applying such methods to real-world images did not meet my expectations. Then I realized that the systematic local behavior of the vector field of plane normals bears much more information than a thin line. The consequence was to develope a region extraction algorithm in which regions are defined as subsections of the vector field where plane coefficients obey some property and relational constraints.

5.1.2 Sequences

In order to track regions through the image sequence, a metric has to be defined in their feature space which allows the algorithm to find the most similar region in a following or preceeding frame. Feature space and metric have to be constructed in such a way that the distance between two regions from different frames is shortest which are projections of the same object surface despite changes expected from motion, such as translation, rotation, occlusion, specular reflection, and shading.

In this approach the features selected to describe regions are essentially distributions of plane coefficient values (e.g., grey value) and differences between adjacent planes (e.g., angle difference). They retain their characteristics even if part of a region is missing due to occlusion. Shape descriptors are not included. One reason is that shape may change drastically in case of occlusion. To cope with this difficulty, one has to add special mechanisms, for example, predictive models [5.5,18,19] or comparison of contour segments [5.6]. Another reason is that the selected region features reflect the interior structure of the extracted area; the border may be ill defined especially in real-world images when no sharp contrast separates regions but rather the characteristics of adjacent regions gradually mix.

The metric is a fuzzy AND (minimum) of normalized comparison results between individual features of both regions. This is an arbitrary choice and there is some work to do in order to find a better metric, perhaps by statistical analysis of performance on region sequences.

After pairwise comparing regions from the current frame with those from the following or preceeding one, each region has a successor and a predecessor. Regions are then linked conservatively to region sequences by requiring that a region is the successor of its predecessor. What to do in any other case has to be explored by means of appropriate heuristics or postponed to a later stage of analysis.

Local or temporal disturbances of the projection of an object surface may be overridden by connecting two or more region sequences to a longer one which then has some time gaps. To do this, one may utilize information, e.g., motion properties, gathered by linking region sequences.

5.1.3 Planning

KELLY [5.39] demonstrated a gain in efficiency by first performing a coarse image analysis to identify interesting parts for a subsequent fine analysis. He called his technique "planning". YACHIDA et al. [5.40] applied this idea to inspection of image sequences (cineangiogram).

My approach provides two kinds of mechanisms for planning. One is to specify tighter limits for the parameters used to extract a region by analyzing the properties of the extracted region. The new specification will usually be more restrictive than the old one and thus speed up extraction of regions in subsequent frames. The other is to let the region extraction be influenced by special a priori knowledge; e.g., if regions are found which originate from shadows on a street, then it is likely that an object can be found above this region. Both planning facilities speed up extraction and linking of regions considerably.

5.2 Vector Field

The first step in the analysis transforms raw image data into a vector field. This is done by fitting planes to small overlapping windows of the grey-value matrix. This section briefly describes the imaging process, the influence of noise and of movement of objects, and the least-squares approximation.

5.2.1 Sampling

The lenses of a TV camera project a real image on the photosensitive target. If we impose Cartesian coordinates on the target plane, the incoming light may be expressed as a function z of x and y. The video signal is sampled every 100 ns and digitized with 8-bit resolution. What an interfaced computer sees is a rastered world, pixels as triples of (z_i, y_i, x_i). In our apparatus, 573 rows are sampled with 512 columns each. With the origin at the upper left corner, the range of pixel components is:

$$z_i \in [0,255], \quad y_i \in [0,572], \quad x_i \in [0,511],$$
$$i \text{ running from } 1 \text{ to } 512 * 573 = 293376 \quad .$$

Sampling density is lower in the horizontal than in the vertical direction. TV standards determine the number of rows, video bandwidth the sampling frequency. Though the aspect ratio of a video image is 4 by 3, the raster is 512 by 573. One aim of the preprocessing described below is to introduce a transformed pixel which represents a square of the optical image, not a horizontally elongated rectangle.

5.2.2 Noise

An important aim of the first processing step is to reduce the influence of noise. Several devices in the sensorial apparatus cooperate to disturb pixel component values.

Amplitude-noise generation in the camera is mostly due to the vidicon or plumbicon and preamplifiers. If an analogue disk stores image sequences, its modulators, demodulators, and playback amplifiers decrease the signal+noise-to-noise ratio. In our setup it is 34 dB after the camera and 27 dB after the disk. The analogue to digital converter adds quantization noise.

The instability of the electron-beam deflection system in the camera and the mechanical wow and flutter of the disk drive are mainly responsible for the uncertainty of coordinate values. A special ADC strobe synchronization reduces the uncertainty to less than two raster points overall. The interlacing of half-frame lines calls for a long-term stability (compared to 10 MHz sampling frequency) in order to lock out incompensable displacements between odd and even lines.

5.2.3 Motion Effects

This interlacing has a detrimental effect when recording moving objects. TV lines which are adjacent in y position are 20 ms apart in time. During this period the projection of a moving object may be displaced several raster units horizontally. Then contours perpendicular to the vector of motion become jagged or fuzzy. If one does not want to throw away half of the spatial resolution, the segmentation method should not be sensitive to that effect; especially simple edge-detector techniques probably get confused. (Illumination by strobe light, if possible in a controlled environment [5.41], avoids the whole problem.)

Another unwelcome phenomenon is the incomplete neutralization during scanning of the charge distribution generated by the photoeffect on the camera. Thus grey-value readings from an area a moving object passes become a mixture of present and past intensities. This is especially true with vidicon cameras with which we experimented at the beginning. The pictures presented here are recorded by a plumbicon where the magnitude of the effect is tolerable. Charge-coupled devices or silicon-photodiode cameras will behave better in this respect, but they are not yet available with sufficient resolution.

5.2.4 Plane Equation

Over a small patch of the camera target the intensity is assumed to be a linear function of the coordinates

$$z(x,y) = A*x + B*y + C \quad .$$

Furthermore it is assumed that a measurement z_i has a Gaussian distribution with standard deviation s_i about the true (but unknown) value $z(x_i,y_i)$. Then the probability P_i of observing the value z_i at (x_i,y_i) is given by

$$P_i = \frac{1}{s_i*\sqrt{2*\pi}} * \exp\left[-\frac{1}{2}\left(\frac{z_i-z(x_i,y_i)}{s_i}\right)^2\right] \quad .$$

The probability of reading N distinct values in our patch where linearity is fulfilled is

$$P(A,B,C) = \prod_i P_i \quad , \quad 1 = 1,\ldots,N \quad .$$

As we do not know the coefficients A, B, and C we estimate them

$$\hat{z}(x,y) = \hat{A}*x + \hat{B}*y + \hat{C} \quad .$$

We have no idea how to determine the individual s_i's, so we set them all to a constant s. Our probability using the estimated coefficients becomes

$$P(\hat{A},\hat{B},\hat{C}) = \prod_i \left\{\frac{1}{s*\sqrt{2*\pi}} * \exp\left[-\frac{1}{2}\left(\frac{z_i-\hat{z}(x_i,y_i)}{s}\right)^2\right]\right\} \quad .$$

A maximum likelihood estimation has to minimize

$$\sum_i (z_i-\hat{A}*x_i-\hat{B}*y_i-\hat{C})^2 \quad .$$

The solution becomes simple if we choose a point-symmetric patch and translate the origin of the coordinate system to the symmetry point so that some terms linear in x and y disappear.

$$\hat{C} = \sum_i (z_i) / \sum_i (1)$$
$$\hat{B} = \sum_i (z_i * y_i) / \sum_i (y_i^2)$$
$$\hat{A} = \sum_i (z_i * x_i) / \sum_i (x_i^2) \qquad i = 1,\ldots,N \ .$$

The number N of pixels participating in this approximation is determined as follows:

- The patch should contain at least two columns and three rows, because then the aspect ratio of these six points is (512/573)*(3/2) = 4/3, the same as that of the TV image, so the patch represents a square of the optical image.
- N should be higher than six to improve noise reduction.
- Intolerable degradation of detail should be avoided. Recall the assumption of linearity.

The final choice was a 2 by 3 core enclosed by a stripe of one-pixel width which overlaps the other patches (Fig.5.1). For one image we have to fit $256*191 \approx 50{,}000$ planes with 20 pixels each.

We may regard the plane as an approximation of the local gradient, thus we express angle and magnitude in terms of $\hat{A}$ and $\hat{B}$. Let us denote the clockwise angle between the positive x axis and the projection of the plane-normal

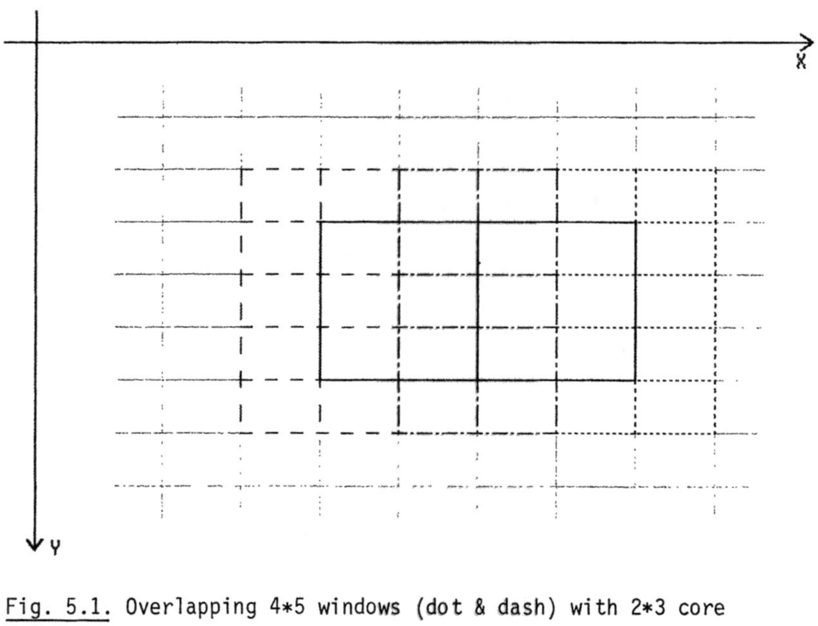

Fig. 5.1. Overlapping 4*5 windows (dot & dash) with 2*3 core

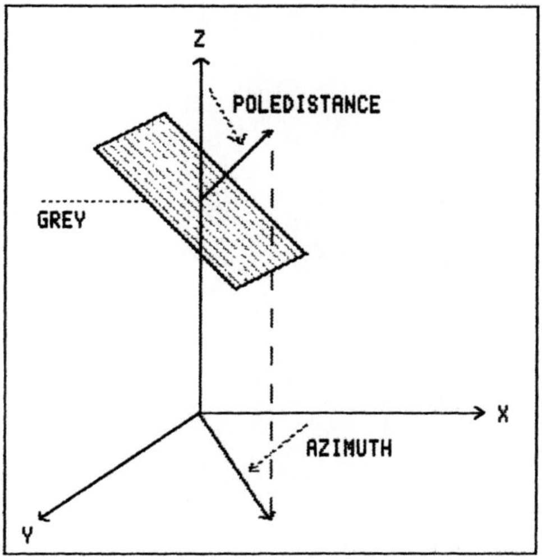

Fig. 5.2. Coefficients of approximated plane

vector as the azimuth (Fig.5.2), and the angle between the z axis and the plane-normal vector as the pole distance. Then

$$\tan(\text{pole distance}) = \sqrt{(\hat{A}^2+\hat{B}^2)}$$

$$\tan(\text{azimuth}) = -\hat{B}/\hat{A} \quad .$$

The azimuth angle increases clockwise starting from the positive x axis. Since the grey value is encoded with 0 for white and 255 for black, plane normals point from dark to light areas.

We are now prepared to define a transformed pixel as a quintuple

(GRY,AZI,POL,Y,X)

where

$X \in [0,255]$, $Y \in [0,190]$ are the coordinates,

GRY $\in [0,255]$ is the mean grey value $\hat{C}$,

AZI $\in [0,180]$ is the azimuth angle $\arctan(-\hat{B}/\hat{A})$ expressed in two-degree units, and

POL $\in [0,250]$ is an approximation of tan(pole distance) as the minimum of $(\hat{A}^2+\hat{B}^2)$ and 250.

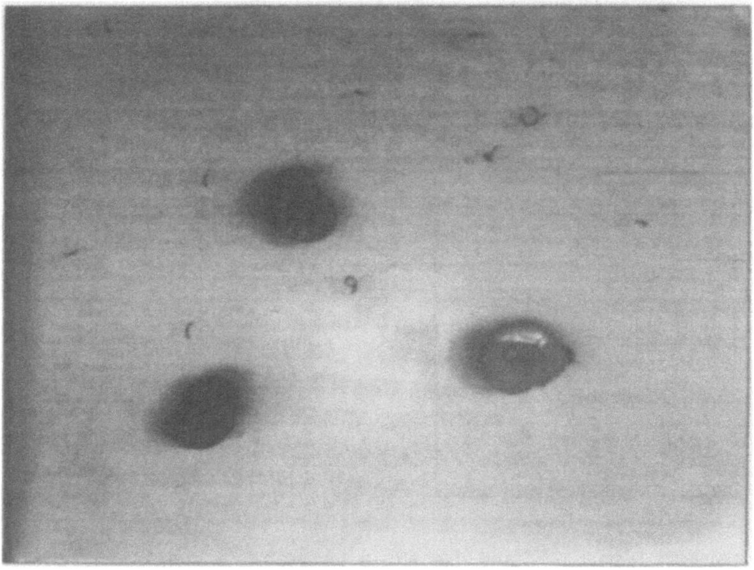

Fig. 5.3. TV image: water snails

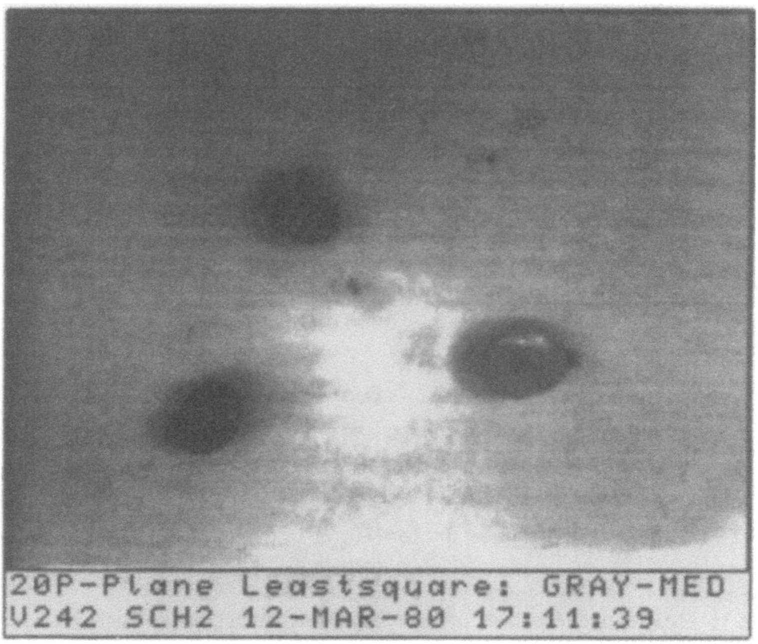

Fig. 5.4. Grey-component: water snails

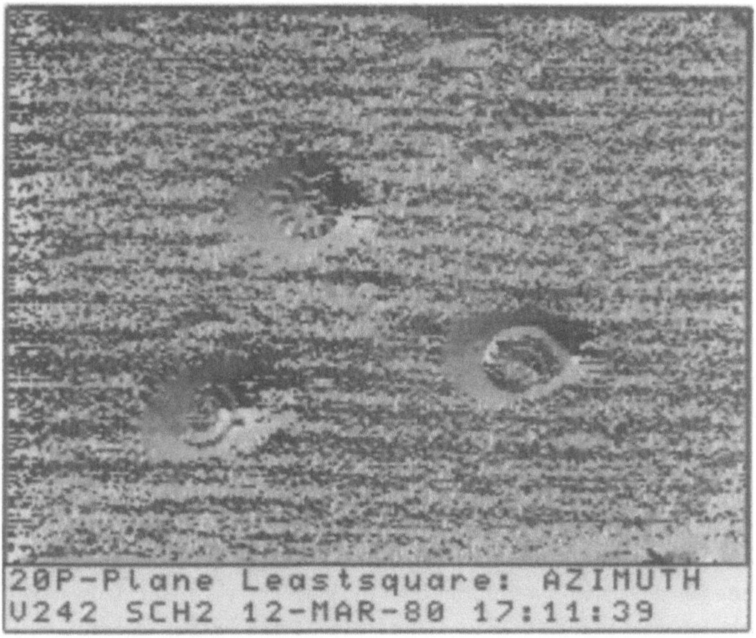

Fig. 5.5. Azimuth-component: water snails. White = 0°, black = 360°

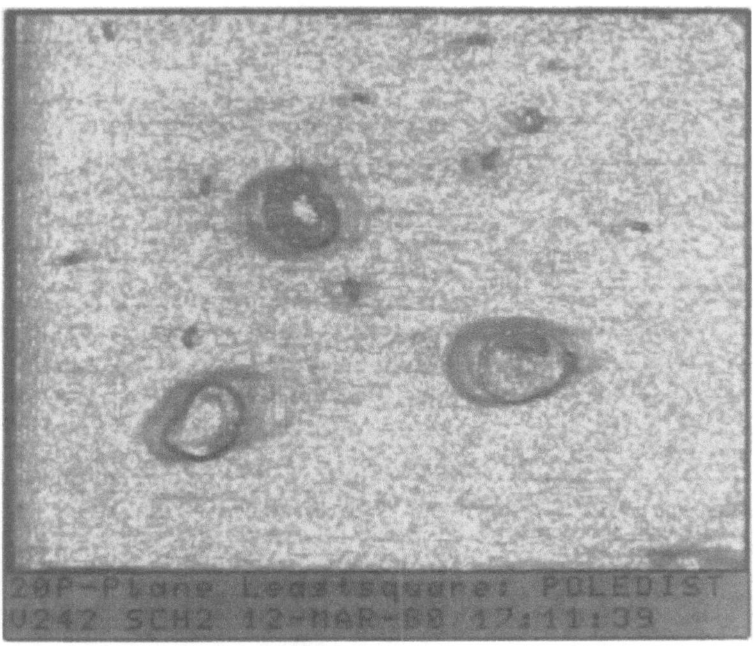

Fig. 5.6. Pole distance-component: water snails. White = flat, black = steep

GRY, AZI, and POL values are stored as matrices of 8-bit-bytes. Figure 5.3 reproduces a digitized TV image. Reduced spatial resolution of the GRY image in Fig.5.4 is the consequence of the averaging process. However a transformed pixel bears more information than only the grey-value average. The other two components describe the orientation of the plane-normal vector. Figure 5.5 is the half-tone representation of the AZI matrix, and Fig.5.6 that of the POL values. As expected, the pole distance is high (dark) at grey-value transitions and low (white) in homogeneous regions. Homogeneous regions usually generate random AZI values, as can be seen in Fig.5.5, because there the values are determined by the noise of the digitized image. When pole distance is high the orientation of the plane-normal vector is better defined and varies systematically, i.e., as in the shadow region of the snails.

5.3 Region Extraction

In Fig.5.7 we see an enlarged subsection of Fig.5.4, where, apart from pixel grey values, the azimuth angle is shown. The idea of the region extraction process is to utilize the systematic behavior of this angle together with grey-value and pole-distance information. The background region – where grey values are more or less constant, pole distance is low, and azimuth angle is randomly distributed – is an example of such regular behavior. Another is the projection of the snail, where pole distances are high and azimuth angles line up. (For this kind of illustration the azimuth angle is rotated by 90° so that it follows contours instead of being perpendicular to them.)

The region-extraction algorithm comprises several steps:

- A vector field is transformed into a graph where nodes are the quintuples (GRY,AZI,POL,Y,X) and arcs go from each node to its 8-connected neighbors.
- A set of parameters is supplied to isolate, by cutting all their arcs, nodes whose component values do not obey conditions prescribed by the parameters.
- Differences between components of connected nodes are calculated and compared with the parameters. Connections are broken if out-of-range values occur.
- The remaining graph is scanned, skipping isolated nodes, to compute properties of isolated subgraphs.
- Resulting properties are tested and in case of success the subgraph is accepted as a region.

These steps may be repeated for each frame with different parameter sets in order to extract regions with different characteristics.

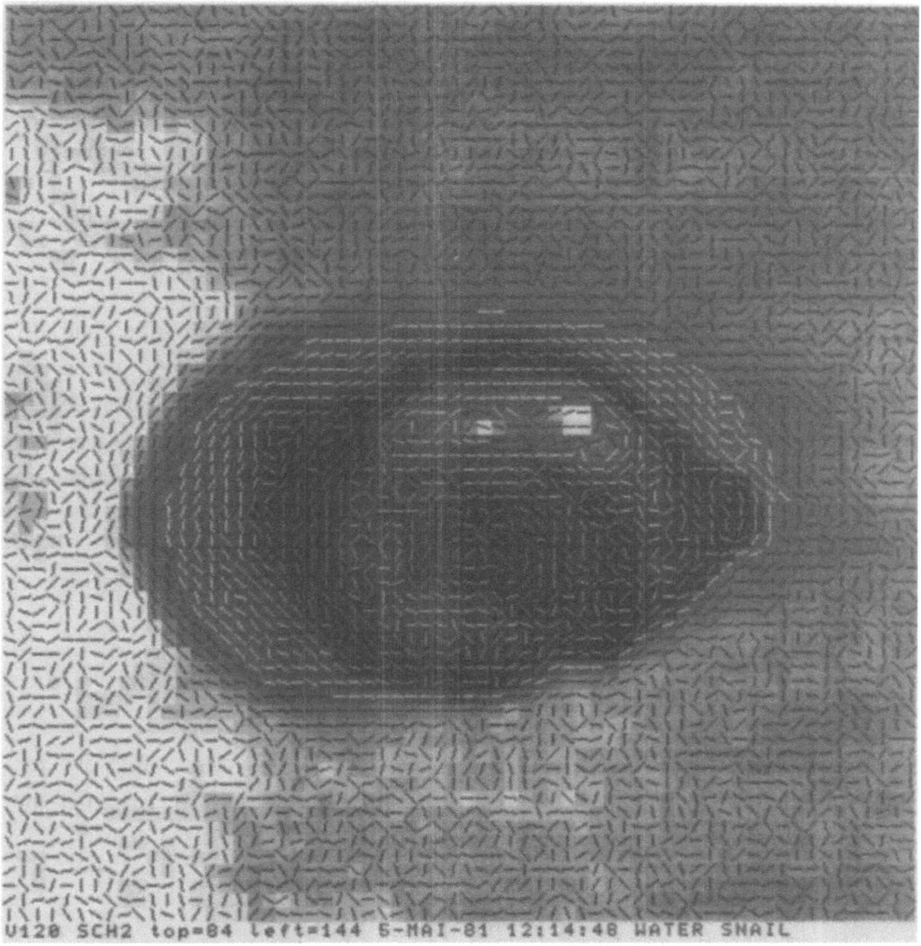

Fig. 5.7. GRY and AZI component: water snail. Subsection of Figs.5.4,5

The whole process was inspired by WALTZ's filter technique [5.42] and may be regarded as a simple case of establishing node and arc consistency in a graph [5.43].

5.3.1 Node Consistency

The graph is defined as G = (NODES,ARCS) of nodes and arcs with

$$\text{NODES} = \{(\text{GRY},\text{AZI},\text{POL},Y,X)\} \quad \text{and initially}$$

$$\text{ARCS} = \{(N_1,N_2)\,|\,0<(X_1-X_2)^2+(Y_1-Y_2)^2<3\} \quad .$$

It is internally represented as a matrix of 32 bit words. Three 8-bit bytes store the GRY, AZI, and POL components, respectively, and the last byte contains the arcs unary coded. The X and Y coordinates correspond to array indices. If two nodes, e.g., $N_1 = (\ldots,Y,X)$ and $N_2 = (\ldots,Y+1,X+1)$ are connected by an arc, then in N_1 the "southeast" bit is set and in N_2 the "northwest" bit (recall that Y=0 is the upmost row and X=0 the leftmost column).

To decide if a node is a candidate for a region, any function f(GRY,AZI, POL,Y,X) might be chosen and tested against a threshold. Here an extremely simple function was used.

When starting region extraction on an image sequence, a file is read which contains as many parameter sets as regions of different characteristics are to be extracted. These parameter sets are stored internally as records. Ten reco-d fields contain minimal and maximal values for the five node components. With an actual parameter record the components of five Boolean one-dimensional arrays are set to TRUE where the value of the array index is inside the range given by the parameter values, and set to FALSE outside, e.g.,

```
FOR I := 0 STEP 1 UNTIL 255 DO
GOODGRY[I] := GREYMIN LEQ I LEQ GREYMAX;
```

(A connoisseur will recognise this as a piece of SAIL [5.44]).

The decision function tests if the values of all five components are inside their prescribed windows. If not, all arcs between the node in question and its neighbors are cut.

```
IF NOT (GOODX[X] AND GOODY[Y] AND GOODPOL[POL]
AND GOODAZI[AZI] AND GOODGRY[GRY])
THEN ISOLATE(NODE)   .
```

This function has two advantages:
- it is fast to compute, and
- the parameters have a simple meaning so that just by inspecting the image one may infer desired values.

Ignoring isolated nodes we arrive now at a modified graph G' = (NODES',ARCS') with

$$\text{NODES}' = \{N \mid N \in \text{NODES} \wedge f(N)=\text{TRUE}\} \text{ and}$$

$$\text{ARCS}' = \{(N_1,N_2) \mid (N_1,N_2) \in \text{ARCS} \wedge f(N_1) \wedge f(N_2)=\text{TRUE}\} \quad .$$

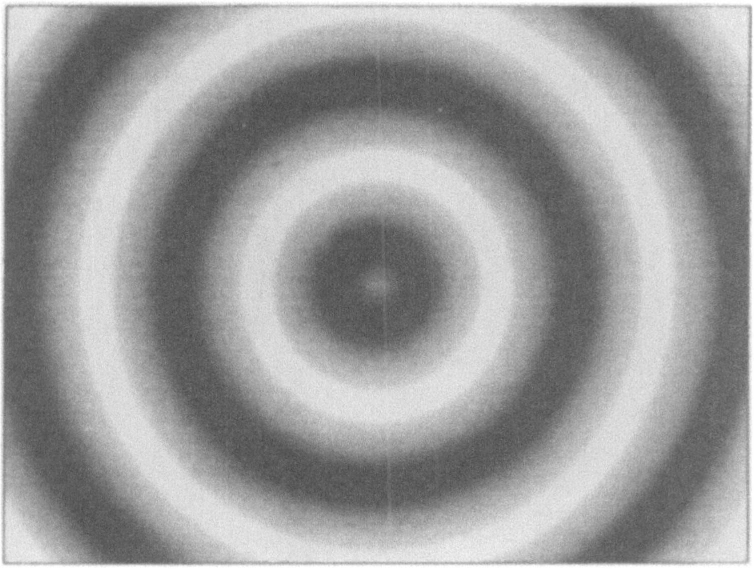

Fig. 5.8. Rotating sine-wave (period-length 111 units)

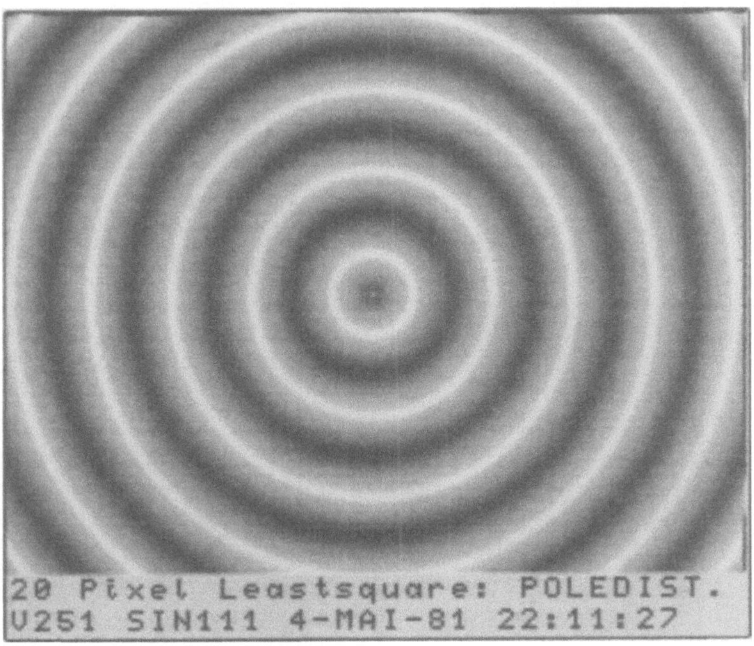

Fig. 5.9. Rotating sine-wave: tan(pole distance)

Fig. 5.10. Rotating sine-wave: azimuth. 0° white, 360° black

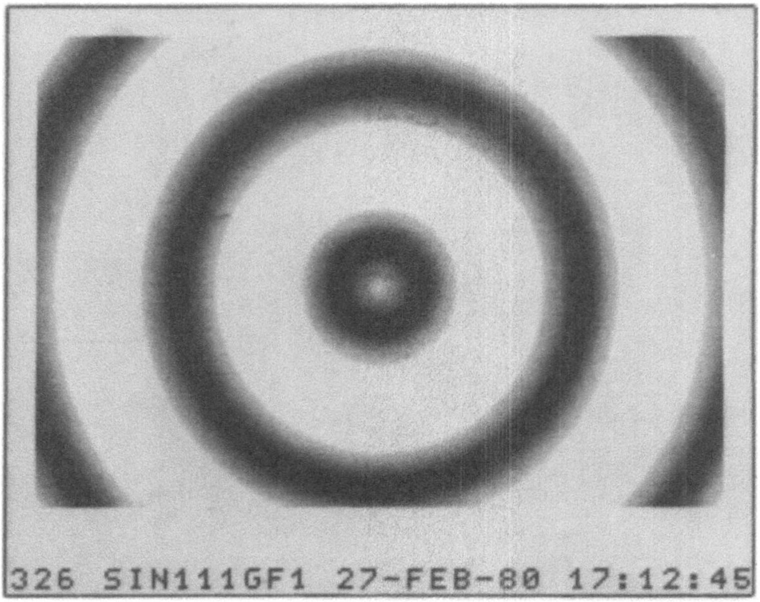

Fig. 5.11. Rotating sine-wave, grey from 128 to 255

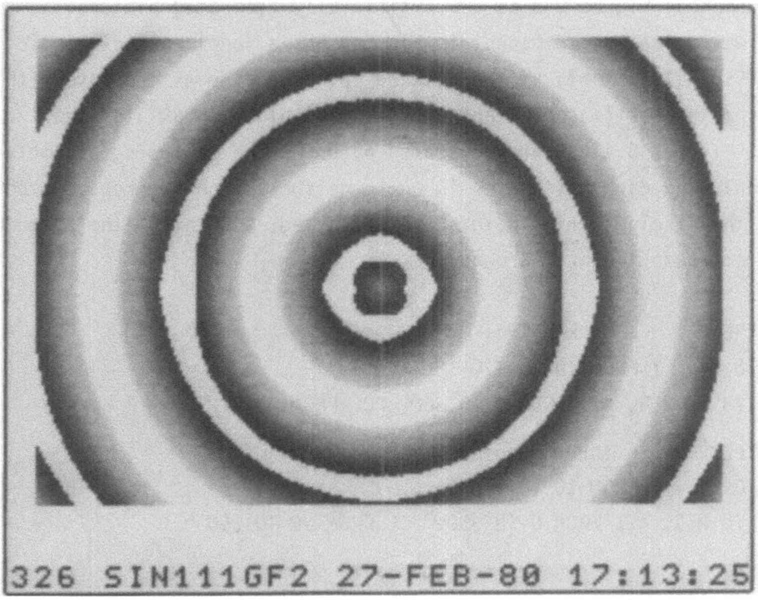

Fig. 5.12. Rotating sine-wave, POL from 20 to 250

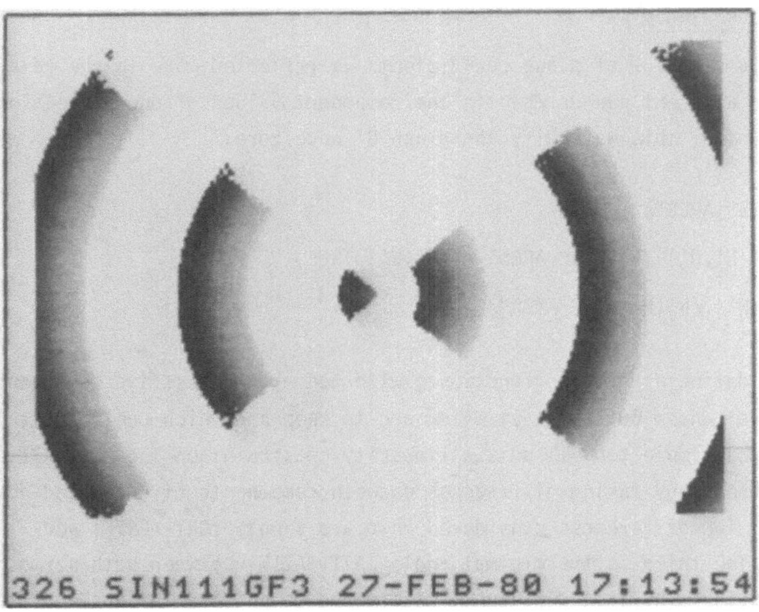

Fig. 5.13. Rotating sine-wave, AZI from 315° to 45°

I give some examples: Figure 5.8 is an artificially generated picture, a rotating sine wave. The POL component in Fig.5.9 has a |cos| characteristic. The AZI plot (Fig.5.10) starts at the outward pointing side of the wave with white (=0°) from the east(+) point and arrives with black (=360°) at the east(-) point. Figures 5.11-13 are generated by using the following parameter file. First, only the dark half-waves in an image subsection are kept; second, the area near the sine's turning points are extracted; and third, the azimuth angle is limited (note the wrap around):

```
PARAMETERTYPE = 1       dark halves
X FROM 10 TO 245, Y FROM 10 TO 170
GREY FROM 128 TO 255, AZI FROM 0 TO 360, POL FROM 0 TO 250
. . .
PARAMETERTYPE = 2       turning points
X FROM 10 TO 245, Y FROM 10 TO 170
GRY FROM 0 TO 255, AZI FROM 0 TO 360, POL FROM 20 TO 250
. . .
PARAMETERTYPE = 3       northeast to southeast
X FROM 10 TO 245, Y FROM 10 TO 170
GRY FROM 0 TO 255, AZI FROM 315 TO 45, POL FROM 0 TO 250
```

5.3.2 Arc Consistency

The systematic behavior of plane coefficients is reflected more in the relations between adjacent planes than in the component values of one plane alone. To take account of this we modify the graph G' once more:

$$G'' = (\mathrm{NODES}'',\mathrm{ARCS}'') \quad \text{with}$$

$$\mathrm{ARCS}'' = \{(N_1',N_2') \mid (N_1',N_2') \in \mathrm{ARCS}' \wedge g(N_1',N_2')=\mathrm{TRUE}\}$$

$$\mathrm{NODES}'' = \{N' \mid \forall N_i' (N',N_i') \in \mathrm{ARCS}''\} \quad .$$

In words, we define a decision function g with ten arguments (five components from each node) whose outcome says which arc to keep and which one to cut; g is chosen to be simple too. It puts a linearity constraint on the GRY, AZI, and POL components by taking differences between components of connected nodes into account. Two differences considered in g are simply $|GRY_1-GRY_2|$ and $|POL_1-POL_2|$. The third is the minimal angle $|AZI_1-AZI_2|$ between both azimuth angles (Fig.5.14). The last difference considered is between the angle of the line which joins the raster locations of the two nodes — given by $\arctan[-(Y_2-Y_1)/(X_2-X_1)]$ — and the azimuth angle. The differences $|JOIN-AZI_1|$

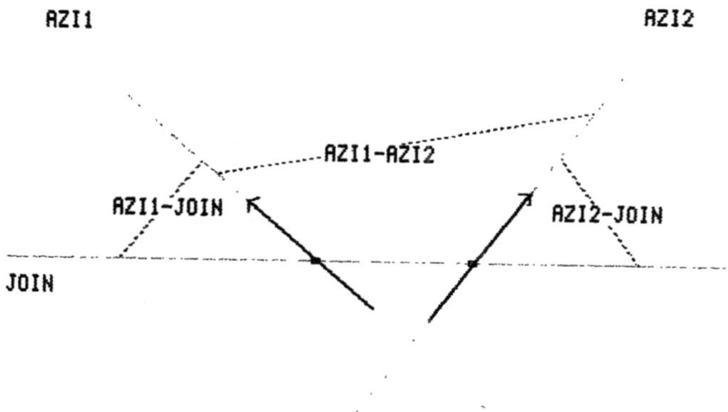

Fig. 5.14. Angle differences

and |JOIN-AZI_2| (Fig.5.14) are taken to be the smallest angle by which one has to turn the plane-normal to line its orientation up with JOIN, clockwise, or anticlockwise. So our parameter set contains four additional range definitions, three for the first three differences and one for the last two differences. As in Sect.5.3.1 definition and computation of g is straightforward and simple. Linear Boolean arrays are filled with TRUE and FALSE according to whether the differences are inside or outside the window given by the appropriate parameter pair, e.g.,

```
FOR I := 0 STEP 1 UNTIL 255 DO
GOODGREYDIF[-I] := GOODGREYDIF[I] := GREYDIFMIN LEQ I LEQ GREYDIFMAX  .
```

The truth value of g is then computed as

```
JOIN := ARCTAN[(Y1-Y2)/(X1-X2)];
G := GOODGREYDIF[GRY1-GRY2] AND GOODAZIDIF[AZI1-AZI2]
AND GOODPOLDIF[POL1-POL2] AND GOODJOINDIF[JOIN-AZI1]
AND GOODJOINDIF[JOIN-AZI2];
IF NOT G THEN CLEARARC(N1,N2)  .
```

The arc between the pair of nodes in question is deleted if g turns out to be FALSE.

Our rotating sine can provide us with some more examples. If we restrict JOIN angle differences to low values,

JOINDIF FROM 0 TO 10,

only those nodes which are close enough to one of the eight join directions remain in the graph (which, roughly speaking, implies that all other nodes are isolated from each other) (Fig.5.15). Sectors would become narrower if we lower the upper JOINDIF threshold, and would join each other if the upper threshold exceeded 23°.

A part of a graph is plotted in Fig.5.16, namely the southeast quadrant. Here the only constraint was

GREYDIF FROM 0 TO 10.

Radial arcs disappear on steep sides of the wave because, there, the grey-value difference exceeds its limit, while concentric arcs remain; along them the difference is always small.

The next example (Fig.5.17) is generated by

POLDIF FROM 0 TO 2.

Fig. 5.15. Rotating sine-wave, JOINDIF from 0° to 10°

Fig. 5.16. Rotating sine-wave, GREYDIF from 0 to 10

Here, extreme points and turning points have radial neighbors because, there, the magnitude of the gradient is constant low or constant high, respectively.

The examples given here demonstrate the wide range of variability of this parameterized technique. So it seems to me justified not to use complicated decision functions but rather to stress the point of fast computability. The process of region extraction beginning from raw data up to the point described here is highly local. The operations of node isolation as well as arc deletion are order independent, and plane fitting and graph editing can be done in parallel by simple processors. Of course one might extend this approach by

Fig. 5.17. Rotating sine-wave, SLOPEDIF from 0 to 2

applying fuzzy logic [5.45], or even choose some iterative process, e.g., relaxation labelling [5.46] which ZUCKER et al. [5.47] applied to enhance line structures, for instance. However, the advantage of low computation time is not negligible when processing image sequences with 10 to 100 frames and 300 kB per frame.

5.3.3 Region Attributes

After filtering the graph by parameterized constraints it usually consists of separated components of two or more nodes, neglecting isolated single nodes.

These subgraphs are considered as regions and their attributes are computed now. The attributes are closely related to the plane coefficients being essentially distributions of them and of their differences. They are specified as follows:

AREA	is the number of nodes in the subgraph.
XLEFT, XRIGHT	are the minimal and maximal x values, respectively.
YTOP, YBOT	are the extreme rows; the last four values define a bounding rectangle.
XSUM, YSUM	are accumulated in order to compute centroid coordinates.

The following distributions are recorded:

D!GREY[0:15]	in bins of 16 grey-value units,
D!GREYDIF[0:15]	and the same for difference.
D!AZI[0:14]	contains azimuth counts in 24° units and
D!AZIDIF[0:14]	the difference which cannot exceed 180° thus binning is 12°.
D!POL[0:15]	and
D!POLDIF[0:15]	are defined like the grey distributions.
D!JOINDIF[0:8]	gives the frequency of |JOIN-AZI| values which cannot exceed 90° therefore one bin is 10° wide.
D!NEIGHBORCOUNT[1:8]	counts occurrence of nodes with one to eight neighbors, more or less is impossible.

There exists some additional bookkeeping information with each region. It is given an individual REGIONNUMBER, the FRAMENUMBER indicates in which image the region was found, and the PARAMETERTYPE identifies the parameter set (already mentioned in Sect.5.3.1) which has generated the region.

Region attributes are computed by a nonrecursive spanning tree algorithm. A standard method to label pixel by region number [5.36] would require more intermediate storage and a high rate of relabelling operations is expected because, in the graph, it is not immediately obvious if two adjacent but not connected nodes are members of different graph components or are connected by a path. The spanning tree algorithm needs only four bits of storage per node. In addition to the 32 bits described in Sect.5.3.1 this amounts to 36 bits, which is fortunately the word length of the PDP-10 where the algorithm is running. Three bits store the parent of a node by indicating in which direction (east = 0 to northeast = 7) the parent is located. One bit flags a node as visited. The program is roughly as follows:

```
FOR ROW := FIRSTROW STEP 1 UNTIL LASTROW DO
FOR COL := FIRSTCOL STEP 1 UNTIL LASTCOL DO
```

```
IF (NODE := GRAPH[ROW,COL]) isnotisolated AND NODE isnotflagged
THEN BEGIN
  XSTART := COL; YSTART := ROW; initialize region attributes;
  GOTHERE := SOUTH;
  ACCUMULATE : compute region attributes from NODE components;
        flag NODE as visited;
        store (GOTHERE+WEST) MOD 8 in NODE;
        COMMENT direction of parent whom we left just;
  FOLLOW:
        FOR GOTHERE :=
        EAST,WEST,NORTHEAST,NORTHWEST,NORTH,SOUTHEAST,SOUTHWEST,SOUTH
        COMMENT try to avoid spiraling around;
        DO IF arc(NODE,NEIGHBOR,GOTHERE)
        THEN BEGIN
          compute region attributes from NODE and NEIGHBOR components;
          IF NEIGHBOR isnotflagged
          THEN BEGIN
            update COL; update ROW; NODE := NEIGHBOR;
            GOTO ACCUMULATE
          END
        END;
        IF COL=XSTART AND ROW=YSTART THEN GOTO READY;
        get location of parent from NODE;
        NODE := parent; GOTO FOLLOW;
        READY: . . .
END;.
```

We used constraints to drop nodes and arcs in the first two steps. Now we enlarge our parameter set by constraints concerning region attributes which allow us to select among these regions. One could prescribe shape of distributions, location of centroid, arc density, etc.; however, this is not fully implemented. The only need was to constrain region area in order to suppress meaningless two- or three-node regions. Thus, the region attributes are kept after the area is found to be within the prescribed range.

5.3.4 Example

The TV image of Fig.5.3 shows three water snails in a shallow dish viewed from above. To transform an image from 300,000 bytes to 50,000 planes takes about 50 s or 1 ms per plane, computed on a DEC-KI10 processor, the program

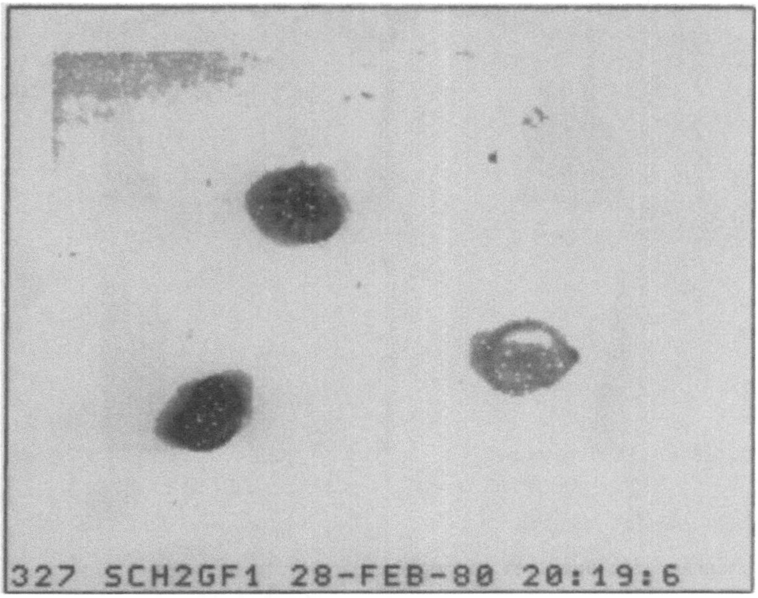

Fig. 5.18. Water snails after filter pass

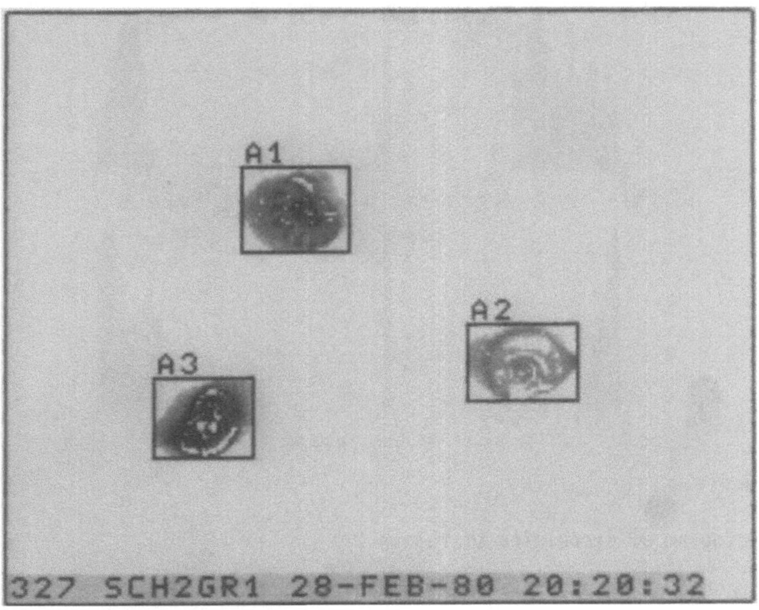

Fig. 5.19. Water snails after region scan

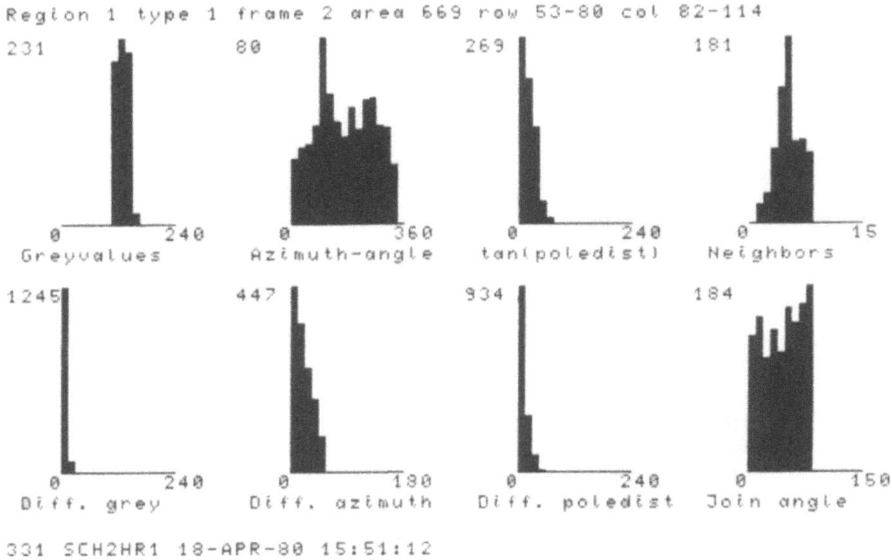

Fig. 5.20. Histogram of properties of region 1

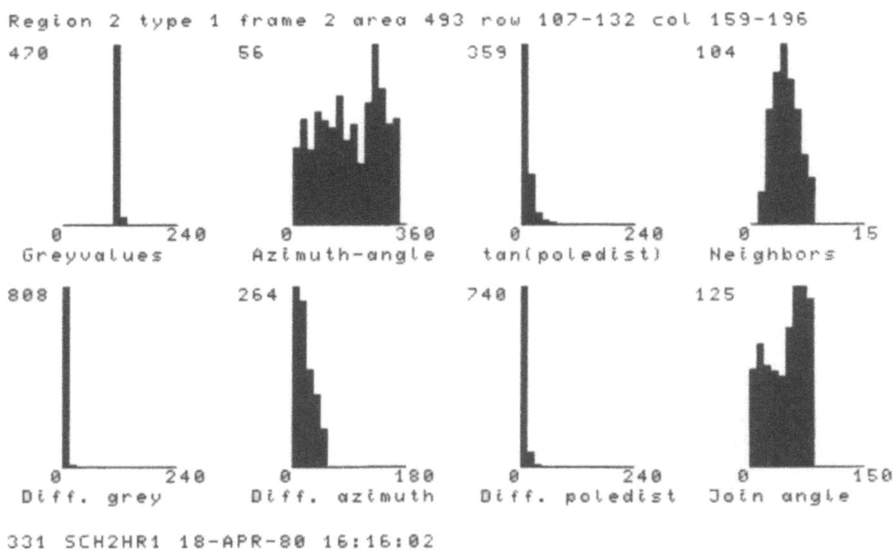

Fig. 5.21. Histogram of properties of region 2

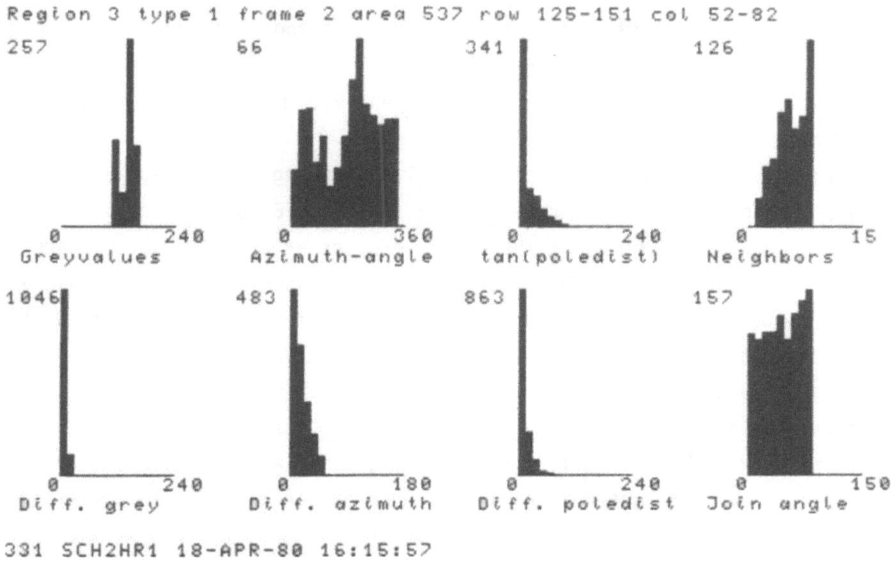

Fig. 5.22. Histogram of properties of region 3

being written in SAIL. Parameters for region extraction have been chosen in order to suppress the more or less homogeneous background. They are

PARAMTYPE 1 watersnails
X FROM 15 TO 250
Y FROM 10 TO 160
GRY FROM 115 TO 250
AZI FROM 0 TO 360
POL FROM 1 TO 250
GREYDIF FROM 0 TO 250
AZIDIF FROM 0 TO 60
POLDIF FROM 0 TO 90
JOINDIF FROM 0 TO 90
AREA FROM 250 TO 1500 .

CPU time for the filter pass, where node and arc consistency is computed, was 4 s which is equivalent to 0.12 ms per node. The result is shown in Fig.5.18. Isolated nodes are displayed as white, the others with their own grey value. As was shown in Figs.5.4-7, the snails are characterized by a darker grey value than their local background, a higher pole distance, and a more regular behavior of azimuth angles. Thus, most of the background is removed by the GRY, POL, and AZIDIF constraints.

To scan the graph and compute region attributes took 5 s per frame. About 6% of the nodes were left from the previous filter pass, a total of 65,000 in the whole sequence. The region scanner spent 2.5 ms on each node, explored 1323 subgraphs and created 95 regions.

In Fig.5.19 each region is enclosed by its bounding rectangle, which is marked by region number and parameter type (A for 1, B for 2, etc.). There seemed to be a larger region in the upper left corner of Fig.5.18. But arc density is low there due to the AZIDIF constraint which requests somewhat parallel vectors. This subsection consists mostly of subgraphs having two or three nodes. It is easily suppressed by the AREA parameter.

Region attributes are displayed in Figs.5.20-22. Let us look closer at the grey-value distributions. Snail 1 is textured; its grey-value distribution is relatively broad. Snail 2 has the same color as its shadow. This leads to a sharp peak, whereas snail 3 is much darker than its shadow (Fig. 5.19) so we get a bimodal histogram. Due to the texture of snail 1, there are more nodes with higher pole distance values than for the other snails. The third remarkable difference is in the azimuth distribution. It reflects essentially the interior structure of the snail images.

5.4 Sequences

Formation of the region sequences starts after regions are extracted from all frames using all parameter sets. Two things are to be defined: similarity between regions and how to pair regions. Sequences are then the transitive pair relation. Members of a sequence are always generated by the same parameter set.

5.4.1 Similarity

Region attributes may be thought of as spanning a multidimensional feature space. Depending on the nature of this space, a wide variety of distance measures is in use. WOLFERTS [5.10] takes the maximum of the cross-correlation of the grey values, MARTIN and AGGARWAL [5.6] compute relative differences (see below) of features like length and slope of line segments, PRICE and REDDY [5.22] include binary positional relations between regions in their similarity evaluation.

In our case, for each individual region attribute a value is computed between 0.0 for "completely different" and 1.0 for "identical". The minimum over all these values is taken as similarity between two regions if both have the same PARAMETERTYPE; otherwise the similarity is set to zero. The formula for the AREA attribute is the relative difference

$$SIMAREA := 1 - |AREA_1 - AREA_2| / (AREA_1 + AREA_2) \quad .$$

It vanishes if one of the AREA values approaches zero and yields 1 if both areas are equal. Distributions are compared by a correlation function which depends essentially on the shapes of both histograms

$$D!SIM := \sqrt{\sqrt{\left\{\left[\sum_i (BIN_{1_i}) * \sum_i (BIN_{2_i})\right]^2 / \left[\sum_i (BIN_{1_i})^2 * \sum_i (BIN_{2_i})^2\right]\right\}}} \quad .$$

This yields 1.0 if one distribution is an exact multiple of the other.

To offer some flexibility, the parameter set can specify whether or not the displacement of region centers should influence the similarity comparison. When this option is selected DISPLACESIM is computed as the ratio of two times the area which is common to both enclosing rectangles and the sum of both rectangle areas.

$$A_i := (XRIGHT_i - XLEFT_i + 1) * (YBOT_i - YTOP_i + 1)$$

$$DX := 0 \text{ MAX } [(XRIGHT_1 \text{ MIN } XRIGHT_2) - (XLEFT_1 \text{ MAX } XLEFT_2)]$$

$$DY := 0 \text{ MAX } [(YBOT_1 \text{ MIN } YBOT_2) - (YTOP_1 \text{ MAX } YTOP_2)]$$

$$DISPLACESIM := 2 * DX * DY / (A_1 + A_2) \quad .$$

This option should be chosen if one suspects that object displacement from one frame to the next will be less than something like its diameter. In other words if the projections of one object in one image and of another object in another image are so far apart that their enclosing rectangles do not overlap, then it is very unlikely that both objects are the same.

The total similarity value is simply the minimum of all individual results. This similarity definition is mostly justified by experimental success. There might be some improvement by deeper analysis; here we tried the simplest approach. One problem seemed to exist, at a first glance, with the azimuth-angle distribution. If, for a region, the pole-distance values are small, the azimuth angles are poorly defined. Fortunately, if the region contains more than some ten nodes, the amplitude noise of the TV image determines the azimuth. Therefore, the azimuth histogram is uniformly populated, and regions of this type can get high similarity scores if they represent the same object.

5.4.2 Identity

An advantage of the region-extraction approach described here is that a limited number of regions is created. Most of them are meaningful in the sense that they locate the desired image characteristic. This is in contrast to typical region merge [5.48] or split [5.49] algorithms. They have to balance between merging semantically different regions and generating meaningless ones. One of the attempts to find a way out of this dilemma was the "interpretation-guided segmentation" by BARROW and TENENBAUM [5.50]. They controlled the region-merging pass by a priori knowledge formulated as constraints on the interpretations (labels) of adjacent regions. This is a technique similar to that which I apply at the lower level of pixels. I admit that in both cases one has to acquire some experience by experimentation in order to get satisfactory results. The point is that usually in each frame the number of extracted regions is low enough to permit computation of the similarity between each region of the current and preceeding or following frame.

Doing this we get two lists ordered by similarity for each region, one for future and one for past. The design detail one has to decide upon is how much to preserve from such a list: the whole, part of it, or only the top element. LOWERRE demonstrated in his HARPY speech-recognition system the advantage of evaluating only a narrow beam of the n best hypothese [5.51]. A congenial technique is the "LOCUS" model of search [5.52]. In a former version of my system [5.53] I kept the top three elements from each list. A pair of regions was chosen (in the case that it existed), such that each region appeared in the appropriate list of the other one; ambiguities were decided in favor of the highest score.

Experiments revealed that most of these pairings – 95 to 100 percent – were between the two most similar regions, the top elements. Therefore, in this version, only the most similar region in the next and in the previous frame is remembered, called successor and predecessor. Another reason to drop the former three-element list is the observation that different phenomena contribute to the exceptional cases. One might be generation of a noise region which has successors and predecessors but should not be part of a sequence. Another reason is a splitting of one region of the current frame into two or more regions in the next frame. Then, eventually, all regions from the next frame have the most similar partner as this region in the current frame, but this region has only one most similar partner in the next frame. It seems to be justified to drop the former heuristic which seems to be too local (in the time dimension), and link just regions which are mutually the best partners of each other to sequences. If such a sequence is broken, one can utilize information concerning whole sequences to attempt to glue pieces together.

5.4.3 Simple Sequences

A sequence is a time-ordered list of region descriptors. Some attributes are computed from this list and stored in a sequence descriptor. Among them is the number of regions in the sequence, the time difference between head and tail region (which corresponds to length, for now), the sum of displacements in the x and y directions of the centroid coordinates, and the sum of the Euclidean distances which the centroid has moved. Velocities are obtained by dividing these sums by the time attribute. Figure 5.23 shows the water snails of Fig.5.3 half a minute later; all three have moved. Three sequences are generated, one for each snail. Figure 5.24 is composed of the following ingredients:

- the background of Fig.5.4,
- the three snails in their first positions surrounded by their enclosing rectangles,

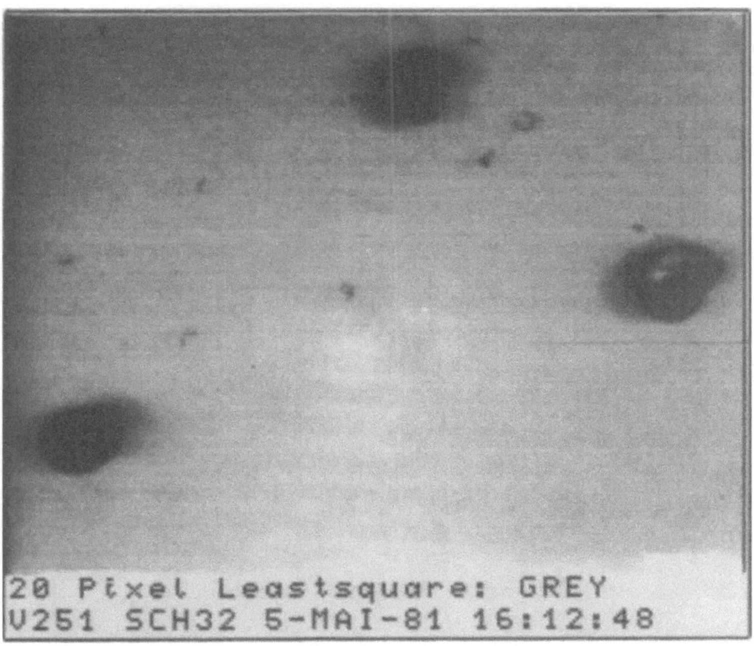

Fig. 5.23. Water snails 32 s after Fig.5.3

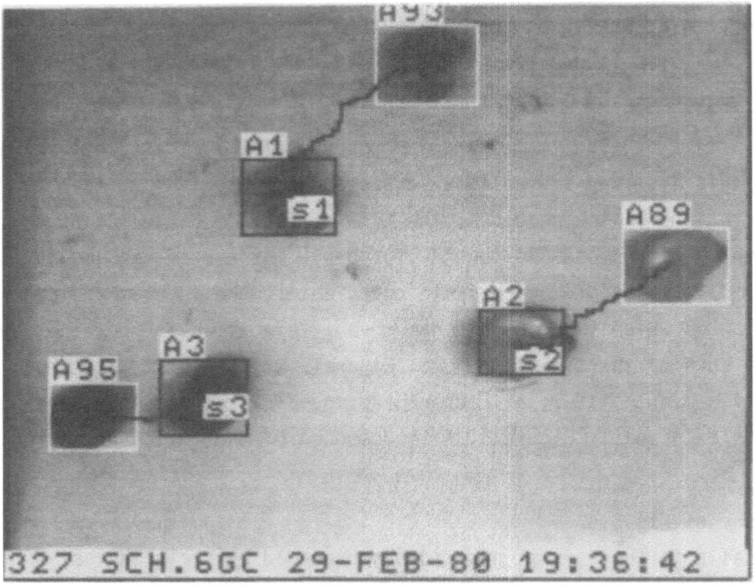

Fig. 5.24. Three moving snails

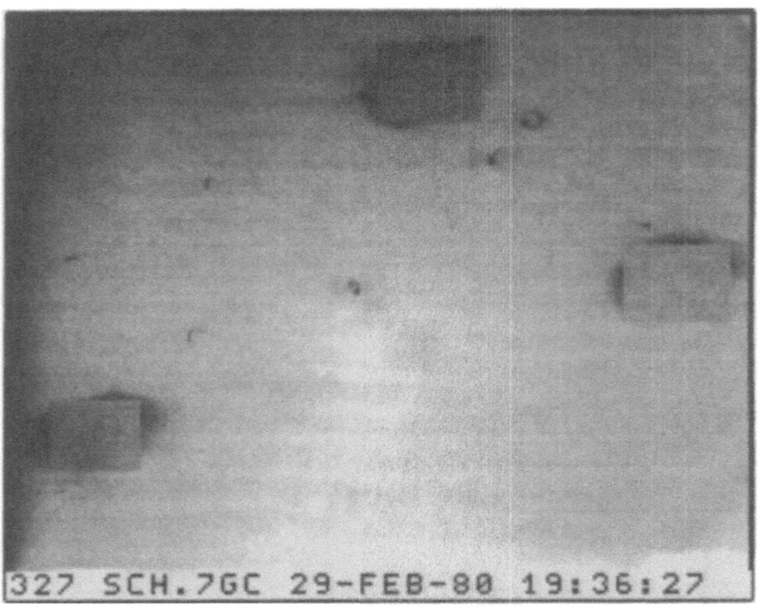

Fig. 5.25. Reconstructed background, snail sequence

- three insets determined by enclosing rectangles of the snails in their last positions, taken from the last GRY file, and
- tracks of the centroids, observed over 32 frames.

The rectangles are marked by region type, "A" stands for PARAMETERTYPE=1, and by region number. Just to play around with the system, I present Fig.5.25. Here, the enclosing rectangles of the first frame are filled by grey values from the last frame and vice versa so that background is reconstructed to some degree. If background reconstruction is a desired application, the system can do it even in more complicated cases. It could copy grey values from nonregion locations into a background frame and add those parts which are uncovered by each region as it moves (and not covered by another one at the same time). Attributes for the sequence marked by "S1" are

LENGTH = 32 regions in sequence
TIME = 32 frame units
X!DISPLACE = 46 raster locations
Y!DISPLACE = -46
TOTAL!WALK = 73.3 raster locations

In this sequence, the time distance between frames was 1 s. The average velocity of the snail which generated S1 is 73.3/32 = 2.3 raster locations per

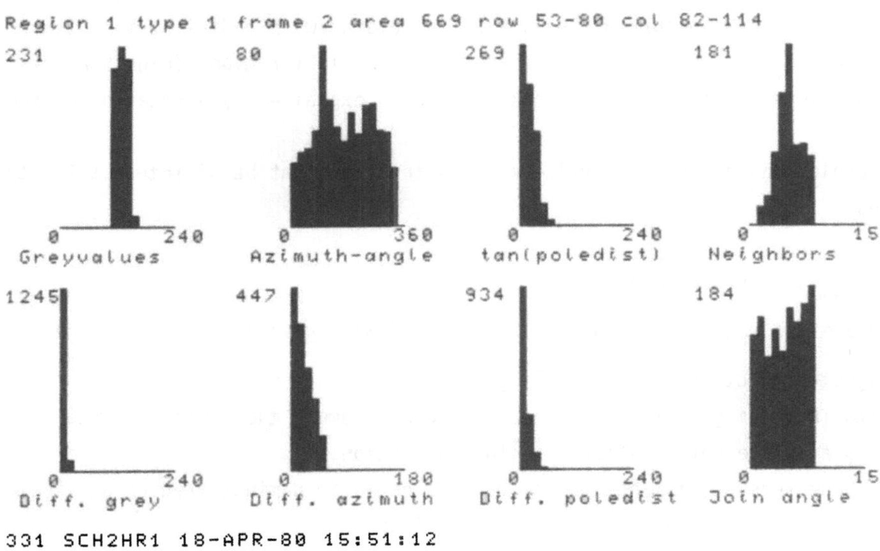

Fig. 5.26. Textured snail in first position

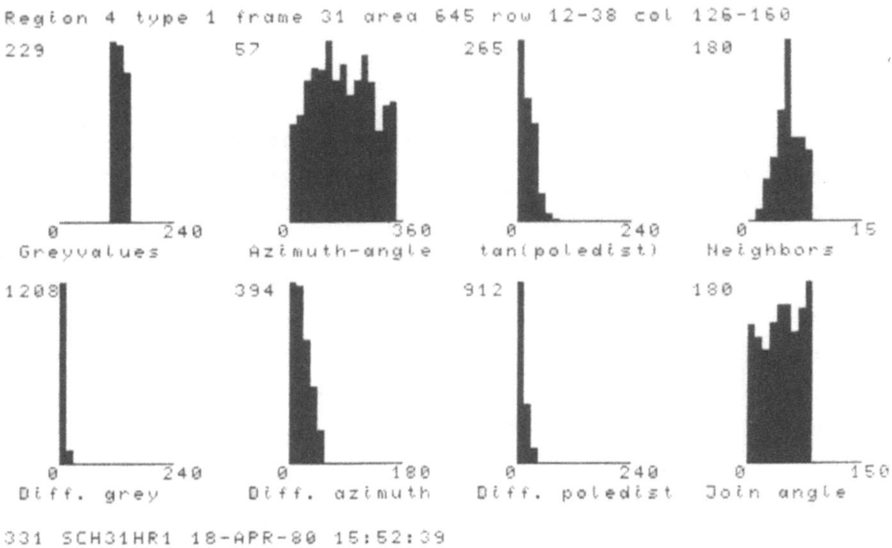

Fig. 5.27. Textured snail rotated

second. From observing that the diameter of the snail is about 25 raster units, one can estimate the real velocity as about one diameter per 10 to 15 seconds.

After connecting regions into sequences by similarity, one may extract further information, in addition to the simple attributes, which reflects changes that have occurred. Snail "S2" is colored with radial strips. If we inspect the azimuth histograms of the first and last regions (Figs.5.26,27) we observe a shift of the two peaks, which is explained by a rotation of the snail.

Development of the grey value or area in time might be of interest in other cases.

5.4.4 Compound Sequences

What are the reasons that a sequence ends? I will give only a few of them:

- object projection leaves the image,
- with increasing distance between object and camera the finite resolution of grey-value matrix affects region extraction,
- with decreasing distance object details begin to dominate region attributes, the object might become only partly visible,
- one object is occluded by another,
- illumination changes drastically, e.g., when an object enters a shadow area,

- region-extraction parameters are chosen marginally, so that minor perturbations result in appearance or disappearance of the region,
- similar objects come close together so that the similarity criterion generates a mixed linkage,
- a lot of other phenomena arise with nonrigid objects, soap bubbles, special illumination, and surface characteristics like specularity.

In some of the above cases it is possible to cure a broken sequence. But because there is such a variety of reasons, one has to apply a variety of remedies depending on what one is able to conclude from the symptoms about the illness. NAGEL [5.54] sketched production rules which indicated how to handle such situations.

A low-level system is not the place to install too much general and domain-specific knowledge. Nevertheless, the system implemented here offers a capability of linking sequences in a simple and partially parameterized manner. The basic idea is to apply the same similarity measure between head and tail regions of two sequences as was used for regions in a sequence. Of course, only those pairs of sequences participate in which the tail region of one sequence has a lower frame number than the head region of the other; the second sequence has to begin after the first has ended. Under this constraint, possible pairings are explored. The forward similarity score and pointer of the tail region is updated if a higher similarity value is detected than was stored before. For a head region, the backward items are treated the same way. After all possible pairs of sequences have been tested, any two sequences are combined to one compound sequence if the tail of one points to the head of the other and vice versa. The principle of building compound sequences is exactly the same as the region pairing process, only the requirement that the regions to be compared have to stem from time-adjacent frames is dropped. Only sequences whose members have the same PARAMETERTYPE can be combined to compound sequences. I emphasize that the similarity values and pointers in the region-describing record are not scratched before this procedure. If the head-tail comparison does not yield a better partner for the end region than was stored from the previous sequence formation pass, a sequence will not be linked at the end in question.

Attributes of a compound sequence are the same as for a simple one. Note, however, that the time difference between head and tail no longer agrees with the number of regions in the sequence.

The formation of compound sequences is influenced by two parameters. They control whether DISPLACE and TOTAL!WALK attributes of both sequences should be ignored. If not, then the relative difference (see Sect.5.4.1) of X!DIS-

Fig. 5.28. Compound sequence (shadow)

PLACEMENT and Y!DISPLACEMENT or TOTAL!WALK is added to the set of individual region attribute scores over which the minimum is taken. In this way a continuity constraint may be formulated which takes into account the more global information a sequence carries.

Figure 5.28 presents a simple example of a compound sequence. Here the shadow of the car is occluded when it passes behind the tree. A white trace denotes the gap in the compound sequence related to the shadow.

One may think of other methods. A typical region may be computed as a representative of all regions in a sequence. Then such representatives may be compared. This corresponds to linking sequences where averaged attributes match. Another way is to extrapolate sequences into the future and the past and to link together those sequences whose extrapolations match best.

5.5 Planning

When KELLY [5.39] introduced his concept of "plan" in picture analysis, he was concerned with only one frame which he explored with a coarse raster in order to locate areas of interest which then are inspected more closely. This idea becomes even more attractive if a sequence of images is processed where

Fig. 5.29. Planning: moving car only

it is assumed that the amount of change from frame to frame is limited. Then knowledge acquired from the first frames can guide the analysis of subsequent frames. The system of YACHIDA et al. which locates the left ventricle in cine-angiograms is built around such planning [Ref.5.40, p.978]:

The analyser, therefore, examines a small number of low-resolution pictures of the record to collect such information and make a coarse model, a sketch, of the process, by which it can estimate which frame and what regions in it are worthy examining, or what type of a feature extractor is most effective at each point in the regions.

Both types of planning – where to look and how to extract – are incorporated in my system. The second type is made easy by the fact that region attributes and extraction parameters are closely related. A region extracted by a tolerant parameter set can easily be used to refine the parameters by automatically converting attributes to window limits. These more specific parameters are then applied to the next frame, where again the parameter set is adapted to the extraction result. The first type of planning is especially important in real-world scenes where objects are not represented by one region of some uniform characteristic. Here, it is desirable to control applications of a second parameter set depending on results from a first region extraction process.

Both types of planning are demonstrated in Fig.5.29. A parameter set is manually formulated and used to look for white roofs of cars in the whole first frame. If one is found, two other things happen. First, the parameter set responsible for the roof is specialized in order to concentrate region extraction on an image window where the roof is expected to be in the next frame. Second, another parameter set is modified and activated which is specialized for sides of cars. Its YTOP, YBOT, XLEFT, and XRIGHT values are adjusted in such a way that the image subsection beneath the roof is selected. If the side is located with this parameter set, a shadow specialist is invoked. This again involves the modification and activation of a preformulated parameter set according to the region scan results from using the side specialist. Note that these specialists are not procedures (as, e.g., in [5.55]), but just easy to manipulate record (data) structures.

All these modifications are repeated for each subsequent frame. Planning results in a gain of computation speed. Total run time to process this 23-frame sequence was 320 s, equivalent to 14 s per frame; 2704 isolated subgraphs have been scanned and 68 regions created. Figure 5.28 was generated without planning using three constant parameter sets. Here processing time was 626 s, that is 27 s per frame; 17334 subgraphs have been scanned and 133 kept as regions. The ability to focus region scanning on interesting objects by describing them in terms of a dependency structure of parameter sets is a powerful tool.

There is a considerable overlap between prediction and planning. Carrying over information which is collected in one frame to guide the analysis of subsequent frames may be considered prediction. Planning consists of first computing what is cheap to do and restricting more expensive analysis according to the results obtained. In this sense adaptation of extraction parameters has some elements of prediction, whereas application of a second or a third parameter set controlled by region extraction using the first set is more like planning.

5.6 Resume

I have presented a multilevel approach for the description of image sequences taken by a TV camera from real-world scenes. The goal was to provide a rich and robust symbolic description of the images on which a high-level system can rely when exploring meaning, action, and three-dimensional structure in a scene. CHIEN and JACOBUS [5.31] expressed the demand for exploitation of low-level features:

The use of high-level information when possible is, of course, to be commended, but when it is used to make up for insufficient low-level feature data, systems begin to 'see' what they want to 'see' rather than what is actually in the scene. To avoid this problem our approach is based on the premise that more work is required at the bottom to extract and order information. To this end we have looked for ways to identify and use more completely the information encoded in picture arrays.

The immense variability of real-world scenes makes it difficult to incorporate heuristics in a low-level system. The alternative is to let high-level information influence the low-level process in an explicitly controlled way. If we regard the described process as computing a hierarchy of relations, the formalism of control by knowledge becomes clear.

5.6.1 Hierarchy

The lowest level relation is the pixel (G,Y,X) which is "computed" by the sensorial front end, and which is a subset of the Cartesian product GxYxX of the sets (Sect.5.2.1)

$G = \{g \mid 0 \leq g \leq 255\}$
range given by analogue to digital converter,

$Y = \{y \mid 0 \leq y \leq 572\}$
range given by TV standard,

$X = \{x \mid 0 \leq x \leq 511\}$
range given by TV bandwidth .

The set of pixels is affected by experimental knowledge: the control of camera parameters.

The pixel set is transformed by a least-squares fit into a quintuple relation of (GRY,AZI,POL,Y,X). This is a parameterless process. The only heuristic involved is the selection of the approximation algorithm together with size, shape, and placement of the image windows for each plane (Sect.5.2.4).

The set of quintuples is converted into a graph by adding the 8-connected proximity relation. The graph is manipulated by a two-pass filter process which is fully parameterized (Sects.5.3.1,2). Design of the function which decides what arcs to remove may be regarded as an implicit heuristic. High-level information has to be expressed in terms of parameter values. They can be supplied from outside (as a priori knowledge by the user) or may be derived from previous interpretation results from the current frame or from past frames (Sect.5.5).

Quintuple values and value differences along remaining arcs of isolated subgraphs are the basis for region attributes (Sect.5.3.3). The next relation is established between regions from time-adjacent frames. The similarity function applied here is essentially heuristic. The only parameter controls whether or not the amount of overlap of region-bounding rectangles should be included (Sect.5.4.1). The relation is a subset of the Cartesian product $R(t) \times R(t+1)$, where $R(t)$ is the set of regions in frame t.

The next higher relation is obtained by requesting transitivity of the former binary relation (Sect.5.4.2). This yields ordered n-tuples $[R_i(t), R_j(t+1), \ldots, R_k(t+n-1)]$. Formally, we may fix this n for each tuple (as the length of the sequence) by substituting the empty region ϕ in place of missing components (frames). Then a region sequence is a subset of $[R(t_1) \cup \phi] \times \ldots \times [R(t_n) \cup \phi]$ where t_1 denotes the first and t_n the last frame.

Compound sequences are formed by fusion of two or more sequences into one. The necessary condition is that only empty regions may be replaced by non-empty ones,

$$[r(1),r(2),r(3),\ldots,\phi,\phi,\phi,\phi] + [\phi,\phi,\phi,\phi,\ldots,r(n-3),r(n-2),r(n-1),\phi]$$
$$= [r(1),r(2),r(3),\ldots,r(n-3),r(n-2),r(n-1),\phi] \quad .$$

The sufficient condition is computed by application of the modified region-similarity function (Sect.5.4.4). Here, explicit knowledge may be used to set two parameters. One controls the inclusion of the x and y velocities in the similarity calculation, the other controls the inclusion of the absolute (Euclidean) velocity.

The system is completely controlled by the parameter sets. This facilitates a top-down flow of knowledge which may come from outside or be collected bottom-up by means of computing the hierarchy of relations.

5.6.2 Outlook

One topic of objections is often the heuristics implemented in a system. One design goal was to reduce heuristics as much as possible and to localize the remaining ones in order to facilitate alterations and experiments. Up until now no evidence has arisen requiring a change of the two essential heuristics: the plane approximation and the similarity function.

An important question in such a highly parameterized system is how to obtain parameter values. To overcome the trial-and-error method, an interactive procedure could be established in order to specify region extraction parameters. A light pen or some similar devide may be used to encircle test regions. For these, distributions of plane coefficients and differences may be calculated from which parameter values can be automatically derived. Here WINSTON's [5.56] ideas of learning structures (parameters, in this case) from examples can be of use. The next step of automation would be the selection of test areas by the system itself, depending on scene domain, application, etc. Another direction for development is the direct inference of parameter values from a scene, illumination, and camera model. In any case, such a system has to incorporate some facilities for adaptation. Feeding back interpretation results is necessary for modification of test-area-selection strategies or scene and illumination models. Here, the system may benefit from existing AI methods.

What is the meaning of interpretation in this system? All relation whose computation is controlled by one or more explicit parameters may be regarded as interpretation. The answer to the question of whether an interpretation in terms of regions or compound sequences is sufficient depends on the application of the system. Moreover, the parameters for a lower level calculation should be provided by higher level results; e.g., to set the parameters for chaining sequences, not from outside, but from within the system, a higher level of interpretation is needed. The relational structure may be naturally extended by introducing relations between compound sequences or by defining sequences whose members are region formations. The latter may describe individual objects which are pieced together from different surfaces corresponding to different regions. The former may express spatial or temporal relations between various objects in the scene. The computation of these relations may lead to pattern matching problems where again AI methods can be applied.

A thorough analysis of data structures (parameters, regions, sequences, etc.), their expressive capabilities (what real-world phenomena they are able to capture), and the operations between them (region linking, parameter refinement, etc.), as well as the meaning of these operations in terms of real-world actions will be important for the development of this system and similar ones.

References

5.1 H.-H. Nagel: "Analysis Techniques for Image Sequences", Proc. 4th Int. Joint Conf. on Pattern Recognition, Kyoto, Japan, 1978, pp.186-211

5.2 J.A. Leese, C.S. Novak, V.R. Taylor: The determination of cloud pattern motions from geosynchronous satellite image data. Pattern Recognition 2, 272-292 (1970)

5.3 S. Ullman: *The Interpretation of Visual Motion* (MIT Press, Cambridge, MA 1979)
5.4 J.K. Aggarwal, R.O. Duda: Computer analysis of moving polygonal images. IEEE Trans. C-*24*, 966-976 (1975)
5.5 W.K. Chow, J.K. Aggarwal: Computer analysis of planar curvilinear moving images. IEEE Trans. C-*26*, 179-185 (1977)
5.6 W.N. Martin, J.K. Aggarwal: Computer analysis of dynamic scenes containing curvilinear figures. Pattern Recognition *11*, 169-178 (1979)
5.7 J. Roach, J.K. Aggarwal: Computer tracking of objects moving in space. IEEE Trans. PAMI-*1*, 127-135 (1979)
5.8 R. Kraasch, B. Radig, W. Zach: "Automatic Three-Dimensional Description of Simple Moving Objects", WCATVI-*79*, pp.42-43 and Int. Conf. on Pattern Recognition, Miami Beach, 1980, pp.1081-1084; "Automatische dreidimensionale Beschreibung bewegter Gegenstände", in *Angewandte Szenenanalyse*, DAGM Symposium Karlsruhe, Oct.10-12, 1979, ed. by J.P. Foith, Informatik Fachberichte, Vol.20 (Springer, Berlin, Heidelberg, New York 1979) pp.208-215
5.9 M. Onoe, N. Hamano, K. Ohba: Computer analysis of traffic flow observed by subtractive television. Comput. Graph. Image Proc. *2*, 377-392 (1973)
5.10 K. Wolferts: "Ein interaktives Verfahren zur teilautomatischen Auswertung von Luftbildern für Verkehrsanalysen", in *NTG/GI*, Proc. Fachtagung Cognitive Verfahren und Systeme, Hamburg, April 11-13, 1973, ed. by Th. Einsele, W. Giloi, H.-H. Nagel, Lecture Notes in Economics and Mathematical Systems, Vol.83 (Springer, Berlin, Heidelberg, New York 1973)
K. Wolferts: "Traffic Analysis", Int. Joint Conf. on Pattern Recognition, 1974, pp.1-2
5.11 H.P. Moravec: "Towards Automatic Visual Obstacle Avoidance", Int. Joint Conf. on Artif. Intell., 1977, p.584
5.12 S.T. Barnard, W.B. Thompson: "Visual Disparity as a Cue for Depth and Velocity in Real World Scenes", IEEE Conference on Pattern Recognition and Image Processing, Chicago, IL, May 31-June 2, 1978, pp.402-404
5.13 J.L. Potter: Scene segmentation using motion information. Comput. Graph. Image Proc. *6*, 558-581 (1977)
5.14 B. Neumann: "Interpretation of Imperfect Object Contours for Identification and Tracking, Proc. 4th Int. Joint Conf. on Pattern Recognition, Kyoto, Japan, 1978, pp.691-693
5.15a S. Tsuji, A. Morizono, S. Kuroda: "Understanding a Simple Cartoon Film by a Computer Vision System", Int. Joint Conf. on Artif. Intell., 1977, pp.609-610
5.15b S. Tsuji, M. Osada, M. Yachida: "Three-Dimensional Movement Analysis of Dynamic Line Images", Int. Joint Conf. on Artif. Intell., 1979, pp.896-901
5.16 D.C. Hogg: "Visual Perception in a Changing Environment: A Paradigm for Real-Time Analysis"; Rpt. 29, Dept. of Comp. Sc., Univ. of Western Ontario (1976)
5.17 A.L. Gilbert, M.K. Giles, G.M. Flachs, R.B. Rogers, Y. Hsun: "A Real-Time Video Tracking System Using Image Processing Techniques", Proc. 4th Int. Joint Conf. on Pattern Recognition, Kyoto, Japan, 1978, pp.1111-1115
5.18 M. Yachida, S. Kitani, M. Osada, S. Tsuji: An interactive system for digital processing of moving images. Trans. Inst. Electron. Commun. Eng. D-*61*, 775-782 (1978)
5.19 M. Yachida, M. Asada, S. Tsuji: "Automatic Motion Analysis System of Moving Objects from the Records of Natural Processes", Proc. 4th Int. Joint Conf. on Pattern Recognition, Kyoto, Japan, 1978, pp.726-730
5.20 T. Tsukiyama, Y. Shirai: "Detection of the Movements of Men for Autonomous Vehicles", Int. Joint Conf. on Artif. Intell., 1979, pp.908-910

5.21 K.E. Price: "Change Detection and Analysis in Multi-Spectral Images"; Dissertation, Carnegie Mellon Univ., Pittsburgh, PA (1976)
5.22 K.E. Price, R. Reddy: "Change Detection and Analysis in Multispectral Images", Int. Joint Conf. on Artif. Intell., 1977, pp.619-625
5.23 N.I. Badler: "Temporal Scene Analysis: Conceptual Descriptions of Object Movements"; Dissertation, Report 80, Univ. Toronto (1975)
5.24 R. Jain, H.-H. Nagel: "Analysing a Real World Scene Sequence Using Fuzziness", IEEE Conference on Decision and Control, New Orleans, LA, Dec.7-9, 1977
5.25 R. Jain, H.-H. Nagel: On the analysis of accumulative difference pictures from image sequence of real world scenes. IEEE Trans. PAMI-*1*, 206-214 (1979)
5.26 S. Tsugawa, T. Yatabe, T. Hirose, S. Matsumoto: "An Automobile with Artificial Intelligence", Int. Joint Conf. on Artif. Intell., 1979, pp.893-895
5.27 M. Nagao, T. Matsuyama: "Edge Preserving Smoothing", Proc. 4th Int. Joint Conf. on Pattern Recognition, Kyoto, Japan, 1978, pp.518-520
5.28 F. Holdermann, H. Kazmierczak: Preprocessing of gray-scale pictures. Comput. Graph. Image Proc. *1*, 66-80 (1972)
5.29 H. Yoda, J. Motoike, M. Ejiri: "Direction Coding Method and Its Application to Scene Analysis", Int. Joint Conf. on Artif. Intell., 1975, pp.620-627
5.30 C. Somerville, J.L. Mundy: "One Pass Contouring of Images through Planar Approximation", Proc. 3rd Int. Joint Conf. on Pattern Recognition, 1976, pp.745-748
5.31 R.T. Chien, C. Jacobus: "Directional Derivatives in Computer Image Processing", Proc. 3rd Int. Joint Conf. on Pattern Recognition, 1976, pp.684-688
5.32 J. Birk, R. Kelley, N. Chen, L. Wilson: Image feature extraction using diameter-limited gradient direction histograms. IEEE Trans. PAMI-*1*, 228-235 (1979)
5.33 F. O'Gorman: Edge detection using walsh functions. Artif. Intell. *10*, 215-223 (1978)
5.34 M.J. Brooks: Rationalizing edge detectors. Comput. Graph. Image Proc. *8*, 277-285 (1978)
5.35 R.M. Haralick: Edge and region analysis for digital image data. Comput. Graph. Image Proc. *12*, 60-73 (1980)
5.36 A. Rosenfeld, A.C. Kak: *Digital Picture Processing* (Academic, New York 1976)
5.37 H. Tamura: "A Comparison of Line Thinning Algorithm from Digital Geometry Viewpoint", Proc. 4th Int. Joint Conf. on Pattern Recognition, Kyoto, Japan, 1978, pp.715-719
5.38 U. Ramer: Extraction of line structures from photographs of curved objects. Comput. Graph. Image Proc. *4*, 81-103 (1975)
5.39 M.D. Kelly: "Edge Detection in Pictures by Computer Using Planning", in *Machine Intelligence 6*, ed. by B. Meltzer, D. Michie (Edinburgh Univ. Press, Edinburgh 1971) pp.379-409
5.40 M. Yachida, M. Ikeda, S. Tsuji: "Plan-Guided Analysis of Noisy Dynamic Images", Int. Joint Conf. on Artif. Intell., 1979, pp.979-983
5.41 J.P. Foith: "TV-Sensor for Top-Lighting and Multiple Part Analysis", Proc. 2nd IFAC/IFIP Symposium on Information Control Problems in Manufacturing Technology, Stuttgart, Germany, Oct.1979
5.42 D. Waltz: "Generating Semantic Descriptions from Drawings of Scenes with Shadows"; Rpt. TR 271, MIT, Cambridge, MA (1972), and in *The Psychology of Computer Vision*, ed. by P.H. Winston (McGraw-Hill, New York 1975)
5.43 A.K. Mackworth: Consistency in networks of relations. Artif. Intell. *8*, 99-118 (1977)

5.44 J.F. Reiser: "SAIL"; Memo AIM-289, Stanford Artificial Intelligence Laboratory (1976)
5.45 L.A. Zadeh: Fuzzy sets. Inf. Control *8*, 338-353 (1965)
5.46 A. Rosenfeld, R.A. Hummel, S.W. Zucker: Scene labelling by relaxation operations. IEEE Trans. SMC-*6*, 420-433 (1976)
5.47 S.W. Zucker, R. Hummel, A. Rosenfeld: An application of relaxation labeling to line and curve enhancement. IEEE Trans. C-*26*, 394-403, 922-929 (1977)
5.48 C.R. Brice, C.L. Fennema: Scene analysis using regions. Artif. Intell. *1*, 205-226 (1970)
5.49 R.B. Ohlander: "Analysis of Natural Scenes"; Dissertation, Comp. Sc. Dept., Carnegie-Mellon Univ., Pittsburgh, PA (1975)
5.50 J.M. Tenenbaum, H.G. Barrow: "IGS: A Paradigm for Integrating Image Segmentation and Interpretation", in *Pattern Recognition and Artificial Intelligence*, ed. by C.H. Chen (Academic, New York 1976) pp.472-507
5.51 B.T. Lowerre: "The HARPY Speech Recognition System"; Ph.D. Thesis, Dept. Comp. Sc., Carnegie-Mellon Univ., Pittsburgh, PA (1976)
5.52 S.M. Rubin, R. Reddy: "The Locus Model of Search and Its Use in Image Interpretation", Int. Joint Conf. on Artif. Intell., 1977, pp.590-595
5.53 B. Radig: "Description of Moving Objects Based on Parameterized Region Extraction", Proc. 4th Int. Joint Conf. on Pattern Recognition, Kyoto, Japan, 1978, pp.723-725
5.54 H.-H. Nagel: "Analyzing Sequences of TV-Frames: System Design Considerations"; Bericht IfI-HH-B-33/77, Fachbereich Informatik, Univ. Hamburg (1977), and Int. Joint Conf. on Artif. Intell., 1977, p.526
5.55 R.C. Bolles: "Verification Vision Within a Programmable Assembly System"; Dissertation, Dept. of Comp. Sc., Rpt. STAN-CS-77-591, Stanford Univ. (1976)
5.56 P.H. Winston: "Learning Structural Descriptions from Examples", in *The Psychology of Computer Vision*, ed. by P.H. Winston (McGraw-Hill, New York 1975) pp.157-209

Chapter 6 Analyzing Dynamic Scenes Containing Multiple Moving Objects*

J. K. Aggarwal and W. N. Martin

With 7 Figures

This chapter provides an insight into the problems encountered in image sequence analysis when the viewed scene contains several objects all of which may be moving. A major emphasis is on the interaction of object images resulting from viewpoint placement and object movement. The interaction that concerns us here is the occlusion of some part of an object by other objects or even by other parts of the same object. Our discussion begins with the problems of interpreting single images containing occluded objects and then turns to the implications of occlusion on image sequence analysis. Further problems encountered in image sequence analysis will then be emphasized through the description of those problems as they have arisen in specific systems. Foremost among these problems is the identification, throughout the image sequence, of objects in spite of their continually changing appearance. Also important are the computational implications for attempting to process the flux of information presented by an image sequence.

6.1 Occlusion in General

6.1.1 Arbitrary Images

Occlusion occurs whenever the image to be analyzed is a projection of some three-dimensional scene onto a two-dimensional plane. In this general case there is always a background obscured by the objects which are considered to be the foreground. For objects widely spaced over a homogeneous background, e.g., paintings on a museum wall or a pair of birds flying in a clear sky, there is no problem. The background is understood to be homogeneous so that the characteristics of the obscured portions are indicated by the visible sections. The foreground objects are assumed to have image characteristics

* This research was supported in part by the Air Force Office of Scientific Research under grant AFOSR 77-3190

Fig. 6.1. Geometric pattern having an ambiguous figure-ground interpretation

which are distinct from the background making the foreground objects readily detectable in the image. In addition, the spacing of the objects assures that the presence of the features of one object will not interfere with the analysis of the remaining foreground objects. However, if the background has a complex structure, e.g., the museum wall has a highly patterned covering, or if the foreground objects are closely arranged in some structure, e.g., a flock of birds flying in the same direction, then the classic "figure-ground" problem arises.

In the figure-ground problem, the spatial relationships between disjoint elements of the viewed scene combine to interfere with the perception of the individual elements. In its full generality, this is a psychophysical problem where the preconceptions and expectations of the viewer play an important part in perception. Figure 6.1 indicates some of the subtleties of this problem. The lowest level figure-ground ambiguity involved in Fig.6.1 is whether the figure depicts dark squares and triangles against a light background or light squares and triangles on a dark background. This ambiguity is inherent in the construction of the figure and when focusing on a single element, i.e., a triangle or square, it is fairly easy to form either interpretation. However, if one focuses on an area containing several elements it becomes more difficult to interpret the figure as being a simple collection of squares and triangles of either color.

The prevalence of pairs of single element edges that are colinear, parallel, or perpendicular interfers with the perception of the individual elements. The lines through which the sides of the squares are colinear give rise to the perception of the figure as having three horizontal and three vertical bands with hourglass holes (or obstructions) along their length. Again bands of either color can be seen. The fact that many element edges can be linked together to form long straight lines reinforces this perception.

Another set of colinearities, the diagonal lines through the sides of the triangles, yields yet another interpretation. In this case the crossings of the diagonal lines emphasize the right angles in the triangles. The triangles are thus grouped into four element sets with each set forming a diamond whose corners correspond to the right angle corners of the constituent triangles. In this interpretation the figure can be seen as a checkerboard of black and white diamonds where each diamond is partially covered by a smaller square of the opposite color.

For the interpretations of Fig.6.1 discussed above, an initial decision is made as to what is the prevalent structure. The remaining parts of the figure must then be related to that structure. For the last of the above interpretations the checkerboard of light and dark diamonds is accepted as the primary structure. The smaller squares interfere with the perception of the checkerboard but can be accounted for by assuming that they are foreground objects occluding the diamonds. In this manner the concept of occlusion is brought into the perceptual process at a very low level in order to make sense of the ambiguous figure. The variety of relationships exhibited by the individual squares and triangles provides the opportunity to resolve the ambiguities into several different interpretations of the figure.

6.1.2 Scene Domain Imposed Constraints

In the abstract geometrical pattern of Fig.6.1, both the quantity and subtlety of the interelement relationships are greater than that occurring in typical natural scenes. The constraints imposed by the three-dimensional structure and distribution of the objects appearing in typical scenes serve to limit the relationships possible in the images derived from such scenes. For instance, the boundary edges of noncontiguous objects are rarely colinear in natural scenes. This consideration makes reasonable the assumption that if the image of a scene contains disjoint edges which are colinear, then those edges correspond to a single boundary in the scene and the discontinuity is caused by the boundary being partially obscured in the given view. BARROW and TENENBAUM [6.1] argue that certain psychological phenomena, such as subjective contour, are the result of the human visual system attempting to use such evidence of occlusion as a cue to apparent depth.

An elegant example of how scene domain constraints can be used in understanding occlusion is the system developed by WALTZ [6.2]. In this case, the domain is that of scenes having a single light source illuminating a set of planar-faced objects whose vertices are trihedral. The distribution of the objects in the scene, the location of the light source, and the orientation of the image plane are restricted only to eliminate certain coincidences which cause unresolvable ambiguities in the resulting images. The images analyzed are actually "perfect" line drawings formed by an orthogonal projection of the scene onto the image plane with a relative brightness associated with each region in the drawing.

The strong constraints imposed by this scene domain are primarily embedded in a junction classification and line labeling scheme generalized from the system first discussed by HUFFMAN [6.3] and CLOWES [6.4]. Junctions are the line drawing representations of the vertices in the scene, thus the trihedral restriction on the object vertices provides extensive constraints on both the types of junctions possible and the allowable labelings of the lines forming those junctions. In particular, certain of the labeled junction types can only arise through cases of occlusion, and thus, when found in the drawings, provide a reliable indication of occlusion.

The so-called T junction is an example of a junction indicative of occlusion. The line forming the bar of the T must correspond to an obscuring edge in the scene. In fact, the edge which forms the bar line must be a convex edge. However, the isolated T junction remains ambiguous in that the post of the T may correspond to a partially obscured edge, or it may be a "crack" along which two objects coincide. In the latter case the bar line is actually the result of an "accidental alignment" of two convex edges and the obscuring object faces occur on the post side of the T junction. In the former case the bar line is generated by the convex edge bounding the obscuring object face opposite the T junction post.

This ambiguity can be resolved in two ways, each of which serves to provide nonlocal information to the labeling process. First, the system may be told that the region opposite the post of the T junction is the background or supporting surface. This insures that the post of the T junction is a "crack" and that the bar line corresponds to two aligned edges. Second, the labeling process may have already determined a legitimate labeling for one of the junctions which are connected to the given T junction. The labeled junction is, of course, connected to the given junction by a common line and thus the currently assigned label for the common line can be used to determine the labels for the other two lines of the T junction or at least to limit the number of possible labels for those lines. For example, the post of a given T junction may also be part of an L junction. This means that the post of the T junction could not possibly be a crack and therefore the bar line must be a single edge bounding the obscuring object face.

This latter method is fundamental to the overall labeling process and is based on another major constraint imposed by the scene domain. For the type of objects allowed in the scenes, a line must retain a given labeling throughout its extent. This constraint is assured by the fact that each edge in the scene is created by the intersection of exactly two planes. The constraint provides, in the actual structure of the input images, a mechanism by which a rather simple labeling process can obtain information that is not local to the junction currently under consideration. The nonlocal information is of prime importance because the ambiguities in the image caused by occlusion in the scene cannot usually be resolved on the basis of information contained at a single junction. Indeed, it may not even be possible to tell initially how far away (in terms of the number of interceding junctions) the necessary clarifying information is. For this reason the labeling process is embedded in a parallel-iterative procedure (since referred to as "relaxation" [6.5]). This procedure allows the necessary information to propagate throughout the interconnected network of junctions, yet requires the labeling process to interrogate no more than two adjacent junctions at a time. Of course, the pairwise comparisons performed by the labeling process are not sufficient to resolve all ambiguous line drawings. Increasing the number of junctions that the labeling process may inspect at a given time will allow the system to disambiguate more scenes. However, for any fixed and finite limit there will always be scenes, albeit exceedingly complex scenes, which will not be resolvable.

From the previous discussion of the figure-ground problem for arbitrary pictures one can see that the removal of scene-domain constraints only worsens the degree of ambiguity caused by occlusion. In particular, many pictures are inherently ambiguous, and no information derived from the image can resolve the uncertainties. Frequently it is not that the image has no consistent interpretation, but rather that there are several mutually exclusive interpretations which are each independently consistent. The choice among such alternatives must be based on the expectations or goals of the viewer, not simply on features actually exhibited in the image.

This discussion has brought to light several factors which are fundamental to the understanding of scenes containing occluding objects. First, the concept of occlusion is used at a very early stage in the human visual system in order to provide interpretations in terms of apparent depth. Second, effective cues to occlusion can be derived from scene-domain constraints. Third, the use of such cues may involve the complex integration of information taken from areas which are widely separated in the image. Fourth, occlusion necessarily results in the loss of information available about the obscure object thus causing uncertainties in the interpretation of the image. And finally, the resolution of some occlusion ambiguities depends on external expectations and goals.

6.1.3 Occlusion in Image Sequences

The discussion up to this point has dealt with the implications of occlusion on the analysis of single images. For the remainder of this chapter the focus will be on time-varying images, that is, sequences of images representing systematic time ordered samplings of scenes. The question addressed is: How is the complexity of the occlusion analysis problem affected by the addition of time variation, i.e., sequences of images? The broad answer to this question is that time variation simplifies some aspects of the problem, complicates other aspects, and introduces several new problems. These points are discussed on a general level in the following, and are described at a detailed level in later sections where specific dynamic scene analysis systems are presented.

The time variation can simplify the initial feature extraction phase of processing through both the redundancy inherent in the dynamic scenes and the opportunities provided for acquiring new information. Typically the sampling rate along the time axis is such that the majority of the scene does not change through short sequences of images. This property has been exploited for data reduction by frame-to-frame encoding of video signals [6.6], but can also be used to attenuate noise and produce more reliable feature values. The new information can be obtained from the changing views of the objects in the scene. For instance, if one of the occluding objects in the foreground is moving, then additional portions of the objects it is obscuring will become visible in each successive image. Similarly, since any three-dimensional object is self-obscuring, the object's motion will usually bring into view previously unseen portions of the object. This concept has been used in a system [6.7] which forms a three-dimensional description of a planar object from a sequence of views taken while the object rotates. The description is in terms of the object faces and their interconnections, which are "learned" as previously hidden faces become visible. New views also result from changes in the orientation of the image plane caused by eye (camera) movement. In these situations, areas of ambiguity in a given image may be clarified by the additional information contained in the subsequent images.

The continual change in the information content of the images, which is an advantage when the change adds information, can be a disadvantage when the change results in a reduction of available information. In each of the information-adding cases discussed above, there can be a complementary aspect in which information is lost. For instance, the moving foreground object is probably proceeding to obscure some other objects or even other portions of the same object that it is elsewhere uncovering. This aspect raises the question as to what can be said about previously visible features once they are no longer visible. If a recently obscured feature is part of an object which is still partially visible, then the relationship of the feature to the currently visible portion, as determined in preceding images, can be used to infer the location and orientation of the feature in the present scene. This type of implication is based on the assumption that the object is rigid and thus that the spatial relationships of the various features of an object will remain constant through time. This is an extremely important scene-domain constraint which will be discussed in more detail in later sections of this chapter.

The information flux in time-varying images also creates new problems at the image segmentation and object identification levels. The problems encountered here involve the additional "semantic noise" [6.8] exhibited in time-varying images. Typical systems for static image analysis must be capable of interfacing with preprocessors which occasionally fail to detect, erroneously produce, or incorrectly locate image feature descriptions. Systems for time-varying images will have similar preprocessing problems but must furthermore be prepared to interpret features which, through time, may take on different values yet signify the same scene component semantically. For example, the effects of shadows on a textured outdoor surface, e.g., a gravel road bed, will vary as the sun angle changes throughout the day.

This problem of identifying "apparently different but semantically identical objects" [6.9] indicates a fundamental concept in the analysis of time-varying images: in order to understand the changes that a given aspect of an entity in a scene may be undergoing, there must be some form of constancy in other aspects of that same entity to serve as the identifying features of the entity. This is particularly important when there are several objects moving about the scene, because the simple detection of change cannot attribute that change to the proper object.

As an illustration, consider the illusion depicted in Fig.6.2. Here four identical disks are attached pairwise to the ends of two cross members which are slightly offset in depth and spin in opposite directions about the center point. They exhibit constancy in both shape and color. These features make it easy to track the disks while they are moving through positions such as that of Fig.6.2a. However, when the position shown in Fig.6.2b is reached, the

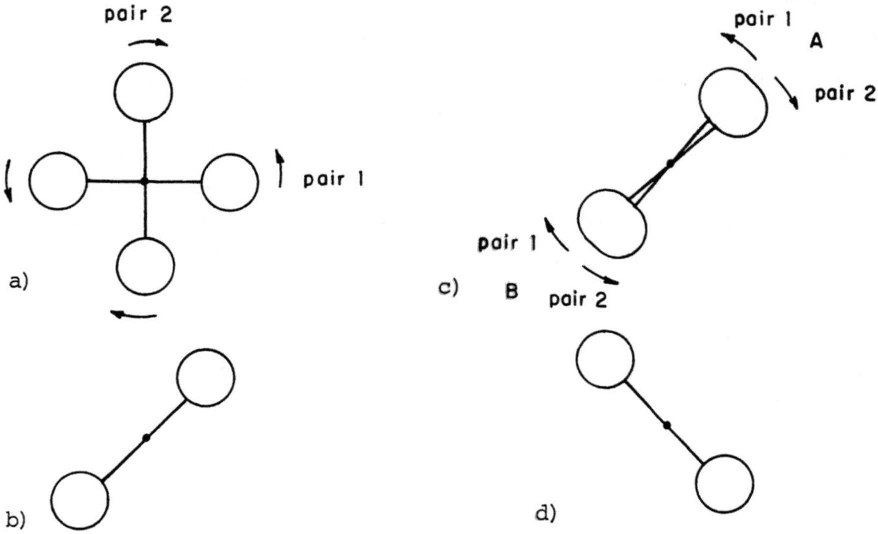

Fig. 6.2a-d. A motion illusion with four spinning disks

constancies no longer serve as identifying features and thus admit an ambiguity to the interpretation of the position displayed in Fig.6.2c.

Is the pair of velocities labeled A in Fig.6.2c the correct interpretation or is the pair labeled B correct? An assumption of minimal velocity change for each object results in a perception according to the velocities labeled A. In such a perception the disks appear to have circular paths and pass completely through one another at positions such as those shown in Figs.6.2b,d. A rather more complicated proximity criterion, which holds that the disk last viewed completely in a given quadrant will return immediately to that quadrant, yields a perception according to the velocities labeled B. In this latter case, each disk sweeps both back and forth through a given quadrant as bounded by the positions shown in Figs.6.2b,d. At these positions the disks appear to "bounce" off each other thus exactly reversing their velocities.

The two cases discussed above can, however, be understood in terms of two different types of constancy, one involving velocity, and the other, occupancy. These constancies can only be used to resolve the ambiguity in an indirect way because the ambiguity occurs when one is trying to understand the progression from an image of a position such as that of Fig.6.2b to the immediately succeeding image. In the constant velocity case for example, the instantaneous velocity is measured as the displacement in disk location between two successive images. But the location of the disk in the image after that of Fig.6.2b is precisely what is in question. Thus the analysis of these two images in isolation cannot resolve the ambiguity. Instead the velocity information must be derived from the preceding images in which the constancies of shape and color can be used to locate each disk, thereby allowing the calculation of its velocity. The velocity information can then be applied to the given pair of images as part of a predictive analysis or as the criterion for a hypothesis and test procedure.

In this introductory section we have discussed several of the general problems in understanding occlusion as they relate to the analysis of time-varying imagery. In the remaining sections we discuss the various problems encountered and the solutions derived in specific systems (for further references see [6.10-12]). We turn first to systems which reduce each image to point patterns and analyze the changes in successive patterns. Then we discuss several systems which operate on the object boundaries. Finally we conclude with a discussion of general representation problems and other areas for further research involving time-varying imagery.

6.2 Dot Pattern Analysis

This section presents several specific dynamic scene analysis systems. These systems preprocess the image sequence so that each image is transformed into a dot pattern, where each dot constitutes a "token" of some significant feature in the image. In addition to spatial location, various attributes of the image features may be associated with their respective dots. In some cases the features represented by the dots are whole objects which, due to the scene domain, do not occlude or otherwise closely interact. For this type of scene, simple one-object tracking procedures (e.g., matching by shortest Euclidean distance) can be applied independently to each dot in a given image in order to identify the represented feature in the next image of the sequence. Identifying a particular feature in every image of the sequence by matching the proper dots in every pair of consecutive images allows the system to form a trace of the positions occupied by the feature throughout the sequence (as an example see [6.13]). Several motion measurements such as linear velocity, angular velocity, and acceleration can be computed from these traces.

6.2.1 Combined Motion and Correspondence Processes

If the represented features are objects which are likely to occlude one another, or are parts of a single object and interact closely, then the simple tracking procedures will not be applicable. In order to elaborate on this point we will discuss a system described in an early paper on cloud tracking by ENDLICH et al. [6.14]. This system represents the clouds by "brightness centers". The centers are obtained by first thresholding the satellite pictures to separate the clouds from the background, and then applying a clustering procedure, ISODATA [6.15], to the designated cloud pixels.

The brightness center representation is appropriate for images of clouds because the detailed description of the cloud region boundaries is quite complex and is continually changing. Through short time intervals these changes along the cloud boundaries have little effect on the location of the resulting brightness centers. Thus the amorphous nature of the clouds can be ignored while retaining a fairly reliable indication of the cloud locations and brightnesses. These attributes do not provide a sufficient basis for identifying the corresponding brightness centers between consecutive images of the sequence. However, the system is capable of successfully matching the centers under the assumption of a fairly uniform yet unknown common motion for most of the centers within arbitrarily selected subimages. The correspondence is determined by hypothesizing for each center in a selected subimage of a given image several possible matches to the centers in the appropriate subimage of the next image of the sequence. Each hypothesis specifies a motion vector so that the procedure initially yields a set of vectors. The most common vector in this set is chosen as the representative motion for the subimage.

Hypothesized matches which generate motion vectors that vary significantly from the representative motion are discarded, thus reducing the number of possible matches. An iterative application of this procedure is used to obtain unique assignments, i.e., no center is matched more than once. Having established the acceptable matches the system can use the vectors specified by those matches to form a vector map of the wind velocities over the area viewed in the image.

In some cases, however, centers will be left unmatched indicating that there is not a center in the second image which when hypothesized as a match for the given center yields a motion vector consistent with the chosen representative motion. It is reasonable to have unmatched centers because clouds tend to both dissipate and gather through time. However, it is also possible that the selected subimage contains clouds from several altitudes which are moving with radically different velocities.

Figure 6.3 illustrates this situation (for a similar example, as processed by the system, see [Ref.6.14, Fig.5]). Two consecutive frames are displayed in Fig.6.3 with the majority of the dots moving down and to the left. There is also a small group of dots moving to the left and slightly up. Due to the

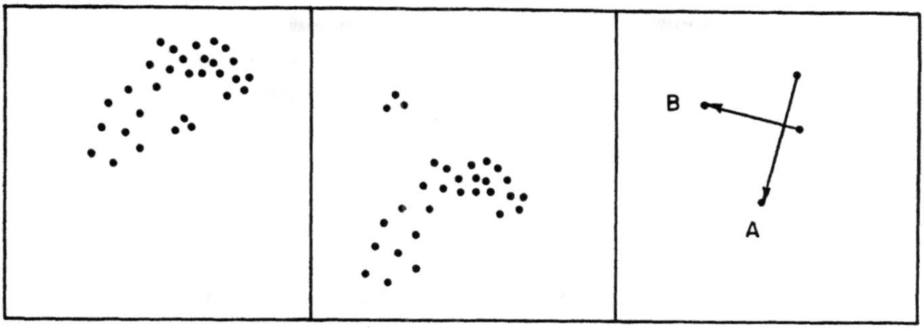

a. b. c.

Fig. 6.3a-c. Dot patterns with interfering motion

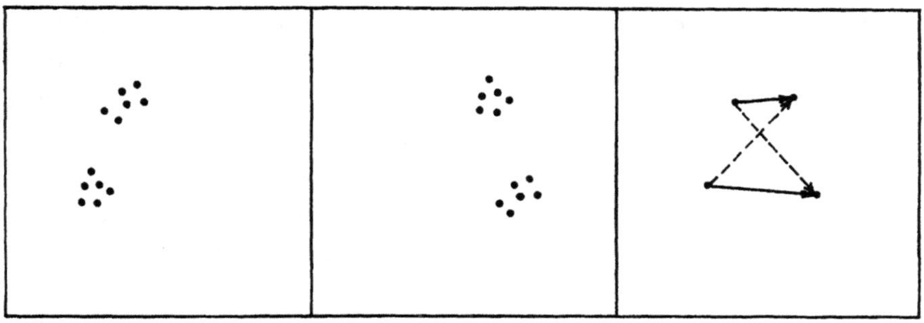

a. b. c.

Fig. 6.4a-c. Dot patterns with dual motion interpretations

statistical weight of the downward moving group of dots, the chosen representative velocity vector is similar to the vector labeled A in Fig.6.3c. This choice precludes the correct matchings for the dots in the smaller group, which would result in vectors such as the one labeled B in Fig.6.3c. Since there are no matches for the dots of the small group that yield vectors similar to A, these dots are left unmatched in both frames.

A more extreme case is displayed in Fig.6.4. In this example two equally numbered sets of dots are moving in perpendicular directions with approximately equal speeds, as indicated by the dashed vectors of Fig.6.4c. These velocities in conjunction with the original locations of the dots allow an alternate interpretation in which a single vector, such as the solid vectors of Fig.6.4c, can be chosen as representative of the motions of all the dots. No dots will be left unmatched, but the chosen vectors will specify an incorrect match for every dot. The problem arises from the essentially circular use of hypothesized motions in determining the dot correspondence. The motion measurements are necessarily based on the derived matches, thus the correspondence must itself be based on some other constancy feature of the moving objects. Otherwise, limitations must be imposed on the types of movement allowed, making the motion constant in some respect. In this system the motion is assumed to be nearly constant over the subimages.

6.2.2 Separate Correspondence Determination

A similar approach to the matching problem is taken in a recent book on motion by ULLMAN [6.16], where it is argued that the "correspondence process is a low-level operation which precedes, or is independent of, the [3D] interpretation scheme." The correspondence process receives each image in the form of a set of tokens and constructs a "minimal" mapping of those tokens to the ones of the previous image in the sequence. It is referred to as a minimal mapping because the computational mechanism suggested creates the mapping by a cost function which reflects the most likely movement of the tokens. "Most likely" is in terms of an assumed probability distribution function for the velocities exhibited by the tokens in the image. In a discussion of human visual behavior, evidence is given for an affinity function upon which the low-level correspondence process could be based. It can reasonably be argued that a typical human response to the example of Fig.6.4 would be that there is only one group of dots and the group is moving horizontally to the right.

This interpretation is consistent with a spatial proximity affinity function. However, the correct interpretation can only be made if information other than the dot displacements between the given two frames is used in the analysis. This information might be in the form of projected movements derived from previous frames in the sequence. Such projections would provide a probability distribution for the motion of each dot in a given frame which had been successfully matched to a dot in the immediately preceding frame. The most likely match for each dot would then depend on its associated distribution rather than a globally assumed distribution. The minimizing function could begin with a much closer initial estimate containing fewer candidate matches to choose from. The problem that would arise is in trying to allow for objects which change their direction or speed of travel. Such movement variations invalidate the previously compiled projections leaving the analysis system with the original problem again. This complication is also encountered in higher level predictive schemes, for example see CHOW and AGGARWAL [6.17].

Other information useful to this analysis but not necessarily dependent on previous frames of the sequence is the spatial relationship of the dots in a given frame. This would involve grouping the dots into another level of tokens with each new token having as an attribute the spatial distribution of the dots grouped under that token. The new tokens could be matched between consecutive frames by this additional attribute, thus removing hypothesized motion measurements from the correspondence process. The problem encountered in trying to use this type of information is that of properly grouping the dots under the higher level tokens.

One obvious grouping is to consider all the dots of a given frame to be under a single token. This grouping is easily made; however, it will clearly be of no utility for scenes containing several moving objects. At the other extreme, assigning one dot to each token would not be a legitimate grouping because the spatial relationship attribute of the resulting tokens would be undefined. The desired grouping would be along the spectrum between these two possibilities, but exactly where would depend on the actual scene being analyzed. This grouping process is analogous to classical segmentation in scene analysis. The process could be quite complicated and depend on information from previous frames in the sequence or from system maintained models of the scene. It is worth observing that ULLMAN contends that the correspondence process operates at a much lower level than could support this grouping process. In fact a computational method [6.16] has been developed that uses the correspondence information from a minimal matching process to derive groupings which have three-dimensional interpretations. A discussion of that system follows.

6.2.3 Motion Analysis Given Dot Correspondence

The input to Ullman's "structure from motion" system is a sequence of images, each formed by taking the orthographic projection of a three-dimensional scene containing identifiable feature points on moving objects. Thus every feature point or token is represented as a dot in each image with an assumed correspondence process identifying the feature points throughout the sequence of images. The transformations exhibited in the resulting two-dimensional dot patterns will, under certain conditions, give rise to a unique interpretation of both the three-dimensional spatial relationship of the feature points and their motions. The conditions are stated in the following theorem [6.16] whose proof constitutes a specification of a computational method to derive the correct interpretation.

Theorem: Given three distinct orthographic views of four noncoplanar points in a rigid configuration, the structure and motion compatible with the three views are uniquely determined.

The most important of the constraints mentioned in the theorem is that the points be in a rigid noncoplanar configuration. The remaining details specify only minimum requirements for the computational method in the sense that more points or views can be used and that an analogous method can be applied to perspective projections.

The rigidity constraint reflects a more fundamental assumption of this system. The assumption is stated as follows: "Any set of elements undergoing a two-dimensional transformation which has a unique interpretation as a rigid body moving in space should be interpreted as such a body in motion" [6.16]. The overall strategy of the system is to find the sets of tokens which can be interpreted as configurations representing rigid bodies. The minimum requirements then prescribe a starting point for the system. The set of tokens for the first view are partitioned into four element subsets. The given correspondences specify the appropriate tokens for the subsets in the second and third views. Thus each subset meets the minimum requirements, and all the system needs to do is determine if the rigidity constraint holds for every subset independently. The test performed, as detailed in [6.16], either determines that the subset can be interpreted as a rigid object by actually computing that configuration, or declares the relationship of the feature points in the subset to be nonrigid. The set of points from rejected subsets, the latter case, can be repartitioned and the test performed again until an interpretation is established for all the feature points.

In a similar manner the system can iteratively test for rigid configurations between previously defined subsets until a minimal, in terms of the number of subsets, covering of the feature points is obtained. The resulting subsets correspond to the rigid objects in the scene and specify, through the successful rigidity tests, the structure and orientation of those objects. It should be noted that due to the orthographic projection the structure is determined up to a reflection about the image plane, while the orientation is resolved to within a translation in depth.

The approach taken by this system is to break the given data, i.e., the tokens in correspondence, into "nuclei" of identifiable features, i.e., four element subsets, which can be independently analyzed by a general knowledge based process. It is important that the analyzing process not depend on specific knowledge about the components of the scene or on disjoint sources of information indicative of the three-dimensional characteristics of the scene. The process should be such that "segmentation, structure, rotation and translation are uniquely determined, although none of them is determined by any 'cue' in isolation" [6.16]. Equally important is that the data are broken into small nuclei which, having been properly analyzed, can be grouped into larger structures. These structures can then be elaborated upon to derive full descriptions of the objects in the scene and their motions.

These considerations return us to the fundamental concept of exploiting the constancies in a changing environment in order to understand the components of that environment and their transformations. At the lower level the extracted tokens have associated features which the correspondence process can treat as locally constant. The correspondence process uses this constancy to identify the tokens throughout the sequence of images. At the higher level are the constancies which reflect what the system considers to be a significant component or object in the scene. The set of identified tokens is decomposed into groupings exhibiting this constancy. The groupings are thus taken to represent the objects of interest in the scene.

This strategy, however, does not depend upon reducing the input images to dot patterns. The tokens can be more complex structures, as we will see in the next section. In that section several systems which use edge and boundary descriptions in the initial analysis are discussed.

6.3 Edge and Boundary Analysis

6.3.1 Straight Edge Domain

We begin this section by discussing a system [6.18,19] which analyzes software-generated scenes containing rigid polygons. These polygons can be arbitrarily complex in shape and can possibly contain holes. Each polygon is restricted to move in a plane parallel to the image plane so that an input frame is formed by taking the orthographic projection of all the object planes onto the image plane. This projection essentially creates the silhouette of the object planes. In this way apparent objects in the image are formed from two or more overlapping actual polygons. The system must be able to derive descriptions of the actual polygons from the sequence of images of the apparent objects in motion.

The overlapping of the actual polygons creates new vertices while removing occluded vertices and edges. The new vertices are referred to as "false" vertices and the visible vertices of the actual polygons are called "real" vertices. One of the main functions of the system is to classify the vertices of the input image into the appropriate one of these two categories. This classification process is facilitated by two characteristics of the input domain. First, no "false" vertex can have an interior angle which measures less than 180 degrees. Second, any vertex which changes its angular measure between two frames must be a "false" vertex. The first characteristic is due to the polygonal nature of the objects, while the restriction to rigid polygons assures the second. However, these two characteristics do not provide enough information to directly classify every vertex. There are vertices with obtuse interior angles which are not "false" vertices and there are "false" vertices which do not change their angular measure. One further restriction is necessary, and it is that no more than one "real" vertex can appear or become occluded between any two consecutive frames. The importance of this restriction is that it allows the system to determine the type of change that has occurred between two consecutive frames. This determination is based on the difference in the number of vertices having acute interior angles along with the difference in the number of vertices having obtuse interior angles.

With the problem domain set in this manner the system begins processing by forming a correspondence between the objects in a given frame and the objects in the immediately preceding frame. This is accomplished by finding in both frames known "real" vertices, i.e., vertices with acute interior angles, which have similar angular measures. The matching of more than one vertex between two objects is restricted by the order in which the candidate vertices appear on each object in question. So the tokens, in this case the vertex points with the attribute of angular measure, are not matched independently on their attribute values. Rather, higher level constraints are imposed on the intertoken relationships.

The ordering constraint combines with the matching of known "real" vertices to provide a cue to which vertices having obtuse interior angles might be matching "real" vertices and should be compared for similarity in angular measure. If the vertices do have matching angular measures then the system assumes that they correspond and are "real" vertices. Of course, if the vertices actually represent a false vertex which is not exhibiting any change in its angular measure then the "real" vertex assumption may be incorrect. In this case, however, the system can either use information from previous frames to determine that the vertex is "false" or accommodate the error until there is a clear indication that the vertex is "false".

The matching of the "real" vertices between two frames provides the system with the correspondence (possibly many-to-one or one-to-many) of objects in the scene. With this correspondence the system can then determine what objects are in which one of the basic types of change, and call special procedures developed to analyze each of those types. The function of these procedures is to create and continually update models of the actual objects in the scene. The vertex classification enables these procedures to decompose the apparent objects into sections comprising the visible portions of the constituent actual objects. The visible portions may simply indicate that the location and velocity components of the models should be updated. Or the models may require modifications such as adding a newly visible vertex or marking as currently not visible a just occluded vertex. In addition, two models might have to be merged or a given model split as more frames are analyzed. In this way the system uses these models not only to track the actual objects, but also to compile complete descriptions of the objects even though the objects may not have been totally visible in any of the given frames. Thus if an appropriate sequence of partial views of an object at some point presents each vertex and edge of that object, then the system will be able to derive a description for the object as a whole.

An example analyzed by the system is shown in Fig.6.5. The input sequence of frames is labeled TIME K for each time K, while the object models resulting from processing the sequence through time K are shown beside TIME K and labeled MODEL K. There are three actual objects in this scene: one large stationary object; a triangle moving to the left; and a smaller triangle, initially obscured, but later visible as it moves more slowly to the left. The portions of the objects which become occluded during the sequence are displayed at their projected positions. These projections are based on velocity estimates made while the particular section was visible. The single apparent object present in frames 2-6 is correctly decomposed into its constituent actual objects. Beginning with frame 3 this decomposition includes a partial object model for the smaller triangle which becomes visible one vertex at a time. This partial object model is updated when the next vertex is seen in frame 5 and is completed by the appearance of the final vertex in frame 7. Also of interest is that each of the basic types of change possible in the polygon domain of this system is instantiated in this example.

This system employs the constancy of angular measure at "real" vertices, as implied by the rigid object restriction, and several general observations about the polygon domain in the successful analysis of complex scenes of moving polygons. The "real" vertex constancy serves as the basis for matching individual vertices between consecutive frames. Higher level constraints are then used to form a correspondence for the objects in the frames. Finally,

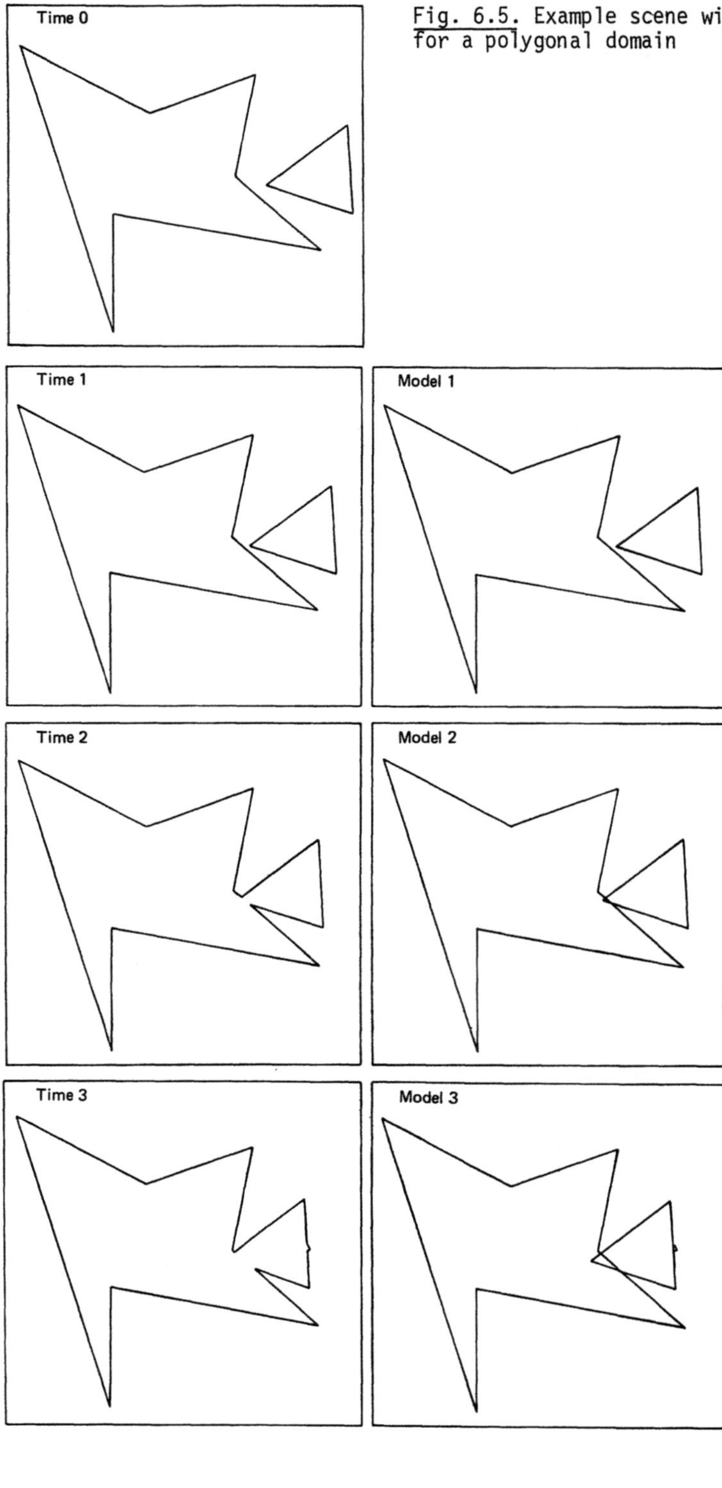

Fig. 6.5. Example scene with derived models for a polygonal domain

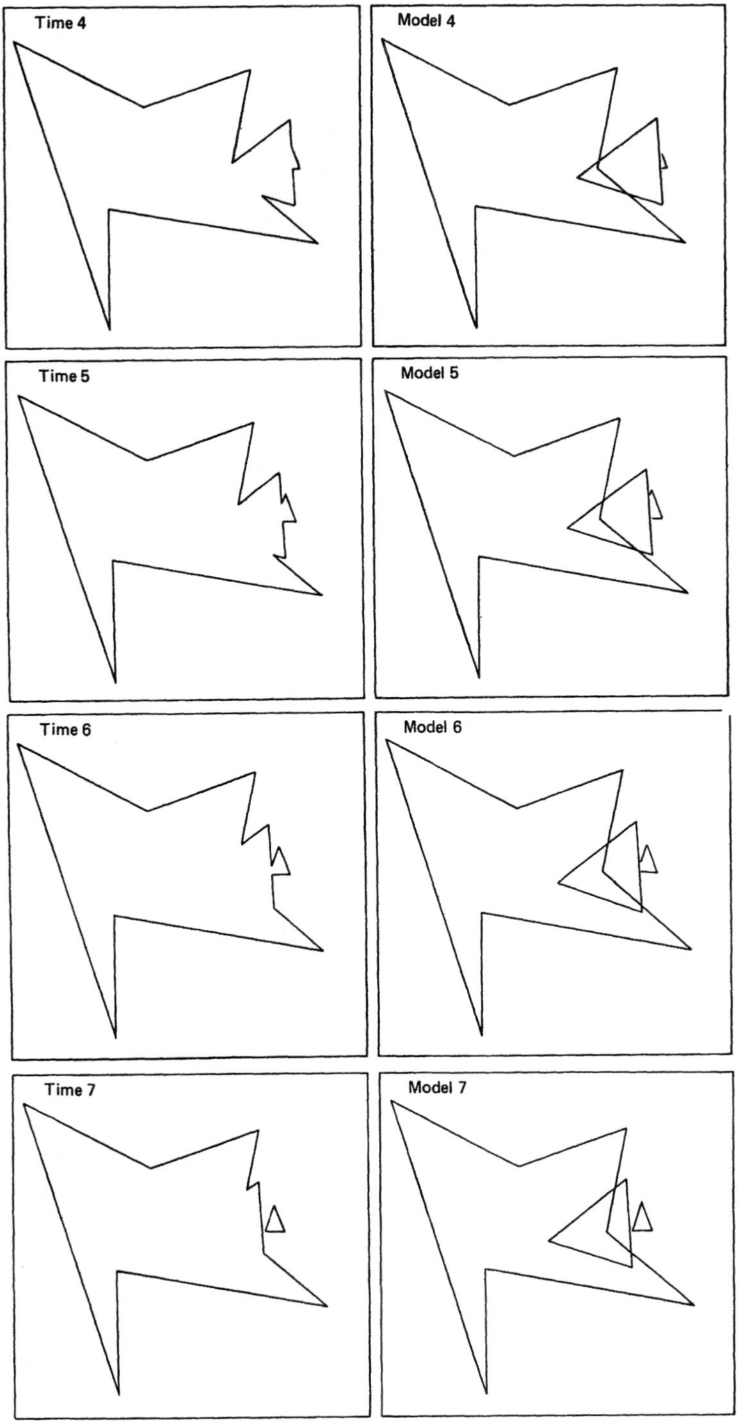

Fig. 6.5 (continued)

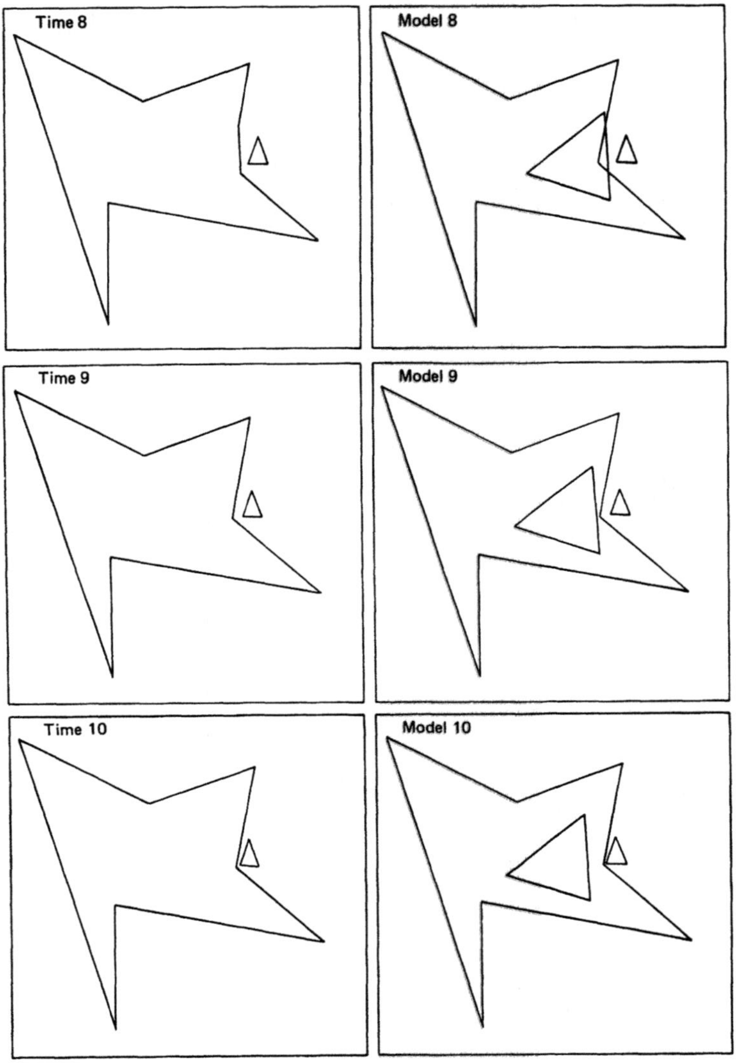

Fig. 6.5 (continued)

the correspondence provides cues, based on general knowledge, which enable the system to correctly interpret the changes as they occur and to use the interpretation to create and maintain detailed models of the actual objects in the scene and their movements.

6.3.2 Curvilinear Boundary Domain

The system of MARTIN and AGGARWAL [6.20], discussed in the following, attempts to apply a similar type of analysis to scenes containing figures with curvilinear boundaries. The input is again restricted so that the objects independently move in planes parallel to the image plane. However, instead of software-generated images, homogeneously shaded, opaque, planar figures are moved in front of an image dissector camera and a sequence of images is made. The camera approximates an orthogonal projection into the digital images which are preprocessed to extract the boundaries of the figures [6.21]. The figure shading and the camera setup form images in which overlapping figures are merged into single apparent objects. The task of the system is thus to derive descriptions of the constituent actual figures and their motions by analyzing the apparent objects of the sequence of images. The analysis of the sequence is performed on pairs of consecutive images from the sequence and is based upon identifying shapes which are common to both images of any given pair. The matched shapes are interpreted as two views of the same object. In this way the moving objects can be tracked throughout the sequence while motion measurements are made from the displacements between the matched views.

For this system, then, the low-level tokens are to be matched on the basis of a shape attribute. Thus the tokens must represent structures derived from the object boundaries having identifiable shapes, i.e., individual edge points are not adequate. The tokens used by this system are circular arcs approximated by portions of the object boundaries. The arcs are derived by analyzing

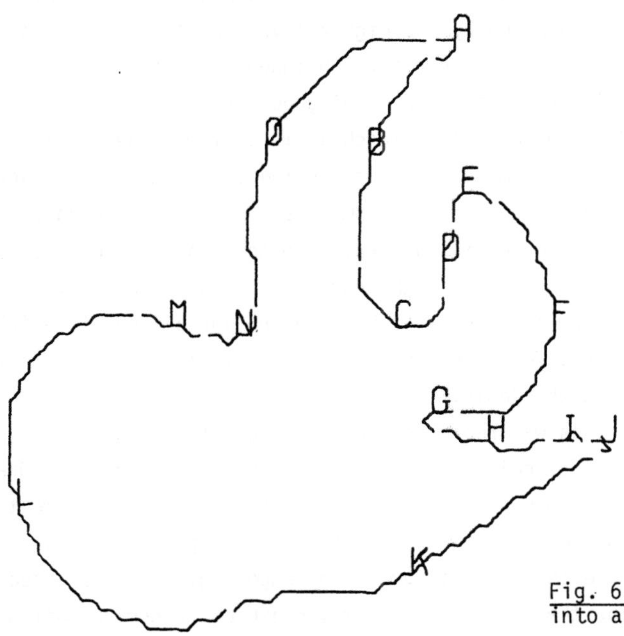

Fig. 6.6. Image as decomposed into arcs

the subtended angle versus arc length, ψ-s, function of a boundary as measured from an arbitrary starting point on that boundary. This function is useful because intervals of constant slope in the ψ-s function correspond to boundary sections of constant curvature, i.e., circular arcs. The appropriate intervals are determined by forming a piecewise straight line approximation of the pictorial graph of the ψ-s function. The set of straight lines in the ψ-s function approximation effectively decomposes the object boundary into a set of arcs. Figure 6.6 shows an object as segmented into arcs by this process.

The shape representation, as entered in the data base which contains all the relevant information derived from the sequence of images, includes the coordinate list of the object boundary, the straight-line description of the ψ-s function, and pointers relating specific boundary sections to the appropriate elements of the straight-line set. This representation separates clearly the information needed for shape matching from the information required in the movement measurement process. In fact the ψ-s function is invariant to translation and rotation (see [6.20] for minor qualifications) and is processed to eliminate the effects of arbitrarily choosing its starting point. This separation is in accordance with the system's use of the constancy in shape of the actual figures in order to interpret the movement of the apparent objects.

The initial correspondence is based on matching the tokens through their shape attributes, but is again aided by the higher level constraint imposed by the token ordering along object boundaries. Contiguous arcs from an object of one image which match, in the same order, contiguous arcs from the second image are grouped into edge segments. This matching is performed by first choosing two arcs, one from each image of a consecutive pair, whose ψ-s function lines have similar slopes and lengths. From these "seed" arcs an edge segment can be "grown" by adding contiguous arcs to either end of the already matched segments until a dissimilarity in the curves is found. The dissimilarity of two curves is measured by the area between the normalized pictorial graphs of their ψ-s functions. Two arcs are declared dissimilar when the measured value exceeds a preset threshold.

Edge segments grown in this way represent the portions of the object boundaries which have retained their shape through the sequence. Thus an edge segment relates two views of some part of an actual figure. The displacement between two such views provides motion measurements for the given edge segment. These measurements are then used to group the edge segments into object models under the assumption that edge segments which exhibit a common motion belong to the same object.

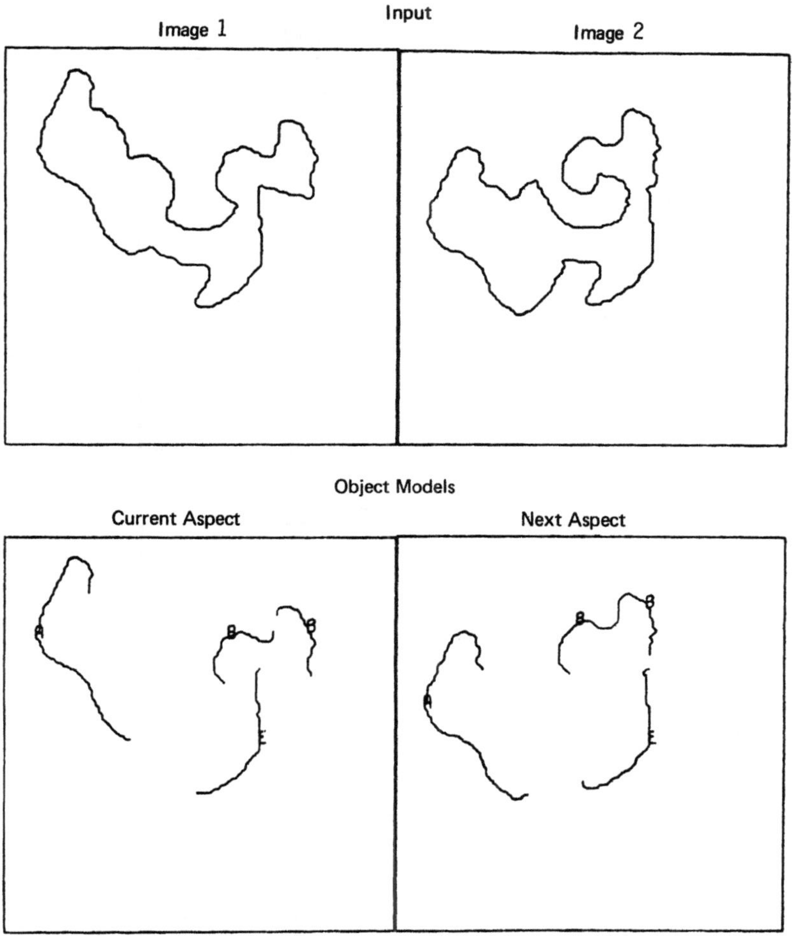

Fig. 6.7

The example shown in Fig.6.7 is taken from a scene containing three actual objects: one central stationary object; one object on the left side moving from top to bottom; and one object on the right side moving toward the upper left corner. The first two images, however, contain only one apparent object. When comparing the shapes of the first image to those of the second, the system forms four edge segments. These edge segments are then grouped into three object models based on motion measurements. The object models formed in this way are inserted into the data base with arbitrarily chosen names. In Fig.6.7 each edge segment is labeled with the name of the appropriate object model. The observant reader will have noticed that no edge segments are formed from the center of the scene when the first two images are compared. This is due to the extensive shape changes occurring in that part of the scene. It should

Fig.6.7 (continued)

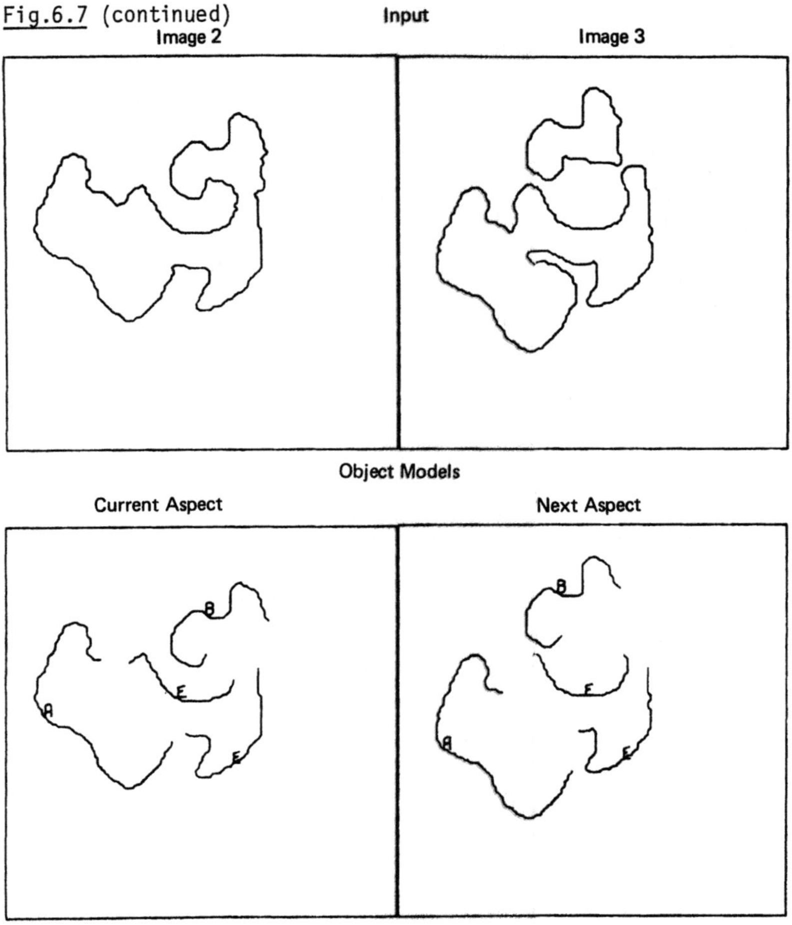

Fig. 6.7. Example scene containing three occluding objects

also be noted that in the last image the upper object no longer overlaps the other object, causing the number of apparent objects to change. The shape matching procedures handle this case making the proper correspondence between the edges of the last image pair.

6.4 Conclusion

This chapter began with a discussion of the general problem of occlusion in scene analysis. Particular attention was brought to the analysis of occlusion in dynamic scenes, i.e., image sequences. Then several motion understanding systems were described in order to elucidate the interaction of change and constancy. Ostensively these systems were developed to analyze the changes which occur in sequences of images. However, prior to the change analysis the systems must determine the features of the scene which remain constant through at least short subsequences of the images. These constancy features are necessary to span the discontinuity inherent in the image sequence representation of the dynamic scene. In particular for each pair of consecutive images a correspondence must be formed to relate the appearance of a given token, i.e., a feature of interest, in one image to the occurrence of that token in the other image of the pair. The correspondence process essentially tracks the tokens throughout the sequence and provides the basis for the initial motion analysis. Convincing experimental results [6.16] have been presented indicating that for certain "competing motion" stimuli the human visual system indeed accomplishes this task at a very early stage in the perceptual process. However, as argued in the introductory section of this chapter, the possibility of occlusion requires that some higher level information be used in forming the correspondence.

In three of the systems discussed, the movement measurements obtained from the tracked tokens played a crucial role in deriving object level interpretations of the dynamic scenes. In this way the changes detected at a low level are used in determining structures which provide constancy features for motion analysis at a higher level. For an example of top-down information flow in a hierarchical matching system see [6.22]. In any case, the inclusion of change information in the derivation of object descriptions has important implications on the data structures used by future scene analysis systems. Not only must the structures allow the descriptions to contain feature values which change in time and to record traces of those changes, but also the structures must provide for features which appear, disappear, and change character. The first two changes are caused by occlusion of the object in question. The latter change, however, is due to the dynamic nature of the scenes being analyzed. For example, a person in a dynamic scene might initially be standing, then leaning slightly forward, then leaning forward and balancing on one foot but still standing, and then finally walking. The person has changed their status from "standing" to "walking" but has done so by gradually varying the value of the posture feature. These representation problems, along with the still important problems of token correspondence, object interpretation, and the interaction of low- and high-level information should form the core of much of the future research in dynamic scene analysis.

References

6.1 H.G. Barrow, J.M. Tenenbaum: "Recovering Intrinsic Scene Characteristics from Images," in *Computer Vision Systems*, ed. by A. Hanson, E. Riseman (Academic, New York 1978)

6.2 D. Waltz: "Understanding Line Drawings of Scenes with Shadows," in *Psychology of Computer Vision*, ed. by P.H. Winston (McGraw-Hill, New York 1975) pp.19-92

6.3 D. Huffman: "Impossible Objects as Nonsense Sentences," in *Machine Intelligence 6*, ed. by B. Meltzer, D. Michie (Edinburgh Univ. Press, Edinburgh, Scotland 1971)

6.4 M. Clowes: On seeing things. Artif. Intell. *2*, 79-116 (1971)

6.5 A. Rosenfeld, R. Hummel, S. Zucker: Scene labelling using relaxation operations. IEEE Trans. SMC-*6*, 420-433 (1976)

6.6 F.W. Mounts: A video encoding system with conditional picture-element replenishment. Bell Syst. Tech. J. *48*, 2545-2554 (1969)

6.7 S.A. Underwood, C.L. Coates: Visual learning from multiple views. IEEE Trans. C-*24*, 651-661 (1975)

6.8 A. Guzmán: "Decomposition of a Visual Scene into Three-Dimensional Bodies," in *Computer Methods in Image Analysis*, ed. by J.K. Aggarwal, R.O. Duda, A. Rosenfeld (IEEE Press, New York 1977) pp.324-337

6.9 R.P. Futrelle, M.J. Potel: The system design for GALATEA, an interactive real-time computer graphics system for movie and video analysis. Comput. Graph. (ACM) *1*, 115-121 (1975)

6.10 W.N. Martin, J.K. Aggarwal: Suvery: dynamic scene analysis. Comput. Graph. Image Proc. *7*, 356-374 (1978)

6.11 H.-H. Nagel: "Analysis Techniques for Image Sequences," in *International Joint Conference on Pattern Recognition*, Kyoto, Japan, Nov.7-10, 1978

6.12 N.I. Badler, J.K. Aggarwal (eds.): Abstracts of the Workshop on Computer Analysis of Time-Varying Imagery, Philadelphia, PA, April 5-6, 1979

6.13 J.O.B. Greaves: The bugsystem: The software structure for the reduction of quantized video dots of moving organisms. Prc. IEEE *63*, 1415-1425 (1975)

6.14 R.M. Endlich, D.E. Wolf, D.J. Hall, A.E. Brain: Use of a pattern recognition technique for determining cloud motions from sequences of satellite photographs. J. Appl. Meteorol. *10*, 105-117 (1971)

6.15 G.H. Ball, D.J. Hall: A clustering technique for summarizing multivariate data. Behav. Sci. *12*, 153-155 (1967)

6.16 S. Ullman: *The Interpretation of Visual Motion* (MIT Press, Cambridge, MA 1979)

6.17 W.K. Chow, J.K. Aggarwal: Computer analysis of planar curvilinear moving images. IEEE Trans. C-*26*, 179-185 (1977)

6.18 J.K. Aggarwal, R.O. Duda: Computer analysis of moving polygonal images. IEEE Trans. C-*24*, 966-976 (1975)

6.19 R. Petermann: "Computer Analysis of Planar Moving Polygons," Masters Thesis, University of Texas at Austin (1975)

6.20 W.N. Martin, J.K. Aggarwal: Computer analysis of dynamic scenes containing curvilinear figures. Pattern Recognition *11*, 169-178 (1979)

6.21 J.W. McKee, J.K. Aggarwal: Finding edges of the surfaces of three-dimensional curved objects by computer. Pattern Recognition *7*, 25-52 (1975)

6.22 J.W. Roach, J.K. Aggarwal: Computer tracking of objects moving in space. IEEE Trans. PAMI-*1*, 127-135 (1979)

Chapter 7 Processing of Medical Image Sequences

W. Spiesberger and M. Tasto

With 41 Figures

Processing medical images has become a large and important application area of digital image processing techniques. Such techniques have been applied to a wide variety of images, namely X-ray images (a review of methods is given in [7.1]), scintigrams, ultrasonic and thermographic images, and microscopic image processing (as presented in [7.1]). A more general description of medical image processing is contained in [7.2].

As in other application areas, time sequence processing has developed relatively late, due to technical problems such as lack of memory and processing power, and probably due to a lack of concepts as well. However, the need has existed for some time [7.3].

Recent activities in time sequence processing in the medical field can be roughly classified into three categories:

a) The determination of size, shape, volume, etc. of certain organs as a function of time. The input is a time sequence of images, and the output usually is a sequence of numbers or low-dimensional vectors, representing the time-behaviour of the measured values. These problems will be discussed in Sect.7.1.

b) Functional imaging. Again the input is a time sequence of images, the output is a single image showing in condensed form the functioning, e.g. the velocity of the blood, etc., in human organs. This topic is presented in Sect.7.2.

c) Image enhancement. The input is a time sequence of images, and the output may be either a single image or a sequence of images, whose quality has been improved with respect to noise, blurring, etc. In Sect.7.3 we will discuss a specific example of generating a single picture from a sequence showing improved noise and blurring properties.

Finally, we shall briefly discuss image sequences that are not time sequences. Although work in this area is mostly in the beginning state, we feel it necessary to at least shortly review it here, because these may have some interesting cross-connection to time sequences. Examples to be discussed will be sequences with respect to spatial coordinates, and frequency characteristics of the image-generating signal (Sect.7.4).

Since most activities as well as our own experience have been in the X-ray field, we will concentrate on X-ray images.

7.1 Extraction of Measurements from Image Time Sequences

7.1.1 Left Ventricular Shape-Versus-Time Determination

In cases of expected severe cardiac disease cineangiograms are frequently taken. These are X-ray motion films showing the cardiac region, where certain

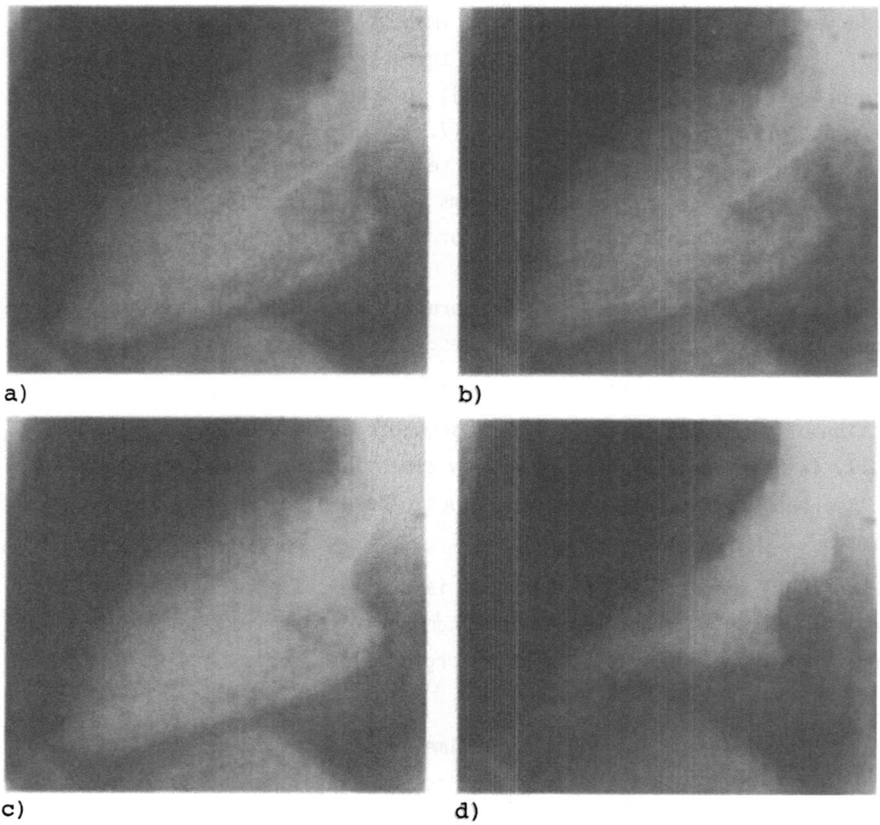

Fig. 7.1a-d. Examples of frames of a film of the human left ventricle filled with contrast medium (cineangiogram). (a-c) Successive frames near the diastolic phase (largest volume of the left ventricle); (d) frame near the systolic phase (contraction of the ventricle)

heart chambers are made visible by injection of contrast medium. Figure 7.1 shows several frames of such a film, where the left ventricle is opacified by contrast medium. Typically, the film speed is about 50 frames per second. One interesting information from such film is the volume of the left ventricle as a function of time as well as certain shape parameters. In [7.4,5] a large collection of research work concerning the use and determination of such parameters is presented.

One way of determining such parameters is to first outline the boundary of the ventricle in each frame, and then to determine the parameters using certain models. In order to reduce the amount of work required to determine the parameters for one heart cycle, which implies evaluation of almost 50 pictures per patient, considerable effort was spent to automate the procedure. The first step was to do the boundary determination manually, using a light pen, and to carry out subsequent calculations by computer [7.6,7]. The next higher level of automation is achieved by manually setting thresholds to separate ventricle boundaries from the environment [7.8]. No information from previous frames is used, and due to the inhomogeneous brightness distribution in the picture such methods have had only limited success. More or less fully automatic methods were described in [7.9-11]. In [7.11] for the first time some simple form of image sequence processing is used; a frame of the film taken before injection of contrast medium is stored and subtracted from the frames showing contrast medium in the left ventricle. The boundary detection algorithm then works on these difference pictures.

If a human observer looks at a sequence of frames of a cineangiogram as shown in Fig.7.1a-c, he will observe hardly any difference between adjacent frames. This suggests utilizing the similarity to apply some sort of motion extraction and prediction techniques to an automatic boundary detection method, where the information gained from one frame is utilized to guide the information search in the next frame. This may be considered as the "attentive" part of the recognition task. Methods in this direction are presented in [7.12-16]. Potential advantages are reduction of computer time, since only fractions of picture must be searched for boundaries, and reduction of errors, as more a priori information is available. The problem left is to determine the first boundary of the sequence. Two possibilities were considered: a pragmatic one, where the first boundary is entered manually by light pen, realizing that this effort is not too large since it needs to be done only once per patient; and a fully automatic way of determining an approximate starting contour. The latter can be realized by utilizing the fact that the ventricle strongly contracts and expands during one heart cycle and that brightness fluctuations

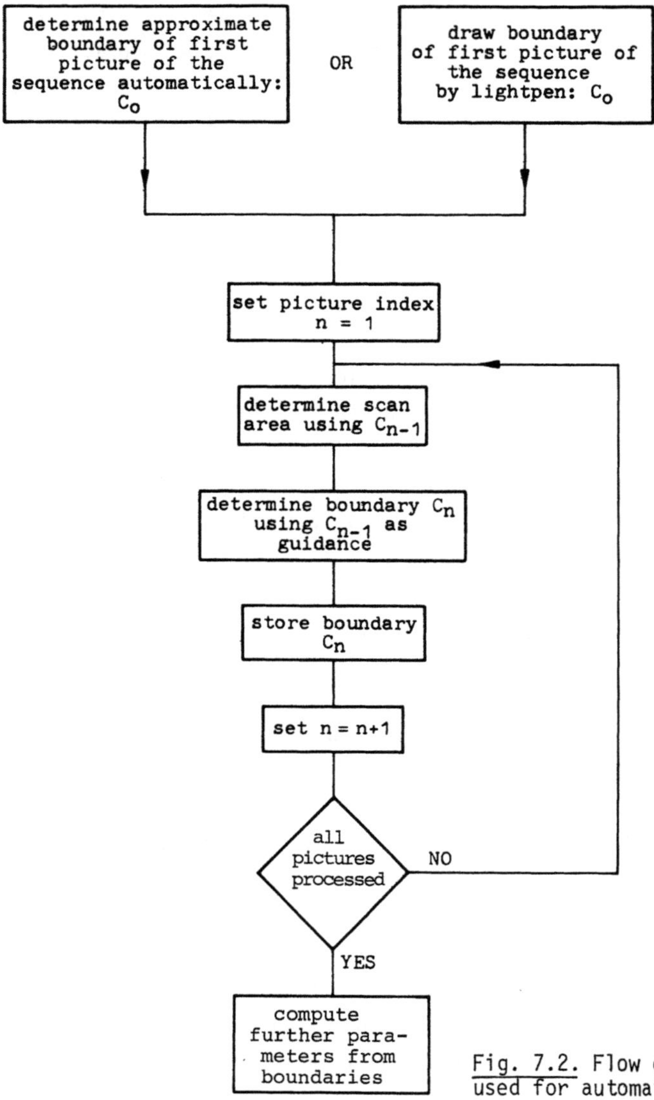

Fig. 7.2. Flow chart of the method used for automatic boundary detection

occur inside the ventricle, and by scanning a sequence of frames covering approximately one heart cycle. Figure 7.2 shows a flow chart of the basic method. In the following sections we shall describe the method in some detail.

a) *Determination of Approximate Ventricular Boundaries by Motion Extraction*

In Figure 7.3, one frame of a cineangiogram of the left ventricle together with brightness-versus-time functions at six selected locations is shown. It

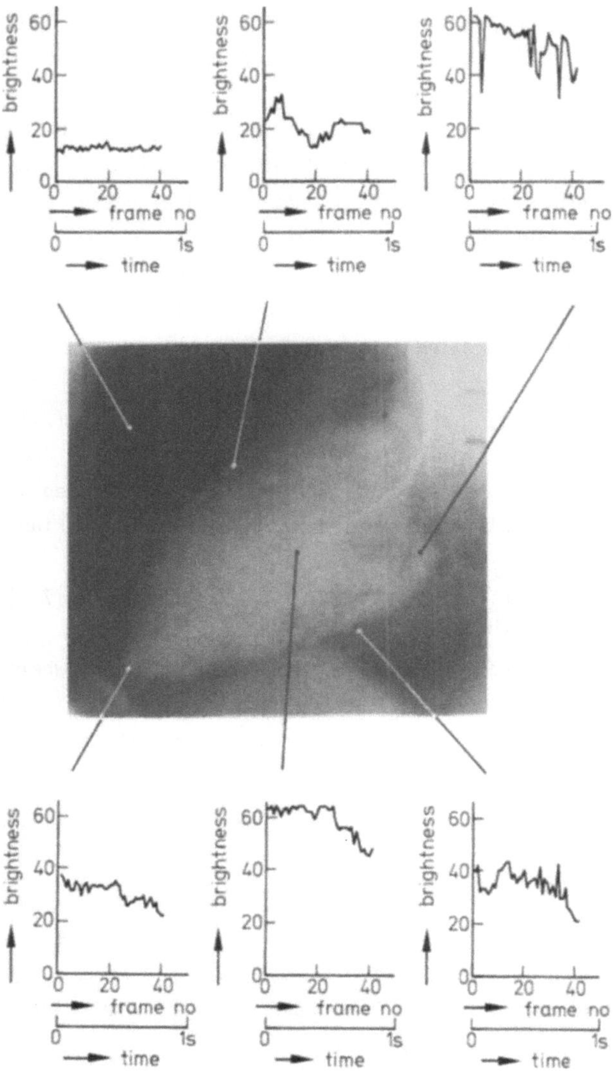

Fig. 7.3. Brightness versus frame number or time for six points of the picture

is apparent that within the area of the ventricle strong brightness deviations due to heart wall motion, change of thickness of the contrast medium layer, blood entering from the left atrium that does not contain contrast medium, and variation of concentration of the contrast medium occur. On the other hand, outside the ventricle and aorta area, only small brightness changes due to noise and possibly some breathing of the patient are visible. Thus, using a suitable measure for brightness change, one can hope to find a boundary that corresponds approximately to that of the ventricle in the phase of its largest extension.

A survey of the steps involved in finding such a boundary is shown in Fig. 7.4. The first step is to determine "motion values". Two possibilities have been considered: the brightness variance, and the "average magnitude of slope" determined from differences of successive frames.

Let $B_{ij}(n)$, $i=1,2,\ldots,K$; $j=1,2,\ldots,N$; $n=1,2,\ldots,L$ be the ij^{th} picture element of the nth frame of the sequence of L frames of digitized pictures, with $K=N=256$. We wish to find a function

$$M_{ij} = f[B_{ij}(1),B_{ij}(2),\ldots,B_{ij}(L)] \quad i,j = 1,2,\ldots,256 \tag{7.1}$$

such that M_{ij} is small for all picture elements outside the diastolic ventricular area, and large inside. This is satisfied by the brightness variance

$$\sigma_{ij}^2 = [1/(L-1)] \cdot \sum_{n=1}^{L} \left\{B_{ij}^2(n)-\left[\left(\sum_{n=1}^{L} B_{ij}(n)\right)/L\right]^2\right\} \quad . \tag{7.2}$$

Figure 7.5 shows an example of a "motion" picture determined from σ_{ij}^2, where the value of σ_{ij}^2 is proportional to the grey level shown.

An alternative method to find a motion picture satisfying the above requirement is to determine the average magnitude of slope of the brightness-versus-time function $B_{ij}(n)$ as follows:

$$\begin{aligned} M_{ij} = {} & |B_{ij}(1)-B_{ij}(1+K)| + |B_{ij}(1+K)-B_{ij}(1+2K)| + \ldots \\ & \ldots + |B_{ij}[1+(P-1)K]-B_{ij}(1+PK)| \end{aligned} \tag{7.3}$$

with P such that $1+P\cdot K \leq L$ and values of K in the order of 6—10. The major advantage of this is a reduction of computer time.

b) *Threshold*

In order to separate motion from no-motion areas, a threshold must be applied to the motion picture. Rather than choosing a specific value of this threshold, it is advisable to use the data M_{ij} themselves to determine a threshold. Figure 7.6 shows a histogram of the values of M_{ij}. A threshold could in the simplest case be derived by using the sample mean, possibly multiplied by some factor. In Fig.7.7 an example of a binary picture is shown as a result of applying a threshold to a motion picture. Most of the random noise points

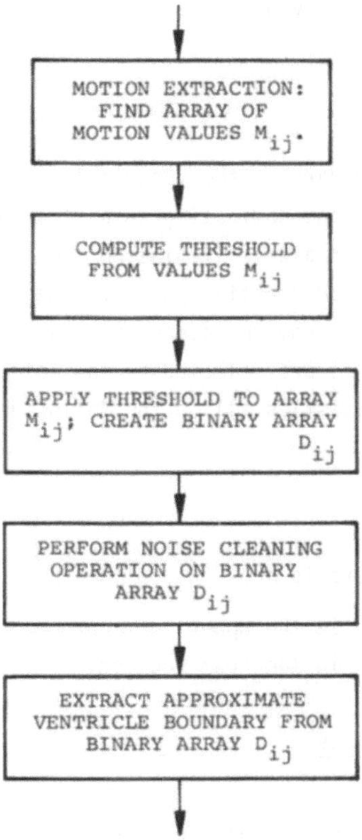

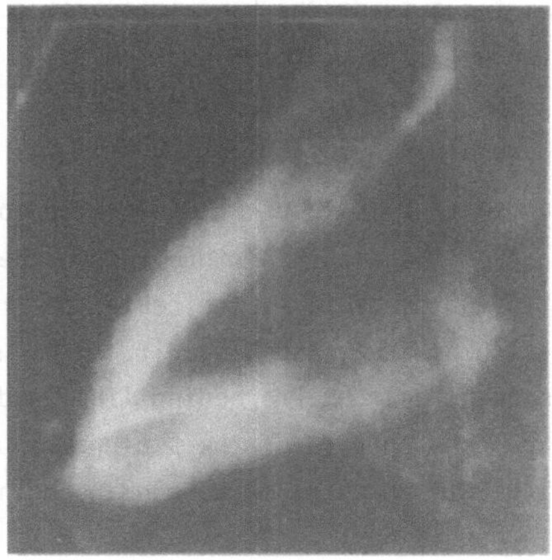

▲ Fig. 7.5. "Motion picture" of the left ventricle determined from the time variances

◄ Fig. 7.4. The steps involved in determining an approximate first boundary using motion extraction

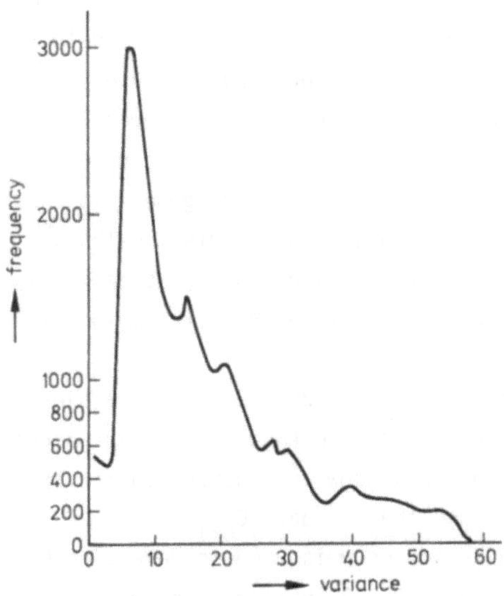

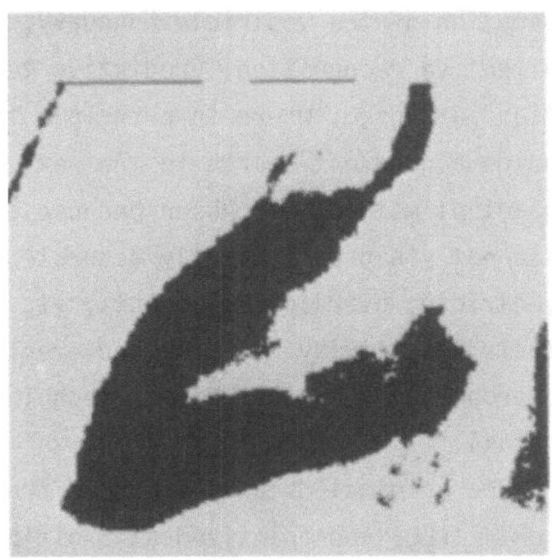

▲ Fig. 7.7. Binary motion picture obtained by applying threshold to the motion picture of Fig.7.5

Fig. 7.6. Histogram of the motion picture

appearing outside the ventricle area can be removed by using neighbourhood criteria [7.17].

c) *Boundary Extraction*

The next task is to determine the approximate boundary of the ventricular area from the binary picture. Since there is only one dominating compact area of "1" in the picture, the center of gravity should always lie inside the ventricular area, and hence it can be used as a good starting point for the subsequent search. Proceeding line- and columnwise from the center of gravity towards the outside of the picture, boundary points are selected by the following rule. A point is a boundary point if it satisfies all of the following three conditions:

1) The point is a binary 1.
2) Its neighbour towards the center of gravity is a 1.
3) Its neighbour towards the outside of the picture is a 0.

The boundary points obtained are ordered starting at the upper left corner of the picture and "cleaned" by methods discussed in the next section.

7.1.2 Determination of Precise Ventricle Boundaries Using Prediction Techniques

Once the recognition system has obtained a rough idea about the approximate location of the ventricle boundary, it can enter the second phase of a more attentive recognition. Predictive techniques called "guided boundary detection" are used, where in principle the boundary from one frame is used to guide a gradient search in the next frame of the sequence of pictures. A gradient method was chosen because other techniques such as a thresholding did not yield sufficiently accurate results, due to the inhomogeneity of the ventricle, overlapping objects, etc. The disadvantage of gradient methods, their sensitivity to noise and overlapping structures of foreign objects, is overcome by the very guiding technique. We shall now describe the method in detail.

The original data is a set of frames digitized to 256×256 picture elements (PEL) and quantized at 8 bit per PEL. Using the knowledge of the boundary C_{n-1} in the previous frame, a rectangular window is constructed for the new frame incorporating a safety zone around the boundary C_{n-1}.

The part of the picture contained in this window is used to determine C_n. The first step is to reduce its resolution to 32×32 picture elements by averaging. This resolution may seem rather low. It was chosen for the sake

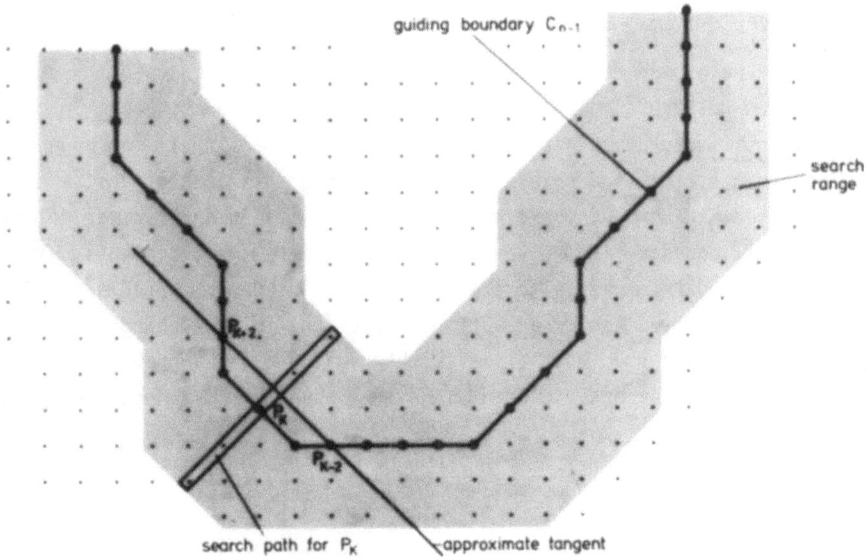

Fig. 7.8. Principle of determining the search range for given guiding boundary

of saving computer time, and it is sufficient for volume determination. For the determination of certain geometric parameters higher resolution may be required. As shown in Fig.7.8, the known boundary C_{n-1} is superpositioned on the new picture by proper coordinate transformation, and a boundary search range and search directions to find C_n are constructed around C_{n-1} as follows. For every point P_K of the guiding boundary, an approximate tangent is first constructed by connecting points P_{K+2} and P_{K-2}. For simplicity, using rounding-off methods the tangent is constrained to take on only angles at 45° increments. Next, a line perpendicular to the tangent is constructed; this is the search direction for finding a new boundary point to replace P_K. Thus the search direction is always approximately perpendicular to the expected boundary direction. In this direction a gradient detector will work best. For the line representing the search direction a search range is now constructed which requires prior knowledge as to how far a boundary point might move from one frame to the next. Taking into account knowledge about heart wall speed and film speed, a range of ±3 picture elements on each side of P_K was appropriate. For each P_K the brightness gradient is found as a function of x along the search path simply by subtracting the brightness of the subsequent picture element from the previous one.

a) *Absolute Gradient Maximum*

Three criteria have been considered to determine the new boundary point using the gradient curve. The simplest one is that of determining the location of the maximum positive gradient in the search range and calling it the boundary point. The human eye considers local brightness gradients as contours, and the method would, therefore, yield the same result as a human observer detecting the sharpest boundary in the specified range, where the brightness change is from bright to dark relative to a path from the inside to the outside of the ventricle. The advantage of accepting only bright to dark changes corresponding to positive gradient maxima is that most overlapping objects such as the diaphragm or ribs are excluded since they usually cause negative brightness gradient maxima.

b) *Local Gradient Maximum*

The above method assumes that the ventricular boundary is always the sharpest in the specified search range. This may not be the case if the concentration of the contrast medium in the left ventricle is low. In that case, the outer boundary of the heart muscle may appear stronger than the inner one. Therefore, another selection rule for the boundary was also considered, where first all positive local maxima exceeding some threshold are found irrespective of the value of these maxima, and then the one which is closest to P_K is selected as the new boundary point. Figure 7.9 shows an example. Two positive local maxima are found, the distances to P_K are D_1 and D_2. The point with distance D_1 is selected as the new boundary because $D_1 < D_2$, even though the value of the other positive local maximum is larger.

c) *Four-Feature Majority Voting*

It is attractive to extend the previous concept from one feature to several. After some experimental work the following features turned out to be best:

a) distance to P_K as before, representing connectivity in time;

b) distance S to the most recently found boundary point P_L in the same frame (Fig.7.10), representing spatial connectivity;

c) sizes of the local maxima of the brightness gradient, shown in Fig.7.11 for the two local maxima as size A and size B; and

d) sizes of the gradient values one step towards the inside of the ventricle from each local maximum. In Fig.7.11 they are shown as size C and size D. A large size of this gradient value gives some indication of the "robustness"

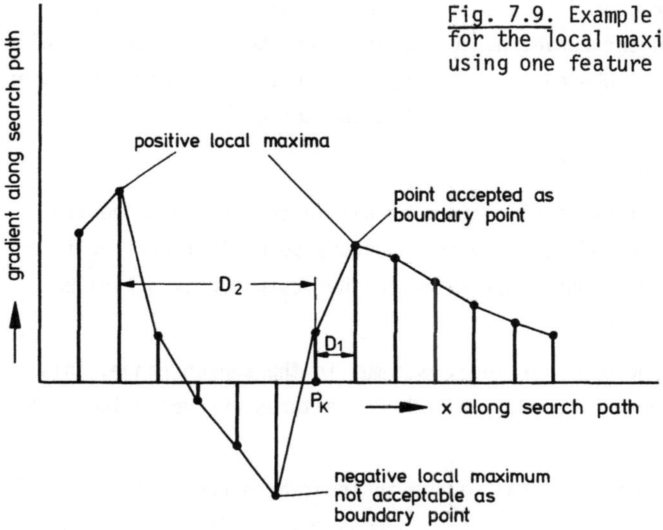

Fig. 7.9. Example of boundary detection for the local maximum gradient criterion using one feature

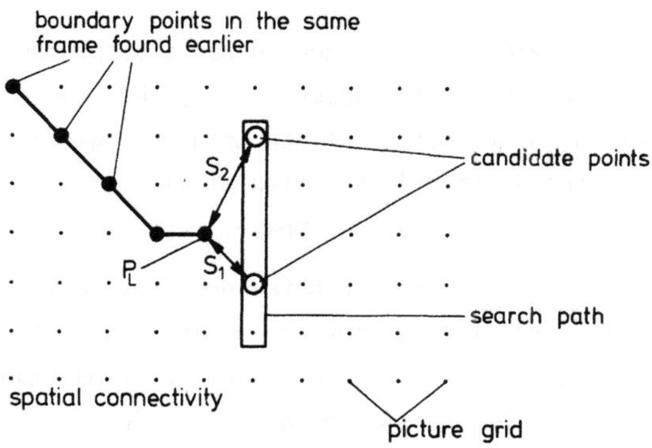

Fig. 7.10. Spatial connectivity as feature for classification of boundary points

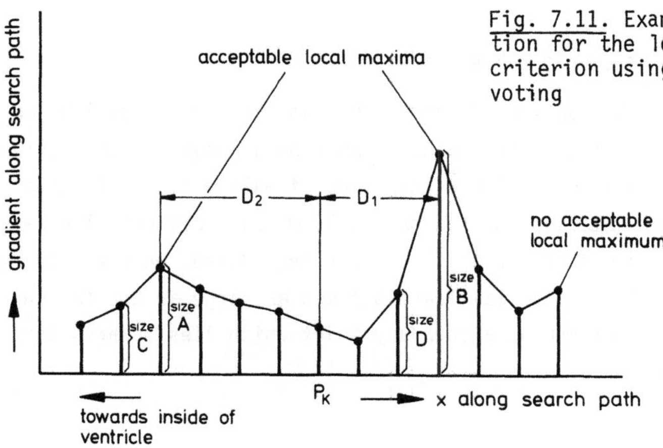

Fig. 7.11. Example of boundary detection for the local maximum gradient criterion using four-feature majority voting

of a contour. A contour caused by a small object or noise tends to yield a narrow peak in the gradient curve, hence the neighbouring values of a local maximum tend to be small, whereas a large object such as the ventricle causes a steadily increasing and then decreasing gradient curve.

The decision process works as follows:

Case a. There is no positive local maximum at all in the search range exceeding the threshold. In this case no new boundary point is found. P_K is simply replaced by a blank, which may later in the postprocessing part be filled by a filling procedure.

Case b. There is only one positive local maximum in the search range. This is considered as the correct boundary point. No features are determined and no decision is necessary.

Case c. There are two positive local maxima in the search range. A decision as to which of the two is the right one is necessary, and the four features must be determined.

Case d. There are more than two local maxima. This is considered a suspicious case by the machine, as experiments show that this happens mostly when the search range has been misplaced into a noisy region. Rather than taking the risk of an incorrect decision, no boundary point is selected at all, and the resulting gap is later filled in the postprocessing phase.

A majority voting method is used as follows. For each feature, a vote is given to that local maximum exhibiting the smallest feature a, the smallest feature b, the largest feature c and the largest feature d. The local maximum collecting the larger number of votes is considered the boundary point. In case of a tie the one towards the inside of the ventricle is chosen.

d) *Special Condition to Ignore Outer Heart Wall*

Occasionally it happens that angiocardiograms show an outer myocardial boundary as sharp or sharper than the inner one, as mentioned above. In this situation and for the additional condition of rapid heart wall motion all three versions of the boundary detection method may yield wrong decisions. Therefore, a special condition matched to this case was introduced: whenever there are two local maxima of large size (at least 5 times as large as the threshold), we take that local maximum as a boundary point which lies towards the inside of the ventricle.

e) *Postprocessing*

Three types of postprocessing are applied to each newly found sequence of boundary points before it is accepted as the actual ventricular boundary:

1) a gap-filling operation;
2) a cleaning operation which removes redundant points, loops and bumps; and
3) a smoothing operation.

The first two procedures utilize context information. Reasons why gaps may occur were stated in the previous section. A very simple gap-filling operation is used which first connects the two end points of a gap by a straight line and then approximates this straight line by grid points lying on the 32×32 grid using round-off methods.

Sometimes, however, the boundary may contain local loops and redundant points, i.e., a boundary point occurs twice in the sequence of points. As

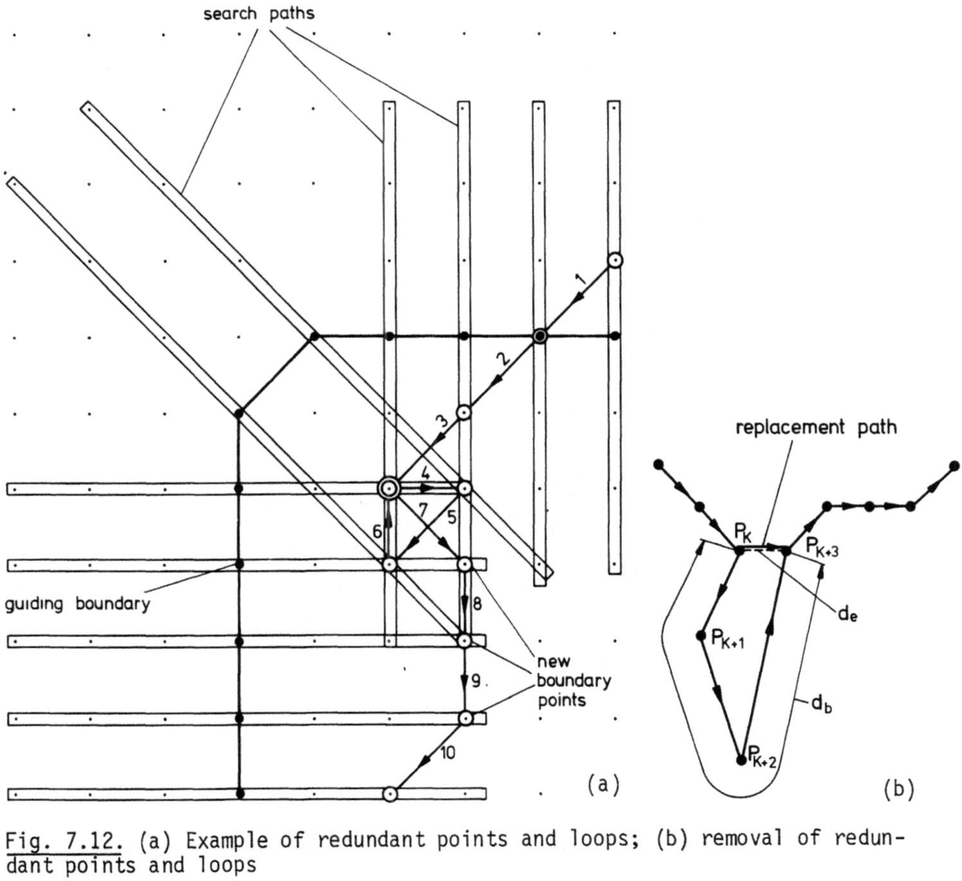

Fig. 7.12. (a) Example of redundant points and loops; (b) removal of redundant points and loops

shown in Fig.7.12a this occurs due to the discrete nature of the search path determination. Redundant points are removed after a simple search procedure, and loops and bumps are deleted by a method sketched in Fig.7.12b. Every point P_K of a boundary is checked relative to a neighbourhood of points P_{K+i} with $-10 < i < +10$, and for every pair of points (P_K, P_{K+i}) the boundary length d_b and the Euclidean distance d_e are compared. If the ratio d_e/d_b is below a certain threshold (values in the order of 0.3) then the part of the boundary enclosed by P_K and P_{K+i} is considered a fault and omitted. The resulting gap is then filled by the gap-filling method.

The final step of the postprocessing is the conversion of the boundary from the 32×32 grid back to the fine 256×256 grid together with a smoothing operation. The smoothing is done in the 256×256 grid by a low-pass operation, i.e., by replacing the x and y coordinates of every boundary point by a weighted average of the x and y coordinates of the point considered and its two neighbours. An example is shown in Fig.7.13. Next, using the gap filling program, artificial intermediate points are constructed such that a connected contour in the 256×256 grid results for both display and comparison with manually determined boundaries.

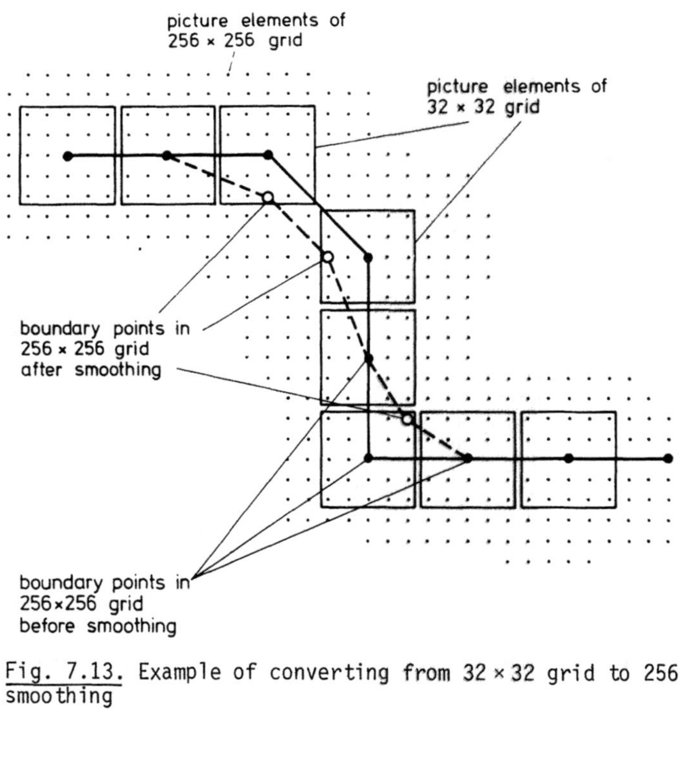

Fig. 7.13. Example of converting from 32×32 grid to 256×256 grid and smoothing

7.1.3 Results

Figures 7.14a-c show examples of boundaries found by the system described. In Fig.7.15 boundaries are shown together with those determined by a physician by manual tracing, without seeing the machine recognition results. In order to gain more quantitative insight into the accuracy problem and the consistency of both human and machine interpreters of cineangiograms, an error measure ε was defined as follows: two boundaries to be compared are shifted horizontally and vertically such that the area between the boundary traces is minimized. Then this area is used as a measure of deviation [7.15].

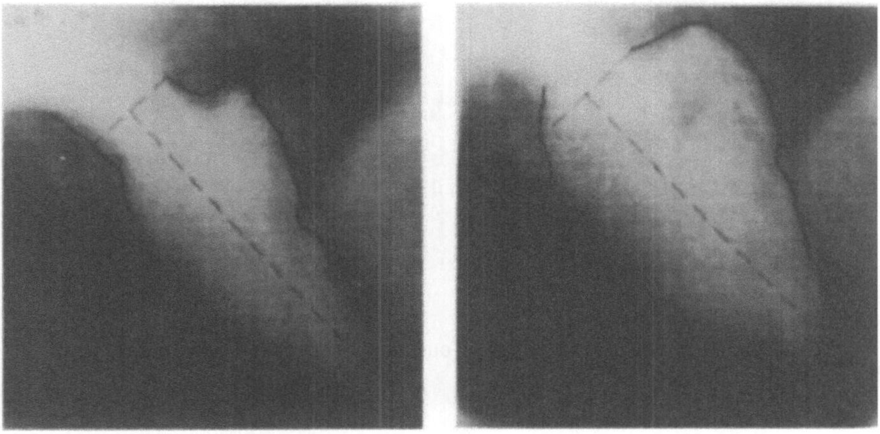

a) b)

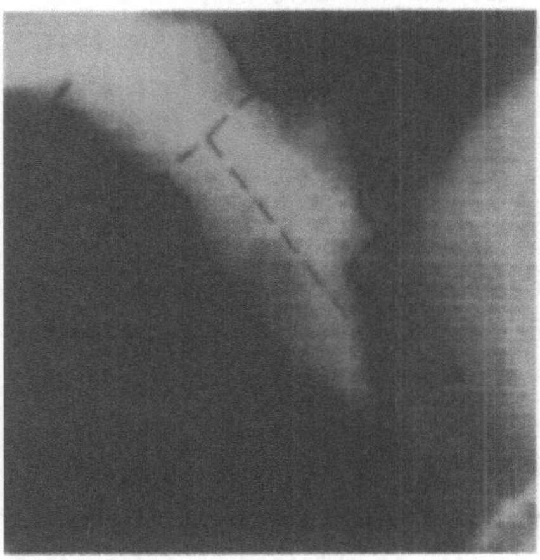

c)

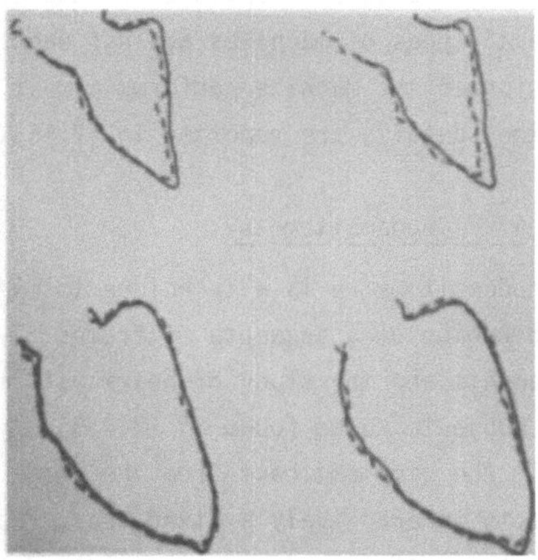

Fig. 7.14a-c. Examples of automatically detected ventricular boundaries. The solid line represents the automatically determined boundary

Fig. 7.15. Boundary traced by Doctor A (solid line), boundary traced by machine (dotted line)

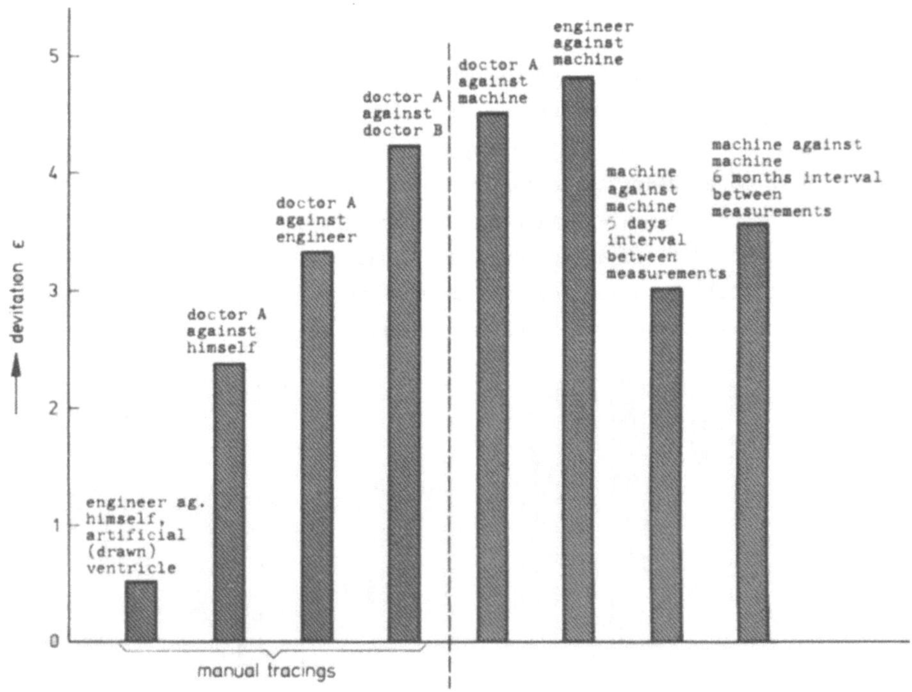

Fig. 7.16a. Boundary deviation for various compared cases and one type of machine

Figures 7.16a,b show examples of the error measure for several persons and several types of machines against each other. It is apparent that the best version of the machine performs almost as well as one doctor against another. Further details are reported in [7.15].

7.1.4 Videodensitometry

Videodensitometry is a technique to extract density information from a specified region of a sequence of frames. Typical applications are blood flow measurements and the study of heart wall motion. A comprehensive treatment of the subject can be found in [7.4,5].

In the simplest case from the image processing point of view an operator selects interactively a fixed, say, rectangular area of the picture. Then for each frame of the sequence considered the density is obtained by integration over the area and usually displayed as a curve. Examples are found in [7.4], the technical realization could usually be achieved by analogue processing of the videosignal. An interesting application is described in [7.18]: Video-

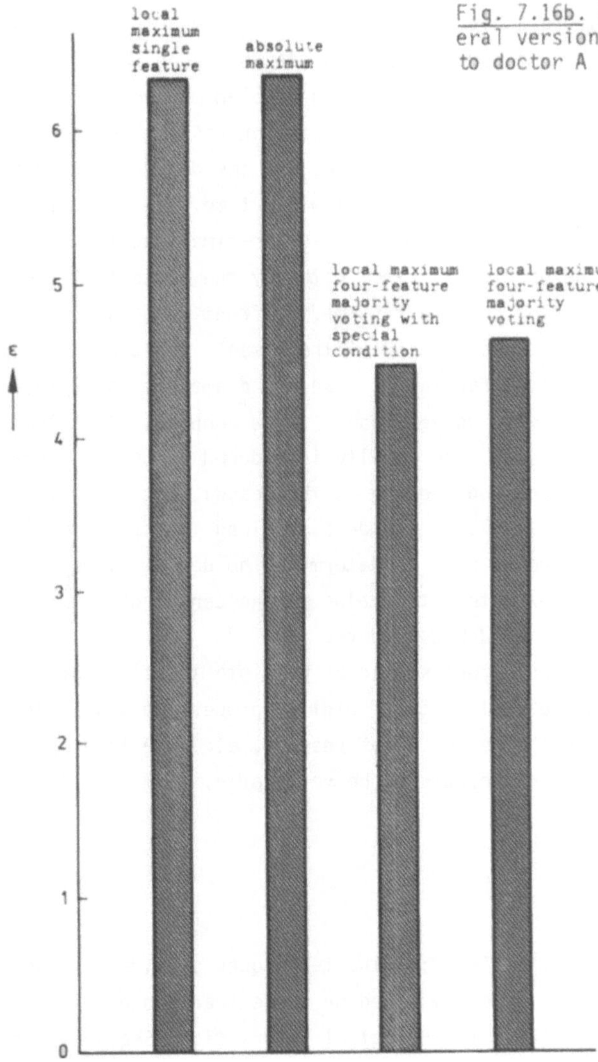

Fig. 7.16b. Boundary deviation of several versions of the machine relative to doctor A

densitometry is used to measure the wall motion of the heart by placing interactively a narrow window over the heart border such that the border remains in the window during all phases of motion. Since the density in the heart region is higher than outside, the density integral over the window is roughly proportional to the section of the heart contained in the window, and this in turn can be extended by using many windows and comparing the phase of motion at various locations.

Slightly more interesting from the technical point of view are cases where the area of measuring the integral density is determined by the picture contents itself. This can simply be achieved by selecting a threshold and using that area within the picture whose density exceeds the threshold value.

For blood flow applications the image processing problem becomes more complex. The task frequently is to detect the arrival of contrast medium at two different locations of a blood vessel, and to calculate the delay time, cross-section of the vessel, and from that the blood flow per time. The arrival times can be determined by monitoring the density-versus-time function at the two locations of interest. The problem is complicated by the facts that the brightness-versus-time function of the contrast medium front changes with time, that it varies across the cross-section of the vessel, and that in many cases the vessel moves by an amount far larger than its diameter. In [7.19] a pragmatic approach is used by simply using windows large enough so that the vessel never moves out of the window. The penalty is reduced accuracy, since most of the area in the window does not belong to the vessel, yet its noise contributes to the measurement. In [7.20] the density along the cross-section is determined, and the peak value is used to determine the density-versus-time function. This yields approximately the value in the center of the vessel, provided the vessel stays in the window considered.

The authors feel that far more effort should be put into the field of videodensitometry, utilizing the full range of digital processing available, and using tracking methods for the detection of vessels, etc. The interest from the application point of view appears to be very large.

7.2 Functional Images

The above-described conventional medical imaging techniques provide an excellent tool for diagnostics which is mainly based on the extraction of size, shape and structure of organs, i.e., morphological information. Sequences of such images recorded as a function of time give information about the dynamical aspects of morphology and are of great interest not only for the detection of abnormalities but, even more, for a detailed understanding of their function.

Similar to the proverb "a picture is worth than thousand words" a picture processing method has been evaluated which condenses the interesting data of a time sequence into one resulting picture. Since such a picture gives insight into the function of the object under investigation, this procedure is called functional imaging. Functional images are in general two-dimensional pictorial representations of a three-dimensional data set where the third dimension is most often, but not necessarily, time (see below).

Early techniques of functional imaging were described in 1969 by KAIKARA et al. [7.21] within the radio-nuclear-medical environment. They described a system to record the amount of activity in small regions of the patient as a function of time in order to calculate the rate constants of all regions separately and to portray the results in form of a functional image. Assuming that the decrease of radioactivity followed the equation

$$Z = A \cdot \exp(-kt) \quad , \tag{7.4}$$

radioactivity was recorded every five seconds. By means of a least-square method decrease of radioactivity was approximated and constants A, k obtained. The washout constant k was then converted into pictorial presentation either by means of a computer line-printer program with 32-grade shadings of black and white, or by modulating the beam intensity of a cathode-ray tube. In the same manner KAIKARA et al. presented a functional image of the type rate constant of accumulation, which is related to the formula

$$R = A[1-\exp(-kt)] \quad . \tag{7.5}$$

A functional image of the cerebral blood circulation has been proposed by TOYAMA et al. [7.22]. Ten minutes after injection of ^{133}Xe in saline, 60 picture frames of the ^{133}Xe clearance curve were recorded for the entire hemisphere by use of a 64×64 pixel matrix from a gamma camera. Four different types of functional image of the brain were displayed using 10 to 13 steps of colour: images of peak count, total count, ^{133}Xe clearance half-time and a calculated regional cerebral blood flow rCBF. In a preliminary phase of their work TOYAMA et al. studied 46 cases with 37 patients.

For comparison Fig.7.17 shows brain scans and colour functional images of both hemispheres in a patient with meningnoma. In the right hemisphere, an abnormal distribution of radioactivity was observed in the peak-count and total-count images. According to the half-time image, regional blood flow was increased in the tumor area, while the surrounding parts showed a perfusion which was remarkably depressed.

Peak-count images as well as total-count images provide useful information about brain anatomy and excessive or depleted initial blood supply to any region of the hemisphere. These two images normally show a concentric pattern, while distortion of this pattern indicates tumors or other focal problems.

Functional images of the lungs have been obtained by NATARAJAN and WAGNER [7.23] who constructed ventilation functional images, perfusion images and Xenon equilibrium images.

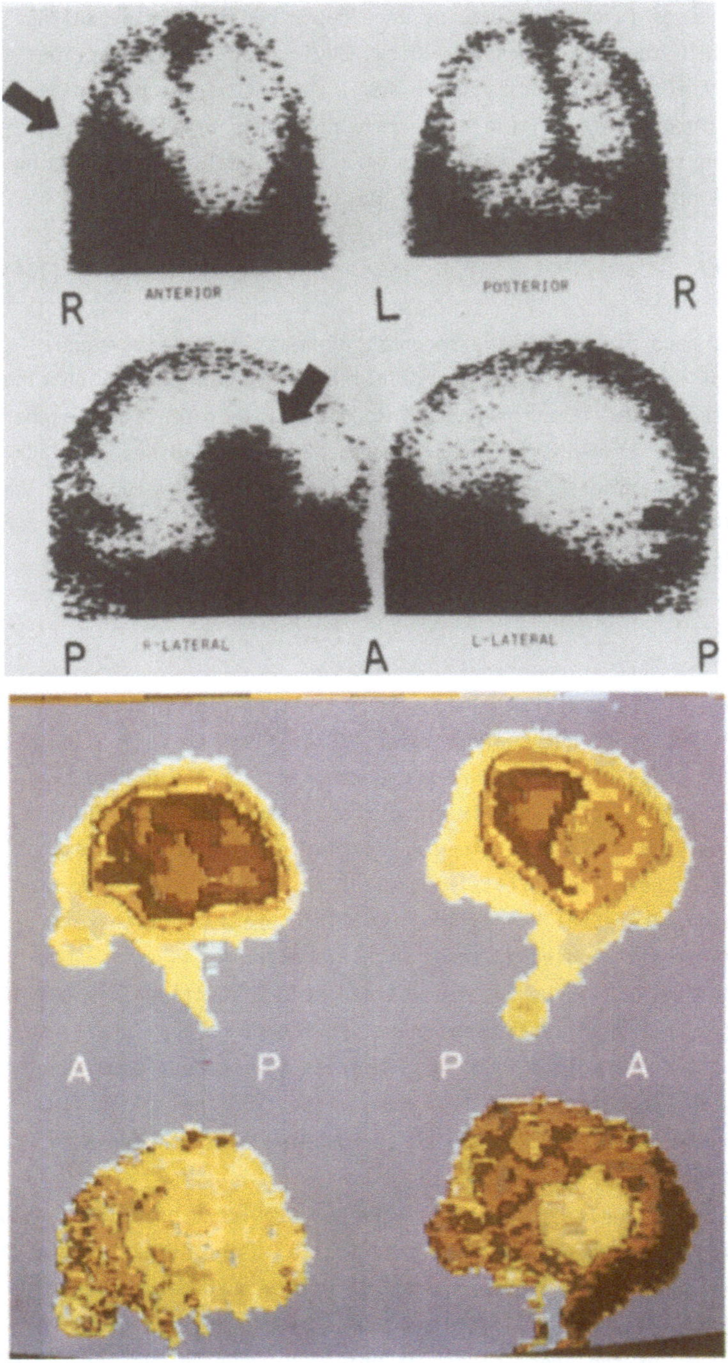

Fig. 7.17.

As far as radiographic techniques are concerned, cineangiodensitometry of the heart (left ventricle) is the most prominent example of analyzing time sequences of medical images. In order to measure the ejection fraction of the left ventricle — this is the difference in end-diastolic and end-systolic volume — it is not necessary to analyze the digital angiographic recordings of the whole heart cycle frame by frame as in Sect.7.1.2, but only to detect the end-diastolic and end-systolic heart phase. Regarding the dynamic behaviour of the ventricle and the injected radio-opaque contrast medium, one can easily define and abstract regions with strong time-varying brightness information which is due to the movement of the heart chamber muscle, the ejection of contrast medium and blood flow.

It is evident that by simply computing the variances of the brightness information versus time pixel by pixel, one can enhance "active regions".

If $B_{ij}(k)$ denotes the brightness information of the kth angioframe $k = 1, 2, \ldots, N$ at location (i,j), the functional image of type variance is given by

$$V_{ij} = \left\{\left[\sum_{k=1}^{N} [b_{ij}(k)-\bar{b}_{ij}]^2\right]^{1/2}\right\} / (N-1) \quad . \qquad (7.6)$$

The result of this type of operation is shown in Fig.7.18, where V_{ij} has been contrast enhanced by applying a histogram equalisation procedure. If the variance picture is thresholded appropriately into binary form one has an excellent estimate for the contour of the ventricle in end-diastolic and end-systolic phase (Fig.7.7). This type of functional image can be useful not only for the determination of the ejection ratio, but also as a preprocessing step for the automatic contour detection as described in Sect.7.1.1a.

The second example also deals with cineangiocardiograms of the left heart ventricle. Consider a set of e.g. 50 extracted heart boundaries (traced by hand or detected by computer program). If one is interested in judging the regional activity of the heart muscle — if there are regions which do or do not contribute to the contraction of the ventricle — the following method proposed by TASTO [7.24] is applicable. Each of the N ventricle contours of the time sequence will be divided into k equidistant cuts between the apex

---

Fig. 7.17. Brain scans and colour functional images of both hemispheres in patient with meningioma. (*Top*) anterior (*upper left*), posterior (*upper right*), right lateral (*lower left*) and left lateral (*lower right*) projections of brain scan. Arrows indicate tumor area. (*Bottom*) Total-count images (*upper*) and half-time images (*lower*) of left (*left side*) and right (*right side*) hemispheres [7.22]

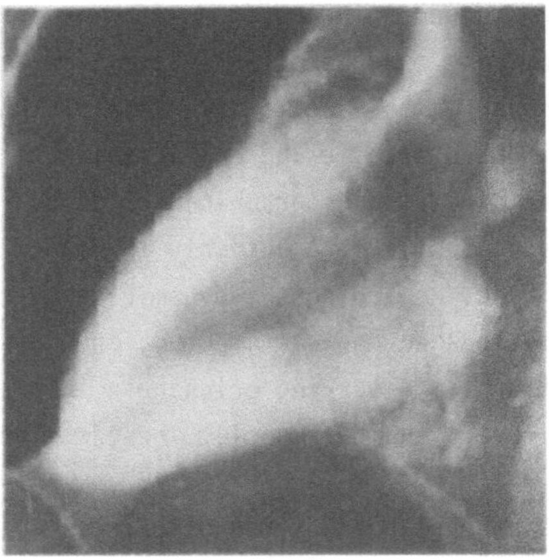

Fig. 7.18. Functional image of type variance with additional histogram equalisation

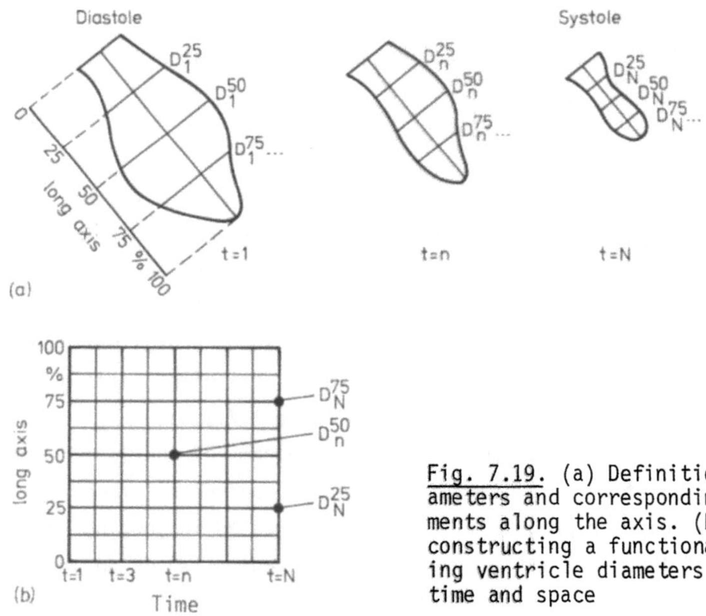

Fig. 7.19. (a) Definition of ventricle diameters and corresponding ventricle segments along the axis. (b) Principle of constructing a functional image representing ventricle diameters as a function of time and space

and the aortic valve area of the ventricle. At each cut the corresponding apparent diameter D_t^l $0 \leq l \leq 100\%$, $1 \leq t \leq N$; will be measured (Fig.7.19a). Because of the equidistant division, a diameter variation versus time at cut l characterizes the dynamic behaviour of the ventricle for a well-defined area of the ventricle muscle. When coding the magnitude of the diameters into grey values and using the spatial distribution along the ventricle axis as one Coordinate and the frame number or the time of the sequence as a second coordinate (Fig.7.19b), a picture can be derived which presents the dynamics of regional contractivity.

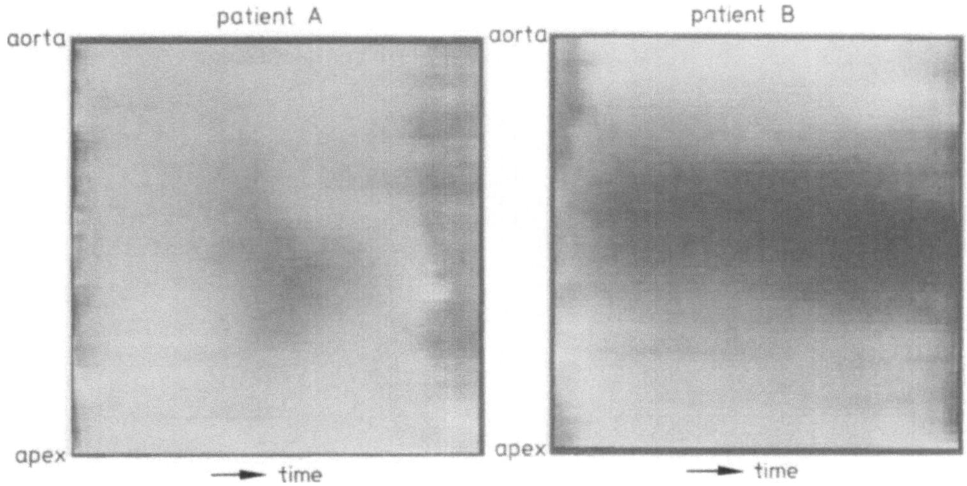

Fig. 7.20. Two examples of functional images of type "ventricle diameter"

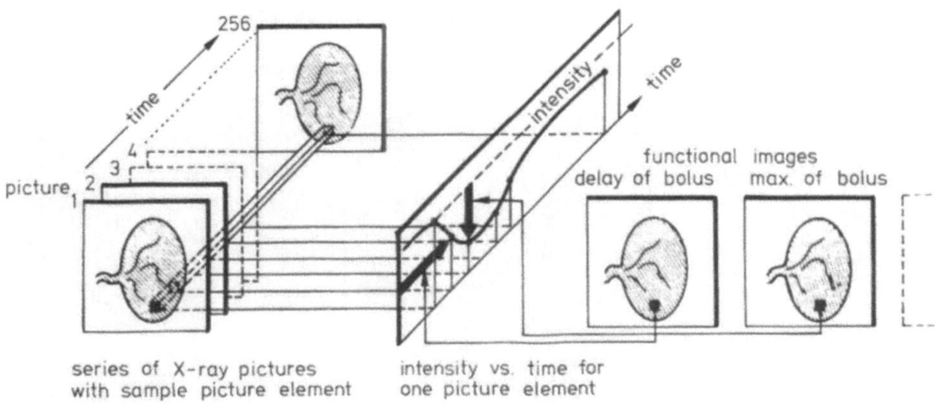

Fig. 7.21. The principle of functional imaging [7.25]

Figure 7.20 shows such functional images, one from a normal and one from a diseased patient. Although the clinical relevance of that type of functional image has not been studied on a larger data base, the benefits of deriving functional images are evident. A dramatic reduction of information is achievable together with easier judgement of time-varying processes in medical imaging.

Extensive work in that field has become known in recent years by HÖHNE et al. [7.25]. They have not only developed new types of functional images especially for the processing of kidney angiograms, but also a highly sophisticated hardware system for real-time acquisition and high-speed processing of such

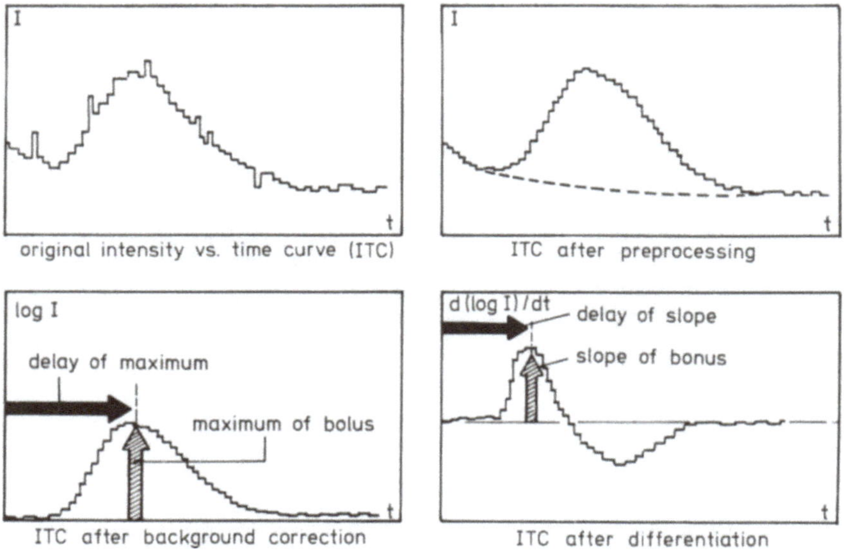

Fig. 7.22. Treatment of intensity-versus-time curves [7.25]

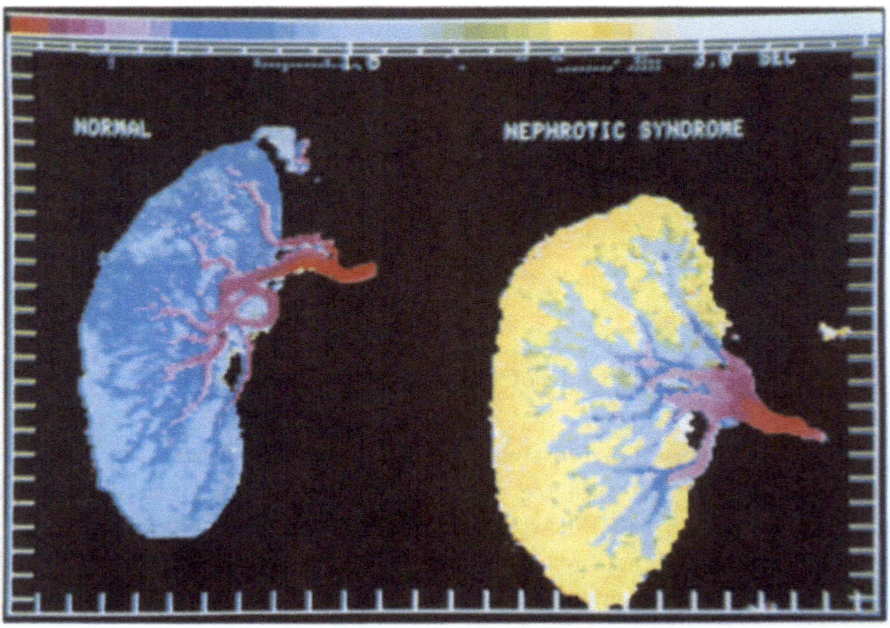

Fig. 7.23. Example of functional image of type delay of slope. A normal (*left*) and a diseased (*right*) kidney is shown. Arrival of contrast medium is coded in pseudo-colour. Speed difference is about 40%-50%. (Courtesy of Prof. K.H. Höhne, Inst. f. Mathematik und Datenverarbeitung in der Medizin, Universitätskrankenhaus Hamburg-Eppendorf, Hamburg, F.R.G.)

series. Following the principle of encoding image series as in Fig.7.21, the brightness information as a function of time of any pixel – determined by the normal radiographic absorption and additional contrast medium flow – is considered as an individual intensity transfer curve ITC. From that curve parameters like slope, delay of slope, maximum, delay of maximum, rate of decay, time of decay, etc. can be derived (Fig.7.22), and presented as functional pictures in grey or pseudo-colour. A picture of the type delay of slope gives completely different information to that of conventional pictures although the coarse morphology is the same. It gives the time needed for the contrast medium to reach any point of the kidney. As information about blood dynamics are presented at a glance, functional abnormalities can now be assessed by looking to morphological abnormalities of the functional image, rather than by sequential viewing of the respective X-ray image series.

In Fig.7.23 two pictures of the type delay of slope for a kidney – one normal and one diseased – are compared. Regions of the same colour describe regions of equal time of arrival for the contrast medium. In the normal kidney comparable regions have larger distances from the injection point than in the diseased kidney, because the blood was faster. From these two pictures one can simply derive that the order of magnitude of speed difference is 40%-50%.

An image of type maximum is shown in Fig.7.24. It looks very similar to the conventional X-ray photograph of a kidney, but the maximum uptake of contrast medium for different zones, which is distributed over several images of the time sequence, is now concentrated in one single image.

We shall now describe a complementary possibility of judging regional heart wall activity by means of incorporating perspective view techniques. This method is again based on a series of extracted ventricle contours, obtained at specific times (Fig.7.25). As it is very hard to gain a true impression of ventricle border changes using this set of contours, a three-dimensional data set is constructed where time is encoded into depth increments (Fig.7.26). The set of ventricle contours then forms an envelope which can be displayed as a surface by use of three-dimensional display utilities, e.g., the general purpose computer graphics display system MOVIE.BYU (developed by U. Stepenson and H. Christiansen). The resulting data can then be displayed in any interesting projection, so that an inspection of all ventricle wall segments is possible. Figure 7.27 shows an example of a 3-D functional image in two discrete projections.

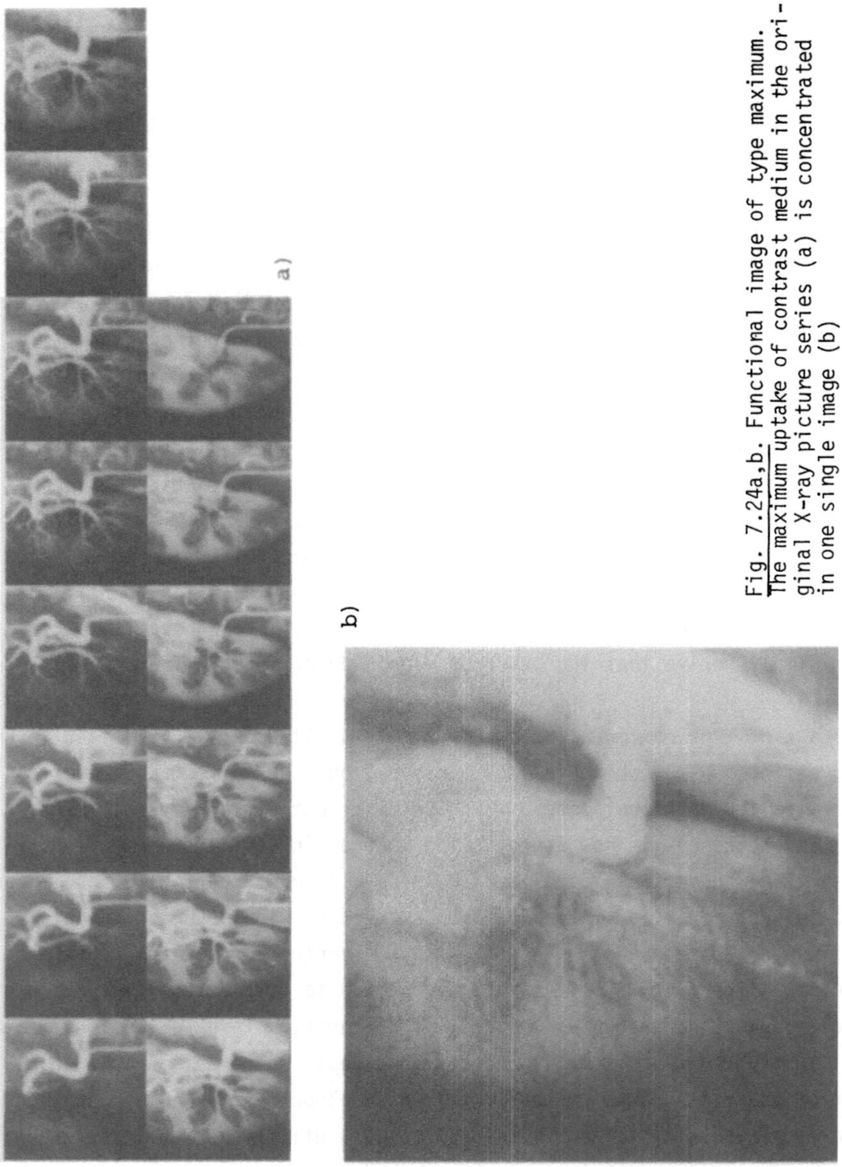

Fig. 7.24a,b. Functional image of type maximum. The maximum uptake of contrast medium in the original X-ray picture series (a) is concentrated in one single image (b)

7.3 Image Enhancement

The well-known concepts to restore single images by linear [7.26] or nonlinear filtering [7.27] can be extended to time sequences of images. Here, additional knowledge about the frame-to-frame correlation of the sequence can be utilized leading to improved restoration results [7.28,29]. Such techniques could be

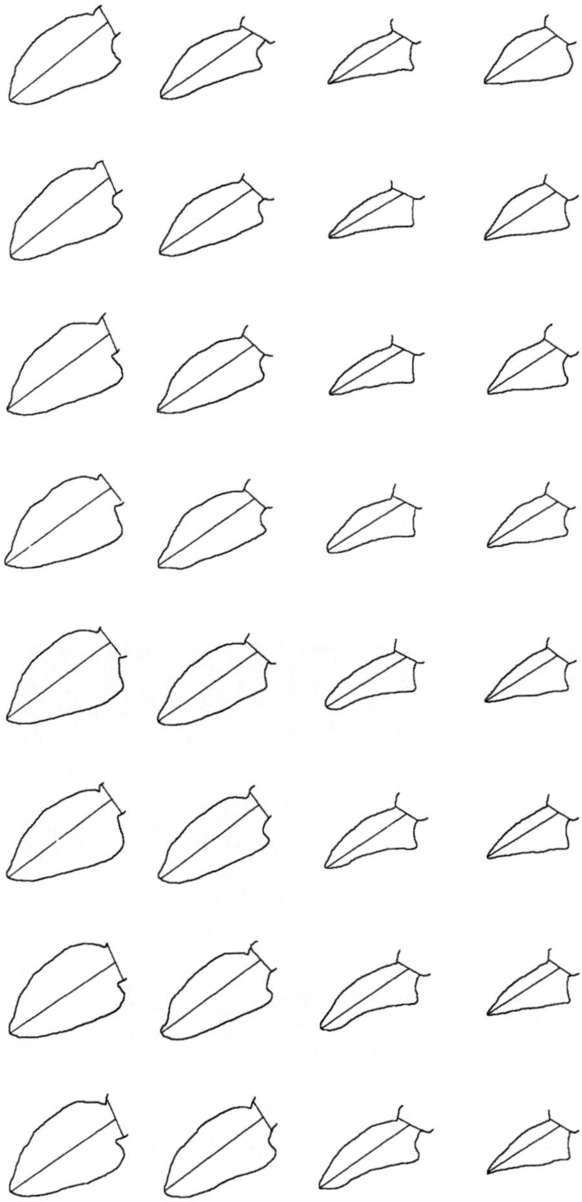

Fig. 7.25. Series of 32 extracted ventricle contours

applied to the restoration of, for example, cineangiocardiograms or coronary angiograms to improve the visibility of small coronary vessels. However, the authors are not aware of actual results in such applications.

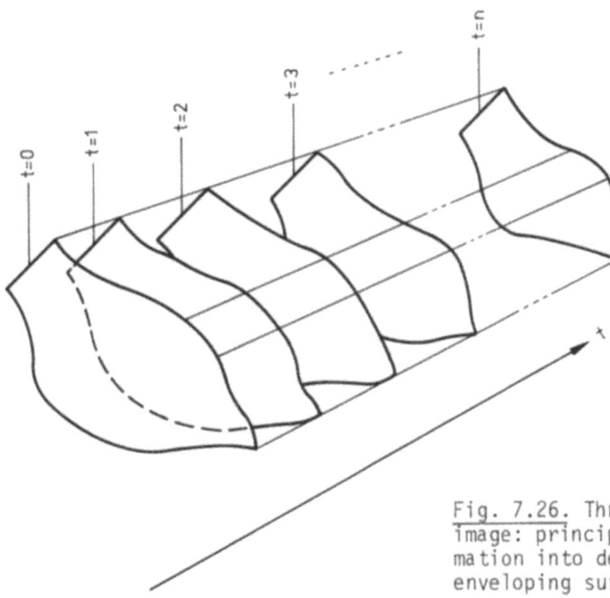

Fig. 7.26. Three-dimensional functional image: principle of encoding time information into depth, and of constructing enveloping surface elements

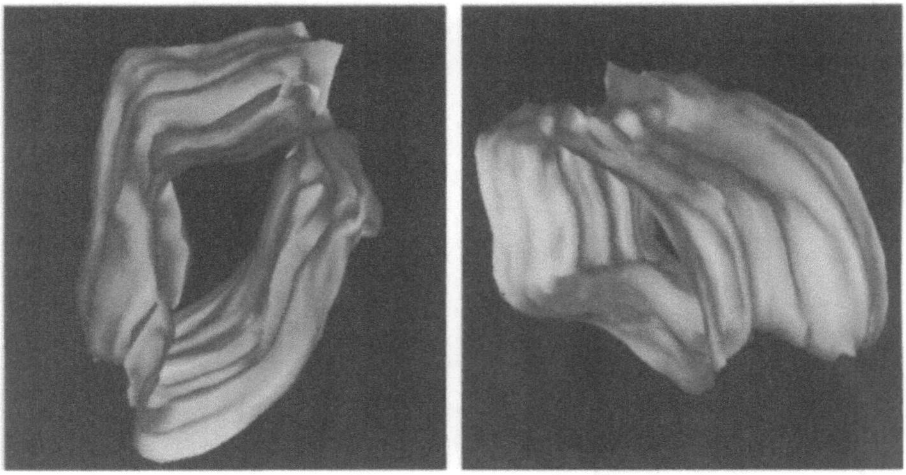

Fig. 7.27. Example of three-dimensional functional image. Two discrete projections are shown

In another application area, that of generating a single X-ray picture from a short sequence of pictures in order to reduce blurring caused by patient motion, etc., some results have been reported [7.30].

7.3.1 Motion Deblurring

When normal shadow X-rays are taken, frequently certain areas of the resulting images are blurred because either the whole patient or some of the organs in the imaged area have moved. Usually, the physician tells the patient not to move and not to breathe, with limited success. Very often the procedure must be repeated, with a resulting higher exposure to X-ray doses, loss of time, and a strong burden on severely ill patients.

A technical countermeasure that first comes to mind is to reduce the exposure time, as one would do with a camera when photographing a fast-moving object. In the case of X-ray images, however, this will result in an increase of noise, as the total amount of X-ray quanta will be reduced. In other words, there is a trade-off between motion blurring and noise.

A better technical solution is as follows. Take the same total exposure time T as before, thus using the same amount of X-ray quanta. However, instead of taking one picture during this time, take a sequence of n pictures with exposure time T/n during the time T, with n = 10, say. Each picture of the sequence will now be far noisier than one taken with exposure time T, but it will be less blurred. By simply averaging the sequence of n pictures, we would again obtain a blurred but less noisy picture. We can now conceive better ways of obtaining a single picture from the sequence by somewhat more sophisticated processing. A condition for this is that the brightness of the image at each location is a continuous function of time, assuming no noise for the moment. Figure 7.28 shows what we mean. In Fig.7.28a the intensity-versus-time function of one image point with additive noise is shown for the special case of no brightness change, which apparently indicates no motion. Figure 7.28b shows (dotted) a continuously changing brightness-versus-time function that is typical for X-ray images because of the translucency of biological objects imaged by X-ray systems. Figure 7.28c shows the brightness-versus-time function of a point of a typical real-life scene, that may have been caused by one opaque object moving over another one. Here brightness is apparently a discontinuous function of time, and such a case would not be appropriate for the method to be described.

We propose to determine for each discrete spatial coordinate separately an estimate of the brightness-versus-time function from the n stored images. Then the single image of interest is constructed from the brightness values of these functions at some time t within the interval, say t = T/2.

One method to determine the estimates of the brightness-versus-time functions is to determine a polynomial regression function, provided that all samples over the time period are available. The higher we choose the order

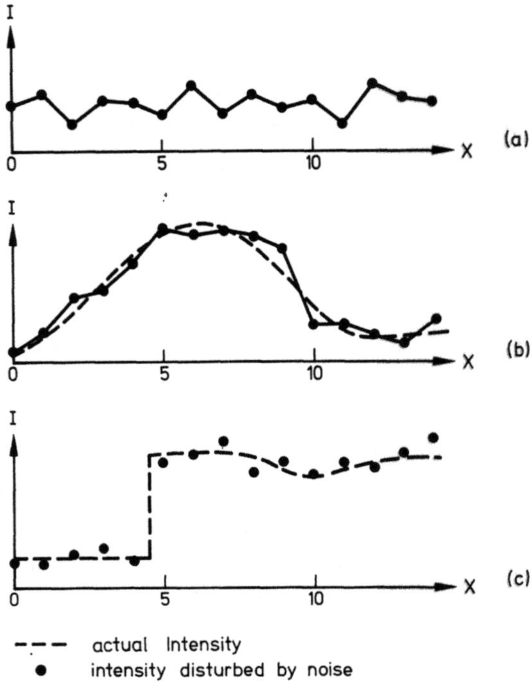

Fig. 7.28a-c. Example of intensities of one picture element as a function of time. (a) No movement, intensity disturbed by random noise. (b) Movement, X-ray image. (c) Movement, opaque object

of the polynomial, the closer rapid brightness changes can be approximated, yet the smaller is the noise suppression.

In order to test the feasibility of the method, an artificial example was used, which allows us to compare the noisy pictures and reconstructions with a noise-free original. A sequence of 9 pictures of the human kidney area during the process of contrast medium injection was used. The motion is so slow that the exposure time could be chosen long enough to obtain an essentially noise-free picture without showing blurring effects. Figures 7.29a-c show three original images of the sequence (no. 1, 5, and 9). This ideal sequence of images was artificially degraded by adding noise, with a noise standard deviation of 64 for an image peak-to-peak signal of 256. The noise in each frame was statistically independent of that of the other frames. Examples of the noisy pictures are shown in Fig.7.29d-f.

Next, we demonstrate the effect of a large exposure time. This is done by averaging all n images of the sequence, i.e., by taking the time average of

Fig. 7.29a-f. Three pictures of a sequence of nine pictures of a kidney angiogram. (a-c) are no. 1,5,9 of the original sequence; (d-f) are the corresponding pictures corrupted by noise

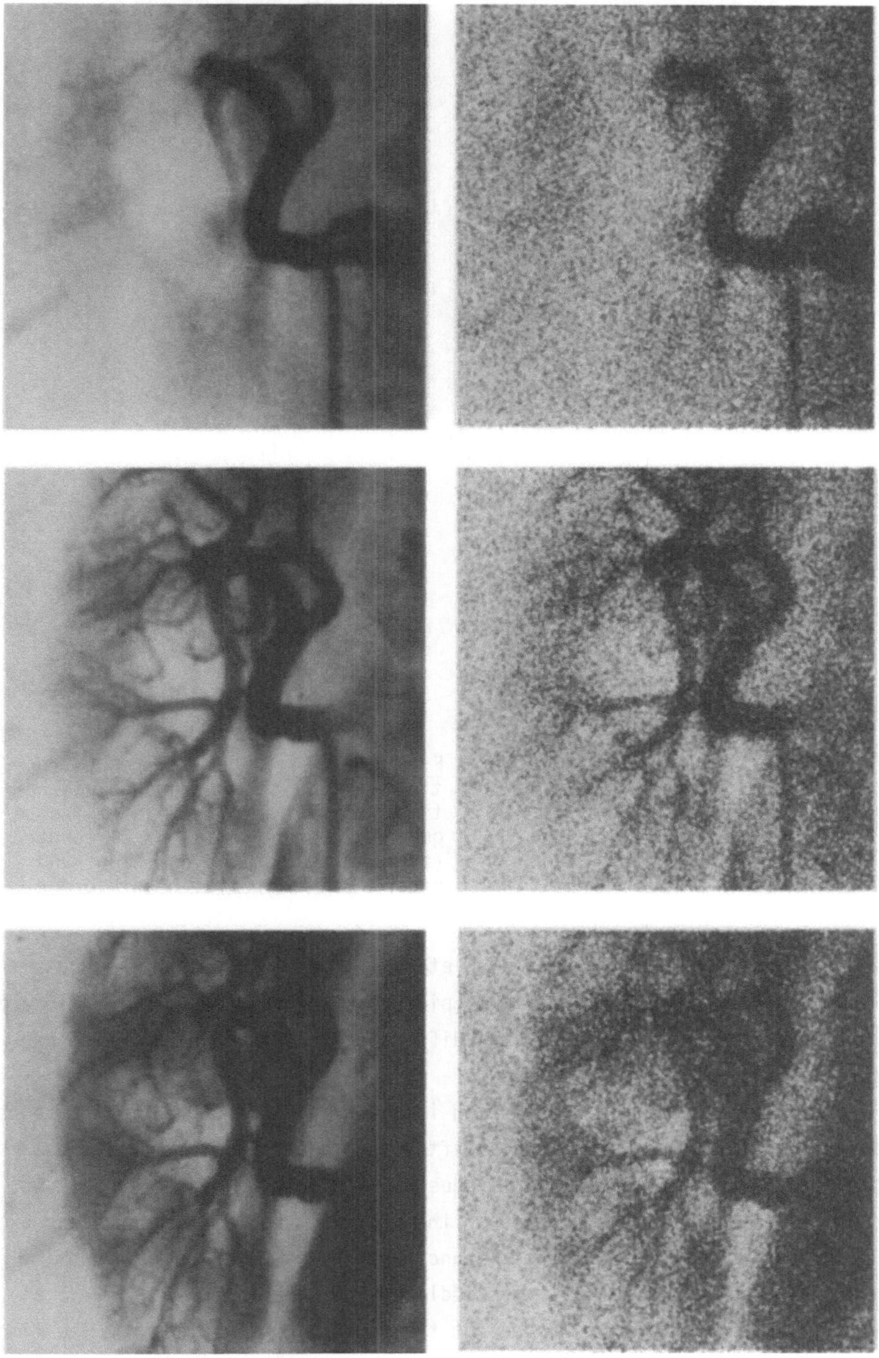

a) d)

b) e)

c) f)

Fig. 7.29a-f.

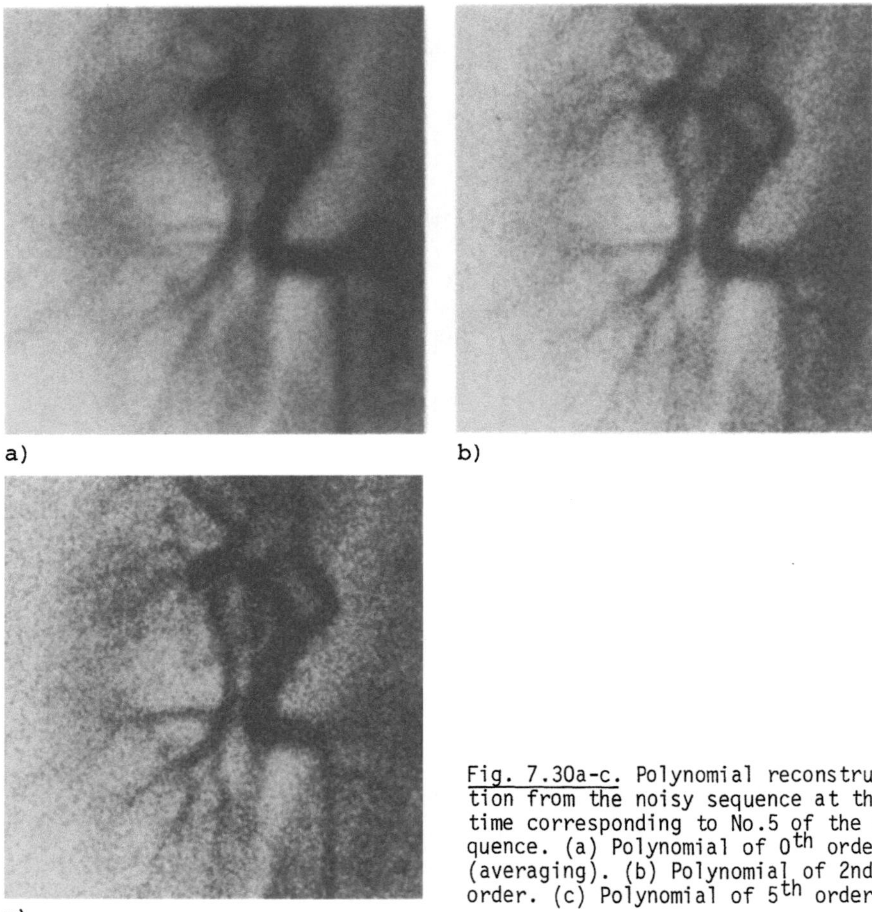

a) b) c)

Fig. 7.30a-c. Polynomial reconstruction from the noisy sequence at the time corresponding to No.5 of the sequence. (a) Polynomial of 0th order (averaging). (b) Polynomial of 2nd order. (c) Polynomial of 5th order

the brightness function for each discrete location of the scene. The result is shown in Fig.7.30a. Comparing this picture with unprocessed noisy picture no.5 of the sequence (Fig.7.29e) the difference between short and long exposure is quite obvious.

The effect of polynomial regression is shown in Figs.7.30b,c with a second-order polynomial in Fig.7.30b and a fifth-order shown in Fig.7.30c. These pictures were constructed from the sequence of 9 noisy pictures as follows. For each discrete spatial location of the picture, the time sequence was used to determine a kth-order polynomial function. The value of each polynomial function is evaluated at, say, the middle of the time interval T, i.e., at T/2. All these values at T/2 represent the picture constructed from the time series. Figure 7.31 shows an example of time series obtained from the sequence at a specific point.

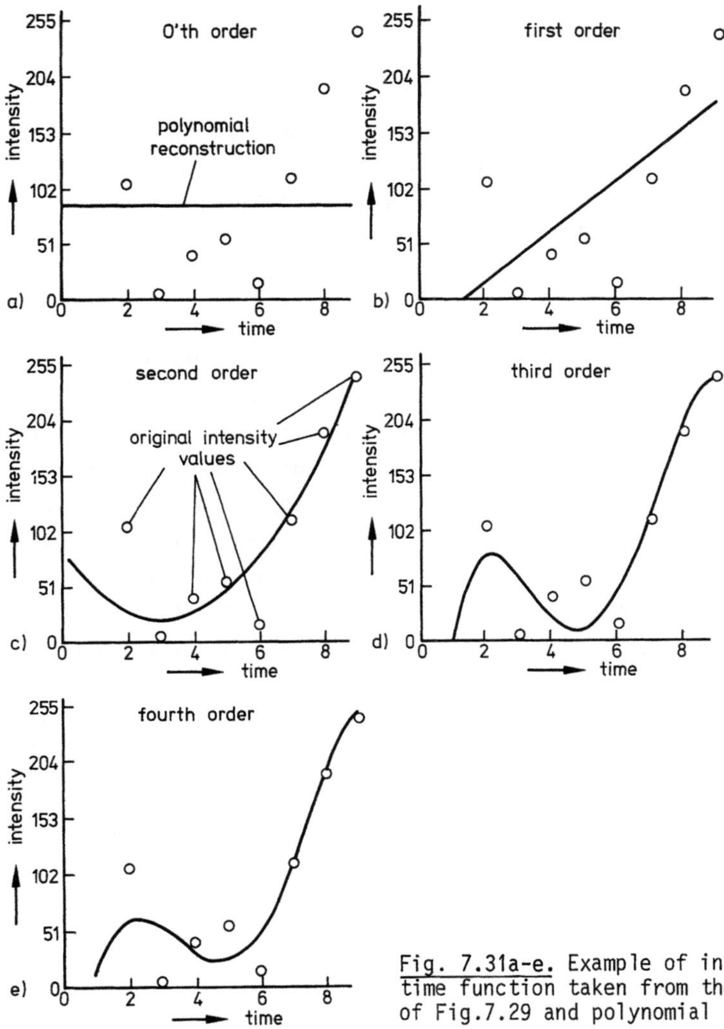

Fig. 7.31a-e. Example of intensity-versus-time function taken from the picture sequence of Fig.7.29 and polynomial approximation

It is quite apparent that the quality of Figs.7.30b,c are superior to that of both Figs.7.30a and 7.29e. In other words, the method described provides advantages. At this point of research, not all problems involved have been investigated. For example, as yet no spatial neighbourhoods have been exploited. Furthermore, the optimal selection of exposure times, intervals between exposure, and number of exposures remain to be exploited for given applications.

A practical implementation of the method in an X-ray system would require a device generating an electronic image signal, e.g. an image intensifier with video camera, a fast A/D-converter, a large mass store capable of storing the sequence of pictures, and a processor to construct the improved picture of the sequence. Furthermore, a hard-copy device capable of producing high-quality grey-scale pictures is required.

It is conceivable that the method described could also be applied to CT-scanners, by using a scanning device which can do, say, 10 scans by rapid rotation. Subsequently a single scan can be determined from the sequence, and hopefully motion artefacts could be reduced this way.

7.3.2 Long-Term Change Detection

So far we have been concerned with the exploitation of rapid motion or the suppression of its side effects by image sequence processing. An important aspect in medical X-ray evaluation is the determination of long-term changes of certain features over weeks or months. A comparison of image sequences taken over such time intervals is difficult, since many of the differences between such pictures are caused by medically insignificant changes such as different position relative to the imaging system, weight changes, different parameter settings (or drifts) of the imaging system itself, etc.

In order to compensate for such irrelevant parameters, a histogram equalization and a correction of geometric distortion can be performed. This implies determination of a raster of points by local correlation of pictures of the sequences and a subsequent correction of the pictures, except the first one, by some "rubber stretching" methods [7.31]. The technique is in its infancy, as it cannot be guaranteed that only irrelevant information will be suppressed by this correction method.

7.4 Spatial Sequence

Besides the well-known time sequences in medical imaging, processing a series of two-dimensional images which represent depth information of the imaged object are becoming more and more important. The medical information inherent in depth series enables the observer to construct a model (in three dimensions) of the original object. This seems to be the best way to study anatomical structures because the objects can be viewed as if they existed in their natural state.

In medical science three main application areas of slicing and reconstructing three-dimensional information exist: electron and light micrograph series, series of ultrasonic data and computerized transverse axial X-ray tomography. The last application has had a revolutionary impact on medical diagnostic imaging in recent years. The idea, however, to reconstruct the third dimension from serial images was first reported in 1957 [7.32] using electron micrographs. In the following sections we will shortly mention the main goals and methods used, and give a list of references for the interested reader in this field.

7.4.1 Electron and Light Micrograph Series

In the research on biomedical ultrastructures, a continuous desire of the anatomist studying the mamilian central nervous system is to understand the branching structure of axonal and dendritic fibres of neurons. These fibres tend to repeatedly branch in tree form, and at the "leaves" or terminals of the trees, synaptic activity occurs between neurons. The tree structure forms a space distribution system, sending electrical potentials to other neurons in different parts of the nervous system. It also forms a time encoder causing action potentials to synapse to other trees. A good understanding of a tree structure requires a spatial visualization of the tree.

One current practical method in use [7.33] for obtaining this understanding, involves an anatomist tracing GOGLI- or HRP-stained trees on a light microscope in a semiautomatic manner.

The coordinates of each point, an order number etc. are recorded and stored in a tree data structure. A three-dimensional display of the entire tree or parts of the tree may be shown with slight rotations and translations which aid understanding of the structure. Figure 7.32 shows a single view of a reconstructed axon tree. It was traced from seven transverse serial sections. SHANZ and McCANN [7.34] first reported a three-dimensional computer graphics system for electron microscopy which reconstructs surfaces from an image sequence. Three-dimensional display techniques including shading and hidden surface removal have been also used by MAZZIOTTA and HAMILTON [7.35] using the THREAD (three-dimensional reconstruction and display) system [7.36].

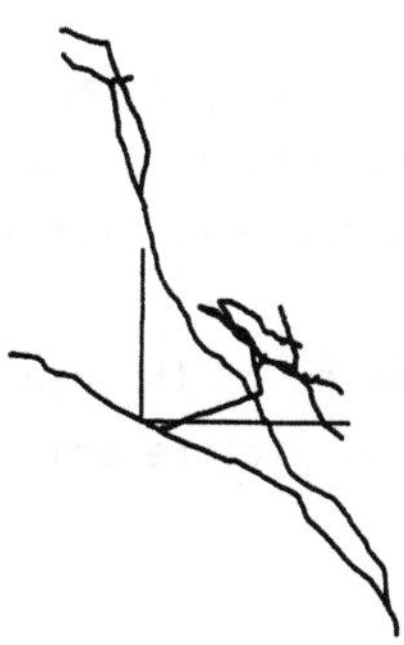

Fig. 7.32. A saggital view of a reconstruction of a delta-hair axon tree from the dorsal horn of a monkey spinal cord. The parent axon, in white matter, runs from the lower right through the tissue origin to the center left. Two main side branches terminating in grey matter are shown. The tree was stained intracellularly with HRP and traced from seven transverse serial sections, each 80 μm thick [7.33]

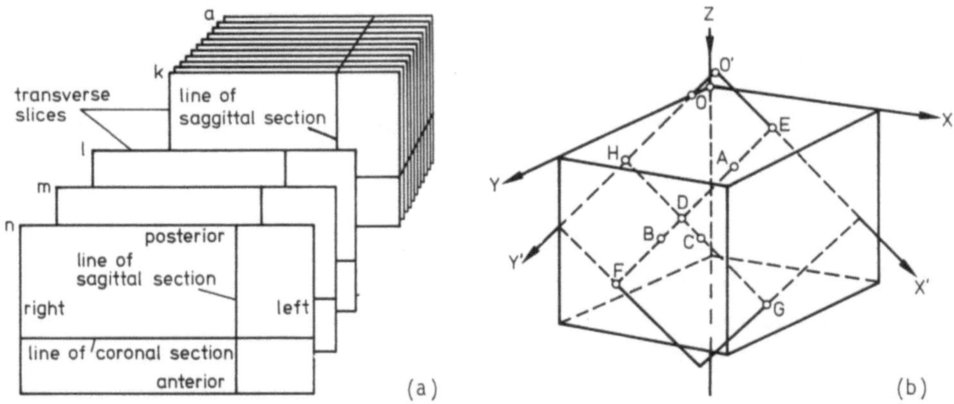

Fig. 7.33. (a) Construction of coronal and saggital sections by processing a stack of transverse slices. (b) Principle of constructing an arbitrarily oriented section

7.4.2 Series of Ultrasonic Data

In digital processing of ultrasonic data only little effort has so far been reported. In most ultrasonic diagnostic methods suggested, the output is in the form of a two-dimensional image, and a serial set of cross-sections is used to give three-dimensional information about the object examined. In 1971 ROBINSON [7.37] proposed several methods to generate additional information from a series of transverse echograms. Figure 7.33a shows schematically how saggital and coronal sections can be constructed. Figure 7.33b shows in principle the definition of any arbitrarily oriented section through a stack of serial echograms. TAMARA et al. [7.38] have described a specialized processing system for three-dimensional display of serial tomograms. They used a representation in which depth is coded by a grey level, i.e., each tomogram is binarized and displayed with some grey level which corresponds to its depth.

7.4.3 Stacks of Computerized Tomograms

During recent years computerized axial tomography (CT) using special X-ray diagnostic machines has become a standard tool in clinical examinations. As far as medical image series are concerned, this technique is the most important example of spatial or serial sequences.

We do not intend to present here the mathematical intricacies of the various reconstruction techniques, but shall restrict ourselves to picture processing and display problems in that field.

Although the reconstructed picture elements in one single plane are measured in HOUNSFIELD units [7.39] and represent a quantitative measure, most processing of CT scans deals with qualitative aspects, like improvement of detectability and display of three dimensions. Only a few approaches have been reported up to now which tackle the problem of quantitative and automatic measurement of brain ventricles or cavities, etc. in CT image series. REESE et al. [7.40] proposed extracting quantitative measures from CT scans, via histograms, whereas WALSER and ACKERMANN [7.41] dealt with the automatic determination of the volume of fluid-filled brain cavities. PENN et al. [7.42] described a system in which, by interactive processing, ventricular volume could be determined. Scene segmentation in the latter case is accomplished by a series of steps based on known Hounsfield values for tissue densities by simple thresholding. Each segmentation is then displayed on a graphics terminal as a line drawing of the boundaries between regions. With a cross-hair cursor, only those regions belonging to the ventricles are identified, and the computer then calculates the volume by multiplying the number of ventricle pixels by the pixel volume. The quality of the results depends highly on the chosen thresholds and on the spatial resolution of the scanner device. When this is too poor there is a further difficulty, the partial volume effect.

An approach for overcoming the restrictions of the bounded slice thickness by averaging the attenuation coefficients of different materials lying within the slice has been proposed by LEMKE [7.43] and STIEHL [7.44].

By analysis of the partial-volume ratios of the pixels information on the three-dimensional density distrbution within the voxels can be retrieved out of the two-dimensional tomogram matrix.

The summation of all partial-volume ratios of the automatically detected ventricles enables the exact determination of the ventricular volume, and by approximation of up to 7 subslices per original slice – dependent on the spatial orientation of the partial-volume ratios within one 10-mm slice – the three-dimensional morphology of the brain ventricles is reconstructed.

Figure 7.34a-d shows four tomographic slices out of a series of eight. The results of the preprocessing and segmentation step for Figs.7.34b,c are shown in Figs.7.35a,b, and a contour plot of the seven subslices between the slices of Figs.7.35a,b is shown in Fig.7.36.

In this particular approach a true cubic resolution is achieved and the 3-D-reconstruction of the morphological structure of the ventricles results from volume determination by partial-volume analysis, and is in no sense an interpolation between abutting slices.

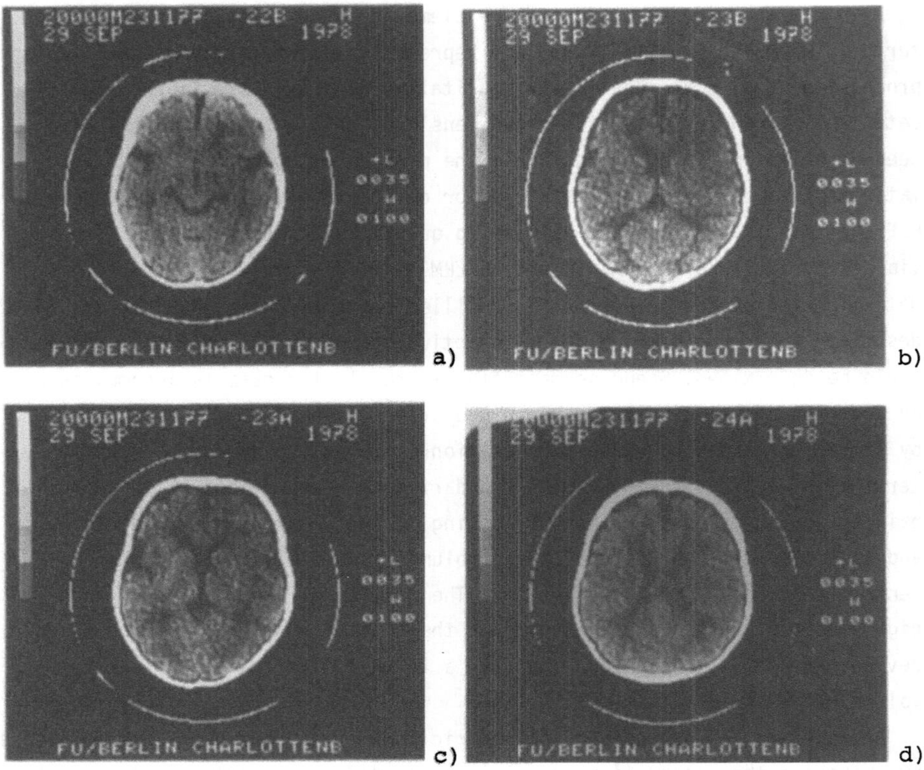

Fig. 7.34a-d. Four CT scans through the head

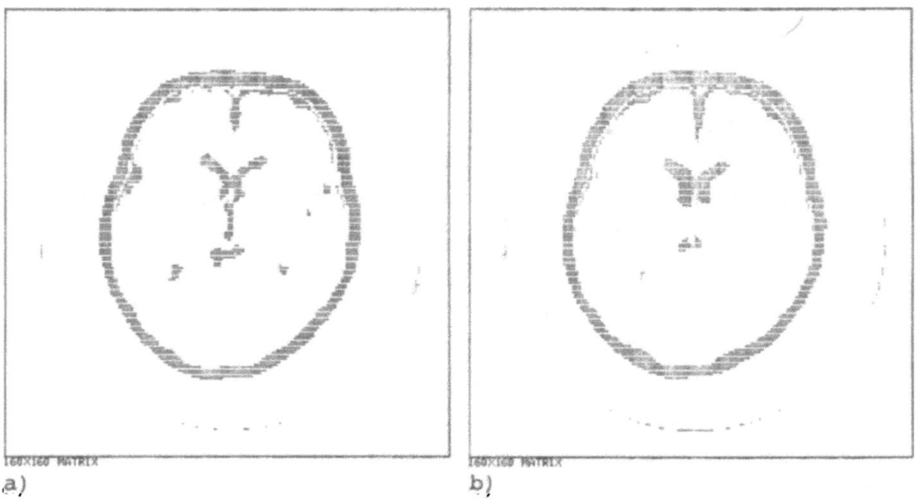

Fig. 7.35a,b. Extracted ventricle sections by use of an automatic segmentation procedure; see Figs.7.34b,c

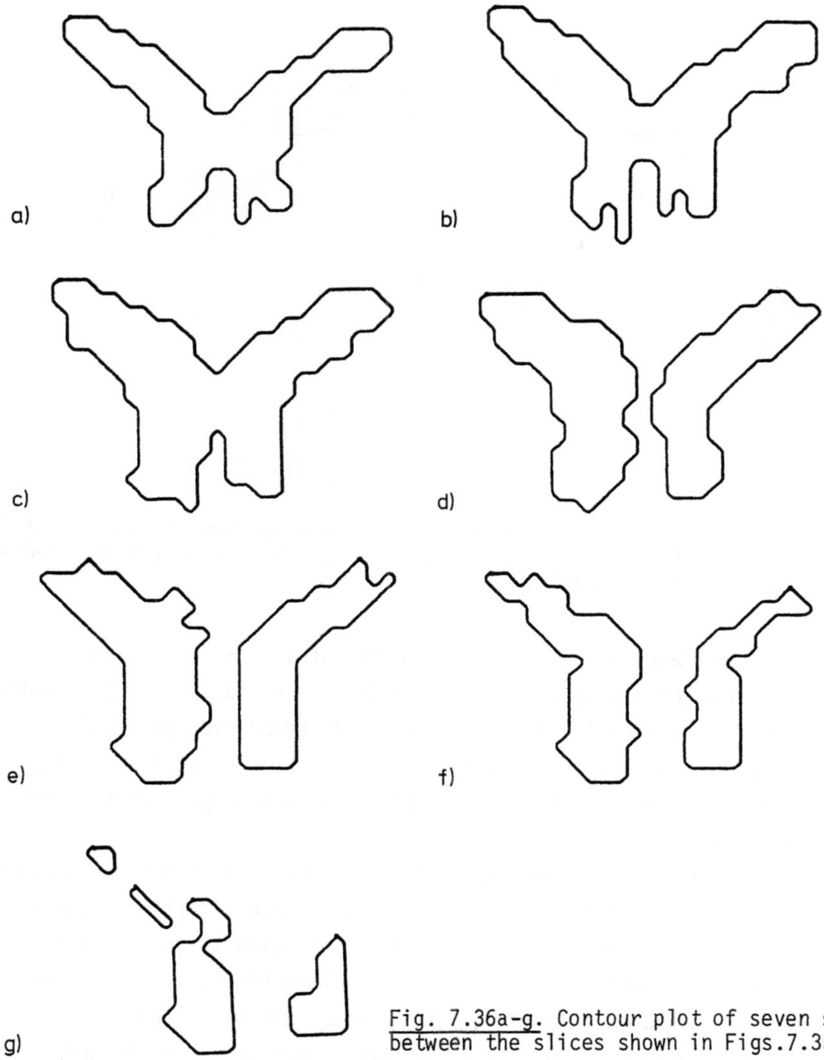

Fig. 7.36a-g. Contour plot of seven subslices between the slices shown in Figs.7.35a,b

Figure 7.37 presents a photograph of a reconstructed ventricular system which has been constructed from layers of Styrofoam.

Besides these quantitative automatic and semiautomatic approaches to processing stacks of computer tomographic layers, several authors have worked on the more qualitative approach of displaying three-dimensional information several ways. SCHULZ et al. [7.45] proposed using the transverse tomographic layers in order to produce additional lateral and frontal views similar to the processing of ultrasonic image series [7.34]. These projections of reori-

Fig. 7.37. Reconstruction of the human head ventricle system. Photograph of a Styrofoam model. (Figs.7.34-37: Courtesy of H. Stiehl, COMPACT Group, Technische Universität Berlin, Berlin, F.R.G.)

ented CT slices contain in one image a composite of all the data from all slices. Hence, a lateral projection corresponds to the familiar lateral radiograph and a frontal projection to the posterior-anterior radiograph. This processing does not require any additional scans to be done on the patient, and requires no additional computer or display equipment beyond that of the computer tomograph.

More advanced and sophisticated approaches deal with the three-dimensional display of organs, etc., reconstructed from serial slices. Most of the proposed methods discriminate the object of interest in each slice, reconstruct the three-dimensional surface of the organ, eliminate hidden surfaces, and shade the visible surfaces in order to give a realistic visual effect.

Automatic scene analysis procedures have been evaluated by HUANG and MAZZIOTTA [7.46] who displayed the three-dimensional information of the heart as a stack of line contours; LEDLEY and PARK [7.47] who used thresholding and automatic boundary detection techniques; and SCHLINDWEIN and VERING [7.48]. The latter applied a region-growing algorithm to detect the boundaries of a part of the skull (bone shell). A very general way of describing complex three-dimensional objects is given by SAROKA and BAJCSY [7.49] using generalized cylinders as primitives. Very elegant and efficient techniques for the reconstruction of a surface from planar contours are presented in [7.50,51]. Figures 7.38,39 show the extracted boundaries, the surface representation by

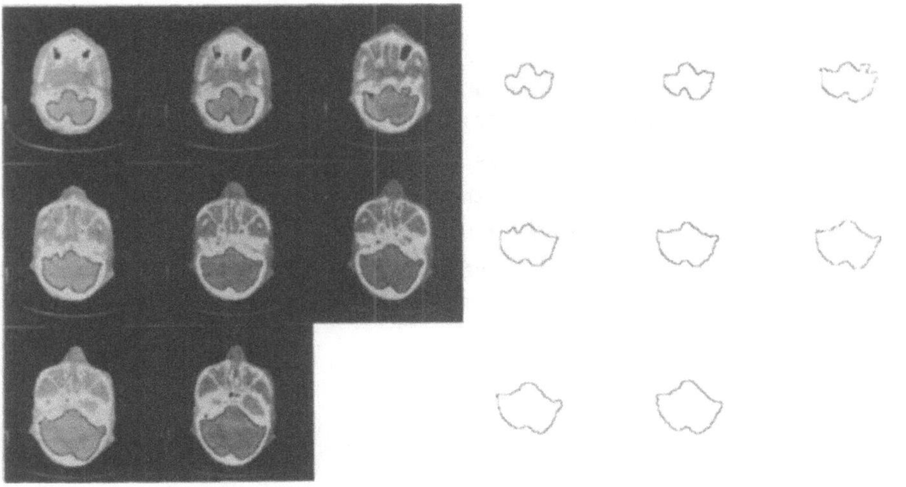

Fig. 7.38. 8 original CT scans of the human head and the respective outlines of the skull [7.48]

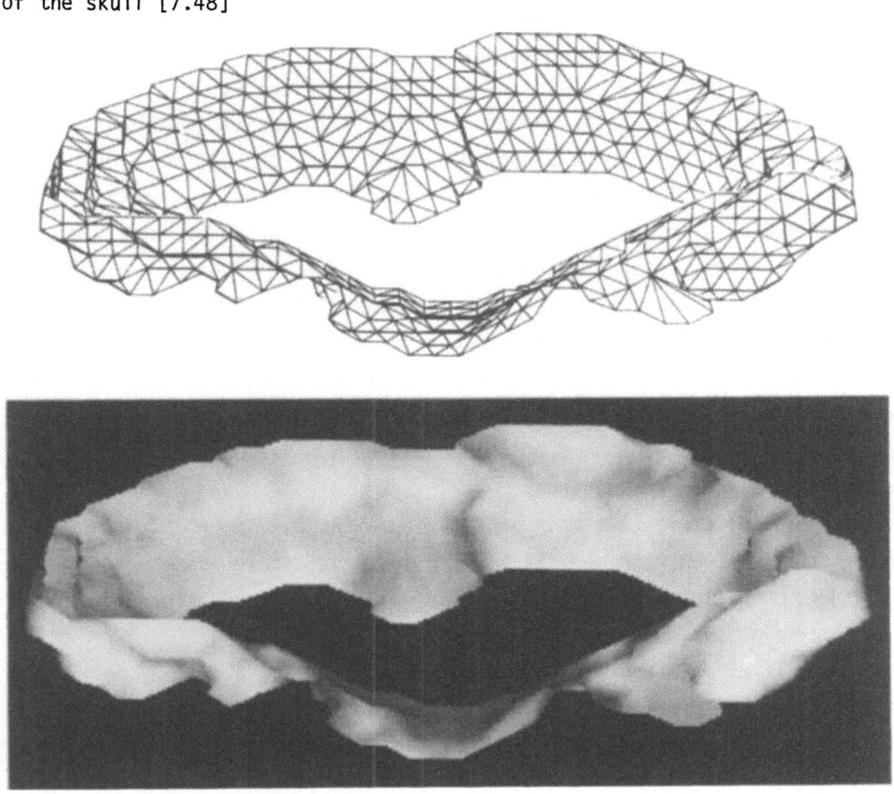

Fig. 7.39. Three-dimensional representation of the human skull including shading and hidden surface removal [7.48]

triangles and the shaded three-dimensional image of the skull as they have been evaluated by [7.48].

The direct determination of the surface of a connected subset of three-dimensional space is treated in [7.52] by ARTZY and HERMAN. They translated the problem of finding boundary faces into the terminology of graph theory. Finally, the techniques of two- and three-dimensional boundary detection [7.53] have recently been extended to the fourth dimension. The idea of determining dynamic boundary surfaces has been presented by HERMAN and LIU [7.54] in order to combine the processing of serial slices (depth series) and time sequences of medical organs.

7.5 Frequency Series

It is a physical necessity that all imaging devices use a carrier, e.g. light, ultrasound, infrared electromagnetic fields and microwaves, which by absorption, reflection, refraction, attenuation, scatter, etc. at the imaged object deliver information which physicians are able to interpret.

The selection of a proper frequency/energy of the carrier influences the type of image, because of the energy-dependent behaviour of the absorption coefficient, refractive index, etc.

By definition we understand a frequency series as a set of recordings with different carrier frequencies/energies.

At the present time, analysis of frequency series is limited to research and plays only a minor role in the area of processing medical image series, compared to the processing of time and spatial sequences. Additionally, frequency series have so far mainly consisted of only two or three different images, whereas time sequences often contain 50-100 frames and spatial sequences 8-50 slices per sequence.

For frequency series two main application areas have been introduced during the last few years in medical X-ray diagnostic: the enhancement of information by absorption edge imaging and the generation of additional information by energy-selective computer tomography.

As is well known, subtraction radiography has become a popular method for the visualization of blood vessels. The usual method involves taking two radiographs of the region of interest, one with radio-opaque contrast material in the blood vessel, a second without contrast material. Structures common to both images (such as bones) cancel out, which permits a better visualization of the vessel under study. In order to increase the sensitivity of the method a subtraction technique has been proposed by ORT et al. [7.55] which takes the energy dependence of the X-ray attenuation of the elements into account. If two X-ray images can be recorded, one with an X-ray beam average energy above and the second one with an energy below the k edge of the particular element to be visualized, very small amounts of the element can be imaged.

A three-spectrum technique which overcomes serious difficulties due to variations in tissue and bone thickness has been proposed by KELCZ and MISTRETTA [7.56] in an analogue electronics realization.

Quasi-monoenergetic beams with mean energies of approximately 30, 40 and 45 keV are formed by filtering a conventional X-ray beam with iodine, cerium and brass filters respectively. A digital version of that technique has been realized and proven by KRUGER et al. [7.57]. The output of an X-ray image intensifier detector is digitized in real time using an 8-bit A-to-D converter, but integration can improve the signal-to-noise ratio of the final images up to a maximum of 13 bit per pixel. With that technique a sensitivity of 1 mg/cm^2 iodine can be achieved, through 20 cm of tissue. A further improved three-spectrum technique has been evaluated by HEINZERLING and SCHLINDWEIN [7.58]. Instead of the common linear reconstruction technique which holds only for monochromatic radiation, or for a certain "equilibrium mass distribution" due to the beam hardening effect, they use a nonlinear reconstruction for this basically nonlinear process. As these investigations are still in their infancy, no quantitative results are yet known.

Energy-selective computer tomographs can be used not only to compensate for the very serious problems of beam hardening [7.59,60] but to extract energy-independent information. In this way one can generate more information for the same dose than a conventional system supplies [7.61-63]. Energy-selective computer tomography (tomochemistry) is based on the fact that for almost all body materials the absorption coefficient can be accurately represented within the diagnostic energy region as

$$\mu(x,y,z,E) = a_1(x,y,z) \cdot f_1(E) + a_2(x,y,z) \cdot f_2(E) \qquad (7.7)$$

where $f_1(E)$ and $f_2(E)$ represent the energy dependencies of the photoelectric and Compton attenuation interactions, respectively. a_1 is a material constant proportional to the electron density and the third power of the atomic number, whereas the material constant a_2 is proportional to the electron density. It can be assumed that $f_1(E)$ is proportional to E^{-3}, and $f_2(E)$ can be described by the well-known Klein-Nishina formula.

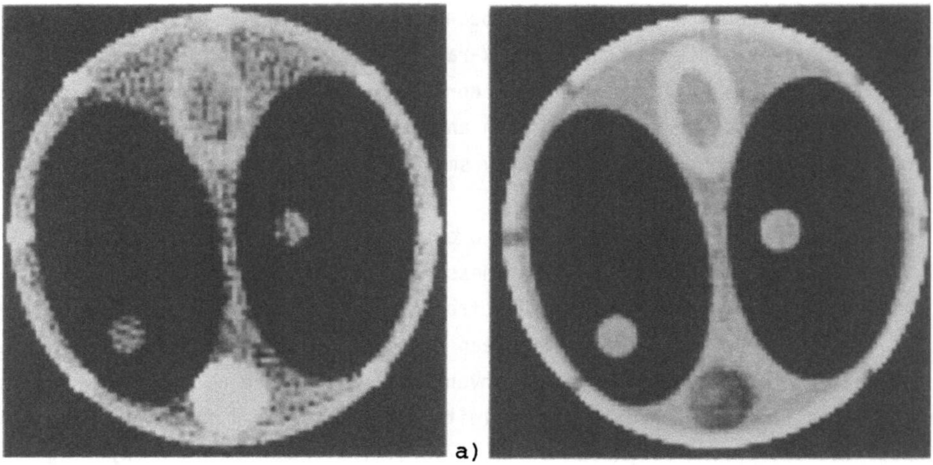

a) b)

Fig. 7.40. (a) Photo picture; $0 < HP < 500$. HP: Hounsfield units photo effect. (b) Compton picture; $40 < HC < 60$. HC: Hounsfield units Compton effect [7.63]

Combining the above formula with the set of measured projection values along path s

$$Q_{1,2}^{s} = -\ln \int dE\ I_{1,2}(E)\ \exp[-\mu(x,y,E)]ds \tag{7.8}$$

the projections

$$A_{1,2}^{s} = \int a_{1,2}(x,y)ds \tag{7.9}$$

can be evaluated from $Q_{1,2}^{s}$ by solving this couple of integral equations by iteration. The sets of projections A_1^s and A_2^s are reconstructed by the convolution method to give pictures of $a_1(x,y)$ and $a_2(x,y)$ in the scanned slice.

Figure 7.40 shows photoeffect and Compton effect pictures of a phantom object (Fig.7.41). Unfortunately, the algorithm is very sensitive to noise. The difference in grey-level structures due to white matter and bone should be noticed.

This technique seems to be a very promising method to get further quantitative information from CT pictures.

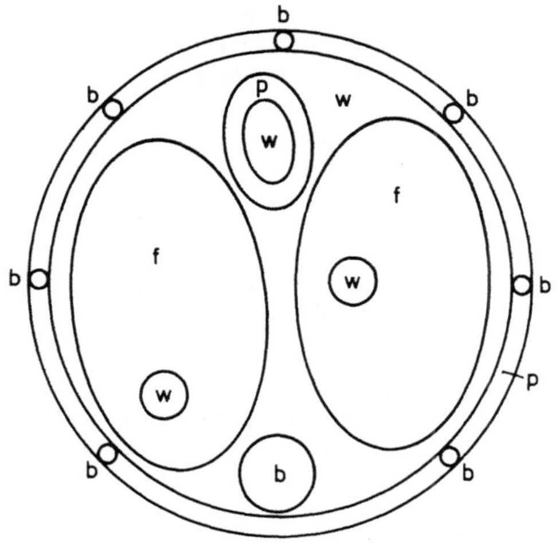

Fig. 7.41. The phantom attenuation values. b = bone, w = white matter, p = pancreas, f = fat [7.63]

Values of the constants

	a_1 $(keV)^3$ cm^{-1}	a_2 cm^{-1}
fat (f)	2 552	0.1588
white matter (wm)	4 792	0.1694
pancreas (p)	5 239	0.1751
bone (b)	20 003	0.1663

7.6 Summary

We have demonstrated that in the field of medical diagnostics there is a huge potential of applications for digital image sequence processing. So far, most techniques used have been simple, and they have more or less been restricted to research environments. One reason for this is certainly a lack of digital processing systems capable of handling image sequences in reasonably short times at low cost. Another reason is the fact that research in image sequence processing has so far not been as active as in the processing of single images. Since considerable progress in both areas is to be expected [7.64], we can hope for rapid advances in medical image sequence processing.

Acknowledgement. The described work was sponsored in part by the German Federal Ministry for Research and Technology (BMFT) under grant no. DVM 113. Only the authors are responsible for the contents of this publication.

References

7.1 A. Rosenfeld (ed.): *Digital Picture Analysis*, Topics in Applied Physics, Vol.11 (Springer, Berlin, Heidelberg, New York 1976)
7.2 M. Tasto: "Maschinelle Bildverarbeitung in der Medizin", in *Erfassung und maschinelle Verarbeitung von Bilddaten*, ed. by H. Kazmierczak (Springer, Berlin, Heidelberg, New York 1980)
7.3 H.H. Nagel: "Analysis Techniques for Image Sequences", Proc. 4th Int. Joint Conf. on Pattern Recognition, Kyoto, Japan, Nov., 1978, pp.186-211
7.4 P.H. Heintzen (ed.): *Roentgen-, Cine-, and Videodensitometry* (Thieme, Stuttgart 1971)
7.5 P.H. Heintzen, J.H. Bürsch (eds.): *Roentgen-Video-Techniques* (Thieme, Stuttgart 1978)
7.6 W.K. Wiscomb: "A Hardware System for Man-Machine Interaction in the Study of Left Ventricular Dynamics", in Ref.7.4
7.7 GRAFOMED, Preliminary technical description, Philips Corp.
7.8 H.R. Schelbert, H. Kreuzer, J. Dittrich, H. Reitsma, P. Spiller: Videometrische Ventrikelflächenbestimmung mit halbhautomatischer Korrektur des Bildhintergrundes. Res. Exp. Med. *158*, 66-74 (1972)
7.9 B.G. Trenholm, D.A. Winter, G.D. Reimer, D. Mymin, E.L. Landsdown, G.P. Sharma: Automated ventricular volume calculations from single plane images. Radiology *112*, 299-304 (1974)
7.10 C.J. Slager, S.H.C. Reiber, J.C.H. Schuurbiers, G.T. Meester: "Automated Detection of Left Ventricular Contour Concept and Application", in Ref.7.5
7.11 C.K. Chow, T. Kaneko: "Computer Calculation of Left Ventricular Volumes from a Cineangiogram", Proc. Quantitative Imaging in the Biomed. Sciences, SPIE, May 1971
7.12 M. Tasto: "Motion extraction for left-ventricular volume measurement". IEEE Trans. BME-*21*, 207-213 (1974)
7.13 M. Tasto: "Guided Boundary Detection for Left Ventricular Volume Measurement", Proc. 1st Int. Joint Conf. on Pattern Recognition, Washington D.C., Oct., 1973
7.14 W. Spiesberger, M. Tasto: The automatic measurement of medical X-ray photographs. Philips Tech. Rev. *35*, 170-180 (1975)
7.15 M. Tasto, M. Felgendreher, W. Spiesberger, P. Spiller: "Comparison of Manual versus Computer Determination of Left Ventricular Boundaries from X-Ray Cineangiograms", in Ref.7.5
7.16 S. Eimo, U. Kuhawara, U. Fujta, S. Sasayama, C. Kawai: "Automatic Processing of Cineangiographic Images of Left Ventricle", Proc. 4th Int. Joint Conf. on Pattern Recognition, Kyoto, Japan, Nov., 1978, pp.740-742
7.17 A. Rosenfeld: *Picture Processing by Computer* (Academic, New York 1969)
7.18 N.R. Silverman: "Videodensitometry and Videokymography for Evaluation of Myocardial Contractibility", in Ref.7.5
7.19 H.C. Smith, R.L. Frye, G.D. Davis, J.R. Pluth, R.E. Sturm, E.H. Wood: "Simultaneous Indicator Dilution Curves at Selected Sites in the Coronary Circulation and Determination of Blood Flow in Coronary Artery-Saphenous Vein Crafts by Roentgen-Videodensitometry", in Ref.7.4, pp.152-157
7.20 D. Decker, E. Epple, F. Heuck, M. Nagel, G. Polony: Anwendung des Mehrfachdetektor-Meßverfahrens in der Cine-Densitometrie. Biomed. Tech. *20*, Ergänzungsband, 265-266 (1975)

7.21 S. Kaihara, T.K. Natarajan, C.D. Maynard, H.N. Wagner, Jr.: Construction of a functional image from spatially localized rate constants obtained from serial camera and rectilinear scanner data. Radiology *93*, 1345-1348 (1969)

7.22 H. Toyama, M. Iio, J. Iisaka, K. Chiba, H. Yamada, K. Matsai, Y. Hoshi, M. Fuse: Color functional images of the cerebral blood flow. J. Nucl. Med. *17*, 953-958 (1976)

7.23 T.K. Natarajan. H.N. Wagner, Jr.: "Functional Images of the Lungs, in *Dynamic Studies with Radioisotope in Medicine IAEA-SM-185/15* (IAEA, Wien 1974) Vol.2, pp.357-367

7.24 M. Tasto, M. Felgendreher: "Verfahren zur Darstellung des zeitlichen Verlaufes einer Bewegungsgröße und Anordnung zur Durchführung des Verfahrens", German Patent P 2447396.9, 1974

7.25 K.H. Höhne, M. Böhm, W. Erbe, G.C. Nicolae, G. Pfeiffer, B. Sonne: Computer angiography: a new tool for X-ray functional diagnostics. Med. Prog. Technol. *6*, 23-28 (1978)

7.26 A. Habibi: Two-dimensional Bayesian estimate of images. Proc. IEEE *60*, 878-883 (1972)

7.27 T.S. Huang, D.A. Barker, S.P. Berger: Iterative image restauration. App. Opt. *14*, 1165-1168 (1975)

7.28 E. Angel, A.K. Jain: Frame-to-frame restoration of diffusion images. IEEE Trans. AC-*23*, 850-855 (1978)

7.29 L. Basanez, P. Brunet: "Linear Filtering Approach to Slow-Varying Image Restoration", Proc. 4th Int. Joint Conf. on Pattern Recognition, Kyoto, Japan, Nov., 1978, pp.747-749

7.30 M. Tasto, W. Spiesberger: "A New Technique for Motion Deblurring of X-Ray Images" (to be published)

7.31 J.H. Kinsey, B.D. Vannelli, R.J. Fontana, W.E. Miller, S.A. Johnson, B.K. Gilbert: "Application of Digital Image Change Detection to Diagnosis and Follow-Up of Cancer Involving Lungs"; Tech. Rpt., Control Data Corp., Minneapolis, MN and Mayo Clinic, Rochester, MN (1975)

7.32 B.G. Bang, F.B. Bang: Graphic reconstruction of the third dimension from serial electron micrographs. J. Ultrastruct. Res. *1*, 138-149 (1957)

7.33 J.J. Capowski: Computer-aided reconstruction of neuron trees from several serial sections. Comput. Biomed. Res. *10*, 617-629 (1977)

7.34 U.J. Shanz, G.D. McCann: Computational morphology: three-dimensional computer graphics for electron-microscopy. IEEE Trans. BME-*25*, 99-103 (1978)

7.35 J.C. Mazziotta, B.L. Hamilton: Three-dimensional computer reconstruction and display of neuronal structure. Comput. Biol. Med. *7*, 265-279 (1977)

7.36 J.C. Mazziotta, H.K. Huang: THREAD (three-dimensional reconstruction and display) with biomedical applications in neuron ultrastructure and computerized tomography. AFIPS Natl. Comput. Conf. Expo. Conf. Proc. *45*, 241-250 (1976)

7.37 D.E. Robinson: Display of three-dimensional ultrasonic data for medical diagnosis. J. Acoust. Soc. *52*, 673-687 (1972)

7.38 S. Tamara, K. Tanaka, K. Yoshida, I. Hiramoto, K. Hirano, M. Matsumoto: "Specialized Processing System for the Three-Dimensional Display Based on Serial Tomograms", Proc. 4th Int. Joint Conf. on Pattern Recognition, Kyoto, Japan, Nov., 1978, pp. 851-853

7.39 G.N. Hounsfield: Computerized transverse axial scanning (tomographie), part 1: description of system. J. Radiol. *46*, 1016-1022 (1973)

7.40 D.F. Reese, P.C. O'Brien, G.W. Beeler, P.R. Gerding, E.C. McCullough: An investigation for extracting more information from computerized tomography scans. Am. J. Roentgenol. Radium Ther. Nucl. Med. *124*, 177-185 (1975)

7.41 R.L. Walser, L.V. Ackermann: Determination of volume from computerized tomograms: finding the volume of fluid-filled brain cavities. J. Comput. Assisted Tomography (Comput. Tomography) *1*, 117-130 (1977)

7.42 R.D. Penn, M.G. Belanger, W.A. Yasnoff: Ventricular Volume in Man Computed from CAT Scans. Ann. Neurol. *3*, 216-223 (1978)
7.43 H.U. Lemke, H.S. Stiehl, H. Scharnweber, D. Jackel: "Applications of Picture Processing, Image Analysis and Computer Graphics Techniques to Cranial CT Scans", Proc. IEEE Conf. on Computer-Aided Analysis of Radiological Images, Newport Beach, CA, June, 1979
7.44 H.S. Stiehl: "Automated Processing and Analysis of Cranial Computed Tomograms", Institut f. tech. Informatik, COMPACT Tech. Rpt., Technische Universität Berlin (1979)
7.45 R.A. Schulz, P.M. Joseph, S.K. Hilal: Frontal and Lateral Views of the brain reconstructed from EMI axial slices. Radiology *125*, 701-710 (1977)
7.46 H.K. Huang, J.C. Mazziotta: Heart imaging from computerized tomography. Comput. Tomography *2*, 37-44 (1978)
7.47 R.S. Ledley, C.M. Park: "Molded Picture Representation of Whole Body Organs Generated from CT Scan Sequences", Proc. 1st Annual Symposium on Computer Application in Medical Care, Washington DD.C., Oct., 1977, pp.363-367
7.48 M. Schlindwein, B. Vering: Three-dimensional display of human organs from computed tomograms. Biomed. Tech. *24*, Ergänzungsband, 219-220 (1979)
7.49 B.I. Soroka, R.K. Bajcsy: "A Program for Describing Complex Three-Dimensional Objects Using Generalized Cylinders as Primitives", Proc. IEEE Comp. Science Conf. on Pattern Recognition and Image Processing, Chicago, May/June, 1978, pp.331-339
7.50 H. Fuchs, Z.M. Kedem, S.P. Uselton: Optimal surface reconstruction from planar contours. Commun. ACM *20*, 693-702 (1977)
7.51 H.N. Christiansen, T.W. Sederberg: "Conversion of Complex Contour Line Definitions Into Polygonal Element Mosaics", Proc. 5th Annual Conf. on Computer Graphics and Image Processing, Atlanta, GA, Aug., 1978
7.52 E. Artzy, G.T. Herman: "Boundary Detection in Three Dimensions with a Medical Application"; Tech. Rpt. No. MIPG9, Medical Image Processing Group, State University of New York at Buffalo (1978)
7.53 H.K. Liu: Two- and three-dimensional boundary detection. Comput. Graph. Image Proc. *6*, 123-134 (1977)
7.54 G.T. Herman, H.K. Liu: "Dynamic Boundary Surface Detection", Proc. Symposium on Computer-Aided Diagnosis of Medical Images, Coronado, CA, Nov., 1976
7.55 M.G. Ort, C.A. Mistretta, F. Kelcz: An improved technique for enhancing small periodic contrast changes in television fluoroscopy. Opt. Eng. *12*, 169-175 (1973)
7.56 F. Kelcz, C.A. Mistretta: Absorption-edge fluoroscopy using a three-spectrum technique. Med. Phys. *3*, 159-168 (1976)
7.57 R.A. Kruger: Digital k-edge subtraction radiography. Radiology *125*, 243-245 (1977)
7.58 J. Heinzerling, M. Schlindwein: X-ray absorption-edge imaging with non-linear reconstruction. Biomed. Tech. *24*, Ergänzungsband, 193-194 (1979)
7.59 S.Ch. Pang, S. Gena: Corrections for X-ray polychromatic effects on three-dimensional reconstruction. IEEE Trans. NS-*23*, 623 (1976)
7.60 R.A. Rutherford et al.: "Quantitative Information from EMI Scanner", Tech. Rpt., Dept., of Medical Biophysics, Univ. of Manchester (1974/75)
7.61 A. Makovski et al.: Energy-dependent reconstruction in X-ray computerized tomography. Comput. Biol. Med. *1*, 325-336 (1976)
7.62 R. Rieckeheer: Biochromatic CT pictures from dual spectrum scanning. Medita, Sonderheft I, 79-81 (1978)
7.63 G. Kowalski, R. Rieckeheer, W. Wagner: New means for picture formation in computer tomography. Acta Electron. *22*, 51-63 (1979)
7.64 M. Tasto: Parallel array processors for digital image processing. Opt. Acta *24*, 391-406 (1977)

Additional References

Chapter 1

J.W. Roach, J.K. Aggarwal: Determining the movement of objects from a sequence of images, IEEE Trans. on Pattern Analysis and Machine Intelligence, Vol.2, No.6, pp.554-562; Nov. 1980
T.S. Huang, R.Y. Tsai: Three-dimensional motion estimation from image-space shifts, Proc. IEEE International Conf. Acoustics, Speech, and Signal Processing, pp.1136-1139, March 30-April 1, 1981, Atlanta, Georgia
R.Y. Tsai, T.S. Huang: Estimating three-dimensional motion parameters of a planar patch, Proc. IEEE Conf. Pattern Recognition and Image Processing, Aug. 3-5, 1981, Dallas, Texas. A more detailed version to appear in IEEE Trans. on Acoustics, Speech, and Signal Processing

Chapter 2

J.K. Aggarwal, N.I. Badler (eds.): IEEE Trans. PAMI-*2*, No.6 (1980) [Special Issue on Motion and Time-Varying Imagery]
A. Arking, R.C. Lo, A. Rosenfeld: A Fourier approach to cloud motion estimation. J. Appl. Meteorol. *17*, 735-744 (1978)
E. Bribiesca, A. Guzman: How to describe pure form and how to measure differences in shapes using shape numbers. Pattern Recognition *12*, 101-112 (1980)
C. Cafforio, F. Rocca: "Detection and Tracking of Moving Objects in Television Images", Int. Workshop on Real-Time Edge Detection and Motion Estimation, Rennes, France, September 1979 (Doc. Tec. CCETT/CTN/T/1/80)
R. DiPaola, A.E. Todd-Pokropek: "New Developments in Techniques for Information Processing in Radionuclide Imaging", Proc. Int. Symposium on Medical Radionuclide Imaging, Heidelberg, Germany, September 1-5, 1980 (IAEA, Vienna 1981)
L. Dreschler, H.-H. Nagel: "On the Frame-to-Frame Correspondence between Greyvalue Characteristics in the Images of Moving Objects", 5. GI-Fachtagung GWAI-81, Bad Honnef, Jan. 26-30, 1981, ed. by J. Siekmann, Informatik Fachberichte (Springer, Berlin, Heidelberg, New York forthcoming)
L. Dreschler, H.-H. Nagel: "Volumetric Model and 3D Trajectory of a Moving Car Derived from Monocular TV-Frame Sequences of a Street Scene", Int. Joint Conference on Artificial Intelligence, Vancouver, Kanada, August 24-28, 1981 (in press)
W. Frei, T. Shibata, G.C. Huth: "Environmental Change Detection in Digitally Registered Aerial Photographs", Applications of Digital Image Processing SPIE Proc., Vol.207 (1979) pp.26-31
W. Frei, M. Singh, T. Shibata: Digital image change detection. Opt. Eng. *19*, 331-338 (1980)
W. Frei, T. Shibata, C.C. Chen: "Fast Matching of Non-Stationary Images with False Fix Protection", Proc. Int. Conference on Pattern Recognition, Miami Beach, FL, December 1-4, 1980, pp.208-212

H. Fuchs, S.M. Pizer, J.S. Cohen, F.P. Brooks, Jr.: "A Three-Dimensional Display for Medical Images from Slices", in *Information Processing in Medical Imaging*, ed. by R. DiPaola, E. Kahn (Editions INSERM, Paris 1980) pp.581-602

U.L. Haass: "Cloud Tracking from Satellite Pictures"; Ph.D. Dissertation, Colorado State University, Fort Collins, CO (1981)

G. Hirzinger, K. Landzettel, W. Snyder: "Automated TV-Tracking of Moving Objects – the DFVLR-Tracker and Related Approaches", Proc. Int. Conference on Pattern Recognition, Miami Beach, FL, December 1-4, 1980, pp.1255-1261

B.K.P. Horn, B.G. Schunck: "Determining Optical Flow"; AI Memo 572, Artificial Intelligence Laboratory, MIT, Cambridge MA (1980), Artif. Intell. (in press 1981)

R.M. Inigo, E.S. McVey: CCD implementation of a three-dimensional video-tracking algorithm. IEEE Trans. PAMI-*3*, 230-240 (1981)

C. Jacobus, R.T. Chien: Intermediate-level vision – building vertex-string-surface (V-S-S) graphs. Comput. Graph. Image Proc. *15*, 339-363 (1981)

C.J. Jacobus, R.T. Chien, J.M. Selander: Motion detection and analysis of matching graphs of intermediate-levels primitives. IEEE Trans. PAMI-*2*, 495-510 (1980)

M.A. Lavin: "Analysis of Scenes from a Moving Viewpoint", in *Artificial Intelligence: An MIT Perspective*, ed. by P.H. Winston, R.H. Brown (MIT Press, Cambridge, MA 1979) Vol.2, pp.183-208

M.D. Levine, M.L. Reisch, W.M. Thurlbeck: Automated measurement of the internal surface area of the human lung. IEEE Trans. BME-*17*, 254-262 (1970)

A.N. Netravali, J.D. Robbins: "Interframe Coding with Recursive Motion Estimation", in *Signal Processing: Theories and Applications*, ed. by M. Kunt, F. de Coulon (North-Holland, Amsterdam 1980) pp.143-148

M. Onoe, K. Preston, Jr., A. Rosenfeld (eds.): *Real-Time Medical Image Processing* (Plenum, New York 1980)

M. Onoe, K. Preston, Jr., A. Rosenfeld (eds.): *Real-Time/Parallel Computing* (Plenum, New York 1981)

M.J. Potel, R.E. Sayre, S.A. MacKay: Graphics input tools for interactive motion analysis. Comput. Graph. Image Proc. *14*, 1-23 (1980)

U. Shani: "A 3-D Model-Driven System for the Recognition of Abdominal Anatomy from CT Scans", Proc. Int. Conference on Pattern Recognition, Miami Beach, FL, December 1-4, 1980, pp.585-591

M. Singh, W. Frei, T. Shibata: A digital technique for accurate change detection in nuclear medical images. IEEE Trans. NS-*26*, 565-575 (1979)

B.I. Soroka: Generalized cones from serial sections. Comput. Graph. Image Proc. *15*, 154-166 (1981)

Chapter 3

1981 Picture Coding Symposium Abstracts, Montreal, Canada, June 1981

E. Dubois, M.S. Sabri, J.Y. Ouellet: Three-dimensional spectrum and processing of digital NTSC colour signals. Digit. Video *3*, 72-84 (1980)

A.N. Netravali, J.D. Robbins: Motion compensated coding: some new results. Bell Syst. Tech. J. *59*, 1735-1745 (1980)

J.A. Stuller, A.N. Netravali, J.D. Robbins: Interframe television coding using gain and displacement compensation. Bell Syst. Tech. J. *59*, 1227-1240 (1980)

Chapter 4

R.H. McMann, S. Kreinik, J.K. Moore, A. Kaiser, J. Rossi: A digital noise reducer for encoded NTSC signals, SMPTE Jour., Vol.87, No.3, pp.129-133; March 1978 (SMPTE=Society of Motion Picture and Television Engineers)

J.R. Sanders: Fully adaptive noise reduction for a television network, the Jour. of the Royal Television Society, Vo.18, No.3, pp.29-33; May/June 1980

Chapter 5

S.T. Barnard, W.B. Thompson: Disparity analysis of images. IEEE Trans. PAMI-*2*, 333-340 (1980)

K.H. Bers, M. Bohner, H. Gerlach: "Object Detection in Image Sequences", Proc. Int. Conf. on Pattern Recogn., Miami Beach, FL, 1980, pp.1317-1319

J.-K. Cheng, T.S. Huang: "Algorithms for Matching Relational Structures and Their Application to Image Processing"; Rpt. TR-EE 80-53, Purdue Univ., School of Electr. Eng., West Lafayette, IN (1980)

L. Dreschler, H.-H. Nagel: "Volumetric Model and 3D Trajectory of a Moving Car Derived from Monocular TV-Frame Sequences of a Street Scene"; Int. Joint Conf. on Artif. Intell., Vancouver, Canada, Aug. 1981

F.P. Ferrie, M.D. Levine, S.W. Zucker: "Cell Tracking: A Modelling and Minimization Approach", Proc. Int. Conf. on Pattern Recogn., Miami Beach, FL, 1980, pp.396-402

C.J. Jacobus: "Visual Recognition of Artifacts by Computer"; Dissertation, Univ. of Illinois at Urbana-Champaign (1980)

C.J. Jacobus, R.T. Chien, J.M. Selander: Motion detection and analysis of matching graphs of intermediate-level primitives. IEEE Trans. PAMI-*2*, 495-510 (1980)

R. Jain: "Peripheral Processes in Machine Perception of Motion", Proc. Int. Conf. on Pattern Recogn., Miami Beach, FL, 1980, pp.1239-1242

A. Korn, R. Kories: "Motion Analysis in Natural Scenes Picked up by a Moving Optical Sensor"; Proc. Int. Conf. on Pattern Recogn., Miami Beach, FL, 1980, pp.1251-1254

M.J. Potel, R.E. Sayre, S.A. MacKay: Graphics input tools for interactive motion analysis. Comput. Graph. Image Proc. *14*, 1-23 (1980)

B. Radig: "Inferential Region Extraction in TV-Sequences", Int. Joint Conf. on Artif. Intell., Vancouver, Canada, Aug. 1981

J.W. Roach, J.K. Aggarwal: Determining the movement of objects from a sequence of images. IEEE Trans. PAMI-*2*, 554-562 (1980)

S.M. Rubin: Natural scene recognition using locus search. Comput. Graph. Image Proc. *13*, 298-333 (1980)

W.E. Snyder, G. Hirzinger, S.A. Rajala: "Image Modeling: The Continuity Assumption and Tracking", Proc. Int. Conf. on Pattern Recogn., Miami Beach, FL, 1980, pp.1111-1114

J.K. Tsotsos: "Temporal Event Recognition: An Application to Left Ventricular Performance", Int. Joint Conf. on Artif. Intell., Vancouver, Canada, Aug. 1981

S. Tsujii, M. Yachida: "Efficient Analysis of Dynamic Images Using Plans", in *Real-Time Medical Image Processing*, ed. by M. Onoe, K. Preston, A. Rosenfeld (Plenum, New York 1980)

M.O. Ward, Y.T. Chien: "Analysis of Time-Varying Imagery Through the Representation of Position and Shape Changes", Proc. Int. Conf. on Pattern Recogn., Miami Beach, FL, 1980, pp.1236-1238

M. Yachida, M. Asada, S. Tsujii: Automatic analysis of moving images. IEEE Trans. PAMI-*3*, 12-19 (1981)

M. Yachida, M. Ikeda, S. Tsujii: A plan-guided analysis of cineangiograms for measurement of dynamic behaviour of heart wall. IEEE Trans. PAMI-*2*, 537-543 (1980)

S. Yalamanchili, W.N. Martin, J.K. Aggarwal: "Differencing Operations for the Segmentation of Moving Objects in Dynamic Scenes", Proc. Int. Conf. on Pattern Recogn., Miami Beach, FL, 1980, pp.1239-1242

Chapter 6

J.K. Aggarwal, N.I. Badler (eds.): IEEE Trans. PAMI-*2*, No.6 (1980) [Special Issue on Motion and Time-Varying Imagery]
B.R. Hunt (ed.): Proc. IEEE *69*, No.5 (1981) [Special Issue on Image Processing]
W.E. Snyder (ed.): IEEE Trans. C-*14*, No.8 (1981) [Special Issue on Time-Varying Imagery]
W.N. Martin, J.K. Aggarwal: "Occluding Contours in Dynamic Scenes", Proceedings of the Pattern Recognition and Image Processing Conference, Dallas, TX, August 3-5, 1981, pp.189-192
S. Yalamanchili, J.K. Aggarwal: "Motion and Image Differencing", Proceedingss of the Pattern Recognition Image Processing Conference, Dallas, TX, August 3-5, 1981, pp.211-216
J.A. Webb, J.K. Aggarwal: "Visual Interpretation of the Motion of Objects in Space", Proceedings of the Pattern Recognition and Image Processing Conference, Dallas, TX, August 3-5, 1981, pp.516-521
J.W. Roach, J.K. Aggarwal: Determining the movement of objects from a sequence of images. IEEE Trans. PAMI-*2*, 554-562 (1980)
J.K. Aggarwal, L.S. Davis, W.N. Martin: Correspondence processes in dynamic scene analysis. Proc. IEEE *69*, 562-572 (1981)

Subject Index

MIX
Papier aus verantwortungsvollen Quellen
Paper from responsible sources
FSC® C105338

If you have any concerns about our products,
you can contact us on
ProductSafety@springernature.com

In case Publisher is established outside the EU,
the EU authorized representative is:
Springer Nature Customer Service Center GmbH
Europaplatz 3, 69115 Heidelberg, Germany

Printed by Libri Plureos GmbH
in Hamburg, Germany